MISSION OF DISCOVERY

ANDREW A. BONAR
and
ROBERT MURRAY McCHEYNE

edited by
ALLAN M. HARMAN

CHRISTIAN FOCUS

Allan M. Harman is Professor of Old Testament and Principal of the
Presbyterian Theological College, Melbourne. He was previously
Professor of Old Testament at the Free Church College, Edinburgh.
He is currently writing a commentary on the Psalms for Christian
Focus. His other writings include *Approaching the Old Testament*
(Auspress) and *The Story of the Church* (with A. M. Renwick, IVP).

Originally published as NARRATIVE OF A MISSION OF INQUIRY
TO THE JEWS FROM THE CHURCH OF SCOTLAND IN 1839. This
edition published in 1996 by Christian Focus Publications.

ISBN 1 85792 258 1

Cover design by Donna Macleod

Printed and bound in Great Britain by
The Guernsey Press Co. Ltd., Vale, Guernsey, C.I.

CONTENTS

INTRODUCTION

This book is the record of an amazing missionary journey undertaken by a group of Scottish clergymen in 1839.[1] It is a slightly abridged account by two of the group, Andrew Bonar and Robert Murray McCheyne, first published in Edinburgh in 1842.[2] It was a journey which was to have considerable impact on Jewish missions, first of all in respect to the Continent of Europe and then afterwards in regard to Palestine itself. They undertook an arduous trip, travelling across southern Europe, then by ship to Alexandria, and finally by camel from Egypt to Palestine. Though the four visitors separated at Beirut, they all travelled through Europe and back to Scotland. A journey of this magnitude excited a lot of interest and also concern. One old woman in Andrew Bonar's congregation at Collace in Perthshire asked how he would go. When it was explained that he would go first to Egypt and then to Palestine, she held up her hands and exclaimed, 'Oh, then, we'll no see him again for forty years!'[3]

The book itself is a tribute to the meticulous care which Bonar and McCheyne took to document their journey. It is a detailed account of all their travels, practically on a daily basis. It is accompanied by maps and many sketches, presumably by McCheyne as it is known that he was gifted with his pen as an artist. It may well be that much of the writing is actually the work of Bonar.[4] It contains many statistics concerning the Jewish people, and gives a picture of the state of missionary activity in all the areas through which they passed. They made enquiries about other places and recorded the information they were given. Throughout they drew attention to biblical passages which had a bearing on the matter in hand. Over a thousand passages, most of them from the Old

---

1. Much of the material in this introduction first appeared as an article entitled 'A Missionary Journey to Palestine with McCheyne and Bonar' in the journal *Mishkan* 15 (1991), pp.42-52 and is used here with permission.
2. The references which are given in this introduction are to the present edition, and they are placed in parentheses in the text.
3. Marjorie Bonar, ed., *Andrew Bonar: Diary and Life* (The Banner of Truth Trust, Edinburgh, 1984), p.78.
4. N.L. Walker, *Chapters from the History of the Free Church of Scotland*, new edition (Oliphant Anderson & Ferrier, Edinburgh, 1895), p.168 calls Bonar 'the historiographer of the mission' and refers to it as 'his narrative'.

Testament, are utilised in this way, and with quite a few there is reference to the Hebrew text. The youthfulness of Bonar and McCheyne can easily be overlooked by a modern reader, but they were only 29 and 28 years of age respectively when they set out for Palestine. However, their biblical and theological knowledge, their linguistic abilities, their spirituality, and their maturity of judgement were exceptional for men of that age.

1. The Scottish Mission to Palestine 1839

A concern for the Jewish people was present in Scotland right from the time of the Reformation. Though neither Luther nor Calvin expected a future conversion of Israel, yet in post-Reformation theology there was a strong concern for the Jewish people.[5] In the marginal notes of the Geneva Bible of 1560 the following comment occurs on Romans 11:15 and 26: 'He sheweth that the time shall come that the whole nation of the Jews, though not every one particularly, shall be joined to the church of Christ'. Many of the Puritans held to this position, and the Westminster *Directory of Public Worship* said that prayer was to be made 'for the conversion of the Jews'. The same viewpoint was set forth in Scottish commentaries such as Dickson's on the Psalms and Ferguson's on the Epistles, or in sermons by such men as Thomas Boston of Ettrick.

This desire for the conversion of the Jews was maintained in Scotland by evangelical ministers down into the nineteenth century. However, the concern for Israel seems to have been heightened by the arrival in Scotland of quite a number of Jewish people in the early part of that century. Missionary vision in general had been stimulated in Scotland in the half-century before the visit and as the theme of revival was coming to the fore, so also as an accompaniment came a desire to reach out to the Jews with the Gospel. From its inception in 1810 the *Christian Instructor* (under the editorship of Dr. Andrew Thomson) carried articles on the Jewish people and activities about endeavours to bring the Gospel to them. This included reports of the meetings of the London Society for the Propagation of Christianity amongst the Jews and its Scottish auxiliaries.[6]

---

5. For an excellent survey of post-Reformation thinking on the conversion of the Jews see I.H. Murray, *The Puritan Hope* (The Banner of Truth Trust, Edinburgh, 1971), especially pp.39-55 and 115ff.
6. The article by Don Chambers, 'Prelude to the last things: the Church of Scotland's mission to the Jews', *Scottish Church History Society Records* XIX, 1(1975), pp.43-58

By the mid-1830s there was a deep concern on the part of many Scottish Christians for missionary work to the Jews. The General Assembly of the Church of Scotland appointed a Committee on the Conversion of the Jews to the Faith of Christ in 1837. The following year various overtures came to the General Assembly on the question of Jewish missions, and it responded by appointing a committee 'to collect information respecting the Jews, their numbers, condition and character – what means have hitherto been employed by the Christian Church for their spiritual good, and with what success -- whether there are any openings for a mission to their nation, and where these are most promising'. During the winter of 1838-39 a series of sermons was preached in Glasgow by ministers of the Church on the conversion of the Jews.[7] One of these sermons was by John Duncan, afterwards to become himself a missionary in Hungary and later a professor in the Free Church of Scotland after the Disruption of 1843.[8]

The committee appointed by the General Assembly decided to fulfil its remit by sending out a commission of enquiry to Palestine and also to Eastern and Central Europe. Two senior ministers were selected, Dr. Alexander Keith,[9] minister of St. Cyrus in Kincardineshire, and Dr. Alexander Black,[10] Professor of Theology in Marischal College, Aberdeen. Mr. Robert Wodrow of Glasgow, who had cherished the idea for many years and who had proposed the visit, was also chosen to go, but he had later to withdraw from the visit. Dr. Robert Candlish made the suggestion that Robert Murray McCheyne and his close friend Andrew Bonar should make up the party.

---

has much useful information yet lacks the theological and spiritual orientation needed for a true assessment. For comment on some aspects of the background to the missionary movement, see G. White, '"Highly Preposterous": Origins of Scottish Missions', *Scottish Church History Society Records* XIX, 2(1976), pp.111-124.

7. *The Conversion of the Jews,* 1839.

8. This sermon is reprinted in J.S.Sinclair, ed., *Rich Gleanings after the Vintage from 'Rabbi' Duncan* (Chas. J. Thynne & Jarvis, London, 1925), pp.330-357. The Disruption was a controversy in Scotland over the autonomy of the Church, and led to the formation of the Free Church of Scotland in 1843.

9. Dr Keith, who wrote extensively on biblical subjects especially prophecy, revisited Palestine in 1844 with his son, Dr. George Skene Keith, who was the first person to photograph the land.

10. Dr Black was minister of Tarves before he was appointed Professor of Divinty in Marischal College, Aberdeen in 1831. After the formation of the Free Church of Scotland in 1843 he became Professor New Testament Exegesis in New College, Edinburgh from 1844 to 1856.

McCheyne was at that time in Edinburgh. His congregation was St. Peter's, Dundee, but because of his prevailing ill-health he was with his family in Edinburgh. When the news became known Bonar wrote him saying: 'His cure for you is the *fragrance of Lebanon* and the balmy air of *Thy land, O Immanuel.*' As for himself Bonar could not at first see how he could leave his congregation at Collace. In the same letter to McCheyne, Bonar explained that the deputation did not need his linguistic skill for they had Dr. Black (a brilliant linguist), and he felt that the three others could attain all the objects of the visit.[11] His concern for his congregation was great, but at length satisfactory arrangements were made and he agreed to go. This was a happy arrangement for two close friends to travel together, and in the end they had to fulfil a major part of the visit. The two older men were forced to abandon the visit at Beirut. Dr. Black's health was a problem, and the climate, together with the rough travelling, sapped his strength. He felt he could not carry through the projected visit to Galilee, and therefore the decision was made that he and Dr. Keith would return to Britain via Constantinople and the Danube. Dr. Black had to stay some months in Vienna, while Dr. Keith was seriously ill at Budapest. Ill-health so delayed their return, that it was not until well after McCheyne and Bonar had arrived back that they finally were able to return home.

The journey was an arduous one. Repeatedly they faced dangers, and, on several occasions, there was the prospect that they would lose their lives. As Bonar and McCheyne were leaving Sidon to head for Galilee, a Greek Christian came and told them that a traveller had been killed by Arabs the day before. However, they committed themselves to God and pressed on. A day or two later they were wakened by a soldier and two Jews who told them in broken French that a Jew had been shot the day before two hours' journey further on towards Zefat. In addition they had to cope with accidents such as when Dr. Black fell from his camel on the way from Egypt to Palestine. This accident contributed towards Dr. Black's inability to fulfil the original plan, though in the providence of God it led to blessing because of the time Dr. Keith spent in Pesth. That city became the site of Jewish mission work from Scotland in 1841. One of the touring party rightly said: 'Dr Black's fall from the camel was the first step towards Pesth'.[12] The plague was

---

11. Quoted in A. Smellie, *Robert Murray McCheyne* (National Council of Evangelical Free Churches, London, 1913), pp.96-97.
12. Andrew A. Bonar, *Memoir and Remains of Robert Murray McCheyne* (The Banner of Truth Trust, Edinburgh, 1973), p.99.

raging both in Egypt and in Palestine at that period, and they had to undergo periods of quarantine. McCheyne took very ill while in Beirut for a second visit, and then was left behind at Smyrna while Bonar and their travelling companion Calman went on to Constantinople. One Sabbath in Poland Bonar, McCheyne, and Calman separated for a time of private devotions. McCheyne went about a mile and a half towards some hills, not realising that this was an area of frequent robberies and murders. Two men approached and tried to drag him into the nearby woods. He struggled violently for fifteen minutes and then completely exhausted he collapsed on the ground. The men talked to themselves for a while and then suddenly ran off. The comment on the incident was: 'We felt that the hand of God, that had delivered us out of so many dangers during our previous wanderings, had been eminently stretched out again.'

2. An Investigative Journey

In the preface to their volume Bonar and McCheyne wrote that they only had one object in view in their journey, 'to see the real condition and character of God's ancient people, and to observe whatever might contribute to interest others in their cause'. Wherever they went they made detailed enquiries concerning the Jewish people in the locality, and they commented on such matters as economic circumstances, educational opportunities, devotion to Jewish belief, and openness to Christian teaching. At the end of a discussion relating to a particular place, there was usually a summary of their findings. Thus they surveyed the situation in France and Italy, and they pointed out that in France the Jews were not gathered in large communities, but spread out throughout the population. Hence an itinerant missionary would be of more value there. However, in Italy the situation was different, and they recommended that as the Jews were so numerous and the government not so interfering it would be good if a missionary was placed there who could minister to the Protestants and also reach out with the Gospel to the Jews.

The major statement concerned the condition of the Jews in Palestine. The committee of the Church of Scotland which sent them out had provided them with a list of questions which they wished answered. The answers are a detailed response to a variety of questions. They reckoned that the total Jewish population of Palestine was 12,000, with approximately 7,000 of these living in Jerusalem. Statistics such as these have been important for Jewish as well as Christian writers when assessing the size and ethnic distribution of the population of Palestine.[13] The Jews in Palestine were supported by collections taken among Jewish people in other countries, with the Amsterdam community providing the largest sums, and not much coming from Britain. The Palestinian Jews came largely from Poland, with a strong representation from Russia. Most of them were the 'elite of the devotional and strictly religious Jews of other countries'. They gave an account of the history of missionary work in Palestine among the Jews from the arrival of a Swiss clergyman by the name of Tschudi in 1820 to the time of their visit. Details regarding cost of living and housing were also provided and their pen-pictures of Jerusalem provide additional information on conditions in the city at that time.[14]

Similarly they gave detailed reports on all the places they visited in Asia Minor and Europe on their way home. For example, there was a detailed report on their visit of 17th-20th September, 1839 to Jassy in Hungary. This report was significant, for the first missionary to the Jews sent out soon after by the Church of Scotland in 1841 went to Jassy. They visited twelve of the Jewish synagogues there, though they noted that there were two hundred synagogues in the town, over thirty of which were large. Their arrival coincided with the beginning of the Day of Atonement, and they described how the greater part of Leviticus 16 was incorporated in the prayers, and how a Hebrew poem was read, but because it was such difficult Hebrew, the worshippers scarcely understood one word. They tried to calculate the Jewish population, and finally estimated that out of a total population of 50,000 about 20,000 were Jews.

Quite often Bonar and McCheyne contrasted what they saw with situations in Great Britain, or else compared geographical features with places well known in Scotland. When they landed at Boulogne '... the demand for our passports, the pacing of the *gens d'armes* along the shore, and the general aspect of the people, reminded us that we were in a less favoured land than we had left'. They were delighted as they

---

13. See, for example, the quotation of the figures from *The Narrative of a Mission* in Dan Bahat, *Twenty Centuries of Jewish Life in the Holy Land: The Forgotten Generations*, p.63.
14. For a full discussion of the re-development of Jerusalem in the 19th century, see the excellent presentation in Martin Gilbert, *Jerusalem: Rebirth of a City* (Chatto, London: 1985).

were making their final approach to Jerusalem to be greeted in English
by a young man in European dress who was riding on a mule. Wherever
they went they tried to make contact with the British Consul, carrying
with them letters to her Majesty's consuls, as well as letters to friends
and merchants in the various countries they visited. In Jerusalem they
found that the professed Christians (Greeks, Armenians and Roman
Catholics) were more bitter enemies of the Jews than the Muslims. If a
Jew was in danger he would flee to the house of a Turk rather than look
to a Christian for help. Instead of showing love to Israel these Christians
displayed great hatred, and even prevented Jews from passing the door
of the church of the Holy Sepulchre. They then had this to say:

> On this account, the kindness of Protestants appears to them very
> striking; and convinces them that here is a real difference in the
> religion we profess. And they are becoming strongly attached to
> British Christians. The fact that a British Consul should be sent
> to the Holy Land, with special instructions to interest himself in
> behalf of the Jews, and having for his district the very region
> formerly allotted to the twelve tribes of Israel! And how much
> more wonderful still, that our first Consul in Jerusalem should be
> one actuated by a deep and enlightened attachment to the cause
> of God's ancient people!

In regard to scenery they compared the bleak and wild hills through
which the river Rhone runs with the hills of Glencoe in Scotland. Other
places did not impress them, including Mount Carmel. When they first
saw it they needed some persuasion that it was really Carmel. Because
it lacked any imposing appearance one of the party exclaimed: 'Is this
Carmel? Lachnagar is finer than this!'

At the same time as they were in Jerusalem, Sir Moses Montefiore,
Sheriff of London and leader of English speaking Jews at the time, was
on a visit, and he received them kindly and gave them cake and wine.
He told them of his visit to other places including Zefat and Tiberias, and
they talked over 'the state of the land, the miseries of the Jews, and the
fulfilment of prophecy'. Later Sir Moses was again to show further
kindness to them when they met up in quarantine at Carmel (the plague
had not reached further north than Carmel and all travellers had to wait
there for 14 days and to wash their clothes in the sea for seven days). Sir
Moses sent them a fine watermelon and two bottles of the wine of

Lebanon. Bonar and McCheyne commented that if this was a fair sample of Lebanon wine then it had lost its excellence since the days of Hosea (Hosea 14:7) for it was not pleasant!

McCheyne also expressed his reaction to Palestine in verse, and in this and other poetical writing he may well have been strongly influenced by Old Testament poetry.[15] Four pieces ('Fountain of Siloam', 'The Sea of Galilee', 'To Yonder Side', and 'On the Mediterranean Sea in the Bay of Carmel') are printed as part of his *Memoir and Remains*.[16] In them he not only draws attention to geographic features but also points forcefully to spiritual lessons. The application was first and foremost to himself.

3. A Missionary Journey

What was proposed as a journey of investigation turned out to be a remarkable missionary journey. Bonar and McCheyne recorded how the four members of the deputation engaged in telling the message of the Gospel wherever they went. Naturally this was done more fully in the case of the authors themselves, especially as so much of their visit was without Dr. Keith and Dr. Black.

The four members of the deputation all had backgrounds which fitted them for their missionary work. Dr. Black was a Professor of Theology, while Dr. Keith had been an ardent student of the prophecies of the Old Testament for many years and had written on the subject. Bonar and McCheyne had developed a love for the Hebrew and Greek Scriptures during student days in Edinburgh. They had been part of an exegetical society which met every Saturday morning at 6.30 am. McCheyne himself attributed to this society much of the knowledge of Jewish literature and geography of Palestine which came in so useful during his trip.[17] Along with Bonar he had a thorough grasp of things relating to the Jews which he was able to put to such good use during the visit.

As soon as McCheyne set out for London his Jewish missionary

---

15. See R.P. Gordon, '"Isaiah's Wild Measure": R.M. McCheyne', *Expository Times* 103, 8(May, 1992), pp.235-237 for comment on the fact that McCheyne's reference to 'Isaiah's wild measure' in his poem 'Jehovah Tsidkenu' may well be recognition on his part that the book of Isaiah was largely composed of poetry.

16. Andrew A. Bonar, *Memoir and Remains of Robert Murray McCheyne, op.cit.*, pp.640-644.

17. *Ibid.*, p.40.

work started. On board the ship on which he was travelling he found a young Jew who did not want his Jewish identity known. McCheyne spoke with him several times and before parting read with him Psalm 1 in Hebrew. Once the deputation crossed the Channel to France, the missionary activity started in earnest. At Boulogne they began to ask about Jewish people, and that first evening on the Continent they had a visit from a Jew of good education and who spoke excellent English. They explained their love for the Jewish people had impelled them to take on this deputation, 'and Dr Keith, with great fervour, pictured the outcast state of Israel, and how plainly it seemed to be on account of some sin lying at their door, urging him to consider what the sin could be'. The Jew in reply spoke of God's general love and mercy, but the visitors showed him the way of pardon and acceptance with God. He was much affected and wished that there were more of the Church of Scotland's missionaries. Immediately he explained that he meant this only in one sense, as he did not wish to see them succeed in their desire to convert his brethren! Their activities on this first day abroad set the pattern for the rest of their time abroad. No opportunity was lost to speak of the Saviour or to turn attention to God's Word. When they visited the home of a sick rabbi in Galilee they spoke in Hebrew and German 'and before leaving had some conversation regarding the pardon of sin'.

It is clear that the members of the deputation were well prepared for their missionary work because they had Bibles and tracts with them, and they distributed them wherever they went. At Dijon they met a young boy and gave him the gift of a book. He went away and got his father, and they were delighted that father and son were Jews! The father looked at their Hebrew Bible and read some verses aloud. They gave him a book and a French New Testament, which he accepted with joy. Another man approached them and asked for a Hebrew tract, for they must have been distributing them too.

Their literature got them into trouble on several occasions. They had heard that Leghorn in northern Italy was a free port and thought that it might be free to receive the Gospel. Hence when eight men carried their luggage to the hotel where they were staying they gave them tracts. An hour or so later an officer appeared and asked them if they were the men who were distributing books, and then he proceeded to seal and carry off their box with books and tracts and their box with Hebrew books. They were sent to Florence for a report from the censor. When they were getting ready to sail to Malta, they were called before the police and given the finding on their books. The censor had condemned the books and they were told to leave Tuscany without delay. Afterwards they learned that a sentence of perpetual banishment had been passed on them. They noted that the Jews were interested in what had happened to them and it showed that Popery was equally the enemy of Protestantism and of Israel. When returning they travelled through Austria and their literature was confiscated there, and they had to undergo an examination from the police because of their interest in Jewish matters – synagogues, Hebrew language, and *tefillin* (phylacteries). At Brody they were sent for by the chief of the police. It was claimed that they were Jews travelling under a false passport. The police had been informed by letter that Bonar and McCheyne had gone into the synagogue at Jaaglinsky and joined in the Jewish prayers, even saying the Shema. They were also asked why they had bought *tefillin*. This is how they recorded their reply:

> We were somewhat perplexed as well as amused by this attempt to shew that we were Jews and not Christians, and were now made aware of the system of jealous espionage maintained in this kingdom of Popish darkness. We answered that we were Protestant pastors from Scotland, and that all ministers in our country are instructed in Hebrew; that we had read in the synagogue only to shew the Jews that we knew their language; and that we had bought the *Tephillin* as curiosities.

The variety of languages which the ministers used is amazing. Driving away from Bar-sur-Aube in the coach, the Scottish ministers threw leaflets in French out the window to people on the streets and in the fields. Bonar and McCheyne started this but they were joined by Dr. Black who, in throwing tracts to those in the fields, said: 'Voila! Un petit livre pour votre enfant!'[18] In the stagecoach travelling from Dijon to Lyons they met a Roman Catholic priest. With him they held a conversation, especially on the subject of peace with God, and the conversation was sometimes in French, sometimes in Latin. In Leghorn they had a long conversation with an Eastern rabbi on religious topics including the nature of the Messiah. They all took part in the conversation but Dr. Black was the main speaker as he was very fluent in Italian. At later times on the trip they used Italian when trying to present the

---

18. Smellie, *op. cit.*, p.102.

Gospel as on ships en route to Alexandria, while travelling from Egypt to Palestine, and in Palestine itself. German was used in Palestine and frequently on their travels in Europe and Latin came in useful on various occasions. There are also examples in the *Narrative* of their use of Yiddish and Rumanian.

Hebrew was frequently used. They were able to read Hebrew inscriptions in the synagogues, to understand much of Hebrew liturgy, and even to make limited conversation in it. On the last stage of their sea journey to Alexandria they talked with four Jews from the Dardenelles. They explained Hebrew abbreviations to them and then surprised them by saying (in Hebrew), 'We too use the word *Amen.*' It would seem that their knowledge of Hebrew had been academic up to this time, but they were ready to attempt to use it in debate over the Hebrew Scriptures, or with children as Andrew Bonar did in Tyre. At times they made mistakes with the Hebrew (as on the last occasion) and also with the spelling of post-biblical expressions.[19] In the town of Zefat in the north a young man met McCheyne in the street, and seeing that he had a staff in his hand, he asked for it as a present. He said (in Hebrew), 'Give me this staff, and if the Arabs come, I will smite them with it.' The comment was added: 'It was strange to hear this youth speaking the language of his fathers on their own mountains.' They even engaged in some elementary comparative philology using Arabic and Hebrew.

The evidence by Bonar and McCheyne in reference to the use of Hebrew in Palestine is further confirmation of the continued use of the language in Palestine prior to the arrival of Eliezer Ben Yehudah in 1882. Part of modern Israeli folklore consists in the view that Ben Yehudah was responsible for the resuscitation of Hebrew as a spoken language among the Jews in Israel. Bonar and McCheyne are among various Christian writers who show that Hebrew was a living language in Palestine last century wherever there were Jews.[20] They have numerous references to its use, and of their realisation that they had to attempt to use it also as a means of confronting Jews with the Gospel.

Several times in their narrative Bonar and McCheyne dealt with the question of the qualifications needed for being a missionary to the Jews.

---

19. For examples see S.G.Reif, 'A Mission to the Holy Land – 1839', *Glasgow University Oriental Society Transactions* Vol. XXIV (1971-72), p.6. This article is an interesting Jewish commentary on the mission.
20. See the important discussion on this general question by T.V. Parfitt, 'The Use of Hebrew in Palestine 1800-1882', *Journal of Semitic Studies* 17(1972), pp.237-252.

They had discussed this with those working in Jerusalem on their visit, and the feeling was that Hebrew was the most necessary language for ministering to the Jews in Palestine. All of them spoke it, but there was also a variety of other languages in use – Arabic, Spanish, German, Italian, Judeo-Spanish, and Judeo-Polish. Seemingly some Italian was understood by almost all the Jews, regardless of background. In addition to this impressive array of languages which a missionary would need they added: 'A knowledge of Chaldee [Aramaic] and Syriac would be very useful!' The missionaries also would need to have a good knowledge of Hebrew literature and especially of the Talmud. In discussing the qualifications with Mr. Pieritz (who was once the Jewish rabbi in Yarmouth in England) he mentioned the name of Wolff, who had been a missionary in Palestine, and said: 'Rather send one good missionary than fifty others. I have come after many missionaries, and have wished that they had never been there. It was pleasant to come after Wolff. All the Jews in the place knew what he wanted with them – viz. that without Christ there is no remission of sin.' That last comment was significant, for Bonar and McCheyne constantly came back to that basic issue in their discussions with both Jews and Gentiles.

In Palestine they found the Jews more oppressed and in greater poverty than in other countries. The expectation of the coming of the Messiah was real though, and Bonar and McCheyne saw this as an opportunity for missionary work: 'The missionary has thus firm ground to stand upon, and, with the Hebrew Bible in his hand, may expound to them, with intelligence and power, all that is written in the Law of Moses, and in the Prophets, and in the Psalms, concerning Jesus.' They concluded that the Holy Land presented the most attractive and most important area for missionary work among the Jews. At the time of their visit an effective work was maintained in Jerusalem by the London Society for the Conversion of the Jews. Hence they suggested that the northern part of the land, the ancient Galilee, with over half of the Palestinian Jewish population, 'still presents an open and uncultivated field'. It was to be almost fifty years before Scottish missionaries were in fact sent to Galilee.

4. The Results of the Mission
The deputation provided a major stimulus to the cause of Jewish missions in Scotland. At the meeting of the General Assembly in May, 1840, a report was received from the Committee for Promoting Chris-

tianity among the Jews, and two of the deputation spoke to the Assembly about their visit to Palestine. The committee was authorised 'to take steps for preparing and sending missionaries to the stations most promising; and the General Assembly recommend that collections be made throughout the Church for this object, in the same way as for the other Schemes of the Church; and renew their recommendation to ministers to remember the cause of God's ancient people in the services of the sanctuary'.[21] This meant that funds would be collected for Jewish missions along with Foreign Missions, Church Extension, Education, and Colonial Churches. The following year the Assembly agreed to send an address to the Jewish people which was drawn up by Robert Wodrow, the man who had first proposed the mission of enquiry to Palestine. While clearly the evangelical party in the Church of Scotland was the driving force behind the cause of the Jewish mission, yet the so-called moderate party was prepared to give assistance and even to agree to waive the normal requirements in regard to the ordination of William Allan and William Wingate.[22]

The first Jewish missionary sent out by the Church of Scotland was Rev. Daniel Edward, who in 1841 was sent to work in Jassy in Moldavia.[23] A few months later he was followed by Dr. John Duncan, with two helpers, William Allan of Glasgow and Robert Smith of Aberdeen, to Pesth. Alfred Edersheim and Adolph Saphir were soon to become two very significant converts of the Hungarian mission, and afterwards they became prominent in British evangelical life. The infant mission was changed by events in Scotland, for with the Disruption of the Church of Scotland in 1843 all four missionaries joined the Free Church. The first report dealt with by the Free Church Assembly in 1843 was Jewish Missions, and work amongst the Jews was an integral part of Free Church missions thereafter.[24]

Bonar and McCheyne in particular were busy in promoting the cause of Jewish missions and telling of their visit to Palestine. In this connection McCheyne went across to Ireland in July, 1840 and spoke in both Belfast and Dublin. A result of this visit was that the first

---

21. *Acts of the General Assembly of the Church of Scotland 1638-1842*, p.1101.

22. For personal details of the early Jewish missionaries of the Church of Scotland see Hew Scott (ed.), *Fasti Ecclesi Scotican*, new edition (Oliver and Boyd, Edinburgh, 1928), vol. VII, pp.712-717. A discussion of the evangelical/moderate support for the Jewish cause is found in Chambers, *op. cit.*, pp.55ff.

23. Jassy is the present city of Iaçi in Romania.

24. For a summary of later Free Church activities in regard to Jewish work, see N.L.

missionaries to the Jews from the Presbyterian Church of Ireland were sent out in the following year.

The establishment of a Scottish mission in Palestine did not take place until 1885. Dr. John Wilson of Bombay came through Palestine when returning from India, and he reported that there was no suitable place for a mission station.[25] It was only when Dr. Hood Wilson visited there in 1883 that a new interest developed and stations, involving medical work as well as educational and evangelistic, were opened in Tiberias and Zefat.

It is hard to estimate the indirect effect of the mission of enquiry. Clearly the report to the General Assembly in 1840, the *Narrative* (of which 23,000 copies were in print by 1847), and the sections in Bonar's *Memoirs and Remains of Robert Murray McCheyne* dealing with the visit to Palestine and with Jewish missions in general, further stimulated interest. The outcome was a deep commitment to Jewish missions so that evangelical Christians in Scotland to this day are known for their concern to bring the news of the Messiah to Jewish people.

Walker, 'The Conversion of Israel', in *Chapters from the History of the Free Church of Scotland* (Oliphant, Anderson & Ferrier, Edinburgh, 1895), pp.168-180.
25 *Ibid.*, p.171.

CHAPTER 1

FRANCE–ITALY–MALTA–GREECE

'Thus saith the Lord of Hosts, I am jealous for Jerusalem and for Zion with a great jealousy, and I am very sore displeased with the heathen that are at ease' (Zechariah 1:14,15).

The subject of the Jews had but recently begun to awaken attention among the faithful servants of God in the Church of Scotland. The plan of sending a Deputation to Palestine and other countries, to visit and inquire after the scattered Jews, was suggested by a series of striking providences in the case of some of the individuals concerned. The Rev. Robert S. Candlish, D.D., Minister of St George's, Edinburgh, saw these providences, and seized on the idea. On the part of our Church, 'the thing was done suddenly' but it soon became evident that 'God had prepared the people' (2 Chronicles 29:36). The Committee of our General Assembly, appointed to consider what might be done in the way of setting on foot Missionary operations among the Jews, was led unanimously to adopt this plan after prayerful and anxious deliberation. Our own anticipations of the result of our inquiries might be described by a reference to Nehemiah (Nehemiah 1:2,4). We thought we could see that, if the Lord brought us home in safety, many people would ask us 'concerning the Jews that had escaped and were left of the captivity, and concerning Jerusalem'; and that our Report might lead not a few to 'weep, and mourn, and fast, and pray, before the God of heaven', for Israel. We have good reason to believe that this has been the effect. In Scotland, at least, many more 'watchmen have been set upon the walls of Jerusalem' (Isaiah 62:6,7), men of Nehemiah's spirit, who keep their eye upon its ruins, favouring its very dust, and who 'will never hold their peace, day nor night, till the Lord make Jerusalem a praise in the earth'.

It was a token for good at the very outset that Dr. Black, Professor of Divinity in the Marischal College, Aberdeen, and Dr. Keith, Minister of St Cyrus, whose writings on the evidence from fulfilled prophecy have been so extensively read and blessed, were willing to give themselves to this work, along with two younger brethren, Rev. R. M. McCheyne, Minister of St Peter's, Dundee, and Rev. Andrew A. Bonar, Assistant Minister of Collace, Perthshire. Mr. Robert Wodrow, an Elder of our Church, whose whole heart had yearned over Israel for many a year, was also appointed by the Committee, but ill health compelled him reluctantly to decline. Being all of one mind in regard to Israel, and eager to seek their good, a few weeks sufficed to have every preparation completed. Those of us who had Parishes to leave behind, felt that, in a case like this, we might act as did the shepherds at Bethlehem, leaving our flocks for a season under the care of the Shepherd of Israel, whose long lost sheep we were now going to seek, nor have we had any cause to regret our confidence, and one at least of our number found this anticipation of the Good Shepherd's care more than realized on his return.

As we went on our way through Glasgow, Greenock and Liverpool, the members of our Church commended us to the Lord. On our arrival in London, the office-bearers and members of the London Jewish Society, and many other Christian friends in the city, shewed us no small kindness. The Religious Tract Society furnished us with their publications in various languages. What we saw of the Jews there, and of the operations of the London Society among them, was very useful to us. Provided with Lord Palmerston's passport, and letters to her Majesty's foreign Consuls, through the kindness of Sir George Grey and Lord Ashley, as well as with letters to friends and merchants in the various countries we expected to visit, we were commended to the Lord in Regent Square Church the night before we set out. Many prayers also followed us, and the prayers of our brethren have not been in vain.

We sailed from Dover on the morning of 12th April 1839. Soon its white cliffs – its chalky hills – were left behind, and after three hours' sail over a boisterous sea we landed in Boulogne. No sooner had we landed, than the demand for our passports, the pacing of the *gens d'armes* along the shore, and the general aspect of the people, reminded us that we were in a less favoured land than we had left. We wished to press on to Paris that night, as we were afraid of not reaching Marseilles before the 21st, the day when the Alexandrian steamer was to sail, but we found that there was no *diligence* till next morning. In this there was a kind design of providence, intended both to encourage and teach us, as we found before the evening had past.

Boulogne is said to contain 25,000 inhabitants, of whom 5,000 are

English visitors. It was not till evening that we were able to ascertain any facts regarding the Jews here. We had been told that two Jews had lately come from Dover, who resided near our hotel, but that they were men of the world rather than devout Israelites. In the evening, however, we were visited by a very interesting Jew, a person of education and agreeable manners, who spoke English fluently. He told us his history. Originally possessed of a small fortune, he had exhausted it in travelling for the sake of his brethren, having gone to North America, to investigate the question whether or not the Indians there are really the descendants of the ten tribes. He had lived a year among the Winebegos and Micmacs, learned the Cherokee and Oneida languages, conformed to their manners, often living almost naked, all in order to ascertain that question, which he did not hesitate to decide in the negative. He was now spending his time in retirement, with the view of being able to recruit his resources, so as to undertake new journeys among his brethren in other parts, and especially in Palestine. The circumstance of our being on our way to Palestine had chiefly induced him to visit us. In the course of conversation, we stated the feeling of love to Israel which had led us to go forth on this journey; and Dr. Keith, with great fervour, pictured the outcast state of Israel, and how plainly it seemed to be on account of some sin lying at their door, urging him to consider what the sin could be. In reply, the Jew spoke of God's general love and mercy; and when we in return exhibited the way of pardon and acceptance, he became much affected, chiefly, he said, because we manifested such interest in him, and such kindness. He added, that he wished there were more of the Church of Scotland's Missionaries; and then immediately explained himself, that it was only in one sense he could express such a wish, for he could not desire our success in converting his brethren – but if any should accomplish this, it would be in the way of kindness. He had been long seeking the truth, and thought he was still doing so, but was not convinced that it lay with us. He argued that the Jews had got their laws *for ever*; but was silent when we pointed to the new covenant promised in Jeremiah (Jeremiah 31:33). In speaking of Jesus, he made some interesting admissions. The character and doings of Jesus Christ were most wonderful, and the success of Christianity in the world was the doing of God, in order to alleviate the misery of men; for had Christianity not existed, he shuddered to think what might have been the state of nations. When pressed with the question, 'Would Jesus, so excellent a character as he admitted him to be, declare himself *Son of God,* if he were not really so?' he was again silent, and seemed confused. He thought that God may possibly have prospered Christianity for the sake of *the Jews*; for *true Christianity* had never persecuted them. He had heard of Dr. Keith's work on Prophecy, expressed delight at meeting with the author, and on being presented with the Doctor's last work on the Evidences, requested him to write his name upon it. When presented with a Hebrew New Testament, on which we had written that we would often pray that he might be brought to light and peace, he shewed much emotion. Once or twice, after rising to go away, he resumed his discourse. On finally taking leave, which he did with tears running down his face, he said with great emphasis, 'If you wish to gain a Jew, treat him as a brother.' From him we learned that there were only eight families of Jews here, and that the children of one of these attend a Christian school.

This being the first night of our inquiries after the scattered sheep in a foreign land, we could not but feel peculiar encouragement from this interview. It seemed as if the Lord was in haste to give us a token of his presence.

Next day (April 13) at ten o'clock we started for Paris, a distance of 140 miles, in the *diligence*, a cumbrous, heavy waggon, enormously loaded with passengers and luggage, and boxes of treasure.

About two in the morning (Sabbath), the diligence arrived at Beauvais where we were delayed for some hours. Our information had led us to expect that we should have been in Paris before Sabbath morning broke, and we felt this violation of the Holy Day very painfully. As morning advanced we saw the people of the villages going forth to labour just as on other days – ploughmen in the fields, women at their cottage-doors, children at play. We soon found that buying and selling, and every sort of amusement, were the chief occupations of the people of France on the holy Sabbath.

On reaching Paris, we refreshed ourselves, and set out for Marboeuf Chapel, where divine service is conducted in English. The streets presented an endless scene of gaiety and show. There was scarcely a shop shut, and the people literally thronged every street, all in their best holiday dress. Our way led through the Champs Elysées, crowded with people of all ranks; each determined to find their Elysium in every form of pleasure, and openly defying the words of the Holy One of Israel (Isaiah 58:13). Even children were there, boys and girls skipping at their games, and amusing themselves on gaudily painted swings. The well-conditioned and fashionable were parading up and down; many eating and drinking; the noblesse riding in all kinds of vehicles. It might be a scene like this that was witnessed in the days of Noah, or when Lot went out of Sodom – eating, drinking, planting, building, etc. Even now the day of Christ would 'come as a snare' upon all the earth (Luke 17:26,30)!

We felt the contrast when we got within the walls of the Chapel. While worshipping there with a devout band we seemed to have exchanged the din and confusion of Babel for the peace and stillness of the Holy Place. In the evening we heard a French sermon from Frederic Monod, in the upper chamber of the Oratoire, on Paul being sent 'to open the blind eyes': the assembly was small, but lively and fervent, and the singing of the Psalms in French was very sweet; it seemed to be with all the heart. In canonical hours the French Protestants use a short liturgy; they have also a short extempore prayer. Out of a population in Paris of 800,000, only 2,000 attend regularly any Protestant place of worship. Still the state of Protestantism is much improved. Not long ago scarcely one faithful sermon was heard in Paris, now fourteen are preached every Sabbath-day; and there are Protestant schools, attended by 800 children, two-thirds of whom are children of Catholic parents. The Popish party are active, bringing to the city some of their best preachers, who have increased the attendance at their churches, but made scarcely any impression on the infidel part of the population. No city seems more to resemble Sodom (Revelation 11:8). Even in our way from the church, we saw some of the horrors of a Parisian Sabbath evening; gambling and other scenes of profligacy being plainly visible from the street.

This morning (Monday, April 15), Mr. Evans from Edinburgh, and other excellent friends to whom we were introduced, assisted us in our inquiries and forwarded all our arrangements. In regard to the Jews, we found that they are not numerous, and are mostly infidels. Frederic Monod said that there had been efforts made for the conversion of the Jews but with no success. He knew of no instance of real conversion among them in Paris. They are scattered through the mass of the population, and thus are lost to the Christian eye – and hence, in some degree, we may account for the comparatively little interest taken in this people by Christians here. The eye of the Christian in Paris rests on the masses of infidelity, and when he sees *these*, 'he is moved with compassion', and can look no farther.

We saw some splendid buildings. The Church of the Magdalene, The Palaces, The Pillar in the Place Vendome, and many others. We had time to walk round the city and see some of its magnificence. But even had this been Babylon with its hanging gardens and walls of brass, we would rather have found out Israel by the riverside, hanging their harps on the willows, than gazed on the trophies of Atheism and the abodes of guilt.

On Tuesday afternoon (April 16) we set out for Chalons-sur-Saone. While riding up the banks of the Seine and across the Marne the country was very pleasant. Beautiful villages seem to be characteristic of French scenery. One or two handsome chateaux appear, with gilded railings according to French taste.

When we awoke next morning, we were approaching Troyes, a decayed-looking town, containing 28,000 inhabitants. The white and red blossoms of the cherry, the apricot and the peach trees met the eye in every garden we passed. Vineyards were now more frequent, the vines just beginning to bud. Bundles of sticks were lying ready to support them, when they should begin to sprout. In the plains, a field of vines and a field of wheat generally alternate, affording the necessaries and luxuries of life, corn and wine. Some of the fields are ploughed in the circular manner, as in the Carse of Gowrie.[1] We then came to the Aube, another tributary of the Seine, within view of some gently rising hills. There were with us in the diligence two young Roman Catholic lads, very open and amiable, with whom we got into free conversation. As we were distributing tracts from the windows to the people that passed by, one of them offered to join us in our employment, and both seemed happy at being presented with tracts for themselves. Indeed, one of them took a good supply with him to distribute in Lyons, where he resides.

About sunset we reached Chatillon-sur-Seine. Walking onward beyond the town, while the postilions were changing horses, we found it a quiet peaceful spot, the scenery resembling the banks of the Jed a little above Jedburgh.[2] In this district, and indeed along all our journey, we observed how carefully in France a church has been attached to every

---

1. *Carse* is a Scots word describing an extensive stretch of alluvial land. The Carse of Gowrie is the fertile belt of agricultural land on the north bank of the Firth of Tay in Scotland which extends from Perth to Dundee.
2. Jedburgh is a town in the border district of Scotland on the banks of Jed Water, a tributary of the River Teviot.

small village. Popery has here allowed none to escape its grasp, nor grudged to bring its ordinances to the door of the poorest villagers.

We reached Dijon about half-past six in the morning, and made up for the uncomfortable rest of the diligence by a few hours' sleep at the *Hotel de la Galère*. The town is marked out by a remarkably slender, tapering spire shooting up from the cathedral. About midday we called upon the Protestant clergyman, M. Alfonse Frontin, a young man labouring patiently for the truth. He has the charge of the Protestant population, who amount to 200 souls, but they are very lifeless. He told us (and we found his information verified by an intelligent member of his congregation), that there are about 400 Jews here. None of the French Protestants in the town have ever turned their attention to Israel but M. Oster, the Jewish missionary from Strasburg, has visited the place. M. Frontin went with us to the house of Moses Israel, the Rabbi, a feeble old man, of no education, and very poor. A young Jew was our guide, who at first bitterly opposed all we said on the subject of religion, but soon became interested, and at parting took some tracts, at the same time positively refusing any remuneration for his trouble in going about with us. When M. Oster was here he visited the synagogue desiring to speak in a friendly way with the Jews; but they treated him very ill, and many even followed him through the streets and threw back his tracts.

In the evening, while preparing to set out, one of us met a pleasant little boy, looking at the diligence, who eagerly accepted the offer of a book suited to his age. Soon after he returned, bringing with him an old man, dressed in a blue frock, for whom he asked a tract. This old man was his father, and the father and son were Jews! The father looked at our Hebrew Bible and read some verses aloud. We gave him the life of Dr. Cappadose and a New Testament in French – both of which he took with as much joy as his little boy, shaking hands with us more than once at the window of the diligence. At the same time, another man came forward and asked for one of our Hebrew tracts: he proved to be a Jew going to Lyons, but sceptical in his views, like most of the Jews in France. With him we had some conversation at various periods of our journey, and gave him the Life of Cappadose on leaving his company.

At the *Table d'Hôte*, the young Roman Catholic had mentioned his conversations with us, and recommended the tracts which we were giving away. The consequence was, that before the vehicle had started a person came running down from the inn, to get some for the use of the company.

At length, fairly seated, we found a Roman Catholic priest in our company. With him we conversed sometimes in French, sometimes in Latin, on various topics, chiefly, however, on the subject of *peace with God*. He received from us, and read the tract *La Bonne Nouvelle*. At sunset, taking out his prayer-book, he requested to be left to himself for a little, and having completed his evening devotions, conversed with us for nearly two hours longer, occasionally with some warmth.

At half-past five next morning, we were at Chalons, where we had to wait two hours for the steamboat at a miserable inn, *Hotel des Diligences*. We heard that there are a few lively Protestants here. At seven we embarked on the Saone, a river that flows so quietly that it is difficult to tell which way it runs. Our voyage from Chalons to Lyons cost no more than 2.5 francs each, though the distance is about 100 miles – there being an opposition steamboat on the river. The group on board was interesting. There were peasants from Grenoble with broad straw hats, frocks, and wooden shoes; soldiers in the showy uniform of France; sailors with the Italian cap, brown or red; three Roman Catholic priests with the three-cornered hat, black bands with white edge black cloak and sash, and buckles in their shoes; and women with the Swiss bonnet, that seemed to be falling over the forehead. The sail was delightful, the day warm and clear. Many of the sloping vineyards on the banks reminded us of Isaiah's expression (Isaiah 5:1), 'My beloved hath a vineyard on a horn the son of oil', i.e. a little hill projecting like a horn, with its soil rich and fertile. Tournou is a picturesque little town, on the right bank of the river, having a cathedral with two fantastic spires. We afterwards learned that the Spirit has lately been quickening a few souls there. Maçon, halfway down the Saone, is a large town with a handsome bridge over the river. It was after leaving this town, that we first saw the snowy ridge of the Lower Alps, and part of the Jura range, in the direction of Geneva. We next sailed past Trevoux, romantically situated; its old walls and battlements hanging over the river, and the church perched upon a rock. The banks are beautifully lined with white stone. It was once the resort of a famous literary society.

About five o'clock, the boat reached Lyons. The approach is very picturesque, and becomes at last magnificent. The river seems to run along a passage cut through high solid rocks into the heart of the town. On one of the high rising grounds that meet the eye in sailing up, stood the Roman amphitheatre where Blandina was put to death. Some remains of it still exist, and the house of Pothinus is pointed out in the city.

We took up our abode in the *Hotel de l'Europe*, and were soon visited by M. Cordes, the devoted Protestant minister, who invited us to spend the day with him. M. Cordes, in going through the town, pointed out the marketplace where the five Swiss young men were burned at the time of the Reformation; and shewed us Peter Waldo's street, which is still called *Maudite*, i.e. accursed. Some streets of lofty houses reminded us of the venerable piles of building in the old town of Edinburgh.

There are 200,000 souls here, and the trade is very great. There are 6,000 Protestants, and several Protestant clergy; but none evangelical or orthodox except M. Cordes. M. Adolphe Monod, now professor at Montauban, was once pastor here, but was expelled from communion by the Neologian[3] pastors. M. Cordes succeeded, and has now a church of his own. He has 400 hearers, very lively Christians; and there have been many conversions under his ministry. God remembers his ancient witnesses in Lyons. 'This Mount Zion wherein thou hast dwelt' (Psalm 74:2) is not an unmeaning or unavailing plea, whether offered for the land of Israel or for other places once visited by the Spirit. There are about 400 French Protestant clergy in the kingdom, but of these scarcely half are orthodox. Of late faithful pastors have been on the increase and Evangelical Protestant congregations have been formed at Chalons, Maçon and Trevoux, the places we passed today. The Jews have a synagogue here. Mr. Wilson, a Christian friend of M. Cordes, told us that he went round with M. Oster, and found fifty Jewish families, most of whom were sceptical in their opinions. He knew of only one convert, a young man, who had gone to Montlimart to follow a trade. There are, however, some Jewish children at the Protestant school, eight at the weekday and three at the infant school. If they had means, the number might be increased.

Next morning (Saturday, April 20) we sailed down the rapid Rhone for Avignon, a distance of about 100 miles. Again the Lower Alps appeared on our left – beautiful in the light of the morning sun – some of them snow-clad at the summit. The scenery on the river is exceedingly beautiful, and continues full of interest, until the frequency of similar views makes the eye weary. There is more majesty in the scenery of this

---

3. The term *neologian* refers to adherents of the theology which arose from the period of the Enlightenment on the Continent. It was greatly influenced by men like Reimarus, Semler and Lessing, and it stressed that biblical revelation must be subject to human reason.

river than on the Saone. Hills and rocks enclose it. The vineyards on its banks are very frequent, raised on terraces, like the steps of an amphitheatre. Sometimes the hills are bleak and wild, reminding us of Glencoe and other of our native mountains. Sometimes there is a fine open country studded with towns and villages, villas and gardens.

Next to the city we had left, we felt deepest interest in sailing past Vienne, close to the riverside on the left, early renowned, along with Lyons, for its martyrs, and its devoted Christians, whose calm and heavenly spirit is so beautifully manifest in their letter to the Church of Smyrna. An intelligent passenger pointed our eye to a very precipitous hill among the Alps: 'It is at the foot of this hill that Provence begins'. We passed the mouth of the Isere, flowing into the Rhone, and came to Valence, pleasantly situated – a place where Napoleon spent a great part of his youth. We next passed in sight of Montlimart, a town resembling Abernethy on the Tay. We were continually sailing under bridges, of which there are seventeen across this river. One of these, called Port Saint l'Esprit, is a very splendid one, and has eighteen arches, each large arch including in it a smaller one, that the water may flow through unimpeded. It spans the river at a very broad point. We often met long trains of horses or mules, perhaps sixty in a train, dragging a chain of boats laden with merchandise up the river; and once or twice an immense haystack was conveyed up the stream in this manner.

It was five o'clock when we reached the celebrated Avignon, an ancient palace of the Popes of France. Indeed, it seems a town of ruined palaces and towers. Everything combined to make us feel the exquisite beauty of its situation. The evening was calm, the air soft, the sky clear; the trees, in which the town is embosomed, wore their most refreshing verdure; the clock sounded from the tower amidst the stillness, reminding us of the vesper-bell. The Alps in the distant background, and the splendid river, completed the scene.

But our object was not to linger over scenery, or enjoy historical memorials. We needed to be self-denied. Accordingly, we sailed on to Beucaire, and there during the night exchanged our vessel, and moved onward to the mouth of the Rhone. In the vessel, we found that the bell had a cross on it with this inscription, 'Sit nomen Dei benedictum' (Blessed be the name of God). It was one of the baptized bells of Popery. We soon reached Arles, an old town, full of antiquities, though none are of much importance. After that point, the scenery becomes totally uninteresting. Our Engineer was an Englishman, who seeing us distributing tracts to the passengers, became very zealous in the same work. He was a steady Protestant by profession, though it was now ten years since he came to this station, and during all that time had been only twice in a place of worship.

When nine leagues from Arles, and as many from Marseilles, at the mouth of the Rhone, about nine o'clock am., the steamer was completely stopped in its progress. A wind, called the Mestrael, which had not retarded the boat for eighteen months before, met us in the face; and the current joining with this adverse force, made the vessel unmanageable. It was immediately resolved to cast anchor close by an island at the mouth of the Rhone – a small, flat island, very barren and sandy. This done, we all landed, waiting till the wind should change. We found no cultivation on the island. About twenty asses were feeding on rushes. The inhabitants consisted of twelve or sixteen families of fishermen; their huts were formed of rushes, each hut surmounted by a cross on the roof, as a protection from storms and other accidents. A few of the huts had vines (though not luxuriant) growing at the door, and forming arbours. There was also one fig-tree on the island, a proof of the mildness of the climate. The language used by the people is neither French nor Italian, but a mixture of both. They have no church nor school nearer than Arles or Marseilles. Only a very few could read French and understand it. However, as these few might be readers to the rest, we were anxious to leave tracts among them. The Engineer made his appearance, offering to go to every house with them. One tract, *Religion de l'Argent* (the Money-Religion) – a satirical exposure of Popery – was got hold of by a French captain, who read it aloud to a crowd of bystanders. The Engineer, not content with his day's work, asked us to send him more from home, and he would distribute them at various times in the course of his voyages. 'What would it be to England,' said he, 'to send a man to preach the truth in every village of France?' Some of us went apart among the grass and rushes for prayer and reading the Scriptures. We did this in the forenoon, and again at evening, with the Rhone at our feet, in the soft air, with a clear sky above, and perfect stillness round. That night we had no other couch than the floor of the cabin.

Before morning the wind changed, and by half-past eight we reached Marseilles, where we found rest at the *Hotel du Pavilion*. The approach to the city from the sea is magnificent – high hills or rather rocks form the west side of the entrance, and deep blue waters, deep even in the midst of the harbour, floated up the vessel to its anchorage. The harbour is formed by the sea running into a natural basin which is always full, the ebb of the tide being less than six feet deep. It is defended by very strong fortifications, and these are splendidly built. Ships from all nations ride at anchor in the harbour, and people of all countries are found in its streets. The population is 150,000 – of these only 2,000 are even nominally Protestant. They have, however, three evangelical pastors, with a Sabbath school attended by 60 children, and a weekday school attended by 50 girls and 40 boys – both of very recent origin. This information was given to us by one of the pastors, M. Monod. We found time to call on the Rabbi, a smart Frenchman. Though a Jew, his opinions are those of the Neologians. He denies the fall of man, believes that the curse on the ground was a blessing, and that a new heart means the improvement of the mind. He rejects the Talmud, and though he does not avow his rejection of the Bible, yet denies the restoration of Israel to their own land; and disbelieves the promise of a Messiah, on the ground that the good of the universe, and not of one nation, is what we are to look for. Most of the young Jews here are quite given up to the world, and cherish infidel views. The Rabbi was willing to take tracts, was proud to shew his synagogue, and said that there were about 1000 Jews in the town. We got more information in the evening; but there is very little to interest a friend of Israel here.

We had by this time ascertained that a steamer had sailed for Malta the day before, and that we must wait ten days for another. We resolved, therefore, to spend the time in visiting as much of Italy as we could. A boat was about to sail for Leghorn called the *Sully*, in which we embarked, enjoying a most beautiful day, and smooth sea. The vessel coasted the shore, which is bold and precipitous. We had a near view of Toulon, the bay of the French navy, and the place where Napoleon first pointed the cannon. Its harbour is shut in by hills, and strongly fortified.

The Isle of Hieres next came in sight, whose salubrious climate draws invalids to its shores. The scenery continued rocky and pictur-esque, the waters deep blue, and calm - 'a glassy sea'. At night the moon rose clear, and the stars were very brilliant; the waters glittered with peculiar brightness under such a firmament. We united in prayer in the cabin, and 'slept in peace, for God sustained us'.

At seven next morning we were on the coast of Italy. Numerous villages attracted the eye, built of stone that seemed remarkably white and clean, especially under the morning sun. Omeglia, Allasio, Albenga, were all successively pointed out close to the water-edge, the olive-clad Alps (Alpes maritimae) pressing hard upon them in the background. Allasio stands on a hill, and the spire of its church is a fine object. The hills round these towns are dotted with villas, and this continued to be the aspect of the coast till we reached Genoa. Italy is indeed a beautiful region, but 'gross darkness covers its people'. The Engineer of our vessel, a pious Presbyterian of the Synod of Ulster, agreed to circulate tracts on board, if we would send a supply, and proposed to give them to the other engineers along this coast, all of whom are Englishmen and Protestants.

We entered the splendid bay of Genoa about midday. The finest view of Genoa is from the sea. The eye is almost dazzled in wandering round the bay, by the irregular tiers of marble palaces, fantastic towers, and spires, the remnants of ancient days. The whiteness of the marble and the bright colouring of many of the houses, has a very striking appearance. Steep sloping hills enclose it from behind, and it is walled and fortified on every side; the cannon pointing down upon the town. Entering the harbours, the galley-slaves loaded with chains attracted our attention. They work in a floating machine, like the treadmill, used for bringing up the mud of the harbour. They are sentenced by fiction of law, not for life, but for 120 years.

On landing we were examined by the Police. Our names and the place where we meant to lodge in the city were demanded, betraying a jealousy which made us feel that we were no longer in a free country. We took up our residence at the *Hotel Croix de St Malte.*

The streets of Genoa are very narrow, and delightfully cool. Originally carriages could not go along them, but now some of them are made a little broader. Most of the houses have pilasters and entrances of white marble. Some are entirely built of marble. One lately built by Paganini was pointed out to us. It is very common to see pictures fixed into the walls on the outside of the houses, in the porches, and even in the interior of hotels. Among these, the picture of Andrea Doria frequently occurs.

The appearance of the inhabitants attracted our notice. The females wear a beautiful veil, which covers the back part of the head and the shoulders, meeting over the breast. Some wear it of a fine white, some of bright variegated colours; to all it gives a clean, tidy appearance. The number of Ecclesiastics here is remarkable. We met twenty-eight in the priests' dress in a ten minutes' walk. Of these many are not priests, but all are connected with the ecclesiastical office. We here also, for the first time met with sandalled monks, bareheaded, rough-looking men, the Dominicans in a brown, and the Franciscans in a black dress; the rude cord round the waist and pendent crucifix, the bare head, and cowl, marking them all.

April 25

We began our inquiries yesterday, but received fuller information this day. We called upon the Swiss Protestant minister, who received us kindly. Genoa contains from 90,000 to 100,000 inhabitants. Of these, only 25 are British residents, and 150 Swiss, and these have one place of worship between them. He told us that they are allowed to worship only by the sufferance of Government: they are strictly watched, and no Italian would be allowed to join their communion, even though convinced of the truth. He appeared to be sadly disheartened. Happy day when Evangelists shall be permitted to stand and proclaim the truth in the streets of Genoa! We waited upon the English Consul, who introduced us to Signor Becchi, the vice-consul, a Roman Catholic, but a very mild, candid, amiable man. He and a young English gentleman, a merchant from Ancona, gave us information regarding the Jews. They have a synagogue here, but there are only about 250 residents. The reason of there being so few is said to be, that 'one Genoese has cunning enough to cheat two Jews'. So they say of Lucca, that 'one Luccese can overreach three Jews'.

The Jews here are not strict in their religious observances, but often do business on their Sabbath, and several of them have become Roman Catholics. Only three or four months ago, a family of seven was baptized with great pomp, simply for the sake of worldly gain. There was also recently a Jewish child baptized in the Protestant church; but the reason was, that the mother was a Protestant, and had made that agreement at her marriage. There are not more than four or five Jewish families of wealth and respectability in the town.

Signor Becchi introduced us to a Jew from Gibraltar, named Moses Parienti, an elderly man, of an amiable disposition, and one who was well acquainted with his nation. His beard was undressed, which he begged us to excuse, as he was then mourning for the recent death of his wife. He told us that in Genoa there are few learned Jews, and most of them are poor. He reckoned about fifty families; but many move from place to place. They are not now, he said, admitted to the *casinos* (clubs), although formerly they were; at which exclusion many of the citizens expressed regret. He knows that, in Italy, Roman Catholics are willing to receive Jewish children and baptize them, if the nurses do (what is sometimes done) carry them off, and take them to a priest; and, according to his statement, throughout all Tuscany the Jews enjoy perfect freedom. He represented Leghorn as the chief place in Italy for them, and thought that there were nearly 4,000 there, with forty managers to take charge of their civil concerns, and a flourishing school for boys and girls. He offered us letters to Signore Abodram and Franchetti who are at the head of the nation there. There are no Jews at Civita Vecchia. The King of Naples allows none to dwell in his dominions. There are none in Sardinia, because that island was part of the Spanish kingdom of Arragon, from which all were expelled. Not long ago, a Jew named Israel went there in disguise, but was at last forced to flee. There are none in Corsica. The French do not forbid it, but the native population are bigoted to excess. At Milan there are 1,500, and some have property in land. At Verona, Pavia, Padua, Parma, and Venice, a good number are found. At Florence and Modena, there are a few; and at Pisa also; but the families there are chiefly from Leghorn. At Ferrara, Becchi reckoned about 4,000 souls. At Turin there are 50 Spanish, and 1,500 German Jews; the latter of whom have a fine synagogue, and use a different liturgy from the Spanish. At Nice there are 400 or 500, and many of them from England. Nine months ago, an order was issued by government to put them in *ghetto*; but the Prussian Consul there being a Jew refused to go, and his remonstrances had the effect of leaving the matter undetermined. At Lucca none are allowed to settle, but many reside for a short time. Every three months they must get from the Duke a new permission to remain. Through all Piedmont they enjoy considerable liberty – and hence Jews are found at Trieste, Cassagli, Asti, Alessandria, Acqui, and Cuneo. At Rome, there are 5,000 or 6,000 who live in ghetto; and though much oppressed, yet still remain, because they make money. At Gibraltar there used to be 6,000 families, but these are now reduced to 2,000. At Corfu there are many. A few at Athens. The Portuguese consul-general there, Signor Pacifico, was a Jew from Lisbon.

Signor Becchi spoke of the contributions made by the Jews for the Holy Land. They keep boxes in the synagogues, over which it is written, *'For Jerusalem'*, or, *'For Saphet '* etc.; and at a certain time, a Commissioner is appointed to see what these contain, and to send the contents to the Holy Land. The Jews of Italy write pure Hebrew, and not Italian in Hebrew characters. He said they write really 'the holy tongue'.

The English gentleman from Ancona gave us much information

regarding the Jews of that city. He thought that there were about 4,000 there, or nearly one-fifth of the whole population, which is 24,000. They are scrupulous about engaging in business on their Sabbath, and as fair in their dealings as any in the town. At Lent and Good Friday, they are shut up in their houses; and their quarter of the town is called *ghetto*, as at Rome. There are other oppressions to which they are subjected; yet still they continue in the town, because they make money, the native population being stupid and indolent. They are not allowed to visit casinos, nor to buy land; but many of them have villas. Mr. Lewis Waye spent six or eight months there, and often visited their synagogues. Most of the young men are deists, and devoted to the world. It is said that occasionally Roman Catholics get hold of their children and baptize them, and then they must be brought up as Christians.

We afterwards mounted up a steep path to the north of Genoa, and came upon a fine view of the Ligurian Hills. A lovely valley watered by a rivulet lay beneath, the hills on all sides terraced for vines. Villages were scattered here and there, and six churches were in sight. At six in the evening, we bade farewell to Genoa. It is a lovely town, but the shadow of death rests upon it. Popery reigns undisturbed, holding all in chains.

April 26
Early this morning, we cast anchor in the harbour of Leghorn. The morning was misty and rainy, unlike the sky of Italy, and the town appeared flat and cheerless. Sailing up a canal into the heart of the town, we soon after found ourselves comfortably settled in the *San Marco Albergo,* a hotel kept by a Scotsman, Mr. D. Thomson, well known to us for the kindness which he shewed to our countryman, Rev. Mr. Martin, minister of St George's, Edinburgh, during his last illness. He and Mrs. Thomson received us most cordially, and we found their house a home indeed. Hearing that Leghorn was a free port, we thought that it might be free to receive the gospel; and accordingly, without reserve, gave tracts to each of the eight men who carried up our luggage, and to some bystanders. Scarcely, however, had an hour elapsed, when an officer appeared at the inn, making inquiry if we were the persons who had been distributing books. Our box of books and tracts, and our bag of Hebrew books, were immediately sealed up and carried off, and the two elder members of the Deputation summoned to appear before the Commissary of Police without delay. After a long examination, it was decided that the books and tracts be sent to the Censor at Florence, and

that until his report be made, we be dismissed.

Leghorn is a flourishing commercial port, visited annually by 300 ships from Britain alone, but the state of religion is very low. There is a handful of Swiss and German Protestants: but not a single instance has occurred of a native Italian openly renouncing Popery. One reason for this may be found in the law of the country, which strictly forbids apostasy from the Romish faith. And another reason, no less powerful, is to be found in the licentiousness of Protestants in Italy. The English in that country are generally gay and dissolute, regardless of all religion. One of the most profligate Italian towns is Florence, and the English residents take the lead in dissipation. Hence it has become an almost universal impression that Protestantism is the way to infidelity.

It is to be feared that a great number of the young Romish priests are infidels at heart, and many are great gamblers. On the other hand, some appear to be conscientious men and exemplary in their lives, and several private persons of their community seem to be really Christians. The sincere priests preach most vehemently against prevailing vices. We were told of one who a few days before, preaching against breaking the Sabbath, spoke in this way: 'Some of you will say, I have a dispensation from the Bishop or from the Pope; but I say this is the word of God, and the Bishop or the Pope is nothing to the word of God.' We heard of another priest who began with the sins of the government, and then spoke of the sins of the priesthood in a most severe manner. He said, 'We should be the light of the world, and what are ye but darkness? We should be the salt of the earth, what are ye but salt without savour, ruining your own souls and the souls of others?'

The priests in Italy are in a great measure losing their hold upon the people, and confession is greatly neglected. We were told of a priest, a fortnight before, who preached to the people that it was lawful for a wife in certain circumstances to steal from her husband; if he was a spend-thrift and neglected her, she should take what she needed. On being afterwards asked by a Protestant gentleman how he could preach such doctrines to the people, and if it would not be better that the wife should tell her case to the church? 'The church!' said the priest; 'they care as much for the church as you do.'

During the time of our visit, the canonization of four new saints expected shortly to take place at Rome, engrossed much of the public conversation. At Monte Nero, three miles from town, there is a famous shrine of the Madonna, to which pilgrimages are made at all times. The

Dominicans lately found an image of the Virgin there, which has brought their order into great repute. When the Pope visited Leghorn several years ago, the great square of the town presented a scene worthy of being noticed. An immense multitude crowded the square to excess. The Pope appeared, and all fell on their knees. His holiness then stood over the kneeling multitude and pronounced his benediction. It was one of those scenes which irresistibly led the spectator to the prophetic words regarding the Man of Sin, 'He, as God, sitteth in the temple of God, shewing himself that he is God' (2 Thessalonians 2:4).

We spent the Jewish Sabbath in making acquaintance with some intelligent Jews, of whose information we hoped to avail ourselves in the beginning of the week. On our own Sabbath (April 28) we attended service at the English Chaplaincy. In the evening, Dr. Black preached in the hotel, in the large room to a numerous audience, chiefly of our own countrymen. All the day long, the town was full of bustle and gaiety. The ringing of bells, and the music of the military, dissipated the Sabbath stillness. Popery has abolished the fourth commandment, as effectually as it has done the second. Instead of teaching 'Remember the Sabbath-day to keep it holy', they teach by precept and by example, 'Remember to keep holy the festivals'.

In passing along the streets to the Chaplaincy, we observed with a shudder criminals at work cleaning the streets, chained one to another, and having their crimes stamped upon their backs. One was marked 'Furto violento' (robbery); another 'Uxorcidio' (killing his wife); another, 'Omicidia in rissa' (manslaughter in a quarrel).

On Friday evening, and frequently during our stay, we visited the synagogue. It is a large handsome building, and reckoned the finest in Europe, with the exception of that of Amsterdam. There are two galleries for women, one above the other, the lattice-work of which is beautiful. The place of the ark is lined with variegated marble; the door veiled with a curtain of black velvet, flowered with silver and having a motto from the Psalms. The reading-desk is also of marble, the velvet cloth bearing the motto, 'The law of the Lord is perfect, converting the soul'. There were perhaps 500 Jews present, but few seemed to take any interest in the service. Close by the ark stood two Orientals, dressed in eastern costume, venerable men, with long grey beards, lately come from Jerusalem. Many came to them to kiss their hand, and get it laid upon their head. Others also gave this benediction.

Near the two Easterns, stood another Jew of some eminence from

Saloniki. Jews from Greece, Barbary, Turkey, Syria and Arabia are often here, as we learned from an English Jew whom we met in the synagogue. At the door, for the first time we observed the box for alms, having the Hebrew word for 'alms' over it, and another with this inscription in Hebrew, 'For the land of Israel, let it (the temple) be built and erected speedily in our days'.

The whole population of Leghorn in 1835, including the suburbs, was 76,397, and the Jews at that time in all Tuscany were reckoned at 6,486. Now (1839), in Leghorn alone there are 9,000 or 10,000 Jews, some of them among the most wealthy men in the land. They have much influence over the government, and most of them are very liberal in their religious opinions.

From the printed statistics of the Tuscan States we gathered the following facts. 'The Papal States having discouraged the Jews, they have flocked into Tuscany. The Duke of Tuscany granted land to the Jews in a marshy district, called Maremne, on condition of their cultivating it. About a thousand *siccate* of land were taken by the Jews for the purpose of colonization, near the town of Follonica, and nearly 300 labourers employed in clearing away brushwood, trees, etc.. It was proposed to divide the district into twelve *podère* or separate estates, and erect a villa, or *fattoria*, to superintend the whole.' The Jewish schoolmaster at Leghorn informed us that this project had not succeeded, and that very few Jews had offered to settle there. It seems vain to try to plant Israel anywhere till they be planted again upon their own land.

There are occasionally conversions to Popery among them. But about three years ago, there occurred a sincere and somewhat singular conversion. A Jew of influence and education declared that he was led to embrace Christianity in a manner that resembles Dr. Cappadose's account of his change. He immediately renounced the world, and is now in a monastery at Sienna, where he occasionally preaches.

On the forenoon of Monday (April 29), we visited an Eastern Rabbi, named Bolaffi, whose acquaintance we had made on Saturday. He was seated on a sofa in the Eastern fashion. His dress was that of the East – his appearance was imposing, and his action and elocution were very striking. We found him frank, intelligent, and learned. He liked better, however, to speak on general subjects than on religion; but at length did enter into some religious discussion. We spoke of the nature of Messiah. Bolaffi said, 'He is to be a king, and a prophet, but not a priest'. We quoted Psalm 110. He denied that to be spoken of Messiah and thought that David was meant. We maintained his divine nature, and among other passages quoted Isaiah 9:6. He admitted that the rendering 'Mighty God' was justified by the Hebrew, but evaded the application, by bidding us notice that the Prophet says only, he shall be 'named' so. He argued that the Protestants ought to return to the observance of the seventh day as their Sabbath, because the change was an act of the Romish church. We came back to more vital questions, and referred to Psalm 51, 'Purge me with hyssop'. He got away from this by turning his remarks to *ruach* (Spirit), arguing that the word applied even to beasts. As to the way of pardon he maintained that repentance was all that was needed, quoting 2 Samuel 12:13, where David said, 'I have sinned,' and Nathan answered, 'The Lord hath put away thy sin.' He had read the New Testament, and his knowledge of it enabled him to object that Christ was not Prince of peace, because he himself says, 'I am not come to send peace, but a sword.' He contended that the Sabbath should be so kept that a fire ought not to be lighted on that day even in Siberia. At parting, he said, 'Christians shut us out of Paradise, but we think that all who do good works may enter, whether they be Catholics, Mahometans, or Protestants.' Each of us in turn had joined in the conversation; but Dr. Black was the chief speaker, being able to use the Italian language very fluently.

We left him and went to see the Jews' Library. Several volumes lay open on the table, and many Jews were in the room. Those present vied with each other in shewing us Hebrew works upon geography, mathematics, and the sciences. They brought out a Hebrew copy of *Euclid*, and a Hebrew translation of *Philo*, and said that they had *Josephus* also translated into Hebrew. When we had taken a sufficient survey of their books, they led us to their School – a large, commodious building. The classes are arranged after the Lancasterian plan, and there is a regular gradation from those learning the letters and the sound of the vowel points, to those who translate Hebrew into Italian. There are masters to teach drawing, music, history, geography, and writing. English and French are given in the upper classes. Each teacher has a large blackboard, and the alphabet, syllables, vowelpoints, and short sentences are taught from large sheets hung up on the wall, exactly as in our own schools. We found 180 Jewish boys and 80 girls attending the school, all educated free of expense. The advanced boys and girls translated Italian into Hebrew, and *vice versa,* in our presence with great fluency. The young men in the Talmudical class read and translated the 1st chapter of Isaiah with Aben Ezra's Commentary.

Next day we paid Rabbi Bolaffi a second visit. He was affable and polite as before. Six or eight Jews were present in the room. One of us happening to sneeze, he immediately exclaimed, 'Santa!' and another Jew 'Felicita!', that is, *good luck*. After a few remarks on a book which he had in his hand, he stated some of the objections he had to the New Testament. They were such as these: Paul advised a man to remain in the religion wherein he was found, whereas he himself circumcised Timothy, contrary to his own advice. And again, Timothy's mother could not have been a pious woman, for she had married a heathen. He told us he had himself written against Voltaire's works; and brought out a map to shew us the absurdity involved in Voltaire's hypothesis of Israel crossing the Red Sea at low tide. His map and his argument were alike curious. We brought him back to the great question. He argued that a man is free in his will, otherwise he could not be judged for sin, and asserted, as before, that *repentance* is the method of procuring pardon, referring to God's promise, that as soon as the seed of Israel repent He will bring them home. Another of his objections to the New Testament was that *First-born* and *Son*, to which terms much importance is there attached, are no more than names of affection among the Jews. He understood Zechariah's words, 'The man that is my fellow', in the same sense; and Micah 5:2, as proving no more than that Messiah was to be of David's line. We said, 'He *has* come of that line.' 'No; even the New Testament does not say that Christ's genealogy can be traced to David; it only gives Joseph's line.' 'The genealogies were fully known in Christ's time, and publicly appealed to by the Evangelists. Are there any in existence now?' 'Yes, there are some who know their genealogy.' 'Are there any of the line of David now known?' He replied with a look of dignity, *'Io sono'* (I am one). Thus ended our interview with this interesting man. He is a fine example of the Jewish Rabbi; a subtle sophist in argument, deeply read in the literature of the Hebrews, yet so ignorant of general knowledge, that he soberly estimated his nation now scattered through the earth at thirty millions. After leaving him we sent for his acceptance several tracts such as *The City of Refuge* and *The Life of Cappadose*, along with the Italian edition of Dr. Keith's work on Prophecy.

In the evening we returned to the Library to meet a polite, active, young Rabbi, Abraham Piperno. He shewed us a copy of Elias Levita, dated 1541, and Zemach David. He brought out a Hebrew copy of *Euclid*; and a Hebrew Encyclopaedia in five volumes, some of its articles written by himself. He told us that they have three printing presses in Leghorn.

In the course of conversation, we spoke of Isaiah 53 and Daniel 9. His answers were very brief and consisted of little more than a reference to what we would find in a book called *Defence of the Faith*. He believes in the restoration of Israel to their own land. He was not aware of any Jews from Leghorn having gone to Palestine; but Chancellor Uzzielli afterwards told us, that occasionally some of the poor and illiterate do so to die there, believing that thus they shall escape purgatory.

Returning to the hotel, another Jew, a teacher of music, waited upon us, bringing with him a servant who carried for his master a heavy manuscript. It turned out to be a work written by himself against Voltaire and Volney. We soon began to see that he had some selfish object in view and that he was more anxious to sell his manuscript than to buy the truth as it is in Jesus.

Next morning we visited a rich merchant, named Abodram, from Spain, with whom and his family, Mr. Neat, once Jewish missionary here, had been on friendly terms. He had heard of our discussion with the Rabbi, which had indeed made a stir throughout the Jewish quarter. He received us politely, and accepted a Spanish copy of Dr. Keith's work, but did not seem to care much about the object of our journey.

We then proceeded to the Jewish burying ground – 'house of the living' – as we found written over the gate. It is large and extensive, and requires to be so, for it is considered unlawful to lay two dead bodies in the same grave. It is a bare, level enclosure; no cypresses wave over the tombs; a few goats were skipping through the grass. The Jews are compelled by law to bury their dead either in the morning, or at night by torchlight. The older part of the burying ground lying toward the west, is full of tombstones, bearing Spanish inscriptions, for the Jews of Leghorn came originally from Spain. With some natural pride, they point out not a few of these monuments having a coronet graved upon them, which they believe to be the tombs of those among their brethren who were Spanish nobles. Upon some of the tombs are carved hands spread out to bless – marking the grave of a priest; upon others a hand pouring water out of a cup – marking the grave of a Levite. At the head of almost every gravestone are these expressive letters, that is, 'Let his soul be bound up in the bundle of life'.

Another epitaph, probably over a rabbi, runs thus:

'Lament over wisdom, which is perished;
Lament over the law, which is a clod of dust;
Lament over light, which is darkened', etc.

In our way home, an opportunity occurred of calling upon a Rabbi from Barbary, who had a large collection of Hebrew books. Most of them were commentaries of obscure Jews and not in good condition. His wife wore the high, sugarloaf cap peculiar to the Barbary Jewesses. The Jew who accompanied us shewed us a Hebrew manuscript, which he says is prohibited by the Rabbis, containing the theory that, when Christ comes again he will be Messiah. We had some reason to suspect that this was an imposture, and did not purchase it.

The Chancellor Uzzielli very kindly called upon us, and gave us information regarding the civil affairs of the Jews. Of such importance are the Jews here that their feasts are marked in the Almanac, and if a bill falls due on any of these days, they are not required to pay on that day. They are governed as a community or corporation by forty men, called 'Elders'. These elders manage any assessment laid on the nation by government gathering it from their brethren in equable proportions. They also manage cases of divorce, which are not frequent. Napoleon allowed polygamy among them, but it is a thing unknown in their community. The office of elder is hereditary in certain families; and when a vacancy occurs, they select two individuals, and present their names to the Grand Duke, who chooses one of the two thus nominated.

The Jews of Leghorn send about £800 to Palestine every year. This sum is gathered in the boxes at the synagogue doors, and sent to the four holy cities, Jerusalem, Hebron, Saphet, and Tiberias, sometimes by individuals going to Palestine, but more frequently through their mercantile correspondents at Constantinople, where there is an agency appointed to manage such sums sent from any part of the world. The Jews in Leghorn believe in the restoration of their nation to the Holy Land; but, added the Chancellor, it is *'pia credenza, che desid rio'*, 'more a belief of the head, than a desire of the heart'.

A Jew who had been our guide, Jacob Mossias, in prospect of our departure, asked us to give him a Hebrew New Testament, which we did, along with some tracts. We bought several books from him; among others, Abarbinel on the Passover, containing a Jewish map of Palestine, and some singular Jewish woodcuts.

'Come from the four winds, O breath, and breathe upon these slain, that they may live' (Ezekiel 37:9).

We had now taken our passage for Malta, and were preparing to sail next day, when all were summoned to appear before the Police to receive the sentence passed upon us and our books. The Censor had examined and condemned our books. The two elder brethren were therefore commanded to leave Tuscany without delay; the two younger, being supposed to act under their direction, were not commanded but requested to do the same. Many of our tracts were restored to us, but all the copies of Dr. Keith's work on Prophecy were detained, because it contained interpretations opposed to those of the Church of Rome. And thus we were dismissed. We afterwards learned that a sentence of perpetual banishment from Tuscany had been pronounced against us all – a sentence we could easily bear, but one that proves Popery to be still the silencer of the witnesses and the deadly enemy of the truth.

The Jews were considerably interested in our case; and perhaps it was permitted in order to shew them that Popery is equally the enemy of Protestantism and of Israel. The return of the Jews and the fall of Popery are two events that seem intimately connected in prophecy. It was therefore well ordered that, in seeking the lost sheep of the house of Israel, we should meet with treatment at the hand of their oppressors, fitted to awaken in us the cry, 'How long, O Lord'? (Psalm 89:46; Revelation 6:10).

On calmly reviewing all that we had seen of Israel in France and Italy, and considering what might be done to carry the gospel to them, we came to the following conclusions.

In France, the state of the Jews seems to call for the labours of an evangelist or itinerant missionary, for the Jews are not gathered together in great numbers in any one town but distributed among many. Such a missionary would not require a great knowledge of the Talmud and of Jewish learning as in other countries, but rather a mind capable of grappling with the sophisms of infidelity; above all, the power of simply and affectionately urging the gospel upon them. Having the command of the French and Hebrew languages he might be an eminent blessing to the Jews scattered over the towns of France. With regard to Italy, there can be little doubt that Leghorn affords the most promising station. The Jews are more numerous there than in any other Italian town, and it seems probable that the government would not interfere with the labours of a prudent missionary, if these were confined to Jews and Protestants. It appears as if God had shut the door upon our efforts to carry the gospel to the poor blinded Papist, but left the door open to carry the message of mercy to the poor despised Jew. If our Church were to maintain a chaplain for the benefit of our own fellow-countrymen resident in Leghorn – a measure which would be hailed with delight by many Presbyterian families there, who sigh for the privilege of pure gospel ordinances administered in the same form as in their native land – it occurred to us all that this labourer might also turn his efforts toward the Jews. If he were to become intimately acquainted with the Jewish families, which he could easily do, he might, by the blessing of God, carry the sweet savour of Christ into many a domestic circle of Israel in that land of the shadow of death.

In the afternoon of Friday (May 3), we embarked in the *Lycurge* for Malta, our kind friends accompanying us to the boat. Upon the deck of the vessel we met with individuals from many various nations. Besides French, English, and Italians, there were an American traveller, a German, and a young Greek, known by his horizontal moustache and the fantastic dress of his native mountains, full of spirit, and proud of his liberated country. In addition to these, we had the newly appointed Bishop of Tripoli, of the Graeco-Romish church in Syria, a mild-looking man, with very fine long hair, beard and moustache, marked features, and a pleasing expression, dressed in a brown mantle over a red gown, with a purple sash, gold chain, and cross. Two younger priests and a servant accompanied him, all of the same pleasing appearance. We had also several soldiers on board, a Romish priest, several monks, and three veiled nuns from Spain, all on their way to Rome.

We sailed over a calm unruffled sea, and passing the small island of Gorgonna, coasted the more celebrated Elba. A white cloud was leaning on its heights as we passed. Had Napoleon never been there, that island might often have been seen with no more notice than an inquiry, 'What is its name?' Now, however, every eye gazes on it with interest as the vessel passes by.

A devout superstitious Roman Catholic, come from Holland on a pilgrimage to Rome, entered into discussion with us. His pronunciation of Latin nearly agreed with ours, so that we were able to converse freely till night separated us. We spoke also with one of the monks from a Spanish monastery, and found him a most bigoted, ignorant devotee. The party from Syria spoke Arabic and a very little Italian, so that our intercourse was limited though interesting. The bishop accepted from us a very small Italian New Testament, raising his eyebrows in astonishment that the whole could be comprised in so small a compass. But when we told him that in our country we were Bishops, his wonder almost amounted to incredulity, as he eyed us from head to foot, observing the youthful countenances of some of us, and our simple attire. The young Greek spoke freely with us in Italian. He is employed as a guide to lead travellers through the scenes of ancient history in his native country. Full of vivacity, his tongue seemed never to rest, but was either singing the songs or describing the romantic scenes of Greece till night came down. Then he spread out his mat on the deck, and after going through his evening devotions, wrapped himself up in his rough, shaggy capote, and resigned himself to repose.

When next morning dawned, we found ourselves not far from Civita Vecchia where we anchored for two hours. We landed and rambled through the town. The country around appeared to be very desolate and mostly uncultivated. The town itself is wretched in the extreme, and the streets are gloomy and dull; the only objects to attract the eye being the carts in the market drawn by oxen, and the cross surmounting every dwelling. This town is the *Centum Cell* mentioned by Pliny and was in his day a port of Etruria.

Re-embarking, we soon lost sight of the Italian shore. Next day was the Sabbath, a silent Sabbath, far from the assemblies of God's worshippers.

May 6

No land appeared till Monday morning when we obtained a distant view of Sicily. Mount Eryx might be one of the heights we saw. By sunset the same evening we came in sight of Gozo, rocky and steep, and as we looked round upon the blue waters, without a bound but the horizon, remembered Paul, having no doubt that this is the part of the sea at the mouth of the Adriatic on which he was tossed.

About ten in the evening, we drew near Malta and soon sailed far up into the splendid harbour of Valetta, formed by one of the creeks in which the island abounds. We cast anchor in the smooth deep water, near some of the ships of war stationed here. The lights twinkling on the heights shewed the direction of the town, while the solemn bells tolled the hours of night. A small boat came alongside, and a voice hailed us in English. It was some individual who held office in the place. He inquired if we were all *'en practique'*, i.e. free from plague, if we had brought any news, and if there were any individuals of rank on board.

Sitting on deck, and feeling joy and gratitude at being thus far brought on our way, we remembered that this island once bent up its hymn of thanksgiving when Paul, Luke, and Aristarchus stood on its shore and praised their Deliverer. Perhaps they sang Psalm 107:23-30. Whether or not the spot pointed out on the other side of the island be the real place of Paul's shipwreck, it is difficult to say; but certainly many spots, and the harbour of Valetta among the rest, correspond to the brief description given in Acts 27:39 – a certain creek with a shore.

Early on the Tuesday morning (*May 7*), we disembarked amid tumult and confusion that baffles description, arising from the greedy anxiety of porters and miserable-looking beggars, all striving to the utmost to obtain a pittance by seizing on the luggage of strangers. Valetta is certainly a singularly-built town. Several of the streets are little else than so many flights of steps, steep and slippery; yet up these the mule can climb with ease, a feat that no horse in our country could accomplish. The heat was very great, so that we were quite oppressed by walking under a burning sun. Strangers from every country under heaven seem to meet here; the Greek gracefully attired, and the turbaned Turk; the dismal priest, and the monk with shaven crown; English sailors next, and then an English officer; the Maltese peasant with ornamented vest, and girdle round the waist; and then the Maltese lady wearing the *onella* (perhaps a remnant of the eastern veil), a black silk scarf drawn over the head, forming an arch, which reveals the face half in the shade.

In Malta there are very few Jews, and these few move from place to place. Not many have wealth, and most of them are wretchedly poor. There is one convert employed in the printing establishment of the Church of England Society's Mission.

We called on Mr. Schlienz, of the Church of England Missionary Society, from whom we received useful information; and at the quarantine station we conversed with the Rev. Mr. Freemantle, a minister of the Church of England, who, with his wife, had just returned from Palestine. They had travelled by way of Cairo to Mount Sinai, and thence to Jerusalem. He told us that we would find far fewer Jews in the Holy Land than is generally reported; and all of them poor and wretched. He stated that the fearful corruptions of the professedly Christian churches in those countries are the most effectual stumbling-blocks to the Jew, and that the exhibition of a pure and holy faith would probably be one of the chief advantages of building an English Protestant Church upon Mount Zion.

We required to be ready to sail early next morning in the French steamer *Eurotas* for Alexandria; and though the tardiness and greediness of porters and boatmen very nearly disappointed us of our passage, we at length succeeded in getting off. It was a bright and beautiful morning when we sailed from the quarantine harbour. Occasionally the reflection of the sun's rays from the smooth surface of a bending wave was like the gleam from a mirror. A few small white clouds appeared in the horizon, but not a speck in the sky above us. Malta was out of sight in a few hours, and during the rest of the day we saw nothing but fields of level water.

At evening the few clouds on the horizon seemed like the hills on some distant land. The swallows kept flying about the vessel till darkness came on; and then the stars shone out singularly bright. The planet Venus was reflected on the water quite like the moon in brilliancy.

Coming down to the cabin, the young American traveller described to us some of the scenes which he had witnessed at Rome during Passion-week. He told us of the Pope blessing 150,000 people, all kneeling before him in the great square of St Peter's, and of his riding into the city in imitation of Christ's entry into Jerusalem.

Next morning (*May 10*) about sunrise, we came in sight of Greece, opposite Cape Gallo (the ancient Acritas). Crossing the Gulf of Coron (anciently the Sinus Messeniacus), we sailed slowly past Cape Matapan (the ancient Tænarus), where the cloudcapped hills of Laconia terminate. The young Greek guide proudly pointed to the mountain range as the seat of the unconquered Mainotes, and to the far distant hills at the top of the gulf (the Sinus Laconicus) as marking where Sparta stood. Many of the summits were capped with snow. The heights of Tænarus were obscured by morning clouds – while their bases reached down to the water edge. Through the glass we could descry many hanging villages with terraced fields and gardens.

Passing the island of Elaphonesia and Cerigo (the ancient Cythera), and the promontory Malea, we entered the Aegean Sea. The numberless islands of the Archipelago now came in view one after another. We remembered that the Psalmist spoke of all this great sea, and may have known something of the islands and countries which it washes. The expression appeared very appropriate, 'this great and wide sea' (Psalm 104:25), or more literally, *this great sea which is broad in its arms*, an

epithet which seems to refer to the waters clasping round these innumerable islands, and pouring themselves into these thousand creeks and
bays.

Our vessel was now directing its course north-east for the island of
Syra, the ancient Syros. At a distance, Spezzia was pointed out to us, and
a little farther off rose Hydra, famous in the warfare of modern Greece,
reminding us of our own Bass Rock. Next we passed near Falconero, an
uninhabited rocky islet. Melos and Anti-melos then came in sight; the
former a large island with a fine harbour, and marked by two lofty hills;
the latter bold and precipitous, descending steep into the water. Far to
the south we saw Dipsis, almost a bare rock, and toward evening
Seriphos. The sun seemed to sink down behind Falconero, leaving a
calm sea and a beautifully spotted sky behind, tinging all the western
horizon with a glorious red.

At two next morning (*Saturday, May 11*), we cast anchor before the
town of Syra. The coast of the island forms a natural harbour. The town
rises up from the shore, and seems entirely to cover the conical hill on
which it is built. The castle or Acropolis is on the top, keeping watch
over houses that seem to creep up the hill toward the Acropolis for
shelter. All the buildings are of a dazzling whiteness, and the hills
around green with olives. We could imagine ourselves riding in the
harbour of one of the ancient cities of Greece, the town smiling below,
and the Acropolis frowning defiance from above. The chief town of
Syra was anciently called Hermopolis, and the books printed here by the
Church of England Missionary Society bear this name on the title-page.

The mail-packets of the French and Austrian companies use Syra as
their station, and from this place vessels are ready to carry the traveller
to Athens, Egypt, and Constantinople. We witnessed much activity in
the harbour, boats loading and unloading. The water was so clear that
we could see the pebbles at the bottom. In the docks we counted thirteen
small vessels on the stocks. The town has a population of 20,000. A
hardy Greek rowed us to the shore, when, after being examined by the
Board of Health, we found our way to the 'Hotel de Gréce' or
Ξενοδοχειον της Ελλαδος (the Greek inn). It was a wretched inn, but
the people were anxious to shew us every kindness. Instead of butter
they brought us Grecian honey.

In walking through the streets it was interesting to find the language
of ancient Greece moulded to express modern inventions. There was the

Βασιλικον δρομειον Συρας, 'the Royal Post-office of Syra'; and again, a board, marking the sailing of the steamers, was headed by the word Ατμοταχυπλοια. We met asses carrying in panniers the ancient amfora, a two-handled jug. A little child came begging for bread and his cry was 'ψωμι ψωμι', (i.e. bread). We came upon three booksellers' shops, in one of which we found Τα θαυμασια συμβαντα του Ροβινσωνος Κρουσου, 'the wonderful adventures of Robinson Crusoe', with a recommendation of it by some of our countrymen: Ο πολυμαθης Χαλμερος και Ταυολρος, 'the learned Chalmers and Taylor'. We saw with greater joy the whole Greek Bible for sale; though beside it stood one of Sir Walter Scott's novels. Occasionally in the streets tumblers of clear cool water were set in rows upon a marble slab for sale and it is no small refreshment in such a climate to receive even a cup of cold water. Looking down upon the harbour from above, the white cotton sails of the small vessels seen upon the deep blue sea appeared very beautiful.

We visited Mr. Hildner of the Church of England Missionary Society. He and his wife are Germans, and have laboured here nine years. Miss Wilcox had lately joined them, her department being to teach the Grecian girls English, drawing, singing and needlework. As yet they have seen little fruit in the conversion of souls, but wait for it. Their efforts have been confined almost entirely to teaching the young: in doing which they adopt the Lancasterian system. In the school-rooms, which are pleasantly situated, we found the whole apparatus of an Infant and Juvenile school. On the walls were boards for the multiplication table, entitled 'Πινακες Αριθμητικαι'. Others had the elementary syllables, 'Πινακες Αναγνωσεως; and others the picture of some object of natural history, 'Αιετος', 'eagle'; 'Ονος', 'ass'; 'Λυκος', 'wolf'; with the description below. There were present 300 boys and 300 girls, all busily engaged. It was curious to hear the boys reading the *Cyropedia* in ancient Greek, and rendering it into Romaic. The girls were writing, and they formed the Greek letters beautifully. Some of them were learning English. Young Greeks are very clever and anxious to acquire knowledge. Want of perseverance is their greatest fault. They read the New Testament daily, and almost every child possesses a copy. On Sabbath mornings, after they have been at the Greek church with their parents, they are assembled for two hours in the school, learn a Bible lesson, and are addressed by the Missionary; but many do not attend, as the parents are anxious only about their temporal welfare, and the acquisition of secular knowledge. The American

Missionaries at Athens conduct a school in all respects similar to this, and some of the inferior clergy there, who seem to be pious men, take an interest in its prosperity. The London Society maintain a similar school at Corfu.

This visit to Syra served to awaken in our bosoms new feelings of interest in behalf of Greece. On our way back to the harbour, observing the rising spire of a new building, we asked what it was, and were told that it was a Roman Catholic church. Popery seems determined to assert her right to the name of *Catholic,* by her untired zeal and universal enterprise.

The same day we left the island with regret in the 'Leonidas', another French steamer, which was to convey us to Alexandria. On leaving the harbour we saw the hills of the island Negropont (the ancient Euboea), to the west, and near us on the left lay Tinos. Before us were Delos and Mycone, on our right Andros and Xiphos. We could see the general aspect of all these islands. Summer clouds rested over the summits of their hills.

On board our new vessel we found a change of company, several passengers having been waiting at Syra for a vessel to carry them to Egypt. Among others were four Eastern Jews and a tall strong Albanian, who spoke only Romaic, but whose gestures were as significant as language. There was also a Turk, of a mild pleasing countenance and his wife with her face muffled in a white veil.

We passed by Naxos, with its town of the same name, of marble whiteness. Opposite to it lie Paros and Olearos. We stretched our eyes in the direction of Icaria and Naxos, that we might obtain a glimpse of highly-favoured Patmos; but in vain. We could only see the waves that were rolling on to break upon its rocky shore.

About sunset, when we were leaving Naxos and Paros behind us, and had left off gazing on their hills, we found the four Jews seated together, finishing their Sabbath prayer. At the moment we had first spoken to them, one was reading Psalm 85:1-2, 'O Lord, thou hast been favourable to thy land', etc. They told us that they had come from Dardanelles, and were now on a pilgrimage to Jerusalem meaning to return home in the course of three months. Two of them were men of learning, and all seemed to know Hebrew well. They spoke Spanish with each other, but understood Italian. In order to gain their confidence, and engage the attention, one of our number brought out Abarbinel on the Passover, and shewed them its map, vignettes, and figures. At the foot of one of these pictures, the abbreviation meaning 'Amen' occurred. These we explained to their great surprise; and when one of us added, 'We too use the word *Amen*', they looked at each other and began to smile and talk. Our friendship was now established, and opening our Hebrew Bibles, we got into close conversation. One of them, at our request, read aloud Isaiah 53, and then listened to us, when we applied it to the atoning Saviour. On telling them that we believed in a first and a second coming of Messiah, they spoke of it to each other, but made no remark to us. A little after we joined them again, all sitting upon the deck. We opened out a map of their country, and as we pointed to the most remarkable places, named them in Hebrew. We had in our hands a small publication of the Tract Society, entitled *Manners and Customs of the Jews.* In explaining to them some of the woodcuts, we took occasion to let them know that we were not Roman Catholics, and had no images in our churches. Of this also they spoke to one another. A little after, opening our Italian New Testament, we read the quotation from Isaiah in Matthew 4:15,16, 'The people that sat in darkness', etc., saying, 'The great Light is Messiah'. One of them replied, 'We believe it is'. They continued for some time looking at the pictures in the book already mentioned, till coming to a representation of Paul preaching to the Jews from the stairs of the Temple (Acts 22), they asked what it was. This led us to explain, and again taking up the Italian New Testament, we read Paul's address. Everything in the passage was suited to awaken their attention. Paul's reference to the law, to his sitting at Gamaliel's feet, and to the traditions of the fathers – the people keeping silence because he spoke in Hebrew – and then the full narrative of his former life, and his conversion to Christ. It seemed a message directed to them by the Lord, and they listened with deep attention. But as soon as it was ended, first the one that seemed most learned, and then another, rose and left us, apparently somewhat displeased. Two still remained, and continued to examine the other pictures, such as the Feast of Tabernacles, and the Deluge, which afforded us further opportunity of speaking to them. Observing one of Peter and John healing the man at the Beautiful Gate of the Temple, one of us said it was the gate *Nicanor*; they immediately looked to each other and said *Saar Nicnor*. After which, we read in their hearing the passage where the miracle is described (Acts 3). During the conversation, they were not a little pleased by our remarking in reference to there being *four* of them and *four* of us travelling to Jerusalem, 'We are brethren' (quoting Genesis 13:8). The two who had stayed with us, then bade us good night with great cordiality. We learned from them that Jacob Baal Turim, a well-known Jewish commentator, is believed to be buried in the island of Scio.

The captain of the steamer informed us that from November to February he has often on board sixty or seventy Jews at a time, going up to visit Jerusalem. Of these not many are wealthy, and they return in the course of a few months.

During the night the wind rose and the sea became boisterous so that we experienced the tossings of the Carpathian Sea, to which we had now come. About sunrise next morning, which was Sabbath, we were passing the eastern point of Crete, opposite Cape Sidro, anciently called Samonium or Salmone (Acts 27:7). A ledge of rocks ran along the shore behind which the country was bold and mountainous. Over all a lofty peak rose in the distance, which may possibly have been Ida. About an hour after, we obtained a view of a part of the southern coast of the island, where, in the days of Paul, was 'the place called the Fair Havens, nigh whereunto was the city of Lasea'. The recollections of the sacred history were a thousandfold sweeter to us than all our classical remembrances. It was interesting no doubt, to look upon the island of which Virgil sung, and whose inhabitants Homer celebrates. But a far deeper and holier feeling of interest was awakened in our breast, when we looked upon it as a region where the Cross of Christ was once so successfully lifted up, and salvation preached with power to the debased idolaters. We read over with a new relish the Epistle to Titus, who was 'left in Crete to set in order the things that were wanting, and to ordain elders in every city'. We remembered how frequently Paul must have visited this island, sailing over the very sea we had been traversing; and we thought of Apollos tarrying at Crete, on his way to his native Alexandria (whither we were bound), along with Zenas, the lawyer, a scribe, well-instructed unto the kingdom of heaven (Titus 3:13).

Next day (*Monday, May 13*) the sea was calm, and we had some farther conversation with the passengers. We offered an Italian tract to a poor monk, a pilgrim on his way to the Holy Sepulchre; but he civilly declined it, saying, *he had a pain in his head whenever he attempted to read!* One deeply interested person on board was the medical attendant belonging to the vessel, a young Frenchman named Darnel. Last evening when nearly all had gone to rest, one of us was led into a close and earnest conversation with him on his hope for eternity. The ship was rolling very heavily, but he lay down on the floor of the cabin, and in broken English on his part, and broken French on ours, we spoke on divine things till past midnight. This morning the conversation was renewed. The doctor declared that religion was dead in France; the follies of Popery had led men of reason to despise all religion, and he believed that there was more morality now than when Popery reigned. His idea of duty was, that it consisted in the practice of such virtues as, concern for the public good, faithfulness to the marriage relation, and charity to the poor. He had no idea that a regard to the will of God was the rule of a man's duty, and honestly confessed, that he had not the least feeling of sin. 'Philosophy', said he, 'has taught me all that is needful for man'. He acknowledged that he was not happy. He ate, drank, slept, and rose every day to his work, yet still was not so happy as he wished to be. 'But where am I to find happiness? The St. Simonians say they are quite happy in their brotherhood, yet their system is absurdity.' We said that we had found happiness, and pointed out the foundation on which it rested, and urged him to put to the proof God's promise through his Son, 'Come to me, and *I will give you rest.*' He put us off by saying he could not pray unless he believed. We rejoined that he refused to turn the mind's eye toward the object to be believed, and therefore could not rationally expect to embrace the truth. Upon this he argued that a man was no more to blame for his hard heart than for a diseased member of

CHAPTER 2

EGYPT – THE DESERT –
SOUTH OF PALESTINE

'Set thee up way-marks, make thee high heaps: set thine heart
toward the highway, even the way which thou wentest: turn again, O
virgin of Israel, turn again to these thy cities'
(Jeremiah 31:21).

When about to land, we were told that the plague had that very day made
its appearance in Alexandria. This was by no means welcome news, for
we saw that in all probability we should now be subjected to the delay
of a quarantine before entering Palestine. Meanwhile, having no alternative, we disembarked. The quay exhibited a strange scene of confusion and noise. A crowd of rough half-naked men and Arab boys, some
with asses, some with camels, lined the beach, all screaming and
quarrelling, determined to press their services on every passenger, and
to take no denial. With some difficulty we got our luggage satisfactorily
disposed of, and then each of the company mounted on an ass, and
guided by an Arab boy, scampered through the gate of the city, and
through the narrow bazaar, till we came to a pleasant square in the other
extremity of the town. Here we took up our abode in an inn kept by a
Frenchman.

With calm delight we were now able to look round upon the land of
Egypt, while many scenes of its eventful history rose up before us. It was
here that Jacob and Joseph sojourned, with their families, for 100 years.
This was the land of Moses and his wondrous deeds. And, more
interesting still, this was the land that gave refuge to 'the holy child
Jesus,' when compelled to flee from the land of Judah. It was the cradle
of Israel, and the cradle of Israel's Saviour – as it is written, 'out of Egypt
have I called my son' (Matthew 2:15).

This city Alexandria was the birthplace of Apollos (Acts 18:24), that
pattern of burning zeal, and scriptural eloquence – the city, too, of
Athanasius – and the scene of the labours of the seventy translators of

the Old Testament. Alexander the Great, Cleopatra, Caesar, and many other names, are associated with the name of the once illustrious Alexandria. With still deeper interest we now pondered over the future history of Egypt, as disclosed in the record of prophecy, and prayed that the time may be hastened, when 'Ethiopia shall stretch out her hands to God' (Psalm 68:31) – When 'the Lord shall be known to Egypt, and the Egyptians shall know the Lord' – 'And the Lord shall smite Egypt, he shall smite and heal it'; 'Saying, Blessed be Egypt my people' (Isaiah 19:21,22,25).

May 14

Every eastern city is infested with dogs that prowl about the streets for food; and during all the night their ceaseless howling reminded us of David's description of his enemies: 'They return at evening; they make a noise like a dog, and go round about the city' (Psalm 59:6). Before breakfast, some of us rambled out to Pompey's Pillar. The only thing remarkable about it is, that the shaft is one stone, a solid mass of red granite, 90 feet long, and 9 feet in diameter. The capital is Corinthian, indifferently carved. The traces of many a traveller's visit are to be found scratched upon its pedestal. The Mareotic Lake lay east of it, but is now dried up, affording no moisture to water the Mareotic vines that once regaled Cleopatra and her luxurious court. The ground around it swarmed with small lizards, and the surface is broken with innumerable holes made by the jerboa. It was curious for us to observe for the first time women wearing the veil that hides the whole face except the eyes. Some carried the earthen jar upon their head in a very graceful manner. Some also were carrying their children on their shoulders, as referred to by the prophet, when he says of returning Israel 'thy daughters shall be carried on their shoulders' (Isaiah 49:22). Some carried them in a still more singular manner, upon their side, a custom also referred to by the prophet, 'Ye shall be borne upon her sides' (Isaiah 66:12).

In the evening we visited the Frank Synagogue. We were guided up a dark stair in an obscure street, and through a long narrow ill-lighted passage into a small room, not more than thirty feet long and ten broad. At the door stood the usual box for alms, and another for 'olive-oil for the lamps'. There were only ten persons present; three of whom were natives of Egypt, dressed in the common oriental costume; the rest from Leghorn, Trieste and other mercantile towns of Europe. They shewed little feeling of devotion, except at one point of the short service, where there was a pause in the reading of the prayers, and all seemed to pray in silence for four or five minutes, turning their faces towards the ark. Before concluding, a box was carried round for contributions. There was not one interesting feature either in the worship or in the place, with the exception of a large frame suspended on the wall bearing the words (in Hebrew): 'May the merciful one bring back the service of the house of the sanctuary to its place, speedily, in our days.' This was like one of the groans of Israel for deliverance in 'the house of bondage'.

As soon as the service was over, the Jews spoke freely to us – opened the ark, and shewed us their copies of the law. One of the best of these we spread out for examination on the reading-desk; and out of their own scriptures discoursed to them of sin and atonement for sin. We told them that we had come from Scotland out of love to their souls. We spoke of Messiah, how he came the first time to die for sin, and is coming soon the second time to reign in glory. They said that there are about 100 families of European Jews in Alexandria, who have only one synagogue; and that there are about 300 families of native Jews who have two, and these they called the Arab synagogues. One Jew who had resided much at Cairo, told us that in that city there were 300 families of Jews, of whom one-third were Caraites. We afterward learned from English residents that this information was not very accurate, and that there are more Jews in Cairo than in Alexandria. In the latter, there may be about 1,000, and in Cairo about 2,000. The Jews of Alexandria are mostly of the third class in trade – the richest of them are all *sarafs*, or money-changers.

We were occupied all next morning *(May 15)* in preparing for our journey through the desert. The plague having appeared in Alexandria, we could not enter Palestine by Jaffa or Beyrout, without submitting to a long and unwholesome quarantine. We therefore resolved to proceed by the way of El Arish; and to do this without delay, as in the course of a few days, orders were likely to be sent to establish a quarantine at El Arish. The Consul's trusty janissary,[1] Mustapha by name, born at Thebes, a useful, clever person, busily engaged himself in providing us with needful articles. We had already furnished ourselves with light dresses at Marseilles and straw hats at Leghorn – and now we purchased travelling implements. We went to the bazaar, and bought carpets to lie upon at night, and a thick soft coverlet to wrap ourselves in. We next

---

1. A Turkish word for a soldier in the foot guards.

procured with some difficulty two tents, neither of them large, one round, the other oblong. Cairo is the proper place for obtaining such articles. An Indian gentleman's canteen and cooking utensils, with a stock of remainder provisions, fell into our hands at a cheap rate. Mustapha procured two Arab servants to attend us, Ibraim and Ahmel, the former able to speak Italian and English, the latter only Italian. They had often journeyed through Syria, and Ibraim had been lately there with Professor Robinson[2] of America. When they came to be hired, Mr Todd said to them in the eastern manner: 'I am as they are,' pointing to us. 'Offend them, offend me.' They replied, 'Their comfort shall be on our heads'. Mustapha added, 'If they do not do what is right, they shall never drink water in Alexandria again'.

Before dinner we had a pleasant ride to the gardens of the Governor, about a mile from town. Passing out of the gate, we observed that every man who went out shewed his hand to the sentinel. This is to prevent desertion from the army, every soldier bearing the Pasha's mark on his right hand. We passed a grove of palms and observed the flowering pomegranates – vines also and figs, tamarisks, and banians.

We stood a little to observe the common manner of drawing water at the wells. A wheel is moved round by oxen or buffaloes, whose neck is yoked to a pole. Everywhere we saw the slow-pacing animal moving round, and heard the creaking of this clumsy apparatus. By the roadside an old sarcophagus was lying in fragments. We alighted and walked through the gardens, laid out with straight walks, after the Egyptian taste. The flowering oranges were beautiful and fragrant, and the vines luxuriant. The grapes are said to be watery. In returning we visited the site of the lake Mareotis, Pompey's Pillar, and the Mahometan burying-ground. We then proceeded through the extensive ruins of the old city to Cleopatra's Needles, two beautiful obelisks, one lying flat, half sunk in the ground, the other still standing erect. Both are covered with hieroglyphics, fresh and unchanged by time. Near the Coptic Convent we examined with much interest the site and remaining traces of the church of the great Athanasius, who was Bishop here in AD 326, God's witness for the truth against many kings and people. Some broken pillars and fragments of the foundation are all that remain. Not far from

2. Professor Edward Robinson (1794-1863) of Union Theological Seminary, New York, undertook a geographical expedition to Syria, Palestine and Sinai in 1838. His findings, published in three volumes in 1841, established him as the foremost historical geographer of the Holy Land of his day.

this is the ancient Jewish burying-ground, but the Jews are now forced to bury outside the walls.

We returned about sunset – one of the Moslem hours for prayer – and observed for the first time the Mahometans bending to pray on the deck of the ship, the retired corners and even in the streets. The same evening, in the Bazaar, we met two of our Jewish friends who had sailed to Egypt with us. They were kinder than ever, and told us that they were going to sail for Beyrout.

Next morning *(May 16)*, before dawn, we were awakened by the arrival of the asses and drivers, that had been engaged to convey us as far as Damietta, the sand of the desert being so far hard and suitable for the asses' feet. Notwithstanding the continued knocking of these drivers, we refused to start so early; and it was not till seven that we were fairly mounted on the nimble little animals, our carpets serving the purpose of a saddle. Our train consisted of sixteen asses. Our servants Ibraim and Ahmet rode by our side, and ten Egyptian lads ran beside the asses that bore the luggage. Soon after, our train received the addition of two more asses, one to carry the water-skins, and another to be ready for service in case of any of the rest becoming exhausted. We soon passed through the Rosetta gate, and bade farewell to Alexandria.

It was the morning of the day on which our General Assembly was to meet in Edinburgh, an Assembly in which the important question of the Spiritual Independence of our Church and the privilege of its Christian people, were likely to be keenly discussed. As we rode along the sands, sometimes meeting the palm-tree, sometimes a cluster of lowly shrubs, with flocks of goats browsing near, we spoke to each other of the day, praying that the crown might be set on the head of the Anointed One, and that the dry land of our parishes might be turned into water-springs.

We thought of the Judges of Israel riding on asses (Judges 5:10), and of the many references to this custom in the Bible. We remembered above all that Zion's King came thus to Zion, 'Meek, and sitting upon an ass, and a colt the foal of an ass' (Matthew 21:5). The palms seemed frequently to spring up immediately from out of the sand, their root no doubt being nourished by unseen moisture. Does the Psalmist refer to this circumstance, when he says, 'The righteous shall flourish as the palm-tree?' (Psalm 92:12). At all events, there is reference to its regular, steady growth, year after year, marked by a new circle upon the bark.

The beautiful waving of the branches also, when moved by a passing breeze, shewed us how they came to be so frequently used in triumphs, a custom alluded to in Revelations (7:9), where the great multitude who have overcome all their enemies and stand before the throne, are clothed in white robes and hold 'palms in their hands'. Lizards were everywhere basking in the heat of the sun, and sometimes in the distance a group of camels were seen feeding on the stunted shrubs of the desert; while the only sounds that broke on the ear were the cries of the driver, *'ruach'* (get on) and *'uzbel'* (stop), or sometimes the voice of the older men calling *'waled'* (boy) to the younger lads. The boys took great delight in teaching us the Arabic for the numbers one, two, three, etc., and for some of the common phrases of life, interpreting them by signs. Dr Keith engaged himself in questioning our servant and guide Ibraim about Petra; for he had been there with Dr Robinson of America. From him we learned that a rough, hairy animal, which we understood to be the porcupine, abounds in Wady Mousa, and that the Arabs call it *kangfud*, which is evidently the Hebrew *kippod*, the word used in Isaiah 34:11, though translated *bittern* in our version.

Our course lay across the head of the ancient Lake Mareotis, and some other salt-lakes, now dried up by the sun. A white crust of salt often covered the hard sand. In the distance, we observed the well-known phenomenon of the *mirage* to which the prophet Isaiah is supposed to allude, 'The parched ground shall become (really) a pool' (Isaiah 35:7). At one time, we saw what seemed to be a calm flowing water, reflecting from its unruffled surface trees growing on its banks, while some object in the background assumed the appearance of a splendid residence amidst a grove of trees. At another time, there appeared castles embosomed in a forest of palms, with a lake of clear water stretched between us and them. Generally the mirage may be known by its continually shifting the view, and by the hazy movement of the atmosphere over the apparent waters.

Suddenly we came upon the Bay of Aboukir and were refreshed by the cool breeze from the Mediterranean. This bay is famous in the warlike annals of our country, and here the Canopic mouth of the Nile used formerly to empty itself into the sea.

About one, we rested, taking shelter from the heat under the walls of a wretched khan,[1] which was so small that we preferred putting up our tent, while the Arabs opened their sacks and gave the asses provender

---

1. An inn or rest house.

– reminding us of Jacob's sons (Genesis 42:27).

At three, we resumed our journey, enjoying the pleasant air from the sea till toward evening, when we left the shore. The road was now marked by pillars, composed of heaps of brick, at distant intervals. The Arabs call these *Ahmoud*, that is 'pillars'. They are peculiarly useful to the traveller, for it is as easy for one to find his way amidst drifted snow that has covered the tracks and lines of a road, as to find it in this sandy desert – and no doubt, to these allusion is made by the prophet (Jeremiah 31:21), 'Set thee up way-marks, make thee high heaps'. When a hurricane has passed over the desert, the traces in the sand are easily obliterated, which may be alluded to by the prophet (Isaiah 3:12), 'O my people, they which lead thee cause thee to err, and destroy (swallow up) the way of thy paths.'

We descried Rosetta about two hours before we reached it, at the extremity of a long flat valley of sand. The rays of the setting sun gave a red tinge to the surface of the desert, and as we approached the town, we entered a beautiful grove of palms, growing luxuriantly out of sandy hillocks. Some of our attendants had got before us, and were waiting for us, in eastern style, at the gate – *El Bab Rashid*, the gate of Rosetta, as they said. All was now truly oriental, and the scenery of the Arabian Nights occurred vividly to our mind, as we rode through streets silent as the grave, with not even a solitary lamp to cheer the eye. The houses seemed nothing else than lofty walls of brick or red granite. Many of them appeared to be wholly deserted, though sometimes a turbaned head was dimly seen at the narrow windows of these ominous-looking dwellings. The darkness of evening, the gloom of the buildings, and the silence of the town, made our entrance into Rosetta peculiarly sombre.

We lodged at the Latin Convent, wearied with our journey, having travelled thirty or forty miles in nine hours. This convent was erected about thirty-five years ago, chiefly with the view of accommodating travellers, and is a large brick building, in the form of a square, with a court in the midst, like all eastern houses. We were guided by the aid of a lantern up a dark irregular stair to the highest story, where we found the apartments for strangers far from being either airy or clean, but very acceptable after a day's journey in the wilderness. There are about fifteen Roman Catholics in the town, and a superior (who was absent at Jerusalem) generally resides in the convent; but at the time of our visit, there were no inmates except a solitary monk – an amiable Italian, with a little native boy attending him.

We were refreshed by a draught of the water of the Nile. It is certainly peculiarly sweet and soft – very palatable at any time, and not less so after the heat of the day. Perhaps the peculiar pleasantness of these waters is referred to by Jeremiah, 'Now what hast thou to do in the way of Egypt, to drink the waters of Sihor' (Jeremiah 2:18). We had scarcely sat down when we heard the sound of music and mirth, and running to the window observed the glare torches in the street. We were told that it was 'the voice of the bridegroom and of the bride' (Jeremiah 33:11). Some of us instantly set out to witness the spectacle of an Eastern Marriage. We wished to see the Parable of the Ten Virgins illustrated, and our wish was ratified. The bridegroom was on his way to the house of the bride. According to custom, he walked in procession through several streets of the town, attended by a numerous body of friends, all in their showy eastern garb. Persons bearing torches went first, the torches being kept in full blaze by a constant supply of ready wood from a receiver, made of wire, fixed on the end of a long pole. Two of the torchbearers stood close to the bridegroom, so that we had a view of his person. Some were playing upon an instrument not unlike our bagpipe, others were beating drums, and from time to time muskets were fired in honour of the occasion. There was much mirth expressed by the crowd, especially when the procession stood still, which it did every few paces. We thought of the words of John, 'The friend of the bridegroom, which standeth and heareth him, rejoiceth greatly because of the bridegroom's voice' (John 3:29). At length the company arrived at the entrance of the street where the bride resided. Immediately we heard the sound of many female voices, and observed by the light of the torches, a company of veiled bridesmaids, waiting on the balcony to give notice of the coming of the bridegroom. When they caught a sight of the approaching procession, they ran back into the house, making it resound with the cry, 'Halil, halil, halil,' and music both vocal and instrumental commenced within. Thus the bridegroom entered in, 'and the door was shut'. We were left standing in the street without, 'in the outer darkness'. In our Lord's parable (Matthew 25:1), the virgins go *forth* to meet the bridegroom with lamps in their hands, but here they only waited for his coming. Still we saw the traces of the very scene described by our Lord, and a vivid representation of the way in which Christ shall come to his waiting Church, and the marriage supper of the Lamb begin. In India and other parts of the East, it is the custom for the friends of the bride to *go out* to meet the company.

There are a few Jews in Rosetta, but no synagogue. The whole population of the town consists of 6000 inhabitants, and about 3000 soldiers. The ancient Canopus stood near the site of the town, but Rosetta is believed to be the ancient Bolbotine, and the branch of the Nile that flows past Rosetta is the *Bolbotinicum ostium*.

The monk in the convent proved very affable. His name was Jeremiah Galazzo, a Franciscan, from Italy. He had never read the New Testament in any language but Latin; and when we offered it to him in Italian, received it with a smile of delight. Shortly after he came back to us, and asked if we really meant to make the book his own; and then requested us to write our names upon it, mentioning that it was our gift to him. This we gladly did, and also left some Italian tracts in his library. Perhaps the Lord may some day make these seeds of divine truth to spring up in his heart, as they did in Luther's within the walls of a monastery.

At one end of the room where we slept, there was a small library, containing such books as these: *Officia Sanctorum; Corpus Christi; Scopa; Grammatica Francese; Jerome's Epistles in Latin; 'La Dottrina' of Bellarmine; Antoine's 'Theologia Moralis'; Pictavii Compendium Historiae Universalis*. There was a work on the Incarnation, in Arabic; a copy of Bellarmine's *La Dottrina* in Arabic and Latin, and Missals in abundance, two large folio copies in Latin, and one in Arabic – but no Bible among all! In the corner of the room was a small cupboard, neither neat nor clean. On the table stood a tinderbox, a vessel of olive-oil, and some cups. On the wall hung a rosary, with the image of the Virgin, bearing this inscription, *Maria concepta senza peccato originale precate pro noi che a voi recoriamo* (Mary, who wast conceived without original sin, pray for us who betake ourselves to thee). On the back of a chair hung a monk's brown, dirty dress; and a skullcap lay on a shelf above.

May 17

Next morning when we rose we gazed for the first time upon the river Nile; and in the forenoon walked along its banks, drinking of the 'water of Sihor', those pleasant waters that were once turned into blood. The fact that these waters were so highly prized must have made that amazing miracle to be the more deeply felt, and gives singular force to the words, 'The Egyptians shall loathe to drink of the water of the river' (Exodus 7:18). So much is the water esteemed down to the present day, that the Turks say, 'if Mahomet had tasted this river, he would have prayed for a temporal immortality that he might enjoy it for ever'.

We visited a rice-mill which is in the course of erection; and found that the principal workmen in it were four Americans employed by the Pasha. They were very happy to meet with us, and invited us to their lodging. One of them begged us to leave any English books which we could spare, as they had read over all their store. They said they kept the Sabbath every week, for when engaging with the Pasha, he allowed them this privilege, that they might take either their own Sunday or the Mahometan Friday for rest. We next went to the Bazaar, a strange scene of filth and wretchedness. The shops were poorly supplied, except in the article of cucumbers; but the miserable objects that were crawling about – sore-eyed children perched on their mother's shoulder, with faces half devoured by flies – old men half blind – and all filthy in the extreme, presented a scene that cannot be described. Water is universally carried in skins of animals, sewed up in the form of a bottle. The women always carry their burdens, however light, upon the head.

At twelve o'clock, the Muezzin, who were standing on the minaret of the Mosque, called the people to prayer, for it was noon. The deep-toned and prolonged cry of these watchmen is heard over the whole city, and if it were a call to the worship of the true God, would have a solemn effect. It is repeated at set hours every day, and is to be heard in every Mahometan town. Did Mahomet think upon the words of the Psalmist when he instituted this practice, 'Evening, and morning, and at noon, will I pray, and cry aloud; and he shall hear my voice?' (Psalm 55:17) As it was Friday the Mosques were all open. Looking into one of them, we observed a row of turbaned worshippers all kneeling at the same time. On approaching too near the door, we were warned to withdraw. Looking into another, we observed a man in a kind of pulpit addressing the worshippers, who were seated in a row upon a marble floor, with their eyes directed toward the preacher. The attitudes of devotion in the East are singularly beautiful.

In returning to the convent, we had an opportunity of witnessing the procession that takes place upon the event of a circumcision. The Arabs, with a reference to their progenitor Ishmael, circumcise their children when thirteen years old, and perform the ceremony with great pomp (Genesis 17:25). The boy, on whose account the ceremony was to be performed on this occasion, was handsomely dressed, and seated upon a white horse, with his head garlanded with flowers. The attendants stopped every now and then, and were entertained with music, firing of muskets, and merriment of various kinds, as in the marriage procession. The women wearing the veil seated themselves on the ground, and sang with shrill voices: sometimes they threw a fragrant liquid over the boy, reminding us of the words of the Psalmist, 'All thy garments smell of myrrh, and aloes, and cassia, out of the ivory palaces, whereby they have made thee glad' (Psalm 45:8). We observed more narrowly the bracelets and ornaments on the forehead worn by the women, and their eyes painted with stibium, and also the silver anklets worn by the children. The men together played at single-stick, keeping time to the music in a very dexterous manner.

At four in the afternoon, we took leave of Rosetta and of our friendly monk, and crossed the Nile, which is here 1,800 feet broad. We and our servants were a sufficient load for one small boat; our luggage occupied another; and our asses a third – and thus we floated slowly to the other side. A rice-field was near the spot where we landed; the rice was springing up through the water, which still drenched its surface. We saw a man ploughing with oxen – the plough seemed nothing more than a piece of wood, shaped so as to be capable of piercing the ground. Some of the women of the villages were using the distaff, and the children were gathering mulberries.

We had now a pleasant ride down the right bank of the Nile, among very rich gardens of melons and cucumbers, with figs and mulberry trees, and the finest palms we had yet seen. The croaking of frogs in all the rice-fields was incessant, and the pigeon, called by the Arabs *Tur*, was cooing among the trees. From time to time we had to cross little canals formed to carry water from the Nile, and supplied by the oxen turning round a wheel. Into one of these one of our baggage asses was pushed headlong by his fellow; and the patient animal lay quietly at the bottom till it was lifted out.

One of our attendants went to drink at a tank by the roadside. At all these tanks there is a small pitcher for the accommodation of travellers; sometimes fastened by a chain, and sometimes without it, but even if left loose it remains untouched. The villages are wretched. The people seem almost naked, and excessively dirty; most of them, too, are old people; very rarely did we meet any healthy young men. The reason is, that all such are obliged to enter the army; and Egyptian villages and lands are left to the care of women and old men. It seems still the case that taskmasters rule over Egypt – it is a *'house of bondage'* at this day. God remembers how Egypt kept his chosen Israel 400 years in slavery, and therefore has poured out upon it the fulfilment of that humiliating prophecy, 'It shall be the basest of kingdoms' (Ezekiel 29:15). If God fulfils so accurately the *threatening* against the *enemies* of Israel, will he not as literally fulfil the *blessing* which he has promised to the *friends* of Israel? And has he not said, 'Blessed is he that blesseth thee?' (Numbers 24:9).

About sunset, we left the rich banks of the Nile, and entered again upon the pathless desert. We could not observe so much as one footprint of man or beast upon the smooth sand. Soon we came upon the seashore, and rode along the margin, the waves washing the asses' feet, while the moon rose to light us on our way. At one point, our drivers being weary, proposed encamping for the night, but Ibraim advised us to advance a little farther. Upon this the young Arabs proceeded without a murmur, and in order to cheer the way commenced a native dance and song. One of them, advancing a little before the rest, began the song, dancing forward as he repeated the words, when the rest, following him in regular order, joined in the chorus, keeping time by a simultaneous clapping of hands. They sang several Arabian songs in this way, responding to one another, and dancing along the firm sand of the seashore, in the clear beautiful moonlight. The response, the dance, and the clapping of the hands, brought many parts of the word of God to our minds. We remembered the song of Miriam at the Red Sea, when 'the women went out after her with timbrels and with dances; and Miriam *answered them*,' that is, 'Miriam sang responsively to them' (Exodus 15:21); and also the song of the women of Israel after David's victory over the giant, 'They *answered* one another as they played, and said, Saul hath slain his thousands, and David his ten thousands' (1 Samuel 18:6,7). The words of the Psalmist were likewise brought to mind, 'O clap your hands, all ye people; Shout unto God with the voice of triumph' (Psalm 47:1); and again, 'Let the floods clap their hands; let the hills be joyful together' (Psalm 98:8) – i.e. in full choir. The responsive form of the 136th Psalm, and others of a like kind, was fully illustrated by this interesting scene.

We slept this night on the seashore. And in putting up our tents, we began to understand better the circumstances attending this manner of life. We learned how to *enlarge the space of the tent* (Isaiah 54:2) by 'stretching out the curtains'. We saw how by 'lengthening the cords', we drew wider the covering and as we drove in the pins 'or stakes' into the

sand, we learned the necessity of 'strengthening the stakes', if they were
to endure the tugging of the wind and weight of the canvas. Israel is yet
to dwell at large, under a tent widely spread but not a temporary abode,
shifted at next morning's dawn. Jerusalem is to be 'a tabernacle that
shall not be taken down, not one of the stakes thereof shall ever be
removed, neither shall any of the cords thereof be broken' (Isaiah
33:20). There may be a reference to the falling of the tent when its cords
are loosed, in Job, 'He hath loosed my cord and afflicted me' (Job
30:11). And perhaps also in the Epistle to the Corinthians, 'If our earthly
house of this tabernacle were dissolved' (2 Corinthians 5:1,4), where
the original word is καταλυθη (loosened). Then verse 4 has this
meaning, 'We groan, not to be left without a tabernacle altogether, but
to have the glory enveloping our tent, to have an additional and far more
glorious covering'.

May 18
We started early next morning, and were soon on our way. We had
already learned how natural were the words, 'Take up thy bed and walk'
(John 5:8); our simple beds costing us no trouble, and serving us for a
softer seat on the asses' back.

About one o'clock we reached the lake Bourlos, anciently lake
Buteo, where the Sebennetic branch of the Nile once discharged its
waters into the Mediterranean. It is a fine expanse of water, communi-
cating with the sea by a narrow outlet. Multitudes of large porpoises
were swimming about, whose playful motions amused us as we sailed
across. They repeatedly darted out of the water in pursuit of smaller fish.
The fishermen on shore were using the αμφιβληστρον, a net resembling the poke-net used in the isles of Scotland. It is circular, and weights
are placed round the circumference. The fisherman holds it by the
centre, gathers it up in his hand, and casts it into the water: he then draws
it slowly to shore by a line fastened to the centre. This is probably the
very kind of net used by the disciples (Matthew 4:18).

Leaving Bourlos, we rode through a pleasant wilderness abounding
in palm-trees. Passing a garden of melons and cucumbers, we observed
'the lodge' in the midst of it, a small erection of four upright poles,
roofed over with branches and leaves, under the shadow of which a
solitary person may sit and watch the garden. To this desolate condition
the daughter of Zion has come as the prophet foretold, 'The daughter of
Zion is left as a lodge in a garden of cucumbers' (Isaiah 1:8). In two

hours we arrived at a paltry village named Balteen, whose wretched houses appeared externally to be masses of brick or of mud. They are built in squares, and the windows look inward. Several families occupy one of these square edifices. At this spot our guides refused to go on, because they said that there would be no more water till four hours more of our journey, and the road was too bad for travelling in the dark. Without any altercation, therefore, and being glad to rest, we pitched our tents in the middle of this village about seven o'clock. The day had been exceedingly sultry; and the faces of some of us were blistered by the hot wind and glowing sands. We had scarcely sat down in the tent-door to enjoy the cool air of evening, when our attention was painfully arrested by the screams of one of our drivers. We rushed to the spot in time to save the poor fellow from a repetition of the unmerciful blows which the chief driver had been inflicting on his head with a staff. Some disobedience in drawing water was the cause of quarrel. We took him into our tent, and Ibraim applied some coffee to the bleeding wound, laughing all the time at his piteous cries. Truly the tender mercies of the heathen are cruel.

May 19

This morning was the Sabbath, and we rested according to the commandment. After worshipping together, we spent the forenoon in a grove of palms. The heat was great, the thermometer being 84°. We soon left the shade of the palm, and seated ourselves under the deeper shade of the fig and tamarisk. A fox started from his lair at our approach, and the native pigeons hovered around us. A threshing-floor was in sight – for our resting-place was on a rising ground – and here the men were busy bruising out the corn, with an instrument which we afterwards found very common in the East. It was no more than a flat board teethed with rows of sharp stones, on one end of which sat the man driving the oxen round and round over the straw.

Some of the villagers found us thus seated. About twenty half-naked, wretched-looking people, gathered round, to gaze at us and our clothing. We felt it painful to be among these ignorant, miserable people, and not able to tell them in their own tongue one word of the great salvation. It stirred us the more to cry, 'Thy kingdom come!' They kindly offered us some fresh garlic, and then their long pipe to smoke. One of them brought a vessel of water, and tasted it first himself to induce us to drink with confidence.

In the evening, the Sheikh or Governor of the place came down to our tent, attended by his Secretary – whom we found to be an Arabic Christian – and by his Pipe-bearer. They drank tea and ate sugar with great good humour, and seemed delighted at the attention paid them. They gladly accepted a pencil-case and knife, and promised to Dr Keith to take Arabic tracts if he would send them. The Governor's brother was next introduced, that we might heal him of blindness. We found that one of his eyes was obscured by cataract, which we assured him it was beyond the reach of our skill to remove. Upon their leaving us, we received a hint to give a small *bacshish*, or present, to the Pipe-bearer, as a token of respect to the Master for the honour he had done us in visiting our tent.

May 20

Owing to the restless impatience of our guides and servants, we were obliged to strike our tents at midnight. The moon was nearly full, and the sky without a cloud as we travelled onward for some hours through a much richer and more undulating country than that which we had passed. The palms and other trees of the desert gave beauty to the scene, while the hoarse croaking of the frogs told us that water was plentiful. Sometimes we came upon Arab huts made of branches of the *belach* or palm, and were saluted by the angry howl of dogs. Arriving at the sea, we rode along the shore, the waves frequently washing the asses' feet. We now felt great difficulty in preventing ourselves from falling asleep, and were often on this account precipitated to the sand, to the great amusement of our Egyptian attendants. Frequently we were roused by the vivid flashes of lightning, which played beautifully from the bosom of the dark clouds above the sea.

After riding ten hours in this manner we came to Assoum, an unsheltered village, consisting of a few wretched huts, and with very bad water. To save time, our tents were not erected; but we cast ourselves down, wearied and sleepy, upon our mats, under the shelter of the coverlets thrown over us, and tried to find a little rest under a scorching sun and upon glowing sand. It was easy now to understand the murmurings of the children of Israel in the desert; for heat, thirst, and a long journey over burning sands, made us experience feelings of misery which we had not known before. After two hours of repose, a dip in the sea, and a sparing meal of rice and dates, we resumed our journey, being anxious to reach Damietta this evening. About three o'clock, as we left the seashore, the Minarets of the town appeared in the distant horizon. We rode through an undulating pass of low sandhills, the air resembling that of an oven. Coming in sight of a well, our guides ran to quench their burning thirst. To us, however, this only afforded a trial of patience for the water was so muddy that we could not drink. In a little time we arrived at Senana, a village on the west side of this branch of the Nile, where the Pasha has barracks for some thousand troops. The troops were exercising as we passed by: some were in drill, and some shooting at a mark. They wear a white cotton dress, with a deep red sash, and are far from being a bold-looking set of men. The Nile here is 800 feet broad; and this was anciently called the Phatnitic or Bucolic branch. We sat down upon the bank, and drank freely of the water, which, when passed through a filter, was pure and delicious. An Egyptian officer brought us out chairs, and sat down with us in the shade of his house. He spoke with deep admiration of Mehemet Ali, and told us anecdotes of his unwearied activity.

The houses and mosques of Damietta looked very beautiful in the evening sun on the opposite bank of the river – a sad contrast to the filth, poverty, and guilt, to be found within. This is the ancient Tamiatis; it occupies a fine situation, and has well cultivated lands in its vicinity. We had sent Ibraim across the river with a letter to the Vice-Consul, the only representative of England in this place, to make known our arrival. He returned with a message from the Vice-Consul inviting us to his house; upon which we immediately embarked, and were soon rowed across the gentle stream, and up one of the canals, till we landed in Damietta, immediately under the Consul's garden. We were received into a large hall, with a stone floor, and a broad divan at the far end. In the one corner, which is the place of state, we found the Vice-Consul, a smart-looking Egyptian, in a Greek dress of dark green, with yellow slippers. He received us very graciously, and made us sit beside him on the divan. Long pipes, highly ornamented, were immediately brought to us by the attendants. We felt it not a little teazing, after all our fatigues and sleeplessness, to be compelled, out of politeness, to go through these eastern formalities, and to recline with him for nearly two hours, until a repast was prepared such as he thought suitable for British travellers. However, we were deeply interested by observing many eastern customs, which we had read of from our youth. We were introduced also to the Consul's brother and nephew, the latter a fine-looking young man, with a pointed moustache, who had singular command over his features.

He spoke to us in the Italian very freely; told us with great *sangfroid* of the poverty and misery of the inhabitants of Damietta, and when we informed him that we were Ministers of Christ, said that he admired our religion very much, because it appealed to reason. An old Bedouin sheikh was brought before us, who promised to do his best to procure camels for our future journey through the desert. At last the repast was served up. It was much after the English fashion, our host shewing us the greatest kindness. After all was over, we were guided by the janissary, carrying a silk lantern, through the dark streets, to rooms belonging to the British consulate. Our mats were spread upon the floor, and we slept soundly, although the mosquitoes annoyed us not a little. A locust also dropped in at one of the lattices of the room. Our chamber was fitted up in the true oriental style, for the part of the room assigned for the bed was about a foot higher than the rest of the floor. We saw the meaning of 'going up to the bed' (Psalm 132:3). The windows were completely shaded by a wooden lattice-work on the outside, which we found universal in Egypt. It is probably the same thing that is spoken of by Solomon, 'shewing himself through the lattice' (Song of Solomon 2:9).

May 21

Early next morning, we settled accounts with the Egyptian donkeymen who had brought us thus far on our journey. Soon after which the Consul's janissary, dressed in white, with red shoes, came to invite us to our forenoon's repast. We then found that it is the custom in the East, to send for the guests when the feast is prepared, saying, 'Come for all things are now ready' (Luke 14:17). The Consul was sitting as usual in the corner of his divan, along with some Egyptian friends, among whom was the Governor of the province – a rough-looking man, with a grisly beard, snow-white turban, and piercing eye. He was very kind to us, and examined all our clothes, even the pockets and lappets of our coats, our watches, outside and inside, with uplifted eyebrows, adding *'Buono, buono,'* at every discovery. The collazione[1] was in the English fashion for our sakes, and the Governor for the first time, as he told us, attempted the use of the knife and fork. After the repast, the servants carried round a brazen basin, and out of a jar poured water on the hands of every guest. We remembered Elisha pouring water on the hands of Elijah (2 Kings 3:11).

---

1. Italian, *conversation.*

Returning again to the hall, and squatted once more upon the divan, coffee was brought in very small cups, each cup being enclosed in a small silver case. The long pipes were next carried in by six attendants. Each servant stood at a reverent distance, and kept his eye fixed upon the hand of the guest whom he was serving, watching the slightest notion. This vividly recalled the allusion in the Psalms, 'Behold as the eyes of servants look unto the hand of their masters' (Psalm 123:2). While we were thus seated, a tall old man came in with a petition in his hand. He took off his shoes, and approached the Governor barefoot (Exodus 3:5). The great man glanced rapidly over the paper, and without speaking a word, gathered his brows into a terrible frown; whereat the poor man retired as if from a serpent.

At parting, we were invited to return to the evening meal. No hour was fixed; but towards evening, we were sent for by the secretary, whose name was Salvator Strigelli, an intelligent young Italian, fantastically dressed, with long black hair curling upon his shoulders. We asked him when his master usually dined; he said, 'About half an hour after sunset,' which proved to be half-past seven. We had an opportunity of speaking to this secretary very directly on the necessity of a personal interest in Christ. He seemed, however, to have a strong leaning to scepticism, and was of a romantic turn of mind.

At the door of the Consul's house were many poor and diseased, hanging about in expectation of getting help from those who visited him. We remembered Lazarus laid at the rich man's gate (Luke 16:20). At dinner we were still more interested in observing a custom of the country. In the room where we were received, besides the divan on which we sat, there were seats all round the walls. Many came in and took their place on those sideseats, uninvited and yet unchallenged. They spoke to those at table on business or the news of the day, and our host spoke freely to them. This made us understand the scene in Simon's house at Bethany, where Jesus sat at supper, and Mary came in and anointed his feet with ointment (John 12:1-3); and also the scene in the Pharisee's house, where the woman who was a sinner came in, uninvited and yet not forbidden, and washed his feet with her tears (Luke 7:36-38). The chief dish at the table was a highly-seasoned *pilau* of rice; but the Consul pressed us much to another, which he described as a dish peculiar to Egypt, made of an herb like clover, called *melahieh*. It has a saltish taste as its Arabic name indicates. Several armed Arabs were serving us, but the favourite attendant was Hassan, who was always summoned into the room by a loud call *'Wa-hassan'*, accompanied by clapping the one hand very sharply on the other. The conversation was of a more serious cast than previously. The Consul, whose name is Michael Suruff, is by birth an Egyptian, and his father was a native of Damascus. He is a Greek Roman Catholic, but so liberal that he declared he believed our Protestant worship to be much nearer the form which Christ would approve. He thought that there were no traces in Scripture of any such orders in the church as their bishops. At the same time he reckoned it a disgrace for any man to change his religion.

Wednesday, May 22

In the pleasant air of morning the flat roof of our house afforded us an opportunity of realizing Peter's position in Acts 10:9, and of imitating his example. Immediately below our apartment was the Graeco-Romish chapel, a very small apartment, filled with the fragrance of incense. Two priests stood at the altar and two monks were reading the Arabic service. Two little boys also were assisting; but we were the only auditors. The half of the population of Damietta is professedly Christian, but most of these belong to the Greek church. In one of the streets we were attracted, by the sound of bawling voices, to a native school. Eight children were seated on the floor, with their books placed before them, not on a desk, but on a sort of hurdle. The children kept up an incessant rocking motion of the body backward and forward at every word they repeated, and all seemed to speak at once at the pitch of their voices. At the corner of another street we were attracted by a similar sound to a school up a stair, attended by about thirty children, with two teachers. They sat in regular rows on the floor, with their books, which were all Arabic, in their hands; their shoes had been left in a heap at the door. Three repeated their lesson at once, rocking to and fro. Quickness and loudness of utterance seemed to be aimed at as the chief excellence of the scholars.

We visited the Consul once more, to thank him for all his kindness and bid him adieu. The common salutation at meeting and parting is to put the hand first on the breast and then on the lips, as if to intimate that what the lips utter the heart feels (see Job 31:27, 'my mouth hath kissed my hand'). But no custom of the East struck us more than their manner of squandering away time: drinking coffee, smoking, and sitting indolently on a couch, seem to occupy many hours of the day.

In the forenoon, our arrangements for traversing the desert being completed, we set out for the lake Menzaleh, about a mile from

Damietta. Reaching the lake, we embarked in a large open boat, spread our carpets on the floor, and formed an awning with our mats. A large sail was raised, and a gentle breath of wind carried us slowly along; the sail and ropes were well patched, and would have fared ill in a gale. Lake Menzaleh is the ancient Mendes, and is in general four or five feet deep. The bottom appeared to be a very rich alluvial soil, and were the lake drained would form a splendid plain. The banks are all cultivated for rice. The thermometer was 74° under our awning, and the vessel moved very slowly, so that we found it pleasant to bathe in the lake. We sailed past two villages that lie close to each other, Ugbieh or Menzaleh, and Maturieh. The former is on the neck of land, and both had a lively appearance, presenting the aspect of more industry than any Egyptian town or village we had yet seen. There were many boats at the quay; some carrying lime, others rice, others fish. The Mosque, rising over the houses and palm-trees, and seen against the deep blue sky, gave a truly picturesque effect to this quiet but busy spot. Towards evening, we observed the shore covered with immense reeds, from ten to twenty feet high; the waterfowl, and the fish leaping out of the water, seemed to be innumerable. The unbroken stillness of the evening scene was strangely solemnizing, and after singing the 23rd and 121st Psalms, we committed ourselves to repose in the bottom of the boat.

May 23

We were roused before sunrise. Our boat had reached during the night a narrow embankment, which divides this part of the lake from the next. The part we had sailed over was anciently the Mendesian branch of the Nile: and the part we were now to enter upon was the Tanitic or Saitic branch, now called Moes. The place was called Sid, perhaps a remnant of the ancient Sais.

While the men were transporting the luggage over the slender isthmus, we wandered along the shore. It was a beautiful morning, and the air was soft and balmy – just such an atmosphere Joseph used to breathe when he was governor over the land of Egypt. We came upon two Arabs sitting by a smouldering fire of camel's dung. The quern or hand-mill, made of two granite stones, was lying by a large cruse of water, and a round iron plate for baking. As we sailed on, the banks on either hand presented fields of very large onions watered by human labour. A half-naked Egyptian stood by a well, into which he dipped a bucket, which was attached to a transverse pole. By means of a weight at the other end of the pole, the bucket was easily raised and emptied into the ditch, which conveyed it over the field (see Deuteronomy 11:10 for a similar custom). There were also many 'sluices and ponds for fish', similar without doubt to those referred to by Isaiah (Isaiah 19:10), which were once numerous on all the branches of the Nile.

About 10 am we landed at the village of San, anciently called Tanis, and in Scripture Zoan, one of the most ancient cities in the world (Numbers 13:22). The fine alluvial plain around was no doubt 'the field of Zoan' (Psalm 78:12,43), where God did marvellous things in the days of Moses; and it is by no means an unlikely opinion, that the well-known Goshen (Genesis 46:29) was in this region. We pitched our tents upon the bank to shelter ourselves from the rays of an almost vertical sun, while the wild Arabs came round, some to gaze upon the strangers, and some to offer old coins and small images for sale. In the cool of the day we wandered forth for solitary meditation, and Mr Bonar, passing over some heaps of rubbish a few minutes' walk from the village, started a fox from its lair. Following after it, he found himself among low hills of loose alluvial matter, full of fragments of pottery, while beyond these lay several heaps of large stones, which on a nearer inspection he found to be broken obelisks and ruins of what may have been ancient temples – the relics of a glory that is departed. But darkness came on, and obliged him to return to the tent. It was a lovely moonlight night, and very pleasant it was to unite in prayer and in singing psalms amid the wild Arabs, in the very region where God had wrought so many wonders long ago. We read over Isaiah 19, 'The burden of Egypt', in our tent, and when we looked out on the paltry mud village of San, with its wretched inhabitants, we saw God's word fulfilled before our eyes. 'Surely the princes of Zoan are fools, the counsel of the wise counsellors of Pharaoh is become brutish:' *'Where are they? where are thy wise men?'* 'The princes of Zoan are become fools' (Isaiah 19:1-13). The people of the modern village are extremely filthy and ignorant, famous for pilfering, and not to be trusted. Our sheikh and servants were a little afraid of them, and insisted on making one or two discharges of firearms, to instil a salutary awe into the villagers. They also kept watch round our tents the whole night (one of them with a naked sabre, which lay by his side gleaming in the moonlight), keeping one another awake by a low Arab chant.

May 24, Friday

At sunrise, we took a full survey of all that now remains of ancient Zoan. We found that the large mounds of alluvial matter which cover the ruins of brick and pottery, extend about two miles from east to west, and one mile and a half from north to south. The whole country round appeared to be covered not with sand, but with soil which might be cultivated to the utmost if there was water. The most remarkable relics of this ancient city lie at the western extremity. We came upon immense blocks of red granite lying in a heap. All had been hewn, some were carved, and some were still lying regularly placed one above another. Here probably stood the greatest temple of Zoan; and there seems to have been an open square round it. Possibly also a stream flowed through the very midst of the city, for at present there is the dry channel of a torrent. Farther to the north, we found ten or twelve obelisks, fallen and prostrate, and two sphinxes, broken and half sunk into the ground. The finest of the obelisks was thirty feet long, the culmen unbroken, and the carving unimpaired. All were covered with hieroglyphics. Several had the symbol of Ibis, others of Anubis and Osiris. One of the sphinxes was thirteen feet long, and nearly perfect, the other was a fragment. Towards the south were the remains of two columns having capitals of the Corinthian order, though in the form of the shaft there seemed to be an imitation of the lotus leaf. Among the mounds we could clearly trace buildings of brick, the bricks still retaining their original place. The remains of pottery, however, were most remarkable, consisting of jars of the ancient form without number, all broken into fragments, many of them bearing the clearest marks of the action of fire, shewing that God has literally fulfilled the word of the prophet, 'I will set fire in Zoan' (Ezekiel 30:14).

Returning to our tents, we found eight camels waiting for us, each attended by a Bedouin. This was our first trial of 'the ship of the desert'. The loading of the camel is a singular scene. At the word of command the animal sinks down upon the sand with its limbs crouched under it. A wooden frame is fastened on the highest part of the back, to which a network of ropes is commonly attached, for the convenience of enclosing luggage. A carpet and covering are then placed above, and form a soft saddle, upon which the rider must sit either astride or sideways, without stirrup or bridle, and balance himself according to the best of his ability. The camel often moans sadly during the time of mounting, and sometimes tries to bite. When it rises there is much danger of being thrown over its head, and then of being thrown the other way; and the Arabs are very careless in warning, for they say no one is hurt by a fall from a camel. All things being ready, we proceeded forward at the slow rate of somewhat less than three miles an hour. The long step of the camel causes a constant monotonous rocking of the body, which is very fatiguing at first, and our patience was tried by their incessantly bending down their swanlike necks to crop the dry prickly herbage of the desert. The Sheikh presented us with some fresh cucumbers to keep us from thirst, and we listened with interest to the short plaintive song of the Bedouins, who responded to one another while they urged on their camels. We passed a small hovel in the sand, where the Arabs made a curious sound expressive of superstitious reverence. They told us it was the dwelling of a *dervish*. Coming upon the dead carcase of a camel, which two men were flaying for the sake of its flesh and skin, our guide remarked that, besides these, the hair also is valuable, being used in making rough cloaks for the Bedouins. No doubt these are the same as the hairy garment worn by Elijah (2 Kings 1:8), and the 'raiment of camel's hair' worn by John the Baptist (Matthew 3:4). All the Arabs wore also a broad 'leathern girdle about their loins'.

We frequently experienced an interesting illustration of a passage in the prophet Isaiah (Isaiah 25:5). About midday, when the heat was very oppressive, a small cloud, scarcely observable by the eye, passed over the disc of the burning sun. Immediately the intense heat abated, a gentle breeze sprung up, and we felt refreshed. 'Thou shalt bring down the noise of strangers (enemies) as the heat in a dry place (a sandy desert), even the heat *with the shadow of a cloud*; the branch (the palm branch waved in supposed triumph) of the terrible ones shall be brought low'. The immediate relief afforded us by the interposition of a small and almost imperceptible cloud, taught us the lesson of the prophet – with what divine ease and speed God can relieve his suffering church and bring low her proudest enemies. Again and again in the course of our journey we had occasion to quote the words, and in the spirit of Bunyan's pilgrim when refreshed, said one to another, 'He bringeth down the heat in a dry place with the shadow of a cloud'.

In four hours and a half we arrived at Menaghee, a poor village, where every house was built entirely of mud, but where there was a wood of fine palm trees and three wells of good water, so that as we pitched our tents we were reminded of Elim (Exodus 25:27).

The evening was pleasant, and we bathed in a part of the old Pelusaic branch of the Nile. The river no longer flows to the sea, and its reeds are 'withered, driven away, and are no more' (Isaiah 19:7). We concluded that we must be near Sin or Pelusium, the key of Egypt in ancient days. Beside this stream we saw great numbers of ravens, called by the Arabs *ourab* (cf. Hebrew, *oreb*), and many a vulture, called *daiah* (doubtless the Hebrew *da'ah*), hovered over us as if desirous to feed upon our flesh. A fine moonlight night succeeded. The Arabs and camels formed a circle round our tents. They fed the camels with chopped straw and bran; in reference to which common food, Isaiah speaks of a better time that is to come, when the provender shall be 'winnowed with the shovel and the fan' (Isaiah 30:24). Talking to Ibraim about the Bedouins, we asked if the Arab sheikh could read. 'No, no (said Ibraim), Bedouin-man neither read nor write; Bedouin-man just like donkey.' There was something in this rude testimony that irresistibly reminded us of the word of God concerning Ishmael, 'He will be a wild man' – or more literally, 'He will be a wild ass man' (Genesis 16:12).

May 25, Saturday

We were mounted on our camels by sunrise, and bade salaam to the old sheikh and his black attendant, who now took leave of us in a very kind manner, committing us to the care of the Bedouins. The sunbeams glanced along the level plain of the wilderness, scorching our hands and faces, for we were journeying nearly due east. Every hour it became hotter and hotter, and this, along with the slow rocking motion of the camel, often produced an irresistible drowsiness – a feeling indescribably painful in such circumstances. About half-past nine o'clock, a loud cry from the guide aroused us all. Our friend Dr Black had fallen suddenly from his camel. We immediately slipped down from our camels and ran to the spot. For some time he remained nearly insensible, but by the use of such restoratives as we had, at last began gradually to recover. It was a truly affecting scene, which we can never forget. Far from our kindred, in the midst of a vast solitude, no living being near except our little company of Arabs, not knowing what might be the extent of the injury received, we felt how completely our times were in God's hand. The Arabs cheerfully erected the tent, and though the water in the skins was scarce and precious, they sprinkled some over the tent to keep it cool – for the thermometer stood at 89° in the shade. The camels couched on the sand under the burning sun, and each of the

Bedouins made a little tent of his cloak and lay down beneath. We were thankful to be able to resume our journey, and proceed onwards the next stage towards the cool of the day, intending to spend the Sabbath there. The desert now presented an unvaried circle of sand as far as the horizon, sometimes gathered into little hillocks, sometimes covered with stunted thorns, 'the heath in the desert' of which Jeremiah speaks (Jeremiah 17:6). The sun went down in the same manner as at sea, and bright moonlight followed. Very weary we arrived at Gomatter about ten o'clock at night. A small fort, or posthouse of the Pasha, and a deep well of cold water, were the only objects of interest in this desolate spot, where we pitched our tents and sought rest.

May 26, Sabbath

The Sabbath dawned sweetly upon us, but soon it became very hot, the thermometer being 92° in the shade. We rested in our tents, and found many of the Psalms, such as the 63rd, full of new meaning and power.

Dr Keith went up to the Post-office, and finding the master very friendly, sat down with him in the shade of his house. Our Arab attendants also seated themselves beside him, while he read several passages of the Bible, Ibraim being interpreter. They listened with the utmost attention, putting in a note approbation again and again. But in the midst of his occupation, Ibraim could not refrain from making his remarks on the Bedouins. Pointing to one man who was staring with unmeaning countenance, he whispered, 'Look, look, now, *is not Bedouin-man just like donkey?*' In the evening we invited the Governor to visit our tent, and seated him on our best carpet in the corner, the Bedouins being all gathered round the tent-door. Dr Black was so far well as to be able to address this interesting congregation. He went over several Scripture narratives, and ended by reading part of John. He spoke in Italian, and Ibraim interpreted, but evidently not so willingly as in the forenoon. The constant remark of the auditors – often, it is to be feared, out of mere courtesy – was *'Taib, Taib'*, 'good, good', or *'Saheia, Saheia'*, 'very just'. Ibraim and Ahmet spoke to us when the rest were gone. One of their great stumbling-blocks seems to be the profligate and irreligious conduct of professing Christians. Ibraim related the shameful manner in which a gentleman at Cairo had treated him. Ahmet started some speculative questions regarding Providence, and mentioned some Frenchmen who believed in no God. We explained the difference between nominal and real Christians; and Ibraim remarked that he had met with good Christians, mentioning with great affection and respect Professor Robinson from America, with whom he had travelled about two years ago. Both of them had met with Joseph Wolff in Mr Gliddon's house at Alexandria, and remembered him with much interest.

When left alone we were led to meditate on that happy time when Israel shall 'arise and shine', and the sons of Ishmael, the untamed wanderers of the desert, shall share in the blessing. 'The multitude of camels shall cover thee, the dromedaries of Midian and Ephah; all they from Sheba shall come'; 'all the flocks of Kedar shall be gathered together unto thee, the rams of Nebaioth shall minister unto thee' (Isaiah 60:6,7).

May 27

We were up with the sun, and soon on our way. This is the extreme part of the desert of Shur, wherein Hagar wandered (Genesis 16:7). It is still overspread with stunted bushes and shrubs; and it was no doubt under one of these that she cast her child (Genesis 21:15). The most common bush is called *'atel'* or *'athle'*, 'the tamarisk'.

Not far from this point of the road stood in ancient days Tahpanhes, or Daphne, and Migdol, whither the rebellious remnant of Judah carried Jeremiah after the destruction of Jerusalem by the King of Babylon (Jeremiah 43:7; 46:14). At a distance on the left, we saw ancient remains, which the men said were the ruins of a city. The infallible word of God has been fulfilled. 'At Tehaphnehes (Tahpanhes) also the day shall be darkened', 'a cloud shall cover her, and her daughters shall go into captivity' (Ezekiel 30:18). We met the Pasha's dromedary-post, travelling at the rate of six or seven miles an hour. We were told that, if he be a few hours beyond his time, he is in danger of losing his head. Before midday we came to a resting-place called Duadahr, which means 'the Warrior', and our camels kneeled down beside a fine well, out of which the water is drawn by a large wheel. This resting at wells called vividly to mind many Scripture events.

On resuming our journey, the character of the desert was altered. Instead of a level plain, our route lay over sandhills, with considerable valleys between. The setting-sun, casting his rays on these, had a peculiarly pleasing effect; and especially when the palm trees adorned the heights, a mild desolate beauty was added to the landscape. We understood that we were approaching the range of desert mountains, anciently called Mount Casius. The moon rose in clear, unclouded splendour, and under its light we often seemed to be journeying over drifted snow. Late at night we reached Catieh, very weary, having spent about twelve hours on the camel's back.

Catieh is the ancient Casium, and not far from the sea. Like Elim it has many wells of water, and many palm trees; though very sandy, we thought it the most engaging spot we had yet seen in the wilderness. Some have supposed that several of the stations of the wandering Israelites were along this track. For example, they say, that Rissa was probably El Arish, and if so, Kehelathah must have been near this place (Numbers 33:22).

May 28

In the morning, while we were seated at breakfast, the postmaster, Osman Effendi, visited our tent. He willingly drank tea, and asked for a little to present to his wife, who, he said, had learned how to make it. Seeing that our bread was very old, he sent for some new bread from his own house, and presented it to us. He gave us also a quantity of salted milk, which, however, we could not drink. We afterwards visited him in return at his house, and found him seated on the ground among some of his younger servants, teaching them to read. His whole manner and appearance recalled to mind the patriarch of the desert. His house was wretched, the floor being loose sand, but the cool shade of the stone walls was pleasant.

We had rested the first part of this day in order fully to recruit our strength. Towards evening we were again mounted, and bade farewell to Catieh. Our last view of our kind friend Osman Effendi was when he was kneeling upon the sand near the tombs, and praying with his face towards Mecca.

The desert was now of a more verdant character; and as we proceeded, many flocks of goats were feeding by the way, some of which had sheep mingled with them; forcibly reminding us of our Lord's parabolic account of the great day (Matthew 25:32). At present, the thoughtless and the hypocrites feed side by side with the children of God in the pastures of this world's wilderness, but the day is coming when He shall separate the righteous from the wicked, 'as a shepherd divideth his sheep from the goats'. The long curling hair of these goats was of a beautiful glossy black, shewing us at once the beauty and propriety of the description in the Song, 'Thy hair is as a flock of goats that appear from Mount Gilead' (Song of Solomon 4:1).

Next morning *(May 29)* we saw at a distance a range of hills running north and south, called by the Arabs *Djebel Khalil*. They form part of 'the hills of Seir'. After wandering so many days in the wilderness, with its vast monotonous plains of level sand, the sight of these distant mountains was a pleasant relief to the eye; and we thought we could understand a little of the feeling with which Moses, after being forty years in the desert, would pray, 'I pray thee, let me go over and see the good land that is beyond Jordan that goodly mountain and Lebanon' (Deuteronomy 3:25).

Before noon, the sudden sight of the sea, or rather of the famous Sirbonian lake, and the sea beyond it, made us cry to one another (in language we had learned from our guides), *'El Bahr, El Bahr'*, 'the sea, the sea', like the joyful shouts of the ten thousand Greeks, $\theta\alpha\lambda\lambda\alpha\sigma\sigma\alpha$, $\theta\alpha\lambda\lambda\alpha\sigma\sigma\alpha$. The lake is referred to by Milton,

> 'A lake profound, as that Serbonian bog
> Betwixt Damiata and Mount Casius old
> Where armies whole have sunk' (*Paradise Lost*, B.II).

The lake is connected with the sea, but the drifting sands keep it in the state of a morass, a sandy morass. It was very shallow at this place; and at the time we bathed in it the water was tepid. When we came out, the salt of the water appeared on our bodies in the form of a thick crust.

Returning to our tent, we gathered specimens of the few flowers of the desert, and in our search found the ground overrun with lizards and beetles. While seated at our midday meal, a company mounted on camels came past us from another quarter of the desert. One of them rode up to us, his face scorched with the sun and his mouth parched, his only cry being, *'Moie, moie'*, 'Water, water'.

Towards evening we journeyed forward through a more verdant part of the desert, cheered by the view of the distant hills, and by the chirping (for there was little song) of the little birds which, for the first time, we observed among the bushes. The moon rose upon us in glorious brightness, and late at night we pitched our tents in a place called Abugilbany.

May 30

In the morning, the desert was really enlivened by the chirping of birds. As a single note of a sweet song will often revive a sad heart, so it seems as if the lively notes of these birds, in a place so desolate and far from the dwellings of men, were a kind arrangement of Providence in order to refresh the weary traveller.

We found the heat more oppressive this day than we had yet experienced it. The hillocks of sand, between which we were slowly moving at the usual camel's pace, reflected the sun's rays upon us, till our faces were glowing as if we had been by the side of a furnace. The hills of Seir occasionally reappeared, and on the left the lake stretched out in full view. At one time a fox started from the bush and fled before us. It was to such an animal the prophet Ezekiel referred, 'O Israel, thy prophets are like *the foxes in the desert*' (Ezekiel 13:4), hungry and anxious to find a prey.

Our track now lay amidst unusual plenty of herbage and tufts of verdant plants, a change which became the occasion of considerable annoyance; for the camels were continually bending down their long necks to crop the shrubs, especially some species which seemed peculiarly succulent. We saw in this an illustration of the description given of the wild ass, 'He searcheth after every green thing' (Job 39:8). Here, too, the sand was occasionally covered with a crust of salt, as if a salt lake had once been there. This also is mentioned in the same passage as a feature of the scenery, 'Whose house I have made the wilderness, and the barren land (in Hebrew "the salt place") his dwelling' (Job 39:6).

Our guide now directed us by a road a little nearer than that by the seaside; though much more irregular, and over endless hills of sand. Perhaps it was through this part of the desert of Shur that Hagar wandered, intending to go back to her native country (Genesis 16:7); and it may have been by this way that Joseph carried the young child Jesus when they fled into the land of Egypt (Matthew 2:14). Even in tender infancy the sufferings of the Redeemer began, and he complains, 'I am afflicted and ready to die from my youth up' (Psalm 88:15). Perhaps these scorching beams beat upon his infant brow, and this sand-laden breeze dried up his infant lips, while the heat of the curse of God began to melt his heart within. Even in the desert we see the suretyship of Jesus.

All this day our guides would not suffer us to pitch our tents. They were anxious to reach the first town on the Syrian frontier before nightfall, and our store of provisions being now exhausted, Ibraim urged us forward, in spite of heat, fatigue, and faintness. One half hour alone we rested and sought shelter under some of the low bushes of the desert, while we satisfied our hunger with a few raisins and a morsel of Arab cheese. The heat was very oppressive. Even the Bedouins begged us to lend them handkerchiefs to shield their faces from the rays of the sun; and often ran before and threw themselves beneath a bush to find shelter for a few minutes. How full of meaning did the word of the prophet appear, 'There shall be a tabernacle for a shadow in the daytime from the heat' (Isaiah 4:6). And again, 'A man shall be as the shadow of a great rock in a weary land' (Isaiah 32:2).

In the afternoon, we came in sight of three wells, situated in a lonely valley. On getting near the spot, there was a general rush down the slope to reach the water. The cameldrivers ran forward to be first there, and we all followed, and even the patient camels came round the wells eager to drink. But to us, the water was *Marah*; we could not drink it, for it was muddy, and bitter too. We tried to get a draught by straining it through a handkerchief, but all would not avail. Thus sadly were the Israelites disappointed, for when 'they came to Marah, they could not drink of the waters of Marah for they were bitter' (Exodus 15:23). The Bedouins seemed to care nothing for the impurity of the water, for they drank largely and greedily. We imagined that thus eagerly Israel rushed forward to the clear, cool waters of the Smitten Rock (Exodus 17:6).

We now passed over a sandy soil, in which small shells abounded, and occasionally heaps of stones that appeared to be ruins of ancient buildings. In these stones also small shells were imbedded. It was near this that *Ostracine* once stood, an ancient town, so called (from σοτρακον, a shell) from the circumstance of the shells found in the soil. The setting sun was pouring its last rays upon the bare and desolate sandhills, as if in vain attempting to clothe them with beauty, when we came in sight of El Arish, the frontier town between Syria and Egypt, the spot we had so anxiously desired to reach before any quarantine should be established to delay our progress. We passed the remains of an old city, the foundations of which we could distinctly trace, though half-buried in the sand. This we supposed to be the ancient *Rhinocolura*. In a little while after, our camels knelt down outside the gate of the small town of El Arish. We encamped under a tree, with a cluster of palms near, and not far from the burying-ground on the North West of the town, and on the road to Gaza.

The town is situated on the gentle slope of a sandhill about two miles from the sea. The castle, a square building, not very formidable to an enemy, stands on the highest part, and the houses, dingy, monotonous-looking buildings, with flat roofs and scarcely any windows, slope down from it. The population of the town cannot be more than 600 inhabitants, many of whom were enjoying the cool breeze of evening on the roofs of their houses. The quarantine established here for all who come from Syria going down into Egypt, prevents the increase of traffic, people being unwilling to come to it from Syria, since they must tarry so long in the Lazaretto[1] near its walls. We were told that, at one time, El Arish was surrounded with beautiful gardens, but these have been completely covered by the desolating sand, and now the only remains of fertility is a grove of young palms which shelter the eastern side of the town. We were rejoiced to find that the quarantine was not yet established for those going to Syria, so that we had attained the object of our journey through the desert. This was a new and special call upon us to give thanks and praise, especially now when we were in sight of the Promised Land, and our eyes rested on some of the hills given to Abraham, Isaac, and Jacob.

We were outside the wall, but we heard the call to prayer from the Mosque, whose minaret rises conspicuous above the common dwellings. The cry of the Muezzin was louder that evening, and more prolonged, because it was Thursday, the commencement of the Mahometan Sabbath. The Mahometans begin their Sabbath, like the Jews, at six o'clock in the evening, and Friday is the day which they keep sacred. The call to prayer is certainly one of the most solemn and affecting parts of their worship; but the Mahometans themselves seem not at all affected by it. Indeed, their whole religious services appear to be empty forms, all voice and gesture, and no feeling.

May 31

In the morning, the place was enlivened by the multitude of little birds that chirped and sung among the trees near our tents. So small is the traffic existing at present between Egypt and Syria, and so little plenty is poured over the borders of the Promised Land, that no articles of food were to be had in the town, except milk and Arab bread. However, in the midst of our difficulties, Ibraim came to tell us that a man had brought a sheep to the tent-door, wishing to sell it to us. We gladly bought it for

---

1. A hospital for contagious diseases.

twenty-five piastres, about five shillings of our money. Our servants appropriated the skin and wool; and what became of the head and feet we know not, only they were not served up to us as they would have been in Scotland.

A more serious difficulty than want of food presented itself in the want of camels to carry us on our way. Our Bedouins had bargained to carry us to El Arish, and this they had faithfully performed. But nothing would persuade them to carry us farther. In this dilemma the Governor of the town sent us word that he would come and visit our tent. There is a degree of real authority suggested by the dress and air and attendants of such a man. He came riding upon a cream-coloured Arab horse, small but fleet, with silvery mane, flowing tail, and rich caparisons. His attendants rode by his side, and even they assumed an air of importance with their ornamented girdles, crooked scimitars, and elegant eastern attire. Their favourite feat of horsemanship was to gallop at full speed along the sand or among the palms, and then suddenly to draw the rein and stop, making the sand fly in all directions. When the Governor was fairly seated in the corner of our carpet, he evidently wished to show his authority and importance, and to get money from us by pretending causes of delay; but after much arguing and annoyance, he at last agreed to arrange with the camel-driver who had brought us thus far, to take us to Gaza for 600 piastres (about £6 Sterling) – a price double what ought to have been charged, but demanded at present as necessary to remunerate the men who would be kept in quarantine on their return. Part of the price was accordingly paid into the Governor's hand, and the interview ended. He afterwards sent us a jar of cold water as a present, for 'a cup of cold water only' (Matthew 10:42) is a real gift in this country. In the afternoon he visited us again, to announce that the Bedouins refused to observe the contract, but that he himself would provide us with camels tomorrow. We suspected some fraud in this, but had no remedy. One of the Bedouins on taking leave of us, showed a good deal of feeling, and while all of them kissed our hands, Ibraim was treated in the true oriental style, being kissed on the cheek half a dozen times ere they parted. The sight of these poor ignorant Arabs, often deeply impressed us with wonder at God's kindness to ourselves. Here is election – sovereign grace alone makes us to differ from them!

Although our desert wanderings had delayed us longer than we could have wished, yet we could see a kind Providence leading us this way to the land of Israel. We were made to sympathize far more than we had ever done with the trials of Israel in the wilderness, and to understand better how they were so much discouraged because of the way, and how they were so often tempted to murmur against God.

How great a blessing 'the pillar of the cloud' must have been! Towering over the camp, it cast a delightful shadow upon the sand over which they moved. But still more, what a gracious pledge it was that their heavenly Guide would lead them in the right way to the place of rest.

Now, too, we were taught the meaning of 'dwelling in tents with Isaac and Jacob' (Hebrews 11:9). Such a life is one of constant dependence and faith. In the morning when the tent is struck, the traveller never knows where he is to pitch it at noon or evening; whether it is to be beside the palm and springs of water, or in solitude and sand. The description of the joyful state of the redeemed given in the Apocalypse (Revelation 7:16,17), seems to be formed in reference to such a life as this. There shall be no more hunger, thirst, nor burning sun, but green shady pastures and living fountains of water, and the Lamb shall dwell as in a tent (σκηνώσει) among them. And all this because they have reached the promised inheritance – their desert life has ended, and the Promised Land begun.

We noticed that when camels are sent out to feed they often stray over a wide surface. At the place where we now were, the reason alleged for keeping us till next day was, that the camels had been sent out to feed and could not be found. A man had been sent upon a dromedary to look for them, but could not discover what direction they had taken. This circumstance reminded us of Saul being sent to seek his father's asses, in days when the pastures of Israel may have been equally free (1 Samuel 9:3).

The evening was beautiful. Indeed, morning and evening here, day after day, have a brilliance such as we never see more than once or twice in a year at home. The flood of light that pours out of the clear, unclouded skies, reminds us of the last words of David, where he compares the reigning of the coming Saviour 'to a morning without clouds' (2 Samuel 23:4), and also of the language of the Psalmist, 'Day unto day *pours out* speech' (Psalm 19:2, *a gushing fount of praise*).

The heat having abated, we wandered towards the town. We observed two very deep wells, arched over to keep out the sun and the sand. Two marble columns were built into one of them, and broken pieces of marble pillars of the Doric order were lying scattered in various places near the town. To the east a kind of garden, surrounded with a hedge of prickly pear, and planted with palms, aloes, and melons, seemed to struggle with the sand for existence. In the town several women in the streets wore the anklet, 'the tinkling ornament about their feet' (Isaiah 3:18). We heard its sound as we passed along. Most of their children had their heads adorned with pieces of money. The Effendi's child was carried at the side, having six or eight gold coins, called *harieh*, strung together round the front of its cap. Most of the houses are built completely of mud. At present they are as hard and as dry as stone, but we could readily imagine how easily the overflowing shower would destroy them, and the stormy wind rend the wall (Ezekiel 13:11). The roofs of the houses are all flat, and communicate with one another. Often they are made of the branches of the palm and other trees, with the leaves remaining on them, and coated over with mud. If the house mentioned by Mark (Mark 2:4) had a roof of this description, how easy it would be to break it up. In the court of one of the houses (for every house, however humble, has its court, 2 Samuel 17.18), we examined the Arab oven, a rude and simple contrivance. It is made of clay like their houses, quite dry and hard. The lower aperture is to admit the fire, a few cinders of charcoal, or some heated stones. Over the fire there is a floor of clay, where the dough is fired. The upper aperture is for putting in the dough when it has been kneaded and divided into cakes. The roof of the whole, surrounded by a parapet, affords a convenient place for the bread gradually to cool. The kneading trough is a large wooden bowl, not unlike that used in our own country.

In the middle of the town there is a very fine well, the water of which is drawn up by a wheel. We drank freely for the first time since entering the desert. No one who has not wandered in arid regions, can imagine the delight which cold water gives to a thirsty soul (Proverbs 25:25). Toward sunset, two of our number crossed the hills of sand which enclose El Arish, till we came to the ancient bed of a broad river, about half a mile east of the town. The channel is about two hundred yards in breadth, distinctly marked by banks on either side. The bed was perfectly flat and dry: but in other days, when Judah's rivers flowed with water, it must have been a majestic stream, not unworthy to form the boundary of the land, if indeed (which is doubtful) this was *the river of Egypt*, so often referred to as the limit of Israel on the south (Genesis 15:18). A little way farther inward, the channel seemed to be filled up by sand, drifted from the hills: but from the spot where we were down to the sea, a distance of two miles, we could distinctly trace its ancient course. We stretched ourselves under one of the bushes that still overhang its banks, and remembering with gratitude that we were now within the border of the Promised Land, united in prayer for Israel, our Church, our distant flocks, and our own souls. We then wandered homeward! that is, to our tents – our only home in this strange land. The hills of El Khalil were full in sight, and toward the sea the Lazaretto attracted our notice by the patches of verdure round it. A few palms, fig trees, aloes, and bushes of prickly pear, also relieved the eye. Darkness came on before we reached our encampment.

Next morning *(June 1)*, we found that our patience must be still further tried, no camels having arrived. We visited an Arab school, and found it very clean, being all whitewashed within, though built of mud. Nineteen boys were present, dirty and ill clad, several of them affected in the eyes, and one blind. Two or three had Arabic books in manuscript; the rest sat in groups, crosslegged, upon the ground, rocking to and fro as they bawled out in one shrill voice words and syllables, which they were reading from a board held in their hand. No master was present, and all went on repeating without any one superintending. One boy brought in a jar of water, from which all in turn drank greedily. On the wall were slates of tin with Arabic traced upon them.

This being Saturday, we remembered in looking across the bed of the ancient river, that on the other side in former days, Israel would have been keeping their Sabbath, and Egypt would hear the praises of Jehovah floating across the stream.

Entering the Fort, we examined an old trough of very hard granite, quite covered with Arabic writing, well engraved. At midday, we went to the gate to enjoy the coolness. The arched roof affords a complete shade at all times, and often a pleasant breeze passes through. Under such a gateway probably Lot was seated, for coolness' sake, when the angels came to Sodom (Genesis 19:1); and for the same reason, the people of old used to resort to it, and it became the market-place (Ruth 4:1,11; Psalm 69:12; Jeremiah 17:19). We saw how the gate became the seat of judgment (Job 5:4; Jeremiah 38:3; Amos 5:15; Matthew 16:18), when a little after the Governor and his Effendi appeared. His attendants having spread a mat and a carpet over it, and a cushion at each corner, he took his seat, inviting us to recline near him.

We took off our shoes and sat down. Our conversation was very limited, as Ibraim was not with us to interpret, but we partook of coffee together, served up in little cups, which are everywhere in use. The Governor was interrogating a native Christian who stood by. This man was a Christian Copt. He told us in broken Italian that he was rejoiced to meet us, because, being almost the only Christian in the place, he is much despised. He wore 'a writer's inkhorn by his side' (Ezekiel 9:2), which intimates that the person is so far superior to the generality that he can at least read and write. The inkhorn has a long shaft which holds the reeds, and is stuck into the girdle, while the place for the ink forms a head at the one end. At our request the Copt took out his reeds and wrote very elegantly. On one of his arms, he shewed us the figure of Christ on the cross and the Virgin Mary, punctured apparently either with *henna* or gunpowder. This is a remnant of an ancient custom (common even among heathens), by which men would shew their anxiety to keep a beloved object ever in mind. There is no doubt a reference to this custom in the beautiful words, 'Behold I have graven thee on the palms of my hands; thy walls are continually before me' (Isaiah 49:16); and also when it is said, 'Another shall subscribe with his hand unto the Lord', or more literally, 'Another shall write upon his hand, *To the Lord*' (Isaiah 44:5) – words intended to express the complete surrender which a believer makes of soul and body to the Lord that bought him.

This day we experienced the effect of the wind raising the sand. The wind was not remarkably strong, but the sand was so fine that it penetrated everywhere. No tent nor portmanteau could shut it out. Our clothes, our food, the water we drank, all were filled with sand. At length eight camels arrived. We joyfully struck our tents, and were conveyed to the Lazaretto close by the shore.

In our way down we passed the rude booths of palm-branches which we had elsewhere seen, and heard the sound of the millstone, coming from one of them, it being now near sunset, the time for the evening meal. In the dry channel of the River many fine palm trees were growing and several luxuriant plants, cultivated in holes dug for the purpose. Several gardens also were laid out with small canals intersecting them, so that streams of water might be conducted to the different beds when needful. These are the 'rivers of water' mentioned by the Psalmist (Psalm 1:3; also Proverbs 21:1). Nearer the shore we saw rushes, a proof that the bed of the ancient river is still occasionally moistened with water. The Governor of the Lazaretto, a pleasant Arab, wearing the hyke or wide mantle, came and conversed with us.

We now exchanged the camels which had brought us from the town for seven camels and a dromedary belonging to the quarantine. The camel and dromedary resemble each other in appearance, but the difference between them is not, as commonly stated, that the one has two hunches on its back and the other only one. It is like the difference between a heavy carthorse and a swift riding-horse. The dromedary is much lighter, swifter, and quicker in its motions; but the Arabian camel and dromedary have both only one hump, though the camel of Bactria and other regions is said to have two. One of our camels had a young one running by its side. Under the conduct of Mustapha – another Bedouin with fine Eastern features – Mahommed, and a boy, we proceeded across the bed of the River, and ascended the opposite bank, entering with joy the Land of Israel.

The country was now very different from the desert. A range of low sand-hills lay between us and the seashore, ready to fulfil God's work of desolation on the land within but the valley through which we were passing had verdure and pasturage, and opened into other valleys of the same character. The ground was full of holes, which we were told were made by the jerboas. Darkness soon came on, and we rested a short time at the command of our Bedouin, who wished to feed his camels. We kindled a blazing fire in the manner of the Bedouins, whose fires we saw in several places round about us. The moon rose most splendidly as we proceeded, and the birds in the bushes round about began to twitter and sing, as if mistaking the bright moon for the rising sun. Though much oppressed with sleepiness, and often in danger of falling from the camel's back, yet the pleasantness of the air, the change of scenery, and the knowledge that we were now traversing the portion of the tribe of Simeon, made our journey comparatively easy. We arrived at Sheikh Juide, once a village, now only a station and a burying-place, marked by the white tomb of a Mahometan saint. It has a good well, some fields of tobacco, and several palm trees. We pitched our tent under a *nabbok*-tree, resembling a plane-tree, and felt how naturally it is recorded, 'Deborah dwelt under the palm-tree' (Judges 4:5), 'Saul tarried under a pomegranate-tree' (1 Samuel 14:2); and of Abraham, who had received the three angels into his tent, that 'he stood by them under the tree' (Genesis 18:8). We spread our mats and fell asleep, thinking over the Promised Land, and how in some part of this very country, God had said to Jacob, as he was stretched out for rest with a stone for his pillow, 'The land whereon thou liest, to thee will I give it' (Genesis 28:13).

June 2, Sabbath

Awaking, we felt the solemnity and privilege of spending a Sabbath-day in the land of Israel. We had worship together in the tent, and sang with joyful hearts,

> 'In Judah's land God is well known,
> His name's in Isr'el great,'
>   (Psalm 76:1, Scottish Metrical Psalter)

With what appropriateness we could look round on every plain and hill within our view and say,

> '*There* arrows of the bow He brake!
> The sword, the shield, the war–
> More glorious thou than hills of prey,
> More excellent art far.'

We had leisure to meditate on those portions of Scripture that peculiarly refer to God's wonders done here. Between us and the range of hills to the east, we had reason to believe, lay the valley of Gerar, the valley where Abraham dwelt (Genesis 20:1), the land where Isaac sowed, and received in the same year an hundredfold, and where he digged so many wells (Genesis 26:12,18). In this region, too, the Avims dwelt till they were destroyed by 'the Caphtorims out of Caphtor' (Deuteronomy 2:23), the ancestors of the Philistines, who in turn yielded to Judah and Simeon. This is the highway down into Egypt; so that by it the Ishmaelites would carry youthful Joseph into Egypt, with their camels bearing spicery, and balm, and myrrh (Genesis 37:25,28); and by this way Jacob would come down with the waggons which Joseph had sent to carry him (Genesis 46:1). This tract was in the portion of Simeon.

The day was very warm, but far pleasanter than in the desert; the breeze not having that dry, scorching feeling which is so overpowering amid the sands of the desert. When the heat of noon abated, we walked to a grassy eminence to the eastward, and found that the country rose into a series of gentle elevations, bounded by a range of hills running parallel to the sea. Herds and flocks of goats and asses were feeding in several places. It was pleasant to think of Isaac and his herdman having wandered here.

We prayed together, feeling that the land was fitted to make us ask much, for from these heavens the Holy Spirit had descended on many a prophet and many a saint. May such men be raised in our day, and Israel be so blessed again, and the same Spirit who visited them visit our land! The evening closed calmly round us in our tents.

June 3

We left Sheikh Juide before 6 am, pleasant clouds veiling the sun. Our course lay northward on the road to Gaza. The same low sand-hills were still between us and the sea, but there was considerable verdure on the undulating plains through which we passed. The road is not like a king's highway with us, made before it is travelled, but is made by the feet of the animals that travel it; and as camels generally follow one another, it consists of many narrow paths mingling with each other, in a breadth of thirty or forty yards. Verdure and wild genista often occurred between the paths, so that the camels were frequently bending their long necks to feed as we journeyed.

At midday we arrived at Khanounes, the ancient Jenysus – its Scripture name is unknown. We had expected to find rest and refreshment here, but a complete hurricane of wind blew the small dry sand full in our faces for about an hour. It was vain to attempt putting up the tent, so that we were forced to shelter ourselves from the combined heat and storm of the sirocco,[1] by wrapping ourselves in our carpets, and lying on our faces at the roots of some large sycamore-trees, till it abated. We thought of Isaiah, 'A man shall be as an hiding-place from the wind, and a covert from the tempest' (Isaiah 32:2); and 'a refuge from the storm, a shadow from the heat, when the blast of the terrible ones is as a storm against the wall' (Isaiah 25:4). An old Arab took special charge of us, asking our names, and leading us through the town in a most friendly manner.

After partaking of some rice and ripe apricots, we resumed our journey about six o'clock in the evening. The camels moved on through a very level and broad plain, which retained more of its grassy verdure than any we had yet passed through. The descending sun shone mildly, the stormy wind had fallen, many flocks were browsing on each side of the road, and there was reviving freshness in the evening breeze. About half an hour North East from Khanounes is a small village called

---

1. A hot oppressive wind beginning in North Africa.

Bennisail, built apparently of mud bricks, but embosomed in trees, among which a solitary palm raised its head. The name of the town is taken from the Arabic name of one of the constellations. It stands upon the summit of a rising ground, and the channel of a stream, which at one time had watered its gardens, but is now dry, can be plainly traced. It may occupy the place of some of Simeon's cities, 'Hazar-Susah', or 'Baalath-beer, Ramath of the south' (Joshua 19:8). Some, indeed, have supposed Khanounes to be *'Ramath of the South'*, but the word *'Ramath'* means 'high ground', a name which could not apply to Khanounes, but would suit well the situation of this pleasant village, for the towers *(Ramoth)* on that slope would glance beautifully in the setting sun, even as do now its figs and solitary palm. The birds were singing very sweetly. Many old and verdant sycamores, with gnarled trunks and branches spreading out toward the east, adorned the plain.

It is said of Solomon that 'he made cedars to be as the sycamore-trees that are in the vale for abundance' (1 Kings 10:27), which shews that in his day the sycamore grew in great plenty, probably in this very plain along the Mediterranean. At present they are far from being abundant. Indeed, trees of any kind are few in the Holy Land. The palm especially occurs only here and there, for it requires cultivation, and has therefore gradually decreased in a country where it was no more attended to. The emblem of triumph has withered away from the land of Judah! The terebinth also (generally reckoned *oak* in our version) is very rare. 'All the trees of the field are withered, because joy is withered away from the sons of men' (Joel 1:12).

We met several of the Bedouin shepherds riding on asses, driving home their cows, sheep and goats. Our guides told us that in all this region they drive their flocks at evening, because of the many wolves, which would render it hazardous to leave them in the open fields at night. Passing up a gentle ascent, there was a village on our left, called Dair or Adair, conjectured by some to be the Adar of Scripture (Joshua 15:3), but as darkness had come down upon us, we could only hear the barking of its dogs.

We had already crossed the dry bed of two torrents, and now came to a third, broader than any of the rest, but quite as dry, called Wady Salga. Perhaps this may be the brook Besor, memorable in the history of David (1 Samuel 30:10), as the place where two hundred of his valiant men remained behind when he pursued the Amalekites. Some hours after we crossed another bed of a river, which the Arabs called Wady

Gaza. The banks were steep and the channel broad at the point where we crossed. When we met with so many dry channels of streams in the south of the Holy Land, we remembered with interest the prayer of Israel, 'Turn again our captivity O Lord, *as the streams in the south*' (Psalm 126:4). These have no water within their banks, except when the rain descends; they wait for rain, like the souls of men of Israel!

We encamped at midnight upon the sand-hills, within half an hour of Gaza.

In the morning *(June 4)* we were told that the plague was raging within the walls of Gaza, and that fifteen persons had died that week. Our cameldrivers now refused to carry us any farther, having completed their contract; and as there had been neither camels nor mules to be had in Gaza for thirty days, the plague having suspended all intercourse with other places, we had to make up our minds to remain here all day. Our servant Ibraim was despatched to lay our case before the Governor, and try to get an arrangement made. The Governor behaved with great politeness, only regretting that we had not a firman[1] from the Pasha of Egypt, in which case he could have compelled the men to carry us forward. This was almost the only instance where we had any reason to regret the want of a firman. As it was, the Governor, finding that we had no other hope of getting away, took it upon him to command the cameldriver to arrange with us and go forward next morning.

Meanwhile, we wandered over the sand-hills on which we had pitched our tents, that we might view the town and adjoining country. Beneath us on the north-west lay the high road to Gaza, the same as in ancient days, but lonely and still, except when the shepherds and their flocks passed by. 'The earth mourneth and fadeth away, few men are left.' Whether the Ethiopian eunuch had come thus far or not, it was this tract of land he was traversing; and it might have been, while his chariot moved heavily and noiselessly over these sands, that Philip had the opportunity of running up to him, and speaking the words of eternal life (Acts 8:26). We sat down on the northern extremity of the mounds of sand, a spot which beautifully overlooks the modern town of Gaza. The evening sun shone sweetly through the beautiful gardens, fine old figs and sycamores, and curious hedges of prickly pear. The minarets and other buildings rose above the trees, and we listened with delight to the

---

1. A decree or order ensuring safety and assistance for travellers.

soft voice of the turtle heard in the land, and the voices of the little children at play. We were told that there are about 3000 inhabitants, though others say above 10,000.

Whilst we gazed upon this peaceful scene, we felt it hard to think that this was a land on which God was 'laying his vengeance' (Ezekiel 25:17). It appeared at first as if there had been no fulfilment of those distinct predictions, 'Gaza shall be forsaken' (Zephaniah 2:4), and 'baldness has come upon Gaza' (Jeremiah 47:5). But when we had completed our investigation, we found that not one word has fallen to the ground.

We separated in order to obtain different views of this interesting spot. Dr Black remained to examine more fully the hills of sand. Dr Keith took the direction of the sea, which is about three miles distant from the modern town, starting the idea, that in all probability these heaps of sand were covering the ruins of Gaza. The ancient town occupied a site much nearer the sea. The rest of us took the direction of the most prominent hill in the landscape lying north-east, and overhanging the modern town.

Returning to our tents, we were now prepared to verify Dr Keith's conclusion, of the truth of which he had been fully satisfied, namely, that these hills of sand, where we had pitched our tents, really covered the ruins of Gaza. Each of us had found the fragments of polished marble in the flat hollows between the sand-hills, the remains no doubt of 'the palaces of Gaza', and also masses of fused stones, proving that God had 'sent a fire on the wall of Gaza' (Amos 1:7). We now saw in a manner we had never done before, that God had fulfilled his own word, *'Baldness is come upon Gaza'* (Jeremiah 47:5). We saw that not merely *mourning*, such as 'baldness' indicated in ancient times, but literally and most remarkably the appearance of baldness has come upon Gaza. No sort of verdure, not a single blade of grass, did we see upon these sand-hills. One solitary tree there was, which only served to make the barrenness more remarkable. This barren bare hill of sand is *the bald head* of Gaza. How awfully true and faithful are the words of God!

During our ramble we had met with some interesting customs of the East. A kind Arab came forward from his tent as we passed, offering us the refreshment of a drink of water, saying, *'Tesherbetu moie'*, 'Will you drink water?' The promise of our Lord, seems to refer to cases like this, where the individual, unasked, seeks out objects on whom to shew kindness. The least desire to bless one who is a disciple shall not lose its reward. At another place we came upon 'the tents of Kedar' (Song of Solomon 1:5). The tents of the Bedouins are of a dark-brown colour, made of goat's hair, and rudely stretched on four poles. In one of the Arab huts the inmates were grinding at the mill, and we helped them to move round the upper millstone. Again, we came upon an Arab cottage, made of branches of trees, and found the whole family seated on the sand before the door. After the usual salaam, they gave us bread warm from their oven, with a look of great kindness, and refused to take any money in return. In one field, the men were ploughing with oxen. In another under the hill, they were winnowing barley, casting it up to the wind with a sort of wooden shovel or fan. The corn lay in heaps not bound in sheaves.

Returning in the evening through fields of melons, we disturbed 'the keepers of a field', the same as those mentioned by the prophet (Jeremiah 4:17). A rude shed made of four upright poles, that supported a covering of twined branches, protected from the weather an old decrepit Arab, who sat watching against any intrusion that might be made by man or beast upon his field. In passing through a large flock of sheep, we remarked how familiar they appeared to be with the shepherd, shewing no signs of timidity at his closest approach. Their large heavy tails are also very remarkable. These are chiefly composed of fat, and are particularly referred to in the Mosaic Law (Exodus 29:22; Leviticus 3:9) as the pieces that were to feed the flame of the sacrifice.

June 5

Early this morning seven camels arrived from Gaza, and Mustapha again took his place at the head of our caravan; but we had to make the condition that our journey should be direct to Jerusalem, instead of by Hebron, as we had previously intended – the cameldrivers pretending that if they went that way, we would be stopped by the people because we had come from a town where the plague was raging. Our morning meal was a spare one, a barley-cake and a glass of pure water. We soon passed the foot of Samson's hill, and then the entrance to Gaza, near the public well, where the women were already assembling with veiled faces to draw water. Several of the houses in the town had tents erected on their flat roofs, which we supposed might be especially intended at present to avoid the infection of the plague. A burying-ground a little way from the gate had lamps suspended over several of its tombs.

We entered upon the Grove of Olives, which is laid down in maps.

The public road passes through it for about three miles. The trees appear to have been planted at regular distances – handsome trees with pleasant shade, reminding the traveller of the days of Philistia's glory. We met many peasants, some riding on asses, some on foot, carrying into town vegetables and fruits. Several women carried baskets of mulberries on their heads. The Bedouins brought us some of these, and we found them much better than those we got in Egypt. On either side of the road, the ground is covered with verdure, so that the grove is not unlike some nobleman's domain. The constant chirping of the grasshoppers, though monotonous, was not unpleasant.

On emerging from this pleasant grove, the country opens out into a fine plain. In the fields all the operations of harvest seemed to be going on at the same time. Some were cutting down the barley, for it was the time of barley-harvest, with a reaping hook not unlike our own, but all of iron, and longer in the handle and smaller in the hook. Others were gathering what was cut into sheaves. Many were gleaning; and some were employed in carrying home what had been cut and gathered. We met four camels heavily laden with ripe sheaves, each camel having bells of a different note suspended from its neck, which sounded cheerfully as they moved slowly on. Perhaps those bells may be a remnant of the 'joy in harvest' (Isaiah 9:3) though this is not the only time when they are used. The practice appears to have been very common in the days of Zechariah, for he makes use of the expression, 'On the bells of the horses shall be, Holiness to the Lord' (Zechariah 14:20) to indicate the holiness that shall pervade the land, descending to the minutest and most ordinary movements of life.

Bet-hanoon, a small village on the right hand, is the first object of interest in this plain. It is composed of brown square huts standing on a rising ground, and surrounded with trees. In 1 Kings 4:9, there is mention made of 'Elon-beth-hanan', or 'the plain of Beth-hanan', in the tribe of Dan, a name which resembles this. A wady runs past in a northerly direction, and joins what we believe might be the brook Sorek several miles farther on. This we conjectured to be the channel of the brook Eschol. Some have supposed that Sorek is the stream, and Eschol the tributary, and this agrees exactly with our observation, for in all this plain we crossed only one channel of a river that communicated with the sea. The tributary stream answering to Eschol must have been Wady Safia, which we crossed soon after. The channel was quite dry, and the road lay through the middle of it for some part of the way. Often the banks were much broken as if by a winter torrent, and very deep. Ten or twelve feet of beautiful soil was sometimes laid bare, so that we could not help exclaiming, 'How fertile this land might yet become, if there were bestowed on it the industry of man and the blessing of God!' About a mile farther on we crossed by a bridge another deep and narrow channel, called by the Arabs Wady Djezed, which runs to the sea, and which we conjectured to be the brook Sorek. Although some fix the position of Eschol nearer Hebron, yet there seems good reason to think that this open vale through which we passed is the true valley of Eschol, where the spies cut down a cluster of grapes so large that they bare it between them upon a staff (Numbers 13:23).

About noon we encamped at the village of Deer-esnait. Our guides remarked that *deir* means a convent or some such building. We could, h wever, find no trace of any ancient building; the houses are all p astered with mud; and the village is surrounded with trees. As we a proached, one of the cameldrivers, pointing to a cluster of six fig-trees, cried out, *'Tacht et-teen?'* (under the fig tree). And soon we felt the pleasantness of this shade for there is something peculiarly delightful in the shade of the fig-tree. It is far superior to the shelter of a tent, and perhaps even to the shadow of a rock, since not only does the mass of heavy foliage completely exclude the rays of the sun, but the traveller finds under it a peculiar coolness, arising from the air gently creeping through the branches. Hence the force of the Scripture expression, 'When thou wast under the fig-tree' (John 1:48), and the prophecy, 'In that day shall ye call every man his neighbour under the vine and under the fig-tree' (Zechariah 3:10). Restored and happy Israel shall invite one another to sit down beneath their embowering shade to recount the glorious acts of the Lord.

Reclining under these six fig-trees we enjoyed a short repose, the servants and camels being gathered round us under the same grateful shade. These immense trees shew plainly that the substantial fertility of the soil is still remaining, but they are almost the only remnants of Eschol's luxuriance. A small village was in sight to the right, called Dimreh, its mud-plastered houses half-concealed by verdant trees. None of the villages we had seen would contain above fifty souls, some not so many, and yet these are spots where Judah and Israel used to be 'many as the sand which is by the sea in multitude' (I Kings 4:20). But now Isaiah's words are verified, 'The cities are wasted without inhabitant, and the houses without man, and the land is utterly desolate with desolation (margin), and the Lord has removed men far away, and there is a great forsaking in the midst of the land' (Isaiah 6:11,12). And the fulfilment is all the more striking, when the traveller remembers that in these ruined cities and villages not one of even the few inhabitants is a Jew.

While the servants were preparing our simple meal, each of us took a solitary ramble, in order to see more of the features of the land. From the top of one of the neighbouring eminences, we stretched the eye to the north-west, to discover Ashkelon's uninhabited ruins; but in vain – the sea was distinctly visible, but the low range of hand-hills which line the coast intercepted our view of the shore. Looking to the east, flocks and herds were seen spreading through the undulating valleys. In one place we saw many of them gathered together under a shady tree, waiting till the excessive heat of noon should be abated. At other times, the shepherds gather the flocks beside a well, as we afterwards saw at Lebonah, where many hundreds were lying down around the well's mouth.

After gathering some of the wild flowers and seeds of shrubs, as memorials of the hills of Philistia, we returned to the encampment through fields where some were cutting down the barley, and others gleaned behind them, like Ruth in the fields of Boaz, not far off; while the feet of oxen were treading out what had been cut. In the village 'the sound of the millstone' met our ears, proceeding from several of the huts. It is a clear ringing sound, conveying an idea of peace and cheerfulness, and is more than once spoken of in Scripture (Jeremiah 25:10; Revelation 18:22). In the courtyard of one house, the grinders accompanied their occupation with a song. Before leaving the poor villagers, we partook of the first fruits of the land in the shape of fine ripe apricots, and drank a little of their *Hemat*, or *Leban-hemat*, a kind of sour milk, which is very cooling and pleasant when well prepared. It was this which Jael gave to Sisera (Judges 5:25), 'She brought forth butter in a lordly dish'; the word in the original being the same as that now applied by the Arabs to this simple beverage. It is made by putting milk into an earthen jar, and letting it stand for a day. The taste is not unlike that of buttermilk, cool and most refreshing to a weary man oppressed with heat. The Arabs say 'it makes a sick man well'.

In less than an hour we came to Bet-Car, a small place, composed of one square of houses for villagers and their flocks, a white tower, and Sheik's tomb, surrounded with some fine trees and hedges of prickly pear. From this point to the ruins of Ashkelon, there was only a single hour's journey. We would have rejoiced to have seen with our own eyes the fulfilment of the prophecy, 'Ashkelon shall not be inhabited' (Zechariah 9:5); and also the place where the remnant of Judah is yet to 'lie down in the evening' (Zephaniah 2:7); but the day was too far gone to admit of our visiting it. The hill country of Judah came in sight this evening. The view was distant, but very pleasing over the vast plain covered with barley. On the right appeared a village, Bet-ima, or house of eggs', and in half an hour after, having crossed the dry bed of Wady Rousad, we came to Doulis, a considerable village, placed upon a rock, and overlooking the open vale through which we had travelled. It stands on the left of the road, and is four hours distant from our last station. Here we encamped for the night.

While the servants were pitching the tents, we wandered through the place, and sitting down by the well, observed that women come to draw water. The well is very deep, and the mode of drawing up the water curious. A rope is attached by one end to a large bucket, made of skin, and let down over a pulley; while the other end is attached to a bullock, which is driven down the slope of the hill; the skin of water is thus hauled up to the top, where a man stands ready to empty it into the trough, from which women receive the water in earthenware jugs. To us this was a novel and amusing sight.

On the way to our encampment, we passed some of the tents of Kedar pitched under a tree outside the village, exactly like those mentioned before – low dark-brown coverings. The wanderers were couching beneath, and not far off a fire of wood was sending up its curling smoke.

The women in all this region wear long veils, which in part cover the lower part of the face, but are not drawn close over it as in Egypt. Long veils seem to have been common, and were used for various purposes, often like aprons.

The incessant sound of the grasshopper both day and night, made us observe how natural was the image used by the spies, 'we were in our own sight as grasshoppers' (Numbers 13:33), for, like us, they must have listened to their perpetual chirping in this very region. Before falling asleep we heard the wild howling of the jackal and the wolf as if hungry for a prey.

June 6

We were awakened before break of day by the voice of Mustapha crying to Ibraim and Ahmet, *'Koom, Koom'*, 'Rise, rise'. The sleepers answered now and then by a groan, till, wearied out by their refusal, Mustapha resolved on forsaking us and actually gave orders to his Bedouins to depart. We all started up, and our tents were down in a few minutes. Mustapha's great anxiety was to get past a certain part of the road, which is infested with flies, before the sun was hot. We were on our camels before five, and the moon was shining sweetly on Doulis as we departed. Instead of going northward, our route now lay directly eastward. We ascended a hilly pass, adorned with wild flowers and perfumed with fragrant thyme. The birds, too, were filling the morning air with their sweet voices. Looking behind us we could see, under the rising sun, the pleasant village we had left, till we arrived at the top of the rocky eminence. The slopes on each side were bare and stony, but evidently well fitted for training the vine in the days of Eshtaol's glory. We supposed that, in the region northward to us, lay Zorah, where Samson was born; and still nearer us the 'camp of Dan', where 'the Spirit of the Lord began to move him'; and not far off, the vineyards of Timnath, where he slew the lion.

Looking nearly due north, we saw a town upon a conical rising ground, surrounded with trees. This the Arabs called Shdood, the remains of Ashdod, where Dagon fell before the Ark of God (1 Samuel 5:3). It is about two hours and a half distant. Suddenly we reached the summit, and a splendid prospect broke upon us. An immense undulating plain was stretched before, lying north and south, and of vast breadth east and west. There were few trees, but the plain was covered with fields of yellow grain, and studded with a goodly number of little towns, the remains of other days. Vast tracts appeared to lie uncultivated, and some parts were covered with sesamine, whose white flowers formed an agreeable variety. In the background, the beautiful hill country of Judah rose tier above tier, and the sun, which was just rising above them, poured a flood of golden rays into the plain. This is the great plain of Sephela, called 'The Plain' (Obadiah 19).

As we descended into the vale, we inquired of the Arabs the names of the different villages in sight, making them repeat the name carefully and frequently that we might not be mistaken. Three villages immediately before us, and not far off, they called Erd Safeen. We now came down upon the three villages, situated as it were at the points of a triangle, and about a quarter of a mile distant from each other. We halted for a few minutes to break our fast with a little barley-bread and fine warm milk. By now we began to experience the annoyance of which we had been forewarned by Mustapha. The air was filled with swarms of small flies, whose bite was very troublesome, so that we were glad to use every means to cover our faces. The camels also, stung by these insects, became very restive, and for the first time almost ungovernable. A wolf here started across our path, and fled before us.

The last of the three villages has marks of antiquity. There is a large well a little out of town, from which the water is drawn up in the same way as at Doulis. The women were all busy drawing the morning supply; some were washing their hands and faces, and their feet, by rubbing one foot upon another. There are also many pits for grain here, large stones and mounds of earth, and a pool of water. A wady winds past, called Wady Safeen, at present dry, but it may have been a considerable stream in winter. The situation and name of these villagers at once suggested to us that this is the valley of Zephathah where Asa defeated Zerah, the Ethiopian, with his host of 'a thousand thousand' (2 Chronicles 14:9). In this vast plain there would be room enough for all that multitude, and ample scope in these level fields for the three hundred chariots. We remembered with fresh interest also, how the ark of God was carried by the two milch kine from the land of the Philistines to Beth-shemesh, across this very plain, probably a little to the north of us (2 Samuel 6:12). Nor could we lift our eyes to the hill country of Judah without remembering the visit of the mother of our Lord to her cousin Elizabeth (Luke 1:39). Once also Mareshah, Lachish and Libnah stood in this vast plain.

At nine o'clock we arrived at Kasteen, where was a well and plenty of water, pits for grain, and mounds of earth. Upon the roof of the houses the inhabitants were spreading out sheaves of corn to dry. A solitary palm rises in the midst of the village. On the left side of the road is Hasur, a small village with many trees, perhaps one of the *Hazors* of Judah.

Half an hour after we rested at Mesmieh, a village surrounded by prickly pear, and interspersed with olive trees. The houses were of a wretched description; but there were deep pits for grain – a large well also at the farther side of the village, and a pool near it, where the oxen were bathing themselves up to the neck to get rid of the flies. We found a scanty shelter under an old decaying olive-tree.

At one o'clock we mounted again – the great heat, the flies, and the bad water, making us very willing to depart. An interesting and lively scene of rural life here presented itself. Close to the village lay a thrashing-floor, where twenty or thirty pair of oxen were employed in treading out corn. One peasant attended to each pair, and another tossed up the straw with a wooden fork, and spread it out again for them to tread. Few of the oxen were muzzled. We remembered the commandment, 'Thou shalt not muzzle the ox that treadeth out the corn' (Deuteronomy 25:4); and how Paul says to ministers, 'For our sakes no doubt this is written, that he that plougheth should plough in hope, and that he that thrasheth in hope, should be partaker of his hope' (1 Corinthians 9:10). The camels, too, were carrying home loads of ripe sheaves, to the sound of the tinkling bell round their neck.

Here we came upon a narrow stream of water called by our guide Wady Maruba, an hour and a half from Mesmieh. The water was very muddy, yet the Arabs drank and bathed in it with the greatest satisfaction. This was the first sight we obtained of running water since entering this land, which was once called 'a land of brooks of water' (Deuteronomy 8:7). We again remembered the prayer of Israel, so applicable at this moment, 'Turn again our captivity, O Lord, as the streams in the south' (Psalm 126:4). As we recalled with a thrill of interest the clear promise by the mouth of the prophet Joel, 'All the rivers of Judah shall flow with waters' (Joel 3:18).

Four hours together this day we travelled through fields of weeds, briars, and thorns, such as we never saw anywhere else. Often there was nothing but weeds. In ploughing, they plough round about them, and in reaping they take care not to cut down the giant thistles. The variety of thistles was very great. We counted ten or eleven different species in the course of the afternoon. There were also large fields covered with the 'hellah' or sesamine, like 'hemlock in the furrows of the field' (Hosea 10:4). Through the whole of the plain the ground is chapped and cracked as if by an earthquake, and to the foot feels hard as iron.

Towards evening we entered among the lower tract of hills behind which rose the mountains of Judah, which appeared very beautiful in the evening sun, the limestone of which they are composed giving a white appearance to all mountain tracks. Here we began to notice the remains of terraces. We turned northward, getting deeper into the hills of Judah. Hitherto appearances had indicated fertility in the soil, but now the hills became bare and rocky on each side for about an hour's ride, though even these shewed many marks of former cultivation.

Wearied with constant motion of the camel, we sometimes dismounted and beguiled the way by culling a few of the choice pinks and wild mountain flowers that grew among the rocks. Here we overtook an

African playing with all his might upon a shepherd's pipe made of two reeds. This was the first time we had seen any marks of joy in the land, for certainly 'All joy is darkened, the mirth of the land is gone' (Isaiah 24:11). We afterwards found that the Jews have no harp, no tabret, nor instrument of music in the Holy Land. In all parts of it, they have an aspect of timidity and rooted sorrow. All the men we met with were strangers; ancient Israel are left 'few in number, whereas they were as the stars of heaven for multitude' (Deuteronomy 28:62). We have not as yet met a single child of Abraham in their own land.

The hills now opened wider, and our path turned north-east to the village of Latroon, strongly situated on a rocky eminence. There can be little doubt that this must have been the site of some ancient fortresses of Judah. A winding path leads to it from the valley below; and here the traveller may stand and catch a wide view of the surrounding hills, all bearing the remains of ancient terraces, though not a vine is trained upon them. There are patches of cultivation round the village, but only to the extent necessary to supply the wants of the villagers and their cattle. The whole scene reminded us of one of the glens in our own Highlands. We kept ascending higher and higher by a mountain path till a little after sunset, when we prevailed on our guides to encamp in a stubble field near Deir-Eyub, a small hamlet of two or three houses. The hills around seemed to form a verdant amphitheatre, the terraces of the ancient vineyards having the appearance of seats. There were many patches of cultivation, and a good deal of brushwood. There were also two fine wells of water.

We were now many hundreds of feet above the level of the plain, so that the air was delightfully cool and soft. Dr Keith, observing one of the adjoining hills to be very verdant, and not very steep, set out with the purpose of climbing it. After a short absence, however, he returned to tell us that he had failed in his attempt. He found the surface overgrown with strong briers and thorns, through which he tried to make his way, but without success: 'Every place where there were a thousand vines at a thousand silverings, it shall even be for briers and thorns. With arrows and bows shall men come thither, because all the land shall become briers and thorns' (Isaiah 7:23,24). We felt a secret joy in beholding the deserted terraces and fields overrun with thorns; for when we saw the word of threatening so clearly and literally fulfilled, our unbelief was reproved, and we were taught to expect without a shadow of doubt, that the promised blessing would be as full and sure. We too felt that it was pleasant to anticipate the time when, as certainly as these thorns and thistles overspread Judea, the Holy Spirit shall be poured out as a flood upon Israel, and both the people and the land shall become a garden of the Lord. As darkness came on, the fire-fly was to be seen moving through the air in all directions. Weary and yet thankful, we committed ourselves to the care of Shepherd of Israel, and lay down in our tents to enjoy a short night's repose.

June 7

This day was to be among the most eventful of our lives, as on it we hoped to reach Jerusalem. We therefore rose very early, and we were mounted by four o'clock. The morning had not yet dawned, but the moon poured its silvery light up the valley, and enabled our guides to find the track. Even at this early hour, the birds had begun their song from the brushwood on the hillside, and increased in number and in fullness of song as the sun arose. At least it was peculiarly pleasant to remember these words in such a spot, so near the place where David learned to sing. We came upon many small mountain streams, on the banks of which grew luxuriant bushes, and from the branches of which the blackbird, lark and others were pouring forth their lays.

About five o'clock we reached the head of the valley in which Latroon is situated, and began to enter a singular mountain defile, called the Pass of Latroon. It is supposed that the 'Descent of Beth-horon' and the 'Ascent' is this defile. Other travellers have found the name Betur in a village not far off, and the entrance is called Bab-el-Wady or 'Gate of the Valley'. The sun rose upon the tops of the mountains soon after we entered this defile, revealing a scene truly wild and romantic. The path is steep and rocky, and especially difficult for camels, whose feet are better fitted for the soft sands of the desert, yet they pressed on with wonderful perseverance. Around and above us were rocks of the wildest description, yet adorned with the richest vegetation. Trees of considerable size occasionally lined the Pass. Pleasant shrubs and flowers also attracted our eye, among which were the oleander, the cistus, the lavatera and wild pink. The fragrance diffused by them was truly delightful, and the voice of the turtle saluted our ear again and again. The eastern attire of Mustapha and the rest of our band as they urged on their camels, corresponded well with the character of the scene. A more suitable fastness for banditti could hardly be found, and it was actually so employed in former times. Indeed, the name Latroon is given to the

Pass in virtue of a monkish tradition, that it was the resort of banditti of which the penitent thief *(latro)* was one.

As the hills opened we began to trace more distinctly the terraces upon their sides, where in former days the vine used to be trained. But we were especially struck with the fact, that on many of the hills these terraces were natural formations; the industry of man in other places had only followed the suggestions of nature. God himself seems to have so formed these hills, that the natural strata of limestone wind round them in concentric circles, and at regular intervals. On these natural terraces they planted the vine and olive. The God of Israel thus taught them thriftily to use every spot of their fruitful land, and to cover the very rocks with the shadow of their vines.

At a step or turn of the Pass, near the ruins of a small building, we looked back and obtained a delightful view of the valley through which we had come. The sight of the terraced hills, with their bright verdure, lighted up by the brilliant beams of the morning sun, made us think how lovely this spot must have been in the days of David and Solomon, when its luxuriance was yet unblighted by the curse of Israel's God.

At length we reached the plantation of olive-trees, and the ruins of a small fort, perhaps the Modin of many travellers, which mark the summit of this interesting Pass. We had been ascending for four hours and a half from Latroon. From this point we obtained a beautiful glance of Ramla, lying to the north-west, in the plain of Sharon. Its tower, houses and minarets were conspicuous. It has long been regarded as Arimathea, the city of the wealthy Joseph, whose noble character is referred to by each of the Evangelists. We felt that perhaps the rich man came by this very route to Jerusalem on the awful day of the crucifixion. Possibly we were in his footsteps, for this is still the Jaffa road. By this route also would Peter (Acts 9:35) go down to the saints who dwelt at Lydda, which is within an hour of Ramla, where he healed Eneas, and drew the eyes of all in that beautiful plain to the Rose of Sharon.

We now began to descend, and came down upon a beautiful village which the Arabs called Karieh or Kurieh. The houses are solidly built of stone, and there are ruins of ancient buildings, especially a large church or abbey in the Gothic style, which Ibraim told us was now turned into a mosque. The village is literally embosomed among olives, pomegranates, and very large fig-trees, and a solitary palm rises above the cluster. The pomegranates were in full bloom, the scarlet flowers shining brilliantly from among their deep green leaves. A flock of goats was browsing beneath the trees. Many of the terraces around were finely cultivated, shewing what these mountains might soon become.

Descending to the bottom of this delightful valley, the hills on either side were terraced in still greater perfection than anything we had yet seen or imagined. These hills are not peaked, but are placed side by side, 'like round balls placed in juxtaposition'. We often counted forty, fifty, sixty, and even seventy terraced from the bottom of the wady up to the summit of the mountain. What a garden of delight this must have been, when, instead of grass making green the surface, verdant and luxuriant vines were their clothing! There seems to be little doubt that the Psalmist refers to the mode of training the vine over these terraces, when he says, 'The hills were covered with the shadow of it' (Psalm 80:10).

We ascended another rocky path, and when arrived at the summit began to descend again into a pleasant valley, overhanging which is the tower El Kustul, a name derived from the Latin *castellum*; but its history is unknown. The pathway was very steep, so that it was safer to leave the camel's back and walk; still the faithful animals never made a stumble. Halfway down this ravine there is a well of fine cold water, from which we drank in a broken sherd. At this point, to our great surprise, a young gentleman in European dress met and passed us riding upon a mule. He saluted us with 'Good morning', the first English words we had heard from a stranger for many a day. He proved to be Mr Bergheim, the assistant medical attendant of the Jewish mission at Jerusalem, on his way to Joppa. Figs and vines were cultivated on many of the terraces here, but when we reached the bottom of the valley, it was one complete garden, or rather orchard of fruit-trees.

We now entered into what is generally believed to be the Valley of Elah. It is called by the Arabs Wady Bet Hanina; but there is a Wady Aly not far off that seems to retain the ancient name. This is believed by many to be the place where David slew Goliath of Gath, the champion of the Philistines (1 Samuel 17:2). Whether it be so or not, the sight of these deep valleys gave us a clear and vivid impression of the memorable conflict. Here were hills on each side, the ravine between being deep and narrow. On the front of these opposing hills the armies were encamped. 'The Philistines stood on a mountain on the one side, and Israel stood on a mountain on the other side, and there was a valley between them'. They could not meet each other hand to hand without descending into the ravine; yet they could speak to each other, and hurl their words of defiance across the intervening space. This explained to us how the giant could stand and cry to the host of Israel, defying the armies of the living God, and yet not come within reach of their weapons. But when David accepted the challenge, he descended into this narrow valley, crossed the small running brook, picked up five of its smooth pebbles for his sling, and began to climb the opposite ascent. Goliath sees him, looks down with contempt, and advances to overwhelm him; but David takes his aim at him, and slings the stone into his forehead. The giant falls forward down the slope, and David with his own sword severs his head from his body, and invites the armies of Israel to cross the brook and assail their blaspheming foes.

A small village lay below us in the bottom of the hollow. Its name is Caglione or Kalonie, supposed to be derived from the Latin *colonia*, but its history is unknown. The voice of the turtle saluted us from its olive-trees. We now ascended a much barer mountain, and by a path the steepest we had yet climbed, yet the camels went up wonderfully. Arriving at the summit, it appeared as if we had left all cultivation behind. A bare desert of sunburnt rocks stretches to the right as far as the eye can reach. We remembered the description given by travellers of these mountains, and knew that we were near the Holy City. Every moment we expected to see Jerusalem. Though wearied by our long ride, which had now lasted seven hours, we eagerly pressed on. Mr McCheyne, dismounting from his camel, hurried forward on foot over the rocky footpath, till he gained the point where the city of the Lord comes first in sight. Soon, all of us were on the spot, silent, buried in thought, and wistfully gazing on the wondrous scene where the Redeemer died. The distant mountains beyond the city seemed so near, that at first sight we mistook them for the mountains that enclose 'the valley of vision', though they proved to be the mountains of Moab, on the east side of the Dead Sea. As yet we were not sufficiently accustomed to the pure clear atmosphere, so that distances were often very deceptive. As our camels slowly approached the city, its sombre walls rose before us; but in these there is nothing to attract or excite the feelings. At that moment we were impressed chiefly by the fact that we were now among 'the mountains that are around Jerusalem' (Psalm 125:2), and half unconscious that it was true, we repeated inwardly the words, 'Our feet shall stand within thy gates, O Jerusalem.' We got a slight view of the Mount of Olives, as we rode toward the Jaffa Gate. The nearer we came to the city, the more we felt it a solemn thing to be where 'God manifest in flesh' had walked.

The feelings of that hour could not even be spoken. We all moved forward in silence, or interchanging feelings only by a word. While passing along the pathway immediately under the western wall, from which no object of any interest can be seen, and entering the Jaffa Gate, we could understand the exclamation, and were almost ready to use it as our own, 'Is this the city which men call the perfection of beauty, the joy of the whole earth' (Lamentations 2:15). Its dark walls, and the glance we got of slippery narrow streets, with low ill-built houses, and a poor ill-clad population, suggested no idea of the magnificence of former days. But we were soon to learn, that all the elements of Jerusalem's glory and beauty are still remaining in its wonderful situation, fitting it to be once again in the latter day, 'The city of the Great King'.

CHAPTER 3

JERUSALEM – HEBRON

'Then said I, Whither goest thou? And he said unto me,
To measure Jerusalem, to see what is the breadth thereof,
and what is the length thereof' (Zechariah 2:2).

Our camels kneeled down in the open space within the gate of Jerusalem, and we rested for a short time while Ibraim sought out the residence of Mr Young, the British Consul, to whom we had letters of introduction. He soon returned to say that the Consul was waiting for us, and would procure a lodging in part of an unoccupied house near the Latin Convent. Our camels and servants moved slowly away to their place of destination, and we followed Ibraim down the steep and slippery street opposite the Jaffa Gate. In a few minutes we were at the house of Mr Young, who received us with the greatest kindness. He told us the general state of matters in Jerusalem. The plague had not yet left the town, but the number of cases was decreasing; and there was no cordon drawn round the walls as had lately been the case. He strongly recommended us not to encamp on the Mount of Olives, as we had proposed, but to live in the town, and use the ordinary precautions of touching nobody in the streets, and receiving all articles of food through water. He then introduced us to two travellers just returned from Petra by way of Hebron, Lord Claud Hamilton and Mr Lyttleton. The former was not a little surprised to meet in Jerusalem with Dr Black, whom he had known in former days as a laborious student and theologian, and unassuming minister in the parish of Tarvis, in Aberdeenshire.

Two large apartments were assigned to us on Mount Acra, floored with stone, with a pleasant open space on the roof between them.

Worn out with incessant travelling, we were thankful to retire, that we might refresh our weary frames and compose our minds, which were not a little bewildered by the multitude of feelings that had passed through them this day. We had not rested long when Mr Nicolayson, Missionary of the London Society for the Conversion of Jews, called to welcome us to the Holy City, as brethren and friends of Israel. He stayed a considerable time with us, talking over our journey, the object of our visit, his own sphere of labour and hopes of success, and many matters regarding the spot where we now were. It was a desultory but pleasant conversation, a conversation about the people and land of Israel while really sitting in their ancient capital. Lord Hamilton called in the evening, and told us much of what he had seen in Petra, and the land of Egypt. When the darkness came down we heard the wailing of mourners over some dead friend, a peculiarly melancholy sound at all times, but doubly so when the plague is raging. Yet we never heard any more joyful sounds in the streets of Jerusalem – so true is the prophetic word, 'I will cause all her mirth to cease' (Hosea 2:11).

It was with feelings that can be better imagined than described, that for the first time in our lives within the gates of Jerusalem, we committed ourselves and those dear to us, our Church, and the blessed cause in which she has sent us forth, to the care of Him who sits as a King upon the holy hill of Zion. We are not aware that any clergyman of the Church of Scotland was ever privileged to visit the Holy City before and now that four of us had been brought thus far by the good hand of our God upon us, we trusted that it might be a token for good, and perhaps the dawn of a brighter day on our beloved Church, a day of generous self-denied exertion in behalf of scattered Israel and a perishing world.

Saturday, June 8

We had spread our mats on the cool stone-floor, hoping for a night of calm repose, but our rest was broken and uncomfortable in the extreme, our rooms being infested with vermin, a kind of trial which travellers in the East must make up their mind frequently to undergo. All our annoyance, however, was forgot by sunrise. We rose early and finding the road to the Jaffa Gate, went a little way out of the city and sat down under an olive-tree. We turned to Psalm 48, 'Great is the Lord, and greatly to be praised in the city of our God, in the mountain of his holiness. Beautiful for situation, the joy of the whole earth, is Mount Zion, on the sides of the north, the city of the great King. God is known in her palaces for a refuge' (Psalm 48:1-3). Reading this with the eye upon Jerusalem, the scenes of former days seemed to rise up as a flood. We could imagine holy prophets and men of God in these fields and within these walls. The vivid associations of the place with all our Bible readings and hours of holy study, made it appear like a spot where we had once met with beloved and honoured friends, whose absence spreads a sadness over all. We read part of Lamentations, and could feel sympathy with the prophet when he cried, 'How hath the Lord covered the daughter of Zion with a cloud in his anger, and cast down from heaven unto the earth the beauty of Israel'. 'He hath swallowed up Israel; he hath swallowed up all her palaces!' (Lamentations 2:1, 5).

In the forenoon, Mr Nicolayson kindly insisted on our removing from our house on Mount Acra, to one of the Missionary houses upon the northern brow of Mount Zion. Mr Pieritz and Dr Gertsmann, the medical missionary, being from home, we were put in possession of their comfortable rooms, with an outer one for our two Arab servants. In this house, one of our windows opened towards the east, having a fine view of the dome of the Mosque of Omar, which rises over the site of Solomon's Temple, and beyond it was the Mount of Olives. That ever-memorable hill, with its three summits, its white limestone rocks appearing here and there, and its wide bosom still sprinkled over with the olive-tree, was the object on which our eye rested every morning as we rose, an object well fitted to call to mind the words of Jesus spoken there, 'Watch ye, therefore, for ye know not when the master of the house cometh, at even, or at midnight, or at the cock-crowing, or in the morning' (Mark 13:35).

The site of the proposed Hebrew church was not far off. It is close to Mr Nicolayson's own house. At the time the foundations were only digging, and builders were preparing the stones, which we saw camels carrying into town. We were told that they were brought from a quarry a few miles north of Jerusalem, near a village called Anata, the ancient Anathoth, where Jeremiah was born. In seeking a solid foundation they had dug down about forty feet, and had not yet come to rock. They laid bare heap after heap of rubbish and ancient stones. It is a remarkable fact, which cannot but strike the traveller, that not only on Mount Zion, but in many parts of the city, the modern town is really built on the rubbish of the old. The heaps of ancient Jerusalem are still remaining; indurated masses of stones and rubbish forty and fifty feet deep in many places. Truly the prophets spoke with a divine accuracy when they said. 'Jerusalem shall become heaps' (Micah 3:12). 'I will make Jerusalem heaps' (Jeremiah 9:11). And if so, shall not the future restoration foretold by the same lips be equally literal and full? 'The city shall be builded upon her own heap' (Jeremiah 30:18). The ancient gates mentioned by Nehemiah (Nehemiah 3) are no longer to be found, and it is quite possible that several of them may be literally buried below the feet of the inquiring traveller.

During the day we began inquiries after the Jews in their own land. We were told that the plague prevailed most of all in their quarter, and that we must be very cautious in visiting their houses. Meanwhile Mr Nicolayson afforded us every information. The difficulties in the way of conversion of the Jews are certainly greater in Palestine than elsewhere. The chief of these difficulties are:

1. That Jerusalem is the stronghold of Rabbinism; the Jews here being all strict Rabbinists, and, as might be expected, superstitious in the extreme.

2. A Missionary has fewer points of contact with the Jews here than in other countries. He cannot reach them through the Press, nor address them in large assemblies; his work must be carried on entirely by personal intercourse, so that it is like wrenching out the stones of a building one by one.

3. The opposition to an inquiring or converted Jew here is much greater than in any other country, for it is regarded as a very awful calamity that any one should become an apostate in the Holy City.

4. All the Jews in the Holy Land are more or less dependent on pecuniary supplies annually sent from Europe. But the moment any one is known to be inquiring after Christ, he is cut off from all share in this fund and is thrown utterly destitute.

Schools for Jewish children have never been established in Jerusalem; and, in the present state of things, it seems impossible that they could succeed; for there are not here, as in Poland and Germany, any worldly inducements to prevail with Jews to send their children to be educated; there being no situations of wealth or distinction open to their young men, which might tempt them to accept of a liberal education for their youth. The London Society have entertained the plan of instituting a school for converts, in which many branches of general knowledge would be taught, and this might perhaps allure some of their brethren to attend.

In regard to Missionaries, a converted Jew is in some respects a better missionary than a Gentile. It is true he meets with greater opposition in the first instance, but in process of time, the fact of his change never fails to make an impression on his brethren, provided they see in him consistency of temper, character and life. A Jew will indeed listen more readily to a Gentile Christian, and shew him more respect;

but then he listens more carelessly and thinks less of what is said, because he thinks it natural for a Gentile so to speak. A Gentile missionary again, has the advantage of more ready access to the Jews, being regarded with far less prejudice but a Jewish convert is more efficient where confidence is once established. Perhaps the true principle in missions to the Jews, is to unite both Jewish and Gentile labourers in the same field.

The importance of erecting a church on Mount Zion, where Protestant worship might be maintained in its purity, is that it may open the eyes of the Jews to see what true Christianity is. At present, they justly regard the Greek and Romish churches as idolatrous and licentious in the extreme, and believe the English to be Infidels, without any religion.

The hope of Messiah's coming is strong in the hearts of many Jews here. Many believed that it would be in the year 1840, as that was the end of a period fixed in the book of Zohar; and some said that if they were disappointed in that year, they would turn Christians; but this is a mere saying, for they have often declared the same before, and when the time came have found out excuses for Messiah's delay.

The fact that Palestine is the stronghold of Rabbinism appears to be a sufficient reason why Christians should direct their most vigorous efforts to send the light of the gospel among the Jews of this land. There have been many tokens for good and encouraging appearances of late years among the Jews at Jerusalem. Their wretched condition in the city where their fathers ruled loudly calls for sympathy. They are poor and despised, and sadly divided amongst themselves. The Consul told us of a Jew who last week was beaten till he died, by order of the Governor. He was not proven to be guilty of the offence laid to his charge, and was not in reality guilty, yet there was none to plead his cause, or avenge his murder.

In the cool of the evening we enjoyed our first walk about Jerusalem, Mrs. Nicolayson accompanying us upon her donkey. Passing by the Armenian Convent, which appeared to be the largest and most substantial in the city, surrounded with a pleasant garden, we went out at the Zion Gate, the only gate now open on the southern wall of the town, and came out upon the open summit of Mount Zion, for one-half of that hill is now outside of the walls. A gloomy ill-shaped building near the gate is an Armenian convent, enclosing what is called by the monks the House of Caiaphas, and nearer the southern brow is a small mosque covering the tomb of David. The minarets of this mosque, and of that on the Mount of Olives, were both destroyed by an earthquake a few years ago. There is a prevailing and much-credited tradition, that within that building is the very tomb of which Peter said in his sermon, 'His sepulchre is with us unto this day' (Acts 2:29).

These are the only prominent buildings upon the unwalled part of Zion. Leaving these on the left, we wandered among the flat tombstones of the Greeks and Latins. The graves of some of the American mission-aries were pointed out to us, and also a small spot of ground which they have purchased and enclosed as a burying-place, though we were told that they were still uncertain whether they would be permitted to bury in it, as the Moslems had found out that the shadow of David's mosque fell upon it at certain hours of the day.

Zion is truly desolate. The only fortified building upon it is the Castle of David, erected on the site of the tower of Hippicus, within the walls, and close by the Jaffa Gate. This alone of all the bulwarks of former days still remains, so that when we obeyed the command, 'Walk about Zion, and go round about her; tell the towers thereof' (Psalm 48:12), we saw in the very absence of all her towers and fortresses the force of the words, 'They that trust in the Lord shall be as Mount Zion, which cannot be removed, but abideth for ever' (Psalm 125:1). Full trust in the Lord Our Righteousness, apart from all human helps and additions, estab-lishes the soul firm as the hill of Zion, firmer far than all its bulwarks and palaces, which are now swept away as if they had never been.

Approaching nearer to the brow of the hill, we found ourselves in the midst of a large field of barley. The crop was very thin, and the stalks very small, but no sight could be more interesting to us. We plucked some of the ears to carry home with us, as proofs addressed to the eye that God had fulfilled his true and faithful word, 'Therefore shall Zion for your sake be ploughed as a field' (Micah 3:12). The palaces, the towers, the whole mass of warlike defences, have given way before the word of the Lord, and a crop of barley waves to the passing breeze instead of the banner of war. On the steep sides of the hill, we afterwards found flourishing cauliflowers arranged in furrows, which had evident-ly been made by the plough; so that this important prophecy, twice recorded (Jeremiah 26:18; Micah 3:12), is most fully accomplished.

From the southern verge of Zion, we looked down into the valley of Hinnom, still called Wady Jehennam, which lies nearly due east and west. It appeared very deep, the opposite side rocky and precipitous, and the bosom of it filled with shady olive-trees. Here Manasseh caused his children to pass through the fire to Moloch (2 Chronicles 33:6); and here Jeremiah uttered that dreadful prophecy, 'This place shall no more be called Tophet, nor the valley of the son of Hinnom, but the valley of Slaughter' (Jeremiah 19:6). From the awful wickedness committed in this valley, perhaps as much as from the Satanic fires kindled in it, the name came to signify the place of eternal sin and woe. To us it appeared a pleasant shady valley, but in other days, when the precipitous sides were planted with thick trees, it may have been gloomy enough.

Instead of descending into it, we turned and went down the steep western side of Zion into the valley of Gihon, which lies nearly north and south on the west side of Jerusalem, to examine the upper and lower Pools of Gihon. We came first to the lower pool, and standing on the edge, were surprised at the vast size of the basin, which is by far the greatest reservoir of the Holy City, though it is much dilapidated and perfectly dry. It is formed in a very simple manner, by throwing a massy wall across the lower end of the valley. This wall answers also the purpose of a bridge, which is crossed in going to Bethlehem. There is a neat fountain at the middle of it, to refresh the traveller, with an Arabic inscription; but we found no water in it. The stones of this wall are closely cemented, and the work is evidently ancient. There are also remains of a wall at the upper end, and on both sides. The bottom of the pool is merely the natural bed of the valley, and is bare and rocky.

We proceeded up the valley as far as under the Jaffa Gate, and then to the north-west, till we came upon the conduit or rude aqueduct of the upper pool, out of which a flock were satisfying their thirst, and shortly after to the upper pool of Gihon itself.

The walls of this pool are in a much more perfect condition than those of the lower pool, the strong walls being unbroken, the cement still remaining, and the steps into it from the corners nearly entire. It was about half-full of pure water. We spent some time here, and plucked leaves from a large terebinth tree which grows close by. It was here that Solomon was anointed king; and these valleys were once made to resound with the cry, God save King Solomon (1 Kings 1:38,39). This is the spot also where the prophet Isaiah stood with his son Shear-jashub, the type of returning Israel. 'Go forth now to meet Ahaz, thou and Shear-jashub thy son, at the end of the conduit of the upper pool, in the highway of the fuller's field' (Isaiah 7:3). The conduit here spoken of is no doubt the same as that mentioned above, which now conducts the water from the pool into the city; and we were told that it carries the water into

Hezekiah's pool, a large tank upon Mount Acra, at the back of the Consul's house, which we afterwards saw. 'The end of the conduit' must be the place where it first appears above ground, so that the highways to the fuller's field probably passed that spot. Beside the same pool where Solomon had been anointed king, did the venerable prophet stand and tell Israel of their coming King and Saviour, 'Behold, a virgin shall conceive and bear a son, and shall call his name Immanuel' (Isaiah 7:14).

It is interesting also to remark that it was here Rabshakeh, the Assyrian captain, stood at the head of a great army, and reproached the living God (Isaiah 36:2,13). And it was from this point that he cried in the Jews' language to the men that sat upon the wall, a fact which goes to prove that the wall of Jerusalem must have extended much farther to the north-west than it does at present.

Around the pool is a burying-place for the Mahometan dead, where tombs were lying broken and scattered about in a most desolate manner. From the rising ground near, we got a view of the plain or valley of Rephaim, lying south-west of the city, and which is still so fertile, that we were assured it is capable of yielding three crops in the year. To this fertility the Prophet Isaiah refers. He says, 'The glory of Jacob shall be made thin' and shall be no more like the rich waving fields of Rephaim, but only like its gleanings; 'it shall be as he that gathereth ears in the valley of Rephaim' (Isaiah 17:5).

In this plain, too, David twice defeated the Philistines, who had penetrated as near as this to the royal city (2 Samuel 5:17-25); and somewhere not far off was Baal-perazim, where the heat of the conflict was greatest – the type of a yet more terrible conflict in the latter days, when 'the Lord shall rise up as in Mount Perazim' (Isaiah 28:21).

By the help of Mr Nicolayson, we now attempted to trace the probable extent of ancient Jerusalem upon the north. There is room for a great city on the elevated ground to the north of the present wall, and there can be little doubt that the Bezetha of Josephus, which Agrippa enclosed with a third wall of great strength, occupied a vast range of that district. It now consists of cultivated fields and olive plantations, but remains of ruins are visible in many parts of it. When the wall of the city was thus stretched out to the north, and included the whole of Mount Zion on the south, it is not very difficult to understand how Jerusalem could contain the millions who are said to have been sometimes gathered into it. In the distant north, we could see the hill Scopus which encloses Jerusalem on the north, where Titus first encamped when he came to besiege Jerusalem, 'from whence the city began already to be seen, and a splendid view was obtained of the great temple'. We returned by the Cave of Jeremiah, a grotto cut in the rock almost due north of the Damascus Gate, lying in the road from Anathoth, his native village, and where tradition says he wrote the Book of Lamentations. We reached our dwelling a little before the city gates were closed for the night.

We thought with joy of the Sabbath that was now drawing on – a Sabbath in Jerusalem. It seemed to us a wonderful privilege to be allowed to worship in the very city where Immanuel died, and where his living voice was so often heard, calling upon Jerusalem-sinners, in accents of more than human tenderness, 'How often would I have gathered thy children together, even as a hen gathereth her chickens under her wings, and ye would not' (Matthew 23:37).

Sabbath, June 9
The morning seemed the dawn of some peculiar season, from the thought that we were in Jerusalem. We sung together in our morning worship, Psalm 84:1-4, 'How lovely is thy dwelling-place'. At 10 o'clock according to agreement, we met in Mr Young's house, where divine service was at that time conducted. It was an upper room, that being generally the situation of the largest and most airy apartments in the East, and also farthest removed from the noise and bustle of the street. Here was gathered together a little assembly of fourteen or fifteen souls to worship according to the Scriptures. How different from the time when in the same city 'the number of men that believed was about five thousand!' After Mr Nicolayson had gone through the service of the liturgy, Dr Black preached on Isaiah 2:1-5. It was very pleasant thus to mingle our services, and to forget the differences between our churches in the place where Jesus died, and the Holy Spirit was given. On our way back to our lodging, we had to pass through a small part of the bazaar. Here all was going on as on other days, and we were forcibly reminded that 'Jerusalem is trodden down of the Gentiles' (Luke 21:24).

Having rested till the noonday heat was passed, we went at four o'clock to the house of one Simeon, a converted Jew, where Mr Nicolayson went through the evening service of the liturgy in German, and preached on Hebrews 12:5,6. At five in the evening we assembled again in the upper room, when Dr Keith conducted the service in our own Presbyterian form, and preached from 1 Kings 18:21. All these exercises were very solemn and reviving; yet still we frequently felt throughout the day that it is not in the power of the place itself, however sacred, to enlighten and refresh a sinner's soul. Compassed about as we were on every side with the memorials of the Saviour's work, our eyes gazing on the Mount of Olives, our feet standing on the holy hill of Zion, we felt that there was still as much need as ever that 'the Spirit should take of the things of Christ and shew them unto us' as he himself declared when sitting with his disciples in such an upper room as this in Jerusalem. 'The glory of God in the face of Jesus Christ' (2 Corinthians 4:6) is not an object within the compass of the natural eye. Associations of place and time cannot open the eye to see it; though such associations as those with which we were now surrounded soften the mind, and suggest the wish to comprehend what 'God manifest in flesh' revealed. Even were Christ already 'reigning in Jerusalem, and before his ancients gloriously' nothing less than heavenly eye-salve would enable us to say, 'We beheld his glory!'

June 10

We met with Lord Claud Hamilton this morning, and obtained from him some information regarding Petra and Sinai. In the forenoon we went to the Consul's house, and met with a Bedouin chief who had come to accompany Lord Hamilton to Ammon and Jerash on the other side of Jordan. He was a genuine son of Ishmael, possessing a commanding figure, with dark and striking features. He wore the yellow shawl of the Bedouins over his head, fastened on by two circles of rope made of camel's hair. His arm was bare up to the elbow, and the motions of his hands and features were graceful and expressive.

We this day visited the Church of the Holy Sepulchre, believed by so many to cover the very spot of Calvary where our Lord was crucified and buried – a visit which awakened in our minds only feelings painful and revolting. The descriptions of this place commonly given in books of travels are perfectly accurate, and indeed the wonder is that the writers should have been so careful in describing what no serious mind can regard but as 'lying wonders'. The church is not remarkable for elegance or beauty, and the pictures, with a few exceptions are far from being of the first order. In the centre stands a marble house enclosing the sepulchre. We entered and examined the sarcophagus, which is of white marble. Even the monks seemed to be a great deal more taken up with the silver lamps hung over it than with the tomb itself. We were then led to a flat stone of reddish marble, on which, say the monks, the Saviour's body was anointed. With lighted tapers we descended to a damp dark place, where Helena is said to have found three crosses. The rock of Calvary, so called by the monks, is only a few paces from the sepulchre. Ascending some twenty steps into a small chapel, the guide lifted up a gilded star in the floor, and shewed what is called the hole in the rock where the cross was fixed. In a dark chapel underneath, lighted by a single lamp, he pointed to the well-known fissure in the rock, pretended to be the rent that was made when Jesus died. We had little patience to go round all the spots accounted sacred under the roof of the Church of the Holy Sepulchre; and each of us felt the blush of honest indignation rising in our face at the mingled folly and profanity of the whole scene. To do the monks justice, they seemed to have as little feeling of reverence toward the holy place as we could possibly have, and Ibraim, our Arab servant who accompanied us, was fully as deeply impressed as any of the party. The fissure in the rock, and the tombs of Joseph and Nicodemus (so called), situated in a dark chapel behind the marble sepulchre, were the only objects which peculiarly drew our attention, both being in the natural rock. As for the rest, if Calvary was really within these walls, then true Popery has contrived to hide the place where the Redeemer died, as completely as she has done the person of the Redeemer himself. The simple work of Immanuel, in its essential native glory, is an idea far beyond the reach of Popery – or perhaps it is perceived, but on account of its innate power, is studiously hid. 'The God of this world hath blinded their minds, lest the light of the glorious gospel of Christ who is the image of God, should shine upon them'.

On the supposition that this spot is Calvary, the only probable reason that can be given for its being so near the city itself is, that 'the place of a skull' was a sort of trench, by the walls, where criminals were executed. But the longer we remained in the Holy City, the more we were convinced that is not the true site of Calvary. We are told expressly in Scripture that 'Jesus suffered without the gate' (Hebrews 13:12). And also that 'the place where he was crucified was nigh to the city' (John 19:20). But the site of the Church of the Holy Sepulchre is a long way within the walls of Jerusalem. We cannot believe that the ancient city was narrower or smaller in any way than the present Jerusalem. On the contrary, there is reason to believe that it was much more extensive. From the church, along the Via Dolorosa, to the western enclosure of the

Mosque of Omar, is but a five minutes' walk, and yet this must have been the whole breadth of the city, if the present Calvary was without a gate. How contrary is this to the description given by the Psalmist, 'Jerusalem is builded as a city that is *compact* together' (Psalm 122:3).

On the whole we found it a relief to our minds to rest in the conclusion that the cleft rock and the holy sepulchre of the monks, have as little to do with the place where Jesus died, and the rocky tomb in the garden where they laid him, as the polished marbles and gaudy lamps by which the place is disfigured.

There is no tradition which may lead the mind to any other spot as the site of Calvary. It struck us forcibly that some place among the tombs on the high ground above Gihon, was far more likely to have been the real situation. We could then understand how 'Jesus bearing his cross *went forth* into a place called the place of a skull', and 'suffered without the gate'. There would be room for 'the garden', and the new sepulchre of Joseph might well be hewn out of its rocks. But it is wisely ordered that a cloud of oblivion should rest over the spot where Immanuel died, and there is something pleasing to the mind in reflecting that the turf that was stained with his blood, and the rocky tomb where be lay, are left unprofaned by the followers of a blind and wicked superstition.

This afternoon we heard again the wailing of mourners; some Arab had died, and his friends were lamenting him. How graphic is the description of this scene given by Solomon, 'Man goeth to his long home, and the mourners go about the streets' (Ecclesiastes 12:5). The cry 'Allah, Allah' and many similar exclamations, were mingled with the loud wailing, and the sound of instruments of music filled up the measure of confusion. We remembered the faithful description of this given in the gospel narrative, 'when Jesus came into the ruler's house, and saw the minstrels and the people making a noise' (Matthew 9:23).

In the cool of the day we enjoyed a delightful ride to the Mount of Olives. Mounted on hardy Syrian horses of very small stature, we rode out at the Jaffa Gate. Here we saw the reapers busy cutting down barley in the valley of Gihon. Turning to the right we went round the northern wall of the city. The road is rough and in some parts difficult. Often the bare rock appears, and the way was covered with loose stones. It is made entirely by the feet of the animals that pass along it; and there is not so much as one road about Jerusalem upon which a wheeled carriage could run. Coming to the north-east corner of the walls, the valley of Jehoshaphat opened to our view, and the Mount of Olives across the valley appeared very beautiful, having much more variety of rocks, gardens, olive-yards, fig-trees and patches of grain upon its sides, than we had expected to find. We now turned due south, riding still under the city wall, which is farther from the brow of the hill than we anticipated. In one point only, namely the south-east corner, does the wall stand on the immediate brink of the valley, in other parts it is forty or fifty yards from the edge. Before reaching St. Stephen's Gate, we came upon a small reservoir half full of water, in which an Arab was bathing. We could not learn its name or history. Near this stands the monument of St. Stephen, where he is said to have been stoned, and the gate called by his name is said to be that out of which they hurried him when 'they cast him out of the city' (Acts 7:58).

We descended the steep side of Mount Moriah by the footpath leading from St. Stephen's Gate, and crossed the dry bed of the Kedron by a small bridge. The path here widens out to a considerable breadth for about fifty yards, and then separates into two, the one leading directly up the face of the Mount of Olives, the other winding gently round the southern brow of the hill. Both of these footpaths lead to Bethany, and between them lies a square plot of ground enclosed with a rough stone wall, and having eight very old olive-trees. This is believed to be Gethsemane. We stayed only to glance at it, for it needs to be visited in quiet and stillness; and choosing the path that leads straight up the hill, urged our little palfreys up the steep ascent. Mount Olivet was far from being a solitude this evening. One turbaned figure after another met us, and, to add to the interest of the scene, we recognised them by their features to be Jews. At one point we came upon a small company of Jewesses, not veiled like the Moslem ladies, but all dressed in their best attire. The reason for this unwonted stir among the solitudes of Mount Olivet was, that Sir Moses Montefiore[1] from London who had come on a visit of love to his brethren in the Holy Land, had arrived at Jerusalem, and his tent was now pitched on one of the eminences of the hill. Multitudes of the Jews went out daily to lay their petitions before him.

We often halted during the ascent, and turned round to view the city lying at our feet, the deep valley of Jehoshaphat, and the surrounding

---

[1] Sir Moses Montefiore (1784-1885) was from an Italian Jewish family. He made his fortune in London and became sheriff there in 1837, in which year he was knighted. He used his influence and his wealth to support oppressed Jews all over the world. On seven occasions he visited Palestine and the Scottish visitors were to meet him on several occasions.

hills. By far the finest and most affecting views of Jerusalem are to be obtained from some of these points. A little after we came to the eminence where Sir Moses Montefiore had pitched his tents. He had fixed a cord round the tents at a little distance, that he might keep himself in quarantine. On the outside of this a crowd of about twenty or thirty Jews were collected, spreading out their petitions before him. Some were getting money for themselves, some for their friends, some for the purposes of religion. It was an interesting scene, and called up to our minds the events of other days, when Israel were not strangers in their own land. Sir Moses and his lady received us with great kindness, and we were served with cake and wine. He conversed freely on the state of the land, the miseries of the Jews, and the fulfilment of prophecy. He said that the Bible was the best guidebook in the Holy Land, and with much feeling remarked, that, sitting on this very place, within sight of Mount Moriah, he had read Solomon's prayer (1 Kings 8) over and over again. He told us that he had been at Saphet and Tiberias, and that there were 1,500 Jews in the latter town, and more in the former; but they were in a very wretched condition, for first they had been robbed by the Arabs, then they suffered from the earthquake, and now they were plundered by the Druses. When Dr Keith suggested that they might be employed in making roads through the land, as materials were abundant, and that it might be the beginning of the fulfilment of the prophecy, 'Prepare ye the way of the people; cast up the highway, gather out the stones' (Isaiah 62:10), Sir Moses acknowledged the benefit that would attend the making of roads, but feared that they would not be permitted. He seemed truly interested in the temporal good of his brethren, and intent upon employing their young people in the cultivation of the vine, the olive, and the mulberry. We explained to him the object of our visit to this land, and assured him that the Church of Scotland would rejoice in any amelioration he might effect in the temporal condition of Israel.

Taking leave, we proceeded to the summit through a plantation of fig-trees. From this the view on all sides is splendid and interesting in the extreme, but it was too near sunset to allow us to exhaust it. Looking to the north-west, the eye falls upon Naby-Samuel, believed by most travellers to be Ramah where Samuel was born, but by others Mizpeh, the rallying place of Israel (1 Samuel 7:5). It seems to be five or six miles distant, and forms one of the highest points of the landscape, crowned with a mosque which always catches the eye in the northern view. To the east and south-east, over the summits of a range of bare and rugged mountains, we looked down upon the Dead Sea, of a deep blue colour. The air was so clear, and every thing seen so distinctly, that our first momentary impression was, that we could ride down to it before nightfall; though in reality a long and difficult day's journey lay between. Beyond it the range of Abarim, the brown barren mountains of Moab, rise steep and high, and bound the prospect. Over a dark rugged chain of hills between us and Jericho we could distinctly trace the valley of the Jordan and the verdure on its banks, but the river itself was hid. The summits of Abarim present to the eye an almost even line, so that we could fix on no particular peaks, and yet some one of the mountain tops we were gazing on must be Bethpeor, and another Pisgah, the top of Nebo; the former ever memorable as the spot where Balaam stood when he wished to die the death of the righteous (Numbers 23:10), and later as the spot where Moses did indeed die that blessed death (Deuteronomy 34:1).

Turning to the west, we looked down upon Jerusalem, its mosques and domes, flat roofs and cupolas, being stretched out beneath us. We could now see the accuracy of the description, 'As the mountains are around about Jerusalem, so the Lord is round about his people' (Psalm 125:2). We obtained a complete view of Mount Moriah, the hill nearest us, occupied by the Haram Sherif, or 'noble sanctuary', with its Mahometan mosques. Here probably is the very hill where Abraham's uplifted hand was arrested when about to slay his son Isaac (Genesis 22:2,9). Here the cry of David stayed the hand of the destroying angel (1 Chronicles 21:17). Here Solomon built the house of the Lord (2 Chronicles 3:1), where God dwelt among the cherubim. Here the lamb was slain every morning and evening for many generations, shewing forth the sacrifice of the Lamb of God. Here in the last day, that great day of the feast, Jesus stood and cried (John 7:37). And here the veil of the temple was rent in twain from the top to the bottom, when Jesus yielded up the ghost (Matthew 27:50,51), and the way into the holiest was made manifest. But now the word of God is fulfilled, 'He hath violently taken away his tabernacle, as if it were of a garden; he hath destroyed his places of assembly' (Lamentations 2:6). 'The mountain of the house is become as the high place of the forest' (Micah 3:12). The mountain on which God's house was built has literally become a place of heathen sanctuaries, like those which in Micah's day were erected in groves and forests.

The present wall of Haram is nearly identical with the enclosure of

Solomon's Temple on three sides. The Mosque of Omar stands in the centre, and probably on the spot where were the holy place and holiest of all. On the south stands the Mosque El Aksa, and there are several other oratories and sacred buildings round the walls. The rest of the area is beautifully laid out with cypress and orange trees, and here the Moslem ladies enjoyed themselves on their holidays. No Christian is ordinarily permitted to enter these enclosures. No foot but those of the heathen is allowed to tread the court of God's holy and beautiful house.

We descended into the Valley of Jehoshaphat by a path farther to the south, which led us past the Jewish burying-ground, and onwards to the monuments of Absalom and Zacharias, cut out of the solid rock, which have been often described, and are well known. It occurred to us that the pillars, pilasters, and other ornaments, may have been added at a recent date, but that the square mass cut out of the rock of the mountain may be very ancient. Again we crossed the Kedron, and by a slanting path, ascended to the south-east corner of the Haram; then, passing round the southern wall of the city, entered the Zion Gate a little before the gates were shut.

We spent the evening at the house of our kind friend, Mr Nicolayson. Here we found a fellow-countryman, who had been invited to meet us. He lives in Jerusalem in complete retirement, joins no church, and has no fellowship with Christians of any denomination, but waits for the coming of the Son of Man. He wears the long beard, turban, and flowing dress of the Easterns. He is a very pious, but singular man. On one occasion imagining that Elijah, 'the watchman of Ephraim' would soon be on the mountains of Israel, he went to seek him, though he knew nothing of the language of the country. He travelled as far as Sychar, keeping in his hand an Arabic list of vegetables, and other articles of food, so that by pointing to the written word, he was able to make himself understood. On another occasion, passing by the Church of the Holy Sepulchre, the monks mistaking him for a Jew, rushed out to him, and pursued him through the streets, into a house where he took refuge, threatening to kill him unless he kissed a picture of the Virgin, in a New Testament which they held out to him. This he did, and saved his life. His object in residing here is that he may be one of the men 'that sigh and cry for all the abominations that be done in the midst of Jerusalem' (Ezekiel 9:4). He is waiting also to hear the cry 'Behold the bridegroom cometh' and to see if the Lord will yet employ him in any work for his ancient people.

June 11

We had agreed to visit the Consul, Mr Young, this forenoon, to receive information from him regarding the Jews. On going to him, he told us that a remarkable circumstance had occurred that morning. The Turkish Governor of Jerusalem had allowed Sir Moses Montefiore and his attendants to enter the tomb of David upon Mount Zion, and to pray over it, a privilege not granted to a Jew for many centuries.

Mr Young gave the following statistics of the Jews in the Holy Land; and having afterwards taken down Mr Nicolayson's information on the same subject we insert both together for the sake of comparison.

	Mr Young		Mr Nicolayson	
Jerusalem	5000 to	6000	6000	7000
Nablous	150	200	200	
Hebron	700	800	700	800
Tiberias	600	700	1200	
Saphet[2]	1500	2000		
Kaipha[3]	150	200	150	200
Sidon	250	300	300	
Tyre	130	150	150	
Jaffa	60		60	
Acre[4]	200		200	
	400	580	400	500

On the whole, Mr Young reckoned that there are in round numbers about 10,000 Jews in the whole of Palestine. The difficulties, however in the way of procuring statistics are very great. The Jews are unwilling to give their true numbers, and they are reduced from time to time by the ravages of the plague. Add to this, that few young men come to the land; so that it is not reckoning accurately to take the usual average of individuals in a family. People who come here are generally elderly, and do not leave families behind them to increase the population or supply its vacancies. There is without doubt, a constant influx of Jews into this country, yet not so great as to do more than supply the annual deaths. Their poverty is great. The contributions from Europe of late have been

---

[2] The modern Zefat.
[3] The present Haifa was called Caife or Kaife from the medieval period.
[4] The modern Akko.

smaller than usual; and when they arrive instead of doing good, are the occasion of heart-burnings and strife. There is no such thing as 'brethren dwelling together in unity' in Jerusalem; no Jew trusts his brother. They are always quarrelling, and frequently apply to the Consul to settle their disputes. The expectation of support from the annual European contribution leads many to live in idleness. Hence there are in Jerusalem 500 acknowledged paupers, and 500 more who receive charity in a quiet way. Many are so poor that, if not relieved, they could not stand out the winter season. A few are shopkeepers; a few more are hawkers; and a very few are operatives. None of them are agriculturalists – not a single Jew cultivates the soil of his fathers. Among other peculiar causes of poverty, they are obliged to pay more rent than other people for their houses; and their rabbis frequently oppress and overreach those under their care.

The professing Christians here – Greeks, Armenians and Roman Catholics – are even more bitter enemies to Jews than Mahometans; so that in time of danger, a Jew would betake himself to the house of a Turk for refuge, in preference to that of a Christian. How little have these Christians the mind of Christ! Instead of His peculiarly tender love for Israel, they exhibit rooted hatred, and thus prove they are *Anti-Christ*. So far do they carry their enmity, that no Jew dare at this day pass by the door of the Holy Sepulchre. On this account, the kindness of Protestants appears to them very striking; and convinces them that there is a real difference in the religion we profess. And they are now becoming strongly attached to British Christians. The fact of a British Consul being stationed here on their account has greatly contributed to this effect. How wonderful that a British Consul should be sent to the Holy Land, with special instructions to interest himself in behalf of the Jews, and having for his district the very region formerly allotted to the twelve tribes of Israel! And how much more wonderful still, that our first Consul in Jerusalem should be one actuated by a deep and enlightened attachment to the cause of God's ancient people! There is also another singular fact, namely, that converted Jews have complete access to their brethren. Five converts are here at present, and the Jews treat them with kindness, allow them to visit their houses, and frequently visit them in return.

In the afternoon we mounted our hardy little palfreys, and with Mr Nicolayson for our guide, set out to visit some of the interesting spots around the city. Going out by Jaffa Gate, we turned to the south, and crossed by the wall of the lower pool of Gihon – that being the usual way to Bethlehem. Crossing Solomon's aqueduct, which we could trace far on its way to Bethlehem, we turned to the south-east, and climbed the hill immediately south of Mount Zion, parted from it by the deep vale of Hinnom. This ridge is named the Hill of Evil Counsel, because upon the summit a ruin is pointed out, which is called by the monks the country-house of Caiaphas, where the priests, scribes and elders met and took counsel how they might kill Jesus. From this we had another pleasant view of the plain of Rephaim, lying to the south-west. The reapers were gathering the ears of corn at the very time. The prominent object to the south is a graceful conical hill called the Frank Mountain, and supposed by some to be Beth-haccerem, a suitable spot 'for setting up a sign of fire' (Jeremiah 6:1).

To the north, we looked across the valley of Hinnom to Mount Zion, descending bold and steep into the ravine. Several parts were ploughed like a field as already mentioned, and on one part sheaves were standing. To the north-east, beyond the high wall of the mosque on Mount Moriah, we obtained the finest view we had yet seen of the Mount of Olives, with its three graceful summits. The depth of the Valley of Jehoshaphat (vale of Kedron) struck us very forcibly, and gave an appearance of great loftiness to Mount Olivet. To the east, we looked down the valley of the Kedron, toward the Dead Sea, with the mountains of Moab beyond.

Descending gradually toward the eastern side of the ridge, we came to the spot pointed out as Aceldama, 'the field of blood' the field bought with the thirty pieces of silver, and 'known to all the dwellers at Jerusalem' (Matthew 27:7,8; Acts 1:19). It lies opposite the south-east corner of Mount Zion. A particular tree is pointed out as the tree on which Judas hanged himself, a mere tradition, or rather a barefaced invention, but interesting as shewing that to this day the awful doom of the Son of Perdition is not forgotten by the dwellers of Jerusalem.

At this point is obtained a remarkable view of the Valley of Jehoshaphat. It is wide and ample, in some parts terraced, and a small portion of it planted with gardens, which are watered from the Pool of Siloam. The village of Siloam hangs over it on the right, and Ophel and Mount Zion slope down into it on the left. Its bosom is extensive enough to contain immense multitudes, such as Joel describes, 'Let the heathen be awakened and come up to the valley of Jehoshaphat'; 'multitudes, multitudes in the valley of decision' (Joel 3:12,14). The scenery of this spacious valley was no doubt before the prophet's eye as he uttered the prediction. Every height and hollow appeared before him thronged with armed multitudes, till he was made to realise the greatness of that last dread conflict, when from the neighbouring hill and city, the Lord's voice shall be heard, confounding his people's enemies; – 'the Lord shall roar out of Zion, and utter his voice from Jerusalem' (Joel 3:16).

From this point also, is seen the gentle hollow that marks the separation between Zion and Moriah. At other points, it seems as if the one hill overlapped the other; but here it is quite easy to trace the line of separation. This hollow is the Tyrop on of Josephus, or Valley of the Cheesemongers, beginning near the Jaffa Gate, and running east to the wall of the Mosque, and then south till it opens out into the Valley of Jehoshaphat. It was no doubt much deeper and more distinct in ancient days. The debris of the ruins of many generations has been long filling it up. Between the Tyrop on and the Valley of Jehoshaphat, outside the walls of the city, stood the tower called in Scripture, Ophel. The ridge ends there in a precipice of solid limestone rock, overhanging the Pool of Siloam, to the height of about sixty feet. Due east from the Mount of Evil Counsel, on the other side of the valley, rises the hill called the Mount of Offence or Mount of Corruption, on which, it is believed, Solomon set up idols to his strange gods. It is just a lower ridge of the Mount of Olives, barren and rocky. We thought we could trace indications of former buildings on the face of the hill, near the top.

Winding down the hill, we reached the lowest part of the Valley of Jehoshaphat, a retired spot, pleasantly shaded with fruit-trees. Here is Nehemiah's Well, or rather, there is little doubt, the ancient En-Rogel, 'the fuller's fountain'. There are the remains of ancient buildings over it, and a large tank beside it. It is 125 feet in depth. Formerly, the water seems to have been drawn up by a Persian wheel, such as we saw at El Arish and many other places, but now an old Arab let down a skin vessel and gave us a drink. The water was delightful. By this well in ancient times was drawn the border between Judah and Benjamin, for it is said with minute accuracy, that 'the border came down (from the Valley of Rephaim) to the end of the mountain, and descended to the Valley of Hinnom, and descended to En-Rogel' (Joshua 18:16). In this spot, so near the city, and yet so completely secluded, the two youths Jonathan and Ahimaaz tarried when Absalom took possession of Jerusalem, that they might carry tidings to David (2 Samuel 17:17). Among these pleasant fruit-trees Adonijah made a feast, at the time he aspired to the throne, when their mirth was so suddenly arrested by the shouts of joy in the city proclaiming Solomon to be king (1 Kings 1:9, 41).

Proceeding up the valley, we passed through a small grove of olives, pomegranates, and figs. A girl came running to us with her lap full of ripe apricots. Her head was ornamented with a circle of silver coins. Here we found people busily employed, some treading out corn by the feet of an ox and the ass, others winnowing what had been trodden out already. We passed the mouth of the Vale of Hinnom, and approaching the rock of Ophel above described, came to an old mulberry tree, whose roots are now supported by a terrace of rough stones, said to mark the place where Manasseh caused the prophet Isaiah to be sawn asunder (Hebrews 11:37). Three Arabs were reclining in its plentiful shade, and seemed to wonder why we gazed.

Passing under the rocky face of Ophel, we came to the Pool of Siloam. We were surprised to find it so entire, exactly resembling the common prints of it. It is in the form of a parallelogram, and the walls all round are of hewn stones. The steps that lead down into it, at the eastern end, are no doubt the same which have been there for ages. The water covered the bottom to the depth of one or two feet. At the western end, climbing a little way into a cave hewn out of a rock, we descended a few steps into the place from which the water flows into the pool. It is connected by a long subterranean passage, running quite through the hill to the Fountain of the Virgin, or more properly the Fountain of Siloam, the entrance to which is a considerable way farther up the Valley of Jehoshaphat. Through this passage the water flows softly from the fountain till it finds its way into the pool, not as generally represented in pictures by pouring over the mouth of the cave, but secretly from beneath. Wild flowers, and among other plants the caper-tree, grow luxuriantly around its border.

We are told that 'the wall of the Pool of Siloam, by the king's garden' (Nehemiah 3:15) was rebuilt in the days of Nehemiah. There can be no doubt that this is the very spot; and possibly the present walls and steps may be as ancient as the days of our Lord. While sitting on the margin, we could imagine the history of the blind man (John 9) realized before us. We had seen that very day a blind man in the streets of Jerusalem as we passed by. Now it was to such a man that our Lord said, 'Go wash in the Pool of Siloam'. The man obeys – comes out at the gate – descends the sloping side of Zion, gropes his way down these steps, and feels for the cool water with his hand; then laves his clay-anointed eyes, and they open! Now he sees the glory of Jerusalem, but above all, comes back to see the face of the Son of God, the light of the world, whose word commanded the light to shine on his dark eyeballs and his darker heart. The water of this pool flows out through a small channel cut or worn in the rock, and descends to refresh the gardens which are planted below on terraces.

Leaving the pool, we turned northward, proceeding up the Valley of Jehoshaphat with the village of Siloam on our right, which literally hangs upon the steep brow of the Mount of Offence. Three or four hundred yards up the valley, we came to the spring or fountain-head of Siloam, beneath the rocky side of Moriah. It is commonly called the Fountain of the Virgin, from a foolish tradition of the monks. We came to a wide cavern partly or entirely hewn out by the hands of man; and descending two flights of steps cut in the rock, worn smooth and white like marble, we came to the water. From this point it flows through the subterranean canal already mentioned, and supplies the Pool of Siloam. But it slows in such perfect stillness, that it seemed to us to be a standing pool, until we put our hands into it, and felt the gentle current pressing them aside. Nothing could be more descriptive of the flow of these waters than the words of Isaiah 8:6: 'The waters of Siloam that go softly.' The calm silent stream of grace and power which flows from under the throne of a reconciled God is, by this simple figure, finely contrasted with the loud noisy promises of Rezin and Remaliah's son.

It was with a full remembrance of this day's pleasant visit to the Fountain of Siloam, that the following lines occurred at an after period, when stretched in our tent under the brow of Carmel.

Beneath Moriah's rocky side
   A gentle fountain springs,
Silent and soft its waters glide,
   Like the peace the Spirit brings.

The thirsty Arab stoops to drink
   Of the cool and quiet wave;
And the thirsty spirit stops to think
   Of Him who came to save.

Siloam is the fountain's name;
   It means *'One sent from God'*;
And thus the Holy Saviour's fame
   It gently spreads abroad.

O grant that I like this sweet well,
    May Jesus' image bear;
And spend my life, my all, to tell
    How full His mercies are.[5]

We now passed farther up the Valley of Jehoshaphat, and observed with interest on the sides of the Mount of Olives, immediately opposite where the Temple stood, the Jewish burying-ground. Innumerable white flat stones overspread the valley, with short Hebrew inscriptions, generally very simple and uninteresting. It is here that the old Jews desire to be buried, that they may reach bliss without needing to make their way underground to the Valley of Jehoshaphat, as others require to do who die elsewhere. They expect to arise from these tombs at the resurrection, and see Messiah among the first.

Here we crossed the Kedron, and examined minutely the supposed tombs of Zechariah, James the Just, Jehoshaphat, and the monument called Absalom's Pillar, mentioned above. This last may possibly occupy the site of 'the pillar which Absalom reared up for himself in the king's dale, and called after his own name, Absalom's Place' (2 Samuel 18:18). The Jews believe it to be so, and cast many a stone at it in abhorrence as they pass. The original pillar seems to have been a square mass hewn out of solid rock, about sixteen feet high. The columns, pilasters and triglyphs which now adorn it, are evidently not Jewish work, and may be of much later origin.

We left the valley, and ascended the southern limb of the Mount of Olives by the Jericho road. We wished to view Jerusalem from the spot where the Saviour is supposed to have stood when he 'was come near, and beheld the city and wept over it' (Luke 19:41). The road to Jericho crosses the shoulder of the hill, so that when a traveller is approaching Jerusalem, the city is brought into full view all at once by a turn of the road. The scene is truly magnificent. The air is so clear and the view so comprehensive. The city lies, not under your feet, but almost on a level with you. You look across the valley to the temple rising full before you, and think that you could count every tower, every street and every dwelling. Jesus saw all this before him, and its guilty people were themselves as fully open to his view in that wonderful moment, when

---

[5] The full text of this poem, 'The Pool of Siloam', is given in Andrew Bonar, *Memoir and Remains of R.M. McCheyne* (The Banner of Truth Trust, Edinburgh, 1973), p.640. A facsimile in McCheyne's own hand is given on p.206.

his tears testified his unutterable love to Israel, and his words declared their fearful doom. Oh that we could stand and look on Israel now, with our Master's love and bowels of compassion! We stood awhile to realize that mysteriously interesting moment, and then rode on towards Bethany. The road slopes gently down the other side of the hill, and you are immediately out of sight of Jerusalem.

Descending and leaving the Jericho road, we came quite suddenly upon Bethany, called by the Arabs Azarieh, from the name of Lazarus. We found this ever-memorable village to be very like what we could have imagined it. It lies almost hidden in a small ravine of Mount Olivet, so much so that from the height it cannot be seen. It is embosomed in fruit-trees, especially figs and almonds, olives and pomegranates. The ravine in which it lies is terraced, and the terraces are covered either with fruit-trees or waving grain. There are not many houses, perhaps about twenty, inhabited, but there are many marks of ancient ruins. The house of Lazarus was pointed out to us, a substantial building, probably a tower in former days. The sepulchre called the Tomb of Lazarus attracted more of our attention. We lighted our tapers, and descended twenty-six steps cut in the rock to a chamber deep in the rock, having several niches for the dead. Whether this be the very tomb where Lazarus lay four days, and which yielded up its dead at the command of Jesus, it is impossible to say. The common objection that it is too deep seems entirely groundless, for there is nothing in the narrative to intimate that the tomb was on level with the ground. A stronger objection is, that the tomb is in the immediate vicinity of the village, or actually in it, but it is possible that the modern village occupies ground a little different from the ancient one. However this may be, there can be no doubt that this is 'Bethany, the town of Mary and her sister Martha, nigh unto Jerusalem, about fifteen furlongs off' (John 11:1,18). How pleasing are all the associations that cluster around it! Perhaps there was no scene in the Holy Land which afforded us more unmingled enjoyment. We even fancied that the curse that every where rests so visibly upon the land had fallen more lightly here. In point of situation, nothing could have come up more completely to our previous imagination of the place to which Jesus delighted to retire at evening from the bustle of the city, and the vexations of the unbelieving multitudes – sometimes traversing the road by which we had come, and perhaps oftener still coming up the face of the hill by the footpath that passes on the north of Gethsemane. What a peaceful scene! Amidst these trees, or in that grassy field, he may often have been seen in deep communion with the Father. And in sight of this verdant spot it was that he took his last farewell of the disciples, and went upward to resume the deep, unbroken fellowship of 'his God, and our God', uttering blessings even at the moment when he began to be parted from them (Luke 24:51). And it was here that the two angels stood by them in white apparel, and left us this glorious message, 'This same Jesus which is taken up from you into heaven, shall so come in like manner as ye have seen him go into heaven' (Acts 1:11).

As we purposed to visit Bethany again, we were contented to leave it the sooner, and following another footpath, ascended to the summit of the Mount of Olives. Near the top is the Tomb of Huldah the prophetess, which we entered and examined. It is a large chamber cut out of the natural rock. On what authority the name of Huldah is attached to it, we do not know. Not far from it we visited the Church of the Ascension, originally built by Helena, the mother of Constantine,[6] AD 326, over the spot where it is said that our Lord ascended from the earth, and where the inhabitants still pretend to shew the print of his last footstep! This tradition, though very ancient, is directly at variance with the words of the Evangelist. It evidently arose from the circumstance of this being the most conspicuous summit of the hill, and perhaps in some measure from the appearance, which does exist, of something like the footmark in the limestone rock. But the simple words of the Evangelist decide the matter, 'He led them out as far as to Bethany' (Luke 24:50). He led them beyond the summit, and down the other side of the hill, as far as the retired village of Bethany; and in the spot where he so often parted with them for the night, he now parted with them for 'a little while' (John 14:19) till the hour should come, when again 'his feet shall stand upon the Mount of Olives' (Zechariah 14:4).

We passed across the face of the Mount of Olives, towards the northern summit of the hill, and there descending into the valley of the Kedron, considerably to the north of the city, crossed over to the Tombs of the Kings. We first clambered down into a large area which has been cut out of the solid rock, and on the west side of which is a wide entrance which slopes under the rock. The band of carved work over the entrance

---

[6] Helena, mother of the emperor Constantine, became a Christian through her son and did many charitable works. In her old age she visited Palestine and her name is linked with the building of churches on sites connected with Jesus.

is very beautiful, representing a vine branch with bunches of grapes. With lighted tapers we crept through the low aperture which leads from the portico into an inner apartment, where are entrances to the chambers of the mighty dead. We examined with interest the remains of the stone doors described by many who have visited the place. The sloping ground at the entrance reminded us of what is said of John at the sepulchre of Christ, 'He stooped down and looking in, saw the linen clothes lying' (John 20:5).

As the sun was nearly down we began to move homewards, and from a rising ground between the tombs and the city we obtained a much more pleasing view of Jerusalem, with its domes and minarets, than is afforded by any of the other approaches on this side. We entered the Damascus Gate before sunset. Spending the evening with Mr Nicolayson, we saw again the custom which had attracted our attention at Damietta, and which illustrates several passages in the gospel. While we sat at meat several persons came in, though uninvited, and seating themselves by the wall, joined in the conversation.

These are specimens of the days we spent in Jerusalem. Every object that met our view was invested with a sacred interest in our eyes, and that interest increased instead of diminishing the more we examined the place. Early one morning two of us set out to visit Gethsemane. The sun had newly risen; few people were upon the road, and the valley of Jehoshaphat was lonely and still. Descending the steep of Mount Moriah and crossing the dry bed of the brook Kedron, we soon came to the low rude wall enclosing the plot of ground which for ages has borne the name of Gethsemane. Clambering over we examined the sacred spot and its eight olive-trees. These are very large and very old, but their branches are still strong and vigorous. One of them we measured, and found to be nearly eight yards in girth round the lower part of the trunk. Some of them are hollow with age, but filled up with earth, and most have heaps of stones gathered round their roots. The enclosure seems to have been tilled at some recent period. At one corner some pilgrim has erected a stone and carved upon it the Latin words, '*et hic tenuerunt eum*' marking it as the spot where Judas betrayed his Master with a kiss. The road to Bethany passes by the foot of the garden, and the more private footpath up the brow of the hill passes along its northern wall. Looking across the Kedron, the steep brow of Moriah and sombre wall of the Haram with its battlements, and the top of the Mosque of Omar, shut in the view. At evening, when the gates of Jerusalem are closed, it must be a perfect solitude. Our blessed Master must have distinctly seen the band of men and officers sent to apprehend him, with their lanterns and torches, and glittering weapons, descending the side of Moriah and approaching the garden. By the clear moonlight, he saw his three chosen disciples fast asleep in his hour of agony; and by the gleam of the torches, he observed his cruel enemies coming down to seize him and carry him away to his last sufferings; yet 'he was not rebellious, neither turned away back' (Isaiah 50:5). He viewed the bitter cup that was given to him to drink, and said, 'Shall I not drink it?' (John 18:11) .

We read over all the passages of Scripture relating to Gethsemane, while seated together there. It seemed nothing wonderful to read of the weakness of those three disciples, when we remembered that they were sinful men like disciples now; but the compassion, the unwavering love of Jesus, appeared by the contrast to be infinitely amazing. For such souls as ours, he rent this vale with his strong crying and tears, wetted this ground with his bloody sweat and set his face like a flint to go forward and die. 'While we were yet sinners Christ died for us' (Romans 5:8). Each of us occupied part of the time alone – in private meditation – and then we joined together in prayer – putting our sins into that cup which our Master drank here, and pleading for our own souls, for our far distant friends, and for the flocks committed to our care.

As the day advanced, we repassed the brook Kedron, visited the spot where Stephen is said to have been stoned, and entered the city by the gate which bears his name. Here we delayed a little to examine the large dry reservoir which is generally called 'the Pool of Bethesda'. The bottom is partly covered with rubbish, and partly planted with a few flowers and old trees. At the farther end are two arches, forming entrances into dark vaults, which are generally believed to be remains of the five porches. There can be little doubt, from the manner in which the sides are cemented, that it was anciently a pool, and it bears the name of a pool among the native population to this day. That the Pool of Bethesda was in the immediate vicinity of the Temple, and also near one of the gates of the city, there can be no doubt; and that it was a large and important reservoir, seems also probable from the narrative of the gospel. But there is no other pool at present remaining in Jerusalem which answers this description; so that it may really be the case that this large reservoir, though used as part of the trench of Antonia, is still the remains of the interesting Pool of Bethesda.

While we were leaning over the parapet and musing over the past, some Moslem boys began to gather stones and throw them at us, calling 'Nazarani'.[7] We had approached nearer the gate of the mosque than Christian feet are permitted to do. An Egyptian soldier who was by took our part, and we quietly retired. Being without a guide, we had the pleasure of losing our way, and wandering up and down for about an hour in the streets of Jerusalem, before we found our home on the brow of Mount Zion.

In the afternoon we spent five hours in receiving from Mr Nicolayson full information regarding the numbers and condition of the Jews in Palestine. The Committee of our Church who had sent us forth, had furnished us with a list of questions to be investigated, and answered. These we shall set down in order, with the information we received in reply to them.

1. *What is the number of Jews in Jerusalem and in the Holy Land?*
We have already set down briefly the answer to this question. A few more particulars may be added. In Jerusalem 1,000 Jews pay taxes, and all of these are males from thirteen years old and upwards. The Jews marry when very young, so that, allowing five to a family, there are 5000 represented by the 1,000 who pay taxes in Jerusalem. Foreign Jews, however, such as Russians, Poles and Hungarians, and many others, continue under the protection of European powers, and pay no taxes. These may amount to 2,000, which would give about 7,000 Jews to Jerusalem. This is the largest statement of the number of Jews in the Holy City that we anywhere received, and is no doubt above the real amount; for the average of five to a family appears to be far too great.

The destruction of Saphet by an earthquake in 1837 occasioned the dispersion of many of the Jews who dwelt there. Of these, some settled at Acre, and some at Jerusalem. In the cities along the coast, the Jews have been increasing of late. In Tyre, formerly a Jew was not allowed to spend a night; but the Pasha's government changed the law, and now a congregation and a rabbi have settled there. They are chiefly from the Barbary coast. The recent occupation of Algiers by the French enabled the Jews of that coast to claim protection as French subjects, and this induced them to leave home more freely for purposes of trade. The same

---

[7] The term 'Nazarene' was clearly used from New Testament times to describe Christian believers (Acts 24:5) and then it became the name for Syrian Christians. Later still it was adopted by the Persians, the Armenians and the Arabs.

class of Jews is found in Sidon and Beyrout. At the utmost, the whole Jewish population of Palestine may be reckoned at about 12,000. This is the largest estimate which we received; yet comparing it with their numbers in the days of Solomon, we may well say in the words of Isaiah, there are 'few men left' (Isaiah 34:6).

2. Has the number of Jews in Palestine been increasing of late years? Their numbers did increase decidedly during the first five years of the Pasha's government, that is from 1832 to 1836 – a time which coincides with the occupation of Algiers by the French. Many came from the Barbary coast, who settled chiefly at Saphet and on the coast. During the last two years there has been little or no increase. There is always an influx, but then the mortality is great, and the number that come do no more than supply the places of those cut off. The change of climate at the advanced period of life in which many come, the new habits which the country forces them to form, their being crowded together in damp, unwholesome residences, all combine to shorten their days. This diminution in the numbers of Jews returning to their own land, seems to be caused by the ravages which the plague has been making for two years past; by the rise in the price of provisions; by the embarrassed finances of the Jewish community, their debt amounting to nearly 8000; and by the oppressions which they suffered from their rabbis. Some have actually left, and several have said that they would gladly leave Jerusalem if it were in their power. Their reasons for coming into the land are:

1. The universal belief that every Jew who dies out of the land must perform a subterraneous passage back to it, that he may rise in the Valley of Jehoshaphat.

2. They believe that to die in this land is certain salvation, though they are not exempted from 'the beating in the grave, and the eleven months of purgatory'.

3. They believe that those who reside here have immediate communication with Heaven, and that the rabbis are in a manner inspired.

4. They expect the appearing of the Messiah. The Jews in Palestine have always cherished the hope of his coming, and of their own restoration. This opinion has now even more weight with them than formerly, for they partake of the general impression that a crisis is approaching. The Jews here, as a nation, are far from infidel, but there are many whose minds are fully occupied with their miseries.

3. *Are the Jews in Palestine supported by their brethren in other parts of the world?*

Generally speaking they are all supported by a yearly contribution made by their brethren in other lands. All foreign Jews residing in Palestine are entirely dependent on contributions from Europe, except a few who have property in Europe. These last either bring their little property with them, or make it over to friends in Europe, on condition of them sending them an annual sum to the Holy Land, upon which they live here. But even these may receive their share, as every Jew, rich or poor, who has been one year in the country, has a share allotted to him if he chooses to take it. The sum received by each individual is very small; much is swallowed up by their differences and quarrels, and much is required to pay the interest of their debt. Five ducats, or about £3.10s. a-head, is thought a good contribution. At present, however, it is even smaller. The way of collecting the European contributions used to be this. Messengers were sent from Jerusalem to the different cities in Europe, where collections were made, and these brought the money to Palestine. This was a very expensive method, for nearly one-fourth of the sum collected was spent in paying the expenses of the messengers. Of late years, however, another plan has been adopted. The money is sent to Amsterdam, where it is received by a rich Jewish merchant and he transmits it to the Austrian Consul at Beyrout, by whom it is conveyed to the Jews at Jerusalem. They are persons who have been specifically named by friends in Europe who sent the money. The largest collections come from Amsterdam; not much from Britain. Some Jews, chiefly Spanish, are supported by being readers in the places devoted to study.

4. *Is there kept up constant and rapid communication between the Jews in Palestine, and those in other parts of the world?*

The rabbis of Palestine maintain a constant communication with their brethren all over the world. In one respect, indeed, it may be said, that Jerusalem is not the centre of Jewish influence; for there is little outgoing from it; the Jews are stationary there; yet, on the other hand, it is true that Jerusalem is the heart of the nation, and everything done there or in the Holy Land will tell upon the whole Jewish world. When conversions take place, although they wish to keep them quiet, still the intelligence is soon communicated, and known and spoken of every where. A Jew said lately to Mr Nicolayson, that he believed that in a short time no young Jews would be allowed to come to the Holy Land, if the missionaries continued to labour as they were doing. They would trust only old confirmed Jews there, who would be able to meet their arguments. The communication, however, is by no means rapid, being carried on by means of messengers. Much mischief has often arisen from this system, for the rabbis sometimes intercept the letters of poor Jews, which they fear may be complaining of their conduct.

5. *From what countries do the Jews principally come?*
The greatest numbers come from Poland and the Austrian dominions. Many come from Russia, and many more would come if they were not hindered. There are some from Wallachia and Moldavia; a few from Germany; a few from Holland; but scarcely any from Britain. All these being Europeans receive the name of Ashkenazim. The native Jews, that is, those Jews who are subjects of the country, are called Sephardim, and are almost all of Spanish extraction. They come principally from Turkey in Europe, from Saloniki, Constantinople, and the Dardanelles. Those who come from Asia Minor are chiefly from Smyrna. Many have come from Africa, especially of late years, from Morocco, and the Barbary coast, from Algiers, Tunis, and Tripoli. These bring French passports, and are therefore under protection. There are a few from Alexandria and Cairo. Mr Nicolayson never saw any Jews from India, though several have gone to India, and returned. They have occasional communication with Yemen and Sennah. There are many Spanish Jews, and several Polish families, who have been here for generations, whose fathers and grandfathers have died here, and who are really natives of Palestine. But most even of these count themselves foreigners still, and they generally contrive to make a tour of Europe some time in their life.

6. *Are there many Rabbis in Palestine?*
There is often a great mistake made about the rank of those who get the title of Rabbi. The truth is, all are included in that class who are not in the class (*am haaretz*), that is, the uneducated. Formerly, the Rabbis were a kind of clergy, and were appointed by laying on of hands, but now there is no such distinction. The official Rabbi does not even preside in the synagogue, but deputes this to another, the Hazan, who is often chosen because of his fine voice. The only part of the duty which is reserved peculiarly for the priest is the pronouncing of the blessing. None but a Cohen, a priest of Aaron's line can give this. In the

synagogue any one may be called up to read. This custom appears to be as old as the days of our Lord. The only distinction made is, that first a Cohen is called up to read, then a Levite, then a common Israelite. Most of the Jews in the Holy Land spend their time in a sort of study or reading. Crowded in their families, however, they cannot really devote themselves to study; and their disputes also are a great hindrance. They study nothing but Talmudical books, and even in this department there is none of them who can be called learned when compared with Jews in Europe.

7. *What are the peculiar characteristics of the Jews in Palestine?*
Their principal characteristic is, that they are all strict Rabbinists, though in this they can hardly be said to differ from the Polish Jews. They are also superstitious in the extreme. Their real characteristic may be inferred from the fact, that those who come are the *élite* of the devotional and strictly religious Jews of other countries. They have so little trade that their covetousness and cheating are turned upon one another.

8. *What are the feelings of the Jews in Palestine towards Christianity?*
9. *What success has attended the efforts hitherto made for their conversion?*
These two questions involve each other. The first effort of the London Society in this country was made in the year 1820 by a Swiss clergymen named Tschundi, who was employed chiefly in distributing the Scriptures to the Jews. Joseph Wolff then made two visits to Jerusalem, and had a good deal of personal intercourse with the Jews. He was always enabled to leave this impression behind him, that Christians were really seeking the conversion of Israel, and that without Christ there is no forgiveness. Soon after, Mr Lewis Waye came to the East with the view of forming a mission, accompanied by Mr Lewis, an Irish clergyman (the same whose kindness and Christian hospitality we afterwards enjoyed), and by several converted Jews. He rented a convent at Antoura, intending to make it a place where missionaries might prepare themselves, but ill health forced him to return home. In 1824, Dr Dalton, a medical man, was sent out to aid Mr Lewis in forming a settlement in Jerusalem; but the latter returned home that same autumn. Upon this Dr Dalton made an arrangement with two American missionaries who had arrived, named King and Pliny Fiske, to rent one of the small convents for their establishment. Pliny Fiske, however, died in November 1825,

before the arrangement was completed; and Dr Dalton was again left alone. It was to aid him that Mr Nicolayson was sent to this country in December 1825. But very soon after his arrival Dr Dalton died, in January 1826, of an illness caught on a tour to Bethlehem. Mr Nicolayson returned to Beyrout, and studied the language more thoroughly during that winter.[8]

In the summer of the same year (1826) a rebellion broke out, and Mr Nicolayson retired to Saphet and lived there till June 1827, having much intercourse with the Jews. Considerable impression was made, and the rabbis grew jealous of him. They threatened to excommunicate the man who let him his house, and the woman who washed his clothes, so that he was forced to return to Beyrout. He then left the country for four years, and travelled on the Barbary coast. In 1832 he returned, and came to Beyrout with his family at the time when the Pasha had nearly taken Acre. The country was now quite open, so that he spent the summer at Sidon, and had intercourse with Christians and Jews. He was beginning to build a cottage there, when the jealousy of the Greek priests threw obstacles in his way.

In 1833, Mr Calman came, and he and Mr Nicolayson made a tour together to the holy cities. Mr Calman's sweetness of temper and kindly manner gained upon the Jews exceedingly. At Jerusalem they consulted with Ysa Petros, a Greek priest, who was very friendly, as to the practicability of renting a house in that city. They visited Tiberias, and had many discussions with the Jews, the results of which were often very encouraging; and last of all spent an interesting fortnight at Saphet. On returning to Beyrout, they found that two American missionaries had arrived on their way to Jerusalem to labour among the native Christians. They all resolved to attempt the renting of a house in the Holy City.

Accordingly, in the autumn of 1833, Mr Nicolayson and family removed to Jerusalem, to the house on Mount Zion where he now lives, and spent a quiet comfortable winter. In the spring of 1834, Mr Thomson, an American missionary arrived, and about the same time the

---

[8] John Nicolayson (1803-1856) was an outstanding early missionary in Palestine. His grave is in the Protestant cemetery on Mount Zion. It contains the inscription: '23 years a faithful watchman on the walls of Jerusalem, fearless in the midst of war pestilence and earthquake. A master of all the learning of the Hebrews and the Arabs. Founder of the English hospital and builder of the Protestant church. Lived beloved and died lamented by Christians, Jews and Mahometans'.

rebellion broke out. One Sabbath morning the missionaries found themselves environed, the soldiers having left the town to the mercy of the Fellahs; and the earthquake happened the same day. They were shut up in their dwelling till the Friday when Ibraim arrived, but remained in a state of siege for five or six weeks. During ten days they had to live upon rice alone. Sickness followed. Mrs. Thomson, of the American mission, died of brain fever, produced by the alarm and other circumstances. Mrs. Nicolayson was ill for three or four weeks, and Mr Nicolayson felt ill soon after, so that they had to leave for Beyrout, and thus lost that summer. In the spring of 1835, Dr Dodge and Mr Whiting, two more American missionaries, arrived. Mr Whiting boarded with Mr Nicolayson in Jerusalem, but Dr Dodge died in the middle of the same year he came out. From this time the Jewish Mission may be accounted as established in the Holy City. In 1835, the subject of a Hebrew Church on Mount Zion was started in England, and in 1836 Mr Nicolayson was called to England to consult regarding it. He returned in July, 1837, and laboured alone in Jerusalem for a year. But in July 1838, Mr Pieritz and Mr Levi, converted Jews, but not in orders, were sent out to strengthen the Mission here; and in December, Dr Gerstmann, and his assistant, Mr Bergheim, both converted Jews, and both medical men, arrived. They have thus made Jerusalem the centre of the Mission to the Jews in Palestine. Mr Young the English Consul, had fixed his quarters here about three months before our arrival.

The efforts made have been blessed to the conversion of some Jews in Jerusalem, though it is still the day of small things. A Jew named Simeon was awakened at Bucarest by reading a New Testament and some tracts which he received from a Jew who did not understand them. He was convinced, but had many difficulties which he could not get over. A converted Jew came and preached at Bucarest, and advised him to go to the Missionaries at Constantinople. He went, but could not find them out. He proceeded to Smyrna, where he met with another inquiring Jew named Eliezer. Mr Nicolayson was in Smyrna at the time on his way to Jerusalem. When Simeon heard that a missionary from the Holy City was there, he immediately came to him, and opened up his mind. Mr Nicolayson brought him as a servant to Jerusalem. During Mr Nicolayson's absence in 1836-37, he was under the care of Mr Calman. His wife for a long time refused to follow him from Wallachia, and bitterly opposed his change; but being induced to come to Jerusalem, and being regularly instructed by Mr Pieritz, and also affected by an illness, she gave good evidence of having undergone a saving change, and now she speaks like a missionary to her countrywomen. The whole family, consisting of Simeon, his wife, a boy, a girl, were baptized in Jerusalem after last Easter. This is the family at whose house we heard the German service last Sabbath Day. Another case was that of Chaii or Hymen Paul, an amiable young Jew, an acquaintance of Simeon, who became intelligently convinced of the truth. He was baptized last Pentecost, and at his own desire sent to England.

The first native Jew awakened at Jerusalem was Rabbi Joseph, in September 1838. He was a learned young man, and so bitterly was his change opposed by the Jews, that the Missionaries were obliged to send him away to Constantinople before he was baptized. Three rabbis have very lately become inquirers after the truth, and seem determined to profess Christianity openly. We afterwards received a fuller account of these last two cases from Mr Pieritz. These are all the known fruits of the Mission in the way of conversion.

When Rabbi Joseph was awakened, a *herem* or ban of excommunication was pronounced in the synagogues against the Missionaries, and all who should have dealings with them. But when Dr Gerstmann, the medical man, came in December, the Jews immediately began to break through it. Another *herem* was pronounced, but in vain. No one regarded it, and Rabbi Israel refused to pronounce it, saying that he would not be the cause of hindering his poor and sick brethren from going to be healed. This interesting fact shews the immense value of medical missionaries.

The more general fruits of the establishment of the Mission have been these:

1. The distinction between true and false Christianity has been clearly opened up before the eyes of the Jews.

2. The study of the Old Testament has been forced upon them; so that they cannot avoid it.

3. The word of God has become more and more the only ground of controversy. The authority of the Talmud is not now appealed to; the only dispute about it being whether it is to be referred to at all, or what is its real value?

The support of inquirers and converts is one of the chief difficulties that meets a Missionary here. The institution of a printing press, to afford them both manual and mental labour, has been proposed. An hospital for the sick has also been set on foot.

10. *What modes of operation have been employed?*
The mode of operation is entirely by personal intercourse. The Missionaries frequently make tours to other towns, and dispose of copies of the Old Testament. Mr Nicolayson has sold about 5,000 Hebrew Bibles. The Missionaries never dispose of the New Testament, except to those in whom they have confidence. They at one time sold a box of fifty New Testaments, bound up with the Old. But they afterwards found the New Testament torn out, and blank leaves inserted instead, with Jarchi's Commentary written on them. The Jews will not take tracts except privately. Many of their Old Testaments have been conveyed to Baghdad and to India.

11. *How far is the health of the Missionaries affected by the climate?*
The climate of Jerusalem is decidedly healthy. The sicknesses and deaths among the Missionaries above mentioned can hardly be attributed to the climate. Dr Dalton was very delicate when he came; Mrs. Thomson died of brain fever; and Dr Dodge's death was occasioned by a hurried journey in which he was much exposed.

12. *What kind of house accommodation is there, and what is the expense of living in Palestine?*
The house accommodation in Jerusalem is tolerably comfortable. In the winter it is difficult to keep the houses dry, the rain causing much dampness; but the sorest privations are want of Christian society, and public means of grace. A Missionary here meets with many trials which he did not anticipate. He must have great patience, and must make up his mind to suffer delays and disappointments, which are much more trying than merely temporal privations, which are really small. A Missionary coming out must not expect full work at once, he must be willing to stand by and wait. Often we may say, 'His strength is to sit still'. The Christian Missionary enjoys perfect liberty to carry on his operations under the Egyptian government, more so, indeed, than under the British government at Malta or in India. No one inquires what he is about.

Provisions are easily got; but the expense of living is rising continually. The price of food is now double what it once was, and some things are four times as high as when Mr Nicolayson first came. In addition to the salaries of the Missionaries, the London Society pay all the travelling expenses of their missionary tours.

The business of the day being over, we enjoyed a walk outside the Zion Gate. As we sat upon the brow of the hill, we were led to rejoice in the thought, that as certainly as 'Zion is now ploughed as a field', the day is coming when 'the Lord of Hosts shall reign in Mount Zion, and in Jerusalem, and before his ancients gloriously' (Isaiah 24:23).

Two flocks were moving slowly up the slope of the hill, the one of goats, the other of sheep. The shepherd was going before the flock, and they followed, as he led the way toward the Jaffa Gate. We could not but remember the Saviour' words, 'When he putteth forth his own sheep, he goeth before them, and the sheep follow him, for they know his voice' (John 10:4).

In the evening we visited the Consul, who had invited the Governor of Jerusalem to meet us. This Turk occupies the house said to have belonged to Pontius Pilate. He came in attired in full Eastern costume, a handsome young man, attended by three servants, one of whom carried his pipe. The servants remained in the room, near the door, and kept their eye on their master. On occasion of a slight motion of the hand, one of them stepped forward and took the pipe, and then resumed his place as before, watching his master's movements, as if to anticipate his wishes. This is the custom which we observed in Egypt as illustrating Psalm 123:2: 'Behold, as the eyes of servants look unto the hand of their masters – so our eyes wait upon the LORD our God, until that he have mercy upon us.' He was very affable, and seemed highly entertained with examining our eyeglasses and watches. He drank wine with us also, probably to shew how liberal a high-born Mussulman[9] can be.

In the evening we planned an excursion to Hebron, and next day (June 13) set out by 7 am, accompanied by the Consul and his lady, Mr. Nicolayson, and Mr George Dalton. Some were mounted on mules, and some on horses; the saddles, as usual, broad and uncomfortable. Crossing the Vale of Gihon, we turned due south, and travelled over the fine plain of Rephaim. About three miles from the city, we came to a well, where tradition has fixed the scene of Matthew 2:10. It is one of the few beautiful traditions associated with sacred places. The tradition is, that the wise men, who for some time had lost the guidance of the star which brought them from their country, sat down beside this well to refresh themselves, when one of their number saw the reflection of the star in the clear water of the well. He cried aloud to his companions, and 'when they saw the star they rejoiced with exceeding great joy'. This

---

[9] Muslim

well may perhaps be *the fountain of Nephtoah* (Joshua 15:9).

We passed the Convent of Elijah, for the monks suppose that the prophet fled this way to Beersheba (1 Kings 19:4), and under a neighbouring tree, they pretend to shew the mark left by his body as he lay asleep on the rocky ground, though it is hard stone. From this point we obtained our first sight of Bethlehem, lying about three miles to the south upon a considerable eminence, and possessing at a distance a peculiarly attractive appearance. We meant to visit it in returning, and therefore at present contented ourselves with a distant view of the place where the memorable words were spoken by the Angel, 'Fear not, for behold I bring you good tidings of great joy; unto you is born this day in the city of David, a Saviour, which is Christ the Lord' (Luke 2:10). About a mile and a half farther to the south we came to a tomb, built like the whited sepulchres of the East, but believed to be *Rachel's Sepulchre*. The tomb is no doubt modern, erected probably by the Mahometans; but the spot may justly be regarded as the place where Rachel died and was buried, 'And there was but a little way to come to Ephrath (i.e. Bethlehem Ephratah, Micah 5:2); and Rachel travailed, and she had hard labour – and Rachel died, and was buried in the way to Ephrath, which is Bethlehem; and Jacob set a pillar upon her grave; that is the pillar of Rachel's grave unto this day' (Genesis 35:16). The Jews frequently visit it, and many (as Benjamin of Tudela says they used to do in his days) have left their names and places of abode in Hebrew inscribed upon the white plaster in the interior walls. To the west of the tomb on the face of a hill stands a large and pleasant-looking village called Bet-Jalah inhabited, we were told, entirely by Christians. May this not be the ancient Zelzah, 'by Rachel's sepulchre in the border of Benjamin' (1 Samuel 10:2), where Saul was told that his father's asses had been found? In other passages of Scripture (Joshua 18:28; 2 Samuel 21:14) the place is called Zelah, from which the modern name might easily be formed by prefixing the common syllable 'Bet' (that is, 'house') and softening the sibilant letter. If so, then this is the spot where they buried the bones of Saul and Jonathan – 'in Zelah, in the sepulchre of Kish his father'.

Leaving Bethlehem about half a mile to the east, and proceeding still in a southerly direction, we came down in a short time to the valley, where lie the three large and singular reservoirs, called Solomon's Pools. They are situated at a short distance from one another, each on a different level, so that the water flows from the upper into the middle

pool, and from the middle in to the lower pool, from which it is conveyed
by a stone aqueduct round the hills to Bethlehem, and from Bethlehem
to Jerusalem. The walls of the pool are of solid masonry covered over
with cement. Close by is a Saracenic fort[10] with high walls and a
battlement, perhaps originally intended to protect the pools. Under the
shade of its walls we left our mules, and proceeded to measure the pools
with a line as accurately as the ground would admit. The result was as
follows:

1. *The Upper or Western Pool*

Length of north side,	389 feet
Length of south side,	380 feet
Breadth of west side,	229 feet
Breadth of east side,	236 feet
Depth at one point,	25 feet

2. *The Middle Pool*

Length,	425 feet
Breadth of west side,	158 feet
Breadth of east side,	250 feet

3. *The Lower or Eastern Pool*

Length,	583 feet
Breadth on west side,	148 feet
Breadth on east side,	202 feet

At all the corners there are flights of steps descending into them. The
water is pure and delightful, and each of the pools was about half full.
Of the great antiquity of these splendid reservoirs there can be no doubt,
and there seems every probability that they are the work of Solomon.
This pleasant valley being so near the spot where his father David fed
his sheep, would be always interesting to the king; but the only reference
to the pools in Scripture, appears to be in Ecclesiastes, where he
describes the manner in which, forsaking the fountain of living waters
– 'the God that appeared unto him twice' – he sought everywhere for
cisterns of earthly joy. 'I made me gardens and orchards, and I planted
trees in them of all kinds of fruits. I made me *pools of water*, to water
therewith the wood that bringeth forth trees' (Ecclesiastes 2:5,6). It is

---

[10] This fortress was probably built by the Turks around 1540.

highly probable, that, besides other purposes, these cisterns were intended to water rich gardens in their vicinity; and in the lower parts of the valley, at present covered with ripe crops of waving grain, there would be a splendid situation for the gardens, and orchards, and nurseries of fruit-trees, which The Preacher describes. In Josephus and in the Talmud, this place is called Etham (see also 2 Chronicles 11:6). The former says concerning it, 'There was a certain place about fifty furlongs distant from Jerusalem (more than six miles) which is called Etham; very pleasant it is in fine gardens, and abounding in rivulets of water. Thither Solomon used to ride out in the morning' (Antiq. 8.7.3). Beautiful insects, especially very large dragonflies, with fine variegated wings, were fluttering round the water. We refreshed ourselves at a fountain close by, on the north-west corner of the upper pool, to which we descended by steps. This is said by tradition to be 'the spring shut up, the fountain sealed', to which the church is compared in the Song (Song of Solomon 4:12). It was usual in former times to cover up the well's mouth for the sake of the precious living water. In the fields around the reapers were busy at barley-harvest. It was somewhere near this very spot that Naomi found them reaping as she returned from the captivity of Moab, 'they came to Bethlehem in the beginning of barley-harvest' (Ruth 1:22), and some of these fruitful fields may have been the field of Boaz, where Ruth gleaned after the reapers, in the same manner as the Syrian women were doing when we passed.

After leaving the pools, the road conducted us for some time over very rocky hills. We came to a considerable valley, cultivated to some extent, at the extremity of which, where the ground begins to rise again, is a village called Sipheer. Can this be a remnant of the name *Kirjath-Sepher*, the city smitten by Othniel, when he gained Achsah, Caleb's daughter (Joshua 15:16)? Perhaps this valley may be the field which she asked from her father; but we had no time to search for the upper and the nether springs that once watered it. Other travellers have found sepulchral caves there. Ruins occasionally met our eye, chiefly on eminences, the remains no doubt of the towns and villages of Judah. On our left one ruin was called 'Bet-hagar', that is, 'house of stone', another 'Bet-Immer', with an ancient pool still remaining. About an hour from Hebron, there is a large, and evidently much frequented fountain, named Ain-Derwa. Many camels were drinking out of the troughs, and our horses and mules were glad to join them. This is possibly *the well of Sirah*, at which Abner was refreshing himself when Joab's messengers found him and treacherously brought him back to Hebron to be slain (2 Samuel 3:26).

We had now spent nearly eight hours on the road, riding very leisurely. About two miles from the town we entered the Valley of Hebron, the way running through vineyards, which make the approach very pleasant. Fig trees and pomegranates in great abundance were everywhere intermixed with the vines, and the hills above were covered with verdant olive-trees. The vines were in great luxuriance, and the flowers just forming into the grape, so that the delightful fragrance diffused itself far and wide. 'The fig-tree putteth forth her green figs, and the vines with the tender grapes give a good smell' (Song of Solomon 2:13). In many of the vineyards we saw the towers, built for protection and for other uses, and frequently referred to in Scripture (Isaiah 5:2; Matthew 21:33).

We encamped about four o'clock on a verdant plot of ground opposite the northern portion of Hebron, pitching our tents under some fine olive-trees. Beauty lingers around Hebron still. God blesses the spot where he used to meet with Abraham his friend. It lies in a fine fertile valley, enclosed by high hills on the east and west. The houses are disposed in four different quarters, which are separated from each other by a considerable space. The largest portion is to the south-east, around the Mosque, the houses running up the eastern slope. The ruins of ancient houses are still higher up. The fourfold division of the town gives it a singular appearance, while the cupolas on the houses, and the vigorous olive-trees that are interspersed throughout the town, add greatly to its beauty. Some miles north of the town we passed four bare walls, which are called by the Jews the ruins of Abraham's house, and the plain around it is called the 'plain of Mamre'. We felt much inclined, however, to believe that the fine valley on the south-east side of the town is the true plain of Mamre.

The Moslem Governor, hearing of the arrival of the English Consul, sent him the present of a sheep, and soon after waited upon us. Mr Nicolayson acted as interpreter. When the Consul thanked him for his kind present, he replied, 'It is all the blessing of Abraham. It is only what should be done in the city of El-Halil. Had Abraham been here he would have sent a sheep or a calf, and we are in Abraham's stead.' The Arabic name of the town is El-Halil, 'the beloved', so called in memory of Abraham, 'the friend of God'.

An old Jew, Rabbi Haiim, who is now blind with age, hearing of the arrival of Mr Nicolayson, sent him an *oka*[11] of wine in token of respect and kindness. This little incident in the city where Abraham dwelt was peculiarly affecting, and shewed in a very clear light the friendly feelings which the Jews of Palestine entertain towards Protestant Missionaries, though fully aware of the object which they have in view. A Greek Christian, named Elias, who was acquainted with our fellow-travellers, shewed us great attention.

When the darkness came down, we saw some fine specimens of the glowworm around our tents. Overhead the sky was splendid; the stars being unusually large and brilliant from the clearness of the atmosphere. For the same reason, many more stars are visible to the naked eye than in our northern sky. We recollected that it was here, in the plain of Mamre, under the same sky, that God 'brought Abraham forth abroad, and said, Look toward heaven, and tell the stars, if thou be able to number them: so shall thy seed be' (Genesis 15:5). The same sight recalled with new power the gracious promise, 'They that be wise shall shine as the brightness of the firmament, and they that turn many to righteousness as the stars for ever and ever' (Daniel 12:3).

We all met for evening worship in one tent. Mr Nicolayson read Genesis 18 and prayed with a full heart for Israel, that they to whom the promises were made might soon enjoy the Redeemer's communion as Abraham enjoyed it here; and that we might receive Abraham's spirit of intercession for a perishing world.

June 14

This morning we awoke early, and tried to realize the feelings of a true child of Abraham in Hebron, meditating over all the Scriptures that relate to it. The deep terraces of the mountain afford sweet spots for retirement.

We had scarcely breakfasted when the Governor paid us a second visit, offering to conduct us to see the mosque, which is believed to cover the cave of Machpelah. The appearance of this man in the midst of his attendants was anything but prepossessing. He was an ill-looking Moslem, an oldish man, with fine grey beard, very marked nose, and dark suspicious eyes. The duty of paying attention to Christian travellers seemed to be a very irksome one to his Mahometan pride. He brought two sheep with him as a present to the Consul, doubling the gift of the previous day.

---

[11] A Turkish word related to the English 'ounce' designating a weight of about 3lbs.

We proceeded toward the Mosque, the Consul's janissary going before. Several Jews joined in the train. As we passed through the streets, the boys and girls cried *Nazarani,* teaching us that 'the Nazarene' is still a term of reproach in this land. The Mosque is a large quadrangular building, with two minarets at the opposite corners. The lower half of the walls is evidently of the highest antiquity; the stones are very large, and each of them is bevelled in the edge, in the same manner as the ancient stones of the temple wall of Jerusalem. One stone which we measured was 24 feet by 4, and another was still larger. On the two principal sides there are sixteen pilasters, on the other two sides ten, composed of these immense stones, with a simple projecting cope at the top. Above this, the building is evidently of Mahometan origin, and is surmounted by a battlement. We were allowed to ascend the wide massy staircase that leads into the interior of the building. The door into the mosque was thrown open, but not a foot was allowed to cross the marble threshold. We were shewn the window of the place which contains the tombs of Abraham and Sarah, beneath which is understood to be the cave of Machpelah. There is none of the sacred places over which the Moslems keep so jealous a watch as the tomb of Abraham. It was esteemed a very peculiar favour that we had been admitted thus far, travellers in general being forbidden to approach even the door of the Mosque. A letter from the Governor of Jerusalem, who had been with us on the evening before we set out, gained us this privilege.

A little farther on, we were permitted to look through a window, where we saw one of the tombs covered with a rich carpet of green silk. This is called the Tomb of Joseph, although we know from Scripture that Joseph was not buried here, but at Shechem (Acts 7:16). The only persons mentioned in Scripture as buried at Machpelah are Abraham and Sarah, Isaac and Rebecca, Jacob and Leah (Genesis 49:31; 50:13). The Jews believe that this remarkable building is one of the works of Solomon; and from the peculiar form of the building, and the great size of the stones, there seems every probability that it is of Hebrew origin. It is by no means improbable, that it was built by the Jews to keep in remembrance the burying-place of the father of their nation and the friend of God. The Jews at present are permitted only to look through a hole near the entrance, and to pray with their face toward the grave of Abraham.

After leaving this, we climbed the highest hill to the southeast of Hebron, to obtain, if possible, that view of the plain of Sodom which

Abraham had on that morning when it was destroyed from heaven. In the valley, we passed with some difficulty through the vineyards, regaled by the delightful fragrance. At one part we came upon a company of villagers treading out their corn; five oxen were employed on one floor. Some of the villagers also were winnowing what had been trodden out, and others were passing the grain through a sieve to separate it from the dust. We remembered Amos 9:9. This valley is called Wady Nazarah, 'the valley of the Nazarenes', for what reason we could not ascertain. The sides of the hill were very rocky and slippery, but the top was covered with vines. We sat down under the shade of some bushes, and calmly contemplated the fine view on every side. The town, divided into four parts, lay immediately beneath us. The pool, the mosque, the flat roofs, the domes, were all distinctly marked. The vineyards stretch up the hills beautifully, and groves of deep green olives enclose it on every side. Hebron is embosomed in hills. The more ancient houses are on the east side of the valley, and there are traces of ruins running up the hill behind Machpelah. The ancient town is supposed by some to have been built more upon the hill where the mosque stands, and if so, the tradition of the rabbis is not altogether absurd, that the rays of the rising sun gilding the towers of Hebron used to be seen from the temple at Jerusalem, and gave the sign of the time for killing the morning sacrifice. Hebron was also one of the Refuge cities, and therefore probably conspicuous from afar. Looking to the south, over a high ridge of hills, the eye stretches into a wilderness-land of vast extent In that direction lay Carmel, where Nabal fed his flocks (1 Samuel 25:2). But the most interesting view of all was toward the east, not on account of its beauty, but on account of its being in all probability the view which Abraham had when he 'looked toward Sodom and Gomorrah, and toward all the land of the plain, and beheld, and lo the smoke of the country went up as the smoke of a furnace' (Genesis 19:28). A high ridge intercepts the view of the Dead Sea, but the deep valley formed by it, and the hills of Moab on the other side, are clearly seen. If Abraham stood on the hill where we were now standing, then he saw not the plain itself, but 'the smoke of the country rising up' as from a furnace. If he saw the plain, then he must have stood on that intervening ridge nearer the Dead Sea.

There can be little doubt that it was in this direction that Abraham led the three angelic men on their way toward Sodom, and we felt it a solemn thing to stand where Abraham drew near and pleaded with the

Lord, 'Wilt thou also destroy the righteous with the wicked?' What wonders of mercy and judgment these mountains have seen!

Returning to the town, we visited the large Pool of Hebron. It is quite entire, of solid and ancient masonry, and measures 133 feet square. This is no doubt the pool over which David commanded the hands and feet of the murderers of Ishbosheth to be hung up (2 Samuel 4:12). There is another pool in the town, but not so large. We then visited the Tomb of Othniel, a sepulchre cut out in the rock, with nine niches. We plucked hyssop from the crevices of the outer wall (1 Kings 4:33). It grows in small stalks, with thickly-set leaves. We visited several other sepulchres near the town; in the town itself is shewn what is pretended to be the tomb of Abner, and of Jesse, the father of David, and even that of Esau. In the streets, mothers were carrying their children on the shoulder (Isaiah 49:22); some of whom had their eyes painted with stibium (Ezekiel 23:40), and all of them had anklets, answering to Isaiah's 'tinkling ornaments about the feet' (Isaiah 3:18).

In the afternoon, we paid a visit to the Jewish quarter. We were told that there are about eighty German and Polish Jews in this place. They have two synagogues; one belonging to the Spanish, the other to the Polish Jews. We first visited the Spanish synagogue, the larger of the two. It is not more than forty feet in length, and though clean, is but poorly furnished. The seats were half broken benches, reminding us of some of our neglected country churches. The lamps were of ornamented brass; the reading-desk nothing more than an elevated part of the floor railed in. There was nothing attractive about the ark, and the only decorations were the usual silver ornaments on the rolls of the law, and a few verses in Hebrew written on the curtain and on the walls. Fourteen children were seated on the floor, with bright sparkling eyes, getting a lesson in Hebrew from an old Jew. The Polish synagogue was even poorer than the Spanish. It had no reading-desk at all, but only a stand for the books. However, it surpassed the other in its lamps, all of which were elegant; and one of them of silver – the gift of Asher Bensamson, a Jew in London, who sent the money for it to Jerusalem, where the lamp was made.

Leaving the synagogue, we stepped into one of the *yishvioth* or reading-rooms. The books were not well kept, not even clean – the dust was lying thick on some of them, and only two persons were studying in the room. There are three more of these reading-rooms in Hebron.

We next found our way to the house of the old blind Rabbi Haiim, who had sent the present of wine on our arrival. We were very kindly received in the outer court of his house, where we were invited to sit down, and had an interesting interview with this aged Jew. He had come to this land when twenty-four years of age, and had spent fifty years in it. Like Isaac, his eyes had become dim, so that he could not see. About a dozen Jews and as many children gathered round us, while several Jewesses stood at a little distance listening in silence to the conversation. Mr Nicolayson conversed freely with them, told the errand upon which we had come, and stated the desire and aim of Christians in regard to their salvation. We were glad to be permitted thus to meet with Israel in their own land. They brought us sherbet and water. We remarked that the dress of the Jewish women is peculiarly graceful, and they have fine pleasant countenances. Many of them wear rich ornaments even when engaged in domestic duties.

In the evening, we rode out of the town to see Abraham's Oak, about a mile to the north-west. It is an immense spreading oak, admitted to be one of the largest trees in Palestine, and very old. Possibly it occupies the site of that tree which Jerome saw pointed out in his days as Abraham's Oak. We found the spread of its branches to be 256 feet in circumference, and 81 feet in diameter. Round the narrowest part of the trunk, we measured 22 feet 9 inches, and at the point where the branches separate, 25 feet 9 inches. It was under such a tree that Abraham pitched his tent, when 'he came and dwelt under the oaks of Mamre which is in Hebron' (Genesis 13:18; see the Hebrew). And it was under such a tree that he spread refreshment for his heavenly guests (Genesis 18:8). The ride from this tree to the town is through vineyards of the most rich and fertile description, each one having a tower in the midst for the keeper of the vineyard. We were told that bunches of grapes from these vineyards sometimes weigh 6 lb, every grape of which weighs 6 or 7 drams. Sir Moses Montefiore mentioned, that he got here a bunch of grapes about a yard in length. Such a bunch the spies carried on a staff betwixt two. In Hebron, there are 1,330 Mahometans who pay taxes, about 200 who do not pay; add to this 700 Jews. At the usual average of Eastern families, this will give less than 10,000 inhabitants.

June 15
We broke up our encampment this morning by the dawn and enjoyed a splendid sunrise. We left the vale of Hebron and its verdant vines with regret, traversing the same road which we had come. In four hours we

came down upon the pools of Solomon. Here we turned off to the right, winding round the hills, and following the course of the old aqueduct that carried water into Jerusalem. At this point, a small but beautiful and verdant valley lay beneath us, called by the Arabs 'El Tos', 'the cup', from its appearance. This may have been one of the spots where David loved to wander with his sheep, and where he meditated such Psalms as the 23rd, 'He maketh me to lie down in green pastures: he leadeth me beside the still waters' (Psalm 23:2). A gentle brook meanders through the bottom of the valley. There is also an ancient village with well cultivated gardens. Due east of us, the Frank Mountain, with its sloping sides and flat top, formed the most prominent object. If this be *Beth-haccerem*, a more suitable place for a signal of fire could not be imagined (Jeremiah 6:1). As we approached Bethlehem, the hills were well terraced, and vines and figs abounded. The towers in the vineyards appeared to us more numerous than usual. Bethlehem stands on the top of a hill, on the south side steep and rocky. The white limestone rocks were like marble, and reflected the sun's rays, so as to be very painful to the eyes. They were also so slippery, that we found it safer to go up on foot.

When near the top we came upon 'the well that is by the gate of Bethlehem'. It is protected by a piazza of four small arches, under which the water is drawn up through two apertures. Several people were under this porch, and one had descended the well to clean it out, so that we longed in vain for a draught of the water which David desired so earnestly. The situation of this well would suit exactly the description given in Chronicles (1 Chronicles 11:17), and the direction of the supposed geographical position of the cave of Adullam, to the southeast of Bethlehem, over the hill of Tekoah. We felt it interesting to realize the scene. The hosts of the Philistines were encamped in the valley of Rephaim; their garrison was at Bethlehem, and David was in the cave of Adullam. In the burning heat of noonday, he looked toward the hill that lay between him and his native town, and casually exclaimed, 'Oh that one would give me drink of the water of the well of Bethlehem, that is at the gate!' His three mightiest captains instantly resolve to express their love to their chief, and their devotion to the cause of God, by putting their lives in jeopardy, in drawing some of the water of this deep well, even under the darts of their enemies. 'And the three brake through the host of the Philistines, and drew water out of the well of Bethlehem, that was by the gate, and took it, and brought it to David'.

The white stone of which the hill is composed, and of which the town is built, makes it very hot, and gives it a dusty appearance. The fig-trees, olives, and pomegranates, and the ripe barley fields which cover the north side, shew that it is still capable of being made what its name signifies, 'The House of Bread'. At present, however, the plague was raging in Bethlehem, and we could not find bread even in the bazaar, so that we had to seek for food at the Latin Convent. This convent is a very substantial building, like a castle. The church, generally supposed to have been built by Helena around 326, is a fine spacious building, and the rows of Corinthian columns are substantial masses of granite. It was delightful to repose a while in the cool atmosphere of this venerable pile; but the monks, who seemed to be ignorant and unpolished men, would have us away to see the sacred places of the Nativity. We descended to the grotto which they call the stable where our Lord was born. Here they shewed a *marble* manger as the place where the heavenly babe was laid; but they had the honesty to allow that 'this was not the original manger, though the spot was the same'. They shewed the stone where Mary sat, and pointed to a silver star as marking the spot where the Saviour was born. The star is intended to represent that which 'stood over where the young child was'. The grotto is illumined by many handsome lamps, and there are several paintings by the first artists. Yet all is only a miserable profanation, like the Church of the Holy Sepulchre, it called up in our bosoms no other feelings than disgust and indignation. If the cave were really the place of the nativity, then Popery has successfully contrived to remove out of sight the humiliation of the stable and the manger. 'The mystery of iniquity' which pretends to honour, and yet so effectually conceals both the obedience of Christ which he began at Bethlehem, and the sufferings of Christ which he accomplished at Calvary, has with no less success disfigured and concealed the places where these wonders were 'seen of angels'. Though the tradition that Christ was born in this cave is of the highest antiquity, yet there seems no doubt, from the simple words of the Gospel narrative, that it cannot be the true place, for it is said, 'She wrapped him in swaddling clothes and laid him in a manger, because there was no room for them in the inn' (Luke 2:7). There is no evidence that the stable of an eastern khan was ever a grotto cut out of the rock.

We were conducted to another cavern in the rock, farther to the east, where the monks said that the Virgin Mary lived. But we enjoyed far more a visit to the roof of the convent, where we could breathe the pure air, and look up to the deep blue sky, and down upon the fields and valleys around Bethlehem. These are still the same as in the night when the angel of the Lord proclaimed, 'Fear not, for behold, I bring you good tidings of great joy, which shall be to all people' (Luke 2:10). It filled us with unmingled pleasure to gaze upon the undulating hills and valleys stretched out at our feet, for we were sure that among these David had often wandered with his flock, and in some of them the shepherds had heard the voice that brought the tidings of a Saviour born. Nearly due south lay a prominent hill about six miles distant, which we were told was the hill of Tekoah, giving name also to the wilderness around. The withered sides of this hill were once traversed by the prophet Amos, along with the herdmen that fed their cattle there (Amos 1:1). But we saw neither flock nor herd. One interesting association connected with this convent is, that Jerome[12] lived and died here. His eyes daily looked upon this scene, and here he translated the Word of God into Latin. We did not, however, find in the convent any one who seemed to have inherited the industry or learning of Father Jerome.

Remounting our horses, we bade farewell to our monkish friends, and wound slowly down the northern slope of Bethlehem, amongst vineyards and barley fields, where the reapers were engaged as in the days when Ruth and Naomi returned from the land of Moab. We soon arrived at the well of the Magi, where the Holy City comes in view. We could not but linger at the spot. Behind us lay Bethlehem, before us Jerusalem – on the one hand, the spot where the love of God was first made manifest; on the other, the spot where that love was completed in Immanuel's death – on the one hand the spot where Jesus was born; on the other, the spot where Jesus died! This is the route by which Tasso's pilgrims are represented as approaching and getting their first view of the Holy City. When they see the minarets, domes and bulwarks of the city, they burst out into a cry of ecstasy:

> Ecco apparir Gierusalem si vede,
> Ecco additar Gierusalem si scorge,
> Ecco da mille voci unitamente,
> Gierusalem salutare si sente.

---

[12] Jerome, biblical scholar and translator, made his home in Bethlehem from 386. There he used his immense scholarship including a knowledge of Hebrew to translate the Bible into Latin. This common version, the Vulgate, became the standard Bible of Christendom for centuries and has exerted a strong influence to the present day.

(Behold *Jerusalem* in prospect lies!
Behold *Jerusalem* salutes their eyes!
At once a thousand tongues repeat the name,
And hail *Jerusalem* with loud acclaim.)[13]

The view of Jerusalem from the south is not nearly so desolate as the view from the western approach; still, when seen from afar, it is 'like a cottage in a vineyard, like a lodge a garden of cucumbers' (Isaiah 1:8). Hardly anything is visible but the bare wall with its battlement, surrounding you see not what. Coming near we were startled by the depth of Hinnom, with its rocks and caves, and by the bold front of Zion.

We had scarcely seated ourselves at Mr Nicolayson's hospitable board, when letters from home were put into our hand, the first that we had received since our departure. It was truly refreshing to hear that all our friends were well, and our flocks not left uncared for. One of our letters brought the news that the Auchterarder case had been decided against our Church in the House of Lords.[14] We all felt it a solemn thing to receive such tidings in Jerusalem. They seemed to intimate a time of coming trial to the Church of Scotland. The time seemed to have come when judgment must begin at the house of God in Scotland; and we called to mind the clear intimations of prophecy, that 'there shall be a time of trouble such as never was since there was a nation', at the very time when Israel shall be delivered. We closed our Saturday evening together, by reading the 2nd chapter of Luke.

June 16, Sabbath

We had agreed beforehand to meet together this day, and join in the communion of the Lord's Supper. It was therefore with feelings of sacred interest that we saw the dawn of a Sacrament-Sabbath in Jerusalem. The solemn scenes which we had witnessed during the week – Calvary, Gethsemane, Bethany and Bethlehem, were well fitted to attune our hearts to partake of the sacred ordinance. In walking through the streets and the crowded bazaar to the Consul's house, which was the place of meeting, we felt a peculiarly vivid reality in the truth, that it was

---

[13] Torquato Tasso (1544-1595) was the greatest Italian poet of the late Renaissance. He wrote a major epic poem *Gerusalemme liberata (Jerusalem Liberated)* which relates the actions of a Christian army coming to free Jerusalem during the First Crusade in 1099. The quotation comes from this poem.

[14] Events in Scotland were moving towards the break which occurred in 1843 when over 470 ministers left the Church of Scotland to form the Free Church of Scotland. The issue

for common sinners such as these now walking in the streets of Jerusalem, and ourselves among the rest, that Jesus died. It was for souls nowise more exalted by nature, or more worthy of his love, than the present inhabitants, that 'God was manifest in flesh'. How strange! How passing knowledge does the love of Christ appear in such a view! How free the way to the Father for the chief of sinners; and how personal the application of redemption! Had Christ met one of us that day upon the streets of Jerusalem, he would have said, 'Wilt thou be made whole?'

We met in the same upper room where we had met last Sabbath. There were fourteen gathered together, including two converted Jews, and a Christian from Nazareth, who had been brought to know the truth under the American missionaries. It was a time of refreshing from the presence of the Lord. After the usual morning prayers of the Church of England, Mr Nicolayson preached on 1 John 1:3, 'Truly our fellowship is with the Father, and with his Son Jesus Christ', with fervent simplicity. Dr Keith joined with him in administering the broken bread and poured out wine. In the evening, Mr Bonar preached from John 14:2,3, 'In my Father's house are many mansions ...' on the believer's desire to be with Christ, and Christ's desire to be with his people. Feelings of deepest solemnity filled our hearts, while we worshipped in an upper room, after such a feast, where we had been shewing the Lord's death 'till he come' (1 Corinthians 11:26) and 'his feet stand upon the Mount of Olives' (Zechariah 14:4). And it was with more than ordinary fervour that we joined in the prayer that Israel might soon have their solemn feasts restored to them, and the ways of Zion no longer mourn, and that even now the Holy Spirit, who, in this city, came down on the apostles, would again descend on us, and on all the churches. After singing together the last part of the 116th Psalm, we separated. On our way to our home on Mount Zion, we gazed upon the Mount of Olives, on which the last rays of the evening sun were pouring their golden lustre, and remembered how, after the first Lord's Supper, Jesus went out there to his agony in Gethsemane; and how from the other side of that mountain he was 'received up into heaven'.

---

was over the right of congregations to call ministers whom they chose, rather than a patron presenting a minister of his choice. A minister, Robert Young, was presented to the parish of Auchterarder in Perthshire but the local Presbytery and the General Assembly rejected him. The patron and the nominee took civil action and the House of Lords ruled that the imposition of such a veto (as agreed by the Assembly in 1834) was illegal.

June 17

This morning at six o'clock, we attended the Hebrew service in the Mission-house. Mr Nicolayson read the Liturgy in Hebrew in a very beautiful manner, Mr Bergheim, Simeon and ourselves responding. It was truly interesting to hear the holy tongue made use of in believing prayer in the name of Jesus. The greater part of this day was devoted to making up our journals and writing letters to Scotland.

In the afternoon, we visited the Castle of David, the only stronghold now remaining upon Mount Zion. It is a little to the south of the Jaffa Gate, and overhangs the vale of Gihon. The lower part of one of the towers is evidently of great antiquity. The stones are very large, and bevelled in their edges, and we were told that it is perfectly solid. This is believed to be the tower of Hippicus, said by Josephus to be one mass (ουδαμου διακενος), and which was spared by Titus when the temple and city were destroyed. May it not be still more ancient, the site at least of 'the stronghold of Zion' which David took from the Jebusites (2 Samuel 5:7)? Or 'the tower of David', to which the neck of the Church is compared, 'Thy neck is like the tower of David builded for an armoury' (Song of Solomon 4:4)? Descending into the vale of Hinnom, we tried to sketch the steep view of Mount Zion; then returning, gathered several specimens of the *Spina Christi*. This plant, called *Nabka* by the Arabs, grows abundantly on the hills of Jerusalem; the branches are very pliable, so as easily to be platted into a crown, while the thorns are very many, and sharp, and about an inch in length. The tradition seems highly probable, that this was the plant of which the Roman soldiers platted a crown of thorns for the brow of Christ (Matthew 27:29).

Towards evening, we visited that part of the Old Temple wall to which the Jews are allowed to go, that they may pray and weep over the glory that is departed. It is a part of the western enclosure of the Haram, and the access to it is by narrow and lonely streets. The Jew who was our guide, on approaching the massy stones, took off his shoes and kissed the wall.

Every Friday evening, when the Jewish Sabbath begins, some Jews may be found here deeply engaged in prayer; for they believe that prayer still goes up with most acceptance before God, when breathed through the crevices of that building of which Jehovah said, 'Mine eyes and my heart shall be there perpetually' (1 Kings 9:3). This custom they have maintained for centuries, realizing the prophetic words of Jeremiah, 'Is it nothing to you, all ye that pass by? Behold, and see if there be any sorrow like unto my sorrow, which is done unto me, wherewith the Lord hath afflicted me in the day of his fierce anger' (1 Samuel 1:12). We counted ten courses of those massy stones one above another. One of them measured fifteen feet long by three broad; another was eight feet square; others farther south were twenty-four feet long. They are bevelled like the immense stones of the mosque at Hebron, and are of a very white limestone resembling marble. Some of them are worn smooth with the tears and kisses of the men of Israel. Above the large stones the wall is built up with others smaller and more irregular, and is evidently of a modern date, affording a complete contrast to the ancient building below.

Later in the evening, Mr McCheyne went to visit the same spot, guided by Mr George Dalton. On the way, they passed the houses where the lepers live all together, to the east of the Zion Gate within the walls. A little farther on, the heaps of rubbish on Mount Zion, surmounted by prickly pear, were so great, that at one point they stood higher than the city wall. The view of Mount Olivet from this point is very beautiful. The dome of the mosque El Aksa appeared to be torn and decayed in some places, and even that of the Mosque of Omar seemed far from being splendid. Going along by the ancient valley of the Tyrop on, and passing the gate called by the monks the Dung Gate, now shut up, Mr Dalton pointed out in the wall of the Haram, near the south-west corner, the singular traces of an ancient arch, which Professor Robinson had discovered to be the remains of the bridge from the Temple to Mount Zion, mentioned frequently by Josephus, and remarkable as a work of the highest antiquity. The stones in the temple wall that form the spring of this ancient bridge are of enormous size. This interesting discovery goes to prove that the large bevelled stones, which form the foundation of the present enclosure of the Haram in so many parts, are really the work of Jewish hands, and the remains of the outer Wall of the Temple of Solomon. Neither is this conclusion in the least contradictory to the prophecy of our Lord, 'There shall not be left here one stone upon another that shall not be thrown down', for these dreadful words were spoken in reference to the Temple itself, which was 'adorned with goodly stones and gifts'; and they have been fearfully fulfilled to the very letter, for the Mosque of Omar, entirely a Moslem building, stands upon the rock of Moriah, probably on the very spot where the Temple stood.

The Jewish place of wailing is a little to the north of this ancient bridge. Here they found a young Jew sitting on the ground. His turban, of a greyish colour peculiar to the Jews here, shaded a pale and thoughtful countenance. His prayerbook was open before him, and he seemed deeply engaged. Mr Dalton acting as interpreter, he was asked what it was he was reading. He shewed the book and it happened to be the 22nd Psalm. Struck by this providence, Mr McCheyne read aloud till he came to the 16th verse, 'They pierced my hands and my feet'; and then asked, 'Of whom speaketh the prophet this?' The Jew answered, 'of David and all his afflictions'. 'But David's hands and feet were not pierced!' The Jew shook his head. The true interpretation was then pointed out to him, that David was a prophet and wrote these things of Immanuel who died for the remission of the sins of many. He made the sign with the lip which Easterns make to shew that they despise what you are saying. 'Well, then, do you know the way of forgiveness of which David speaks in the 32nd Psalm?' The Jew shook his head again. For here is the grand error of the Jewish mind, 'The way of peace they have not known'.

The same evening we visited all the synagogues of Jerusalem at the time of evening prayer. They are six in number, all of them small and poorly furnished, and four of them under one roof. The lamps are the only handsome ornaments they contain. The reading-desk is little else than an elevated part of the floor enclosed with a wooden railing. The ark has none of the rich embroidery that distinguishes it in European synagogues. As it was an ordinary weekday, we found in every synagogue the Jewish children who had been receiving instruction in reading; and in one of the largest, a group by themselves was pointed out to us as being orphan children who are taught free. After examining the synagogues we paid a visit to a Rabbi, whose house, like that of Justus, 'joined hard to the synagogue' (Acts 18:7). We walked with him upon the roof, looking down upon the city. The roof had a railing or battlement, as commanded in the Law, 'Thou shalt make a battlement for thy roof' (Deuteronomy 22:8). There are thirty-six *yishvioth*, or reading-rooms, for the study of the Law in the Holy City. In one of these close by, some old men were busy at evening prayer. The evening prayers in general seemed not to be well attended. Our guide, who was a Jew, on coming to his own synagogue, immediately left us and went up to the front of the ark, praying very devoutly, but with much ostentation. We were much impressed with the melancholy aspect of the

Jews in Jerusalem. The meanness of their dress, their pale faces, and timid expression, all seem to betoken great wretchedness. They are evidently much poorer than the Jews of Hebron; and 'the crown is fallen from their heads; woe unto them that they have sinned' (Lamentations 5:16).

At night we had another opportunity of obtaining information as to the experience of Missionaries in labouring among the Jews of Palestine. The principal subject of conversation was – *the literary qualifications of missionaries for Palestine*. The Hebrew is the most necessary language for one who labours among the Jews in this country, and it is spoken chiefly in the Spanish way. A Missionary should study the character and elements of Arabic in his own country, and the more thoroughly he is master of these the better, but the true pronunciation can be acquired only on the spot. Yet Arabic is not so absolutely necessary as Hebrew. Spanish, too, is useful, and also German, and he must know Italian, for the purpose of holding intercourse with Europeans in general. Judeo-Spanish is the language of the Sephardim and Judeo-Polish of the Ashkenazim (*i.e.* Jews from Europe). All of them know a little of Italian. All Jews in Palestine speak Hebrew, but then they often attach a meaning to the words that is not the true meaning or grammatical sense, so that it is absolutely necessary to know the vernacular tongue, in order to be sure that you and they understand the same thing by the words employed. A Missionary ought to be well grounded in prophecy, and he should be one who fully and thoroughly adopts the principles of literal interpretation, both in order to give him hope and perseverance, and in order to fit him for reasoning with Jews. It is not so much preaching talents as controversial that are required; yet it is to be hoped that both may soon be needed. He ought to have an acquaintance with Hebrew literature to the extent of understanding the Talmud, so as to be able to set aside its opinions. Acquaintance, too, with the Cabbala is necessary, in order to know the sources of Jewish ideas, and how scriptural arguments are likely to affect their minds. Zohar is one of the best Cabbalistic commentaries. A knowledge of Chaldee [Aramaic] and Syriac would also be very useful. In a mission to the Jews there ought to be both Jewish and Gentile labourers; the Gentile to form the nucleus, the other to be the effective labourers. If a converted Jew go through a course of education, and be ordained, he would combine the advantages of both; still a Gentile fellow-labourer would always be desirable. Faith and perseverance are the grand requisites in a missionary to Israel. He should never abandon a station unless in the case of absolute necessity. He may make occasional tours in the country round about, but he must have a centre of influence. It is of the highest importance to retain his converts beside him, and form them into a church; for two reasons:

1. Little is done if a man is only convinced or even converted, unless he is also trained up in the ways of the Gospel.

2. The influence of sincere converts belonging to a mission is very great. It commends the cause of Christ to others. At the same time it ought, if possible, to be made a rule to give no support to converts, except in return for labour, either literary or agricultural.

June 18

Early next morning some of our company set out to make a farewell visit to Bethany, and the more notable scenes on the east of the city. We passed through the bazaar and narrow ruined streets, and purchased some articles as memorials of Jerusalem. Issuing forth by St Stephen's Gate, we crossed the Kedron, and once more visited Gethsemane, a spot which called forth fresh interest every time we saw it, and has left a fragrant remembrance on our mind that can never fade away. Passing the northern wall, we went up the face of the Mount of Olives, stopping every now and then and looking round upon 'the perfection of beauty'. Jeremiah says that 'all her beauty is departed' (Lamentations 1:6). How passing beautiful, then, it must have been in ancient days!

Crossing by the north of the Church of the Ascension, and standing on the summit of the Mount of Olives, we once more enjoyed the commanding prospect of the Dead Sea, stretching to the south, calm and of the deepest blue, and the mountain range of Moab beyond. From this point of view we could see the full meaning of Ezekiel, where he says, 'Thine elder sister is Samaria, she and her daughters that dwell *at thy left hand;* and thy younger sister, that dwelleth *at thy right hand,* is Sodom and her daughters' (Ezekiel 16:46). And as we turned from the view of that mysterious lake, under whose heavy waters lie 'Sodom and Gomorrah, and the cities about them, set forth for an example, suffering the vengeance of eternal fire' (Jude 7), and looked down upon the place where Jesus 'came near and beheld the city, and wept over it', we felt that the recent sight of Sodom's doom may have kindled into a flame the Redeemer's unutterable compassion, when he seemed to manifest in his person the tender words of the prophet, 'How shall I give thee up,

Ephraim? how shall I deliver thee, Israel? how shall I make thee as Admah? how shall I set thee as Zeboim? Mine heart is turned within me, my repentings are kindled together' (Hosea 11:8).

From the same height we took our last view of the course of the Jordan, marked only by the strip of verdure on its banks. Beyond lay the valley of Shittim, in the plains of Moab, a wilderness of pasture-land, said to be fifteen miles long by ten miles broad, affording ample room for the goodly tents of the many thousands of Israel (Numbers 22:1; 25:1). Not far from that spot Elijah ascended to heaven in his fiery chariot, and his mantle floated down upon his holy successor. And from the same open sky, at another time, the Spirit descended like a dove, and abode upon the Saviour when he was baptized by John in Jordan.

Another prominent object in the scene is the remains of an ancient village on the height nearly south from Bethany, and about half a mile distant; it is called Abu-Dis. May not this be the remains of Bethphage, the village *over against* the Jericho road, where the disciples obtained the colt and brought it to Jesus? No other trace of Bethphage has ever been found, neither has any traveller found an ancient name for Abu-Dis that has any probability of being the true one.

Leaving the summit, we descended, over a lower brow of the hill, upon 'the town of Mary and her sister Martha', concealed by terraces, and rocks and fig-trees. We lingered here for a considerable time, occasionally attended by some of the simple country people, and reading over to ourselves the 11th chapter of John. It is a fragrant spot; the name of Christ was poured forth here in his wonderful deeds of love and tenderness, like Mary's pound of ointment of spikenard very costly, and the fragrance is as fresh to a true disciple's heart as on the day when it was done.

We left Bethany with regret, and proceeded to Jerusalem by the broad and rocky pathway, which appears to be the ancient road. It was along this way Jesus rode upon the ass's colt, here they spread their garments in the Way, and cut down branches of the trees and strewed them in the way, and cried Hosanna! You first obtain a distant view of part of Jerusalem before leaving the ridge on which Bethany stands, again you lose it, descending into a ravine; then ascending, you wind round the Mount of Olives, with the Mount of Offence beneath you, when suddenly the whole city comes into view. We read over the 11th chapter of Mark as we traversed this interesting road. It was by this road Jesus was walking when he said to the fig-tree, 'No man eat fruit of thee hereafter for ever'; and the next morning they saw it dried up from the roots, and Jesus said, 'Whosoever shall say unto *this mountain,* Be thou removed, and be thou cast into the sea, he shall have whatsoever he saith' (Mark 11:14,20,23). Many such fig-trees now line the road, and we pulled some of their leaves for a memorial.

Leaving the track, and descending the steep of the Mount of Offence, we tried to find our way into the valley of Jehoshaphat through the hanging village of Siloam. With great difficulty we succeeded, for the houses, many of which are ancient sepulchres hewn in the rock, are placed one above another in a very singular manner. As we sat at the Pool of Siloam, the deep shade of the rock was truly refreshing. We read over John 9 and 7:37. We also paid a last visit to the fountain farther up, and gathered some of the white pebbles from beneath its soft-flowing waters. We then ascended to the wall of the city, and entering by the Zion Gate, once more passed through the Jewish quarters, and looked upon the miseries of Israel in the city where David dwelt. 'How hath the Lord covered the daughter of Zion with a cloud in his anger!' (Lamentations 2:1). They are by far the most miserable and squalid of all the inhabitants of Jerusalem, and if we could have looked upon their precious souls, their temporal misery would have appeared but a faint emblem of the spiritual death that reigns within. 'Ah sinful nation! a people laden with iniquity! The whole head is sick, and the whole heart faint' (Isaiah 1:4,5). May we never lose the feelings of intense compassion toward Israel, which these few days spent in Jerusalem awakened; and never rest till all the faithful of the church of our fathers have the same flame kindled in their hearts!

CHAPTER 4

GIBEON – SYCHEM – SAMARIA – CARMEL

'Blow ye the cornet in Gibeah, and the trumpet in Ramah: cry aloud at
Beth-aven, after thee, O Benjamin. Ephraim shall be desolate in the
day of rebuke; among the tribes of Israel have I made known that which
shall surely be' (Hosea 5:8,9).

In the cool of the afternoon, all the preparations for our departure being
completed, we mounted our horses and wound our way through the
streets of Jerusalem, slowly and reluctantly. We felt deep regret at
leaving both the city with its holy associations, and the kind friends who
had given us such Christian entertainment in this strange land. The
communion of saints had been inexpressibly precious, though enjoyed
here only for a few days. Mr Nicolayson, whose truly Christian and
brotherly kindness we can never forget nor repay, rode some miles with
us, and then bade us farewell.

A Latin Christian, Giuseppe, asked leave to travel in our company.
He lived at Bethlehem, and had visited us several times in Jerusalem,
selling the beads, inkhorns, and mother-of-pearl ornaments, which are
made at Bethlehem. On his arm he had the Virgin Mary and the Holy
Sepulchre punctured with the Al-henna dye, a custom which appears to
have been in use in ancient times (Isaiah 49:16; 44:5).

We journeyed north-west, and soon passed the Tombs of the Judges,
but had only time to glance at them. Descending by a very rocky path,
we came to the bottom of the deep valley, called by travellers the Valley
of Elah. Luxuriant vineyards were on either hand, and the sun's rays
poured down with great power into the deep ravines. We soon began to
ascend the high ridge on which Naby-Samuel stands. Several villages
appeared among the hills both on the right and left, and the remnants of
ancient terraces were distinctly to be traced on most of the slopes.

In two hours from Jerusalem, we arrived at Naby-Samuel, situated
on the highest point of a terraced hill of considerable height, having a
few wretched houses and an old ruined church, said to have been built

by the renowned St George, but now converted into a mosque, whose spire or minaret attracts the eye on every side. For many centuries this spot has been regarded as the ancient Ramah, where the prophet Samuel was born; where he lived and mourned over the land and its apostate king as he looked down from this eminence on its populous tribes; and where also he was buried (1 Samuel 1:1; 8:4; 25:1). There appears to be no good reason for doubting the accuracy of this ancient tradition. The ruins stand on the most elevated point of the whole region, commanding a magnificent view on every side thus answering well to the name *Ramah*, which means *a height*, and to its other name Ramathaim-Zophim (The heights of the watchmen)'. The conjecture that it is the ancient Mizpeh, the gathering-place of Israel, is without any solid foundation.

We ascended to the roof of the deserted mosque and surveyed the country round and round with unmingled pleasure. We could count twelve towns or villages within sight. To the south, Jerusalem, sheltered by the Mount of Olives, was distinctly visible; and still farther south, about twelve miles distant, Bethlehem and the Frank Mountain. We were now in a situation to understand the prophecy of Jeremiah in reference to the massacre of the infants of Bethlehem, 'In Rama was there a voice heard, lamentation, and weeping, and great mourning, Rachel weeping for her children, and would not be comforted, because they are not' (Matthew 2:18). The tomb of Rachel suggested the figurative representation of the mother of Benjamin and Joseph rising up to lament her slaughtered little ones, and the import of the passage is as if he had said, That the tide of woe rolled from Bethlehem to the hill whereon Rama stands. Rachel from her sepulchre begins the note of woe, and it spreads all around even to the distant hills that shut in the plain.

Quite near us in the same direction stood a village in the mountains called Lifta, and still nearer Betiska, which may possibly be the ancient Sechu, where there was a great well (1 Samuel 19:22). To the south-east was another village, Kephorieh, which we fancied might possibly be the site of Chephira (Joshua 9:17), since the other cities of the Gibeonites, Beeroth, Gibeon and Kirjath-jearim are all in this region. Emmaus must have been like one of these secluded villages and probably in this direction. We could easily imagine the two disciples traversing the rocky pathway between the vineyards, by which we had that evening passed, and Jesus himself drawing near and going with them, talking with them by the way, and opening to them the Scriptures, while they perceived not the difficulties of the road nor the lapse of time, for 'their hearts burned within them by the way' (Luke 24:32). Looking to the east a fine hilly scene lay before us, bounded by the mountains of Moab. Upon a height near at hand stood Bet-hanina to the north-east, on another hill, Ram; and still farther north, Kelundieh. In the same direction, though not within our view, lay Gibeah of Saul, and Michmash, not far from each other, both of which remain unto this day. Due north we saw Ram-Allah in a very notable position; a little to the west, Beth-hoor, believed to be the Upper Beth-horon; and on the hill above it Betunia. To the west, we looked down from the hills of Ephraim upon the vast plain of Sharon, bounded by the Mediterranean Sea, into which the evening sun was pouring a flood of golden rays.

But the most interesting of all the ancient towns at this time within sight was El Geeb, lying at our feet, directly north, and about a mile distant. This is the ancient Gibeon whence came the wily Gibeonites who beguiled Joshua and the congregation of Israel (Joshua 9), described as, 'a great city, as one of the royal cities, greater than Ai, and all the men thereof were mighty' (Joshua 10:2). It is situated on the top of a remarkably round hill, the sides of which are so completely terraced, not by art but by nature, that they present the appearance of a flight of steps all round from the top to the bottom. The buildings are mostly on the western brow of the hill, the rest of the summit being covered with fine olive-trees. Many of the terraces also are set with vines and fruit-trees. From the foot of the ridge on which Ramah stands, a fine plain or shallow valley stretches past Gibeon to the north for two or three miles. From Gibeon it stretches westward for about a mile, bounded by a low hilly range, except in two points, where there are openings towards the western plain, the one of which is the 'descent of Beth-horon'. The fields of this valley were distinctly marked out, some of them bearing grain, but most lying waste. In one place, the vineyard stretched quite across, with a verdure most refreshing to the eye. This valley the muleteers called Ajaloun. Again and again we put the question to them, to make sure that we were not mistaken, and they still answered Ajaloun. Since our return, we have not been able to find that any previous writer has found this name still remaining, and applied to this valley, and we therefore fear that the muleteers may have picked it up from the inquiries or conversation of some traveller. However this may be, the scene of Joshua's miracle was at that time vividly set before us. The glorious sun was sloping westward, about to sink in the Mediterranean Sea, and his horizontal rays were falling full upon the hill of Gibeon; at the same moment the moon was rising, and soon after poured her silver beams into this quiet vale. Such probably was the very position of the sun and moon, in that memorable day when Joshua prayed and 'said in the sight of Israel, Sun, stand thou still upon Gibeon; and thou, Moon, in the valley of Ajalon' (Joshua 10:12). We are plainly told that the battle between Joshua and the five kings of the Amorites was 'at Gibeon'. It lasted probably the greater part of the day, till toward evening, the bands of the Amorites began to give way, and Israel chased them as far as the descent to Beth-horon. At that steep defile the Lord cast down great hailstones from heaven upon them, so that they died. But it seems to have been before that, and before they were out of sight of Gibeon, that Joshua uttered the singular prayer above narrated; and in confirmation of this view, it is interesting to notice that Isaiah calls the scene of that day's wonders, 'The Valley of Gibeon' (Isaiah 28:21). There was a peculiarly mellow softness in the evening light, that gilded both tower and Valley at the moment, and it was strangely interesting to look upon the scene where 'the Lord hearkened unto the voice of a man'.

It was at Gibeon also, that Abner and Joab met on either side of the pool, and that the young men began the contest which ended so fatally (2 Samuel 2:12). We were afterwards told that the pool remains there to this day on the north side of the hill. Here, too, 'at the great stone which is in Gibeon', Joab murdered Amasa, and 'shed the blood of war in peace, and put the blood of war upon his girdle that was about his loins, and in his shoes that were on his feet' (2 Samuel 20:8; 2 Kings 2:5). In the same place, Johanan, the son of Kareah, found Ishmael 'by the great waters that are in Gibeon'. It was here also, that 'God appeared to Solomon in a dream by night, and said, Ask what I shall give thee' (1 Kings 3:5). It is thus hallowed as a place of prayer, and yet more, as a place where God shewed to the world before the Redeemer came, how unlimited was his bounty to his people – all a prelude to the unspeakable gift, his beloved Son, which has made all other wonders lose their glory by reason of the glory that excelleth.

Leaving the height of Ramah, we descended into the plain, but did not enter Gibeon, because the sun was setting. Journeying still north, we passed near two other villages, both finely situated on rocky terraced heights, the name of one of which was Raphat. It was here that Dr. Keith missed his favourite staff, which had a mariner's compass on the top of it. A muleteer rode back in search of it, but in vain. The darkness was coming down, so that we had to hurry on. Our view was beginning to be obscured, but we could perceive that Benjamin (whose borders we were traversing) had a pleasant portion.

In two hours from Ramah, we reached Beer, the ancient Beeroth. Our servants had gone before us and erected the tent, and now stood at the tent-door to welcome us, Giuseppe helping us to alight with great kindness. It was a fine moonlight evening; the ground was sparkling with the light of the glow-worm, in a manner similar to what we had seen at Hebron, and the fire-flies glittered through the air in great numbers. Our tent was pitched immediately in front of a gushing fountain that emptied its waters into a large trough, above which was a Mahometan place of prayer falling into decay. We lay down to rest, with the remembrance that it was here that Jotham took up his abode when he fled from Shechem for fear of his brother Abimelech (Judges 9:21). There is a pleasing though fanciful tradition associated with the place, that it was here Joseph and Mary, on their way back to Nazareth, first discovered that the child Jesus was not in their company, and turned back again to Jerusalem seeking him (Luke 2:44). It was probably near this, too, that Deborah the prophetess dwelt 'under the palm-tree of Deborah, between Ramah and Bethel in Mount Ephraim' (Judges 4:5).

June 19

We were up before the sun, and enjoyed the luxury of washing ourselves at the full flowing fountain of Beer. It is from this fountain that the town receives its name, both now and in ancient times. The Moslem women came out to draw water, and the well soon presented a lively scene. The remains of the town lie on the rising ground to the northeast of the fountain. Beeroth was one of the cities that belonged to the Gibeonites, and afterwards fell to the lot of Benjamin (Joshua 9:17; 18:25). It was to this place, also, that the murderers of Ishbosheth originally belonged (2 Samuel 4:2).

We journeyed to the north-east, through a pleasant pasture country. On our left, we passed a cave in the hillside, running a considerable way into the rock, which suggested to us the nature of the retreat of the five kings of the Amorites, who fled from the battle of Gibeon, and 'hid themselves in a cave at Makkedah' (Joshua 10:16).

In a little time we approached the district of Beth-aven or Bethel. The hills around, as well as the ruins of the town, are called by the Arabs, Beteen. This name is, in all probability, the remains, not of Bethel, but of Beth-aven. It would seem, that in the days of Joshua, this region was called 'the wilderness of Beth-aven' (Joshua 18:12), and perhaps the hill on which the town afterwards stood, Beth-aven (Joshua 7:2). When the town was built it was called Luz, but Jacob, grateful for the visit of mercy which he there received, called it Bethel, 'the house of God'. In later days, it became the seat of idolatrous worship, and the indignant prophet of Israel, to awaken the people to a sense of their sin, recalled the ancient name (Hosea 5:8) 'Beth-aven', or 'house of vanity', and sometimes only 'Aven'. From this seems to have been formed the present name Beteen.

Turning off the path, a little to the right, we rode into the middle of the ruins, on the summit of a considerable rising ground. A ruined tomb on the nearest eminence guides to them. There are not many remains of edifices that can be traced, but here and there heaps of ancient stones, the foundations of a wall, and a broken cistern, indicate former dwellings. The whole summit of the hill is covered over with stones that once composed the buildings, and there is space enough for a large town. We looked with deep interest across the ravine on the right to the gentle hill considerably higher, on the east of Bethel. Probably this was the very spot where Abraham pitched his tent, when first he came a lonely stranger to the land of Canaan; for, it is said, he removed to 'a mountain on the east of Bethel, having Bethel on the west, and Ai on the east, and there he built an altar unto the Lord', which he afterwards returned to visit (Genesis 12:8; 13:3); shewing with what holy boldness he trusted himself to the Lord's keeping, though bitter foes on either side enclosed him. Nor could we forget, that on the hill where we stood Jacob spent that solemn night, when he took of the stones of that place, and put them for his pillows, and beheld a ladder 'set upon the earth, and the top of it reaching to heaven'. We read over the passage and applied the prayer to ourselves (Genesis 28:11,12).

It was here, too, that Jeroboam set up one of the golden calves. And here he stood beside the altar, burning idolatrous incense. Perhaps there was a double scheme of wicked policy in his choice of this place, for we observed that it must have been within sight of the highway to Jerusalem, that the people might be intercepted on their way up to the house of the Lord; so that his object was at once to allure them from God, and obliterate Bethel's hallowed associations with Jehovah's gracious discoveries of himself to their fathers Jacob and Abraham. The success of this plan may be conjectured from the children that here mocked Elisha, and taunted him with Elijah's ascension, saying, 'Go up, thou bald-head'. The prophet who came out of Judah, and warned Jeroboam, probably travelled the road over which we had passed. Deborah, Rebecca's nurse, died here, and was buried probably in the ravine on the south, for it is said to have been 'beneath Bethel', under an oak tree; and Jacob shewed his tender remembrance of her, by calling it *'Allon bachuth'*, 'the oak of weeping'.

Few places are so full of interest. The shapeless ruins scattered over the brow of the hill are themselves silent witnesses of God's truth and faithfulness. He had said, 'Seek not Bethel, nor enter into Gilgal; for Gilgal shall surely go into captivity and *Bethel shall come to nought'* (Amos 5:5). This word has been fulfilled to the very letter. We did not at the time remember the prophecy of Hosea, 'The high places of Aven, the sin of Israel, shall be destroyed; *the thorn and the thistle shall come up on their altar*s' (Hosea 10:8); but we have no doubt, from the desolate nature of the ground, and the abundance of thorny plants in that region, that some other travellers will discover that thorns and thistles are waving over the altars of Bethel, in fulfilment of the word of Him who cannot lie. We ourselves saw sufficient marks of the curse, of which the thorn and the thistle are the emblems.

Leaving the ruins, we returned to the road, and proceeding northward, came in less than an hour to a village on our left, Ain Yebrud, finely situated upon the summit of a very rocky hill, whose sides were terraced and planted with vines. A little after, we saw upon the left another smaller village of the same name, situated upon a similar hill, whose sides were entirely uncultivated, presenting little more than a barren rock. The contrast was very striking, and shewed us at once the change produced by the slightest cultivation in this land, and how, by the blessing of God, in 'a very little while Lebanon may be turned into a fruitful field'. Another village farther on, and also upon a hill, was called Geeb, conjectured by some to be the ancient Gob, famous in the wars with the Philistines (2 Samuel 21:19), though others suppose it to be Gibeah in Mount Ephraim, the burying-place of Eleazar the son of Aaron (Joshua 24:33, Hebrew text). These villages on the tops of the hills had not only the advantage of being easily defended, but must also have been highly salubrious, having the cool breezes playing around them.

We now entered a narrow defile called Mezra, and descended rapidly among the finest vines and fig-trees which we had yet seen. The terraced hills of Ephraim shut us in on both sides, and often the rocks were entirely concealed by the bright green leaves of the vines. At the bottom of this defile we came into a wider ravine running from east to west, in which was a broad channel of a brook now dry. We conjectured that this may be one of the brooks of Gaash (2 Samuel 23:30; Joshua 24:30) in Mount Ephraim. Crossing the dry channel we ascended by the ravine of a tributary, like the former finely planted with fruit-trees; and came upon a building, which is reckoned halfway between Jerusalem and Nablous. It was once a fortress, and is said to have been the headquarters of banditti. There is a singular cavern near that may have favoured their designs.

This road must have been often traversed by our Lord in going from Jerusalem to Sychar and Galilee. The reflection of the sun's rays that now beat upon us from these rocks, may have been felt by him on that very day, when, 'wearied with his journey', about noon he sat down on Jacob's Well. In about an hour we ascended into a pleasant fertile little plain spreading to the east, having Singeel, a village on the hills, on our left hand, and Turmus Aya, upon an eminence in the middle of the plain, on our right. It was at this point that we should have turned to the right, to visit Seiloun, the remains of ancient Shiloh. Our guide promised at setting out to carry us that way, but unwilling to lengthen the fatigues of the journey, he allowed us to proceed north without letting us know till it was too late to return. We afterwards found that it lay about an hour distant to the right. Mr Calhoun, an American Missionary, told us that he had visited it, and found it situated upon an eminence, having fine valleys on every side of it, except towards the south – valleys that could have contained multitudes at the great feasts. Higher hills rise behind these valleys. Our servant Ibraim had visited it with Professor Robinson, and told us that they had found nothing but ruins. The words of the prophet are still full of meaning; 'Go ye now into my place which was in Shiloh, where I set my name at the first, and see what I did to it for the wickedness of my people Israel' (Jeremiah 7:12). We could also see the minute accuracy of the description of its situation given in Scripture, 'Shiloh, a place which is on the north side of Bethel, on the east side of the highway that goeth up from Bethel to Shechem, and on the south of Lebonah' (Judges 21:19). The region round is all fitted for such vineyards as are described in the same chapter (Judges 21:21).

We now ascended to the highest ridge of a rocky mountain, having a very deep valley on our left. Below us on our right lay a picturesque plain of small extent embosomed in hills. Into this we descended by a dangerous pathway, and came first to an old ruin called Kahn-el-Luban, and then to a fine flowing well, Beer-el-Luban. The water was cool and pleasant. Some Syrian shepherds had gathered their flocks around the well. At the north-west end of this valley, on the height, we could see the village of Luban, the ancient Lebonah (Judges 21:19).

Having travelled more than five hours without intermission, we were glad to rest and refresh ourselves for a little under some pleasant olive-trees. Scarcely had we resumed our journey, when we met at the northern entrance of the plain, the Bedouin Sheikh whom we had seen at Jerusalem, and who was to conduct Lord Claud Hamilton to Ammon and Jerash. He had faithfully fulfilled his engagement, and was now returning, having left his charge at Nablous. Three fine young Bedouins rode behind him, and all were attired and armed in the manner of their country. He at once recognised us with joy, and shewed us with no little vanity the presents he had got from Lord Hamilton. Bidding them salaam, we wound out of the valley to the right under a small town. Leaving this vale we descended into another running from east to west, very deep and rocky. Crossing the dry channel, and ascending to the very summit of the opposite ridge, a noble prospect burst upon our view. From the foot of the mountain on which we stood, a beautiful plain stretches to the north apparently for five or six miles. It seemed about two miles in breadth, bounded on either side by lofty and finely intersected hills, studded with villages. The farthest of these hills on the west side was Gerizzim, with a white tomb upon the summit, and Ebal beyond it, the two hills that embosom Sychar. The plain itself was cultivated in a style very superior to any thing we had yet seen in Palestine, and was beautifully variegated with fields of different colour, some bearing *dhura*[1] of a bright green, some ripe barley. We descended into this interesting plain, and followed the track close under the western hills.

The country people were engaged in their harvest. Indeed, this was the busiest part of the country we had yet visited. Several times we came on a band of reapers at their work, and met camels laden with sheaves. In one of the villages the treading and winnowing were going on in a lively manner. On the eastern range of hills there are three villages perched in very romantic situations, the name of the northmost was

[1] Indian millet.

Raujeeb. Probably these were flourishing towns in the days when Joseph's portion was blessed with 'the chief things of the ancient mountains, and the precious things of the lasting hills' (Deuteronomy 33:15). While we gazed upon these villages of the Samaritans one of the most touching narratives of the gospel was vividly recalled to us. Once when our Lord was going up to Jerusalem, he sent messengers before his face, and 'they went and entered into a village of the Samaritans to make ready for him, and they did not receive him'. His disciples wished to command fire to come down from heaven; but he gently rebuked them, saying, 'Ye know not what manner of spirit ye are of'; and they went to another village (Luke 9:52-56). It is probable that this was the road by which the Saviour was travelling, and some of these may have been the villages here spoken of.

In about two hours we left this fertile plain, and came round the eastern shoulder of Mount Gerizzim, ascending up a path worn deep in the rock, till we found ourselves in the entrance of the Vale of Sychar, running east and west between Mount Gerizzim and Mount Ebal. We did not know at the time, but an after visit made up for the omission, that it was at this very turn of the road, where it bends toward the city, that Jesus rested; for Jacob's Well was there. Entering a little way within the vale, we rested for a while beside a flowing fountain, called Beer-el-Defna, at which the shepherds were watering their flocks. The water flows into a large reservoir, from which it is conducted to irrigate a delightful garden of herbs. The ride up this valley was indeed beautiful. The plain stretches about two miles long to the town of Nablous, the ancient Sychar, and the average breadth appeared to be nearly half a mile. The sun was beginning to sink in the west, and was pouring his beams directly through the valley as we approached. A fine grove of old olive-trees extends for about a mile to the east of the town. Through this we passed, and then under the northern wall till we came to a grassy spot on the banks of a winding stream, where we pitched our tent on the west side of Sychar. We had often read of the verdure and beauty of this scene, but it far exceeded our expectations. The town with its cupolas and minarets is peculiarly white and clean, and is literally embosomed in trees. In the gardens beside us, we saw the almond-tree, the pomegranate, the fig, the vine, the carob-tree, and the mulberry; orange-trees also, with golden fruit, and a few graceful palms. The singular prickly pear is the common hedge of these gardens.

Sitting at our tent-door, we surveyed calmly the interesting scene.

Mount Ebal was before us, rising about 800 feet from the level of the plain. It appeared steep, rocky and barren. A few olives were sprinkled over its base, but higher up we could observe no produce save the prickly pear, which seemed to cover the face of the hill, much in the same way as the prickly furze on many of the hills of our own country. Viewing it from another point farther to the west the next day, it appeared entirely without verdure, frowning naked and precipitous over the vale. Mount Gerizzim was behind us, rising to a similar elevation. Although precipitous in many parts, it has not the same sterile and gloomy appearance which Mount Ebal has. It has a northern exposure, and therefore the midday sun does not wither up its verdure with its scorching rays. On the sides of one of its shady ravines we saw fields of corn, olives, and gardens, giving it altogether a cheerful appearance. In some places the precipices of Gerizzim seem to overhang the town, so that Jotham's voice floating over the valley, as he repeated the Parable of the Trees from one of the summits of Gerizzim, might easily be heard by a quiet audience eagerly listening in the plain below (Judges 9:7-20).

It was here also, upon the sloping sides of these confronting hills, that the blessing and the curse were so solemnly pronounced in the days of Joshua (Deuteronomy 27:12). Six tribes were stationed on the sides of Gerizzim, and six on the sides of Ebal, while in the valley between was placed the ark of God, with the priests and Levites standing round. When all was thus arranged, and every man of Israel held in his breath in anxious suspense, the Levites in a clear loud voice uttered the curses in the name of Jehovah. At every pause, the six tribes on Ebal responded 'Amen!' Then the blessings were uttered with the same deep solemnity, and the six tribes on Gerizzim responded to every blessing 'Amen!' It is not difficult to understand how the united voices of the band of Levites in the valley would be heard by the multitudes that lined the hills on either side, when we remember that the sound floated upwards amid the stillness of an assembly awed into deepest silence. This lovely valley formed a noble sanctuary, with these rocky mountains for its walls, and only heaven for its canopy. And where can we meet with a scene of more true sublimity than was witnessed there, when a covenanted nation bowed their heads before the Lord and uttered their loud Amen, alike to his promise and his threatening?

In our evening worship, we read John 4, with feelings of new and lively interest. We had scarcely committed ourselves to repose, when the jackals and wolves, which in great numbers find covert in the neighbouring hills, began their loud and long-continued howling; the dogs that prowl about the gates of the town immediately sent back a loud cry of defiance, and for several hours there seemed to be a regular onset between the parties. The ropes of our tents were occasionally shaken by some that were pursuing or pursued; and the valley continued to resound with their mingled cries till the depth of midnight.

June 20

Mr Bonar, waking before sunrise, wandered through the grove of fruit-trees toward the gate of the town. Finding it already open, he entered. Wandering alone in the streets of Sychar at this early hour seemed like a dream. A Jewish boy whom he met led him to the synagogue. It was small but clean, and quite full of worshippers. They meet for an hour at sunrise every day. There were perhaps fifty persons present, and every one wore the *Tephillin*, or phylacteries, on the left hand and forehead, this being the custom at morning prayer. They seemed really devout, for they scarcely looked up to observe the entrance of a stranger till the service was done. At the close several came and spoke to him. He spoke a little Italian to one, and then tried German with another, finding that there were Jews from many different places. Some were from Spain, some from Russia, one from Aleppo, and a few were natives of Sychar. After conversing for a short time they separated, going home to breakfast.

Mr Bonar engaged a very affable Jew to shew him the road to *Jacob's Well*, who, after leading him through the town, gave him in charge to another that knew the place. They went out at the Eastern Gate and proceeded along the Vale of Sychar, keeping near the base of Gerizzim for nearly two miles, till they arrived at a covered well, which is marked out by tradition as the memorable spot. It is immediately below the rocky path by which we had travelled the day before, at that point of the road where we turned from the spacious plain into the narrow vale, between Ebal and Gerizzim. The guide removed a large stone that covers the mouth of the low vault built over the well, and then thrusting himself through the narrow aperture, invited Mr Bonar to follow. This he accordingly did; and in the act of descending, his Bible escaping from his breast-pocket fell into the well, and was soon heard plunging in the water far below. The guide made very significant signs that it could not be recovered, 'for the well is deep'.[2] The small chamber over the well's

---

[2] The Bible was eventually recovered in July, 1843 by Dr John Wilson of Bombay who employed a Samaritan to go down into the well.

mouth appears to have been carefully built, and may have been
originally the ledge which is often found round the mouth of Eastern
wells, affording a resting-place for the weary traveller. But the well
itself is cut out of the rock. Mr Calhoun, who was here lately, found it
seventy-five feet deep, with ten or twelve feet of water. In all the other
wells and fountains which we saw in this valley the water is within reach
of the hand, but in this one the water seems never to rise high. This is
one of the clear evidences that it is really the Well of Jacob, for at this
day it would require what it required in the days of our Lord, 'αντλημα',
'some thing to draw with, for it was deep' (John 4:11). On account of
the great depth, the water would be peculiarly cool, and the associations
that connected this well with their father Jacob no doubt made it to be
highly esteemed. For these reasons, although there is a fine stream of
water close by the west side of the town, at least two gushing fountains
within the walls, and the fountain El Defna nearly a mile nearer the
town, still the people of the town very naturally reverenced and
frequented Jacob's Well. This may in part account for the Samaritan
woman coming so far to draw water, even if the conjecture be disre-
garded that the town in former times extended much farther to the east
than it does now. The narrative itself seems to imply that the well was
situated a considerable way from the town. He who 'leads the blind by
a way which they know not', drew the woman that day by the invisible
cords of grace, past all other fountains, to the well where she was to meet
with one who told her all that ever she did – the Saviour of the world and
the Saviour of her soul.

The Romish hymn seemed peculiarly impressive when remembered
on this hallowed spot:

> Quærens me sedisti lassus,
> Redemisti crucem passus,
> Tantus non sit cassus!

> (Weary – thou satst seeking me;
> Crucified – thou setst me free;
> Let not such pains fruitless be!)

But nothing can equal the simple words of the Evangelist, 'Jesus
therefore being wearied with his journey sat thus on the well.'

About a hundred yards off, to the north of the well, is Joseph's Tomb,
a whited sepulchre, believed to mark the place where Joseph's bones

were buried (Joshua 24:32). The Jews frequently visit this tomb; and many Hebrew sentences are inscribed upon the walls. Whether by design or accident, we could not ascertain, a luxuriant vine had made its way over the wall that encloses the tomb, and was now waving its branches from the top, as if to recall to mind the prophetical description of this favoured tribe, given by the dying Jacob, 'Joseph is a fruitful bough, even a fruitful bough by a well, whose branches run over the wall' (Genesis 49:22). The beautiful field around it is, no doubt, 'the parcel of ground that Jacob gave to his son Joseph', taking it out of the hand of the Amorite, 'with his sword and with his bow' (Genesis 48:28). And this plain is the plain of Moreh, near to Sychar (Genesis 12:6; Deuteronomy 11:30). Some have fancifully conjectured the name to be derived from Jacob's exploit, as if it meant, 'the plain of *the Archer*'.

About eight o'clock, the rest of our company paid a visit to the town, to visit the Jews and Samaritans. Under a spreading nabbok-tree near the gate, we came upon five or six miserable objects, half-naked, dirty, and wasted by disease. Immediately on seeing us, they sprang up, and stretched out their arms, crying most imploringly for alms. We observed that some had lost their hands, and held up the withered stump, and that others were deformed in the face; but it did not occur to us at the time that these were lepers! We were afterwards told that they were so – lepers on the outside of the city gate, like the ten men in the days of Jesus, who lifted up their voices, and cried, 'Jesus, Master, have mercy on us!' (Luke 17:13). Our Master, had he been with us, would have stood still, and said, 'I will; be thou clean'. On the nabbok-tree were hung many rags of cloth, of different colours. These are intended as sacred offerings, in accordance with a superstition of the Mahometans, which was never fully explained to us, and which we saw frequently in other parts of the country.

We passed through the streets, and found a good example of the Eastern bazaar. It is a covered way, with a few windows in the roof; abundantly dark, but very cool and pleasant. There is a deep pathway in the middle unpaved, about three feet in breadth, along which mules or camels are allowed to pass. On each side of this, there is a raised stone pavement, very smooth and slippery, which is used as a place for the shopkeepers to sit or to display their goods. When not thus occupied, it may be used for walking. It is a strange sight to walk along, and observe the turbaned and bearded sellers sitting cross-legged, and smoking in every doorway. The presence of a stranger excites little curiosity among them in general. Often they disdain to lift their eyes. Finding out the Jewish quarter, we went to the synagogue, into which several Jews followed us. The little children also came round us, and the women looked in at the door. Our Hebrew Bible was soon produced, and the prophecies concerning Messiah formed the subject of our broken conversation. Daniel 9, Isaiah 9, 53, Ezekiel 36, 37 and Jeremiah 23 were the passages read and commented on. The men were most willing to hear, and some of the children clung to us; but the women seemed displeased and impatient. At one turn of the conversation, Ibraim, our servant, who understood what they were saying, cried out, 'Hear how that woman is cursing you.'

While we were thus engaged, a Samaritan came into the synagogue and sat down. He was much better dressed than the poor Jews; his scarlet mantle and tidy appearance shewing plainly that he was better off in the world. He invited us to visit the Samaritan synagogue, an invitation with which we willingly complied. The Rabbi was seated on a carpet in the stone court, a clean pleasant place close by the synagogue. He was a reverend-looking old man, with large uplifted eyebrows, handsomely attired; he received us kindly, and conversed with great freedom.

Mr Bonar having missed the rest of us, and hearing that we were gone to the Samaritan synagogue, persuaded a Jew to guide him thither. He led him to a shop in the bazaar, where a fine-looking man, tall and clearly dressed, was sitting. The Jew's look was that of contempt, as he pointed out this man, saying he was 'a Samaritan'. The Samaritan kindly left his shop, and leading the way through many streets, arches, covered ways, and lanes, brought Mr B[onar] to the Synagogue. The old priest having made sure of obtaining a handsome present from us, now unlocked the door, and we, after taking off our shoes, were permitted to enter the synagogue, a clean airy apartment, having the floor covered with carpets. One half of the floor was raised a little higher than the rest, and seemed to be used for sitting on during the reading of the law. On one side, there was a recess which we were not allowed to enter, where the sacred manuscripts are kept. After long delay, and the promise of a considerable sum (for he told us the sight was worth 150 piastres at any time), the priest agreed to shew us the copy of the Torah, or five books of Moses, which is so famed for its antiquity. They said that it was written by the hand of Abishua, the son of Phinehas, and is 3600 years old. It was taken out of its velvet cover, and part of it unrolled before us. The rollers were adorned with silver at the extremities, and the back of the manuscript was covered with green silk. It was certainly a very ancient manuscript. The parchment was much soiled and worn, but the letters were quite legible, written in the old Samaritan character. If this was the real copy so much boasted of, the Samaritans have lost some of their superstition regarding it, for they allowed us to touch it. Several of their prayer-books were lying about, all written with the pen in the Samaritan character.

The Samaritans can speak very little Hebrew; their language is Arabic, but by means of our servant Ibraim, and a Jew who kept by us, we got our questions answered, and a good many remarks were made on both sides upon passages of Scripture. The son of the priest was an interesting young man, candid, and anxious to hear the truth. He admitted that the prophecy regarding 'the seed of the woman' referred to the Messiah, and said that they still expect a prophet 'like unto Moses'. The Samaritans do not believe in the restoration of the Jews. They told us that there are about forty who attend the synagogue, and about 150 souls altogether belonging to their communion. The enmity between the Jews and the Samaritans is not now so great, nor so openly manifested, as once it was; but we could perceive that it still existed. We had seen a Samaritan sitting in the Jewish synagogue, and the Jew who accompanied us was now seated in the Samaritan synagogue; yet it was easy to see that the Jew was jealous of the attention which we paid to the Samaritans. After taking leave of the priest and his son, we were conducted again to the Jewish quarter. We found a Rabbi, an old grey-haired man, sitting in the synagogue, reading the Talmud. We spoke a good deal with him in Hebrew, chiefly pointing out 'the Lord our righteousness'. It was pleasant to speak even a word to a Jew, in the city where Jacob often dwelt; and to a Samaritan in the very place where Jesus said, 'Lift up your eyes and look on the fields, for they are white already to the harvest' (John 4:35). Our Jewish guide next led us to a handsome fountain of water at the west end of the town within the walls. It seemed to be supplied from Mount Gerizzim. He said that Jacob had built the walls of it.

A little Jewish boy, named Mordecai, with sparkling bright eyes, had for some time kept fast hold of Mr McCheyne's hand. He could speak nothing but Arabic; but by means of most expressive signs, he entreated Mr M[cCheyne] to go with him. He consented, and the little boy, with the greatest joy, led him through streets and lanes, then opening a door, and leading the way up a stair, he brought him to the house of the Jewish

Hazan.[3] The room into which he was led was very clean, delightfully cool, and neatly furnished, in the Eastern mode, with carpets and a divan with cushions all round. The Hazan was not at home, but his wife soon appeared, and received the stranger with all kindness. She was dressed in the peculiar attire of the Jewish female, and carried a long pipe in her hand, which she occasionally smoked. Her only language was Arabic, for the females in Palestine appear to be strangers to the Hebrew, and are thus entirely shut out from understanding the Word of God which is read in the synagogues. She ordered rosewater to be brought – and then coffee – and seemed gratified to be permitted to entertain her unexpected guest. On taking leave, the little guide urged him to pay another visit. He led the way to the Bazaar, and there stopped beside the shop of a merchant, a venerable-looking man, saying *Yehudi*, 'a Jew'. Sitting down on the stone pavement, the Hebrew Bible was produced, and the passage read was 'the dry bones' of Ezekiel. Several Jews gathered round who could speak Italian or the *lingua franca*, and all joined in the discussion by turns. The merchant himself seemed to be a worldly Jew, and cared little about divine things; but some of the rest were interested. Leaving this group, the little Jew proposed to guide Mr M['Cheyne] to the Well of Jacob, which he said he knew. But the day was too far spent, as we had agreed to leave Sychar at noon. With difficulty, Mr M['Cheyne] now prevailed upon little Mordecai to come with him to our tents, to receive a reward for all his kindness. Giving him a Hebrew tract for the Hazan, another for the old Jew in the Bazaar, and a third for his father, and putting a silver piece into his hand, which seemed to fill him with wonder, we bade farewell to little Mordecai.

We felt sorry to part so soon from such a scene as this. The twice-repeated blessing of fruitfulness put upon the land of Joseph lingers about the vale of Sychar still, 'Blessed of the Lord be his land, for the precious things of heaven, for the dew, and for the deep that coucheth beneath, and for the precious fruits brought forth by the sun, and for the precious things put forth by the moon' (Deuteronomy 33:13,14; Genesis 49:22). It seemed almost as if the Lord remembered still the kindness of its former people, and kept this natural beauty around it as a memorial.

We were in the act of preparing to mount our horses when the four interesting Jews with whom we had sailed from Syra to Alexandria

---

[3] In modern Judaism the hazan is the cantor in the synagogue. In former times he had a wider range of duty, including care of the synagogue and the religious education of Jewish children.

arrived at the very spot of our encampment. We could scarcely believe our eyes; but so it was. They were mounted on horses, and had proceeded thus far on their pilgrimage to Jerusalem. After we left them in Egypt they had sailed from Alexandria to Beyrout, endured the sixteen days' quarantine there, and were now accomplishing the object of their journey. We met like old friends; they all saluted us with great heartiness, and were willing ere we parted to receive Hebrew tracts from us. We delayed a short time conversing with them, and then about one o'clock bade farewell to them and to Sychar.

The road from this to Samaria is perhaps the best we travelled in all Palestine. It is a level, broad highway at the base of hills – no doubt once much frequented by the kings of Israel, who would keep the highway to their capital in good repair. The direction it takes is north-west for about one hour, and then over a ridge which may be regarded a continuation of Ebal. The vale down which we rode was well watered everywhere; a fine stream meanders through it, and there are many wells; forming a complete contrast to the south part of the land (Psalm 126:4). The gardens on every hand are very luxuriant, the trees wearing their richest foliage; the fig, olive, and orange trees laden with fruit. We observed gardens of onions which seemed to rival those of Egypt. Many villages embosomed in trees also came in sight. A small village on the left was called Bet-Ouzin. Another on the hill Bet-Iba. Below this an old aqueduct having eleven arches crosses the valley, the water of which turns a mill. Before leaving the Valley of Nablous, we looked back and obtained a view of Ebal, strikingly rocky and sterile.

Our route now lay north-west over a considerable ridge, during the ascent of which we obtained a view of many distant villages; and among others Ramia, on an eminence. When we had gained the summit, the hill of Samaria came in sight, rising out of the plain to the height of about four hundred feet. It is an oblong hill sloping up toward the west, and has a considerable extent of tableland on the top. The plain, near the head of which it stands, stretches far to the west, and the mountains that enclose it are lofty. It is a hill in the midst of higher hills; a noble situation for a royal city. A grove of olives covers the plain, and the lower part of the southern side of the hill. On the mountain to the right stands a picturesque village called Nakoura, and on the summit a white tomb of a Moslem saint. We read over the prophecy of Micah (Micah 1:6) regarding Samaria as we drew near to it, and conversed together as to its full meaning. We asked Dr Keith what he understood by the expression 'I will make Samaria *as an heap of the field*?' He replied, that he supposed the ancient stones of Samaria would be found, not in the form of a ruin, but gathered into heaps in the same manner as in cleaning a vineyard, or as our farmers at home clear their fields by gathering the stones together. In a little after we found the conjecture to be completely verified. We halted at the eastern end of the hill beside an old aqueduct, and immediately under the ruin of an old Greek church which rises on this side above the miserable village of Subuste. Herod rebuilt the city and called it *Sebaste*, which means 'august, or venerable', in honour of Augustus Cæsar but God had written its doom centuries before. The ruin is one of the most sightly in the whole of Palestine. We ascended on foot by a narrow and steep pathway, which soon divides into two, and conducts past the foundations of the ruined church to the village. The pathway is enclosed by rude dykes, the stones of which are large and many of them carved, and these are piled rather than built upon one another. Some of them are loose and ready to fall. Many are peculiarly large, and have evidently belonged to ancient edifices. Indeed, the whole face of this part of the hill suggests the idea that the buildings of the ancient city had been thrown down from the brow of the hill.

Ascending to the top, we went round the whole summit, and found marks of the same process everywhere. The people of the country, in order to make room for their fields and gardens, have swept off the old houses, and poured the stones down into the valley. Masses of stone, and in one place two broken columns, are seen, as it were, on their way to the bottom of the hill. In the southern valley, we counted thirteen large heaps of stones, most of them piled up round the trunks of the olive-trees. The church above mentioned is the only solid ruin that now remains, where the proud city once stood. In the houses of the villagers, we saw many pieces of ancient columns, often laid horizontally in the wall; in one place, Corinthian capital, and in another, a finely-carved stone. Near the village, and in the midst of a cultivated field, stood six columns, bare and without their capitals, then seven more that appear to have formed the opposite side of the colonnade; and at a little distance about seventeen more. Again, on the north-east side, we found fourteen pillars standing. But the greatest number were on the north-western brow. Here we counted fifty-six columns in a double row at equal distances, all wanting the capital, many of them broken across, and some having only the base remaining. These ruins may be the remnant of some of Samaria's idolatrous temples, or more probably of a splendid arcade, which may have been carried completely round the city. And these are all that remain of Samaria, 'the crown of pride!' The greater part of the top of the hill is used as a field; the crop had been reaped, and the villagers were busy at the threshing-floor. Part of the southern side is thickly planted with figs, olives, and pomegranates. We found a solitary vine, the only representative of the luxuriant vineyards which once supplied the capital. At one point, a fox sprang across our path into the gardens, a living witness of an unpeopled city.

It was most affecting to look round this scene of desolation, and to remember that this was the place where wicked Ahab built his house of Baal, where cruel Jezebel ruled, and where Elijah and Elisha did their wonders. But above all, it filled the mind with solemn awe to read over on the spot the words of God's prophet uttered 2,500 years before: 'I will make Samaria as an heap of the field, and, as plantings of a vineyard; and I will pour down the stones thereof into the valley, and I will discover the foundations thereof' (Micah 1:6). Every clause reveals a new feature in the desolation of Samaria, differing in all its details from the desolation of Jerusalem, and every word has literally come to pass. We had found both on the summit and on the southern valley, at every little interval, heaps of ancient stones piled up, which had been gathered off the surface to clear it for cultivation. There can be no doubt that these stones once formed part of the temples, and palaces, and dwellings of Samaria, so that the word is fulfilled, 'I will make Samaria as an heap of the field.' We had also seen how completely the hill has been cleared of all its edifices, the stones gathered off it as in the clearing of a vineyard, the only columns that remain standing bare, without their capitals, so that, in all respects, the hill is left like 'the plantings of a vineyard', either like the bare vineshoots of a newly planted vineyard, or like the well-cleared terraces where vines might be planted. Still farther, we had seen that the ruins of the ancient city had not been left to moulder away on the hill where they were built, as is the case with other ruined cities, but had been cleared away to make room for the labours of the husbandman. The place where the buildings of the city stood has been tilled, sown, and reaped; and the buildings themselves rolled down over the brow of the hill. Of this, the heaps in the valley, the loose fragments in the rude dykes that run up the sides, and the broken columns on their way down into the valley, are witnesses; so that the destroyers of Samaria (whose very names are unknown), and the simple husbandman, have both unwittingly been fulfilling God's word, 'I will pour down the stones thereof into the valley.' And last of all, we had noticed that many of the stones in the valley were large and massy, as if they had been foundation-stones of a building, and that in many parts of the vast colonnade nothing more than the bases of the pillars remain. But especially, we observed that the ruined church had been built upon foundations of a far older date than the church itself, the stones being of great size, and bevelled in a manner similar to the stones of the temple wall at Jerusalem, and those of the mosque at Hebron; and these foundations were now quite exposed. So that the last clause of the prophecy is fulfilled with the same awful minuteness, 'I will discover the foundations thereof.' Surely there is more than enough in the fulfilment of this fourfold prediction to condemn, if it does not convince, the infidel.

We examined the old church at the east end of the hill. It is a massy substantial building, supposed to have been built in the times of the Crusades, as there are many crosses of the Templars on its architecture. The Moslems have broken away one of the limbs of each of the crosses in their zeal to shape them into the form of a crescent. Within the area of the church, there is a tomb where tradition says that John the Baptist was buried. Having obtained lights, we descended twenty-one steps into a handsome vault, the floor of which was tessellated with marble. There were five niches for the dead. The centre one was said to be that of the Baptist, and the door had a hinge of stone like the remarkable doors in the sepulchres of the kings at Jerusalem. 'Now', said our friend Giuseppe with great gravity, 'Tell your father when you go back to your own country, that you have seen the tomb of John the Baptist!'

But the natural scenery of Samaria had greater charms for us. The situation of the city is worthy of particular notice. The sun, about two hours from setting, was gilding the whole country with his mellowed rays, while we stood and gazed around. We could plainly see the meaning of Isaiah's description, 'Woe to the crown of pride, to the drunkards of Ephraim, on the head of the fat valleys of them that are overcome with wine' (Isaiah 28:1). The valley near the head of which the hill of Samaria stands is even now rich in olive-trees, and probably abounded in vineyards and gardens in former days, while the hill itself, covered with palaces and towers, rose over it like a glorious crown. The natural strength of the position of the city at once suggested the true force of the words of Amos, 'Woe to them that trust in the mountain of Samaria' (Amos 6:1).

Within half an hour's distance of the hill on the north and south, and still nearer on the east, the ring of lofty hills which enclose the valley of Samaria begins to rise. These are what the Scripture calls 'the mountains of Samaria'. They encompass the city, so that in the days of Israel's glory, when they were all clad in vineyards, the capital would appear encircled by plenty and luxuriance. The days are coming, when these same 'mountains of Samaria' shall again be clothed more luxuriantly than ever, and cultivated by the hands of ransomed Israel, for the same unerring word that foretold the present desolation, has foretold the coming glory, 'Thou shalt yet plant vines upon the mountains of Samaria; the planters shall plant, and shall eat them as common things' (Jeremiah 31:5).

We remembered the history of the siege of Samaria by Ben-Hadad, the king of Syria (2 Kings 6:24), and observed how easy it would be to shut in such a city on every side, so as to cut off the supplies; and it occurred to us that probably the unbelieving lord, who was trodden to death in the gate, was thrown down by the stream of people rushing *down the hill* toward the Syrian camp (2 Kings 7:17).

As we had still a journey of several hours before us, we were compelled to leave Subuste before sunset. Regaining the public road, we proceeded due north to the foot of the hills which enclose the valley of Samaria, having high on our right a village called 'Bet-emireen', 'the house of Emirs'. In about half an hour we began to ascend, and came to a romantic village called Bourka, halfway up the mountain. The peasants were all actively engaged at the threshing-floor; their houses were built entirely of mud, but pleasantly surrounded by olive-trees, out of which the voice of the turtle sounded sweetly as we passed. Looking back we saw the whole of 'the fat valley' beautifully illumined by the last rays of the setting sun. A very steep and difficult ascent soon brought us to the summit of the ridge, when a magnificent scene burst on our view. To the west lay the Mediterranean Sea, and that part of the plain of Sharon which stretches to ancient Caesarea; to the north, immediately beneath us, Wady Gaba, a fine valley or undulating plain, which seemed like a Paradise, watered by a winding stream, and abounding in olive-trees. This stream we afterwards conjectured to be the brook Kanah mentioned in Joshua (Joshua 16:8; 17). To the north-east rose the hills of Galilee, among which we thought we could distinguish Mount Tabor in the distance. At the head of the valley below appeared a sheet of water, the first we had yet seen in this country.

Slanting down the mountain side, which the Arabs called Jebel Gaba, in a north-easterly direction, we passed through the small village Matalish, and then through the village of Gaba; the latter may possibly indicate the position of the ancient Gibbethon, where Nadab, the son of Jeroboam, was slain by Baasha (1 Kings 15:27; 16:15), for that town seems to have been near Tirzah, and Tirzah was near to Samaria. The moon rose with great beauty, and the noise of the grasshoppers quite filled the valley. The glowworms and fire-flies were scattering their light around us. At length we encamped on the plain opposite Sanour. The time in which the servants were occupied in putting up the tents generally afforded us a profitable hour for meditation and retirement under the shady trees. In our evening worship together we read 2 Kings 6, which recounts some of Elisha's deeds in Samaria.

June 21
We set out at six next morning and passed by the foot of a steep rocky hill, upon which stands the ruined castle of Sanour, a relic of crusading times. We were now within the borders of the half-tribe of Manasseh, and remarked the abundance of streams and the remnants of fertility, far exceeding any thing we had seen in the southern parts of the country – as if the blessing put 'upon the crown of the head of him that was separated from his brethren', had not yet passed away.

We came upon two men ploughing with oxen, and noticed that they held the plough only with one hand. The soil appeared rich and fertile. Thousands of a blue star-shaped flower, the name of which we did not know, decked the ground, mingled here and there with the pink anemone, a very large species of convolvulus, and the tall plants of the lavatera. The beautiful hills all round the plain were clothed with brushwood, with olives and fig-trees sometimes running up a short way from their base.

Leaving this pleasant vale, we soon came to a height from which the hills of Galilee again came in view. From this we descended a rocky pass into a rich olive valley, with yellow cornfields beyond, and found the large Arab village of Gabatieh. Some of the houses were well built of stone, others were entirely of mud. They had no windows except loopholes, and these generally looking into the court of the house; the doors also were very low, perhaps for the purpose of defence. Emerging from the olive-grove we got a full sight of its beauty, and again remembered the many Scriptures which compare the soul of a thriving believer to a green and vigorous olive-tree. Two things seem invariably united in this land, namely, the voice of the turtle wherever there is an olive-grove, and a village wherever the eye discerns verdure.

We met here, and often afterwards throughout the day, camels carrying home the harvest, with tinkling bells hanging from their neck. Many splendidly coloured butterflies were on the wing, and lizards without number were seen basking upon the rocks. Descending a ravine, still to the north-east, on the banks of a small stream running in the same direction, we reached Jenin in three hours from Sanour. This is the frontier town of the great plain of Esdraelon in this direction, so that it must always have been a place of some importance. We halted for a short time under the shade of a spreading tree, while our servants went into the town to buy provisions.

Turning now to the north-west we began to move along the edge of the plain of Esdraelon, the ancient valley of Jezreel. Very large fields of ripe barley occasionally occurred, sometimes a grove of olive trees, but oftener the plain was waste and given over to thorns. It is melancholy to traverse the finest spots in this land, and to find them open and desolate. Even the highways are gone, along which the chariots of the kings of Jezreel used to run. The times of Shamgar are returned – 'In the days of Shamgar the son of Anath, in the days of Jael, the highways were unoccupied, and the travellers walked through byways' (Judges 5:6). The threatening of Moses is fulfilled, 'The land shall rest and shall enjoy her Sabbaths, while she lieth desolate' (Leviticus 26:34). We felt the heat of the sun very intense, while it poured its rays down upon the plain. Sometimes we sought a moment's shelter under a shady tree, and sometimes we rode briskly forward to create a refreshing current in the air. It was over these level fields that the Canaanites used to drive their iron chariots in the days of Joshua (Joshua 17:16); and it was in these plains that Sisera was defeated with his multitude and nine hundred chariots of iron: 'The kings came and fought, then fought the kings of Canaan in Taanach by the waters of Megiddo' (Judges 4:15; 5:19). We saw how easily Ahab could ride in his chariot from Carmel to Jezreel, while Elijah ran before him, there being no obstacle in all the plain (1 Kings 18:44); and also how Jehu 'could drive furiously' (2 Kings 9:20) as he came up from Jordan toward Jezreel. It was in another part of the same valley that good king Josiah came to fight with Pharaoh Necho in the valley of Megiddo, when the archers shot at him and wounded him in his chariot, and he died (2 Chronicles 35:23).

Leaving the plain we entered among the low swelling hills on the west near a village, Bourkeen, in less than three hours from Jenin, and arrived at Ramouni, (that is, 'pomegranate',) a village finely embosomed in fig-trees, olives, and pomegranates, from the midst of which came the voice of the blackbird and turtle-dove. Could this be Haddad-rimmon of which Zechariah speaks and which was near the valley of Megiddo (Zechariah 12:11)? There is space for a large town here, and there are many reservoirs of water, which shew that it has been a place of some importance. Flocks of goats were couching by the well, and the Arab women were milking them, while a boy drew water in a skin and poured it into the trough. Our way lay westward over the slope of low undulating hills, covered with the carob-tree, and evergreen oak, a finely wooded wilderness. Immense thistles, having heads of a rich violet hue, Spina Christi, lavatera, convolvulus, and our common holyhock, were the most abundant plants. We encamped at noon under the deep shade of a carob-tree of unusual size, and employed ourselves in writing up our notes and gathering wild flowers. Leaving at three o'clock, we rode through a fine sylvan solitude, hills and dales, all wild and seemingly untrodden, yet frequently having ruins and traces of ancient terraces, which shewed that once it had been a peopled land.

The first village we came to was called Am-el-Fehm, that is, 'mother of charcoal', probably from the abundance of wood which clothes the hill on which it stands, and the whole neighbourhood. Soon after, an opening in the hills gave us a rich prospect to the north-east over the plain of Esdraelon, as far as the hills of Nazareth, which seemed to be not many hours distant. Riding still north-west, the hill began to assume a more barren aspect, and the valleys looked sad and waste. Thistles, browned and withered, held undisputed reign, and the white stones covering the side reminded us of the valley of dry bones. Toward sunset the mountains opened to the west, and we looked down upon the Mediterranean Sea – the great plain of waters – and the line of coast near Cæsarea. Here our guide missed the track, but after passing a poor miserable hamlet, we reached a convenient spot for encamping near another village called Dalee. The frogs kept up an incessant croaking in the wady below, and the fire-flies glistened in the dusky air. Ibraim brought a plentiful supply of rich goat's milk from the village, a refreshing accompaniment to our evening meal. We had this day been passing through a portion of the land whose luxuriance used to be proverbial, and yet we had seen little else than a labyrinth of thorns and briery plants. Isaiah 32:13 again came to mind, and the remembrance, was soothing, for as certainly as the curse has been fulfilled, so shall the blessing – 'the Spirit shall be poured out from on high, and the wilderness be a fruitful field'.

June 22

Next morning, as we left the poor village of Dalee, we noticed the women carrying their children, some on their sides and some on their shoulder. We were now traversing the portion of Issachar, whose 'land was pleasant', and out of which princes came to the help of Deborah: yet now the pasture was scorched and withered, and the only traces of fertility were a few patches of barley and tobacco. As we approached the sea a cool breeze sprang up, which tempered the excessive heat of the morning. For about an hour after resuming our journey, the same features as before prevailed over the country, the only variety being a few Bedouin tents, 'tents of Kedar'. In about an hour we began to descend towards the west, and the country became much more fertile, assuming the appearance of the hill country between Bethlehem and Hebron. The swelling hills were covered with verdant brushwood, out of which issued the cooing of the dove. The deep thickets of evergreen frequently suggested to us the idea of the ancient groves of idolatry where they 'inflamed themselves with idols under every green tree'.

We turned to the right into a wild pass between wooded hills, which in a short time became a rocky defile, with a single sharp-pointed rock overhanging the entrance. Climbing up to this rocky pinnacle, we found some deep natural caves, which may have afforded a shelter to the prophets in the days of Elijah. The defile down which we had come issues suddenly into the narrow plain along the seashore, which is a continuation of the plain of Sharon. From the rocky height this plain lay stretched at our feet, and on the shore there were heaps of rubbish without any definite ruin, which mark the situation of Tortura, the ancient *Dor*, nine miles north of Caesarea, one of the towns out of which Manasseh was not able to drive the Canaanites (Joshua 17:11,12). On the rocks above us we saw the vulture perched looking out for his prey. After slanting across the plain, which was covered sometimes with fields of barley, sometimes with sesamine, and still oftener lay waste, our road lay parallel to the shore, and within view of it; at length we came upon the shore of the Mediterranean, happy again to meet its deep blue waters. Proceeding north, we came in about an hour to a small stream which here runs into the sea; its banks were skirted with tall oleanders in full bloom, and as we forded the stream many tortoises dropped into the water from the banks. Soon after, looking back we saw on a projecting point of the shore some conspicuous ruins of pillars and ancient buildings. The place is called by the Arabs Athlete, and anciently Castellum Peregrinorum.[4] We were anxious to press forward, and therefore did not turn aside to examine the ruins.

We remembered with interest that we were now in Paul's footsteps, when he travelled with a few friends in the opposite direction from Ptolemais to Caesarea (Acts 21:8). Four miles farther north we came under the sloping sides of Mount Carmel, but it was some time before we could be persuaded that it was really the hill we had read of from infancy. It did not present an imposing appearance; but, on the contrary, seemed low and almost uninteresting. One of our number exclaimed, 'Is this Carmel? Lachnagar is finer than this!'[5] We had been expecting to see a majestic mountain towering high over the sea, and felt not a little disappointed to find the real Carmel a moderately high ridge, becoming less lofty and conspicuous as it approaches the sea, till it terminates in a point about 900 feet in height. Before we left Carmel, however, and especially after viewing the whole extent of it from the heights above Acre, this feeling of disappointment was entirely done away.

At its northern extremity, it comes very near the sea, so that there is but a narrow strip of land between the steep rocky side of the mountain and the shore. Upon this narrow strip were pitched a multitude of tents of all shapes and sizes, while men of different costumes were couching round them, or wandering along the beach. It was an animating scene, and would have been more so had we not known that this was the station where we must perform quarantine. The plague had been for a long time prevailing in several parts of the south of Palestine, but it had not spread to the north of Carmel. Accordingly, all travellers from the south were obliged to rest here in quarantine for fourteen days, or, if they consented to have all their clothes bathed in the sea, for seven days. We pitched on the shore, the waves of the sea almost washing the cords of our tents, and an Egyptian soldier, a simple good-natured man, was appointed our *guardiano*, to see that we touched nobody; for should it happen that any

---

[4] 'Castle of Pilgrims', the present day Atlit.
[5] The reference is to a mountain ridge south of the River Dee in Scotland. It is a ridge with eleven summits over 3,000ft. (900m.) and it was made well-known last century by Lord Byron's poem 'Dark Lochnagar'.

one touch the person, or clothes, or cord of a tent, of any other party in quarantine, they are obliged to begin their days of quarantine anew.

The view which we enjoyed from our tent-door was every way splendid. The deep blue Mediterranean was in front of us, bounded only by the horizon. On the right was the beautiful Bay of Acre, round the whole sweep of which the eye could wander, uninterrupted except by the distant battlements of the town, or by small native vessels sailing past. In the distant background rose Jebel Sheikh, the ancient *Hermon* (Deuteronomy 3:9), which 'the Sidonians called *Sirion*, and the Amorites *Shenir*'; a noble mountain, where were 'the lions' dens and the mountains of the leopards' (Song of Solomon 4:8). The sea-breeze was pleasant and refreshing, and we had the pleasure of bathing daily in the cool waters; but the sand often glowed like a furnace, and the thermometer was generally 86°F. day and night. It was here that Giuseppe, the native of Bethlehem who accompanied us from Jerusalem, took leave of us. He insisted on our giving him a *backshish*,[6] which we could not refuse, although we considered that the favour was all on our side. He kissed our hands again and again, bidding us *Addio*.

The next morning was the Sabbath (*June 23*) and we welcomed the day of rest. Quietly seated in our tents, we read over and meditated upon the history of Elijah, especially his sacrifice on this mountain and his prayer, when seven different times he said to his attendant, 'Go again' (1 Kings 18:43). In the cool of the evening we wandered far from the tents, and had delightful leisure and retirement, and every assistance from association, to spread before God the case of our own souls, our people, our land, and our journey in behalf of Israel. We longed for the effectual fervent prayer of a righteous Elijah.

The greater part of Monday was occupied in dipping our tents, clothes, etc. in the sea, while our books and papers were all fumigated – inconveniences to which we willingly submitted that our quarantine might be shortened to seven days.

The remaining days of this week were spent in extending our notes, writing letters to the Committee of our Church, and to friends at home, in preparing ourselves for farther inquiries concerning Israel, and in solitary meditations while we rambled along the shore. The heat was uniformly great. Before dawn, indeed, and toward sunset, there was generally a pleasant breeze, but on account of the nearness of the sea,

---

[6] A Persian word for a tip or gratuity.

the heat was as great at night as through the day. The food furnished to us was simple and wholesome. The inhabitants of the neighbouring town of Khaifa[6] brought watermelons, and cusas, and fruits in abundance. Water, however, was sometimes scarce, there being but one well to supply the quarantine, and that one not very plentiful. We had long been strangers to the luxury of sitting upon a chair, and now felt the want of that accommodation less than we should otherwise have done. Still, the uneasy position of sitting upon the sand with our writing-desk supported on our knees, made the labour of writing in such a climate much greater than any one can imagine who has not made the same attempt.

Lord Hamilton and Mr Littleton were fellow-prisoners with us; and in a tent at some distance from us, Lord Rokeby, an English nobleman, who also had been travelling in these countries. Stretched upon the sand at respectful distances, under the eye of our guardiano, we held friendly conferences on the wonders we had seen. Dr Keith frequently applied and expounded the prophecies of the Word of God. On one occasion, in speaking of the wild animals that are found in the land at present, Lord Hamilton mentioned that his servant had seen during the preceding night two lynxes from Mount Carmel, with bright glaring eyes, quite near the tents. Near the Jordan, too, they had seen many wild boars and lynxes; and at Jenin, before dawn one morning, his servant had seen sixteen hyenas at one time.

Sometimes when the tide retired (for there is an ebb and flow of a few feet at this place), we gathered shells and sponge among the rocks. We saw some of our neighbours seeking for specimens of the shellfish from which, in ancient times, used to be extracted the famous purple dye. We did not see them find any specimens, but were told that still this is found here. It used to be found in all parts of the Bay, and there were two kinds of it. One of these yielded a dark blue colour, the other a brighter tint, like scarlet; and by mingling together these two juices, the true purple colour was obtained. It was thus that Asher, whose rich and beautiful plain supplied viands fit for the table of kings, yielded also the dye of their royal robes, conveyed to many a distant court by the merchants of Tyre and Sidon. And thus we see the full meaning of Jacob's blessing on Asher, 'he shall yield royal dainties' (Genesis 49:20).

We enjoyed the view of several magnificent sunsets here. One evening especially the sun went down behind the great waters, tinging

---

[7] The modern city of Haifa.

a vast array of fleecy clouds with the most gorgeous crimson. In the course of the week, Sir Moses Montefiore and his company arrived in quarantine, pitching their tents a little way to the south of us. He kindly sent us a present of a fine water melon, and afterwards two bottles of the 'wine of Lebanon', procured from the convent on Mount Carmel. If this was a fair sample of that famous wine, it must have lost much of its experience since the days of Hosea (Hosea 14:7), for it is not very pleasant to the taste. It has the same peculiar flavour with the wine of Cyprus, a flavour said to be communicated by the tar put upon the thread with which the skins containing the wine are sewed. Sir Moses and Dr Keith frequently walked on the beach, conversing on the prophecies that had been fulfilled in the desolations of the land, a subject to which the former had evidently paid a good deal of attention; but he positively declined all reference to the New Testament. During the greater part of Saturday, although the heat was very great, he and his lady, and a medical attendant, who was a very bigoted Jew, went through the Jewish service with scrupulous attention.

On Friday evening (*June 28*), a party of Egyptian Arab soldiers of the Pasha came into quarantine, and encamped beside us. They were rude undisciplined barbarians, having nothing but their pikes and muskets, which they fixed by sticking the bayonets into the sand. They had often noisy quarrels with one another, and sometimes as we passed their tents, half in jest, half in earnest, would level their muskets at us, crying, *'Nazarini'*. At night, we heard them chanting their Arab songs in the same way as we had heard our Egyptians do in the desert – a single voice leading, and a chorus responding with clapping of hands.

On the Saturday, a woman and her two children, in a tent within a few yards of ours, were declared by the physician to be ill of plague. This was a solemn intimation in such circumstances; but we remembered the 91st Psalm, and entrusted ourselves more entirely to Him who had brought us hitherto. None of the cases proved fatal during our stay. We had a longing desire to ascend the summit of Mount Carmel, that we might see the place from whence Elijah's servant saw the cloud no bigger than a man's hand, and that we might fully understand the Scripture references to it, several of which did not at that time appear so exactly suitable as we had found the references in regard to other places. But the regulations of quarantine would not permit us to wander to so great a distance. For the present, therefore, we were satisfied to skirt the foot of the hill and to examine the large caverns which are to be found there. The limestone rock of this mountain abounds in them; and in some such cave Obadiah hid the Lord's prophets, and fed them with bread and water (1 Kings 18:13). We were assured that there are no caves on the summit of the mountain, so that it cannot be in reference to them that Amos speaks of sinners hiding 'in the top of Carmel' (Amos 9:3).

On Sabbath morning (*June 30*), after worshipping together in our tent, we had separated for the day to pass the forenoon in retirement, when suddenly we were roused by hearing loud cannonading from the opposite side of the bay and, looking up, saw the town of Acre enveloped in smoke. This continued for nearly an hour. What it meant we could not imagine but at last a courier arrived from Acre, to announce that the Pasha's army had gained a great victory at Nezib,[8] and that he had commanded all the large towns to celebrate it by rejoicings during three days. This information was good news to us, and for a time set our minds considerably at rest. Our days of quarantine were now expired, though we did not intend to leave till Monday; but the question with us was – Are we to cross the country to Galilee, to inquire into the state of the Jews in that interesting region, or must we give up this fondly-cherished hope, and proceed by water to Beyrout? This had occupied much of our consideration the preceding day. The reports of the state of the country were very contradictory, some affirming that the Arabs, in absence of the Pasha's troops, were infesting the roads, plundering and murdering in every direction; others declaring that there was little danger. Now, however, we joyfully concluded that the news of the victory would overawe the Arabs, and open our way into Galilee. This gave us more rest of mind for enjoying the Sabbath, till the evening, when the Vice Consul of Khaifa paid us a visit which overthrew all our hopes. He came to say that the state of the roads towards Galilee was so dangerous that he would not provide horses for us on the morrow, since in that case he would be held responsible for our safety. Our course was now decided, and we made up our minds to sail along the coast to Beyrout.

Meanwhile, in the cool of evening, we ascended Mount Carmel by a deep and rocky ravine a little way to the south. We conversed together on Elijah's wonderful answer to prayer obtained on this mountain, and felt that we could well spend the evening of the holy day in such a place.

---

[8] Nezib (or Nizip) is in southeastern Turkey. On June 24, 1839 the forces of the Pasha, Viceroy of Egypt, defeated the forces of the Ottoman Empire at Nizip. The Ottoman Empire was only saved through the intervention of Great Britain, Austria, Russia and Prussia.

Having soon reached the summit, a considerable way above the Latin Convent, we sat down at a point commanding a full view of the sea to the west and to the north. Near this must have been the spot where Elijah prayed when he went up to the top of Carmel and cast himself down upon the earth and put his face between his knees, and said to his servant, 'Go up now, look toward the sea. And he went up, and looked, and said, There is nothing. And Elijah said, "Go again," seven times' (1 Kings 18:42,43). There we united in praying for abundance of rain to our own souls, our friends, and our people, and for the progress of our mission, which seemed for a time impeded. It was awfully solemn to kneel on the lonely top of Carmel. The sun was going down beyond the sea, the air was cool and delightfully pure; scarcely a breath of wind stirred the leaves, yet the fragrant shrubs diffused their pleasant odours on every side. A true Sabbath stillness rested on the sea and on the hill. The sea washes the foot of the hill on each side, and stretches out full in front till lost in the distance. To the east and north-east lies that extension of the splendid plain of Esdraelon which reaches to the white walls of Acre, and through which 'that ancient river, *the river Kishon*', was winding its way to the sea, not far from the foot of Carmel. These are the waters that swept away the enemies of Deborah and Barak (Judges 5:21), and that were made red by the blood of the prophets of Baal, after Elijah's miraculous sign of fire from heaven. To the south is seen the narrow plain between the mountains and the sea, which afterwards expands into the plain of Sharon. And along the ridge of Mount Carmel itself is a range of eminences, extending many miles to the south-east, all of them presenting a surface of tableland on the top, sometimes bare and rocky, and sometimes covered with mountain shrubs. On some of these heights the thousands of Israel assembled to meet Elijah when he stood forth before them all and said, 'How long halt ye between two opinions!' and from this sea they carried up the water that drenched his altar; and here they fell on their faces and cried, 'Jehovah he is the God, Jehovah he is the God!'

The view we obtained that evening on Mount Carmel can never be forgotten. No scene we had witnessed surpassed its magnificence, and the features of it are still as fresh in our memory as if we had gazed on it but yesterday. It was, moreover, a most instructive scene; we saw at once the solution of all our difficulties in regard to the Scriptural references to this hill. Carmel is not remarkable for height; and is nowhere in Scripture celebrated for its loftiness. At the point overhanging the sea, we have seen that it is less than 900 feet high. To the south-east it rises to the height of 1200 feet, which is its greatest altitude. But then the range of hills runs nearly eight miles into the country, and was in former days fruitful to a proverb. Indeed, the name Carmel, signifying 'a fruitful field', was given to it evidently for this reason. And when this vast extent of fruitful hills was covered over with vineyards, olivegroves, and orchards of figs and almond-trees, not on the sides alone, but also along the table-land of its summit – would not Carmel, worthy of the name, appear an immense hanging garden in the midst of the land? In the days of its pristine luxuriance, before the curse of God blasted its glory, 'the excellency of Carmel' (Isaiah 35:2), of which the prophet speaks, must have been truly wonderful! How easy at that time it would have been 'to hide in the top of Carmel' (Amos 9:3); for embowering vines and deep shady fig-trees would afford a covert for many a mile along the summit. And would not the beholder in other days at once understand the meaning of the beautiful description of the Church given in the Song, 'Thine head upon thee is like Carmel' (Song of Solomon 7:5)? Would not the jewellery and ornaments, or perhaps the wreath of flowers, around the head of an Eastern bride, resemble the varied luxuriance of the gardens of Carmel seen from afar? There are at present in the convent garden on the hill a few vines that produce excellent grapes; but these are all that now remain to testify of the spot where Uzziah had his vinedressers (2 Chronicles 26:10). With the exception of these, which are not properly on the summit of the hill, we could not descry a single fruit-tree on the top of Carmel. A few verdant olive-trees grow at the northern roots of the hill, and some extend a short way up the side; but the extensive summit, which was once like a garden, was covered as far as our eye reached with wild mountain shrubs and briery plants, all of stunted growth, except where the rock lay bare and without verdure under the scorching sun. The same God who said, 'Zion shall be ploughed like a field', and 'I will pour the stones of Samaria down into the valley', said also, *'The top of Carmel shall wither'* (Amos 1:2); and that word we saw before our eyes fulfilled to the letter.

Refreshed in spirit, we descended through a deep ravine, each side of which was fragrant with sweet-smelling briers. We reached the shore before it was dark.

Early next morning (*July 1*) we saw an interesting scene. About twenty Jews from Khaifa came along the shore to the tent of Sir Moses Montefiore to shew him respect before his departure. They were of all ages, and most of them dressed in the Eastern manner. It was affecting to see so many of them marching in a body in their own land.

Having determined to sail from Khaifa to Beyrout in a coasting vessel, we struck our tents, passed the barrier, and bade farewell to the quarantine and our kindly guardiano. We proceeded through the little plain of Khaifa, by the foot of Carmel on the north, rich in vegetable gardens, with some fine figs and olives. The entrance to the town is between hedges of prickly pear. Here we met an old Jew, originally from Vienna, who had been unable to keep up with the rest in their visit to Sir Moses, and was lingering near the town; he wore the broad-brimmed German hat and black Polish gown. We spoke to him in German, and found him very affable. He took two German tracts and one in Hebrew, and after briefly telling him, in Scripture language, his need of pardon, and that it came through Messiah, we separated, never to meet till the day of Christ.

A simple incident here vividly recalled a Scripture narrative (Matthew 21:18,19). A young Jew who had been out at the quarantine was returning before us; and he had come away, probably, before the morning meal and now felt hungry, for he stopped under a spreading fig-tree, and, looking up, searched the branches for a ripe fig, but in vain.

Khaifa is enclosed with walls, and appeared a neat little town. We found our way to the synagogue, and by this time most of the Jews had returned from their visit to Sir Moses. There were about thirty in the synagogue, all wearing the *Tallith* or shawl with fringes, and the *Tephillin* or phylacteries, because this was the hour of morning prayer. We conversed a little with three or four Russian Jews who spoke German, and told them our object in coming from Scotland. On our asking what they expected Messiah would do at his coming, one of them said nobody could ever know that; and this he proved by turning to Daniel 12:9 – 'The words are closed up and sealed to the time of the end'. In this way he evaded the subject of a suffering Messiah. We shewed them from Isaiah 1:15, 'When ye make *many* prayers I will not hear', that their many prayers would not justify them before God. They answered, 'We do not make many prayers; our prayers are very few'. We pressed them also with Ezekiel 36:26, to shew them that Israel at present have a heart of stone, and that they need a change of heart. Altogether they were most friendly.

There were several boys present, and they too wore the *Tephillin*. Several of the little children came up to us, kissed our hands, and laid them on their heads, that we might bless them in the Jewish manner.

They little knew how truly we longed that God would pour out his blessing upon Israel's seed, and his Spirit on their offspring. One fine little boy followed us to the boat and lingered on the shore till we had fairly sailed. When we reached the shore, the men were busy in getting ready the vessel – a large open boat without cabin, and even without an awning. A man and a boy had the management of it, a poor remnant of the Phoenician sailors so famous of old. As we sailed the town looked well from the sea, adorned with some graceful palm trees. The flags of Britain and France were floating together on the roof of the Vice-Consul's house, and the Egyptian flag, bearing the crescent and star on a blood-red ground, waved over the fort. Behind rose Mount Carmel, stretching into the country in what seemed an unbroken range, bare and withered; and we could now understand well the prophet's description, 'Carmel by the sea' (Jeremiah 46:18), for its northern extremity seems to descend into the very waters. The swell of the sea soon became unpleasant, the vessel rocked with every breeze, and we were exposed unprotected to the burning rays of the sun. We sailed past Acre, presenting a fine but not a formidable appearance. It is the ancient Ptolemais, where Paul abode one day (Acts 21:7). The men soon after pointed to Zeeb, the ancient Achzib, one of the cities of Asher, from which he could not drive the Canaanites (Joshua 19). It stands upon a slope near the sea. By sunset we were opposite Tyre, 'the strong city', and could distinguish clearly the part that was once an island. Here the breeze died away, and we were becalmed for many hours. We spent a painful night exposed to the heavy dew; but remembering how our Master slept in just such a vessel as this, we were still. At break of day we found ourselves opposite Saida, the ancient Zidon, and could hear the distant sound of the rejoicings in the town in honour of the recent victory. Soon the range of Lebanon appeared, rising up to the clouds in tranquil majesty. About eleven o'clock the promontory called Ras-el-Beyrout came in sight, and in a little time we sailed into the harbour of Beyrout. We were thankful to land and escape the discomforts of a Syrian boat, which we had been experiencing for twenty-eight hours.

The town has a fine appearance, the rising ground behind being studded with villas, and completely clothed with verdant gardens and mulberry plantations. A dilapidated castle runs out into the sea, in the midst of a singularly beautiful bay, and over all rise the towering heights of Lebanon.

The public rejoicings were going on; the inhabitants were all dressed in their finest clothes; some moved through the streets with instruments of music, singing and clapping of hands; some were carried in palanquins, and some had mockfights to the sound of music. We were glad to find refuge in the inn of Giuseppe, a Greek Christian, the first inn we had met with since leaving Alexandria.

We were soon waited on by two of the American Missionaries who are stationed here, Mr Thompson and Mr Hebard, who shewed us every kindness. They seemed to be earnest, devoted men, and have been blessed with considerable success. They have a regular Arabic service every Lord's day, attended by sometimes more than a hundred hearers, who are chiefly Christians of the Greek, Latin, and Armenian Churches. They have very efficient Sabbath schools for the young, and their weekday schools are attended by sixty boys and forty girls. In addition to these, they have a seminary for raising up native teachers, attended at present by about twenty Syrians. At this institution they first make trial of the boys for two months, and if in that time they do not evince sufficient aptitude or talent, their instruction is not carried farther. Some of those attending are Arabs; one is an Armenian, one a Maronite, one a Druse; and a few belong to the Greek Church. The Missionaries have baptized eighteen persons since the commencement of their labours in this country. The Roman Catholics, and still more the Maronites, are their most implacable and bigoted adversaries, throwing every obstacle in their way. The priests of both these sects would burn the Bible if they found it in possession of any of their people. Still, by means of native agency, the Bible is distributed, preserved, and read. The Greeks, and next to them the Armenians, have far less of a bigoted and persecuting spirit. Mr Hebard labours here in the winter season, but generally in summer visits Mount Lebanon and labours among the Druses. These are a singular people, supposed to have been originally Mahometans, but having now scarcely any religion. They worship in secret places, and have doctrines which they make known only to the initiated. They are very ignorant, but much more open to the words of the missionary than the prejudiced Maronites.

Several of the resident merchants also shewed us much attention, especially Mr Heald, Mr Kilbee, and some of our Scottish countrymen, among whom was Mr Kinnear, who has since given so interesting an account of his sojourn in the East. By a kind providence also, we now met with Erasmus Scott Calman, a believing Jew, newly arrived from England. We had become acquainted with him in London, and were now providentially brought together, for he was destined to be our kind companion and fellow-traveller from that day till we arrived in England. We had also much joy in meeting with Mr Pieritz, once Jewish Rabbi at Yarmouth, now Missionary of the London Society, along with Mr Levi and Dr Gerstmann, both converted Jews and labourers in the vineyard, the former laid aside for a time through bad health, the other, the medical missionary at Jerusalem. Some of the Syrian young men belonging to the American seminary were very kind and attentive to us, especially two who could speak English very well, named Abdallah and Habib. The latter said, 'My Name is Habib, that is, "friend," so when you want anything you must call Habib'. Frequently during our stay at Beyrout, we visited the residences of the American Missionaries, delightfully situated on the high ground to the south of the town, and about half a mile distant, in the midst of mulberry gardens.

From the roof and windows of Mr Thompson's house we enjoyed a splendid prospect. The coast of Syria, indented with numerous bays, stretched far to the north. But we were chiefly occupied with the view of majestic Lebanon. It is a noble range of mountains, well worthy of the fame it has so long maintained. It is cultivated in a wonderful manner by the help of terraces, and is still very fertile. We saw on some of its eminences, more than 2,000 feet high, villages and luxuriant vegetation, and on some of its peaks, 6,000 feet high, we could discern tall pines against the clear sky beyond. At first the clouds were resting on the lofty summit of the range, but they cleared away, and we saw Sannin, which is generally regarded as the highest peak of Lebanon. There is a deep ravine that seems to run up the whole way, and Sannin rises at its highest extremity to the height of 10,000 feet. The rays of the setting sun gave a splendid tint to the lofty brow of the mountain, and we did not wonder how the church of old saw in its features of calm and immovable majesty an emblem of the great Redeemer, 'His countenance is as Lebanon' (Song of Solomon 5:15). The snow was gleaming in many of its highest crevices, reminding us of the prophet's question, 'Will a man leave the snow of Lebanon?' (Jeremiah 18:14). In coming through the bazaar we had seen large masses of it exposed for sale. The merchants slice it off the lump, and sell it to customers for cooling wine and other liquors, and it is often mixed with a sweet syrup and drunk in passing as a refreshing beverage. Not far from Sannin the ancient cedars are found, a memorial of the glory of Lebanon. Cedars of smaller size are found also in other parts of the mountain.

There are nearly 200,000 inhabitants in the villages of Lebanon, a population exceeding that of all the rest of Palestine. This may give us an idea of the former 'glory of Lebanon' (Isaiah 35:2), and may explain the ardent wish of Moses, 'I pray thee, let me go over and see the good land that is beyond Jordan, *that goodly mountain* even Lebanon' (Deuteronomy 3:25).

Not many miles east of Beyrout, over the ridge of Lebanon, lies the beautiful vale of Cæle-Syria (hollow Syria) between Lebanon and Anti-Lebanon. It is said to be most fertile, and abounds in plentiful springs of water, which may perhaps be some of the 'streams from Lebanon' (Song of Solomon 4:15). At the northern extremity of that vale there is a considerable town called Hamah, supposed to be the ancient Hamath. The narrow entrance of this fine valley may be 'the entrance of Hamath', in the northern portion of the land which God gave to Israel. Ezekiel 47:16 joins it with Berothah, the very Beyrout where we then stood. Mr Thompson informed us of the death of the well known Lady Hester Stanhope, which had taken place a few days before at her own residence in the mountains near to Sidon. He had attended her funeral and read the service over the grave in her own garden. No Christian was near her when she died, and not a *para* of money was found in the house.

Nothing can surpass the softness of the Syrian sky at evening. At such an hour we used to see many of the citizens with their children on the roofs of their houses, enjoying the cool evening air. Some even sleep upon the roof at this season of the year. Beyrout is one of the hottest towns in all Syria. The thermometer stood generally at 85° or 90° F. during the day, but often rose to 96° during the night. The reason of this seems to be that there is little or no land breeze, owing to the proximity of the mountains, so that there is perfect stillness in the air till morning, when the sea breeze commences.

There are about 200 Jews in Beyrout. We visited them and their synagogue on Friday evening at the commencement of the Jewish Sabbath. We found them generally ignorant men, with little of peculiar interest in their character.

From Mr Pieritz, the missionary mentioned above, we received much important information. Speaking of the best STATIONS for the labours of a Jewish missionary, he mentioned the Grand Dutchy of Posen as one of the most promising fields in the whole world. There are nearly 100,000 Jews there, among whom the London Society have sent three labourers; but there is room for thirty. The Jews there have been enlightened so far as to be loosened from the Talmud, and yet they are not Rationalists. This may be accounted for by their situation among Protestant Christians. Nearly one-half of all the Jewish converts are from that country, among whom are three of the Jerusalem labourers.

In Moldavia and Wallachia there is another great field, hitherto untried. The cheapness of living there is extraordinary, and the resources of commerce are great and unoccupied, so that Jewish inquirers and converts could easily support themselves independently of their brethren. Judeo-Polish and Judeo-German are the languages they speak.

From personal observation, he also mentioned Gibraltar as a desirable missionary station. On one side lies the coast of Barbary, all lined with Jews, each of its towns having several thousands, and these men of singular industry. On the other side are Spain and Portugal, where are many called 'New Christians', who are all baptized Jews, to whom a prudent missionary might find access. In Gibraltar itself are about 2,000 Jews, speaking Hebrew and Spanish; many of whom at present allow their children to attend Christian schools there. A knowledge of the Arabic language is required by a labourer on the Barbary coast, and Judeo-Spanish on the European side.

Mr Pieritz spoke further upon the subject of *Tracts for the Jews*. The most useful tract for a Jew is a plain Christian tract, such as one would give to a careless professing Christian, setting before him the simple truth of his lost condition, and the death and atonement of Christ. This is much better than a deficient controversial tract. If it is controversial, it ought to be complete, for otherwise a Jew, accustomed as he is, by studying the Talmud, to acute reasoning, will soon see its deficiency and throw it aside. The tract *Helps to Self-examination* is good because it sets before them the law that convinces of sin, and closes with prayer for light. 'The City of Refuge' is another that Mr Nicolayson considered useful.

Some of Mr Pieritz's anecdotes regarding the Jews in Palestine were very interesting. In Jerusalem, a Jew named Munsternetze, when pressed much to read the Bible for himself, replied, 'But I am afraid'. 'Why?' 'Because (said he) I have a wife and children'. He meant, that if he were to study the Bible, he would be convinced of the truth and would, through the enmity of the Jews, reduce his family to poverty. Six weeks after Mr Pieritz came there, a learned Jew named Joseph visited his house to converse with him, and remained from ten in the morning till five at night; and the result was, that he would not read his rabbinical books any more. Not long after, he came secretly every day, and they read over together most of Isaiah, and all Matthew critically. One day he said that it had occurred to him that, as Messiah *should* have come just at the time when Christ appeared, it might be the case that Christ, knowing this, had taken advantage of it, and by the force of great genius had brought all the prophecies to meet in himself. Mr Pieritz gave him Isaiah 53, Daniel 9 and Zechariah 12 to compare and meditate upon. When he had read the first of these chapters, he returned, saying that he understood it; at the same time he applied it partly to the Jews, and partly to the Messiah as one of the Jews. Mr Pieritz set him to read all the three chapters. He sat very thoughtfully for a while; then burst out into the exclamation, *'How to understand is easy enough, but how not to understand is the difficulty!'* From that time he became really anxious about spiritual things. One Friday evening, talking of veracity toward God and man, reference was made to one of the Talmudical prayers which says, *'I thank thee for commanding'* such and such things, although no command has been given for it in the Bible. He felt the force of this at once, and on going home, finding the table spread to usher in the Sabbath, declined the service. His friends became suspicious of him; but his change became public in an unexpected way. A Mahometan was in the room one day, to whom Mr Pieritz said, 'that the unbelief of the Jews was no objection to Christianity, as many of them did believe', appealing to Joseph, who boldly assented. The Mahometan told this to the Jews, and Jerusalem was turned upside down. An excommunication was pronounced upon Joseph, so awful that the whole synagogue were in tears. They then forced him to divorce his wife and, by repeated solicitations, to leave Jerusalem for Constantinople, whither he went seeking Christian baptism.

On another occasion, a public controversy was held in which Rabbi Benjamin was spokesman in favour of the Talmud. It did not last long, but three months after, he came to Mr Pieritz to say that though convinced at the time that he himself had the best of the argument, yet, on going home, he had been led to reflect and inquire. Another day, he and Rabbi Eleazar came both together with a list of questions written, but went away without proposing them after hearing Mr Pieritz's statement of the truth. They began to read the New Testament together. One evening, while thus engaged in one of their houses, Rabbi Abraham came in unexpectedly; they tried to hide their books, but he insisted on seeing them. Upon a vow of secrecy, they shewed their New Testaments. He was very angry, but agreed to go with them to visit Mr Pieritz. He came full of fire against Christianity. He began by shewing the inaccuracy of the quotation about Bethlehem-Ephratah in Matthew 2, and said many acute things; but Mr Pieritz kept to the statement of the gospel. Rabbi Abraham soon became the most earnest of the three in his love for Christianity, and all determined to make an open profession. Two of them belong to the best Jewish families in Russia. Chaii or Hyman Paul, a young man, became convinced of the truth and was baptized. He used to go to the convent and argue with Roman Catholics, telling them that they could not be true Christians because they did not care for the Jews, but hated them. On one occasion, they ordered him out.

On the subject of *prophecy*, Mr Pieritz agreed in the sentiments of Mr Nicolayson that it is quite necessary for a missionary to hold the literal interpretation of prophecy. He mentioned that some Jews in Poland condemn parts of Abarbinel for spiritualizing. The Jews feel their dispersion to be literal; and therefore if you explain unfulfilled prophecy by saying it is spiritual, they reckon you a kind of infidel. If you say that 'a wolf' does not mean a wolf but a bad man, that 'Zion' means the church, and 'redeeming Israel' not redeeming Israel but something else, and yet try to convince them of the truth of Christianity from the Bible, they think that you yourself do not believe the Bible. In arguing with the Jews, it is sometimes of importance to shew the similarity between Rabbinism and Popery, and that they have the same author. One day a Jew referred to the follies transacted at the Holy Sepulchre, and said, 'that religion cannot be true'. The missionary replied, 'They do just as you do, they add to the New Testament, and you add to the Old'. Like the Papists, the Jews do not approve of a man reading much of the Bible, because it leads him to speculate, and they say the Rabbinical commentaries contain as much as it is proper to know. The parts of scripture read in the synagogue are generally passages that do not directly instruct in doctrine. For example, they read the 52nd and 54th chapters of Isaiah, but omit the 53rd.

In speaking of *the Holy Land as a Missionary field*, Mr Pieritz gave us the smallest estimate we had yet heard of the numbers of the Jews. He reckoned that in Jerusalem there are only 3000 Jews, in Saphet 2000, in Tiberias 1000, in Hebron 700, and in other towns and villages 1300, making in the whole land only 8000 Jews. During the last year he thought there had been a decrease in the Jewish population; for the plague carried away more than those born during the year, and the

Jewish emigrants who came to settle at Jerusalem during that time were not more than twenty. As to their *means of support*, the Ashkenazim depend wholly on the contributions from Europe, except in isolated cases. The Sephardim are not so entirely dependent on this source, as they have a little trade. If the contributions were withheld, they would all be forced to seek support by their own industry, and this would be infinitely better for them. Every intelligent friend of Israel we met agreed in this opinion. There are no Rabbis properly speaking among the Ashkenazim, that is, the Rabbi is supported in no other way than as a member of the congregation; but among the Sephardim there are *Hachamim* or 'Wise', for they do not call them Rabbis. These are all who are raised above the lower class, and have reached a certain standard of learning. Above this is the class of the *Hacham Morenu* or 'Teacher'. Him they regard with unqualified respect, and submit to him as a kind of Pope. He is well supported by them, and often lives in affluence. The Ashkenazim do not pay any such respect to their Rabbis. The Polish and German Jews are generally better scholars than the native Sephardim; but, on the other hand, the latter have more knowledge of the Bible. On the Barbary coast, it is not uncommon to meet with very unlearned Jews who are well acquainted with their Bible. There is a mixture of the customs of different countries among the Jews of Palestine, but a general inclination prevails to yield to the manners and laws of the Sephardim; as, for example, in the rites of burial. There is much more of Pharisaism among the Sephardim than among foreign Jews, and much less morality. Polygamy is not unfrequent among them, but is not allowed among the Ashkenazim. There are several in Jerusalem at present who have two wives, and some who have even four. Divorce occurs every day. Mr Pieritz mentioned one case of a Jewess in Jerusalem, not above thirty years old, who was then married to her fifth husband. In how affecting a manner does this illustrate the question put by the Pharisee to our Lord, 'Is it lawful for a man to put away his wife for every cause?' (Matthew 19:3) and the touching answer of Jesus.

The Jews here are far lower in morals than those in Europe. Those living in Saphet are worse than those in Jerusalem; those in Hebron are the most respectable of all. Their misery also is very great. It is not true, as some have supposed, that though the houses are outwardly poor, they are well-furnished within. Yet the Jews are more open and friendly in this land than in any other, because of their misfortunes. The Bible shews that affliction will be one way of humbling them, and it is so here.

In other lands, where they are involved in business, or rich and comfortable, they will not attend to the missionary.

The Jews here will take an Old Testament willingly, but often they will read the historical parts only, and not the prophets; for it flatters their national pride to read the story of the wars of their fathers. To remedy this, the London Society have published The Prophets separately, and these are often sold to them.

The Karaites, or Jews who keep by the text of the word of God and reject traditions, abound most in the Crimea, and hence some erroneously give that country the honour of originating the name. They are generally very ignorant, having no literature of their own. In the Crimea and Turkey they are said to repeat their prayers in Turkish. Their prayer-book is a beautiful compilation, being taken almost entirely from Scripture, with some hymns: and they do not omit any book of the Bible in the Scriptures, as some have asserted. The other Jews hate this sect more than they do the Gentiles.

In regard to the *literary qualifications of missionaries*, the remarks of Mr Pieritz have been mostly anticipated. He shewed the necessity of a Missionary's knowing more languages than Hebrew. If he speak to them only in Hebrew he must quote the Scripture simply as it stands in the Hebrew text, which they often understand in a different sense from what he does. For the sake of perspicuity, therefore, he must explain himself in the vernacular tongue: Judeo-Polish or German for the Ashkenazim, and Judeo-Spanish or Arabic for the Sephardim. The study of the Talmud sharpens the intellect much, so that a Missionary who has not studied it deeply ought to have passed through an academical education. The only way of learning it is by the help of some learned Jew. The parts that are not controversial are the most easy. But one who is a Talmudist and nothing more will never do for a Missionary. One advantage of Talmudical knowledge is that it enables the person to argue by Talmudical logic, which is much shorter and more striking than scientific logic. Jews cannot follow a long argument.

The concluding words of our conversation with this interesting person were worthy of remembrance. 'Rather send one good Missionary than fifty others. I have come after many Missionaries, and have wished that they had never been there. It was pleasant to come after Wolff. All the Jews in the place knew what he wanted with them viz. that without Christ there is no remission of sin.'

July 5

In the streets of Beyrout, it is common to meet Druse women wearing the tantour or 'horn' of silver, with the white veil thrown over it. It is far from being a graceful ornament, and is adopted only by the women of Lebanon. It is likely that this fashion was borrowed originally from the language of Scripture, and not that Scripture refers to a fashion which existed long before. Probably the truth in regard to this custom is the same as in regard to several practices in use among the Abyssinians; they have grafted customs on a literal application of Scripture expressions. Such passages as 'I have defiled *my horn* in the dust' (Job 16:15), may have suggested this singular head-dress to the people of Lebanon. The horn to which the words of Scripture refer was simply, as among the Greeks, the horn of animals – that being their principal weapon of defence, and therefore the natural symbol of power.

We met a man carrying a wooden key hanging over his breast, and an iron key over his shoulder hanging down his back; and we found that it is common for merchants, when they carry more than one key, to suspend them in this way over the shoulder. It was once the custom in Judah; 'The key of the house of David will I lay upon his shoulder' (Isaiah 22:22). Everybody also seems to carry in his hand a string of beads, keeping his fingers in constant employment. Christians, Jews, and Mahometans seem equally wedded to the practice.

We had been deliberating for some time as to our future movements in the important Mission with which we had been entrusted; and now, after much anxious and prayerful deliberation, came to a unanimous conclusion. Our valuable fellow-traveller, Dr Black, had for some time felt the climate of Syria and the rude manner of travelling too much for his bodily strength, and feared that he would not be able to undergo the farther fatigue of a journey into Galilee. In these circumstances, it was considered right that he and Dr Keith should proceed homewards by Constantinople and the Danube, making inquiries into the condition of the Jews in all the most important places through which that route would take them; whilst the two younger members of the Deputation should remain to visit the Jews of Galilee, and return to England by a land journey through Europe. To aid us in our inquiries, Mr Calman, a Christian Israelite, of whom we have already spoken, a man of tried integrity, who had formerly laboured five years in Palestine, and was master of the Arabic and German languages, was engaged to accompany us.

July 6

On Saturday afternoon, we were present at the Arabic service in the house of Mr Hebard, the American Missionary. About twenty Syrian converts were present, and among the rest a venerable old man, named Karabet, who had been twenty years Armenian Bishop in Jerusalem, but had now renounced the errors of that church at the cost of sacrificing all his worldly interests. A prayer meeting was conducted in English, and then an address and prayer in Arabic followed. In the evening, the heights of Lebanon were here and there blazing with fires kindled by the Maronites in honour of the feast of St John.

July 7, Sabbath

Early this morning the missionaries came to take us to the house of the American Consul where their forenoon service is conducted. Here, in a large commodious room with stone floor, the open windows of which commanded a splendid view of the sea, the old castle, and Lebanon, was assembled a congregation of more than 100, consisting of English residents and their families, and many turbaned Syrians who understood English. The singing of the hymns was very sweet in a foreign land. Dr Black preached from Romans 5:1. At three o'clock we parted with our esteemed fellow-travellers and saw them set sail in the Austrian steamer for Smyrna. It was solemn and painful to separate from our brethren, 'not knowing the things that were to befall us'.

We now went to the mission-house above the town; and round the door found several of the Syrian boys waiting for the commencement of the Arabic service. Sitting down under the shade of the mulberry-trees, we conversed with them. Two of them spoke English remarkably well and went over the Old Testament history most accurately, as far as the wanderings of Israel, accompanying every answer with most expressive looks and actions. One of them especially was full of liveliness, and on asking him the story of Moses wishing to see Lebanon, related it fully, pointing to the lofty mountain towering before us. Three others sitting by occasionally added a remark, while old Bishop Karabet and many others looked on from the steps above. Soon after, the Arabic service commenced in a large airy room, divided by a partition, except at the place where the Missionary stood. The women sat on the one side of the partition, the men on the other, according to the custom of the Christian churches of this country, the preacher standing within sight of both parts of the congregation. Mr Thompson preached in deeply-toned Arabic, to an attentive audience of about 130, gathered out of many different countries. There were two Armenian bishops, with clean venerable beards, Karabet, and Jacob Aga; there were Greeks and Greek-Catholics, an Abyssinian Christian, and a Druse, converted Jews, American Presbyterians and Congregationalists, and Ministers of the Church of Scotland – all different in name, and yet, we trust, one in Christ. This service closed and we removed to a more convenient upper chamber to partake of the Lord's Supper. The American manner of administering this sacrament differs little from ours, except that they give thanks a second time before giving the cup, in close imitation of our Lord. One of us sat between two believing Jews, the other between the two Armenian Bishops. Many of the others also participated, so that it was an emblem of the meeting of the great multitude gathered from nations and kindreds at our Father's table above. This was a well of living water at which we were strengthened for our coming journey, and refreshed after the departure of our elder brethren. When they were gone, we felt as if we were beginning our journey anew in circumstances of more responsibility than before. But we hoped for Asher's blessing, 'As thy days so shall thy strength be.'

CHAPTER 5

SYROPHENICIA – GALILEE

'Thy land, O Immanuel' (Isaiah 8:8).

In the afternoon of Monday, July 8 we set out for Galilee with a small cavalcade of six horses. Ibraim and Ahmet took leave of us. The latter felt little, but Ibraim exhibited very affectionate feelings. He followed us a little way beyond the gates, then took farewell, burst into tears and rushed out of sight. We felt it very sad to leave this Arab for ever, not knowing how it is with his soul.

Our road lay nearly south through a grove of pines, with mulberry gardens on all sides. Pleasant wild flowers adorned our path; the oleander in full bloom skirted the banks of two small streams which we crossed; and often also our own modest white rose appeared amongst the fragrant myrtles in the hedges. We crossed a bar of sand which is here blown across the promontory of Beyrout and is two hours in breadth. The muleteers said that this sand was blown all the way from Egypt, but we heard that the shore is composed of a very soft sandstone which accounts for its origin. Between us and Lebanon lay a splendid olive-grove, stretching north and south, said to be the largest in Palestine, which it was refreshing to the eye even to look upon. But Lebanon itself chiefly attracted our admiration, for every part of its lower ridge seemed covered with villages. From a single point we counted twenty-one villages, all appearing at once on the brow of the mountain, each village having considerable cultivation round it. In the days when these stupendous heights were crowned with forests of pine and cedar, how deeply expressive must have been the words of the prophet, 'Lebanon is not sufficient to burn, nor the beasts thereof sufficient for a burnt-offering' (Isaiah 40:16).

We reached the southern side of the promontory before sunset and came upon the rocky seashore, along which our course now lay. Just as the sun went down we passed a small khan. Some were unloading their asses, some spreading their mats for the night. One man was opening his sack to give his ass provender, and forcibly reminded us of Jacob's sons arrived at their inn (Genesis 42:27). They invited us to stay with them, saying, 'You will be plundered if you go on.' We had not gone far when darkness overtook us, and we lost our way just as we came upon the bank of a broad stream that comes down from Lebanon called Damour, the ancient Tamyras. Here we wandered among mulberry gardens, till at length we found a ford near the ruins of a bridge. The roots of the mountains here stretch out into the sea, forming rocky promontories. We crossed over one and another of these by what appeared to be an ancient Roman road, and came down through a village to a khan on the seashore called Naby-Younes, 'the prophet Jonah'. There is here a small bay which a Mahometan tradition makes out to be the spot where Jonah was cast ashore by the whale. The keeper of the khan offered us accommodation, but, after taking a little of his salt bread and *leban*, we judged it preferable to encamp on the open shore near the sea.

The servants who now formed our party were all of different persuasions. Botros, Mr Calman's attendant, was a Greek Catholic; Antonio, who waited upon us, was a young Syrian of the Latin Church and spoke Italian. The muleteers were Mansor, a Druse, and Tanoos, a Maronite lad, of a most gentle disposition. Sometimes at night Antonio and Botros 'poured water on our hands' to wash away the dust, reminding us of 2 Kings 3:11. With these around us, and the waves of the Mediterranean almost at our tent-door, we slept in peace.

We left this bay at six o'clock and gaining the height of the next rocky promontory, obtained a view of the coast, indented with deep sandy bays, and of Sidon itself two hours distant. The view of Sidon as we approached was very fine and exceedingly like the representations commonly given of it in the sketches of Syria. The town stands on high rising ground which projects a considerable way into the sea. It is enclosed by a high fortified wall on the eastern side, and two mosques tower over the other buildings of the town. The most striking object is a fortress built upon a rock in the harbour and connected with the town by a bridge of nine arches, said to be a remnant of the times of the Crusades. There is also a ledge of low rocks in the offing, near which two small vessels lay at anchor. Between the town and the mountains lie richly cultivated gardens with tall verdant trees. Behind these the mountains appear, and we counted five distinct ridges of the range of Lebanon rising one above another. Altogether, 'Great Sidon', though fallen from her ancient glory, occupies a noble situation. Into the bay to the north of it flows a considerable stream, another of the many which are fed by the snows of Lebanon.

Mr McCheyne rode on before the rest, and arriving at the gate inquired of the sentinel the way to the Jewish synagogue. He pointed to a Jew who was standing beside his shop-door at the entrance of the bazaar. The Jew, shutting up his shop, took the stranger kindly by the hand and led him away to his house. He tied up the horse in the courtyard, took off the carpet and bridle, and ushered him into his best room, where both sat down on the divan. After some preliminary questions, the Hebrew Bible was produced, and the first part of Ezekiel 37 read, from which Mr M[cCheyne] shewed him his state by nature. He seemed a little offended, yet not wishing to shew it in his own house, tried to change the subject of discourse and offered coffee.

On leaving the house, another Jew led Mr M[cCheyne] to the synagogue, a substantial building having the roof vaulted in the Gothic style. An old man sat on the ground surrounded by some Jewish children whom he was teaching to read portions of Hebrew. Here the rest of our company met, and the old Rabbi, whose house joined hard to the synagogue, came in, followed by some twenty or thirty Jews. Several of them recognised Mr Calman and received him in a very friendly manner. They seemed well inclined to enter into controversy on divine things. Two lads maintained an animated conversation with Mr Bonar, during which he produced his Hebrew New Testament and asked one of them to read a chapter. They began very readily to read Matthew 2, but when nearly finishing it, an elder Jew looked over their shoulder and whispered to them the name of the book which they were reading. They immediately closed the book and one of them started from his seat.

We told the Rabbi that we had come from a far country to visit Israel; that we had seen God's Word fulfilled in the desolations of Jerusalem; and we asked for what cause Israel were now like the dry bones in the open valley? The old Rabbi appeared to be a man of perverse spirit. He went to his house and brought out a Hebrew New Testament, one of those printed by the London Society, a good deal worn. He turned up to Mark 13:32 where Jesus says that he did not know the day of his second coming, and asked how then could he be God?

One bitter Jew made signs to have us thrust out of the synagogue; but the rest shewed greater kindness, especially one young Rabbi from the coast of Barbary, who spoke a little French. He shewed us their manuscripts of the law, one of which he said was three hundred years old, written at Bagdad and now much worn. It had cost them 200 dollars. This man afterwards received us politely into his house, entertained us with lemonade and coffee, and at parting accepted a Hebrew tract called 'The City of Refuge'. He told us that there are 300 Jews in Sidon.

We now proceeded through the bazaar to a handsome khan or caravansera possessed in former days by the Franks. It is a large square, built round on all sides, with a fine fountain and pool of water in the centre, over which a vine was trained; a few orange-trees grew around. While sitting by the pool waiting till one of our mules was shod, a string of camels arrived, heavily laden with furniture, which proved to be the property of the late Lady Hester Stanhope, which, we were told, was to be sold at Sidon. Here also two Druse women were sitting wearing the *tantour*, or horn upon the forehead. On the finger they wore a massy ring, having a seal on it. In the streets we met several Greek ecclesiastics neatly attired. The town is solidly built, and the bazaars are in a thriving condition. A public bath is one of the few modern buildings; but frequently we stumbled upon broken pillars and fragments of carved stones, the memorials of departed greatness.

All the magnificence of Sidon is gone for 'God has executed judgments in her' (Ezekiel 28:22). Again and again have its inhabitants been 'judged in the midst of her by the sword on every side'. There are no more any merchants worth mentioning here. In two or three shops, fishing-rods were exposed for sale, but there are no signs of trade. 'Be thou ashamed, O Zidon; for the sea hath spoken, even the strength of the sea, saying, I travail not nor bring forth children, neither do I nourish up young men, nor bring up virgins' (Isaiah 23:4). The city, and the sea that laved its walls, now lament the want of its once crowded and stirring population. It no more can boast of a king. 'All the kings of Zidon' have been made to drink the wine-cup of God's fury, even as it was foretold (Jeremiah 25:22).

Before leaving the town, a Greek Christian who acts as a consular agent came to us and advised us not to proceed, for a traveller had been killed by the Arabs the day before, three hours on the way to Tyre. We had no reason to suspect this person's veracity, and yet we hoped that his information might be untrue; and committing ourselves to God, left the gate of Sidon an hour after noon.

The gardens and groves that shelter the east side of the town, afforded a pleasant shade. There the rich merchants of Sidon enjoyed their wealth and revelled in that luxury and ungodliness which made the Saviour fix on them as eminent instances of guilt: 'It shall be more tolerable for Tyre and Sidon at the day of judgment than for you'

(Matthew 11:22). Our way lay directly south, through the fine plain which stretches beyond Tyre.

In three hours we came upon many fragments of marble pillars scattered on the shore. These and other similar remains appear to be the remnants of ancient villas, if not of some town. In the days when Tyre and Sidon enjoyed their greatest splendour, this midway situation would be most favourable for the country-seats of the princes and merchants. Here, far removed from the noise of the city, they might be refreshed by the sea-breeze tempering the heat of summer, while, from the neighbouring heights, they enjoyed the view of their stately vessels sailing past.

At this midway point stands Sarfend, the ancient Zarephath or Sarepta. It formerly spread toward the shore, but now is on the heights. The hills are here about a mile from the shore, and the village is pleasantly situated upon the steep brow of one of them, overhanging a ravine filled with fine olive-trees, and commanding a wide view. The vine once grew upon its hills in great luxuriance.

But it was matter of far greater interest to us that it was hither that Elijah came from the brook Cherith, and here he was nourished out of the widow's barrel of meal and cruise of oil, and here he raised her child from the dead by prayer. These simple facts invest the place with a sacred interest. It was the theatre where God displayed his amazing sovereignty. The Lord passes by the many widows that were in Israel – he passes by all the princes of Tyre and Sidon, and fixes on one who dwells unknown in Sarepta, 'a woman that was a widow'; teaching the world that he chooses his vessels of mercy where and when it seems good in his sight. Elijah may often have walked along these shores, and it was pleasant even to imagine that we were treading in his footsteps. There is reason to believe that this fertile plain, which may well be called 'the borders of Tyre and Sidon' was also the scene of one of the most affecting of the gospel narratives, shewing the same sovereignty and grace as the wonders of Sarepta. For it was toward this plain that Jesus directed his steps from the Sea of Galilee, when the woman of Syro-Phenicia came and fell at his feet (Matthew 15:21-28; Mark 7:24-30).

More than an hour to the south of Sarfend, we diverged from the shore to visit the caves and tombs which occur in the precipitous face of the low hills. We climbed up into one large cavern, apparently natural, about sixty feet deep by thirty broad, and from twenty to thirty feet in height. From the mouth of the cave we could count about twenty sepulchres cut in the face of the rock, probably part of the ancient works of Tyre, the tombs of her rich men and princes.

Two hours farther south, we arrived at the largest stream we had yet seen in the land. The banks were skirted with the red blossoming oleander, and many tortoises were creeping in the shallows. This is the Kasimieh, believed to be the ancient Leontes, which has its source from Baalbec, flows through the splendid Vale of Coele-Syria, and empties itself into the sea, an hour and a half north of Tyre.

We crossed the stream by a substantial bridge, upon the side of which we found sitting a cluster of Bedouins, wild, suspicious-looking men, with a little yellow shawl over the head, encircled by a rope of camel's hair. They seemed to be looking out for a prey, and our servants evidently did not like their appearance, but we saluted them peaceably and passed on. On the high bank overlooking the river stands an old dilapidated khan; and here, as the sun was going down, we resolved to encamp for the night. Perhaps the story we had heard at Sidon of the danger of the way made us think more of 'perils of robbers' than we should otherwise have done; nor was it any addition to our prospects of a peaceful night's rest to be told that the ground here was full of scorpions, and that even the floor of the old khan was not free from them. However we decided to go up to the khan and seek shelter within its walls. Here, as the brief twilight came on, there arrived first one company and then another of mules, with tingling bells, till the square of the building presented quite a lively appearance. We pitched our tent on the roof of the old ruin where the grass had been allowed to grow; and committing ourselves to Him that keeps Israel, lay down to sleep in peace. Occasionally we heard the cry of the jackal, but nothing else disturbed our rest till the rising sun shone with intense brilliancy into our tent.

July 10

We were soon on our way to Tyre, an hour and a half distant, through a fine plain, covered mostly with thorns, with here and there a field of dhura. Tyre appears a long promontory stretching into the sea. Halfway between the town and the hills, there is a conical rising ground surmounted either by a khan or a tomb, and nearer Tyre appear the remains of the ancient aqueduct.

Arriving at the gate, we were detained some time under the shade of some fig trees till the Governor had fully ascertained that we came from the north, and not from places where the plague prevailed. We entered, and with some difficulty rode through the bazaar, which was shaded with mats and vines, till we arrived at the khan, a large half-ruined building, where we put up our horses.

Tyre is but the wreck of a town. You cannot traverse its streets without meeting at every turn fragments of other days. Thus, at the gate there are two fallen pillars; in the bazaar, another prostrate pillar helps to complete the pavement; and on the shore of the peninsula (once The Island), broken columns lie on all sides, over which the sea dashes its waves. We stood awhile amidst the ruins of the old Christian church at the south-east corner of the town, where Eusebius[1] is said to have preached, and looking over, observed the waves break on two large columns with their capitals that lay close under the wall.

From this point, and from the summit of a tower to which the Jews led us to the south-west corner of the town, we surveyed the whole extent of what was Insular Tyre, once densely covered with the palaces of Tyrian merchants. The island appears to have been of the shape of a prolonged diamond, stretching nearly a mile from north to south. The breadth is not easy to estimate, as we cannot tell where Alexander's causeway commenced. We observed a chain of low rocks in the offing, all a little under water, which may very possibly have been built upon in former days. The modern town or village is thinly scattered over the eastern part of what was formerly the island; the part next the sea is cultivated and bears good tobacco. The little harbour of Tyre lies on the north side of the peninsula and is nearly enclosed by a wall, the ruins of which are standing here and there. It would not now vie with the harbours of any of our fishing-villages, we counted some ten open-decked fishing-boats riding in it; but larger vessels cannot enter. The island was originally nearly half a mile distant from the shore; but across the intervening gulf Alexander, with amazing labour, formed his famous causeway, using for that purpose the stones and the very dust of ancient Tyre, scraped from off her. During the lapse of ages, the sea has washed up the sand on each side of this causeway, so that it is now a broad neck of land with fine sandy bays on each side. Ruins of ancient walls and foundations are still to be found in different parts of it. The houses, or rather cottages of Tyre, are built of good stone, with many

---

1. Eusebius, bishop of Samosata from 361, was a champion of the expression given to the Christian faith in the Nicene Creed.

palm trees, vines, figs, and pomegranates interspersed, giving the place
a cool and pleasing aspect. The modern name is Sour and there are about
1,500 inhabitants. There is some probability that the sea has advanced
upon this coast, and materially affected the size of the ancient island;
and if this be the case, we can have no difficulty in understanding how
the almost impregnable fortifications, of which history speaks, and the
palaces of the Tyrian merchants, were once crowded together upon this
interesting spot.

In order to understand fully the accomplishment of the divine
predictions against Tyre, it must be borne in mind that though the island
may have been very soon occupied as a stronghold, yet the most ancient
city, called by historians Palæ Tyrus, or Old Tyre, was situated on the
mainland, at a distance of nearly four miles south from the island. This
was 'the strong city Tyre' mentioned in the days of Joshua (Joshua
19:20), and the 'stronghold of Tyre' in the time of David (2 Samuel
24:7). As many travellers have done before us, we stood upon the ruins
of insular Tyre, and stretching our eye round the bay to the south,
conjectured where old Tyre may have been situated; and afterwards on
our return from Acre we traversed the coast and sought with the utmost
care for any remains of the strong city, but in vain. The word of the Lord
has come to pass, 'Though thou be sought for, yet thou shalt never be
found again, saith the Lord God' (Ezekiel 26:21).

About eight miles south from the island, a high rocky promontory
appears, forming a precipice over the sea, called Cape Blanco, from the
whiteness of the rock. The road passes over it, and there are singular
steps cut in the rock, supposed to be the Tyrian Ladder of the ancients.
Now, between Cape Blanco and the island, there is a spacious bay, with
one or two lesser curves. It occurred to us that, in the days of Tyre's
glory, when they took 'cedars from Lebanon to make masts for her, and
oaks from Bashan to make oars, and fine linen from Egypt to be spread
forth as her sails', when 'all the ships of the sea with their mariners were
in her to occupy her merchandise', this vast bay may have afforded her
an anchorage, where the forests of masts would present to the eye a
spectacle not less noble than any which can be seen in the harbour of the
very greatest of our commercial cities, and this in a region of surpassing
beauty.

Indeed, it is not unlikely that Old Tyre may have extended as far as
the precipitous summit of Cape Blanco, from which its name Tsour, that
is, 'a rock', may have been derived. Tyre on the Island may have been

at first, as Jowett has conjectured, the harbour of the original city, connected with it, as the remaining aqueducts testify, although four miles distant from its gates. If there be truth in this conjecture, it would at once explain the vast circumference of the city as described by Pliny, and would illustrate the glowing description of Ezekiel when he describes how 'her builders had perfected her beauty'.

Keeping both the Tyres in view, we could not fail to notice with what awful accuracy the word of God has been verified concerning them. The word of Amos has been fulfilled, 'For three transgressions of Tyrus, and for four, I will not turn away the punishment thereof. But I will send a fire on the wall of Tyrus which shall destroy the palaces thereof' (Amos 1:9,10). Not a vestige of her palaces remains, except the prostrate granite pillars over which the wave is ever beating. We remembered, too, as we looked along the bare shore, the minute prediction of Ezekiel, 'They shall destroy the walls of Tyrus, and break down her towers: I will also scrape her dust from her, and make her like the top of a rock. It shall be a place for the spreading of nets in the midst of the sea; for I have spoken it, saith the Lord God' (Ezekiel 26:4). Alexander the Great seems actually to have scraped away the very rubbish as well as the stones of Old Tyre to construct his causeway; and now the bare rocks along the shore, on some part of which the ancient city must have stood, are literally a place for the spreading of nets. The first man we met in the gate of Tyre was a fisherman carrying a load of fish, and the fishing-boats in the harbour we have already mentioned. If, indeed, the sea has made an advance upon the coast, then the very rocks where Old Tyre stood may be now under water, and the nets of the fisherman may thus also be literally spread over them. And this, also, would give new meaning to the expression, 'Thou shalt be broken by the seas in the depths of the waters' (Ezekiel 27:34); although at the same time the ruin of her fleets and merchant-ships will completely satisfy the terms of this prophecy. How interesting, too, is the very uncertainty that hangs over the true situation of ancient Tyre, some placing it on the shore, some at Ras-el-Ain farther inward, and some on a rocky eminence called Marshuk, to the north-east – all combining to shew how awfully the thrice-repeated curse has been fulfilled, 'I will make thee a terror and thou shalt be no more' (Ezekiel 26:21; 27:36; 28:19); and how true to the letter, 'Though thou be sought for, yet shalt thou never be found again.'

Looking to the bare rock of the island, or to the village that stands upon it, without a remnant of the triple wall and fortress once deemed impregnable, a traveller is ready to ask, in the very words of the prophet, 'Is this your joyous city, whose antiquity is of ancient days?' 'Who hath taken this counsel against Tyre, the crowning city, whose merchants are princes, whose traffickers are the honourable of the earth? The Lord of hosts hath purposed it, to stain the pride of all glory, and to bring into contempt all the honourable of the earth.' 'He stretched out his hand over the sea: he shook the kingdoms; the Lord hath given a commandment against the merchant-city, to destroy the strongholds thereof' (Isaiah 23:7, 8, 9, 11). But a brighter day is yet to dawn upon Tyre, when it shall be a city of holiness. For the same sure word of prophecy declares, that though after its ruin it should return to its sinful gains, yet a time is coming, when 'her merchandise and her hire shall be holiness to the Lord, it shall not be treasured nor laid up; for her merchandise shall be for them that dwell before the Lord, to eat sufficiently, and for durable clothing' (Isaiah 23:18). May not this allude to some event connected with Israel's restoration; for it is they who shall be in a peculiar manner the people 'that dwell before the Lord'? Perhaps as Hiram supplied cedars and other materials for the Temple in the days of Solomon, Tyre may again send her supplies to assist Israel on their return home.

The first Jew whom we met in Tyre was from Algiers. He had there acquired a little knowledge of French from the army, and told us that there were about a hundred Jews in Tyre; of these, five families had come recently from Algiers, and the rest from Saphet on occasion of their dwellings being destroyed by the earthquake on 1st January, 1837. He led us to the synagogue, one of the poorest and most wretched we had yet seen, having a solitary lamp burning beside the ark. Several Jews gathered round us. The Hebrew Bible was produced and we soon entered into conversation on divine things. One interesting young Jew seemed a little impressed and often carried his difficulties to the elder ones, seeking from them an answer. Under a verandah, outside the synagogue, an elderly Jew sat on the ground teaching some children. Mr Bonar tried the children with a few simple sentences in Hebrew, and they in turn asked him in Hebrew the names of several Scripture characters, putting such questions as 'who was the father of Moses?'

We next visited the Rabbi of Tyre at his own house. He seemed a sagacious-looking man, kind and polite in his manners. In discussing passages of Scripture, when Mr Calman pushed him hard, he invariably resorted to his commentators, taking down from a shelf some old thin folios. As we sat looking out at the open window upon the bright blue sea, we observed that 'the earth shall yet be full of the knowledge of the Lord, as the waters cover the sea'; upon which he made this interesting remark, that as there are many caverns, and inequalities of depths in the sea, and yet the surface of the water is all smooth and level; so shall it be then, people will still possess unequal capacities of knowledge and enjoyment, yet all will present one common appearance, because each will be filled up to his measure. He asserted that the purpose for which the Jews are now scattered over the world is to diffuse the knowledge of the true God; but was at a loss for a reply when we referred to Ezekiel 36:23, 'My great name, *which ye have profaned*, among the heathen.'

We now retired to the khan, and spread our carpets for a little repose before leaving Tyre, but our visit excited curiosity throughout the Jewish community, and many whom we had not seen before came to visit us. With our back to a pillar of the khan, and the Hebrew Bible in our hand, we maintained a broken conversation, often with half a dozen at a time, some going away, others coming. One, as he departed, cried, 'Come away from that Epicurus'. Some were a little angry, but most were kind and good-natured. We shewed that Isaiah 1:7 had been fulfilled before their eyes: 'Your country is desolate, your cities are burned with fire, your land strangers devour it in your presence'; and, therefore, verse 3 must be true of themselves: 'Israel doth not know, my people doth not consider.' We proved to them from Zechariah 13:1 that, as a nation, they did not at present know the way of forgiveness; for God says, '*In that day*, there shall be a fountain opened to the house of David, and to the inhabitants of Jerusalem, for sin and for uncleanness.' Several of them remained with us to the very last, conducted us through the narrow bazaar, and parted with us outside the gate, with expressions of kindness.

As we moved slowly round the fine sandy bay on the southern side of the peninsula, we remembered the solemn scene which that very shore had witnessed, when the Apostle Paul visited Tyre on his way to Jerusalem, as recorded by Luke. The Tyrian disciples 'All brought us on our way, with wives and children, till we were out of the city; and we kneeled down on the shore and prayed' (Acts 21:5).

Not far from the town, our mules stopped to drink at a well where the trough was of beautifully carved stone, and seemed to have been an old sarcophagus. We passed a small grove of fragrant lemon-trees, and then crossed an old aqueduct, with water running in it. Several of the gardens had watchtowers in them, in one of which we saw two men sleeping on a sort of loft. We soon began to ascend the heights which form the eastern background of the plain around Tyre, and often looked back to enjoy the magnificent view of the sea, the coast of Syro-Phenicia, and Tyre itself, with its rocks stretching south from the end of the peninsula.

Reaching the summit of the ridge, our road lay south-east as it penetrated into the interior of the country. In crossing the hills, we noticed in them another capability of this wonderful land, distinct from any we had seen in the southern parts. The sides, and even the summits, were sprinkled over with vigorous olive-trees. Some of these hills were no doubt 1,000 feet high, yet their tops were frequently crowned with groves of olives, shewing how fertile and how suitable for the cultivation of the olive this range must have been in former days. This was the more remarkable because we were now in the tribe of Asher; and the prophetic blessing pronounced upon Asher, was, '*Let him dip his foot in oil*' (Deuteronomy 33:24). His hills appear to be suitable neither for the vine nor for pasture, but for the olive, whose berries yield the finest oil. To this also, as well as to Asher's luxuriant plains in the south of his possession, the words of Jacob may refer, 'out of Asher *his bread shall be fat*' (Genesis 49:20). Nor is it unlikely that the promise, '*Thy shoes shall be iron and brass*' (Deuteronomy 33:25) may have a reference to these hills that were his defence against his hostile neighbours in Tyre and Sidon. In days of quietness and peace, his hills yield him oil in which he dips his feet; in war, his hills are to him as shoes of iron and brass.

In an hour from the ancient monument, we came to a kind of basin in the bosom of the mountains – a gentle hollow, with a thriving village in the midst. It was surrounded with luxuriant cornfields and verdant olives, and the villagers were all busy at the corn-floor. We asked an old peasant the name of the village, he said, 'Kana'. The name thrilled to our heart, so strange and pleasant was it to hear a Scripture name from the lips of an ignorant Moslem. It is every way probable that this is the Kanah of Asher mentioned in Joshua (Joshua 19:28). Near it are some caves or tombs, and there is a heap of stones on a hill to the right which caught our attention, but which we had no time to investigate. The situation of the village is retired and peaceful. In the last cottage we passed, some Jews, who seemed to be travellers, were much surprised when we saluted them in the holy tongue.

Leaving Kana, we proceeded up a steep ascent, on the summit of which was another village called Sedeekin, that is 'The faithful', so called by the Moslems because none but Mahometans dwell there. It is beautifully situated in the midst of fields of tobacco and fig-trees in abundance. It may be the site of some one of the towns named along with Kanah, 'Hebron, and Rehob, and Hammon'. The inhabitants were all in the field reaping their harvest. The climate on the high hills of Galilee we found to be delicious. The hills around, as far as we could see, were covered with a carpet of green, not of grass, however, but brushwood and dwarf-trees. Crossing over a low hill, and descending a very steep declivity, we came to the entrance of a deeply shady glen, called Wady Deeb, that is, 'Valley of the Wolf', no doubt from its being a favourite resort of that animal. Here we met a Moslem returning from cutting wood with his axe in his hand, while his wife followed carrying the bundle of wood upon her head, an example of the degradation to which women are subjected in eastern countries. The steep hills on each side of the pass rose to the height of 800 feet and were finely clothed with tall shrubs and trees. The road winds through by a footpath, which in winter is probably the bed of a torrent. Nothing could exceed the romantic beauty of this ravine. Every kind of tree and shrub seemed to shew themselves in turn, the beech-tree and valonea oak, the wild rose, the broom, and many others; while the white flowers of the woodbine and clematis clustered like garlands round the stronger shrubs, loading the evening air with their fragrance. We pressed on for an hour and a half till we reached a large natural cave on the left side of the valley where the pathway became very steep and rocky; yet it was wonderful to see how the little Syrian horses clambered up.

The darkness had now settled down upon us, and the fireflies were sparkling through the air in all directions. Reaching the summit, we discerned our nearness to a village by the scent of the straw, peculiar to Arab villages. The name of it was Jettar, and we were directed to the khan, an enclosure at the end of the village, which had a roof and one wall made of the boughs of trees. Under these we spread our mats, thankful to find a place of rest. The villagers were very kind, and so many of them came to visit us that our lodging was full of strangers till a late hour. About forty families live here, all of them Mahometans. Fifteen houses were destroyed by an earthquake in 1837. There is a large pond of water beside the village, and to this herds of leopards and wolves come to drink at night. Wolves and wild boars abound in the valley we had passed through; and gazelles are numerous. The villagers told us, that near this place are the ruins of several old towns, some of them extensive. They mentioned the names of three, Mirapheh, Mar-Yamin, and Medinatnahash ('city of brass'). The name Jettar, and the striking features of the valley Wady Deeb, up which we had passed, suggested to us that this may be the valley of Jephthah-el mentioned in Joshua (Joshua 19:27). It is above five hours distant from Tyre.

July 11
We were awakened early in the morning by the sound of horses' feet, and starting up saw a soldier, armed with gun and pistols, looking in upon us. Along with him were two Jews from Tyre, whom we immediately recognised as friends. One told us in his broken French that a messenger had brought word to Tyre of a Jew having been shot by the Bedouins two hours farther on the road to Saphet, and they were now going to find his body. Whether this was a true report or not we never ascertained, but it made us feel that our way through Galilee was not unattended with danger. The villagers, too, seemed alarmed; they were going to a market at some distance, somewhere in the direction of Saphet, and were very anxious that we should accompany them, either out of kindness to us or through desire of protection to themselves. We thought it better, however, to journey forward by ourselves, as we could not have reached Saphet by the proposed bypath the same night. Their advice reminded us of the days of Shamgar, 'when travellers walked through byways' (Judges 5:6). We read Isaiah 26 in our morning worship under a tree at a little distance from the village, and rode on our way through the tribe of Naphtali.

On a hill nearby were the ruins of a small fortress, and caves that may have been used as sepulchres. The Arabs called the place Bedundah. In a little while a deep valley came in sight lying beneath us, with a fine pass winding to the east, the hills beyond appearing wooded to the top. The mouth of the pass was shut up by a conical hill, completely wooded. In winding round this hill, we came upon a well and a watering trough where several shepherds had gathered their flocks together to drink. The quietness of the valley contrasted with the rumours of danger from the Bedouins, reminded us of Judges, 'They that are delivered from the noise of archers in the places of drawing water' (Judges 5:11). For some time hill and valley alternately presented themselves, covered with shrubs and trees. At one place, a large snake glided away from us among the shrubs, and once or twice an owl was seen perching on the trees

(Psalm 102:6, 'An owl of the desert places').

Leaving this beautiful plain, our way led us through mountain passes of a similar character to those already described, only here we observed the remains of ancient terraces, and remarked that the natural rock is frequently in the form of terraces, as in the hills of Judah. About midday we came in sight of a village on the summit of a rocky hill, to which we gladly turned aside to enjoy a little rest. Throughout all the morning we had expected to fall in either with the Bedouins, or our Jewish friends; and many a lurking-place suitable to the designs of the robber we passed, but no evil came near us. The name of the village to which we had come was Kefr-birhom; its inhabitants, about 200 in number, are all Maronite Christians. They received us very kindly, and introduced us to their priest, a gentle and venerable-looking man. His dress was a dark caftan or cloak, and a high black turban. He pressed us much to take up our lodging in an upper room which he pointed out to us; but we preferred the deep shade of a spreading fig-tree. He sat down with us, and many of the villagers at a respectful distance; and, through Mr Calman, we had some discussion on points of doctrine. One of us, wandering through the village, entered into the cottage of a Maronite, and sitting down read a little of his Syriac prayer-book, to the infinite delight of the poor man, who thereupon welcomed the unknown traveller as a brother. Soon after, when we were all reclining under the fig-tree, this man came with a present of four eggs; and on being presented with a pencil-case, ran back to his house and brought us two pigeons. Contrasting this gift with the present of a sheep which the Governor of Hebron brought us, we saw in a very clear manner the considerateness of the command in Leviticus 1:10,14, where the rich man was expected to bring a sheep for an offering, and the poor man two young pigeons (compare Luke 2:24; Leviticus 12:8). While seated under the fig-tree, several Jews arrived on their way from Tyre to Saphet, among whom we recognised the young man who had been a little impressed in the synagogue. He soon came and spoke with us, and taking up the Hebrew Bible, he put his finger on Joshua 2:1 where Joshua is described as sending out two spies to view the land, 'Now (said he) you are these spies.'

We found in the village traces of former greatness, especially in the north-east, where are considerable remains. The principal ruin is that of an ancient synagogue. The doorway and two windows (one on each side of the door) was still in good preservation, but half sunk in the rubbish.

The upper part of the door is ornamented with a fine wreath of vine leaves and bunches of grapes carved in the stone, and in beautiful preservation. The windows are also adorned with carved work; three columns are still standing, and several fragments lie scattered through the village. The Maronites and Jews both called it a Jewish synagogue and connected it with the name of Isaiah. We were told also that the Jews sometimes go there to pray. In a field about a quarter of a mile distant stands another doorway, said to be not so elegant, but bearing an inscription over it. We regretted much that our time did not permit us to visit it and endeavour to decypher the inscription.

In the afternoon we set out again, having the Jews in our train, and conversing with them by the way. A fine spreading mountain now came in sight, two hours distant on the right hand, commonly supposed to be Mount Naphtali, resembling Queensberry Hill in Dumfries-shire. There is a considerable plain around its base, which may be part of the plain of Zaanaim, where Heber the Kenite dwelt, and where Barak gathered his army (Judges 4:10,11). The hill would serve as a mark easily seen far off by 'all Zebulun and Naphtali', and so would render this spot the better suited for a rendezvous. The town at which they met was Kadesh, the birthplace of Barak, and also a City of Refuge. If Kadesh stood near this hill, it would be well fitted for a city of refuge, as the hill would point out its situation at a great distance to the fleeing manslayer, while the plain made his flight easy. In this respect it would resemble Sychem and Hebron, which were also cities of Refuge.

On the left hand, we passed, without seeing it, the village of Gish, supposed to be the site of Gischala, which Josephus says was mostly peopled with agriculturists, and near which (he says) was Kydessa, which may be the modern village Kadyta, a little to the south-east. Mr Calman had visited Gish immediately after the earthquake by which it was totally destroyed. In one place he mentioned that the rocks were torn asunder to a considerable breadth, and no one could tell the depth of the fissure. About half a mile farther on we turned off the road to the left to visit a singular pool called Birket-el Gish. It bears evident marks of having been at one time the crater of a volcano. It is of an oval form, and about 1,100 paces in circumference. This we ascertained by walking round as near to the edge as the sharp projecting rocks would allow. The rocks are all black, evidently composed of lava, and it is singular to notice that to the south and east the fields are covered with black stones of the same description, while there are none to the north and west. A considerable quantity of water was collected in it, and the flocks are driven down to the edge to drink. The neighbouring plain is called Sachel-el-Gish, or 'Plain of Gish'. The plain, the pool, and the village all bearing the same name, shew that it must have been a place of some importance.

Returning from this pool, we obtained our first glimpse of a small part of the Sea of Galilee, by looking past the shoulder of Mount Naphtali. Saphet also was full in sight, its snow-white houses perched on the summit of a lofty hill, gleaming under the rays of the setting sun. This is believed, though without any positive evidence, to be the 'city set on a hill' to which our Lord referred, and perhaps pointed, in his Sermon on the Mount; and certainly no place in all Palestine could better answer the description. We were not able to ascertain even from the Jews the name of any Scripture town situated there. The name Saphet may be derived from the capital of a pillar (1 Kings 7:41), alluding to the appearance of the town which surmounts the hill, very much in the way that a capital surmounts a pillar. Before coming to Saphet, we passed a village called Saccas, on a high rugged hill. Descending this hill, Mr Bonar's mule entangled its foot in a fissure of the rock, and rolled upon its side. Its rider was precipitated to the ground, without suffering any injury; but the poor animal's foot was sorely crushed, and the muleteer led it along, pouring out incessant lamentations, and often kissing it like a child.

After crossing several ravines, all running south toward the Sea of Galilee, we climbed the hill on which Saphet stands by a very steep path worn deep in the white limestone rock. Mr McCheyne rode up by the path, on the east side of the hill, and came upon ruins made by the earthquake, which on that side are very appalling. Arriving at the house of a Jew, he was kindly entertained, and requested by his host to tell the news of the war. Another Jew kindly guided him to the rest of our company. Mr Calman, being well acquainted with the place and with the Jewish inhabitants, soon obtained for us a comfortable lodging in the cottage of a German Jew, who willingly removed to make way for us. He lighted up the lamp filled with olive-oil, and we spread our mats upon the floor. We found all the Jews here living in a state of great alarm. The troops of the Pasha had been withdrawn, being engaged in the war, and the Bedouins were every day threatening an attack to plunder the town. Only four soldiers had been left to defend them, and these, along with ten Jews, used to patrol the town all night to give alarm in case of an assault. We observed how poorly clad most of the Jews seemed to be, and were told that they had buried under ground all their valuable clothes, their money, and other precious things. It was easy to read their deep anxiety in the very expression of their countenances: they were truly in the state foretold by Moses more than 3000 years ago. 'The Lord shall give thee a trembling heart, and failing of eyes, and sorrow of mind: and thy life shall hang in doubt before thee; and thou shalt fear day and night, and shalt have none assurance of thy life' (Deuteronomy 28:65,66). And all this in their own land!

The Jews wondered that we had travelled so safely when we did not even carry firearms. But 'the Lord had gone before us, and the God of Israel had been our rereward'. We felt deeply thankful for the mercies of this day, and slept quietly in our Jewish cottage, the loud cry of the jackals being the only sound to break the silence of the night.

July 12

The morning air was cool and delightful in this elevated region. The hill on which Saphet stands appears to be of great height, not inferior even to Tabor. The town is built upon two heights, of which the northern and upper is occupied almost entirely by the Jews, the lower by the Mohametans. On the highest point are the ruins of the castle. All its houses are built of a pure white limestone which gives them a dazzling appearance. The ruins of the town, caused by the earthquake 1st January 1837, are everywhere to be seen, and in some places are literally heaps upon heaps; for the town having been built on the slopes of the steep hill, one range of houses actually hung over the other, and hence, in the earthquake, the houses were cast one upon another. The Jews have rebuilt a great part of their quarter, out of veneration for the Holy City, but the Mahometan quarter is still an appalling ruin.

The situation of Saphet is singularly beautiful. Looking west from our cottage door, the noble mountain of Naphtali met the eye, verdant to the top, and the fine undulating plain stretching east and west at its base. Looking down the hill on which the town itself stands, we saw pleasant groves of olives, and vineyards supported by terraces, while footpaths and tracks in the white rock wind up in all directions, along which the country people were moving slowly with mules and camels, this day (Friday) being the market-day. Close to the town, in the north-west. is a village – a small suburb – called Ain Zeitoun, 'well of olives'. Farther off, in the same direction, is the village of Kadyta, and on a height nearly due west, Saccas. And upon the side of the hill of Naphtali, the white tombs of Marona are dimly visible – a highly venerated spot, because of the rabbis buried there.

Walking round to the southern brow on which the Mahometan quarter is built, we sat down among the tombs in full view of the Lake of Galilee – solemn, calm, and still – and meditated over the scenes that had been transacted there. Returning by the bazaar, we had an opportunity of witnessing the market which is held here weekly. All was bustle and noise, very like a market at home. The Bedouin Arab was there, fully armed, with his long firelock under his arm; for, though he is known to be a robber, yet he attends the market in peace, no one laying a hand upon him, in wonderful fulfilment of the prophecy, 'His hand will be against every man, and every man's hand against him, *and he shall dwell in the presence of all his brethren*' (Genesis 16:12). Here, too, were the Syrian women wearing the nose-jewel alluded to by Isaiah (Isaiah 3:21), fastened by a hole bored through the nostril, not so large or uncomely as we had expected. A much more unpleasant yet common custom is the staining of the chin and under the mouth with dots of henna. In many of the shops the only weights in the balance were smooth stones, which we learn from the book of Proverbs (Proverbs 11:1; 16:11; see the Hebrew) were also used in ancient days.

The custom of drying corn and other articles on the roofs of houses here appears to be as common as it was in the days of Rahab (Joshua 2:6). The houses in the streets have their flat roofs so connected that nothing could be easier or more natural in case of any alarm than to walk along the whole length of the street on the housetop, without coming down (Luke 17:31). Indeed, there are some yet remaining where the roofs of the lower row of houses form the pathway of the row above. This was very generally the case in Saphet before the earthquake, and in reference to it a well-known story is current among the inhabitants. A camel-driver passing along the street suddenly observed his camel sink down. It had been walking on the roof of a house, and the roof had given way. The owner of the house was filled with alarm and anger at seeing the animal descend into his apartment. He carried the case to the Cadi,[2] claiming damages for the broken roof of his house. But he was met by the camel-driver claiming damages from him for the injury his camel had sustained by the fall, owing to the roof not being kept in good repair. We did not hear the decision of the Cadi in this difficult case.

---

2. Cadi or qadi – a Muslim judge who interprets and administers Islamic law.

Towards evening, we clambered through a vineyard to the shapeless ruins of the castle, which surmounts the highest peak of the hill of Saphet, and commands the finest view of the Lake of Galilee. Here we disturbed several serpents of considerable size which darted out of sight at our approach, or glided down the slope. Large vultures also were hovering over our heads in great numbers.

We climbed up to the highest part of the untenanted walls, and sat down. Immediately below us was the Governor's house and the Mahometan quarter, and part of the hill clothed with fig and olive trees. Three ridges more intervene, and then the Lake of Galilee appears. It did not seem more than two miles off, though in reality four hours distant, so much does the clear atmosphere deceive the sight. The greater part of the lake was in view, nearly in the form of an oval – a deep blue expanse of calm, unruffled, silent waters. Through part of the middle of the lake, we could discern a streak like the track of a vessel that had lately cut the waters. This might possibly be caused by the current of the Jordan passing through it; but of this we were rather sceptical, for at other times we could not discover anything like this appearance. On the eastern side the mountains are lofty and bare, descending abruptly on the shore. We could not descry a single village or town on that side, although smoke was rising from one or two points. On the western side the hills are not so lofty nor so close upon the lake; but there is more variety. We remarked that there was no part of the margin which shewed anything like a plain except that part in the north-west, where a verdant plain extends apparently three or four miles along the shore, and seemed to be a mile or a mile and a half at its greatest breadth. We concluded at once that this must be the plain of Gennesareth, of which Josephus speaks in such glowing terms (*Wars*, III.10 §8), and the land of Gennesareth, so often mentioned in the Gospel narrative, where stood Capernaum, and other cities, whose very site is now unknown.

South of the plain, two rocky promontories run out into the lake. Over the nearest, a few buildings, dimly discernible, indicated the site of Tiberias; but a little farther a white building attracts the eye upon the shore. It is the hot baths of Tiberias. Over the second promontory a distant village is visible, probably Kerak, the ancient Tarichoea; and there the view of the lake is bounded. The whole extent of the lake may be about fifteen miles in length, and nine miles at the greatest breadth. The view of the hill country to the west and south-west of the lake is very beautiful. The heights of Huttin, commonly fixed on by tradition as the

Mount of Beatitudes, appear a little to the west of Tiberias. Over these the graceful top of Mount Tabor is seen, and beyond it the little Hermon, famous for its dews; and still farther, and apparently higher, the bleak mountains of Gilboa, on which David prayed that there might fall no dew nor rain (2 Samuel 1:21).

A view of the position of Tabor and Hermon from such a situation as that which we now occupied, shewed us how accurately they might be reckoned the *umbilicus terroe* – the central point of the land – and led us to infer that this is the true explanation of the manner in which they are referred to in the 89th Psalm: 'The north and the south thou hast created them; *Tabor and Hermon shall rejoice in thy name*' (Psalm 89:12). It is as if the Psalmist had said, North, south, and all that is between – or, in other words, the whole land from north to south, to its very centre and throughout its very marrow – shall rejoice in thy name.

We could imagine the days when Jesus walked down by the side of that lake and preached to silent multitudes gathered round him. It seemed at that moment unspeakable condescension, that God in our nature should once have stood on some of these slopes and stretched out his hand to sinners as he spoke in the tone of heavenly love, 'Come unto me and I will give you rest!' And it was strangely solemn to be gazing upon rocks that echoed to his prayers by night, and desert places where he was alone with his Father: 'He departed again unto a mountain himself alone'; 'and his disciples went down unto the sea' (John 6:15,16). All sides of the lake are now comparatively bleak and dreary; yet they suit the stillness of the scene. Not a tree is to be seen on the mountains; and even the land of Gennesareth, so famous in the days of Josephus for the amazing variety and luxuriance of its trees and shrubs, is now only a wilderness of reeds and bushes. 'Behold your house is left unto you desolate!' (Matthew 23:33). The house remains, but it is desolate. The rocks and mountains around the sea continue unaltered; the water of the lake is as pure and as full as in ancient days; and yet the place is most desolate. Its cities are gone, and the vast population that once thronged its shores are now reduced to a few miserable inhabitants of mud-walled villages.

Returning from this solemn scene, we bent our steps toward the Jewish quarter. They reckon Saphet a peculiarly holy city because Simeon, author of the Zohar, and many other eminent rabbis are buried in its vicinity. We entered a synagogue, where several persons were reading the Talmud and the Commentators. A young man was reading a commentary on 1 Chronicles 29, where the dying words of David are recorded. This led us to speak of what a man needed when death arrived, and we came at length to the question, How can a sinner be righteous before God? We were speaking in a mixture of Hebrew and German. The young man was very earnest, but several gathered round and stopped the conversation by asking 'From what country do you come?' Before leaving, Mr Bonar read out of a German tract the story of Salmasius, who on his deathbed wished that he had devoted his life to the study of the Holy Scriptures. In another synagogue, a young man who spoke Hebrew and German conversed with us, and three old men joined us for a short time, but all of them looked suspiciously upon us, and soon went away. We learned in the course of the day that they had heard from some of Sir Moses Montefiore's attendants that we were come for the purpose of making them Christians, and had been warned to enter into no discussions.

In the evening toward sunset, we could observe the preparations going on in every Jewish dwelling for the Sabbath. The women brought out of the oven the bread they had baked, beautifully white wheaten bread, the first we had seen among the natives of Palestine. The houses were all set in order, the table arranged, and the couches spread; in every dwelling the Sabbath lamp was lighted, and a low murmur was heard, while the father of the family repeated the appointed benediction. 'Blessed art thou, O Lord, King of the World, who has sanctified us by thy commandments, and commanded us to light the Sabbath lamp'. Soon after, all hurried to the synagogue, to bring in the Sabbath there.

There are two synagogues of the Ashkenazim, and two of the Sephardim in Saphet; and six of those places for study called *Yishvioth*. We visited one of the former, and found it very neat and clean, beautifully lighted up with lamps of olive-oil. Several very venerable men were seated all round; more than half of the worshippers had beards verging to pure white, and grey hair flowing on their shoulders. It was indeed a new scene to us. In reading their prayers, nothing could exceed their vehemency. They read with all their might; then cried aloud like Baal's prophets on Mount Carmel; and from time to time, the tremendous voice of some aged Jew rose above all the rest in earnestness. The service was performed evidently as a work of special merit. One old man often stretched out his hand as he called on the Lord, and clenched his trembling fist in impassioned supplication. Some clapped their hands, others clasped both hands together, and wrung them as in an agony of distress, till they should obtain their request. A few beat upon their breasts. One man, trembling with age, seemed to fix on the word 'Adonai', and repeated it with every variety of intonation, till he exhausted his voice. All of them, old and young, moved the body backward and forward, rocking to and fro, and bending toward the ground. This indeed is an important part of worship in the estimation of strict Talmudists, because David says, *'All my bones shall say, Lord, who is like unto thee?'* (Psalm 35:10). When all was over, one young man remained behind prolonging his devotions, in great excitement. We at first thought that he was deranged, and was caricaturing the rest, but were assured that, on the contrary, he was a peculiarly devout man. Sometimes he struck the wall, and sometimes stamped with his feet; often he bent his whole body to the ground, crying aloud, 'Adonai, Is not Israel thy people?' in a reproachful tone, as if angry that God did not immediately answer. The whole service seemed embodying to the life the description given by Isaiah, 'Wherefore have we fasted, say they, and thou seest not? wherefore have we afflicted our souls, and thou takest no knowledge?' 'ye shall not fast as ye do this day, to make your voice to be heard on high' (Isaiah 58:3,4).

We never felt more deeply affected at the sight of Israel. It was the saddest and most solemn view of them that we had yet obtained – sincere, anxious, devout Jews 'going about to establish their own righteousness'. None seemed happy; even when all was over, none bore the cheerful look of men who had ground to believe that their prayers had been accepted. Many had the very look of misery, and almost of despair.

We had just time to look in upon two other synagogues before they broke up. The devotions in all seemed to be conducted in one spirit of vehement and intense excitement. Yet it is said that the Jews of Tiberias exceed them in the earnestness of their religious services. All the Ashkenazim here belong to the sect called 'Chasidim',[3] who are by far the most superstitious and pharisaical sect among the Jews.

---

[3] The Chasidim form a pietistic movement within Judaism which had its origin in 18th century Poland. It was a reaction to over-insistence on ritual observance of the law and as the movement developed shouting, singing, and dancing became notable marks of it. The Chasidic movement, though still in existence, was decimated by the large number of Jews killed during World War II.

On Saturday morning *(July 13)*, walking out a little way, we came to part of the hill where are some small vineyards, with vines trained on terraces, affording a specimen of former times. It is a surface of rock with a thin sprinkling of earth that has been thus cultivated. Frequently the rocky terraces are entirely concealed by the verdant vines which hang over them, and often we passed through rows of vines, where the road was covered from view by the spreading luxuriance of the branches. To such a fruitful and spreading vineyard, where the very roads were overspread by luxuriant boughs, Job referred when he said of the wicked's final ruin, 'he beholdeth not *the way of the vineyards*' (Job 24:18).

We had planned a journey to explore the upper end of the Lake of Galilee, and see if any marks could be found to decide the position of Bethsaida; but difficulties came in our way. Some assured us that the journey would occupy only two hours; others said that it would require seven, and that the Bedouins had taken some horses there a few days ago, so that we must be accompanied by a guard. The uncertainty as to distance determined us not to go, for we did not wish to risk breaking in upon the Sabbath-day. We accordingly resolved to visit Marona, whose white tomb was in sight, the burying-place of many illustrious Jews, and also a village named Jurmah, higher up the mountain, whither many Jews had fled from the present danger. Every year Jewish pilgrims visit the sepulchres of Marona, and after many prayers burn precious shawls dipped in oil in honour of the dead rabbis. This very year Sir Moses Montefiore had gone on a pilgrimage to it, the Jews of Saphet accompanying him in a body. They sung as they went, and clapped their hands in concert with the song. They prayed at the tombs and returned.

Mr Calman preferred remaining in Saphet, both in order to see some of his old Jewish friends, and not to give needless offence, which would have been done had they seen one of their former brethren travelling on the Jewish Sabbath. Descending from the hill of Saphet, we crossed a rocky wilderness and passed through a fine olive-grove. Here we met a large train of mules carrying merchandise on their way from Nablous to Damascus.

Soon after, we began to ascend Mount Naphtali, and in less than two hours from Saphet came to Marona. It must have been an ancient place, for there are the ruins of terraces; also many caves and excavated tombs, some of them large and very curious. But the most remarkable object is a beautiful gateway, like the one we saw at Kefr-birhom. The carving appeared to be after the same pattern. The stones are very large, and the whole space occupied by the edifice can be accurately traced by the large foundation-stones that are distinctly visible. A pillar said to belong to this building lay among the ruins in the village. Below this spot are situated the tombs of the holy men of the Jews, having a white-washed oratory built over them, and enclosed within walls. We entered by a narrow gate and found ourselves in a court, in the centre of which grew a spreading fig-tree. From this court is the entrance to the white oratory, a cool pleasant spot, having an ostrich-shell suspended from the roof. There is a desk with prayer-books for the use of Jewish pilgrims, among which we left one of our Hebrew tracts. The devout Jews have left their names scrawled over the walls. Beneath repose the ashes of Jewish saints, and the most distinguished of all, the author of Zohar, lies here. A little lower down the hill, we entered a large cave, having seven vaults hewn out in it, containing many places for dead bodies, all empty. At the entrance lay four singularly carved stones, probably intended for lids of the sarcophagi. Some of the Jews of the place were absurd enough to assert that this village, Marona, is the *Shimron-meron* of Joshua 12:20, and they called the channel of a small winter-torrent close by 'the waters of Megiddo'. They proved the former merely from the likeness in the name, and the latter from the circumstance of Kedesh, Megiddo, and Taanach, all occurring in the history of Barak's expedition against Sisera, and then occurring along with Shimron-meron in Joshua 12:20, 22. The village itself is poor and wretched, adorned by a solitary palm-tree. It belongs to the Maronite Christians, who have such respect for the chief man among the Jews there that they give full protection to all his brethren.

We now ascended an hour higher up the mountain to Jurmah. The road was wild and beautiful, and the atmosphere at this elevation pure and delightful. The myrtle-trees were in full blossom, and the whole way was lined with shrubs and evergreens, till we reached the village. It is situated upon a level brow of the hill just where the view opens out towards the Lake of Galilee. Here we had been directed to inquire for the house of Rabbi Israel. We found him sick and in bed, but his family and the other Jews of the place received us very kindly. About fifteen reside here, principally Russians, who had left Saphet on account of the unsettled state of the country. The table was spread with a clean white cloth; bread, cheese, milk, and a kind of spirit, were produced, and we were pressed to partake. We conversed in Hebrew and German, and before leaving had some conversation regarding the pardon of sin. We felt it deeply interesting to partake of Jewish hospitality in one of the villages of the land of Israel, and they seemed friendly and not at all offended by our words. From the door of the house, they pointed out Bet-jan, a village half an hour from this, in which several Jewish families had taken refuge; and told us of a village three hours farther up the mountain called Bukeah, where twenty Jews reside, and where they cultivate the ground like Fellahs. If this be true, it is the only instance we heard of in which the Jews till the ground in Palestine.

Descending the hill, we returned to Saphet in time to visit the synagogues of the Sephardim. On our way we met an old Jew, carrying his prayer-book in his hand, in the same manner as our old Scottish peasants carry their Bibles to church. O that Israel had the same light upon the Word of God that the Holy Spirit has granted to many of our peasants in Scotland!

The synagogues of the Sephardim are both within a small court, in which fig-trees are planted; and both are clean, white-washed, and well lighted up. Here we got into converse with the same interesting young Jew who had followed us from Tyre. When we were speaking on Psalm 32, the blessedness of being forgiven, he said, 'But I obtained forgiveness long ago, by taking four steps in this holy land'. And referring to Isaiah 53, he said, 'Yes, it applied to Messiah, who is now sitting at the gate of Rome among the poor and the sick' – a singular legend which exists in the Talmud, and is one of the ways by which the Jews evade the force of that remarkable prophecy. Whenever any entered into converse with us in the synagogue, they were forbidden by the frown and authority of elder Jews. At last they cut off all further debate by beginning the public prayers. The same young Jew afterwards meeting Mr McCheyne in the street, and observing a strong staff in his hand, requested him to give him a present of it. He made his request in Hebrew, 'Give me this staff, and if the Arabs come, I will smite them with it.' It was strange to hear this youth speaking the language of his fathers on their own mountains.

This evening, we heard that a party of Bedouins had come down upon the little village of Mijdel, on the border of the Lake of Galilee, and plundered the villagers of all their goods and cattle. This news spread fresh alarm through Saphet.

July 14

We spent a pleasant Lord's Day. We sat in the open air enjoying 'the shadow of a cloud' (Isaiah 25:5), and the cooling breeze that swept over the hill. In the forenoon, beneath the shade of an olive-grove, with Mount Naphtali full in view, we read together the Epistle to the Philippians, and worshipped. In the afternoon we joined again in social worship on the southern brow of the hill among the Mahometan tombs, with the lake of Galilee at our feet. While walking down the face of the hill, we came upon a cave where the Jews had thrown aside, from religious scruples, leaves of Hebrew Books, and many manuscripts written on parchment rolls, in which some defect had been found. This cave was amidst the flat gravestones that whiten that part of the hill. On the tombs, few of the inscriptions were interesting. Almost all ran in the same terms, beginning generally with the common formula, 'Here is buried'; and then the individual's name and character, 'A man perfect and upright.' One quaint inscription quoted the words of the prophet Habakkuk, and applied them to a dead rabbi, as one whom even the inanimate objects would lament, 'For the stone shall cry out of the wall; and the beam out of the timber shall answer it' (Habakkuk 2:11).

In returning to our dwelling in the afternoon, a Jew constrained Mr Calman to go into his house. It turned out that the man was intoxicated, and that he was a Russian who had become a Jew. Such cases of apostasy on the part of professing Christians sometimes occur. Mr Calman knew two others who had become Jews in a similar manner.

It was here that we first observed the *Eruv*, a string stretched from house to house across a street, or fastened upon tall poles. The string is intended to *represent a wall*, and thus by a ridiculous fiction the Jews are enabled to fulfil the precept of the Talmud, that no one shall carry a burden on the Sabbath-day, not even a prayer-book or a handkerchief, or a piece of money, except it be within a walled place. How applicable still are the words of Jesus, 'In vain do they worship me, teaching for doctrines the commandments of men' (Matthew 15:9).

In the evening, our servant Antonio, a simple kind-hearted lad, read with us in the Italian Bible. He was much struck with Christ's words on the cross, *'Dio mio, Dio mio, perche m'hai lasciato'*, 'My God, my God, why hast thou forsaken me?' He had for several nights, at the end of the day's journey, sat down alone to read a little. Mr Calman began to address the muleteers, but one of them, when he heard how the Sabbath ought to be sanctified, said, 'He did not like that, for it was the only day he had for *fantasies*', that is, amusements.

Thus our last evening in Saphet came to a close. We could not help desiring that the time would come when our beloved Church should be permitted to establish a Mission here. When the Deputation was unbroken, we had often spoken together upon the subject, and had always turned toward this spot as probably the most desirable situation in Palestine for a Mission to Israel; and now that we had visited it, our convictions were greatly strengthened. The climate of Saphet is very delightful even in the heat of summer. The thermometer immediately before dawn stood at 58° F.; at 8 o'clock, 64°; at noon, 76° in the shade. The mountain air is pure, and the hills are finely exposed to every breeze that sweeps by. A mission established in Galilee would have this great advantage, that the headquarters might be at Saphet in summer, where the cool atmosphere would enable the missionary to labour without injury to health, and at Tiberias in winter, where the cold is scarcely felt. There is no missionary at present resident in either. The missionaries at Jerusalem visit both places occasionally, but by no means frequently. The Jews of Saphet have intimate communication with those of Jerusalem, and of the coast, so that all the motions of our English brethren at Jerusalem, and even our movements as we travelled through the land, were well known to them. They are also quite accessible to the efforts of a kind and judicious missionary, though many of them were shy to us, because they had been warned from an influential quarter to have no dealings with us. Still the Sephardim were quite willing to hear; and all were friendly. In the village, where no external influence had been used, they were kind and attentive. They here have little or no employment, and have therefore abundant leisure to read and discuss. They are also in deep affliction, 'finding no ease, neither has the sole of their foot rest', a state of mind more favourable than carnal ease for affording opportunity to press upon them the truths of the gospel.

If it were thought advisable to engage converts in agricultural pursuits, it would be much more easily accomplished here than in any other part of the land. They might settle in a village among the mountains, and till the ground, or train the vine, like the Jews at Bukeah of whom we heard. The Jews both of Saphet and Tiberias are most interesting, from the very circumstance of their extravagant devotion and bigotry. They have a peculiar love for these two places, being two of their four holy cities, and many of their saints being buried near. They say that Jeremiah hid the ark somewhere in the hill of Saphet, and that

Messiah will come first in Galilee. This notion is probably derived from Isaiah, 'Galilee of the nations, the people that walked in darkness have seen a great light' (Isaiah 9:1,2). That remarkable prophecy was fulfilled when our Lord Jesus, the great light of the world, came and dwelt beside the lake of Galilee (Matthew 4:13); and who can tell whether He may not choose the same favoured spot to make light spring up again on them who sit in the region and shadow of death? If the Spirit of God were poured down upon Saphet, it would become a city that might shine over the whole Jewish world. 'A city set on a hill cannot be hid.' Such were our feelings upon the spot in 1839. The blast of war has passed over the country since then, and the reins of government of Syria have been wrenched from the hand of Mehemet Ali and transferred to the feeble grasp of the Sultan. At present (1842), the country is said to be so unsettled, that no missionary would be safe in Saphet or anywhere in the interior of Galilee. But if tranquillity was restored, the desirableness of the place as a missionary station would be as great as ever.

July 15

We were up before the sun and by six o'clock took leave of our Jewish host and his family. Many Jews saluted us as we passed through the town. We proceeded south, with the Lake of Galilee fully in view, and descended into a deep valley, with a remarkable range of high and precipitous rocks, composed of reddish sandstone, on the left hand. In the bottom was a fresh stream of running water, issuing from a copious well, the oleander blossoming all around. The name of the valley was called Wady Hukkok. It may be the spot mentioned in Joshua, 'The border of Naphtali went out to Hukkok, and reached to Zebulun on the south side' (Joshua 19:34). The name has evidently been given in reference to its steep precipitous sides. It seems probable that the border of Naphtali ended at this point.

Descending still farther south, we observed on the right a singular rock of considerable height, in which were many caverns, and one part of which seemed to indicate excavations made by art, capable of containing a large number of men. We did not ascertain the name of this place, but afterwards conjectured that it might be the site of Jotapata, the city of Josephus, for it answers well to the description of that fortress given by him *(Wars, 3:7)*. 'Jotapata is almost wholly a precipice, abruptly enclosed all round on the other sides with immense valleys, whose depth wearies the eye of the beholder, and affording an access only on its northern side'. The caves of Arbela (supposed to be the Betharbel of Hosea 10:14) in the valley of Doves, south-west of the plain of Gennesareth, appear, from the descriptions of travellers, to be very similar.

Leaving this spot on our left, we crossed over a pleasant hill to the south-east and came down into the fertile Plain of Gennesareth, near a fountain called 'Ain-el-Tin', 'the fig-tree fountain', supposed by some to be 'the fountain of Capernaum' mentioned by Josephus. We did not search out the ruins of the city, but there were pointed out to us heaps among the luxuriant bushes of the plain, which some have thought to be the remains of Capernaum. The land of Gennesareth is a beautiful little plain, extending along the shore nearly four miles, and about two miles from the lake to the foot of the hills at the broadest part. It is in the shape of a bow and string at full stretch, and there is a gentle slope from the hills to the water's edge all round. It seems highly probable that part of the hills which enclose it may have been included in the territory of Gennesareth in the days of its splendour. Gardens and orchards could not find a better soil than these declivities, and it must have been on the different steps of this amphitheatre that the variety of trees yielding the fruits of different seasons found each its appropriate climate, as described by Josephus.

Moving on southward we crossed a fine stream flowing through the plain, the same which we had seen gushing from its fountain among the hills below Saphet. Its banks were adorned with the oleander and other flowers. A fine flock of goats were watering here, and a rich crop of dhura was springing green and beautiful. The reeds and thistles were growing to an amazing height beside the water. Soon after, we crossed another stream from the mountains, full and rapid. On the left bank upon the height, there were the remains of an ancient tower, in no way interesting, and the name of which we could not learn. In the middle of the stream stood a ruined mill. Many tortoises were seen dropping into the water as we approached. The plain opens out considerably, affording spots of pasturage where we observed several Bedouins feeding their horses; but still there was a vast profusion of reeds and shrubs and thorny plants, the most common being the tree called *nabok* by the Arabs. In almost an hour from Ain-el-Tin we came to Mijdel at the southern extremity of the plain.

Such is the present condition of the Land of Gennesareth – once a garden of princes, now a wilderness. We have seen that the remains of Capernaum, which is called the Saviour's *own city* (Matthew 11:1), are scarcely to be found; and the traces of Chorazin and Bethsaida are still more doubtful. There seems every probability that they were also within the limits of this little plain, but where, no one can tell. It seems evident that there were two towns called Bethsaida, on opposite sides of the Sea of Galilee. One was the town of Philip, Andrew, and Peter (John 1:44), associated with Chorazin and Capernaum (Matthew 21:20-24), and belonging to the land of Gennesareth (Mark 6:45,53). This town was clearly on the west side of the sea. The other is associated with the towns of Caesarea Philippi (Mark 8:13,22,27), and with the desert place where Christ fed the five thousand (Luke 9:10). It was on the east side of Jordan, probably an hour north of the lake, where the ruins of a town on a hill still remain. The solemn 'woe' pronounced by the Lord Jesus on these three cities, in whose streets He so often spoke the words of eternal life, has fallen with silent but exterminating power. It is more tolerable for Tyre and Sidon than for them. 'And thou, Capernaum, which was exalted to heaven, art brought down to hell' (Matthew 11:20-24). He took out his believing remnant from the midst of them (as he took Lot out of Sodom), Peter, Andrew, and Philip, three worthies from Bethsaida – and three from Capernaum, the nobleman, the centurion, and Jairus; and then swept the unbelieving cities away with the besom of destruction. An awful voice rises from these ruined heaps of Gennesareth, warning the cities of our favoured land that a despised Gospel will bring them as low as Capernaum; 'He that believeth not shall be damned.'

It was in Capernaum that Jesus healed so many upon one Saturday evening, when the Jewish Sabbath was over and the cooling breeze of sunset was favourable to the journey of the sick (Mark 1:32-35). We could imagine them coming, some up the side of the lake, others from its northern towns, or down the valley of Doves from the interior of Galilee, till all meet in this very plain, where they hear that Jesus is in the city, and forthwith pour in to find him. He receives them, heals many that were sick of diverse diseases, and casts out many devils; for 'he did most of his mighty works' there. And being left alone, 'he rose a great while before day, and went out and departed into a solitary place', wandering up the valley of Doves on the west, or the deep ravines of Saphet on the north, and there prayed till Simon Peter and a multitude of anxious souls found him out among the rocks and said unto him, 'All men seek for thee' (Mark 1:37).

We found the small village of Mijdel[4] quite deserted. We had already

---

[4] The current spelling is Migdal.

met in the village several poor plundered peasants on their way to Saphet, with all that remained of their property. We examined at leisure their wretched mud-huts; the habitation of man and beast seemed to have been not only under one roof, but sometimes in the same apartment, separated merely by a slender partition. Their little gardens were full of cusas and cucumbers and other thriving vegetables. It is not unlikely that this village occupies the site of Migdal-el mentioned by Joshua as one of the towns of Naphtali (Joshua 19:38); and is also generally believed to be the site of the Magdala of the New Testament (Matthew 15:39), the town from which Mary Magdalene got her name. But this latter supposition is doubtful, for there seems to have been another place of the same name on the eastern side; and the name which signifies 'a tower' was not an uncommon one in Palestine. We sat down to rest under a shady nabbok-tree, and then wandered to the edge of the lake through oleanders and reeds. Many curious insects people the leaves of these shrubs; one species especially abounded, shaped like a frog, and green as the leaves on which they sat. We washed our hands and faces in the soft water, and gathered many shells from the beach as memorials of the spot.

From this point of view is to be seen the whole of the upper margin of the lake, which appears like a semicircle. We could easily trace the point where the Jordan enters, by the opening of the hills. The eastern mountains in the region of Bashan appeared still more steep and lofty. The ridge of Hermon on the north, sprinkled with snow, formed the grandest object in sight. There was deep serenity and calm and a bright sun playing upon the waters. How often Jesus looked on this scene, and walked by the side of this lake! We could *feel* the reason why, when harassed and vexed by the persecution of enemies, 'Jesus withdrew himself with his disciples *to the sea*' (Mark 3:7). The rabbins spoke more truth than they intended when they said, 'God loved that sea beyond all other seas!'

From Mijdel, the margin of the lake takes a turn to the south-east, and as the hills approach close to the shore, the pathway is often a considerable height above the water. Sometimes a wady descends from the hills, and the shore forms a gently sloping cove, with a pebbly beach, and then, again, becomes abrupt. It was probably on one of these pebbly spots that Jesus was walking, when the people gathered round him, till the pressure of eager listeners was so great, that he had to enter into a ship, from which he spoke the parable of the sower, 'and the whole multitude stood on the shore' (Matthew 13:1, 2). And perhaps it was during a solitary walk round some of these retired coves that he came on James and John with their father and servants mending their nets by the shore (Mark 1:19).

The largest of these open spaces running up toward the hills was cultivated and seemed very fruitful, and we noticed on the shore a large circular well enclosed by walls that were much dilapidated. The pathway ascends the promontory beyond this, and now the south part of the lake came fully in view, with the dark walls and towers of Tiberias at our feet. The hills of Bashan on the opposite side appeared a steep unbroken wall, descending into the lake, and giving a shade of deeper blue to the waters beneath. We could not distinguish a single tree on the opposite hills, and on this side very few. We passed a single fig-tree, the only fruit-tree we saw till we came in sight of the few palms that adorn Tiberias. In approaching Tiberias, the eye rests on the ruins of towers and walls; and as the greater part of the stones are black like lava, the place wears a dismal and melancholy appearance. The wall, which nearly surrounds the town, has been at one time massy and solid; but the town and much of its walls was ruined by the same earthquake which overwhelmed Saphet, and has never been properly rebuilt. They call the town Taberiah, by a corruption of its ancient name.

We intended to take up our quarters in the old church of St Peter, a relic of the earliest ages of Christianity, but soon found that we could enjoy more cleanliness and coolness by pitching our tent between it and the lake, our cords almost dipping in the water. In passing through the town, our compassion was excited by observing the wretched booths in which most of the people live. Many of them were nothing better than boughs of trees plastered over with mud, and their common fuel was the dung of horses and cattle, such as we had seen used in Saphet.

We walked over several ruined arches in our way to the Jewish quarter. Here we came first among the Ashkenazim, Germans and Russians, with their black broad-brimmed hats, or large fur-caps, and soiled black Polish gowns, of all dresses the most unsuitable for such a climate. Tiberias (as mentioned before) is one of the four cities which the Jews account peculiarly holy. In it are three synagogues of the Ashkenazim and two of the Sephardim, besides several reading-rooms – very clean and airy buildings, especially those of the Sephardim. The first synagogue which we entered was one belonging to the Ashkenazim in which were seated three old men, with beards white as snow, one nearly deaf, and all nearly blind, yet poring over volumes of the Talmud. It was truly a sight fitted to move in us the feelings of our Lord when in Galilee he saw the multitude 'as sheep without a shepherd'. No sooner did we begin to speak with them than they were warned by a young Jew pressing his finger on their arm, and were immediately silent. They seemed lost in studying the Hebrew page, and soon one and another rose and left the place. The veil is upon their hearts while they are at the very brink of eternity! This synagogue was cool and pleasant, with a good many Hebrew books in it. In another synagogue, we found a good number of younger Jews sitting, who at first had some freedom in conversing, but, being also warned, turned more shy. When we were here, a respectable Jew named Haiim came in and suddenly recognised Mr Calman. He was an amiable, intelligent man, possessed of a little money, and practising as a physician. On a former visit, Mr C[alman] and Mr Nicolayson had met with much kindness from him, and had left with him a Hebrew New Testament. When he recognised Mr Calman, he started, and did not speak very freely, for a reason which he afterwards explained. But before leaving us, he quietly invited us to come to his house, which we promised to do.

We then visited a synagogue of the Sephardim, from whom we experienced a much kinder reception. We found an old Jew seated on the ground, with twenty children whom he was teaching to read Lamentations 1, with proper intonation of voice. Several Jews gathered round us, and with them we had an interesting discussion for about an hour. It began by the teacher putting questions to us as to our knowledge of Hebrew. He and Mr Calman carried on the conversation in Arabic. Meanwhile, the Jewish boys gathered round Mr Bonar and read part of Lamentations 1, translating it into Arabic as they went on. They also amused themselves by putting many questions to him in Hebrew. A group of young men stood with Mr McCheyne at the door. He spoke to them regarding Israel's ignorance of the fountain of forgiveness, as proved from Zechariah 13:1. They soon brought two of their rabbis, really venerable-looking men, and asked them to answer the questions that had been put. The rabbis were very friendly, but not liking the discussion soon went away.

On the opposite side of the court, they conducted us to one of the best of their *Yishvioth*, divided into three apartments, in which was a large collection of Hebrew books. It was pleasant to look out upon the blue waters of the lake immediately under the windows. They told us that there were at that time only 600 Jews in Tiberias, owing to the calamitous state of the country. Like those of Saphet, they are in daily terror on account of the Bedouins. We made special inquiry after any traces of the ancient Jewish Academy, where the compilers of the Mishna and Gemara carried on their labours – the once famous seat of the School of Tiberias – but in vain. We inquired if there were remains of any ancient building connected with it, but no one knew of anything of the kind, nor did any of the Jews appear to be acquainted with its history. After leaving the synagogue, we found under an arch of the ruined buildings a parchment roll, being a manuscript of part of the book of Esther, cast out amidst many fragments of other books because of some error in the transcription.

We now visited the Jewish physician, Haiim, who had recognised Mr Calman in the synagogue. We were guided to his house by a little Jewish girl who spoke German. As we went, we asked her about her parents; she replied, 'They were both buried in the ruins by the earthquake'. How truly might she be taken as representative of a large class in Israel, of whom the prophet writes, 'We are orphans and fatherless!' (Lamentations 5:3). We found the doctor's house very clean and comfortable. He told us that he had not spoken to us in the synagogue because he was very much suspected by his brethren. Some time ago, during his absence from home, some of the Jews had discovered the Hebrew New Testament lying in his house, and, on his return, he found them in the act of tearing it to pieces, leaf by leaf. He shewed it to us; it was a Hebrew Bible with the New Testament affixed. He had saved part of it, but as far as the Epistle to the Corinthians had been destroyed. He was a kind pleasant man, with great leanings toward Christianity.

In the evening, while walking along the shore, we saw a boat anchored close by; and on making inquiry, found that it belonged to a Jew, who had likewise another of a smaller size, both of which were used in fishing; and being told that on the coast, directly opposite, where the hills seemed very steep and close upon the water, there were many tombs cut out of the rocks, our desire was excited more than ever to cross the lake. We were sure that the opposite side was 'the country of the Gadarenes, which is over against Galilee'; and from a comparison of all the circumstances, it seemed likely that the scene of the amazing miracle wrought upon the man possessed by Legion was directly opposite, the steep place of which they spoke being possibly the hill down which the herd of swine ran violently into the sea. We accordingly bargained with the boatman to take us over, which he thought he could do, with the aid of the breeze, in an hour. We got on board, furnished with our cloaks and a few mats, in case the wind should fall and prevent us from returning that night; but all of a sudden, without assigning any reason except that the wind might change, and that then we could not get back till next morning, the boatman refused to go, so that we were obliged reluctantly to give up the pleasure of crossing the Sea of Galilee. Soon after we saw him move his boat down the lake.

We returned to our tent upon the pebbly beach. Our servants had procured for us some excellent fish from the lake, resembling the carp, which they broiled, and we recalled to mind, as we partook of it, that this was the scene of John 21. It may have been here, or not far off, that Jesus stood on the shore that morning when he said to the disciples, 'Children, have ye any meat?' and then prepared for them the 'fire of coals, and fish laid thereon, and bread', saying, 'Come and dine'. And on the same spot he left the touching message, first addressed to Peter, but equally addressed to all who, like ourselves, are shepherds of a flock of Christ 'Lovest thou me? Feed my Lambs – Feed my Sheep'. We all felt the deep solemnity of the strain in which one of our number, as he sat on the shore, concluded a song of Zion:

> O Saviour, gone to God's right hand,
> Yet the same Saviour still!
> Graved on thy heart is this lovely strand,
> And every fragrant hill.
>
> Oh! give me, Lord, by this sacred wave,
> Threefold thy love divine,
> That I may feed, till I find my grave,
> Thy flock – both thine and mine.[5]

While we were thus engaged, Dr Haiim came to the tent. He had waited till it was dark for fear of the Jews. Mr Calman had much conversation with him. On our asking him regarding the lake, if there were ever storms upon it, he said, 'Yes, and, in winter, *the storms are worse than those of the Great Sea.*' This quite corresponds with the

---

[5] These are the concluding verses of McCheyne's poem 'The Sea of Galilee'. For the full text see Andrew Bonar, *Memoir and Remains of Robert Murray McCheyne, op. cit.,* pp.640-641.

testimony of Mr Hebard, one of the American missionaries at Beyrout, who visited the lake in April; and who told us that he and his party had encamped at evening close by the lake, when at midnight, all at once, a squall came down upon the lake, so terrible that they had to hold by their tent-poles for safety. Such, no doubt, was the tempest that came down, when the little ship in which the Saviour and his disciples sailed 'was covered with the waves' (Matthew 8:24); and it is not then to be wondered at that the disciples were so alarmed and cried, 'Lord, save us, we perish'; for such a squall coming in fury from the hills is more dangerous than the storms of the Great Mediterranean Sea. The thermometer was 91° F. during the day, and 76° during the night. All night long innumerable fish and wild fowl were dimpling the waters; and the beautiful moon shone above as in one of those silent nights when it was 'Left shining in the world, with Christ alone'.

Some of us awoke at midnight, and for a short time sat by the edge of the lake. The darkness had completely enveloped the waters, and now the Saviour's midnight prayers on these neighbouring heights and shores seemed a present reality; and the remembrance of the time, when 'in the fourth watch of the night, Jesus went unto the disciples walking on the sea', spread an indescribable interest over the sleeping waters. No place excepting Jerusalem is so deeply and solemnly impressive as the Sea of Galilee.

July 16

Early in the morning we bathed with delight in the pure water of the lake, and observed a peculiar pleasantness and softness in the water – resembling that of the Nile. While we were thus employed, a fisherman passed by with a hand-net, which he cast into the sea. The net was exactly the net called in the Gospel of Matthew αμφιϖβληστρον (Matthew 4:18), the same kind of net which we had seen used at Lake Bourlos in Egypt. The simple fisherman little knew the feelings he kindled in our bosoms as he passed by our tent, for we could not look upon his net, his bare limbs, and brawny arms, without reflecting that it was to two such men that Jesus once said by this sea, 'Follow me, and I will make you fishers of men.'

We then resolved to ride down to the baths, about two miles south of Tiberias, and if possible to get a nearer view of the foot of the lake. As we passed through the town we observed some of the inhabitants rising from their bed which had been spread on the top of the house-like

Saul, when Samuel called him on the top of his house at Ramah (1 Samuel 9:26). The Jews were met in their synagogue for morning worship; and one unusual sight was three women sitting under a verandah with large folios before them, apparently prayer-books. Several of the children whom we had spoken with yesterday recognised and saluted us. Might not an opening be found into the bosom of Jewish families by shewing kindness to their children?

We made our way over the southern wall of the town through one of the breaches occasioned by the earthquake. On the outside the country people were already busily engaged in threshing and winnowing their wheat harvest. We rode smartly along the smooth edge of the lake for about two miles till we arrived at the *Hammam Taberiah*, or 'hot baths of Tiberias', a white building which we had seen from Saphet. It is supposed to occupy the site of a fenced city called Hammath mentioned by Joshua (Joshua 19:35), and which stood near the town Cinnereth that gave its name to the lake. An attendant came forward and held our horses while we were ushered into a commodious apartment. The building, which was erected by Ibraim Pasha, is handsome, the floors being all of marble. The bath is open to the public gratuitously, only the bathers pay the attendants, who furnish them with every thing needful. There are small baths of white marble in private apartments, and the common bath is in the centre – a large circular basin built of marble and continually supplied with hot water from hot springs without. We found it about five feet deep, and it was with difficulty that we could at first bear the heat of the water. After swimming round and round for some time, it became exceedingly pleasant, and every pore of the body seemed to be freely opened. We afterwards enjoyed the luxury of free and copious perspiration as we sat in the ante-room and were refreshed with watermelons and coffee. We examined two of the principal springs from which the water boils up so hot that we could not keep our hand in it more than a second. Between the springs and the lake are many curious petrifactions. The stump and roots of some old olive-trees, over which the water from the spring flows, were completely petrified.

We were anxious to obtain a view from the last promontory on this side of the lake, and accordingly rode a little farther south along the shore, finding the banks fringed with beautiful oleanders and reeds, among which one solitary palm raised its head. Two deep ravines in the mountains on the opposite side were from this point distinctly visible, but we obtained no fuller view of the southern end of the lake. We would gladly have gone farther down and explored the remains of Tarichæa and the place where the lake discharges its waters into the Jordan; but a long day's journey lay before us, so we turned back to the town, struck our tent, and about eleven o'clock issued from the gate of Tiberias. Two German Jews shook hands kindly with us at the gate.

It was with real regret that we bade farewell to the blessed shores of the Sea of Galilee. Our course lay due west, up the steep hills which enclose the little plain on which Tiberias stands; and as we turned back to gaze on this sea, it lay at our feet serene and bright, reflecting the deep blue sky as peacefully as on that day when Jesus stilled its waves, 'and there was a great calm'. The rocks over which we travelled were black and of volcanic origin. Reaching the summit of the hill, the beautiful plain of Huttin lay on a lower level on our right hand, extending to the brink of the hills which enclose the lower plain of Gennesareth. On our left was a still higher plain, nearly all cultivated and chequered with fields of green and yellow. The plain of Huttin was also variegated with wild flowers and occasional patches of cultivation, giving it the appearance of an extensive carpet. Here we saw the gazelle bounding on before us over shrubs and rocks and every obstacle, and felt the exquisite fulness of meaning in the church's exclamation, 'Behold, he cometh leaping upon the mountains, skipping upon the hills! My beloved is like a gazelle or a young hart' (Song of Solomon 2:8,9). It is the very nature of this lively animal to bound over the roughest heights with greatest ease; it seems even to delight in doing so.

Looking back, we obtained a distant view of the northern part of the lake from which we were gradually receding; the white summit of snowy Hermon appeared more majestic than ever, and Saphet with its white buildings could not be hid. Our way lay through large fields of splendid thistles, having purple flowers, and very fragrant. The stalk was often six or eight feet high, bearing twelve or fifteen heads. Again we were reminded of the oft-recurring threatening, 'There shall come up briers and thorns' (Isaiah 5:6). But there is a different day approaching of which the same prophet writes, 'The nations shall rush like the rushing of many waters; but God shall rebuke them, and they shall flee far off, and shall be chased *as the chaff of the mountains before the wind, and like thistle-down before the whirlwind*' (Isaiah 17:13; see AV margin). At the very moment, on a neighbouring height before us, a husbandman was tossing up his wheat into the air that the brisk mountain breeze might carry the chaff away; and often by our side the wind caught up some of the loose thistle-down and whirled it rapidly over the plain. With the same ease and rapidity shall Israel's enemies be swept away: 'Behold, at eventide trouble, and before the morning he is not! This is the portion of them that spoil us, and the lot of them that rob us'. In a short time we came in sight of Mount Tabor, called by the Arabs Jebel Tor, in the distant south, while near us, on our right, appeared the Horns of Huttin, a rocky hill with two conical tops. The latter is the hill called by tradition 'the Mount of Beatitudes', being supposed to be the scene of the Sermon on the Mount, for which reason it is also sometimes called the hill of Toubat or Blessings. Another tradition supposes it to be the place where Jesus fed the five thousand with five barley loaves and two fishes (John 6:3-14). It is not impossible that one or both these traditions may be true; but there is no positive evidence of their truth, and it seems too probable that they arose from the hill being so prominently marked by two peaks.

Turning to the south we soon came to a village called Lubiah, situated high on a limestone ridge, commanding a full view of Tabor. Here we encamped till the heat of the day was past. The village is large and surrounded with the fig tree and prickly pear, which gives it an aspect of plenty and pleasantness. Most of the houses have a place for sleeping on the roof, as at Tiberias, and we observed here one of the most interesting examples of the stair from the roof down to the street (referred to in Matthew 24:17). From Lubiah we descended into the valley of Jezreel, now the plain of Esdraelon; and having directed Antonio and the muleteers to carry our luggage to the village Dabourieh at the western foot of Tabor, accompanied by Botros only we rode smartly forward over the plain, intending to climb Mount Tabor before sunset.

The plain (extending about thirty miles in length and twenty in breadth) is singularly level, cultivated in some spots, but for the most part a wilderness of weeds and thorns. There is the appearance indeed of varied produce upon it, but this is caused merely by the different colours of the thistles and briers which cover it. It is reckoned that not more than one-sixteenth of the whole is under cultivation; and at this part the proportion is certainly still smaller. How strikingly are the words of Isaiah fulfilled, 'They shall lament for the teats, and for the pleasant fields' (Isaiah 32:12). The eye is much deceived in judging of distances over this vast plain. From the heights of Lubiah it appeared to us that we might reach Tabor in less than an hour, and yet it occupied fully two hours, though we rode nearly at full speed. The weeds were often as high as our horses, and scarcely a tree was to be seen on the plain till we approached Tabor.

Tabor is a truly graceful mountain, but presents a very different appearance when viewed from different sides. This accounts for the great diversity in the representations given of it. From the north it had the appearance of the segment of a sphere, and appeared beautifully wooded on the summit, affording retreats to the animals for whom 'the net was spread on Tabor' (Hosea 5:1). From the west it is like a truncated cone, appearing much steeper and higher, with the southern side almost destitute of trees. But on all sides it is a marked and prominent object, as the prophet intimates when he says, 'As Tabor is among the mountains' (Jeremiah 46:18). We passed through several flocks of goats, and near the hill came to a ruined khan, and beside it a fortress with towers at the corners which bore marks of having been built by the Franks in crusading times. Close by was the tomb of a Moslem saint under a fine spreading tree with a jug of water upon the grave, according to the practice of Mahometans. The lower branches of the tree were covered with votive rags of different colours.

We stopped a little to examine a plough, which lay thrown aside under a tree. It was made entirely of wood, the coulter only being sheathed in a very thin plate of iron, and was therefore exceedingly light and fit to be guided by a single hand. We at once saw how easy a matter it would be literally to fulfil the words of the prophets, 'They shall beat their swords into ploughshares' (Micah 4:3 and Isaiah 2:4). The approach to Tabor is through a wide and shallow wady regularly wooded with fine oak-trees, so that it was more like the entrance to a nobleman's policy than an open wilderness. The Balut and the common oak were the most frequent. Tabor itself and the low ridge which connects it with the hills of Nazareth were both covered with the same; not brushwood, as on the hills of Judah, but trees, and these growing at regular distances, as if planted by the hand of the forester.

We had ascertained that the village Dabourieh, to which our baggage was to be carried, lay west of the hill, close under its base, and we ought to have gone to that village for a guide, or at least we should have ascended the hill by the plain path on that side of the hill, as is usually done. But the day was far spent and we had no time to lose, so we resolved to press up the northern face of the hill from the point where we were. Leaving the road and penetrating by a narrow footpath through a beautiful grove of oaks, we crossed to the proper base of the hill and began the real ascent. We soon lost all traces of a path and were involved in mazes of tangling shrubs and briers, and strong trees. The acclivity, too, was very steep, and occasionally a projecting rock or a smooth precipitous ledge nearly baffled the efforts of the mules to ascend. At length we dismounted, the closely twined branches of the trees frequently forcing us first to thrust through our own persons and then to drag on the animals. Anxious to reach the summit before sunset, and now not a little perplexed and wearied, we again sought for the smallest track – but in vain. We had no alternative, therefore, but to press upwards without delay. Our attendant Botros, whose clothes as well as our own had by this time suffered considerably from the trees and thorns, finding it no common labour both to ascend in face of such obstacles, and also to drag up the mules, kept muttering angry curses on us in his own language.

At one time we had almost concluded that we must make up our minds to spend the night where we were, on the wooded mountain side, and surrounded by its wild beasts, for we appeared to be still far from the summit. The sun was beginning to sink in the west, and to retrace our way to the foot through the same intricate passage would have been as difficult as to ascend. However, we asked guidance of Him who keepeth Israel, and pressed on. Suddenly and much sooner than we expected, we came upon ancient stones which were evidently the remains of some building. By this sign we knew that we must be now close to the summit, which to our great joy turned out to be the case. The sun had just disappeared, but we had still light enough to see the chief points of the magnificent landscape. We climbed up upon the ruins of the old fortifications on the south-east corner, which appeared to be the highest point on the summit, and looked around. To the north and north-east we saw the plain over which we had travelled, the heights of Huttin, and the deep basin of the mountains enclosing the Sea of Galilee. Other travellers have seen a part of the lake; this we did not observe, but the hills of Bashan, steep and frowning, appeared quite at hand. To the west and south-west lay the largest part of the great plain of Esdraelon, bounded by the long ridge of Carmel and watered by the full-flowing Kishon, making its way through it toward the Mediterranean. To the south, and immediately in front of us, was the graceful range of Little Hermon, and behind it the summits of Mount Gilboa. Between us and Hermon lay stretched that arm of the plain of Esdraelon which encircles

Tabor, beautifully variegated with immense fields of thistles and wild flowers, giving the whole plain the appearance of a carpeted floor. How great must have been its beauty when its wide open surface was adorned with thriving villages planted amidst fields of waving grain and gardens of blossoming fruit trees, and closed in by the fertile hills that gird its horizon! At the foot of Hermon, Mr Calman pointed out to us Endor, where Saul went to consult the woman who had a familiar spirit on the last night of his unhappy career (1 Samuel 28); and a little way to the west of it the village of Nain, still marking the spot where Jesus raised the widow's son to life (Luke 7:11).

Tabor is about a thousand feet above the plain, answering well to the description 'an high mountain apart'. Its level top, about a mile in circumference, covered with groups of fine trees and brushwood, affords a spot of complete retirement in the very midst of the land. If this was really the scene of the Transfiguration, there is a difficulty arising from the fact that both a fortress and a village once stood on its top, though otherwise it would not be easy to find a spot in this world more suitable for that heavenly transaction. It is a solemn thing to feel that you are treading the very ground on which holy beings have walked; and here we believed we were on ground called by Peter 'the holy mount' (2 Peter 1:18), hallowed by the visit of Moses and Elias, by the presence of the transfigured Saviour himself, and by the voice of God the Father, when he spake from the excellent glory, 'This is my beloved Son, in whom I am well pleased; hear ye him'. Barak assembled his 10,000 men on this hill (Judges 4:14), in company with Deborah, and in the plain at its foot, not a few learned men have supposed that the armies of Antichrist (gathered together to the place called Armageddon, Revelation 16:16) are to be destroyed by the Lamb when the great day of his wrath is come.

We would gladly have lingered long upon the summit of Tabor to meditate over the history of the past and the future, for even when we had nothing but the associations connected with it, we felt it 'good to be here'. The darkness, however, was rapidly descending and shutting out the view, so that our stay was very short. The moon rose, and by her light our servant guided us down a steep and rocky footpath on the south side, so that we were able, though with some difficulty, to ride down the whole way. But where we were to find Dabourieh we did not know. On reaching the foot of the hill, six or eight men sprang up from the ground on which they were lying and advanced towards us, each carrying a large club in his hand. We were somewhat alarmed, but were soon relieved by finding out that they were friendly villagers watching their heaps of corn by night, like Boaz in the history of Ruth (Ruth 3:2-7). They on their part imagined that we were plundering Bedouins against whose depredations they were watching, and were overjoyed to find that we were mere harmless travellers. It was only now that we began to learn how wonderfully our God had preserved and guided us. The villagers could scarcely believe that we had come over the mountain, for they told us that a band of Arabs were lurking among the woods and had killed several persons the day before. We knew not how much or how little to believe, but it was evident that we had been saved from danger and had escaped the hands of the Bedouins simply in consequence of our leaving the direct road and climbing a part of the hill seldom visited. The darkness, too, which prevented our making a complete circuit of the hill, had providentially kept us from approaching the retreat of the plunderers. Two of the villagers agreed to conduct us to the village of Dabourieh, which they faithfully performed for a small reward.

There we found our servants anxiously looking out for us. They had put up the tent and set a light within it that we might see the white curtains from a distance; but both they and the villagers had begun to conclude that we had fallen into the hands of the Arabs. Perhaps never before had we felt such gratitude for a deliverance as we did that evening when seated in our tents in peace and comfort after the anxieties and alarms of the day. Had we gone round by Dabourieh at first, to obtain a guide, we would then have heard of the danger, but now, without knowing of it, we had been permitted to visit the summit of Tabor in peace. We could see plainly that every step of our way had been graciously overruled, and that our very difficulties and vexations which had troubled us at the time were made the means of our safety. The simple villagers of Dabourieh gathering round expressed great astonishment at our escape. We sang praise in our tents with a full heart, in the words of Psalm 124, 'Had not the Lord been on our side', etc.

July 17
During the greater part of the night the wolves and jackals kept up a loud and angry howl which was responded to by the bark of the village dogs. At morning the clouds were hanging beautifully on the top of Tabor and the adjacent hills, and the sky was covered with a veil of fretted clouds, the first of the kind we had seen in Palestine. It was easy now to

understand why Tabor had been so often made a place of rendezvous from the days of Barak and downward (Judges 4:6), the hill being so commodious as a place of defence, with a copious supply of water on the very summit, even when the enemy spread themselves on the plain below.

From our tent-door we saw across the plain the villages of Endor and Nain at the foot of Little Hermon. Endor lies under the brow of the hill, and Saul would have an easy road from it to the fountain of Jezreel at the foot of Gilboa, where his army was encamped (1 Samuel 29:1). Nain is further west and appears to lie still closer under Hermon. We observed cultivated fields, and verdure round it; and it was here that Mr Calhoun, our American friend whom we met at Alexandria, found many tombs cut out of the rock, one of which may have been the intended sepulchre of the young man whom Jesus met as they carried him out dead, and restored to the weeping widow. Jesus must have known this spot well, for he would often pass it on his way to the Lake of Galilee. No place in all this land furnishes more remarkable illustrations of the sovereignty of God than do these two villages. At Endor you see a king in the anguish of despair, consulting with a diviner, and warned by the dead that the Lord had departed from him and become his enemy. But on the same plain, a few miles from Endor, a thousand years after, you see at Nain 'God over all' coming in our nature and wiping away the tears of a poor widow.

Over the western shoulder of Hermon lies Solam, the ancient Shunem, and farther south, near Gilboa, Zerin, the ancient Jezreel; but these we did not see. In the village of Dabourieh itself one of the first sights that attracted our notice was a group of Bedouins, near kinsmen, no doubt, of the very robbers who had been ranging the hill and keeping the neighbourhood in alarm. Yet here they were sitting at their ease smoking their long pipes, the passing villagers giving them a suspicious glance that indicated no good will, but nobody daring to challenge them. Could there be a simpler or more striking illustration of the prophecy mentioned before, 'His hand shall be against every man, and every man's hand against him; yet he shall dwell *in the presence of all his brethren*?' (Genesis 16:12). One good-natured Bedouin approaching our tent permitted us to sketch him and smiled when he saw his own likeness. The little yellow shawl over the head and the twisted rope of camel's hair that binds it are the chief peculiarities of their dress. Close by the village of Dabourieh a small stream flows from the north to join the Kishon. They called it by the same name as the village. This name may possibly be derived from Tabor, at the foot of which it lies; others conjecture that Deborah's exploit in this region, when she accompanied Barak to the hill, may have given name to the town and stream; but still more probably it is the same as the Levitical city Daberath which belonged to the tribe of Issachar (Joshua 19:12;21:28).

We left our encampment about nine o'clock, descending from the height on which Dabourieh stands and travelling in a north-west direction. We soon entered a defile, finely wooded with oak-trees and brushwood, often looking back to admire the graceful tapering cone of Mount Tabor. On the top of a hill to the right, appeared a village, Ain Mohil. Our road now lay over limestone hills of a much barer character, until, about two hours from Tabor, we began to descend the slope that leads into the vale of Nazareth.

The town of Nazareth lies on the west side of the valley, on the acclivity of one of the many hills that meet here. The valley has sometimes been compared to a cup; and the hills have all a whitish appearance from the limestone of which they are composed. There are numerous tracks worn deep in the calcareous rocks, leading from the town in different directions to neighbouring villages on the other side of the hill. The houses are of a very white stone and appeared to be more substantial and regularly built than those of other towns of Palestine. The buildings of the convent are massy, and there is a mosque in the town, adorned with cypress trees. There were no ruins visible except the remains of an old khan near the entrance of the town. Fig trees and olives abounded in the gardens, hedged in with prickly pear. The women at the well also appeared to be better dressed and in more comfortable circumstances than in most other places of the land; and, on the whole, we found Nazareth a more thriving place than we had anticipated. We put up our horses at the khan, which is one of the best specimens we met with of the Eastern inn. The Bazaar, however, was poor, having no great show of things for sale. Cusas and cucumbers, cloths and red shoes, formed the staple commodities. A great many bony-featured Bedouins, with the rope of camel's hair round their head, were loitering about the street.

The situation of Nazareth is very retired, and it is said that on account of this seclusion the worthless characters of Galilee resorted thither, till at length the town became a proverb for wickedness. In this town, among such a race of men, did the blessed Jesus live thirty years in calm submission to his Father's will, obeying in obscurity for us.

We visited the convent and saw all its pretended wonders. We were shown the chamber of the Annunciation where the angel Gabriel saluted Mary, 'Hail, thou that art highly favoured'; also, the house of Joseph cut out of the rock and the pillar curiously (the inhabitants say miraculously) suspended from the roof. They wished to take us to another part of the town to see the stone table from which Christ dined with his disciples, both before and after his resurrection – a visit which procures seven years' indulgence to the deluded pilgrims of the Romish Church; but we were no way inclined to see more of their follies and grievously offended our guide by declining to go. One or two of the paintings in the convent are good, especially a large one of the Annunciation, but it has the painful profanation of representing God the Father as an old man. There is also a curious ancient picture of Christ, said to be the very one sent by him to the King of Edessa, on which is inscribed, *'Hoec vera imago Domini'*,[6] etc.

From the convent garden the monks pointed out to us the Mount of Precipitation, regarded by them as the hill from which the angry Nazarenes wished to cast the Saviour headlong, about a mile and a half distant from the town. This is a tradition which disproves itself, being contrary to the express words of the Gospel narrative, 'They rose up, and thrust him out of the city, and led him unto the brow of the hill *whereon their city was built*, that they might cast him down headlong' (Luke 4:29). We next visited the place which Dr Clarke conjectured to be the true precipice, immediately above the small church of the Maronites. This is really a continuation of the hill upon which the town is built. It is composed of limestone rock forming several precipices, so that a person cast down from above would without doubt have more than one dangerous fall. We had no hesitation, when standing there, in concluding that the brow of that hill was the very spot where the men of Nazareth rejected the Lord of glory.

The white rocks all round Nazareth give it a peculiar aspect. It appears dry and tame, and this effect is increased by the trees being powdered over with dust during the summer season. The heat was very great and the glare from the rocks painful to the eyes. There is a good fountain near the entrance of the town, called the Fountain of the Virgin, because it is said that Mary and her Son were in the habit of drawing water there.

[6] 'This is the true image of the Lord.'

We were detained in this town longer than we intended by the abrupt departure of the muleteer whom we had engaged at Saphet to accompany us to Acre, but who had set off to join a caravan that was collecting near the town and bound for Damascus. On discovering this, we went to the *Cadi* to lay our complaint before him, and found several people waiting at the door of his house, who, when he made his appearance, kissed the hem of his garment – an act, like the kissing of the image of Baal (1 Kings 19:18; Hosea 13:2), indicating respect and reverence. Perhaps also there may be an allusion to the same custom in the words, 'Kiss ye the Son lest he be angry' (Psalm 2:12). The *Cadi* could do nothing for us, and sent us to the *Muteselim*; and he again said it was not a cause to be laid before him, but before the *Sheikh*! By this time, however, the man was out of reach, and we had no thought of remaining till search was made for him. We therefore proceeded on our journey without him.

We left Nazareth by a well-worn track leading over the rocky hills to the north-west, passing on our right a village called Reineh. Beyond this lies Kefr Kenna, generally supposed to be Cana of Galilee where Jesus made the water wine. In an hour and a half we reached Sephourieh, the ancient Sepphoris. The name, which means 'a bird', seems to be derived from the position of the town; the town being on an eminence, like a bird perched on a hilltop. Its castle is in ruins, but still occupies the summit of the hill. The village is small, but many fragments of pillars and other ruins lie scattered about. Having so lately visited Tiberias, lying low upon the edge of the Lake of Galilee, we could now see the force of the saying of a rabbi who wished 'his portion to be with those who began the Sabbath at Tiberias and ended it at Sepphoris'. The sun lingers of course longer upon the hill of Sephourieh, and makes a longer day than is enjoyed in low-lying Tiberias. Rabbi Judah, the holy, who completed the Mishna, was born in this town.

The people of this village were kind and affable. Some of them offered us *leban*, of which we gladly sat down in a courtyard to partake. Beside us were women and children busily employed in arranging and binding the leaves of the tobacco plant in bundles. A large threshing-floor was also near and we put many questions to the peasants in regard to their farming operations. A flat board, which is drawn over the corn to bruise it, is called *loah*. It is made of two or three boards firmly united, and the bottom is spiked with stones arranged at regular distances, not unlike the nails in a ploughman's shoe. It is drawn by two horses or oxen, a boy sitting upon it, and driving them round and round. This instrument is universally used and is probably 'the threshing instrument' mentioned by the prophet (Isaiah 28:27). The wooden fork for throwing the bruised corn up in the air is called *midra* and the flat, hollow wooden shovel next used for a similar purpose is called *raha*. The latter is evidently *the fan* of the New Testament. When this implement is used the wheat falls down in a heap on the threshing-floor, while the chaff is carried away by the wind and forms another large heap at a little distance. The peasants do not burn it, they give it to their cattle; but it is so perfectly dry that were it set on fire it would be impossible to quench it. In how striking a manner do these simple customs illustrate the words of David, 'The ungodly are not so, but are like the chaff which the wind driveth away' (Psalm 1:4); and those of John the Baptist concerning Jesus, 'Whose fan is in his hand, and he will throughly purge his floor, and gather his wheat into the garner: but he will burn up the chaff with fire unquenchable' (Matthew 3:12).

Leaving Sephourieh we proceeded still north-west and after half an hour of a rough undulating road entered upon a vast plain, stretching far to the north and east, bounded by gently swelling hills. Here and there we came upon fields of dhura, but by far the greater part was covered with weeds and thistles. The ground was very hard so that although there seems to be a good deal of travelling upon this road, it was not at all cut up, but smooth and good. No wheels ever pass over it. Here we missed our servant Antonio and found that, erroneously supposing that he had left a cloak behind at Sephourieh, he had gone back without our knowledge to recover it. Approaching the north-west corner of the vast plain where the hills come near to one another and form the entrance to the fine pass of Abilene, we arrived at a well and a ruined khan where we halted for a little time to wait for Antonio; but as he did not appear, we prepared to go on without him. Meanwhile an old man came up to the well riding on an ass and immediately warned us not to proceed farther, for there were eight armed Bedouins in the valley who had stopped and threatened him and had allowed him to escape only because he was old and his ass worth nothing. They were lurking for the very purpose of waylaying travellers that might be passing on to Acre.

On hearing his account we were considerably alarmed and hesitated what to do. One proposed that we should encamp in the old khan and proceed under cloud of night; and another that we should cross the plain to a village in sight. While we were deliberating, some other men came up, who were leading camels to Sephourieh. They had met nobody in the valley and conjectured that what the old man took for Arabs might be the Pasha's soldiers. Our muleteers, who were much afraid and anxious to turn back, said that these men wanted us to be taken because we were all Christians. At length, considering that we had no place of safety in which we might encamp and that the road to Acre might be as dangerous on the morrow as that day, we decided to go forward, committing ourselves once more to Him who keepeth Israel and who had helped us hitherto. Accordingly, we left the well and soon entered the pleasant valley of Zebulun, now called Wady Abilene, connecting the plain above described with the plain of Acre. Sometimes the valley was broad and level, like a small plain, well cultivated, and enclosed with steep wooded hills; sometimes it narrowed almost to the straitness of a defile. At one of these narrow passes one of the men picked up a stick which we recognised as belonging to Antonio. This circumstance excited many conjectures. We hoped that he had in some way got safely on before us; although some of the men started the suspicion that he must have fallen into the hands of the Arabs. We journeyed on, and about sunset met with a company of Bedouins, of a dark and formidable appearance, but not armed. They were riding on asses and each carried a massy club in his hand. They looked closely at us, but passed quietly on, returning our salutation. Our servants supposed that when they saw that we were Franks they had imagined that we must be carrying firearms. To us it seemed like the deliverance of Jehoshaphat, when 'God moved them to depart from him' (2 Chronicles 18:31). We met no other travellers during the rest of our way. The valley is long, and declines very gently toward the west; the hills on either side are often finely wooded, sometimes rocky and picturesque. The road is one of the best in Palestine and was no doubt much frequented in ancient days.

Issuing from the valley, we saw with the last rays of evening, high upon a hill on our left, the town of Abilene, a fine-looking place. There is little doubt that this is the ancient Zebulun on the border of Asher (Joshua 19:27), the modern name being a corruption of the ancient. Travellers who have visited it have found there the remains of arches and other buildings. We only saw it at a distance and in the twilight. Josephus says that on account of its populousness it was called Ζαβουλων αφνδρων (i.e. well-mannered, or well-peopled, Zabulon).

Still farther on is a village called Chamforeh. In half an hour after, we left the road and crossed the valley to the right to a small hamlet called Fatria, with two other villages, Damoun and Ruesh, on the right hand lower down the slope. We encamped by full moonlight, with many camels and flocks all sleeping round. In the tent, we felt again called to peculiar thankfulness, and all the more on account of the painful uncertainty of our minds regarding the fate of poor Antonio. There seemed great force in the words of the Psalm, 'Keep me, O Lord, from the hands of the wicked; preserve me from the man of violent deeds' (Psalm 140:4).

July 18

We struck our tents by sunrise and pressed on toward Acre, now in sight. From the height we obtained the finest view of the whole extent of Mount Carmel which we had yet seen. An intervening swell hid the river Kishon, but the fine range of Carmel stretching eight miles into the country, rising higher as it recedes from the sea, the monastery on the northern point, the white walls of Khaifa at its foot, the Bay of Acre between us and it, and the blue Mediterranean beyond, were all gleaming in the morning sun. There are many mounds of earth in the plain of Acre, apparently artificial, cast up probably in crusading times, and used in war. The plain itself is said to be eighteen miles in length and six in breadth, beautiful and well watered. We crossed the dry bed of a stream which flows into the sea a little way south of Acre. This is the ancient Belus or Sihor-Libnah, that is, 'Sihor of the white promontory'. The Palus Cendovia in which it rises is said to be found six miles in the interior. In another part of the channel, nearer the sea, we found the water flowing in it. Before entering Acre, we passed through a large encampment of the Pasha's troops. The tents were all arranged in military order, but the men seemed to be under little discipline.

Entering the gate of Acre we proceeded through the crowded and well-furnished bazaar. Everywhere soldiers were parading the narrow streets, and it seemed to be the most lively eastern town we had yet visited. The fortifications of Acre appeared to us by no means very formidable, although there were many strong forts and other buildings. No doubt, its walls and towers must have been much stronger in former days and its remarkable situation, as the key of this part of the land, has ever made it a post defended and attacked with desperate obstinacy.

We were conducted to the Latin Convent as the best place for refreshment; and as we had hitherto seen almost nothing of the monks of Palestine, we were not unwilling for once to pay a visit to their secret recesses. Our visit to them was not like that of Paul to the Christians of Ptolemais when he 'saluted the brethren, and abode with them one day' (Acts 21:7). The main object of the visit, on either side, was that of giving and receiving a traveller's fare. No price is exacted, but the visitor is expected to leave behind an adequate remuneration for the provision furnished. The monks we found to be coarse men, with no appearance of seriousness or even of learning. The news of the day seemed to form the whole of their conversation. We were led into a large hall, with a plain wooden table and benches round. Here half a dozen of the fraternity sat down with us while two of them served. One repeated a Latin grace in a coarse irreverent manner, and then many dishes of solid food, fowls, meat and vegetables were brought in on a large board and handed round. The polite invitation to take our place at the table was *Favorisca noi* (Do us the favour). After dinner, one of their number left us to embark in a vessel that was to take him to the convent on Mount Carmel, the rest sat with us a while and talked over our providential escape from the Bedouins.

Meanwhile, to our great joy, our servant Antonio made his appearance. The story of his adventure was very much what we had suspected. Having gone back to Sephourieh in search of the cloak, and not finding it, he rode quickly after us in order to regain our company. But meeting a woman on the road of whom he inquired the way, he was directed to a route different from that which we had taken. He had entered the valley at the very time when we were waiting for him at the old khan and had not proceeded far when six or eight Bedouin Arabs, fully armed and mounted on horseback, rushed out upon him. They demanded who he was – what he was doing there – where he was going – and where his company were. Antonio forged a story in reply, saying, that he was servant to a scribe who had gone on before with a company of twelve men and would be out of their reach. The Arabs said that he must come with them; and immediately with their long lances pricked his horse up to the hills. When they had got him out of sight of the road, they tied him hand and foot, and led away his horse, after asking such questions as, 'Can it stop suddenly in the midst of a gallop?' They then stripped him of every article of dress, and one brought out a large club stuck with nails, threatening to beat him to death. But he entreated them to spare him, crying out that he had given them everything, and that his death would do them no good. At length they left him bound in this state till the sun went down. While all this was going on, we had passed in the valley below; and the fact of their attention being occupied with our poor servant was thus in the hand of Providence the means of our preservation. After sunset they came and loosed him and led him a little way farther up among the hills that he might not soon be able to find his way to the public road and give information against them. Then bidding him find his way home, they left him. The poor lad, in a state of nakedness, sat all night upon a tree to escape the wild beasts. He said that his face and upper part of his body were as if bathed in water, the perspiration pouring down in streams from the effects of fear. From the same cause, his mouth was filled with bile and his voice almost inaudible. As soon as the light of morning dawned, he came down from the tree and found out the road to Acre. The first person he met was the Pasha's dromedary post, who gave him a small piece of clothing, and then he reached a village where the people supplied him with more. After this he made out his way to Acre and sought for us at the convent, where he found us to his unfeigned joy and ours. We could not but perceive the special providence of God in our escape, and again we had reason to sing as at Mount Tabor, 'Our soul is escaped as a bird out of the snare of the fowlers; the snare is broken and we are escaped'. Even the monks seemed to acknowledge the hand of God in it. At night, we heard Antonio and the other servants of our company singing a song of vengeance on the robbers. It was in the style of those songs we had usually heard from Arabs, a single voice leading, and then a chorus responding, with clapping of hands. It was to this effect –

> Single voice –   'The curse of Allah rest!'
> Chorus –   'Upon the Bedouins'.
>   Clapping hands
> Single voice –   'The sword of Allah come!'
> Chorus –   'Upon the Bedouins'
>   Clapping hands.

In style, this resembled Psalm 136, though in sentiment it was the reverse of its strain of thankful love.

We visited the English Vice-Consul, Mr Finch, an intelligent Jew, who speaks German, Italian, and a little English. He shewed us every attention, and when we told him the whole matter, his remark was, 'that surely we were upon God's errand; otherwise God would not so protect us'. He conducted us to the Governor, or Aga, a mild, placid old man with an immense turban and long beard, seated in state upon a carpet in one corner of his chamber. Taking off our shoes at the door, we sat down on the floor and related our story, Mr Calman and Antonio being the narrators. He caused his secretary to write it down and promised to send twenty soldiers to the Wady Abilene to find out the robbers. Probably, he thought no more of the matter after we had left him. While we were in the court, a poor man came in to complain that his garden had been plundered by the Arabs. The days are not come when 'violence shall no more be heard in thy land' (Isaiah 60:18).

We were anxious to visit the Jews of Acre. Meeting one in the bazaar, we invited him to partake with us in some melons with which we were refreshing ourselves. He consented, and three others soon joined us. They then led us to their synagogue, a very humble one, with a short inscription on a pane of glass above the door. About a dozen Jews gathered round, one of whom recognised us, having seen us at Tyre. They said that there are sixty of their brethren residing here. We had some interesting conversation with three young men, one of whom eagerly read a chapter in the New Testament, though his companion stood by watching us very suspiciously and apparently uneasy at seeing his friend so employed. An old man then came into the synagogue and mounted the reading-desk. He placed a jar of water beside him, then opened his prayer-book, washed his hands, and put on his *Tallith*. We were informed that he meant to spend six hours in prayer that day and the jar of water was intended to keep his throat from becoming dry during his exercise of bodily devotion. How remarkably this illustrates the words of Christ, 'Woe unto you, scribes and Pharisees, hypocrites! for ye, for a pretence, make long prayer; therefore ye shall receive the greater damnation' (Matthew 23:14).

The same afternoon we left the walls of Acre behind us little thinking how soon they would be laid in ruins. We halted for a time at an aqueduct on the north of the town which is evidently an ancient work and is still used, having a hundred arches entire. Passing a small village called Ismerieh, we came to Mezra, where a fine stream from the hills runs into the sea, and where is a beautiful garden belonging to Ibraim Pasha. It is enclosed by a row of tall cypresses, while within the lemon and other fruit-trees of the East were clothed with the richest foliage, and fragrant shrubs and richly coloured flowers diffused their delightful odours. Many small villages are scattered over this beautiful plain. On the right, a little off the road, stand Sheikh Daud, once a Christian village, and

Zeitoun. In the plain where is the spring of water by which the aqueduct is supplied, is El Capri, and on the hill Tersecha, and not far off a monumental pillar, Kulat Jedin. After these we came to El Hamsin. Still farther north, and on the shore, lay Zeeb, three hours from Acre. It is the ancient Achzib. It has a high situation near the sea and is surrounded with palm trees. A shepherd in the neighbourhood of this place was playing on his pipe at the head of his flock – a sweet, soothing sound in the stillness of evening, and all the sweeter because so rarely heard in Palestine.

After one hour more we came to Boussa, situated in carse ground and bordered with trees. Here the fertile plain of Acre ends, and the low range of swelling hills that form its eastern boundary for twelve or thirteen miles run out into the sea, forming a high rocky promontory. Looking back from the height, the view of the plain, enclosed by the hills on the one hand and the sea on the other, was rich and beautiful. The plain along the coast south from Carmel, the plain of Tyre, and the plain of Acre, are all very like each other, although the last seems to be the most fruitful.

The sun went down behind the Mediterranean Sea as we passed a small ruined fort or khan on the highest point of Nakoura. The khan of Nakoura is nearly an hour farther north and we made haste to reach it before dark. The graceful gazelles were sporting along the shore and bounding on the rocky heights above us. Sandys mentions that, in his time, leopards and boars used to come down from the brushwood of these hills, but we neither saw nor heard of any. We slept that night in a stubble-field near the khan of Nakoura; and early next morning were on our way, journeying north by the edge of the sea. The shore in this vicinity is often grand and picturesque, the white rocks being worn into curious forms by the incessant dashing of the waves; and in addition to the natural beauty of the scene, the associations of the past invest the very waters with a profound interest. One of our company thus expressed the impressions of the moment:

These deep blue waters lave the shore
Of Israel, as in days of yore!
Though Zion like a field is ploughed,
And Salem covered with a cloud –
Though briers and thorns are tangled o'er,
Where vine and olive twined before –

Though turbaned Moslems tread the gate,
And Judah sits most desolate –
Their nets o'er Tyre the fishers spread,
And Carmel's top is withered –
Yet still these waters clasp the shore
As kindly as they did before!
Such is Thy love to Judah's race,
A deep unchanging tide of grace.
Though scattered now at Thy command,
They pine away in every land,
With trembling heart and failing eyes –
And deep the veil on Israel lies –
Yet still Thy word thou canst not break,
'Beloved for their fathers' sake'.[7]

In a short time we came to a well-built and copious fountain where we obtained a plentiful draught of delicious water. It had a pointed arch and Arabic inscription, and still bears the name of the great conqueror of Tyre, 'Iscanderoon'. Soon after leaving it we found ourselves on the remains of an ancient causeway, said to be the work of Alexander the Great. This is the Scaloe Tyriorum, leading over a high rocky promontory of limestone, which here descends precipitously into the sea, the Album Promontorium or Cape Blanco, about eight miles from Tyre. The steps on the northern side are cut out of the rock with immense labour, and a solid parapet is left along the margin over which we looked into the clear deep waters of the Mediterranean. We saw fish swimming about in great numbers at the base of the rocks and over our heads the owl perched on solitary cliffs as in the days of the Psalmist (Psalm 102:6). From this point we began to search along the shore with deep interest for any remains of ancient Tyre. About half an hour from Cape Blanco, we came upon the ruins of some ancient place where were several cisterns, but no distinct remains. These were the only traces we could find of any thing like a city along the bay south of Tyre.

Within an hour of Tyre, we turned aside from the shore to the right to visit the famous pools said to have been made by Solomon for Hiram, King of Tyre. The place is called Ras-el-Ain or 'Head of the Fountain',

---

[7] The full text of this poem by McCheyne, 'On the Mediterranean Sea in the Bay of Carmel', is given in Andrew Bonar, *Memoir and Remains of R. M. McCheyne, op. cit.*, pp. 643-644.

evidently because it was the source from which Tyre was anciently supplied with water. It is about three miles from the gate of modern Tyre. There are four large and remarkable reservoirs, three of which we examined. They are considerably elevated above the plain by means of solid mason-work, and you ascend by steps to a broad border on which you may walk round the water. The fountains springing up from beneath keep them constantly full. Two of them are connected with each other; the one measuring 17 yards by 15 at the water edge, the other 13 yards by 10. The third is a regular octagon, measuring 81 yards on each side. From the first two the water is conveyed by a fine old aqueduct to the rocky hill Marshuk, and from thence anciently to Tyre; but the only use that seems to be now made of the water of the largest one is to turn a mill for grinding corn. The work is beautifully executed and the abundance of water makes everything around look verdant and beautiful, so that we lingered near enjoying the pleasant situation.

While we were refreshing ourselves with bread and *leban*, a man from Tyre joined our party who told us that a few days before, a number of Jews from Saphet had come to take refuge in the town till the disturbances of the country should pass over. So truly are the words of Moses still undergoing their fulfilment, 'Thou shalt find no ease, neither shall the sole of thy foot have rest' (Deuteronomy 28:25).

It was after midday when we set out again. We did not enter Tyre, but passed at a distance, nearly in the course of the old aqueduct. We came near the hill of Marshuk which some have supposed to mark the site of Palæ Tyrus; though this cannot be the case, for Strabo says that it lay thirty stadia to the south of the island whereas Marshuk is less than a third of that distance to the east of modern Tyre. Crossing the plain, we soon came upon the same track by which we had travelled in a contrary direction a fortnight before. At the bridge of Kasimieh we were refreshed by a draught of goat's milk which some shepherds gave us. An hour before sunset, we came to that part of the plain overlooked by Sarfend, the ancient Sarepta. Two of us rode up the steep hill on which the modern village is built by a path worn deep in the rock. We visited the mosque, said to be erected over the widow's house where Elijah dwelt, and the cave beneath it, where a lamp is kept continually burning, and where miraculous cures are reported to have been performed. The view from the village commands the plain and the sea, and is very fine. A deep ravine on the south is clad with an olive-grove, and the hills around bear marks of having been at one time covered with the vine, for the terraces still remain. We passed through a village on the shore immediately opposite to Sarfend, called Ain-teen ('the well of the fig'), which some believe to be the true site of Sarepta.

The sun being set, we now pressed forward toward Sidon. The gazelles were gamboling on the rocky shore. Seven large stones stand on the roadside, of which a curious legend is told. It is said that these are seven Moslems turned into stone for pursuing a Christian, whose companions were guilty, but who himself was innocent. A little farther on is a *cairn* or heap of stones raised over the tomb of a slave who was executed on this spot for murdering and plundering passengers. It is customary for travellers to add a stone to the heap as they pass. Arriving at a khan called Ain-el-Burak, the owner, who was on the roof, invited us in (see Proverbs 9:14,15), but we thanked him and pressed on. The near approach to Sidon seemed peculiarly beautiful in the soft moonlight. A sweet fragrance was breathing from shrubs and flowers, and our road conducted us through groves of luxuriant trees, while the eye was not pained by the sight of dry dusty fields. We reached the gate of Sidon by ten o'clock, having been fifteen hours on horseback. We were too late for admission into the town and had to encamp on the outside of the walls. The ground was so rocky and uneven that it was with difficulty we managed to drive in the pins of our tents, but this did not prevent us from enjoying a refreshing sleep.

We rose early next morning *(July 20)* and saw the Moslem ladies, all swathed in white, moving out of the town to visit the graves, as much for recreation as from respect to the dead. These are in a pleasant grove of cypresses and other trees which shelter the eastern side of the town. The English Vice-Consul waited on us at our tent and brought us the news of the death of the Sultan of Constantinople. We were soon mounted, and leaving the walls of Sidon far behind us, we rode along the bay of Naby-Younes again, crossed the Damour, and passed through the mulberry gardens where we had lost our way. On leaving the shore, instead of crossing the bar of sand, our servants guided us by a very pleasant road, through the vast grove of olives that stretches along the foot of Lebanon. In one of the gardens is a khan which they call a 'Sunday-khan' because it is regularly frequented on Sunday afternoons by the Greek priests and their people, who spend the day in amusements and dissipation. We were anxious to reach Beyrout in time to visit the Jewish synagogue, for that was the day set apart for the commemoration of the destruction of the Temple, a remarkable occasion among the Jews. But in this we failed. We arrived, however, before the sun went down, and rode in at the gate filled with joy and thankfulness to God for permitting us to visit Galilee, and bringing us back in safety and peace.

July 21 Sabbath

In the forenoon, Mr Bonar preached on John 7:37 to a respectable audience in the spacious apartment of the American Consul. We afterwards attended the Sabbath-school in one of the Mission-houses and had the pleasure of addressing a class of young Syrians who understood English. In the evening, Mr McCheyne expounded Acts 9 in a large prayer meeting at which the American brethren and their families were present. And thus we drank of 'the streams from Lebanon', in a dry and thirsty land.

We now found that the next Austrian steamer would sail for Smyrna in a week; so that we took up our abode again at the inn of Giuseppe who paid us every attention. We occupied ourselves during this time, chiefly in making up our journals and writing home, and in the cool of the evenings enjoyed a quiet walk along the rocky beach. One evening we saw the funeral of a poor native. The body was carried out of the town, not in a coffin, but on a bier, like the widow's son at Nain (Luke 7:14). A few mourners followed, lamenting him with occasional cries. Another evening, we paid a short visit along with one of the merchants of the town to Sir Moses Montefiore and his lady, who were here waiting for a vessel to carry them to Egypt.

In the middle of the week, Mr McCheyne was seized with fever. Dr Gerstmann of the Jerusalem Mission, himself a converted Jew, waited upon him with all kindness and ordered him to be removed to a house upon the height above the town where the atmosphere was cool. The disease seemed to abate a little on the Saturday, so that the physician recommended us to make preparations for sailing next day. He thought that there would be greater hope of Mr M[cCheyne]'s recovery by enjoying the cool breezes of the sea, than by remaining three weeks longer in the confined atmosphere of Beyrout. On 23rd August 1841, little more than two years after, this worthy young physician died of a similar fever at Constantinople, to which station he had been removed. He was a man of an excellent spirit, one who loved Christ with all his heart, and was very bold in recommending him to others. One day Lady

Montefiore said to him with great vehemence that she would rather lose her head than forsake the faith of her fathers; his answer was, 'If you do not turn and believe on Christ, you will never see the kingdom of heaven.'

Accordingly, on the afternoon of Sabbath, July 28, we bade farewell to our many kind friends and embarked in the Austrian steamer called *Schnell-Segler* (Swift Sailer) which sailed from the harbour at five o'clock. The four Jews from the Dardanelles, with whom we had sailed into Egypt, and whom we now met for the third time to their surprise and ours, were the only faces we knew on board. There was one young man in the vessel who could speak a little English. It was a solemn and almost melancholy Sabbath evening to us. Mr McCheyne was laid down upon the deck, and we kept our eye upon the majestic brow of Lebanon (the emblem of the Redeemer's countenance, Song of Solomon 5:15), till it faded from our view in the dim and brief twilight of evening.

But here let us for a moment review all that we have seen and heard in regard to the condition of Israel in their own land. We visited every city and village in Palestine where Jews are to be found (with the exception of Jaffa and two small villages upon Mount Naphtali), and we have been led to the conclusion that the Holy Land presents the most important and interesting of all the fields of labour among the Jews.

1. The Jews are in affliction in the land of their fathers and this makes them more friendly there than in other lands. In other countries, where they are wealthy and comfortable or deeply engaged in worldly business, we found that they care little to attend to the words of the Christian missionary. But in Judea, the plague, poverty, the oppression of their rabbis and the insults of the heathen have so humbled them that they cling to any one who offers to shew them kindness, however averse to the doctrine which he teaches.

2. They are strictly Rabbinical Jews, untainted by the infidelity of France or the neology of Germany. They hold the Old Testament to be indeed the Word of God. They have a real expectation of the coming of the Messiah; and this expectation is certainly greater now than it was formerly. The missionary has thus firm ground to stand upon and, with the Hebrew Bible in his hand, may expound to them, with intelligence and power, all that is written in the Law of Moses and in the Prophets and in the Psalms concerning Jesus.

3. Moreover, Judea must be regarded as the centre of the Jewish

world. Every Jew, in whatever country he sojourns, turns his face toward Jerusalem in prayer. It is the heart of the nation and every impression made there is transmitted to all the scattered members. We afterwards met a poor Jew at Ibraila, a small town upon the Danube, who told us of conversions that had taken place at Jerusalem. In this way, whatever is done for the Jews in Palestine, will make a hundred-fold more impression than if it were done in any other land.

4. Another important consideration is that in Palestine the Jews look upon the English as friends. Three months before our arrival in Jerusalem, an English Consul had been stationed there – a true and zealous friend of Israel, whose jurisdiction extended over the country once given to the twelve tribes, and whose instructions from the British Government were that he should to the utmost of his power afford protection to the Jews. The recent changes in Syria have no doubt for a time interfered with these arrangements; but still, is not the hand of an overruling Providence visible in them? And is it not our duty to improve to the utmost the interest we have in the affections of the Jews by being the friends of their never-dying souls?

5. In addition to all this, there is no country under heaven to which Christians turn with such a lively interest as Immanuel's land. 'God's servants take pleasure in her stones and favour the dust thereof.' But especially those who love Israel bear it upon their hearts, because its name is inwoven with the coming conversion of Israel. It is upon *'the house of David, and upon the inhabitants of Jerusalem'* that God has said he will pour his Spirit (Zechariah 12:10). *'On the high mountains of Israel shall their fold be'* (Ezekiel 34:14); and *'they shall feed in Bashan and Gilead, as in the days of old'* (Micah 7:14); and God himself has said, *'I will remember the land'* (Leviticus 26:42).

On these grounds, we rest our conviction that the Holy Land presents not only the most attractive, but the most important field for missionary operations among the Jews.

In the south of the Holy Land, the London Society for the Conversion of the Jews has maintained for several years an effective Mission. Jerusalem is their headquarters, so that the southern parts may be fairly regarded as pre-occupied. But the north of the land, the region of ancient Galilee, containing nearly half of the Jewish population of Palestine, still presents an open and uncultivated field.

In that beautiful country, the town of Saphet at once commends itself as the most favourable point for the centre of a Jewish Mission. It is one of the four cities regarded as holy by the Jews, and therefore they cling to it in spite of the awful convulsions of nature and the ravages of war. Before the earthquake on 1st January 1837, it is said that there were 7,000 Jews residing there. It has again gradually been raised out of its ruins, and there were at the time of our visit about 2,000 Jewish inhabitants. A ride of six hours from Saphet brings you to Tiberias on the margin of the Lake of Galilee, another of the holy cities, and containing 1,500 Jews. Saphet is also within a few days' journey of Tyre, Sidon, Acre, Khaifa, Beyrout and Damascus; in each of which there are many Jews – so that it forms the centre of a most interesting field.

The climate of Saphet is peculiarly delightful, owing to its lofty situation. In one of the hottest days of July, the thermometer rose no higher in the shade than 76° F. In Tiberias, again, the winter's cold is scarcely felt at all.

If the Church of Scotland were privileged to establish a Mission in Saphet, what an honour would it be to tread, as it were, in the very footsteps of the Saviour, to make the very rocks that re-echoed his 'strong crying and tears' and the very hills where he said 'Blessed are the peacemakers' resound with the cries of believing prayer and with the proclamation of the gospel of peace! And if God were to own and bless our efforts, would not the words of the prophet receive a second fulfilment, 'The land of Zebulon and the land of Nephthalim, by the way of the sea beyond Jordan, Galilee of the Gentiles; the people which sat in darkness, saw great light; and to them which sat in the region and shadow of death, light is sprung up' (Matthew 4:15,16)?

CHAPTER 6

SMYRNA AND CONSTANTINOPLE

'And they that are left of you shall pine away in their iniquity in your
enemies' land, and also in the iniquities of their fathers shall they pine
away with them' (Leviticus 26:39).

July 29
At seven in the morning we found ourselves approaching Cyprus. Here
we anchored for some hours off Larnica, which is near the ancient
Citium. There seemed at this point little to interest a traveller in the
island itself; a ridge of bare limestone hills formed the prominent
feature of the scene, while a dry, parching sun glowed over us like a
furnace. The town itself, however, looks well, its mosque and white
houses peering through tall and graceful palm-trees. At a former period,
Cyprus must have been remarkably productive and well peopled. Mr
Thompson, from whom we so lately parted at Beyrout, had travelled
through the interior of the island, and in his journey visited not fewer
than sixty villages, which had remains of ancient churches now ruined
and desolate; and everywhere he found wide plains left uncultivated,
which might yield abundant harvests. It is an island which no Christian
can gaze upon without remembering the days of the apostles. For this
was the native country of Barnabas (Acts 4:36), who sold his estates and
brought the money to Jerusalem for the use of the infant Church, and
who afterwards, in company with Paul, traversed its whole extent from
Salamis to Paphos, preaching the unsearchable riches of Christ. Here,
too, Sergius Paulus had his residence, and Elymas the sorcerer; Mnason
also, 'the old disciple', spent his youth amidst its hills and plains. But,
there is no Barnabas nor Mnason in Cyprus now, for no Jew dare plant
his foot upon its shores because of the furious bigotry of the Greeks, who
have persecuted without remorse every wanderer of that nation that has
visited or been cast upon their coast ever since the reign of Trajan. To
ourselves Cyprus is associated with some of our severest trials. For it
was here that Mr McCheyne's illness increased, the fever burning hot
within his veins, while there was no medical help on board, nor any

remedies that we could apply. A cooling drink or a fresh breeze were the only means of even momentary relief.

Next day we were sailing off the coast of Pamphylia, and at six in the morning of the succeeding day *(July 31)* were anchored off Rhodes. On the left hand of the harbour is a range of very precipitous hills. The town is on the shore, with green hills rising gently behind, and many gardens on every side. All around the sandy edge in the vicinity of the town the shore is lined with windmills, which seem to be much in use throughout this region. It is said by recent travellers that at the entrance of the ancient harbour there are still remains of buttresses, the distance between which is twenty-seven yards, a space sufficiently wide to have afforded room for the famed Colossus. We thought upon Paul sailing past Rhodes as he hasted to Jerusalem (Acts 21:1), and we wished to land, for there are here about 1000 Jews; but this was impossible on account of Mr M[cCheyne]'s illness. It was here the well-known commentator Aben Ezra died, commanding his bones to be carried to the Holy Land.

After leaving the harbour in the afternoon, we found ourselves sailing close to the shore of Caria, the water apparently deep to the very edge, with steep rocks and hills lining the shore. Often it seemed as if we were sailing close under the base of some of our own Highland mountains, while the waves gently weltered round the base of the rocks. At a turn of the coast Cnidos was pointed out to us. A creek running up a considerable way into the land forms a complete harbour; but a ruined tower was all that we could distinctly discern of the ancient town.

We now saw before us Stanchio, the ancient *Coos*, and felt pleasure in gazing on it, because Paul had once done the same (Acts 21:1). On reaching the harbour the vessel made a short stay, giving us opportunity to get a sight of its chief town, which is beautifully situated in the midst of gardens. The buildings are all of white stone, and the hills form a green acclivity behind. The physician Hippocrates gave this island its renown in ancient times.

Once more afloat on the Icarian Sea, we passed an English frigate in full sail, welcome to us as being in a manner a relic of home, and in itself a very imposing object on these seas. But a far more interesting sight engaged our attention a little before sunset. An intelligent traveller on board pointed out to us the island of Patmos, now called Palmosa. It lies sixteen miles south-west from Samos, and is about eighteen miles in circumference, stretching from north to south. We saw the peaks of its two prominent hills, but our course did not lie very near it. Still it was intensely interesting to get even a glance of that remarkable spot, where the beloved disciple saw the visions of God – the spot, too, where the Saviour was seen, and his voice heard, for the last time till he comes again. It is the only spot in Europe where the Son of Man shewed himself in his humanity. John's eye often rested on the mountains and islands among which we were now passing, and on the shores and waves of this great sea; and often, after the vision was past, these natural features of his place of exile would refresh his spirit, recalling to his mind how 'he stood on the sand of the sea' (Revelation 13:1), and how he had seen that 'every island fled away, and the mountains were not found' (Revelation 16:20).

Long after sunset some of us sat on deck under the clear brilliant firmament, 'sown with stars', whose bright rays glittered on the blue waters like beams of the moon. We conversed of God's providence – 'his way is in the sea, and his path in the deep waters' – and of Patmos, where the fall of that empire through whose dominion we were now passing, was long ago foretold.

August 1

Next morning we were on the shores of Ionia. We had passed Icaria, and were sailing by Samos, the birthplace of Pythagoras. We thought of Paul touching at Samos a few days before he gave his memorable address to the elders from Ephesus (Acts 20:15). Soon after Chios (see Acts 20:15), now Scio, came in view, and arriving at the port, the vessel anchored for a few hours. The eye rests on many buildings on the shore, dilapidated and empty, monuments of the awful scenes of massacre that devastated this beautiful island during the revolution. The town is very finely situated, embosomed in orange-trees. There was a considerable bustle in the harbour; and boats filled with Greek sailors soon surrounded our vessel. There were on board some Jews, who, as we left the harbour, pointed to Scio as the burying-place of a famous rabbi, Baal Turim. Among these were our four Jewish friends whom we met first at Syra and then at Sychem, and who were now returning from their pilgrimage to their home on the Dardanelles. On observing that Mr M[cCheyne] was ill, they kindly inquired after him and continued to show their sympathy till we parted from them at Smyrna.

At six in the evening we anchored at Smyrna. Many interesting objects met the eye in sailing up the splendid gulf, and none more beautiful than the town itself, lying close to the shore, set round with tall dark green cypress-trees, with beautiful hills behind. There is one eminence that the eye falls upon near to the entrance of the harbour, dotted over with white flat stones. This is the Jewish burying-ground.

On anchoring, our first care was directed to get medical advice for Mr McCheyne. But we found that we were too late that evening to get any medical help in the town, the best physicians always retiring to the country at night. On that account, and as the town itself was oppressively close and sultry, Mr McCheyne, though so little able for any journey that we feared every moment he would sink under the fatigue, urged us to proceed at once to Bouja, a village three miles off, where we were assured of finding an English physician. The innkeeper soon furnished us with asses and agreed to be himself our conductor. The road was pleasant, rows of cypress-trees often meeting our eye in the gloom. The air, too, was fresher than in the town, yet even here it was sultry. On arriving at the inn of Bouja, we found the surgeon of an English frigate in the house at the moment, and soon after a Greek physician, named Dr Dracopoli, well skilled in the diseases of the country, was recommended to us. Later in the evening, Mr Lewis (formerly a labourer in the Jewish cause, and now chaplain to the English Consulate in Smyrna), visited us, and not only most readily aided us in our perplexity, but insisted on all of us removing next day to his own residence. Never did any in our circumstances meet with more unremitting attention and true Christian kindness than we did during our stay under the roof of Mr and Mrs Lewis. Perhaps Mr McCheyne's recovery was, in the good providence of God, to be mainly attributed to their care. The Lord grant to them the blessing that Paul sought for Onesiphorus who so oft refreshed him; 'May they find mercy of the Lord in that day' (2 Timothy 1:18)!

Our first Sabbath *(August 4)* was spent at Bouja. We worshipped in the English Chapel recently erected there, a beautiful and commodious building, in which Mr Lewis and Mr Jetter (the latter sent out by the Church Missionary Society) officiate alternately. That day, in our peculiar circumstances, Mr Lewis' sermon from Psalm 46:10, came home to the heart, 'Be still, and know that I am God'. There was singular power also in the words that were written over the pulpit of the chapel, 'Be thou faithful unto death, and I will give thee a crown of life' (Revelation 2:10). We felt them the more, remembering that we were within a short distance of the city where the Church used to assemble to which these words were first addressed, and the spot where Polycarp, so long 'the angel of the church of Smyrna', obeyed the exhortation and received his reward. To us this was 'a day better than a thousand'.

Our next Sabbath was not so still, but it, too, had its peculiar enjoyments. It was spent in Smyrna. Early in the morning the sound of bells ringing loudly in the town caused not a little surprise, till we ascertained that it proceeded from the Romish churches in the city. For the Roman Catholics, everywhere zealous, have here erected three large and splendid churches, and already number 5000 members in Smyrna. They have also a flourishing school, to which they give the name of a College *'di Propaganda'*. We worshipped in the forenoon in the English chaplaincy and Mr Bonar preached upon Acts 8:8, 'There was great joy in that city.' Pleasant it was to pray and then proclaim the Gospel in a place to which the Lord had once spoken by name. In the afternoon, we joined the worship of the American Missionaries in the Dutch Consulate, and then reached Bouja in time to enjoy part of Mr Jetter's evening service. These Sabbaths in a foreign land were seasons of peculiar refreshing. On more than one occasion also we enjoyed a weekday evening service in the village, maintained by our American brethren, and attended by an audience of about fifty individuals. Mr Bonar preached one evening on Isaiah 12; and these pleasant meetings brought vividly to mind the similar services in our own parishes at home.

Bouja, where we resided, is a beautiful village, much frequented by English residents. The houses are generally built apart from each other, with a garden and shrubbery round them. But even the common streets of this village have wide-spreading trees shooting up between the houses. Here, too, we remarked how frequently the villagers at evening sit in social companies, to enjoy the evening air before the door of their dwellings. This is the custom referred to by Ezekiel, 'the children of thy people are talking against thee *by the walls and in the doors of the houses*' (Ezekiel 33:30) – that is in the midst of their easy, thoughtless, self-pleasing companies. The evening breeze is sweet, and the nightingale's song is not uncommon.

Oftentimes during our stay Mr Lewis gave us interesting information in regard to his labours among the Jews at a former period. One evening, telling us of his residence in Italy, he related the case of a young Jewess of Ancona whose name was Sarina. She was a teacher, and being the only Jewess of any education in the town, even boys were put under her tuition. Besides Italian she knew Latin and some other languages and could teach geography and other branches of education. Though occupied with the children from eight in the morning till eight at night, she used, as soon as her work was done, to come to the house of Mr and Mrs Lewis to converse with them. They found her a most amiable and intelligent young woman, willing to listen to the teaching of a Christian instructor. She read Christian books which they lent her; translated them into Italian; and told them frankly the ignorance and wretched state of Jewesses in Ancona. On their departure, the grief of Sarina was extreme; indeed, she would gladly have accompanied them, but she had an aged mother depending on her exertions for support. They heard no more of her till recently, when they received notice of her death. She died about two years ago; and the last book she was found translating was one 'on the Truth of Christianity'.

Once or twice we met with a young American traveller, who was in the inn when we arrived. His information about the Karaite Jews confirmed what we had elsewhere heard of that sect. He had just come from the Crimea, where he saw them in their chief town called Joofud Kallah, 'the fortress of the infidels'. He thinks that there were about 1,500 in that town; and in the whole Crimea about 5,000. They are the most respectable of all Jews, men of character and intelligence, very cleanly and industrious in their habits, and much favoured by the Government. It is said that the *word* of a Karaite is more trustworthy than the *bond* of another Jew. One day while making inquiries regarding the Jews at Mr H. Barker, a merchant of the town, he told us a recent instance of the insults and oppression which Jews not unfrequently meet with at the hands of both Turks and Greeks. He saw a Greek go to a Jew who was walking before him and strike him so violent a blow that the poor Jew burst into tears, but made no resistance. Mr B[arker] went up and asked the Greek why he had been guilty of this unprovoked outrage? *'Because he is a hater of Christ'*, was the cool reply of the Greek. A few days ago, also, a Jew was bathing in the sea along with a Turk. In plunging into the water, the Turk struck upon an anchor, which caused his death. The Jew was immediately imprisoned on the charge, *that perhaps he was the cause of the accident*; and no one could tell what might be the result. How truly did Moses foretell of Israel, 'thou shalt be only oppressed and crushed alway' (Deuteronomy 28:33).

Our most important information regarding the Jews was obtained from Giovanni Baptist Cohen, a converted Israelite, who is employed by the London Jewish Society to labour among his brethren in Smyrna. Not long after our arrival we called upon him, when he kindly offered to visit the Jews along with us. Accordingly, on Saturday *(August 10)* we set out at six o'clock in the morning. As we went along we met a considerable number of Jews at that early hour returning from synagogue worship. These, we were told, had already finished their morning service; for, being more devout, or at least adhering more rigidly to the letter of the Scriptures than their brethren, they have service before sunrise, referring to Psalm 62:5 as their authority, 'they shall fear thee *before the sun*' – that is, before the sun rises, as they understand the Hebrew. We met also more females on their way to the synagogue than we had usually observed in other places. All the synagogues were clean and commodious, with porches before the entrance for the sake of coolness. These were often shaded by the spreading vine, and many of the worshippers were reading their prayers under its shelter. There appeared to be sincere devotion among them, for their attention was not diverted from the service by the entrance of strangers.

The Jewish population of Smyrna is about 9,000, and that it is on the increase is proved by the fact that they are at present building an additional synagogue, although they have already ten or twelve. The only missionary here is Mr Cohen, mentioned above, a native of Constantinople, who is a great linguist, and able to speak with some ease, Italian, French, Spanish, Greek, English, Turkish, Armenian, and Hebrew. His wife is a Sciote by birth, one of those who was rescued from the massacre, and educated in England. He has free intercourse with all the Jews, and they return his visits.

While we were with him in the forenoon, three intelligent and respectable Jews called, who spent fully three hours in conversation. He led them to speak of Isaiah 53. Turning up the works of Jarchi (or Rashi), they were very free in their remarks on that commentator; and one of the three on going away, said that 'he was more than two-thirds persuaded that Christianity was true'. Mr Cohen told us after they had gone that their state of mind was not an uncommon one among the Jews of Smyrna. He knew at least five families in the town who were inclined to leave Judaism to this extent that they would admit Jesus as Messiah, but keep up their national rites and customs. Most of these were careless till he visited them; but now they diligently read the Old Testament and allow him to read to them out of the New.

In the evening, a great many Jews called; they sat in the lower room and at the door which stood open to the street. One of them, a very liberal-minded Jew, called our attention to a Roman Catholic priest who was passing by and remarked, *'Our rabbis and these priests are alike impostors.'*

Mr Cohen has been ten years here and has found great freedom of inquiry among the Jews. At the same time, no sooner is a baptism proposed than the Jews stir up the Government and the convert is obliged to leave the place. Several, however, have been baptized in the Greek and Romish churches, because the members of these communions have means of protecting them.

The Jews have many schools, but their system of teaching is most deplorable. No enlightened attempt has ever been made for the instruction of the Jewish children under fourteen years of age. Missionaries might establish schools with good hope of success, because these children are cruelly used, as well as ill instructed, under their present teachers; and the Old Testament being made their schoolbook, the teacher might explain it and ground the whole truth thereon. The inducements of a solid education in Hebrew grammar, and perhaps in some of the modern languages, would lead them to come. The common people among the Jews are simple, not very superstitious, and easily affected by kindness. It would be important to instruct the Jews in the grammar of the Spanish; and a cheap edition of a Spanish dictionary and grammar would be of great use. They have about thirty libraries in the town, all on a private footing, and of no great importance. Several individuals, well qualified to judge, spoke much regarding the want of good tracts suited to the capacities and modes of thinking of those for whom they are intended. Mr Lewis mentioned the case of an English tract translated into Italian so literally that it was unintelligible; and many are unacceptable because not idiomatic. On the other hand, a polished Italian will frequently be induced to read a tract, if only it be written in elegant Italian, for the sake of the language.

From various individuals we heard of Saloniki, the ancient Thessalonica. Drs Black and Keith had proposed to visit it, but were not able to accomplish their intention. The Jewish community there are very exclusive, quite a nation by themselves. They have great influence in the city, and their numbers are reckoned at 50,000. Their real condition could be known only by long residence among them, for they are reserved and keep aloof from all strangers. On this account, the reports of merchants cannot be very accurate. They are very strict Jews. Many poor people among them spend their time in reading and study, receiving money for their support by charity. They publish many books, almost every Jew there aspiring to be author of some treatise. They study astronomy, and publish the best Jewish Almanacs, both in regard to seasons and changes of weather. It is asserted that their almanac for 1837 had put down that there would be an earthquake on 1st January of that year, and another on the 21st. Both of these actually occurred, and by the first of them the town of Saphet was destroyed. From this supposed prediction they acquired great fame among the Jews. It is also a curious fact, and characteristic of the people, that the famous impostor, Sabbathai Sevi, who was born at Smyrna, has still many followers at Saloniki.

On another occasion, Mr Calman spent a whole day in town visiting the Jews along with Mr Cohen. He was led by him to visit the families who are disposed to admit Christ as Messiah but would still retain national rites, such as the Passover and the Jewish Sabbath. All these are rich, possessed of large magazines or stores, and under European protection, so that they are not affected by the common inducements of a worldly nature; but they are weary of the bondage of the rabbis. They said that they have read the New Testament and found in it nothing against keeping Saturday as the Sabbath; and the Saturday they will not consent to renounce, for they believe that they would be traitors to their people if they threw off this mark of nationality. They proposed to keep their feasts also as memorials that Jehovah, whom they now worship as Messiah, is the same God who redeemed them of old. They would call themselves *Believers in Messiah*, but not *Christians*, because all whom they have ever known under the latter name are given to idolatry and immorality. If a church were formed on these principles, and had the sympathy of influential friends in England, they have no doubt but hundreds would soon join them. Mr Calman thought them well versed in Scripture, but that they did not feel the burden of sin. Their assent to Christianity is intellectual; they would embrace it as a deliverance from a superstition of which they are weary. The same feeling begins to prevail among the Jewish females. An old Jewess named Medina, whom Mr Cohen was instrumental in arousing to a concern about her soul, has become very zealous in doing good to others, delights in reading the Scriptures, visits other Jewesses, and has succeeded in leading many of them to her views.

August 5

We were able to devote a day to visiting the Jewish schools. One of them meets in an extensive building, having an open square in the midst, but close and dirty. It contained ten apartments, with about forty children, and a separate teacher in each. Some of the children were further advanced than the others, but there seemed to be no regular gradation in the classes. Few of them had books, not one in ten had a Bible. They are fine interesting children, but miserably taught; kept in fear by the lash of their teacher who tyrannises over them. As we entered one room, the teacher was in the act of applying the bastinado to a boy. On seeing us, the rest of the scholars cried out in Spanish, 'Franco, Franco, salvanos', 'Help us, Frank, help us.' The bastinado is applied by twisting a rope, fixed on a short stick, round the feet of the culprit, who is laid on his face; and then a strong whip made of oxhide, is smartly applied to the soles of his feet. Each schoolmaster had two of these thick whips hanging in his room, along with this miniature bastinado. The whips seemed well used, being worn to fibres at the end. We saw also the stocks, ready for fixing the feet of those who were to be less severely punished. The boy whom we rescued from punishment was guilty of absenting himself from the school – a line of conduct we did not much wonder at when such was the teacher and his discipline. We bought from one of the teachers a whip and a bastinado, as memorials of Jewish darkness. The rabbi who taught the highest class, where the Talmud is the textbook, put many questions to us about the Jews in Palestine and said, 'he himself was a poor man, but had sent already 200 piastres to them'.

In reviewing the information we obtained regarding the Jews here, we feel convinced that Smyrna presents much to invite the attention of a missionary. Independently of the interest attached to the place as having been the seat of a Jewish community since the Christian era – independently, too, of its being a place whose associations with the Apocalypse, and with the history of Polycarp, give it a peculiar interest in the eyes of every Christian, it deserves regard on account of the large population of Jews residing in the city and neighbouring villages, and the vast numbers from other countries who visit it from time to time. Jews call at this port from all parts of Asia, as well as from Constantinople and its vicinity. It might yet become the door of access even to the hitherto secluded Jews of Saloniki, some of whom occasionally visit Smyrna.

The literary qualifications needful for a missionary to this city are not very formidable. Acquaintance with the Spanish and Italian languages, joined to a thorough knowledge of the Hebrew Scriptures and moderate attainments in Jewish literature, would fit the missionary for his work. The climate is one which was highly esteemed by the ancients, who have celebrated the air of Ionia, and many of our countrymen who reside there for the sake of trade have found it by no means unhealthy or unpleasant.

The only obstacles in the way of a mission are the difficulty of supporting converts, and the danger of the Government interfering in the event of the Jewish community remonstrating against the baptism of any of their brethren. But these obstacles are to be met with everywhere, and are such as a devoted missionary is entitled to disregard if 'the fields are white for harvest'. We are convinced that the Presbyterian form of our Church would present no obstacle, and especially that the want of a liturgy would rather be an advantage than otherwise. It is the expressed feeling of many among the Jewish converts that a liturgy reminds them of their former bondage. The field is nearly unoccupied, and yet it is most inviting. We would look for interesting results from the efforts and prayers of thorough Christian labourers in this place who would not needlessly offend Jewish prejudices on the one hand, and who, on the other, would be as far from trifling with the awful truths of the gospel by letting men suppose themselves Christians on any other ground than thorough conversion. Oh that another Barnabas could be sent to Smyrna, and another Apollos, fervent in spirit and instructed in the way of the Lord!

Smyrna must ever possess attractions to all who are interested in ancient Asia, or in the churches of the East. Being the chief city of this region because of its commerce, it forms a very important centre for missionary labour. There are, accordingly, missionaries from several societies established in it. With one of these, Mr Jetter from the Church Missionary Society, we became intimately acquainted during our stay at Bouja, and received much interesting information from him. He told us that the messengers of the gospel have carried on their labours in this part of the world for thirty years, and yet that little success has attended them. Not a single instance of the conversion of a Mahometan has occurred. The eye of man can discern few real followers of the Lamb among native Christians, whether of Greek or Armenian churches, in Smyrna. But to revive the truth among them is the main effort of all the missionaries that have laboured here. The Spirit seems at present withheld, and the opposition of man is great.

We repeatedly sought for information in regard to *the seven churches of Asia*, though we had no opportunity of visiting any of them but Smyrna. In regard to Smyrna, we have already given some details. It has a population of 120,000, of whom 9,000 are Jews, 1,000 Europeans, 8000 Armenians, and perhaps 20,000 Greeks. Many of the latter are falling under the sway of Rome. The Armenians and Greeks form the nominal church of Smyrna, the degenerate successors of the tried but richly endowed Christians of the days of John; yet it is the most flourishing of all the cities where the seven churches stood, perhaps because God remembers his faithful witnesses who here poured out their blood for his cause. May it not be for a similar reason that Pergamos, where Antipas was his faithful martyr, is still a prosperous town? It is now called Bergamo, and contains 1,500 Greeks, and 200 Armenians, amidst 13,000 Mahometans. It is the only town of the seven besides Smyrna that retains any Jewish population; and of these it has a hundred. There are in it remains of an ancient church called St John's, and many extensive ruins of theatres, temples and walls. It stands in a magnificent plain, with a strong acropolis, occupying a majestic hill above the city. This was the place where 'Satan had his seat', commanding the whole of the gay and rich city at his will, more effectually than did the frowning battlements of the acropolis. It was the most warlike of all the cities, being the capital of the kingdom of Attalus, and hence is addressed in a warlike strain by him who had the sharp two-edged sword.

Ephesus, on the other hand, has disappeared from being a city, and its 'candlestick is quite removed out of its place'. It is not the ruins called Aisaluk which mark the true site but some remains near that spot, at the foot of the hills Corissus and Prion. This latter hill is said to be the burying place of Timothy, and the place where the Seven Sleepers enjoyed their long repose. There are traces of a stadium 700 feet long, and of a large theatre, no doubt the same as that into which 'the multitude rushed with one accord' (Acts 19:29). But there are no remains of the temple of the great goddess Diana, silver models of which, mentioned under the name of 'shrines' (Acts 19:24), used to be cast and sold to her votaries. Each pillar of this temple was a single shaft of pure Parian marble, and the whole building cost the labour of 220 years, yet all is now buried out of sight under the soil. A few peasants, all of them

Mahometans, have their huts here. God has left the city for 'its salt had lost its savour'. The fervent love of Onesiphorus (2 Timothy 1:18) was not imitated in the next generation. Paul's glowing words to 'the saints which were at Ephesus', exhibiting Christ's love in order to keep theirs alive, were forgotten (Ephesians 3:13,19). The elders did not imitate his tears and labours (Acts 20:31); the hearts of the people were no more stirred by the fervour of Apollos (Acts 18:25); and even the Epistle from Patmos, and the residence among them of the beloved disciple till the day of his death, could not prevent their falling from their 'first love'. All her faithful ones have long ago been removed to 'eat of the fruit of the tree of life that is in the midst of the Paradise of God' (Revelation 2:7).

Thyatira, called now Akhisar, or 'white castle', stands in a plain embosomed in groves, and is still, as in former days, a busy scene of manufactures. The dyers of the town are noticed in ancient inscriptions, and our friend Mr Calhoun had very lately verified what has been observed by other travellers, that to this day the best scarlet dye in all Asia is produced here, and sent to Smyrna and other places for sale. Lydia's occupation (Acts 16:14) remains characteristic of the place to this day. Two churches, one belonging to the Greeks, the other to the Armenians, keep up the memory, though they do not retain the living faith of the primitive Christians.

Philadelphia is now called Alah-Sher, 'the high city, or city of beauty', because of its splendid situation in the midst of gardens and vineyards, with the heights of Tmolus overhanging it, and in front one of the finest plains in Asia. Its comparatively retired situation might be one of the means used by God in fulfilling the promise, 'I will keep thee from the hour of temptation that shall come upon all the world' (Revelation 3:10). It has five Greek churches and its one solitary ancient pillar has been often noticed, reminding beholders of the promise, 'Him that overcometh will I make a pillar in the temple of my God, and he shall go no more out' (Revelation 3:12). Mr Calhoun remarked that the Greek Christians there were peculiarly hospitable, as if 'brotherly love' ($\phi\iota\lambda\alpha\delta\epsilon\lambda\phi\iota\alpha$) were the characteristic of the place in reality as well as in name.

Sardis, now Sart, has no Christians even in name. Pliny Fiske found one Greek at the spot, who was so true a Sardian, 'having a name to live while he was dead', that he was using the Lord's day for grinding his corn. All that were worthy have long since gone to walk with Christ in white (Revelation 3:4) and have left no successors. It stood partly on a hill; the river Pactolus flowed through its forum. Among its many ruins, two ancient churches can be traced – perhaps remnants of those edifices within whose walls the throng of formal worshippers – who had only 'a name to live' – used to assemble.

Laodicea, now Eski-hissar, or 'old castle', stands upon a hill. Some interpreters discover a literal fulfilment of the words, 'I will spue thee out of my mouth' (Revelation 3:16), in the earthquakes which often occur here, and the fire that then bursts up from the ground. But even the utter emptiness of a place once so populous is an exact fulfilment of the threatening on the city; though it is only that eye which penetrates the shades of death and sees the self-satisfied Laodicean cast out as vile into utter darkness, that can discern how full has been the accomplishment. It has remains of three theatres, and of a circus that could contain 30,000 people – places, perhaps, occasionally visited by the lukewarm Christians there, who saw not the sin of tasting the world's gaieties, while they also 'drank the cup of the Lord'. In Paul's days, they were a people separate from the world, a people for whom he had much wrestling in prayer (Colossians 2:1; 4:15,16); but the current of the world was too strong for the generation that succeeded.

Besides these seven churches, we find in Scripture mention made of Hierapolis (Colossians 4:13), seen from one of the ruined theatres of Laodicea, now Pambouk Kalasi, i.e. 'cotton tower', in allusion to the white rocks on which it is built, without a single Christian inhabitant. Colosse is now called Konas, where a band of about thirty Greek Christians are found. Antioch of Pisidia, now Isbirta, is a town remarked as being peculiarly supplied with gushing fountains, and still possesses several Greek churches. Tarsus, the birthplace of Saul, is said to be a poor decayed town. Iconium is well known under the name Konieh, and is a flourishing city; but Derbe, the birthplace of Gaius and of Timothy (Acts 20:4), and Lystra, where Paul was stoned, have not yet been described by any traveller.

With our friends at Bouja we enjoyed many pleasant and profitable walks, breathing the soft 'Ionian air'. The whole district is interesting. Mount Corax rises in the neighbourhood of the village, and beyond this range appear in the distance the splendid heights of Tmolus, now called Bous-dag. On the north is Mount Sipylus, at whose feet stood the town of Magnesia where Antiochus met with a signal defeat. Dr Keith visited this town during the few days that he and Dr Black spent in Asia Minor, and there he met with an interesting young Jew who seemed in search of the truth. South of Bouja, and not far off, rises the range of Dactyle; and from a rising ground may be seen Sedikoy, a village on the direct road to Ephesus. The road from Bouja to Smyrna is exceedingly pleasant, through a fine valley called the Valley of St Ann. Two tiers of ruined arches remain which anciently formed an aqueduct across it; and many other ruins indicate how great the extent of Smyrna must have been in other days when it was the crown of Ionia. The valley is adorned with fine old olive trees and many red Turkish villas, and there is a beautiful view of the bay and mountains on the other side. Approaching Smyrna, you cross the Caravan bridge, thrown over a narrow and shallow stream. This stream is the ancient river Meles, on whose banks Homer is said to have been born and from which he got the name 'blind Melesigenes'. A cave is shown where, it is said, he used to seek retirement. Water flows in this channel during all the summer, but its course is very short; its source being in the neighbouring hills, from which it flows through the town into the sea. The most picturesque object about Smyrna is the splendid grove of cypresses which wave over the large Turkish burying-ground near the town. These handsome trees shoot up majestically to the sky and cast their dark shade around. Beneath them, as far as the eye can reach through the sombre light of the grove, are innumerable small figures above the graves. These are short pillars about two feet high (reminding one of the figure of the Roman god Terminus) on whose top is carved the head of the deceased, with the coloured turban or fez that characterized him in his lifetime. The most frequent colours are red and yellow. Those painted green cover the graves of Moslems who were descendants of the prophet. The inscriptions on the tombs are commonly written in an oblique direction for the convenience of the passer by, that his eye may more easily run along the lines. Many of them are adorned with gilding, reminding us of the practice of the Pharisees, '*Ye garnish* the sepulchres of the righteous' (Matthew 23:29). Mahometans never bury more than one body in a grave, so that the number of gravestones is immense. At such a spot there is awful solemnity in the thought of the resurrection, when those myriads of sleeping dead who once worshipped the false prophet in their blindness, shall 'hear the voice of the Son of God, and come forth'.

We used to enter the city by a street which is watered by a branch of the Meles, or an artificial canal supplied from it. In this street the water occupies the place of the causeway; trees grow on each side of it and the houses are behind the trees. Coolness is thus secured to the inhabitants at all hours of the day. We thought of the street, river, and trees mentioned in Revelation (Revelation 22:2); and of the words of David, 'There is a river, the streams whereof shall make glad the city of God' (Psalm 46:4). The constant peace and refreshment afforded by God's love and favour are faintly shadowed forth by these images, which an Eastern could fully appreciate. In one street we passed a fountain erected by some benevolent Mahometan long ago, as the Turkish inscription indicates. The water gushes plentifully into a trough; and for the greater convenience of passengers there is a large spoon-like cup attached to the well by a chain. No-one injures or thinks of removing this. The 'bowl is not broken, nor its cord loosed' (Ecclesiastes 12:6) at the fountain. The houses are built sometimes after the Italian and sometimes after the Eastern fashion. A luxuriant vine is ofttimes trained over the portico, and a spreading fig-tree occupies the middle of the court. The inhabitants need every such means of refreshment, for the town in summer is very hot. There is, however, a pleasant breeze called *Inbat* (that is $\varepsilon\mu\beta\alpha\tau\iota\varsigma$, 'incoming') which generally visits the town in the afternoon, and affords a time for refreshment in the hottest part of the season.

In one of our walks, Mr Riggs gave us some illustrations of Scripture from what he had seen in Greece. There every shepherd uses a large wooden crook with which he guides and defends the sheep. This is the shepherd's rod mentioned in the Psalm and by the prophet (Psalm 23:4; Micah 7:14). It is a common mode of expression among the Greeks to say 'such a thing happened *three days ago*', when they mean that a day only intervened. They include the two extreme days as if they had been complete – a mode of speech which illustrates the words of our Lord in Matthew 12:40, 'The Son of Man shall be three days and three nights in the heart of the earth.' Throughout all Greece the natives seldom take any food before eleven o'clock, at which hour they have $\alpha\rho\iota\sigma\tau\sigma\nu$, which we translate dinner; then about eight or nine in the evening they have $\delta\varepsilon\iota\pi\nu\sigma\nu$ or supper, which is the chief meal (John 21:12, see the Greek $\alpha\rho\iota\sigma\tau\eta\sigma\alpha\tau\varepsilon$). This explains the invitation of our Lord to the disciples on the Lake of Galilee, 'Jesus saith unto them, *Come and dine*', that is, come and partake of the morning meal.

On another occasion Mr Riggs gave us his views in regard to the prospects of missionaries in this part of Turkey. Their chief discouragement is the want of any opportunities of speaking freely to the natives, either Greeks or Armenians, on the things of eternity; a painful state of things, brought about by the watchful jealousy of the priests. In Turkey, the priests have far greater influence over the people than they have in the new kingdom of Greece. The Patriarch is allowed by the Turkish Government to do what he pleases, so that he may use his arbitrary power to procure the death of any persons opposed to his authority. In Greece, however, Mr Riggs found that at Napoli, where he was formerly stationed, and indeed throughout the whole kingdom, the Greeks are far less under the control of their priests and are often anxious to be taught the truth. Occasionally at Napoli the Bishops came to hear the preaching of the word, and a few of them seemed to have real concern for their own souls. There is nothing of this kind in Turkey. The candlestick has been entirely removed from Smyrna as far as vital religion among the Greek Christians is concerned. They are thieves, liars, and immoral in a thousand ways. The American Missionaries print a Penny Magazine in the Greek and Armenian languages, which has a considerable circulation; but this is an instrument of little value in the way of saving the souls of the people, as its pages contain only general and scientific information.

On Saturday morning *(August 9)*, in company with Mr Riggs, we enjoyed a pleasant walk up the hill that rises behind the city, where are ruins of the old castle, and where, in the opinion of many, was the original site of Smyrna. We visited the Stadium where Polycarp was martyred for the truth in AD 167. It stands on the face of a hill, the sides of a concave valley forming a natural amphitheatre for the accommodation of spectators. The space may be about 500 feet long on each side, at either end of which rose the seats for the spectators. Near it is a range of broken arches which formed part of the vaults where the wild beasts were kept. From one of these the people urged the Asiarch to let loose a lion against Polycarp. In the midst of this stadium the aged man of God was fixed to a stake and the fire kindled around him; but the flame leaving him unconsumed, he was despatched by the sword of the Roman *confector*. This very stadium was the spot whence his soul ascended up to heaven, 'receiving his portion', according to his own prayer, 'in the number of martyrs in the cup of Christ'. After serving his Lord and directing his flock 'by his step as well as by his voice' during eighty and six years, he was found 'faithful unto death, and received the crown of life' (Revelation 2:10). The Epistle to the Church of Smyrna was to us doubly interesting now. A voice seemed still to echo round the spot,

'Fear none of those things which thou shalt suffer!' A grave close by, over which a tall cypress grows, is said to be the grave of Polycarp.

In the narrative of the martyrdom given in the Epistle by the Church of Smyrna, it is recorded that the Jews distinguished themselves by gathering fuel for the pile; and it is a singular fact, coinciding with this notice, that at present the Jewish quarter lies close under the hill where the stadium stands, and the Jews are much employed in gathering and selling torchwood.

We wandered on to the ruins of a theatre. A fine arch, forming the gateway, remains in tolerable preservation. We could distinctly trace the walls that enclosed a wide circular space; and near the stadium some remains of the ancient wall of the town are still found. Part of the castle also is of great antiquity, and on the hill to the south of it is the Temple of Esculapius.

The prospect from this hill is very splendid. The town below is seen to the greatest advantage. The houses are mostly red-tiled, but the tall dark cypress grove, and the clusters of the same tree shooting up in different quarters, with the calm sea beyond, give the town a rich and noble appearance. There is a full view up to the very top of the gulf, with Bournabat and other villages on the opposite side. In the distance, the island of Lesbos is discernible, and the place where the Hermus enters the sea, at the head of the gulf. On our way back to town we overheard a curious conversation. Two boys came along, one riding upon an ass, the other running by his side. The one on foot was eagerly pressing his companion to let him mount the animal for a little while, offering as an inducement, 'that, if he did so, he would pray for the souls of his deceased mother and sister'. The boy on the ass agreed, on condition that he would remember the soul of his little brother also. At the gate some Tattars with public despatches were riding out very merrily. On a wall we saw an ancient Greek inscription which has been often noticed, but is of little importance. A labourer was returning from the country with his pruning-hook in his hand, a long piece of iron curved toward the point. This pruning-hook might once have been a spear, and could easily be converted into one again. The prophets attended to the nature of things when they said, 'They shall beat their spears into pruning-hooks' (Isaiah 2:4); and again, reversing the command, 'Beat your pruning-hooks into spears' (Joel 3:10). We entered one of the Greek churches at the time when the people were assembling for worship; for all the Eastern churches begin their Sabbath at six on the

Saturday evening. The worshippers were summoned together, not by the ringing of bells (for this privilege is not enjoyed by any of the Christians here except the Roman Catholics), but by beating time on a plank of wood, somewhat in the same way in which our workmen in towns are summoned to their meals. As the people entered one by one, they kissed the pictures on the wall of the church and crossed themselves with three fingers. Near another church we met many Armenians on their way to worship. The most remarkable part of their costume is the head-dress worn by the men, called the *kalpack*. It is like a four-cornered cushion surmounting their cap, and appears very singular to a stranger.

On reaching our dwelling, we received intelligence of an awful conflagration which had taken place in Constantinople, by which 30,000 or 40,000 persons, it was said, had been made houseless. We were the more interested in this information as we were making preparations for visiting that great city. During the second week of our stay at Bouja, Mr McCheyne's health was much improved; yet it was thought advisable that Mr Bonar and Mr Calman should leave him, in the mean time, under the care of our kind friends, and should themselves proceed together to Constantinople by the first steamer to carry on their inquiries there, till by the blessing of God their brother should be enabled to join them.

It was not without melancholy apprehensions that we parted for a season, and with unfeigned regret we took leave of our truly kind and never-to-be-forgotten friends at Bouja. But remembering how the Lord had helped us hitherto, we trusted Him again and went forward.

In the afternoon of *August 17*, we embarked in an Austrian steamer called the *Stamboul*. On the deck, we found ourselves in the midst of people of all nations, but the most were Turkish soldiers, and Greek and Armenian merchants. Many Turkish women sat apart with their faces veiled, and a group of poor Israelites were seated between the cabin door and window, a part of the vessel so frequently occupied by Jews that we began to call it the Jewish quarter. Pacing up and down the deck were two American officers belonging to a vessel near at hand; next were three Englishmen, then two Maltese, some Germans, and two or three Frenchmen. The engineers were from our own land, one an Irishman and the other a Scotchman, and both had their wives on board with them. A Hungarian, with a large beard and whiskers, and a broad brimmed hat, kept himself in perpetual motion. Three Moors also, and four Persians, who wore high sugarloaf caps, attracted our attention, and still more, two Turkish Dervishes, marked by their conical white hats. There was something indescribably saddening in the thought which often rose in our mind, that of all this company perhaps not one knew the Saviour. There is a 'veil spread over all nations'. Yet in such a state of things is the light suddenly to shoot from Zion over the whole world, 'For, behold, the darkness shall cover the earth, and gross darkness the people: but the Lord shall arise upon thee, and his glory shall be seen upon thee and the Gentiles shall come to thy light, and kings to the brightness of thy rising' (Isaiah 60:2,3).

August 18, Sabbath

About three in the morning we were off Lesbos, now called Mytilin, where Sappho and Alcæus sang. The vessel anchored for a short time in the harbour of the town, Mytilin – perhaps the very harbour where Paul's vessel anchored in its voyage (Acts 20:14). In about an hour and a half we were opposite Cape Baba, the ancient Lectum. It is the extreme point of the Ida range, and one of the hills within our view was that renowned Ida, which looked down upon the Trojan plains. It is impossible to sail along this shore without being irresistibly attracted by scenes that have excited the interest of thousands in every land. Many an eye has gazed on these hills and plains, and many a foot explored these ruins. Yet there is to a Christian another and a more delightful feeling called forth by the thought that Paul walked on foot (Acts 20:13) from Troas to Assos along the sands of that seashore, meditating on 'the depth of the riches both of the wisdom and knowledge of God'. Toward the top of this same gulf stood *Adramyttium* (Acts 27:2), one of whose vessels bore Paul to the coast of Lycia in his voyage to Rome. About 7 am we were opposite the Island of Tenedos, and our early classical recollections came here fresh to mind –

Est in conspectu Tenedos, notissima famâ
Insula, dives opum, Priami dum regna manebant. (Virg. Æn. 2.21)
('In sight of Troy lies Tenedos, an isle,
While fortune did on Priam's Kingdom smile,
Renowned for wealth.')

It is six miles from the coast of Troy and is considerably elevated above the sea, rising at the north-west extremity into an eminence. At the time we passed, many vessels lay at anchor wind-bound and unable to enter the Dardanelles. We continued sailing along the coast off Troas, the morning being calm and cool, with a bright sunshine and a deep blue sky. Soon we found ourselves in the midst of the combined English and French fleets, consisting of about twenty ships of the line – more majestic than those of Greece, which once carried its thousand warriors to Ilium. They lay there watching the movements of Russia on Constantinople. The large island of Lemnos was toward the west on our left, and before us to the north-west Imbros, behind which lies Samothrace (Acts 16:11). But still a deeper interest was excited in our mind when Eski-Stamboul was pointed out – the site of Troas, the place where Paul saw in a vision a man of Macedonia that said, 'Come over to Macedonia (across the Aegean Sea) and help us' (Acts 1:8,9), and where he preached till midnight and raised Eutychus from the dead. Here also was the residence of Carpus, the friend with whom Paul left his cloak, books, and parchments (2 Timothy 4:13). We were gazing on it on the Sabbath Day, 'the first day of the week' (Acts 20:7), and the remembrance of Paul's wondrous labours there helped us to enjoy this blessed day, even when so far removed from ordinances. Very near this point are two celebrated promontories, Rhoeteum, where Ajax was buried; and Sigeum, called now Jenesherry, where Achilles was buried. We are told that Alexander the Great stood here upon the tomb of that hero and longed for another Homer to record his own deeds. On the plain of Troy we saw two of the ancient tumuli, each in the form of a small conical hill; the one probably that of Antilochus, the other that of Patroclus. They meet the eye like 'wrecks of a former world'. The mouth of the Scamander, and the point of its junction with the Simois, were shown to us. An obliging young officer kindly pointed out the different localities, and added, that at present English officers might be found fishing every day in these classical streams.

In a few hours we entered the Hellespont, now called the Straits of the Dardanelles, and passed between the far-famed Sestos and Abydos. Near this, the strait is said to be seven stadia, or not quite a mile in breadth, so that two mighty continents seem to approach and gaze upon each other. The modern castles of Romania and Natolia, which have come in place of the ancient towns, are of no great height; their situation is in low ground near the water-edge; but under skilful management their command of the strait would be complete. Each fortress is furnished with more than 100 pieces of cannon. It was here that Leander immortalised himself by his adventurous exploit. It was here, too, that

Xerxes, the king that 'stirred up all against the realm of Grecia' (Daniel 11:2), built his bridge of boats joining Asia to Europe in order to transport his enormous hosts. When he surveyed them lining the shores of both continents, he wept in the vexation of his proud heart because in a hundred years not one of all that multitude would remain to swell the pomp of his power. How unlike the tears of Him who wept over perishing Jerusalem!

The average breadth of the Dardanelles is three miles, and it is about sixty miles long. A delightful breeze and a smooth sea made our sail pleasant and easy; and we were able to spend much of the day in retirement and meditation. While we were reading in the cabin, two Turks came down from the deck to pray, spreading out their mat, and then prostrating themselves to the ground repeatedly till their head touched the floor.

Some of the Jews on board were frank and simple. One had a Hebrew Bible which he had got from Mr Cohen at Smyrna, and on our showing them our Hebrew Bibles, they took them into their hands, examined them, and then held up some of the leaves between them and the sun, to see if there was not a cross stamped on the paper!

About evening, we came to Gallipoli (which stands opposite the ancient Lampsacus), not in itself interesting, but it gives name to the straits, and is situated not far north of the banks of the stream Ægospotamos, at the mouth of which Lysander gave a fatal blow to the power of Athens. The Sea of Marmora, the ancient Propontis, opened upon us; but night came on, and we sailed through it in darkness.

At half-past five in the morning we came in sight of Constantinople, and every moment as we advanced nearer the scene broke upon us with increasing magnificence. The situation is splendid. Having the Straits of the Dardanelles for its gate on the south, and the Bosphorus for its gate on the north, it could rest securely on its seven hills, and look around on all its prosperity undisturbed by the fear of an enemy. The morning sky was cloudy, but this of itself was delightful to us, who had scarcely seen a cloud for nearly four months. It was like a pleasant summer morning in Scotland, when the mist is still lying on the hills, and the clouds are lingering on the face of the heavens. The first part of the city which meets the view upon entering the Bosphorus from the south is called Stamboul. Here the massy dome of St Sophia, and graceful minarets of every kind, crowd upon the sight. Palaces, mosques and baths seem to be without number in this renowned capital. And then the rich verdant trees that surround so many of the white marble buildings, and the clear blue sea which like a deep full river laves the shore and flows up the harbour, combine to give Constantinople a gorgeous beauty, which is perhaps unrivalled by any city in the world. Old Sandys truly says of the view from the sea, 'It seemeth to present a city in a wood to the pleased beholders'. We anchored in the well-known harbour called 'the Golden Horn', so called from its resemblance to the shape of an ox's horn, and this so filled with merchandise that it is a true *cornu copiae*. It is so deep that in many places the largest vessels (it is said) could touch the houses with their prows, while the stern is still floating in the water. We were conveyed to the shore in a *caique*, a light skiff, in breadth generally three feet, and above twenty in length, resembling a canoe, hundreds of which are seen shooting along in all directions with amazing swiftness. We landed at the part of the city called Galata, on the northern side of the harbour, intending to proceed to Pera, and there to take up our quarters in Romboli's inn, to which we had been directed. The inn, however, was already more than full; the recent conflagration and an overflow of travellers having united to fill it, so that no vacancy was left for us. Alone in this great city, we allowed a young man, a Maltese, to guide us to a lodging in Galata, two porters (here called *hamals*) bearing our luggage. It was by no means a desirable locality. The American Missionaries, however, Mr Goodell and Mr Calhoun, on hearing of our arrival, sought us out that same day and insisted upon our taking up our residence with them in Pera. These American brethren and their families were full of kindness and brotherly love; and under their roof we enjoyed all the comforts of a home. From their fellow-labourers also, Mr Adger and Mr Hamlin, we received unremitting attention.

We went out in the afternoon to visit the English Consul, riding up the steep streets on horseback, as the day was excessively hot. Somewhat to our surprise, the state of the public mind in the city was calm; Ibraim Pasha's recent victory at Nezib had made no impression. Indeed, the Turks seem to take everything with apathy. Sometimes an order is issued on occasions of political excitement, forbidding two people to be seen together in the streets talking *about the weather*; in other words, about the state of public affairs. But at this time there was less excitement in Constantinople than in Smyrna, and less known in public of the real state of things.

In the streets we noticed the Turkish carriages for ladies, called *arabah*, drawn by two horses, and not much raised above the ground.

The windows have no glass, but curtains, resembling veils. Within, it is said, the sides are often ornamented with mottoes and curious devices, by which some have illustrated the description given of the chariot in the Song, 'the midst thereof being paved with love' (Song of Solomon 3:10). Waggons drawn by oxen are as common on the streets here as at Smyrna. We saw melons growing on the housetops in the very heart of the town, and many vines trained up the walls of houses. The buildings are in general miserable. Often the lower part of the house is of marble (brought like common stone from the neighbouring islands), while all above is a clumsy shed of wood. We passed one of the Dervish establishments, resembling that of a monastery. It was that of the *Dancing Dervishes*; some of whom were sauntering in the court, wearing the round, high cap, a mark by which they are easily known.

In the evening, we walked among the ruins occasioned by the fire. Several tents, chiefly of Armenian merchants who had lost their all, were pitched among the smoking ruins. One of these was overheard to say as a funeral passed by, 'Would to God that I too had been carried to my grave' (Job 3:20,21). In the bitterness of his soul, he unconsciously imitated the impatient burst of Job.

On our way home, we observed several persons wrapt in their hyke, preparing to sleep under the open sky. Indeed, it is a frequent custom here and in all the East to sleep in the open air all night, and this may explain the case of the young man who followed Christ, 'having a linen cloth cast about his naked body' (Mark 14:51).

August 20

We were visited by Mr Farman, the Jewish Missionary of the London Society, who brought along with him a converted German Jew named Merkuson. Another Jewish convert, since dead, named Jeruschalmai, was prevented by domestic circumstances from accompanying them. From them we received much valuable information with regard to the Jews. But as yet, no one has been able to obtain accurate statistical information as to the numbers and condition of the Jewish population of Constantinople. They reckon their numbers, including the Jews of Scutari, Ortakoy, and the suburban villages, at 80,000 souls. Rabbi Bibas of Corfu, whom we afterwards met, reduced the number to 20,000, but without stating any evidence to induce us to credit his assertion. He may have meant the Jews of the city without those of the suburbs. Most of these are originally Spanish Jews whose fathers took refuge here when expelled from Spain. They, therefore, speak the Spanish and Turkish languages. There are about 600 German and 200 Italian Jews. The great mass of the Jewish community here are ignorant and unlearned. Mr Farman, as well as the two Jewish converts, agreed that schools for the children of the German Jews might succeed well. But in order to induce the parents to send their children, it would be needful to offer to teach them French and Italian. The expense of an Italian master could not be less than £3.10s. a month, and a French master the same. It would also be needful to teach the boys and girls in separate apartments. A Hebrew teacher could easily be found. It would not be very difficult to find some liberal-minded Jew who would teach Hebrew from the Old Testament, and who would not object to a missionary's visit to the schools. Mr Farman even thought that the New Testament might be introduced. If such a school were to be established, probably fifteen boys and as many girls might be persuaded to attend it at once. These remarks apply only to the German Jews.

In regard to the Spanish Jews, who constitute the mass of the population, they are very bitter in their enmity to Christianity. But if the experiment was tried with the others, it is possible that they also might be induced to follow the example set them by their German brethren.

The reason why the German Jews would be willing to send their children is that they have brought with them to this country some of the spirit and principles of Germany – they know the value of education and wish for it. If a German Christian lady was appointed female teacher of the school, it would not be objected to by the Jews. The expenses of a missionary in Constantinople are necessarily great; it is not uncommon to pay £400 as the rent of a moderately-sized dwelling. But the great hindrance in the way of carrying the gospel to Israel here is the total want of protection to converts and inquirers for the Jews, being recognised by Government as a community, have power to get any one of their brethren banished if they desire it. If a Jew is converted and receives baptism at the hands of a Protestant minister, the Greeks and Armenians immediately withhold all employment from him so that he is cast upon the missionary himself for support. Mr Farman fixed his residence at Beyukdere, and one object he had in view in living so far from the city was that he might get protection and employment for inquiring Jews, that village being inhabited chiefly by Franks. Sometimes he has been visited by twenty Jews at one time, all desiring Christian baptism, provided only they could be protected. He told us that he knew of many in that condition at that very moment, and a Jewess had come to him very lately asking baptism. It is true, their motive is not always good. Perhaps there are not many of them who care about Christianity itself, or feel burdened with a sense of sin. It is rather a desire to be free from the yoke of Judaism that influences them. Still, such a desire is not to be lightly treated, and may, by the blessing of God upon the teaching of the missionary, be made the beginning of a saving change. There is a strict adherence to the Talmud among the Spanish Jews. They universally expect Messiah and many of them had fixed the year 1840 as the era of his appearing.

Almost all the large synagogues have a school attached to them and at Ortakoy there are some large schools unconnected with the synagogues. In that quarter, they have frequently purchased Bibles from the missionary for their schools.

Mr Farman told us that he had laboured here about four years; Mr Schauffler, the American missionary to the Jews (and the only one, we believe, that America has hitherto sent to the house of Israel) had laboured longer, but had hitherto turned his attention chiefly to translation. To him, the Jew Merkuson owes his knowledge of the truth. Mr Wolff was the first to visit his brethren in this great city. Then Mr Farman and Mr Nicolayson came and decided upon its claims to be one of the stations of the London Jewish Society.

The Jews here have been superseded as bankers by the Armenians, and so have lost much of their influence with Government. They are poor and unlearned; making money is their great object. They have this remarkable feature that they are very stationary, not moving from place to place. In Ortaktoy alone reside 6,000 Jews; in Scutari, 3,000; in Ismid, the ancient Nicomedia, there are 1,000, and in Brousa, 6,000 or 7,000. The whole population of Constantinople is generally reckoned to be 500,000.

The same evening we walked out with Mr Calhoun and saw on the hill opposite to us the aqueduct of Valens, and the place where Mahommed, the conqueror of Constantinople, entered the city. We traced also what had been the course of the ancient city walls, and returned homewards through the now ruined houses of Pera.

Early next morning *(August 21)* we enjoyed a sail up the Bosphorus in one of the light caiques to pay a short visit to Mr Farman, the converted Jew Merkuson accompanying us. His residence was at the village of

Beyukdere, twelve miles, or almost the whole extent of the Bosphorus, from Pera. As we set sail the caiques were shooting across the harbour in all directions and the scene varied every moment. We kept near the shore in order as much as possible to avoid the strong current from the Black Sea and yet we were so retarded by it that though we set sail at half-past seven it was half-past eleven before we reached Beyukdere. On our left the winter-palace of the Sultan, though irregularly built, had a striking appearance. We counted forty columns in front of one wing of the building and another wing had eight Corinthian pillars. The roof has an elegant battlement, and the rows of windows are light and graceful. The steps in front came down to the water edge, and several Turks were pacing backwards and forwards on them with their usual solemn gait, reminding us of the poet's description –

'The bearded Turk that rarely deigns to speak,
Master of all around, too potent to be meek.'

In the interior, we could see a square enclosing fountains and a well laid out garden. Nearly opposite this, on the other side of the Bosphorus, stands the Golden Palace, so called because ornamented all over with gilded work, where the young Sultan was residing at the time. The line of buildings on the European side is scarcely ever interrupted, there being almost one continuous line of houses for ten or twelve miles. The chimneys of many of them are in the form of a well-shaped pillar, which gives them an air of superior neatness. They are built close upon the water, and often there seemed not above a hundred yards of level ground between the sea and the steep hills that sloped up behind. On the brow of these hills gardens and cypress-trees were waving, which give freshness and beauty to the scene, while the sea flows up to the very steps of many of the houses.

We came to Ortakoy – that is, 'middle village' – a large suburb of the city, poor and ill-built, inhabited by Jews, but generally of the lower class. Beyond this is one ledge of sunken rocks, marked by an elegant marble fountain erected above them, and two other similar ledges of rocks, marked by groups of trees planted on them. The English Admiral, Sir R. Stopford, passing the Seraglio, was saluted by twenty guns, the sound of which echoed deep among the surrounding hills. The water was all the time clear and the channel pebbly to the very edge, the current often so strong as to compel the men to leave the caique, and instead of rowing, to drag the boat with ropes round the point where the current met it. We were met by a steamer from Trebizond coming down from the Black Sea. The sea-fowl were flying round us and innumerable porpoises were sporting beautifully in the water. A breeze from the Black Sea and some overhanging clouds gave a grateful coolness to the air. White towers occasionally meet the eye perched on the surrounding heights, and small forts, defended with cannon, stand close upon the shore. One remarkable fortress occurs near the head of the strait, said by some to be of Genoese origin, and by others to be the work of Constantine. Its towers are not round but sharp-cornered, and the walls surmounted with a battlement. If it be the work of Constantine, it would be valuable and interesting, for no remains of that illustrious Emperor are to be found in his own city. Passing Therapia, where Lord Ponsonby, the British Ambassador, was then residing, we at length reached Beyukdere, pleasantly situated within sight of the opening into the Black Sea. After visiting Mr Farman and hearing more of his labours, both among the Jews and European residents, we returned to the city. The sail back occupied only two hours, the current being with us, and the whole trip cost us only thirty piastres.

In the evening one of the American Missionaries, Mr Hamlin, once assistant to the devoted Dr Payson, but who has now consecrated himself to missionary labour, gave us some account of the Armenians of Constantinople. They are a social community enjoying much domestic happiness. Their feelings against Protestantism are very bitter and they hold no open communication with the missionaries. Still there seems to be a secret work of the Spirit begun in the hearts of some of them. One young priest is decidedly pious and labours silently among his brethren. A rich banker, who had done all he could for the schools, continues to be enthusiastic in that object and friendly to the missionaries. There used to be about sixty young men attending the missionary schools; and all these still manifest great kindness to the missionaries.

This night we remarked at the howling of the dogs that prowl about the city. All foreigners are struck with their noise and unsightly appearance. They wander about the streets with fierce hungry looks, and occasionally even attack the lonely passenger in the night. They answer precisely to the description given in the Psalm, 'At evening let them return, and let them make a noise like a dog, and go round about the city: let them wander up and down for meat, and grudge if they be not satisfied' (Psalm 59:14,15).

Next day *(August 29)*, accompanied by Mr Calhoun, we took a caique at Tophana, and crossed the Golden Horn, hoping to get a sight of the interior of the famous Seraglio in the train of the British Admiral, Sir R. Stopford, who was that day to be admitted within its walls. In this, however, we were disappointed, as the Admiral had left the place before we reached it. From without, its appearance is extensive and splendid, adorned with many gilded minarets, shooting up amidst tan and verdant trees. It has been the scene of many a deed of horrid cruelty.

The part of the city where it stands is called Stamboul, and is the most ancient. As we walked on we observed in various places small pieces of paper collected together and thrust into openings of the walls. This is done by Mahometans, who are careful to preserve pieces of paper with any writing on them, because possibly the name of Mahomet or of Allah may be on some of them. We passed the old divan which was burned down some years ago. Its elegant gate is arched in the form of an expanded leaf and is said by some to have given its name to the Sublime Porte whose sittings were held here.

We then visited the mosque of St Sophia, whose dome is the largest in the world. It is a magnificent building, but the Turks have added many of the present portions of the edifice. The mosque of Achmet stands adjoining it, having six minarets, covered, not with gilding, but with gold itself, which retains its lustre unimpaired. There is first an outer court, a space set round with trees; then, an inner court, or square, adorned with eight-and-twenty pillars, some of marble, others of granite, and the capitals of each finished off in the form of fringes. The pavement of the court is all marble, and in the centre a fountain pours forth its refreshing streams. Through the open windows we got a glance of the interior also, though a surly Turk from within commanded us to withdraw. The roof is supported by immense pillars and is compacted of layers of stone; the walls are finely ornamented and the floor spread with clean mats and carpets.

We then visited the bazaar, which occupies a wide space. It consists of many streets and rows of shops, all roofed over for shade and coolness. In one street there is a row of tentmakers; in another, shoemakers; in another, sellers of pipes; in another, shops exhibiting every variety of rich cloth; then a row of silks and furs; so that almost every article of common use has a row of shops for itself. At one shop-door we asked for a dish of *yaout* – that is, meat boiled with sauce and *leban*, and eaten with toasted bread. We did not find it possible to visit the slave-market.

In the afternoon, we crossed over to Scutari, the ancient Chrysopolis, which was the seaport of Chalcedon, on the Asiatic side of the Bosphorus. Our chief object was to visit the *howling dervishes*. They were beginning their devotions as we entered. At first they prayed moderately, in a kind of chanting voice. In about half an hour they formed a semicircle round their chief, to whom each went up before taking his place, doing obeisance, while he took off the cap he wore, and replaced it with a lighter one, more fit for the part he was to act. They prayed with every imaginable gesture and movement, the body, head, and hands all being in motion at once. From time to time their chief seemed to excite them to greater vehemence by crying out with a loud scream *'Ullah, Illah!'* in a tone that made us shudder. In a short time the whole company were engaged in the most frantic movements. Some of them, nearly overpowered with their intense efforts, were gasping for breath, and all uttering a sound, 'ocha, ocha', like one panting and ready to sink under exhaustion. A *dancing dervish* then entered the room, who sat down and played calmly on a pipe, while the rest kept time to the tune in the violent gestures of their bodies. Then three more appeared, and kept whirling about in a circle for twenty minutes without ceasing. The whole scene was a frightful exhibition of human impiety and fanaticism, and yet we were told that it is often much more extravagant and revolting. The missionaries at Brousa lately saw one of these dervishes work himself up to such a frenzy that the foam came from his mouth, his face grew pale, and he fell on the ground, like the demoniacs mentioned in the New Testament, till one of his company restored him by beating on his breast, and using other restorative processes. We observed hanging on the wall the instruments with which they used to torture themselves, like the priests of Baal (1 Kings 18:28). There were hooks and sharp-pointed instruments, and wires that used to be thrust through their cheeks from side to side; balls also, attached to sharp-pointed spikes. These balls were made to strike the ground, and to recoil in such a way, that the spike struck its point into their breast. It required a decree of the late Sultan to put a stop to these self-torturing practices. Many persons came in *to be blessed* by the dervishes. As they entered, they kissed the hands of the chief. Two soldiers were among the number of the dervishes, and several soldiers came in to receive a blessing. One man, who had sore eyes, came forward to the chief, who prayed over him and sent him away. Clothes also and sick children were carried in to receive a blessing. And yet these dervishes are exceedingly immoral in their lives, being guilty of the grossest licentiousness. We witnessed this painful scene for about two hours, and learned to cry with more intense desire, 'Have respect unto the covenant, for the dark places of the earth are full of the habitations of cruelty' (Psalm 74:20).

Close to Scutari stood the ancient Chalcedon, now called Kadikoy, 'the village of the judges', in allusion to the famous Council once held within its walls, the Council which condemned the opinions of Eutyches who held that there was but one nature in Christ. Crossing to Galata, we enjoyed a splendid sail and the view of a magnificent sunset. The rich beams of the sun were playing on the waters, while innumerable caiques were skimming gaily over them. A Greek vessel was leaving the harbour, *a pilgrim vessel*, setting out for the Holy Land. It was a small brig and the passengers were miserably crowded together, all eager to pay their vows at the Holy Sepulchre. Such vessels as these, manned by ignorant sailors, are often wrecked by sudden storms.

The same evening we applied to the Russian Chancellor to get our passport signed for Warsaw. This he refused to do, assigning as his reason that no ecclesiastic is allowed to pass through Russia, unless he has obtained from St Petersburg the special consent, both of the Synod and of the Emperor. We noticed that, as he spoke, he was all the while noting down our names and appearance from the passport, no doubt intending to send them before us to prevent us from making any attempt to cross the Russian frontier. Had he known that we were sent on a mission of love to Israel, he would no doubt have been still more determined in his refusal for Russia holds Israel with a grasp as firm as that of Pharaoh; though the day is at hand when God 'will say to the north, Give up' (Isaiah 43:6). We were thus obliged to give up the hopes of returning by Warsaw and to make up our mind to shape our course through Cracow. Meanwhile, we occupied our time in fresh inquiries into the state of Israel in the city of Constantinople.

August 23

Setting out for the Jewish quarter, we met two strong Circassians wearing the caftan and conical Persian cap. We also met a Roman Catholic funeral, that of a young person. The priest walked before in his black dress reading the prayers, many boys following him joined in the chant, and the bier was covered with flowers. We sailed up the Golden Horn, passing by a wooden bridge and a dockyard in which we saw no more than two ships building and a few under repair. We landed at the

Jewish quarter called Huski and soon got a pleasant young Jew named Nisim who spoke Italian to be our guide. He knew no Hebrew and had little of an Israelite in his character. He said he was anxious to be away from his countrymen and to get to England. We asked what he hoped to find in England; and, in reply he shewed us that the sum of his expectations was 'that he would get freedom to do as he liked', and wear *nuovo capello*', 'a new hat'. He took us to a school attended by about eighty boys. Here the bastinado and the whip hung on the walls as at Smyrna; yet the children did not appear to be so much oppressed. Scarcely any had books from which to read; but a few leaves were handed from one to the other. In another school we found thirty children, who were reading extracts from the Old Testament, but they also had few schoolbooks. As we entered, they were reading the passage, '*For a small moment have I forsaken thee, but with great mercies will I gather thee*' (Isaiah 54:7). The syllables and sounds of this they repeated over and over, but did not seem to understand the sense. How little they knew the depths of gracious love to their nation which that verse contains! We visited two other schools of the same kind and found that the accommodation in all was wretched and the teachers illiterate.

We came to a synagogue standing on an eminence and enclosed within a wall. It was not unlike one of our churches, well built, airy, and clean. The drapery in front of the ark was embroidered in a beautiful manner, and the lamps were handsome lustres of brass. There were sixteen synagogues in this quarter alone and three in Pera. The Jews seemed very suspicious of us; they scarcely entered into conversation at all, but stood silent, and sullenly noticed what we did and where we went. With some difficulty we now found our way to the synagogue of the Karaite Jews, of whom there are about a hundred families here, all living together in one quarter, being despised and hated by the other Jews. Their synagogue is built in a low situation. You descend a stair, over which a vine is spreading its branches, and there find yourself in the area where the synagogue stands. Perhaps it is a satire on their fondness for the literal meaning of Scripture, but it is said – that the Karaites always have their synagogue low, that so they may literally use the Psalm, '*Out of the depths have I cried unto thee, O Lord*' (Psalm 130:4). The apartment was neat and clean, the floor covered with mats and carpets. We examined their copies of the Bible and found one of the London Society's edition among them. They wear 'the fringes' or *Tsitsith*, according to the commandment in Numbers (Numbers 15:38),

of a different form from those of other Jews. It is with them a sort of sash
or girdle, at the two ends of which are fringes of white and blue – not
merely white threads, like that of the other Jews. We saw also the
mezuzah at the door of the synagogue so that they are not altogether free
from pharisaical traditions. But they have no *Tephillin* or phylacteries;
on the contrary, they deride them, and call them *donkey-bridles*. They
have only one school for their children. Inquiring for the rabbi, we
learned he was absent in Stamboul, so that we resolved to return on the
morrow to get better acquainted with this interesting people, *the
Protestants* of the house of Israel. We made inquiry at many Jews about
the place which Joseph Wolff calls 'the Valley of Job' and which he said
that some Jews thought was 'the land of Uz'. There is such a spot, but
none of the Jews connected it with that patriarch. It gets its name from
a famous Saracen named Yob, who was killed in the valley in the great
assault on Constantinople and whose tomb was erected there. It is said
that the spot of his burial was discovered in a miraculous manner, and
a mosque has been built over it, called, after him, the Mosque of Yob,
which is much frequented by devout Moslems.

August 24

A little after five in the morning we again sailed up the Golden Horn to
Huski and soon reached the Karaite Synagogue. The Jews were already
met, in number about eighty persons. Their shoes were all piled up at the
door and they themselves seated upon the ground. A few who came in
late seemed to show some reverence to the *mezuzah* on the doorpost. All
sat while reading their prayers; but when the Law was produced, all
stood up in token of reverence and then sat down again (see Nehemiah
8:5). After reading the usual portion, in which two boys took the chief
share, the rabbi, who had invited us to sit by his side, read a passage in
Deuteronomy and gave an oral exposition, of which Mr Calman took
notes. The passage was Deuteronomy 21:10-23. 'From verses 10 to 15',
the rabbi said, 'there are given directions regarding the captive woman
who was to be married to her Jewish conqueror; her hair was to be
shaved, her nails pared, and her raiment changed'. 'Now (said he), the
heart is to be kept with all diligence, for if we allow our hearts to think
upon an object, then the desire to have it springs up.' This he applied to
the case of the conqueror and the captive woman. 'To prevent this snare,
she was to be deprived of all her attractions, such as her fine hair, and
her showy raiment; and her glowing spirit was to be brought down by

making her mourn for her parents thirty days. If, even after this, the conqueror persisted in his purpose, and chose her for his wife, then there was need of directions for him how to act toward her. Accordingly, verses 15-18, Moses speaks of "the woman hated"; for a marriage such as this, not grounded in the fear of God, might be expected to produce strife and hatred. And even this is not all. This heathen woman would possibly prove ungodly and ungodly mothers will train up their children in ungodliness. Hence, verses 18-22, Moses is led to speak of "the rebellious son".' After thus ingeniously tracing the connection of the verses, the rabbi spoke at some length of the responsibility lying upon parents. He exhorted them 'to take special care in training up their families, and not to admit persons into their houses of whose piety and integrity they had no evidence. The captive woman was obliged to make a profession of the religion of her conqueror before she could be married to him; but you see (said he) the chain of misfortunes that succeed when the profession is not a true one'. He referred, in conclusion, to the wise provision of the Karaite Jews, that none be admitted into their communion who have not passed through a probation of five years, during which time they are instructed, and their manner of life watched. If they are found to be sincere and faithful, then, at the end of that time, they are received as brethren and married into one of their families.

There was no greater appearance of real devotion in the Karaite congregation than in other Jewish synagogues. They often spoke to each other even during prayer; and we observed that some of them fell asleep as they sat on the ground. When service was over, the rabbi, Isaac Cohen, invited us to his house – a clean and airy habitation – and after entering, according to the custom of the country, a servant brought us water and jelly. The rabbi is an elderly man, of some intelligence and learning – able to speak Hebrew fluently. He admitted the ignorance of his people and highly approved of the proposal that Christians should institute schools among them, saying that he would send his own son to be a scholar. He remarked that their sect had suffered less from Christians than from Jews, and had no enmity at all to the followers of Jesus. He had been told that some Christians believed them to be descendants of the ten tribes who had no part in the death of Christ. He said that it was 1,260 years since they separated from the other Jews. The rabbi of the Karaites must always be a *Cohen*, that is, a priest, or lineal descendant of the family of Aaron. Our host himself was one as his name indicated. Their sect has no influence with the Sultan, and the Hacham

Pasha of the other Jews has frequently attempted to get them banished from Constantinople, and yet they have been able hitherto to maintain their ground and resist the attempts of their brethren to expel them. He told us that he was himself the author of a Translation of the Pentateuch into Turkish, of which he had only four copies remaining; the rest had been all disposed of to Karaites. Before taking leave, we purchased from him at a moderate price, the following works, all of them very rare and connected with the Karaite Jews.

1. A Hebrew Prayer-book, used by the Karaite Jews.
2. A Hebrew Pentateuch, with a translation into the Tartar and Osmanli Turkish language, used by the Karaite Jews. This is the work above mentioned of our friend R. Isaac Cohen.
3. A Commentary on the Books of Moses by rabbi Joseph Solomon, a Karaite Jew.
4. A Commentary on the Prophets, by rabbi Aaron, a Karaite Jew.
5. A Commentary on all the Commandments of the Old Testament, by rabbi Elijah Bsitzi, a Karaite Jew.

All these are now deposited in the Library of the General Assembly of our Church.

We were highly gratified that we had been permitted to visit this interesting community; and all the information that we received concerning them confirms the report which we had previously heard, that they are a peculiarly upright and respectable class of Jews. The Karaites of the Crimea are so highly esteemed that on one occasion, when the Emperor wished them to serve as soldiers, they asked him to inquire if ever during 600 years any public crime had been laid to the charge of a Karaite and pleaded, that if they were sent to the war, he would lose some of his best subjects. The Emperor admitted the truth of their plea and desisted from his demand. Many of them carry on trade at Odessa; and it is said that there is a colony of them in Lithuania, by the side of a beautiful lake, where they are agriculturists and cultivate the cucumber. Our friend Mr Calman also met with Karaites in the village of Heet near Baghdad.

August 25
We enjoyed a Sabbath-day not unlike one of our quiet Sabbaths at home. Even the Roman Catholic bells sounding through the city did not disturb

us, for they reminded us the more of our own privileged land. At ten o'clock forenoon, Mr Bonar preached in the room of the American missionaries, and again at half-past seven in the evening. The audience was composed of the American missionaries and their families, and several European residents. At four o'clock we had a Bible class, in which all the missionary families joined. It was interesting to be so engaged in the midst of the heathen, in the city of the first Christian Emperor, and not far from the place where Peter may have preached; for within view, on the other side of the Bosphorus, stood Mount Olympus, marking out the region of Bithynia. In the region of Bithynia were to be found some of those scattered Christians to whom Peter wrote both his Epistles, encouraging them to bear 'the fiery trial' (1 Peter 4:12) which came upon them under the governor Pliny, in the reign of Trajan.

We were ready to depart on the morrow, having completed our arrangements during the preceding week. We had discovered that to ascertain accurately the state of the Jewish mind in Constantinople, one must take up his residence there, and gradually penetrate the mass. No missionary has ever done this; so that this great city is yet an unexplored territory. Mr Schauffler from America and Mr Farman from England may be said to have laboured on the outskirts. Any efforts hitherto made have been effective, at the most, only on the German Jews residing here, whereas the Spanish Jews form the immense bulk of the vast community of the children of Israel. No aggressive effort has been made on this mass; and yet the spontaneous visits made to the two missionaries who have resided here are enough to show that there is some stirring among the dry bones in this open valley. Oh for an Elijah, 'very jealous for the Lord of Hosts', to go forth on the work of salvation to these untold thousands of Israel who are sitting in the region and shadow of death! He would require the same qualifications as a missionary at Smyrna, but not more; for the ancient learning of the Jews of Constantinople is nearly gone. The obstacles, too, are the very same as in Smyrna, with the addition, perhaps, of greater political power and more bitter and watchful jealousy on the part of the rabbis. But many of the people are weary of the bondage in which their rabbis keep them. It is of consequence, also, to remember that any impression made on the Karaites of this city, whose friendliness to Christians seems like the Macedonian cry, 'Come over and help us', would soon reach their brethren of the same community in the Crimea, and other parts of the world. Indeed, we may well ask, Why have not special advances been made to this class of Jews ere now? They are far less bewildered by tradition and prejudice than their brethren, and the veil seems not to be so closely drawn over their heart as over that of their brethren. Oh that God would raise up some devoted missionary to carry to them the good tidings of the Gospel! *'Oh that the salvation of Israel were come out of Zion!'*

CHAPTER 7

WALLACHIA – MOLDAVIA

'Who shall bemoan thee? or who shall go aside to ask how thou doest?'
(Jeremiah 15:5).

Early in the morning of *August 26*, the steamer from Smyrna arrived in the harbour of Constantinople, and, with heartfelt gratitude and joy, we found Mr McCheyne on board, wonderfully recovered, and able to proceed on the voyage. A few hours after, we took farewell of our kind American brethren, who had made their house our home, and sailed for the Danube. The steamer in which we sailed was named *Ferdinando Primo* and though belonging to an Austrian company was commanded by a kind, intelligent Englishman. The well-known Prince Piccolomusci was on board on his way home to Germany from Abyssinia, from which country he had brought a ransomed female slave and several Nubian boys. As we left the harbour, we enjoyed our last view of this wonderful city. The marble towers and dark green cypresses of the Seraglio, the ample dome of St Sophia, the towering mosques, and the crescent on at least ninety minarets that rise over the red-tiled houses of the city, were all glowing beneath the rays of a noonday sun. We were able to sit on the deck and enjoy the scenery all the way up the Bosphorus; but soon after entering the Black Sea, a headwind sprung up, and we experienced something of the storms that led the ancients to call it $\alpha\xi\epsilon\nu o\varsigma$, 'the inhospitable sea'. We did not, however, experience any of those thick dark fogs which often envelope its bosom and are said to have suggested the modern name. We forgot to look for the famous rocky islands about two miles north of the entrance, known to the ancients by the name of Cyaneae or Symplegades. It was fabled by the unskilful and therefore timid navigators of those days, that these rocks used to dash on each other; and the renowned ship *Argo* ran no small risk in passing between them. Our vessel, however, knew none of these dangers, although, in search of the lost sheep of the house of Israel, we were traversing the same dangerous seas which Jason and his band explored when they sought the Golden Fleece. These shores used to be thickly set with altars and other devout tokens of gratitude for deliverance which seamen erected in honour of their gods.

Next morning the sea was like a sheet of glass and we found ourselves rapidly sailing along the western shore. The coast was low and the country nearly flat, so that the eye wandered over plains partially wooded, without any marked object to arrest it. We passed Cape Emineh Bourun, which is the termination of the range of the Balkan – the renowned Hoemus of ancient days. Between this range and the Danube lay the country called Moesia. At noon, we anchored opposite the town of Varna, which occupies the site of the ancient Odyssus. It is 128 miles from the Bosphorus and stands on the flat shore of a fine bay. The houses are all of wood, low-built and red-tiled, with eight minarets rising over them; and a white wall, with musket-loop holes, surrounds the town. We landed, and after going through the ceremonies of fumigation for a few minutes, entered the town and wandered through its half-deserted streets. There was pointed out to us the pass in the neighbouring hills where the Russian army was attacked by the Turks. In the streets we met some Jewish children, and a little after, three German Jews, one of whom was bitterly complaining of having been left here by the captain of the last steamer, contrary to promise. 'The precious sons of Zion, comparable to fine gold, how are they esteemed as earthen pitchers, the work of the hands of the potter!' (Lamentations 4:2).

At three o'clock we re-embarked and left the bay of Varna. It was a fine calm evening and the eye could see to a great distance. No land appeared to the east, but a few distant sails lay on the line of the horizon. The western coast now became elevated and picturesque. A range of bold white cliffs overhung the sea, terminating in Cape Kalacria, the ancient Tiristria; and the highest point of the promontory was surmounted by the ruins of an old Genoese castle. The bay is called Kavarna, and this is the course of that Pontus which the Roman poet Ovid has made famous by his letters. We must have passed soon after near the place of the same poet's exile, Tomi in Sarmatia; and by this time we were prepared to understand the description of his voyage, given in his Elegies (Trist. I.10).

Next morning *(August 28)*, the Euxine was still calm like an inland lake. Multitudes of porpoises were playing in the water near the vessel, no doubt the dolphins described by Ovid (Trist. III,X,43). About seven o'clock the Five Mountains came in sight. They are situated about thirty miles from the coast and south of the Danube, are of a regular shape, and stand in a line, not unlike a few porpoises following one another. A little farther on we passed the south-west mouth of the Danube, and soon after another of its mouths, marked only by the deep woods upon its banks. The sea now exchanged its clear deep blue for a clay colour, being tinged by the muddy waters of the river; and the depth was only five fathoms. The coast was flat and low, marked by nothing but the tall reeds that skirted it and the trees beyond. Two large flocks of pelicans were dipping themselves in the water. About midday our vessel entered the Danube by the mouth called Seluna. A Russian village was near, at which several vessels were anchored. The rapidity of the stream and the shallowness of the channel make the navigation at the entrance very dangerous, so that many vessels are wrecked here. Indeed, it is said that the chief dangers attending the navigation of the Black Sea are to be attributed to the rivers that flow into it. There are nearly forty rivers which empty themselves into it, and these are continually altering the channel by the large deposits of mud which they carry down. Here the 'dark-flowing' Danube appeared to be about the breadth of the Forth immediately above Alloa, but much more rapid. The territory on the right hand was Bessarabia, under the dominion of Russia. A few wretched huts of reeds plastered over with mud appeared on the bank, before which some Russian sentinels were patrolling to guard the frontier. A vessel lay at anchor near, bearing the Russian flag. As we sailed slowly up the river, the banks continued flat and uninteresting, covered with reeds and bordered by marshes. Before sunset we got a near view of the Five Mountains, which, after all, owe the notice taken of them chiefly to the level plains which surround them, for they are not very high.

We anchored for half an hour at Tultsha, a Turkish town on the Bulgarian or southern bank, fixing the anchor to a tree. The vessel was now in the branch of the river called the St George's branch, which forms the limit of the Russian dominions, and there expands into a lake. The vapours from the river made the full moon appear very large, and its rays fell with a peculiar glare upon the water. Mosquitoes became every hour more harassing; indeed, one of the most painful trials in sailing up the Danube is occasioned by the myriads of these annoying insects. The veils which we had brought with us for the purpose failed to answer the end of keeping out these unwelcome visitors, and sleep was driven from our eyes.

During this voyage we had many interesting conversations with the captain of the vessel and with the Prince. The latter told us that he had been educated when a boy at a Moravian seminary and that he used to weep at the story of the sufferings of Jesus; but he had afterwards attended one of the Neologian Universities of Germany where the seeds of infidelity were sown in his heart. And now he had cast off the authority of the Bible, seemed scarcely to believe in a God and held Pythagorean notions as to the transmigration of souls. We were enabled to bear an honest testimony to this bewildered man, showing chiefly from what we had so lately witnessed of fulfilled prophecy, that the Bible was the Word of God, and proving from that Word his ruined condition and the great salvation.

August 29

Before daybreak we had reached Galatz, the part of Moldavia near which we intended to perform our quarantine. We were not allowed to land, but, leaving the steamer, sailed down to the quarantine station two miles below. Here, in an elevated situation, we found a large enclosure of wood with many wooden cottages in the centre, one of which was to be our place of confinement for a week. It formed a striking contrast to our quarantine at the foot of Carmel, but the atmosphere was cooler, and we felt that we were on European ground. The only objects visible around were the low dusty hills between us and Galatz, and on the west the hills of the Little Balkan and the Five Mountains on the opposite side of the Danube.

As night came on we were at a loss how to procure necessary articles of food; no *guardiano* had been yet appointed to serve for us, and the keeper of the *locanda* or store, where provisions are supplied to those in quarantine by means of a board on which they are placed, could speak no language but Romaic and Wallachian. Besides, not being aware of the difficulty of procuring articles of comfort in a quarantine station, we had provided nothing for such an emergency, except mats for the night, which we brought from Constantinople. We now found the benefit of being inured to the rude life of those who dwell in tents.

Next morning, however, we were visited by a countryman of our own, Charles Cunningham, Esq., British Vice-Consul at Galatz, who, with the utmost kindness, procured for us all we needed. We, and all that we had, underwent a thorough fumigation, our clothes being suspended in the smoke for twenty-four hours. We were then removed into a more comfortable apartment and a guardiano was appointed to take charge of us, a poor Russian named Costandi, very devout in observing the usages of the Greek Church.

We had now leisure to look around and think upon the region which we had entered. We had entered the ancient Dacia; the river before us was the Ister, and the people who were driving along their clumsy vehicles, dressed in linen frock-coats with broad leathern girdles, and Roman sandals of skin on their feet, uncombed hair hanging over brow and neck from under broad-brimmed black hats, are descendants of the barbarians who so often troubled the Empire of Rome. We saw large herds of dun[1] cattle on the wide pasture land, and on the roads clumsy carts drawn by oxen creaked loudly as they went along. Occasionally ships coming up the river gave a pleasant variety to the scene. A soldier guarded the quarantine, wearing a European coat and trousers of clean white fustian,[2] with a black belt and black cap, his musket on his shoulder. Between us and the town lay the rude tents of a company of Zingans or Gipsies, engaged in making bricks. Before sunset some heavy drops of rain fell, the first that had refreshed us since we left the moist shores of England. It was accompanied with loud thunder.

Sabbath came on, and brought with it its holy peace. We worshipped together in our apartment, and in the evening spoke with a Jew from Jerusalem who had arrived in the quarantine.

In the evenings, our guardiano Costandi, good-natured but slow in every motion, used to light a fire on the floor and smoke the room to free us from the mosquitoes and then came in to pour water on our hands. Our only walk during the day was within the limits of the quarantine, commanding a view of the river. We often sat watching the varied shades and colours on its surface, or the course of some skiff passing up or down, or sometimes the leaping of the fish and the wild fowl floating on the stream. The air was generally pleasant and the heat not very great. Sometimes at sunset the people on the opposite heights appeared to be of gigantic stature.

The Vice-Consul visited us a second time to make arrangements for our leaving quarantine, and from him we received much important information regarding the province of Moldavia. It is an interesting

---

[1] Dun colour often designates a brownish-grey.
[2] Fustian is a strong cotton or linen fabric used for clothing and bedding.

country, but far behind in civilization. It is only lately that Galatz has got anything like an inn. The Government oppress the people by taxes; and every landed proprietor is allowed to exact from the peasants eighty days' labour in the year, besides receiving one-tenth of all they possess. Labour, however, brings a good price; a labourer may earn six piastres a-day, and a piastre here will purchase 2 lbs. of meat. The country is very fertile if cultivated; indeed, it is called 'The Peru of the Greeks'; but many of its vast plains are lying waste. There are 400,000 oxen killed annually for the production of tallow, and about 250,000 sheep are carried every year to the market of Constantinople. The languages used by the higher classes are chiefly Modern Greek and French. The Wallachian is the native dialect, and is used by all the common people. The religion of Moldavia and Wallachia is that of the Greek Church. A few strangers in Galatz, who are Roman Catholics, have lately erected a chapel for their own use.

There are many Jews in Galatz, but most of them in a very degraded condition. The English Consul's duty here is to protect the mercantile interests of British subjects, and these are chiefly Greeks from the Ionian Islands. The Gipsies or Zingans (a name, according to some, derived from Zoan the ancient capital of Egypt, though others trace it to the famous Tartar conqueror,) are in this province about 18,000 in number, and in Wallachia there are 80,000. They are almost all slaves bought and sold at pleasure. One was lately sold for 200 piastres; but the general price is 500. Perhaps £3 is the average price, and the female Zingans are sold much cheaper. The sale is generally carried on by private bargain. Their appearance is similar to that of Gipsies in other countries, being all dark, with fine black eyes and long black hair. They have a language peculiar to themselves, and though they seem to have no system of religion, yet are very superstitious in observing lucky and unlucky days. The men are the best mechanics in the country, so that smiths and masons are taken from this class. The women are considered the best cooks, and therefore almost every wealthy family has a Zingan cook. They are all fond of music, both vocal and instrumental, and excel in it. There is a class of them called the Turkish Zingans, who have purchased their freedom from Government, but these are few in number, and all from Turkey. Of these latter, there are twelve families in Galatz. The men are employed as horse-dealers, and the women in making bags, sacks, and such articles. In winter they live in town, and almost underground; but in summer they pitch their tents in the open air, for though still within the bounds of the town, yet they would not live in their winter houses during summer.

The Boyards or nobles of the country are not men of education and spend their time chiefly in idle amusements, such as balls and playing cards. The Greek priests of Moldavia are low in character; so much so, that half a dozen of them may be found openly drinking in a tavern at any hour of the day. Though they are priests, yet they often carry on business, and they oppose the Bible.

September 5
Early in the morning we left our quarantine, glad to be once more at liberty. On our way to Galatz we got a nearer view of the colony of Zingans. Their whole appearance reminded us of the poor villagers on the banks of the Nile. They were clothed in rags, and their little children were carried naked on the shoulder, or at the side, in the very manner of the Egyptians. They were toiling in the sun at the laborious work of making bricks. The sight at once recalled the days when their fathers 'made the children of Israel to serve with rigour' in the same way; 'The Egyptians made their lives bitter with hard bondage in mortar and in brick, and in all manner of service in the field' (Exodus 1:14). If these are really the descendants of the people of Pharaoh, as their name, features, and customs, seem clearly to prove, they are an example of the retributive justice of God in his dealings with the nations that afflict Israel. It seems every way probable that these long-despised wanderers are fulfilling the thrice-repeated prophecy, '*I will scatter the Egyptians among the nations, and will disperse them through the countries*', '*and they shall know that I am the Lord*' (Ezekiel 29:12-16; 30:23-26). May it not be worthy of the consideration of those benevolent persons who have taken up the cause of the gipsies in our own land, whether it might not be possible to extend their labours so as to send the light of the gospel to these benighted exiles in other countries? Their numbers, their ignorance, their degradation, call loudly for the help of a Christian missionary.

The appearance of the country was quite new to us, and Galatz, embosomed in acacia trees, appeared pleasant to our eyes, accustomed to the dismal walls of the quarantine. No tree is so frequent in this region as the acacia-tree, and we were told that, at Galatz, Odessa, and some other places near, no tree thrives so well. Everywhere we met patient oxen, and sometimes strings of small horses, four or even eight at once, dragging unwieldy waggons which go creaking along the highway. The driver guides the oxen by striking them on the head.

Galatz contains above 10,000 inhabitants. Many of the streets are paved with wooden planks laid across, something after the manner of American *corduroy*. Many are totally unpaved, and consequently dusty in summer and miry in winter. The houses are chiefly built of wood, white-washed, and covered over with clay. Even the churches are wooden edifices. Brandy-shops abound in every street. In the market we saw the cusa, so common in Syria, exposed for sale. We were interested in the number of Jews we met, and the numbers we saw busy in their shops. All wear the broad German hat or Russian fur-cap and Polish gown. All have the mustach, beard, and ringlets, and all appeared to be either mechanics, or money-changers, seated at little tables on the street. The people seem very industrious, not, as in the East, sitting lazily with the pipe in their mouth. The women share in the general industry. They spin from the distaff even when walking to and fro. Their dress is not very peculiar, except the head-dress, which is generally a shawl over the head, fastened under the chin. It is often white, resembling that of the Genoese women. The soldiers oppress the people. A few days ago, a party of soldiers came to a man who had got leave to fish for an hour on the river, entered his boat, took away his written permission, and then laid claim to all the fish he had caught.

On the top of one of the steeples we observed a large stork's nest. These are often seen also upon the chimney-tops of the houses, for the chimneys are built with a covering on the top, and open at the sides. The natives do not often allow these to be disturbed, as that would be considered unlucky. These remarkable birds come regularly on the 16th of April; 'Yea, the stork in the heaven knoweth her appointed time' (Jeremiah 8:7), so that you may calculate upon their appearance to a day.

The burying-grounds are near the entrance of the town; and not far from the fosse[3] that surrounds Galatz is a mound of earth that marks the spot where, during the late Greek revolution, Ypsilanti and 600 Greeks bravely defended themselves till they were cut in pieces by 5,000 Turks.

In the afternoon we set out to visit the Jews of Galatz. We entered the shop of a respectable money-changer, who, after making our acquaintance, put on his best broad hat, and conducted us to the Rabbi, whom we found in the court of his house. He was a mild intelligent man, with the

---

[3] A canal or ditch forming a barrier against an enemy.

eye of a student; at first he seemed suspicious of us, because (as we learned afterwards) the Greek Church persecutes him, and hearing that we were Christians, he supposed that we were Greeks. We told him our object in coming from Scotland to visit the lost sheep of the house of Israel, and our desire for their salvation. We were then conducted to the synagogue, a poor, small edifice, with a still smaller one adjoining. Two or three Jews gathered round us; and one old Jew was busily engaged in devotion – an ignorant man, but of a serious cast of countenance. At the door was a collection-box, with this inscription in Hebrew, 'Alms – a gift in secret pacifieth anger.' This started a conversation in regard to the manner of pleasing God and turning away his anger. They spoke of their brethren in other places. We asked if the Jews here collected for those in the Holy Land. They said that they did at all their marriages. They have no school for their children, but as a substitute, they put several children under the occasional instruction of one of their number. The Jew who acted as our guide said that he heard there were now 'Epicureans (that is, unbelievers) even at Jerusalem, and that they had built a synagogue there'. He referred no doubt to the Christian church now building on Zion and the few converts already gathered in Jerusalem. They said that they could not but hate Christians, for they were everywhere oppressed by them. For example, the preceding year, some Jews had caricatured the Greek priests and their religious service in a play – in consequence of which, twelve of their number were cast into prison, and forced to pay 5,000 ducats to save their lives. The Ionian Greeks also burn a Jew in effigy every year at Easter, though the Government has at last forbidden it. They asked us, 'if we belonged to the Epicureans' – and on hearing us quote Hebrew texts, they would scarcely be persuaded that we were Christians. They have no idea of a Christian possessed of feelings of kindness and love towards them. Few of them speak Hebrew, all use German, and they also know the Wallachian language. They said that they had no want of employment and that every one had a trade. Most of the money-changers are Jews. The rabbi said that there were 500 Jews in Galatz; but the Vice-Consul thought that there must be 2,000.

In the evening, Mr Cunningham conveyed us in his *brisca*[4] to Ibraila, the port of Wallachia, three hours distant. The drive was interesting, more because of the novelty of our circumstances than because of any

[4] A light wagon without springs.

peculiar beauty in the country. The fields seem often uncultivated; and many parts of the wide level plain were for the most part unenclosed and waste, sometimes covered with reeds, which show that it is frequently under water. We passed some peaceful cottages that forcibly recalled the scenes of home to mind. At one cottage a woman was churning butter; at some others, some 'Dacian mothers' were sitting at the door, talking together and observing the strangers. Another woman met us, driving home her cow, while she held the distaff in her hand. The people seemed industrious and peaceful – but has 'the Son of peace' been here? Immense herds of oxen, all of the same dun colour, were feeding in different places, and large handsome dogs, between the greyhound and sheepdog, often sprung out from a cottage door as we passed. We came about twilight to the river Seret, a tributary of the Danube which is crossed by a boat drawn across by a rope. This is the boundary between Moldavia and Wallachia, as we soon learned by the trouble which the custom-house officer wished to give us, although we had got a written permission from Galatz. Like all such petty officers in these countries, he wished to extort money, but the Consul's authority at last quelled his interference, and we crossed over to the Wallachian territory. It was dark when we reached Ibraila, where we were comfortably quartered in the apartments of Mr Lloyd, the Wallachian Vice-Consul.

September 6

We had made preparations for starting by daybreak on our way to Bucarest. When we awoke we found that the rain fell heavily. This was like meeting an old friend, for we had not seen a rainy morning since leaving Scotland; but the time was not the most suitable for us. The ordinary way of travelling in this country is by a post-cart, which is a vehicle rude in the extreme, being entirely of wood, the frame slight, the sides made of coarse wicker-work, the wheels small. The harness is made of ropes or cords, some of which on this occasion had given way, but were retied for further use. The interior is filled with straw, among which the traveller sits or lies as he best can. Three of these carts stood at the door, each having four small Wallachian horses. We were ready to start; but Mr Cunningham prevailed on us to defer our journey, as the sky was dark and lowering, and one of our number was little able to bear the hardships to which we would be exposed. With the most disinterested and considerate kindness, Mr C[unningham] sent back to Galatz for his *brashovanca*, a covered travelling carriage without springs, capable of holding four, and this he insisted upon our using until we reached Jassy.

Throughout the day we visited the town. It is clean and airy, with broad streets, of which a few were causewayed. Many of the houses were of brick, but the most were only one storey high. Acacia-trees were planted round them, and here, too, we saw for the last time olive-trees full grown. The ornamented double cross on the Greek churches attracts the eye by its glittering in the sun, being either gilded or made of polished tin. Alas! they hide the divine glory that shines from the true cross of Christ, and try to make up for what they hide by dazzling the carnal eye with its gilded image. The stork's nest was common here as in Galatz, and in one courtyard two or three tame storks were walking about, no one venturing to injure them. In the bazaar, stones were used for weights, as in the East. The Danube flows deep and full past the town. The trade in grain is increasing, and the town rapidly rising into importance. It has at present a thriving population of 6,000.

The dress of the Wallachian is similar to that of the Moldavian, but as the day was wet many of the peasants wore a coat made of rough sheepskin with the wool inside, and a cap of the same. We met several Russians in the streets, known by their long high hats, peculiar physiognomy, and light blue eye. The peasantry take off their hats when they meet you, and a *boyard*[5] in his carriage saluted us in the same fashion. There are not many violent crimes committed in these provinces; but scarcely anything can exceed the deep and widespread immorality in private.

Near the entrance of the town there is an ancient Roman fort, situated on a small rising ground. There, too, is a village of the *Lipuwanni*, or eunuchs, a sect of Christians expelled from Russia. We entered the shop of a Jewish watchmaker, a pleasant gentle young man from Odessa, who had settled here to escape being taken as a recruit into the Russian army, the *ukase*[6] having ordered twelve men to be taken out of every hundred, including both Jews and Christians. He told us that there are thirty Jewish families here who have an old synagogue which is very small; but that eight German families from Vienna are building a new one for themselves, because, few as they are, there is a disunion among them. They have no rabbi, and hence every one tries to be above the other, and does what is right in his own eyes. He said that he had in his possession two tracts

---

[5] A noble.

[6] A proclamation or order by a Russian emperor.

addressed to Jews, distributed by missionaries at Jerusalem and brought here by a travelling Jew for no missionary had ever visited this country. This simple account convinced us of the vast importance of furnishing our missionaries with abundance of clear, spiritual, and pungent tracts addressed to the Jews. Who can tell to what bosom the good seed may be carried, and there be made to spring up? He had also heard that in England several Jewish students had become Christians and that Christian tracts addressed to Jews had found their way into Russia.

By this time about a dozen Jews had gathered round who conducted us to the synagogue. Among them was a mild young man, a Spanish Jew, of a remarkably fine appearance and very kind to us; but he could not speak any language except Spanish, though he understood a little German. Along with him was a friend, a German Jew, equally interesting and very affable. We were standing at the spot where the new synagogue was being built, while the Jewish workmen were sitting down to their midday meal at our side. They asked Mr Calman if he wore the *tsitsith*. In reply, he told them that '*they* wore none, for the real *tsitsith* should have a fringe of blue, and not white strings'. They then said they believed Messiah would come yet; and that many in Smyrna and other parts of Turkey thought he would come next year. On this, Mr Calman told them that the main thing to be known was the *object* of his coming, which was to take away sin; whereas, the Jews have at present no way of pardon. 'You keep Sabbath,' said he, 'that you may be forgiven – you go a pilgrimage to Jerusalem, that you may be forgiven – you think whoever walks four yards on the Holy Land will be forgiven – you eat three meals on Sabbath, pray over graves, keep the Day of Atonement, all in order to find forgiveness; and yet you are never satisfied that you have found it. Your conscience is never at rest, which it would be, if that were the true way of pardon. Would God leave his people without some atonement for sin, after Jerusalem was destroyed and sacrifices done away? No; he left them *Messiah*. You yourselves offer a cock and a hen on the evening before the Day of Atonement, which proves your own conviction that you still need a sacrifice. Now, Christians have peace, not terror, during life, and can die without fear, knowing that they are going to a reconciled Father – not like you, who are so uncertain of your state that even in the hour of death you engage the prayers of rabbis and of your children to be made for you *after you are dead.*' The young German Jew heard with great interest and then said, 'That the Jews now had more faith than Abraham for they believed

God's word, without *having seen* miracles.' Mr Calman replied, 'That to believe *these things* merely would not save them; the devils also believed, and were devils still.' Another Jew standing by said, 'We have no sin; for we keep Sabbath, eat no pork, drink no wine which a *Goi* (a Gentile) has touched, never eat without washing our hands; and we wear the *tsitsith*.' Mr C[alman] turned to him, 'God wishes something more than all this – the heart. Is your heart right with God? Do you dare to say that you love him at all times? Even while you are putting on the *tephillin*, do not your thoughts wander? Therefore, you are sinners, and where are your sacrifices? You have none even on the Day of Atonement.' The Jew answered, that repeating or reading the passages of the Torah that describes sacrifices was as good as offering the sacrifices themselves. Mr C[alman] replied, 'God has never said so; and you yourselves are not satisfied that it is so; for if you were, you would not go away to seek pardon still by pilgrimages.' He then told him of those Jews at Smyrna who are willing to be Christians, only retaining their Saturday and festivals.

This Jew, who seemed so interested, followed us along the streets and told us of his brethren. He said that 'their ignorance here was lamentable and their pride excessive. Every one wished to be head. They needed to be taught their own language, for none could speak Hebrew and few understand it. If a school were instituted, he believed it would be well attended. At present, parents who are able send their children to be educated at Vienna.' He then told us much of Rabbi Bibas from Corfu, whom he called 'a grand rabbi', who lately passed through Ibraila on his way to Bucarest, travelling to seek the reformation of his brethren, and who had preached to the Jews here on Isaiah 11:1-5, the Spirit resting on Messiah. He said that 'the seven wisdoms, or sciences, are meant, such as music, astronomy, etc. When a man is well, if he take medicine it will do him harm; but if he be ill, then he must put away bread and take the medicine. Now, the law is bread; but the Jews are sick, they are ignorant and degraded. You must therefore lay aside the study of the law and take the medicine, which is the seven wisdoms or sciences spoken of here.' This rabbi had left a deep impression upon the Jews here and elsewhere. The young man spoke with great admiration of him and of his sentiments, and especially of this one, that the Jews must be instructed in science and in arms that they may wrest the land of Palestine from the Turks under the conduct of Messiah, as the Greeks wrested their country.

The Jews think themselves better treated in Wallachia than in Moldavia, where lately an additional tax was attempted to be imposed on them; and this may account for the great freedom with which they spoke to us. Yet even here they suffer. A Jew going down to the river will often be ridiculed by the porters and waggoners. We were told the number of Jews at Bucarest, and that at Pitesti, a village twenty miles from it, were seventy Jewish families.

It was nine in the evening when we left Ibraila for Bucarest, the capital of Wallachia, a distance of 120 miles. Mr Cunningham's kindness was unremitting to the last, and we endeavoured to repay it in the only way within the reach of ministers of Christ, whose best description is to be 'poor yet making many rich'. The *brashovanca* or covered carriage (so called from Brashova, a town near Cronstadt in Austria, where it was invented) proved of the greatest value to us. As we had hired twelve horses for our three post-carts, the postilions insisted upon all being employed, so that they formed quite a cavalcade. These little horses were attached to the vehicles by ropes, and urged on at full speed by the wild cry of the postilions, and loud cracking of whips. At the end of the first stage, we were roused up from sleep by a voice, in Wallachian, '*Domne, da Menzil*', 'Sir, give your Menzil'; that is – your agreement with the postmaster to carry you through. A paper accompanying it is called the *Poderosne*: that is, your permission to travel from the Prince. At every stage the same demand is repeated; and every time you must give a small coin to the man at the post-house who examines these documents. The post-houses are no more than solitary cottages, containing one or perhaps two unfurnished rooms; and the horses with which a traveller is to be supplied, are generally in the adjacent fields, only caught on the arrival of a vehicle. Many a time we had to wait long till the straggling ponies were brought in from the fields. And it was anything but pleasant to sit sleeping in the brashovanca in the cold night-air, conscious that we were making no progress, yet unable, from ignorance of the language, to urge on the drivers. Frequently, too, the postilions would stop of their own accord in order to run to a house to get their pipe lighted. At the end of the second stage our horses were reduced to eight, a more manageable number, the foremost pair of the team having a bell attached to their necks to give notice to passers-by of the approach of some vehicle over the soft ground.

September 7

When morning dawned we were in the midst of a vast uncultivated plain, in many parts soft and marshy, with a few rude cottages near us. The drivers were waiting at the post-house until the horses should be brought in from the grass. We resolved to make use of this interval; and having brought with us all the provisions we needed till we should reach Bucarest, we left the carriage and entered one of the cottages. It resembled somewhat the interior of an Irish cabin, consisting of a single apartment, and a sleeping place lower than the ground. The peasant and his wife, good-natured, but most uncivilized-looking people, were seated at the fire. Knowing that we were in the region of ancient Dacia, and that their language was derived in part from that of the Romans, we began by trying of what use our Latin might be. The man said to us that the morning was *frig, frig*, that is 'cold, cold'. They called their fire (which was made of cowsdung) *foco*. We pointed to their cow and called it *vacca*, he smiled and said *vac*, and called the cattle *boi*. We asked for milk, *lac*; he corrected us, and said *lapte*. They brought us a refreshing draught of milk and having boiled a little water on their fire we made tea. They stood by in respectful astonishment, yet apparently much amused, and expressed no small joy on our giving them a trifling present for their hospitality. We learned a little more of their language during breakfast. A horse is called *col* – evidently derived from *caballus*; a cottage is *cas*; water is *apu*. A dog began to bark; we said, *canis latrat*; the man corrected us, *cuin latra*. Bread is *puin*; a pitch-fork, *furc*; a kettle for boiling water *caldare*. Many other examples of the derivation of their language from the Latin we met with afterwards. On our journey, on one occasion the driver asked if we had *fune*, 'a rope', which he said was to tie *ligar*, the pole. Coming to a village, we asked a woman for milk, she replied, *non est*, 'there is none', and another said, *aker, ni dulsh est*, 'there is sour, not sweet', bringing out a large bowl of sour milk. A porter who carried some articles for us said, *Nosti Romanisti, domne?* 'Do you know Romaic, Sir?' and often the people used *spoune*, that is 'tell me', in conversation with one another.

Leaving the cottage, we entered the carriage and swept along over what appeared to be an endless extent of level plains without a single eminence to relieve the flatness, or a tree on which the eye might rest. We saw scarcely any marks of cultivation, but tracts of pasture land, with here and there an immense herd of dun oxen, or sometimes buffaloes; horses also, and sheep, and large flocks of geese. Occasionally the cottages displayed a little neatness, being made of wicker-work, plastered over with clay, white-washed – and the roof thatched with reeds. One object that meets the eye in these vast plains is a stone-cross at various intervals. This may be intended to remind travellers of Him who died for us; but certainly the people shewed it no reverence. Seldom could we discover even the appearance of devotion among them. In the morning, indeed, one of our rough postilions, before mounting his horse, crossed himself three times, stooped down, and said a few words of prayer; but we rarely saw even this attention to religious duties. Mounds of earth occasionally appeared between us and the horizon, artificial elevations probably used in ancient times as watchtowers and beacons. In some places, the lavatera, the foxglove, the hollyhock, and a few other flowers, were abundant in the fields. The soil appeared in general to be fertile and soft, and seldom did a single stone occur on the road. The postilions drove well, each having four in hand; and often they plucked hair from the horses' mane to improve the lash of their whips. The horses, which were small, lean, and active, seemed to prefer the gallop as much as the riders. When any part of the road was cut up, they immediately took a new course – so smooth and level is this country.

About eight o'clock in the morning we passed within sight of a small lake with rocks overhanging it – a rare sight in these plains. At the fourth post, horses were treading out corn, and in the gardens was a sort of gourd that is hard as a turnip and much used for food. Wells now began to be common, having a tall upright pole, over the top of which lay a transverse bar, with a weight at one end to act as a lever in drawing up the bucket. We had seen this before in Egypt and it is commonly used in Poland and Russia. The poor drivers never failed to stop once in a stage to get their pipe lighted, which they continued to use even when riding at full speed.

About midday, we came to a village (the first since leaving Ibraila) called Slobodzi, having a Greek church and a convent. No monks reside in the convent, but only a superior and his two deacons, to carry on the church service. Here we crossed a stream by a bridge of boats; and on the other side, the country rises about thirty feet, after ascending which we came upon a new extent of flat country on a higher level. This is one of the *steppes* which are the characteristic formation of this region. As before, crosses were frequent on the roadside, and herds of oxen in the pastures. Passing a field of Indian corn which had no enclosure, our postilions stopped the vehicle and deliberately supplied themselves with an armful. Quails and bustards occasionally started up from the cornfields as we rode past.

Towards evening we drove past a large village called Obeleshti, situated on the banks of a small lake. The people seemed all busily employed, and vast herds of oxen were coming round the sides of the water. The setting sun shed a pleasing light over this scene, which was peculiarly refreshing to our eye after the tameness and monotonous level of the preceding part of the journey. The two villages named above are the only places of the least importance which we passed in our long journey of 120 miles.

It was three o'clock in the morning *(September 8)* when we reached Bucarest. We should have arrived at nine the preceding evening, but lost several hours at the different post-houses from our ignorance of the language and inexperience in this mode of travelling. We went first to the Khan Rosso, to which we had been recommended; but after knocking and waiting half an hour, our answer was *Nui loghi*, 'no places' – 'no room'. Our drivers next found out the Casino di Martin; but no-one would reply to our knocking. While we were lingering cold and weary in the open street of this strange city, we heard the loud hum of many voices, and saw a large upper room lighted up – it was a Jewish Synagogue, for this being their New Year season, the devout portion of them spend the greater part of the time in continual prayers. The watchmen on the street and our postilions imitated their loud cries in ridicule of their devotions; so true are the words of Moses, 'Thou shalt become an astonishment, a byword, and a proverb, among all the nations whither the Lord shall lead thee' (Deuteronomy 28:37). Many Jews were now hastening through the dark streets to the synagogue, and one seeing our dilemma offered to conduct us to a khan. No other help being at hand we thankfully accepted his services and followed him through several streets till he brought us to a very large caravansera called Khan Manuk, overhanging the muddy stream Dembrowitza, where we found an empty room in which we spread our mats, and, thankful for the mercies of the past day, sought repose.

Sabbath

A strange scene presented itself to us when we looked out in the morning. The khan was of large dimensions, covering apparently an acre of ground, with high buildings all round. The ground floor was occupied with horses and carriages of all kinds. The second floor was devoted to passing travellers, and the third to those who were to stay above six months. The second floor had a wide promenade all round, and on it were gathered groups from many different countries, especially Russians, Hungarians, and Greeks. A mixture of strange barbarian languages filled our ears. We sighed in vain for the holy quietness of a Scottish Sabbath, and being determined if possible to find a more peaceful residence, we removed in the forenoon to a much smaller and cleaner place, called Khan Simeon, kept by a Greek. Here we enjoyed the rest of the holy day and worshipped together in peace and comfort. In the evening the British Consul-General, R. G. Colquhoun, Esq., of Fincastle, found out our dwelling and welcomed us to Bucarest with all the kindness of a fellow-countryman.

Next morning *(September 9)* we waited on the Consul, from whom during our stay we received much information as to the state of the country and experienced the utmost attention and hospitality. He insisted on our dining at the Consulate every day, which, in as far as our inquiries would permit, we agreed to do. Among his servants were three from Scotland, whose faces were lighted up with joy to see fellow-countrymen in this strange land.

Wallachia is a fine country, and, if fully cultivated, might support twelve million inhabitants; whereas at present there are not much above two million. The immense wastes through which we passed might easily be put under cultivation, and would yield ample returns; but there are no hands to hold the plough. Population is not encouraged and the vices of the inhabitants keep it down. Nearly three-fourths of the land in this province and in Moldavia are in the possession of the monasteries. Many estates belong to monasteries in other countries, such as the convent of Mount Athos and that of Mount Sinai; in which case the property is let and farmed by the natives of the country at a reasonable rent. The western part of the province, called Little Wallachia, is entirely a mountainous region, and very different from that part through which we travelled. Crayova, which used to be the rendezvous of the Crusading Knights on their way to the Holy Land, is situated there. Whole tracts of the country are occasionally devastated by the ravages of the locust. Bucarest contains 120,000 inhabitants. The Greek churches alone amount to no fewer than 366. There are also two Roman Catholic churches, one Lutheran, and one Calvinistic. There are no mosques, for, by the treaty of Adrianople in 1829, no Mahometan is allowed to possess property or hold a domicile in either province.

All the *Boyards* or nobles of Wallachia reside in the capital. They seldom visit their estates, and some, it is said, have never seen them, so that their property is left entirely in the hands of agents who take good care to enrich themselves. The Prince, Alexander Demetrius Gike, is believed to be much under the influence of Russia and is not equal in talent to the Prince of Moldavia. There is a Chamber here, elected by men of certain rank and property, who assist in carrying on the government. But the *employés* of government are not men of the best character and the tribunals of justice are lamentably corrupt, so that the only sure way to gain a cause in this country is to go with a bag of money to the judge.

One of the most fruitful sources of crime in this country and one of the most revolting symptoms of its depravity is the frequency of divorce. This is easily obtained, is accounted no disgrace, and the separated parties are soon married again to others. We were often during our sojourn in this country reminded of the awful description given by Jeremiah; 'From the least of them even unto the greatest of them, every one is given to covetousness; and from the prophet even unto the priest, every one dealeth falsely. Were they ashamed when they had committed abomination? nay, they were not at all ashamed, neither could they blush' (Jeremiah 6:13-15).

From the top of the Consul's house we obtained a fine view of the city. It is built upon a marshy plain, and a few years ago was all paved with wooden planks thrown over canals of water, which continually sent up the elements of fever and ague. The Russians, however, destroyed these and drained the city. The churches here are not beautiful within, but appear showy from without. The number of spires is very great and many of them are covered with polished tin, which dazzles the eye in the sunshine. This is a recent mode of adorning; anciently the spires were all of brick, but it was found safer to dispense with these on account of the frequent earthquakes which shake the country. The buildings are beautifully interspersed with luxuriant gardens, containing vines, apricots, and splendid walnuts. Many of the houses being built of wood, fires are frequent and dangerous. We saw a tower on which a man is stationed, watching night and day to give alarm in case of fire breaking out. Not unlike the duty of this man is that of the faithful pastor!

In regard to the Jews, we were told that they are better treated in this province than in Moldavia, for there an attempt was made to overtax them; but not so here. Every Jew must bring a certificate that he can earn a livelihood by some trade before he is allowed to settle. As to the number residing here, we found it impossible to ascertain the truth with accuracy. The highest estimate was made by themselves at 7,000, the lowest by the Consul at 2,800. Some Jews stated the number at 5,000; and the aspect of their synagogues led us to think this to be nearest the truth. There are seven synagogues belonging to the Polish Jews, who are mostly all mechanics – tailors, shoemakers, carpenters, workers in gold-trinkets, etc. Those who belong to the same trade keep by the same synagogue. There is one handsome Spanish synagogue, which is frequented by the wealthy and influential men. The majority of the Jews here are corrupt to such a degree, that about three years before our visit, when one of their rabbis attempted to reform them by preaching against their vices, they never rested till they got him expelled, even stirring up his own wife and children against him. On our asking, if all the Jews here believed the Scriptures (*tanach*[7]) to be the word of God, the reply was, '*Andere glauben, andere nicht*', 'Some believe, some do not'.

The first synagogue which we visited was one belonging to the Polish Jews. This being the festival of Rosh Hashanna, that is, New Year's Day, the place was crowded to excess, no Jew who can possibly attend venturing to absent himself on such a high day. All wore the black Polish gown and fur cap and all had on the *Tallith*, the front of which was ornamented with a band of silver work. The old rabbi wore a white ephod or shirt, having the collar richly embroidered with silver and gold. This is called *halukah rabbonim* (the shirt of the rabbis), a dress which they wear in imitation of the writers of the Talmud who are said to have worn the same, and in which all rabbis are buried. This rabbi commenced, and soon all joined in repeating the 47th Psalm seven times over. The rabbis think that the verse, 'God is gone up with a shout, the Lord with the sound of a trumpet', gives some countenance to the peculiar ceremony of the day, namely, *the blowing of a trumpet*. They also believe that every New Year's Day is a kind of day of judgement. 'Every year, on the festival of Rosh Hashanna, the sins of every one that cometh into the world are weighed against his merits. Every one who is found righteous is sealed to life. Every one who is found wicked is sealed to death.' Accordingly, they imagine that Satan at this season

---

[7] This is an acronym formed from the initial letter of the three Hebrew words by which the Hebrew Bible is designated, the Law, the Prophets, and the Writings.

comes before God specially to accuse every soul. In order, therefore, *'to confuse Satan'*, and prevent him from bringing forward his accusations, and *'to change God's attribute of judgment which was against them into mercy'*, their wise men of blessed memory have ordained that the trumpet should be blown on the first day of the month Elul every year.

The old rabbi made use of a small ram's horn, which he had some difficulty in getting to sound. One rabbi chanted the word of command, at which the other blew through the horn. Nine times this was repeated, and the last was a long blast; then all present shouted and imitated the sound with their hand and mouth. They resembled exactly a company of children imitating a military band, and but for the heartrending fact that these very follies form part of the strong delusion to which God has given up his ancient people, the whole scene would have been irresistibly ludicrous. The prayers that followed were offered with great vehemence, and a rabbi and three young men sang well the Psalm which does not now apply to Israel, 'Blessed is the people that know the joyful sound.'

In another Polish synagogue close by we saw the same ceremony. We also visited the Spanish synagogue, where the Jews present were handsomely dressed, and the Jewesses whom we saw at the gate were enveloped in silk mantles edged with fur. They were engaged in the same ceremony, only they did not seem to be so zealous, and went through it with greater dignity. Alas, Israel, 'children are thy princes, and babes rule over thee!' (Isaiah 3:4). 'The Lord hath taken away from Judah the stay and the staff, the judge and the prophet, the prudent and the ancient.'

In the afternoon we went to the synagogue again, in expectation of seeing the Jews march down to the riverside, and 'cast all their sins into the depths of the sea' (Micah 7:19), which they do by shaking their garments over the water as if casting their sins out of their bosom. But we were too early, and were told that they wait till it is dusk when the people of the town will not observe them.

Mr Calman pointed us to a proof of the degraded character of the Jews here, as we were passing a common eating-house. On the walls of it many German sentences of a jovial character were written in Hebrew letters. Thus,

> 'To-day I have money,
> Tomorrow none –
> In the (Jewish) year 5098.'

The Jews here, in gaining their livelihood, are employed by persons of all religious persuasions, so that they do not depend on their brethren for supply of work. Perhaps nine out of every ten carpenters are Jews; and no questions are asked in employing them, except regarding their capacity as workmen. This is a most important fact, which would remove entirely the difficulty so often felt by Jewish missionaries in the support of inquirers and converts.

The Consul was of opinion that a missionary in Bucarest would require £250 a year. He must have a house with four rooms, which would cost £25 or £30 of rent. He must maintain several servants, for each will do only his own peculiar work; and the state of the streets is such in winter, that he must keep a carriage and two horses, as every respectable person does. Provisions are cheap; a lamb may be got for two shillings, a sheep for four shillings and sixpence, and an *oke* of meat (that is 2½ lbs.) for one piastre, that is about twopence. But firewood is very dear. A large family often pay £50 a year for this article alone. The expense of travelling from England to Bucarest, the Consul estimated at £30. As to the prospects of success, he thought that any direct attempt to convert the Greeks would be immediately fatal to any mission. A Jewish missionary must confine his labours to the Jews and not interfere with the natives. The light will spread indirectly. The only danger to a mission is, that the priesthood, fearing its indirect influence, might bring in the arm of Russia to put it down: and Russia could easily do this in their own secret way if they had the will.

September 10
In the forenoon, we set out to call on Samuel Hillel, a Jewish banker, who was to introduce us to Rabbi Bibas of Corfu. By mistake we were led to the house of a wealthy Spanish Jew and ushered into a fine suite of apartments. Several Jewish ladies came in fully dressed for the festival of the season. They received us very politely, and after discovering our mistake, directed us to the banker's house. He was not at home, but we found his son (who said that he had seen us at the synagogue), and his three daughters, richly attired, wearing diamonds on their head – for the daughters of Judah, even in their captivity, have the same love for gay apparel that they had in the days of Isaiah (Isaiah 3:18-24). In conversation with the son, we soon discovered that he was one of those Jews who care little about Palestine and do not expect a Messiah, believing that education and civilization alone can exalt the Jews, to

which he added – 'a knowledge of arms, that they may defend their land when they get possession of it.' We afterwards saw his father, who conducted us to the house where the rabbi of Corfu was lodging. Rabbi Bibas received us politely. He spoke English with great fluency, told us he was a native of Gibraltar, and was proud of being a British subject. He has a congregation of 4000 under his care in Corfu. On our entrance he excused himself for not rising, a slight indisposition and the fatigue of travelling obliging him to lie on the sofa. We said, 'The Eastern manner became one of his nation.' He replied, 'No! no! the Jews are not Easterns.' We said, 'Abraham came from the distant East.' 'True; but you are not to reckon a nation by their first parent.' Immediately he began to speak of the situation of the Promised Land, asking us to say, Why God chose Israel for his peculiar people, and that portion of the earth as their land? Much conversation arose on these points, and as often as we tried to break off and introduce something more directly bearing on our object, he stopped us by affecting great logical accuracy, and holding us to the point, if we had any pretensions to the character of logical reasoners. He denied that God ever meant the Jews to be a people separate from other nations, asserting that He intended them to enlighten all the earth, a duty which they must still perform whenever it shall be in their power. If they had means like the English they ought to send out missionaries. When we gave this reason why God chose Israel to be his peculiar people, 'that the Lord wished to show that he was a sovereign God', he disputed this, because His sovereignty was already known to the heathen. He thought we must be content to reckon it among the secret things that belong to God. He then suddenly started another speculative question, 'Where Eden was, and how four such streams as Moses described could have existed, since they are now nowhere to be found.' On this point he at length rested satisfied with the remark that it must be true because declared in the Word of God. After this he signified to us that it was the hour of prayer and we must excuse him from farther conversation at present. He shewed great craftiness and skill in keeping the conversation from turning upon matters of experimental religion; for that was evidently his aim. On our rising to take leave, and mentioning that love to Israel had brought us to visit him, he declared that he loved Christians exceedingly and that no Christian loved the Jews more than he did the Christians. He said that he was travelling for the sake of his degraded brethren, to see what might be done for them; and was anxious to meet with Sir Moses Montefiore on his return from the Holy Land. He disliked our reference to Scripture. Thus, on his remarking that the Jews must have been a very holy people since God so preserved them, we replied in the words of Ezekiel, '*Not for your sakes* do I this, saith the Lord God, be it known unto you' (Ezekiel 36:32). But he hastily changed to another topic.

September 11

In the morning we went to the church of the Metropol, to witness the *Fête* of the Prince of Wallachia, on occasion of his birthday. It is a splendid building and the walls very showy within, being covered with gilding and paintings of apostles and saints without number, with a rich silver chandelier suspended from the roof. The splendid pulpit, which had the appearance of being seldom or never occupied, was adorned with gorgeous gilding – a poor substitute for 'the words of eternal life'. The Prince himself was not present, being unwell: but all the principal *Boyards* of Wallachia were present, and also Milosh, the exiled Prince of Servia, a man of dull, heavy-looking aspect, dressed in a rich purple uniform with a costly diamond girdle. His son stood by his side. Consuls of different nations stood around, wearing their respective uniforms; and an immense crowd of well-dressed people, all standing, filled the church. The priests, arrayed in beautiful robes, surrounded the table. The Bishop wore a splendid mitre with a diamond cross on the top, and his garments were stiff with gold embroidery. He is said to be an amiable man; and we could not but honour him for this, that he has permitted the free circulation of the Holy Scriptures in Wallachia. The service consisted chiefly of prayers for the Prince, followed by the responsive chanting of men and boys, not very melodious. At the end, the Prince and Nobles came forward to the Bishop, kissed a cross in his left hand, the Bible on the table, and the Bishop's hand, receiving from him a small piece of bread. This seemed to be the sacramental bread – a miserable profanation of the holy ordinance of the Supper.

When the pageant was done and most had withdrawn, we remained behind to see the rest go through their devotions. In different parts of the church the worshippers were choosing out the picture of their favourite saint, and after many crossings and prostrations on the ground, they kissed the feet and hands of the picture. In one corner an open coffin was exhibited, containing we were told the remains of St Demetrius, the patron saint of the Prince. A frank Wallachian who was with us said, somewhat archly, 'This was not the old St Demetrius, but a new one.'

The body was buried in the channel of a river and the spot was disclosed to a pious young woman, before whom the waters of the river were miraculously divided. The coffin was highly ornamented with silver, and the dead body wrapped in cloth of silver and gold. A shrivelled hand was all that was left exposed; and this was the great object of attraction. The worshippers approached in great numbers, men and women, rich and poor, officers and soldiers. First they kneeled to the ground three times, crossing themselves and kissing the pavement. Then they drew near and reverently kissed the withered hand and a cross that lay beside it, dropping a piece of money into a little plate which lay at the feet. The priest touched their forehead with a little cross in his hand and muttered some parting blessing. With three prostrations more the worshipper retired. One poor boy, more intense in his devotions than the rest, made about twenty prostrations, being often disturbed by the crowd; and we could not see that after all he ever got a kiss of the skinny fingers. A rustic, with long uncombed hair, and his wife, brought their little baby in their arms to be blessed beside the holy coffin. The priest laid the crucifix upon its brow.

It was altogether a scene of the grossest idolatry, and it was melancholy to see so many respectable, intelligent-looking people engaged in it. What a stumbling-block are such Christians in the way of the conversion of the Jews! And yet there are about 200 Jews in Bucarest who have been baptized into the Greek Church. But of these we were told that only three had made the change from any real concern about their soul.

We visited again our friend Rabbi Bibas, and resolved this time to take the start of him in the topics of conversation. Mr Calman at once began by showing the wickedness and folly of several things taught in the Talmud. The rabbi's first answer was, that the Talmud was written by those who composed the Sanhedrin, and that God commanded us to bow to their decision on pain of death (Deuteronomy 17:11,12). Then he explained away its apparently immoral precepts; but, in defending its errors in history and geography, plunged into gross absurdities by endeavouring to prove from the Bible that the Holy Land was of immense extent and that Jerusalem once contained many millions of people. In proof of the latter point he referred to a passage, where so many thousands are said to have been '*at* Jerusalem'; but he insisted that it must be rendered '*in* Jerusalem'. He wished to show us that Messiah must be a *mere man*; and directed us to the description of Ezekiel's temple where 'the Prince and his sons' are mentioned (Ezekiel 46:16). We explained that Messiah was not there spoken of, but the Prince over Israel under him. His only remark to this was, 'Oh, then, you give us two rulers!' He admitted the state of his people at present to be most wretched. In Poland especially, he said, they were grossly superstitious, for they understood everything in the Talmud literally. Indeed, he had not gone to speak with the Polish rabbi, believing that it would be useless on account of his ignorance. The first remedy was to remove their ignorance. He would have the Jews gathered and educated in schools, where they should read and learn the Bible till ten years of age; the Mishna from ten to fifteen, and the Talmud from fifteen to twenty. He thought that the Collections for the Holy Land ought to be given up, and that the Jew there ought to be obliged to work even were it by the bayonet. Sir Moses Montefiore's plan of purchasing land for them in Palestine he considered useless, as long as there is no security for property there. The people must first be educated and taught the sciences. He believed from Zechariah 14:14, which he translated *Judah also shall fight against Jerusalem*, that many of the Jews are yet to fall into infidelity and fight against their brethren. We now attempted to speak still more closely to his conscience, but he refused to argue on the Messiahship of Jesus except in writing. We shewed him the end for which we had left our country and were seeking after Israel. He asked, 'For what good?' We answered, 'To send teachers to Israel.' 'The moment they begin to teach Christianity, all Jews will turn away from them.' 'No (we said), some will receive the truth', and we pointed to Mr Calman. The rabbi started and looked quite surprised, for he had not suspected that our friend was an Israelite; then added, 'Ah! well, there are one or two.' We then pressed upon him to compare the blind and wretched state of the dry bones of Israel described in the prophets, with what *he knew* to be the real condition of his people, and solemnly urged him to inquire if the blood of Jesus, which they were rejecting, might not be the very 'fountain for sin' by which Israel was to be saved. He seemed surprised by our earnestness, evidently felt our sincerity, and we parted good friends.

Mr Calman called on an interesting and very respectable young Jew, lately baptized into the Greek Church, named Alexander Rosiski, a teacher of music. Mr C[alman] asked him how a conscientious Jew could ever become an idolater, as the Greeks were. He said that he never worshipped their pictures, though he attended service in their church.

He had felt a want in his soul and, from what he heard of Jesus, thought that in Him he would find his want supplied. This first led him to the Greek Church; but he confessed that his ignorance was still so great that he could not meet his brethren in argument and therefore avoided them. When Mr Calman explained Isaiah 53, expounding to him the work of Christ and 'the way of God more perfectly', the young man was overjoyed and delighted; for the instruction thus imparted was more than all he had got among the Greeks. He had a Hebrew New Testament, but understood little of it, and owned that often he had asked himself, Why he had become a Christian? But now he saw the truth in a way that convinced and established him. He longed for an instructor, and rejoiced at the idea of a missionary coming to settle there and teach his brethren. What an interesting scene does this open up, and how many 'hidden ones' God may have among the scattered thousands of Israel who, like 'prisoners of hope', are waiting for someone to direct them to the stronghold!

September 13

Having parted with our kind friends at the Consulate on the day before, we bade farewell to Bucarest at nine o'clock am, and set out for Foxshany, a distance of eleven posts. The postilions drove like the wind, raising up clouds of dust which annoyed us sadly. Looking back, we observed how the city lies in a singular plain, marshy all round. A well, surmounted by a tall pole and cross beam, is the most frequent object that meets the eye. Fine brushwood and low trees line the road on both sides for many miles. When we had nearly completed our first stage, the axle-tree of the brashovanca broke and left us helpless in a wilderness. After long delay, a woodcutter, who happened to be by the roadside, made two young trees fall for us and we contrived by their means to support the axle, till we drove gently to the next post, where the broken part was taken to a *Zingan*, who repaired it. After a detention of three hours we set off again, swiftly as ever, through woods and shrubs. There was something quite exciting in this mode of travelling. The two postilions, with their Wallachian vest, loose shirt sleeve, large boots, small fur-cap, and unshorn locks flowing behind, cracking their strong whips and making the woods reverberate their cries, were most pictur-esque objects. The air also was delicious and the flat plains seemed to fly past. At mounting, each postilion springs into the saddle crying *Hee*, when all the horses start off simultaneously. Their loud, wolf-like cry is very singular. One begins very low, gently swelling his voice, till it becomes a scream, then it dies away. Before he is done the other commences, and so on. They crack the whip at every turn of the hand in setting off or coming near a post or town.

Near the second post, first one flight of quails passed us, and soon after another. We descended a *steppe*[8] into a wide platform and twice crossed a calm flowing stream on bridges made of wood. Towards evening we began to see hills in the distance, and came on a sweet village called Buseo, with its church, from which the evening bells were sounding deep and calm. It reminded us of Longforgan in the Carse of Gowrie, and called our flocks vividly to remembrance. During the night we forded a broad but shallow stream and, as morning broke, reached a village called Rimnik. For a short space the country was beautiful, with wooded hills on the south-west. But soon the road again became level as formerly. As we proceeded, a wheel of our vehicle rolled off, but by means of a rope, the postilions contrived to bind it. We next crossed a stream and ascended a steppe to the platform where stands Foxshany, which we reached about ten o'clock am.

This town is situated pleasantly among trees and adorned with glittering tin spires, which give it a fine appearance. It has a tolerable khan dignified with the name of 'Hotel de France', kept by a little Spaniard who is also the French Consular agent, and this khan we were glad to make use of, instead of sitting as hitherto to eat our meals in the carriage or on the grass. But our patience was not a little tried on finding that no post-horses could be got; Prince Milosh and the Russian Consul had so overwrought them that they were too wearied to set out again at present. We engaged a Wallachian peasant, who had four horses, to carry us forward next day to Birlat, for a considerable sum. Meanwhile we visited the town and lighted upon a large school assembled in the open air under a verandah. At the close, we observed that all prayed and made the sign of the cross.

We visited the Jews, of whom there were about sixty families in the town, all Polish, ruled by a rabbi who is maintained by his brethren and carries on no trade. We were told that they have four teachers, each attended by a few children, and supported by the high remuneration which is given by parents for their education. One man gave 12 roubles, or £2, 10s. a month, for two children; and another paid £13 for five

---

[8] An extensive relatively treeless plain.

months for his family. And yet these children learn very little. The Jew who took us to the postmaster, spoke to us on the object of our visit and we explained to him the only way of salvation. Most of the Jews here are mechanics; very many are tailors and shoemakers. We found such a measure of sincere devotion among them that no one would lend us his horses or accompany us on the morrow simply because it was the Jewish Sabbath. They have two synagogues and one *Beth-midrash* (public room for study).

This evening was the commencement of the 'Day of Repentance', a name given to the Sabbath immediately preceding the Day of Atonement. On the morrow the rabbi was to preach a sermon urging them to repentance; and this is one of the two occasions during the year whereon they have a regular sermon, the only other sermon being at the Feast of the Passover. In the ten days between the New Year and the Day of Atonement, the Jews abound more in almsgiving and prayers than during all the rest of the year. Accordingly, both their synagogues were full of worshippers, loud and active in their devotions; even the little boys were rocking to and fro and reading prayers with great earnestness, their gestures resembling those of the Jews of Saphet more nearly than any we had seen. When the service was over, a crowd came round and asked who we were and whence we came. We said that 'we came from a far country out of love for Israel, to tell them the way of forgiveness'. Not knowing what to make of us, they at last demanded 'whether Messiah had come, or was to come?' We answered, 'that both were true, that he had come once to die and was to come a second time in glory'. Many turned away on hearing this and would listen no more.

Foxshany being the frontier town of Wallachia and Moldavia, we were harassed a good deal in getting our passports rightly signed, having to go first to the Governor of the town, then to the Wallachian police, next to the Moldavian police, and lastly to the British Vice-Consul. A narrow stream running through the town divides the two provinces. At the Wallachian office a man was in attendance with the knout in his hand, a large thick whip, often applied without mercy to those who are in the least degree disrespectful or unruly.

September 14

We bade adieu to the obliging little Spaniard, the keeper of the Hotel de France, and started at three o'clock in the morning. On reaching the frontier gate, however, the soldier on guard could himself neither read

nor write; and the examiner of passports being asleep, we were forced
to wait till he chose to rise, sighing in vain for the liberty of our native
land. It was nearly sunrise before we were fairly clear. We were now
riding briskly, in a misty cool morning, on our way to the river Seret,
which we soon crossed by a bridge of boats at a deep and rapid part
where lives have frequently been lost. Nearly forty yoke of oxen,
dragging heavy laden waggons to the market, were waiting on the other
side, and crossing one by one after paying toll. We then ascended a
steppe into a fine plain of vast extent. Soon the country became more
undulating and better wooded. Several pleasant villages appeared with
scattered white cottages. The name of one of these was Taoutchy. Most
of the houses in the villages we came to are built, not continuously, but
at small intervals, with trees round each, giving them a picturesque and
cleanly appearance. The churches are frequently white-washed and
surmounted with glittering spires. The tall poles at the well and the large
haystacks affording provision for their long winter are characteristic
objects; while the large ugly swine, with immense bristles on the ridge
of the back, and the handsome shaggy dogs that rush out as you
approach, enliven the scene to a passing visitor.

About nine o'clock we stopped and set the horses free to feed and
rest, while we got a supply of milk at a cottage and sat down upon the
grass to breakfast, adjourning afterwards to the wooded banks of a
stream that wandered through the wide vale that we might taste the joy
of the Psalmist, 'My meditation of him shall be sweet.' We then
proceeded, and having at midday reached the *podovino* (as our drivers
called it in Russian), that is, 'halfway', our horses were again turned
loose on the grass, while we climbed a woody eminence commanding
a wide view of the country. The scenery during the rest of the day was
much like the preceding, only it had more of hill and dale. We reached
Birlat about five o'clock in the evening, being five posts from Foxshany.
We occupied the upper room of the khan and spreading our mats on the
wooden divan, enjoyed a pleasant Saturday evening, writing home, and
preparing for the Sabbath that was drawing on.

Birlat is pleasantly situated, occupying, like all Moldavian towns, a
large space of ground, and having a population of 10,000. The principal
church has three handsome tin spires, surmounted by four gilded
crosses, much ornamented, as the crosses of the Greek church always
are. The outside of their churches, especially where there are Russians,
have pictures on the walls. In the churchyard, instead of gravestones

they have black wooden crosses; and by the wayside there are stone crosses, the same as we observed before, often two or three together.

September 15 (Sabbath)

We enjoyed a comfortable Sabbath in the upper room of the khan, though it was with difficulty we procured necessary food, as the people at first told us that we could have none without going out to the bazaar to buy it. The atmosphere was pleasant, the thermometer standing at 74° in the shade, as in a summer day at home.

In the afternoon, we went first to the principal church, and found only the priest and three deacons, without an audience, hurrying through the prayers, and chanting without feeling or even melody. We next went to a smaller church, built entirely of wood. Here the priest had six or eight boys, in ragged clothes, who repeated the responses, while two old men and half a dozen of old women made up the audience. The walls of both churches were covered over with pictures and other ornaments, and when all was done, every one kneeled down with the head to the floor three times, crossed themselves between every prostration, kissed the pictures and retired.

The morning service commences at eight or nine, and at that time all the churches are crowded; but after that is over, the whole day is spent in amusements, cards, billiards, and drinking, the priests themselves setting the example. May not a Jewish missionary be blessed to shed some light even on these dark abodes of a heartless superstition? The synagogues of Corinth and Thessalonica brought salvation to the Gentiles in their respective towns; and it may again be so in these regions, if the Lord answer our prayers and prosper our missionaries.

We had seen Jews in the streets on Saturday when we arrived; and now we met one who led us to their synagogue. There are 130 Jewish families from Russia, Austria and Germany who live quietly here and, generally speaking, suffer no persecution. In the synagogue two lads entered very eagerly into conversation with us in German. We began by telling them how different Christians in England and Scotland were from those in their country. They wondered much and asked, 'If we wore *Tephillin*', i.e. phylacteries. We said, 'No, for this is not commanded in the Word of God, but only in their traditions.' We then spoke a long time on the Scriptures being the Word of God, whereas the Talmud was the word of man. We referred to their prayers, showing that they did not procure pardon, but that Messiah only could do this by becoming surety for us. Both of the young men were very attentive, and greatly surprised that we believed the Scriptures as firmly as the Jews do.

Meanwhile, a group gathered round Mr Calman. They told him that they all believe in the divine authority of the leader of the Chasidim in Russia, a rabbi of wealth who used to have attendants and a band of music following him whenever he rode out in his carriage. He had a chamber in his house where it was believed that Messiah will stay when he comes; and at the beginning of each Sabbath went into this chamber, pretending to salute Messiah and wish him 'Good Sabbath'. He had two fine horses, on one of which Messiah is to ride and himself upon the other. Not long ago, being accused before the Emperor by the Jews who are not Chasidim of sending great sums of money to the Holy Land and teaching that it is no sin to cheat the Government by smuggling, he was imprisoned at Kiow, and, though large sums have been offered for his release, he is still in prison. They also spoke of another rabbi of the Chasidim at Navoritz in Poland who had been warning the Jews against the belief that Messiah would come that year or next year, being afraid that they would turn infidels if Messiah did not come. When they spoke of their present misery, Mr Calman said that they should inquire whether the cause of it was not their rejection of Christ? They said, they still expected Messiah and that he is to come when their nation is either *very corrupt or very pure*, even as the leper was counted clean either when his whole body was white, or when there was no sign of leprosy at all (Leviticus 13:6). Therefore, said they, there is no need of our repenting before he comes. We gave them some tracts and left them.

On leaving Birlat next morning, we prevailed on the keeper of the khan, though with great difficulty, to sell us a picture of Christ on the Cross, surrounded by devils, which hung on the wall as a charm. On the wall of an inn upon the road we saw a small picture of the Virgin, having the frame set round with lamps that bore the marks of often being kindled in her honour. Passing some country waggons, we examined minutely the large clumsy yoke which is fastened on the necks of oxen. It is a large wooden frame, so heavy and stiff that the animal cannot put down its head to feed unless the side pins be taken out and its neck released from the yoke. This opened up to us the meaning of the prophet, 'I was to them as they that *take off the yoke on their jaws, and I laid meat unto them*' (Hosea 11:4). Windmills and acacia trees were the common objects that varied the scene on the road. A small lake occurs not far

distant from the town, and near it a pillar on which is represented St Peter
with the keys. There are several neat wells with seats round them for the
accommodation of travellers, in the Eastern fashion, introduced into
this region by the Turks. Farther on we passed an encampment of
Zingans, near a stream, on the opposite side of which people were
dressing flax.

At midday, we rested two hours in a pleasant khan called Tata-
maresti. While there, a sick Jew coming up in a cart, we spoke to him
and gave him a little medicine which relieved him. The poor man was
so grateful that he sent back a messenger with the offer of money as a
recompense. Meanwhile another interesting Jew spoke with us. He
could not believe that we were Christians because we knew Hebrew. We
told him about the Christians in England and the duty of searching the
Scriptures. He said that many Polish rabbis forbid the reading of the
Bible; that he had a fine boy whom the rabbis wanted to begin the
Talmud, but he was resolved not to permit him; and spoke of a Jew in
Jassy, who was called an Epicurus by the Jews, because he studied the
Bible so much. He said that there were fifty families of Jews at the
village of Nacoush near Jassy, and more at Waslui.

As we proceeded, the character of the country became more varied.
Our way lay through a fine open valley with meadow land enclosed by
wooded hills. A smooth river flowed through the vale. Late at night we
arrived at Waslui and found one Jewish khan already fully occupied
with Jews, on their way to Jassy to keep the Day of Atonement there. In
another we found a wretched lodging, though the poor people gave us
their best apartment and slept in the verandah themselves. We spread
our mats on the clay floor and attempted to sleep, but in vain. We cared
less for this, however, because it was the night preceding the Day of
Atonement, and we had thus an opportunity of seeing the curious
ceremony which then takes place. On the eve of that solemn day, it is
the custom of the Jews to kill a cock for every man and a hen for every
woman. During the repetition of a certain form of prayer, the Jew or
Jewess moves the living fowl round their head three times. Then they
lay their hands on it, as the hands used to be laid on the sacrifices, and
immediately after give it to be slaughtered. We rose before 1 am, and
saw the Jewish *Shochet*, or 'slayer', going round the Jewish houses,
waking each family and giving them a light from his lantern in order that
they might rise and bring out their *Cipporah* or 'atonement', namely, the
appointed cock and hen. We walked about the streets; everywhere the

sound of the imprisoned fowls was to be heard and a light seen in all the dwellings of Israel. In two houses the fowls were already dead and plucked. In another, we came to a window and saw distinctly what was going on within. A little boy was reading prayers and his widowed mother standing over him with a white hen in her hands. When he came to a certain place in the prayer, the mother lifted up the struggling fowl and waved it round her head, repeating these words, 'This be my substitute, this be my exchange, this be my atonement; this fowl shall go to death, and I to a blessed life.' This was done three times over, and then the door of the house opened, and out ran the boy carrying the fowl to the *Shochet*, to be killed by him in the proper manner.

How foolish and yet how affecting is this ceremony! This is *the only blood* that is shed in Israel now. No more does the blood of bulls and goats flow beside the brazen altar, the continual burnt-offering is no more, even the paschal lamb is no more slain; a cock and hen killed by the knife of the *Shochet* is all the sacrifice that Israel knows. It is for this wretched self-devised sacrifice that they reject the blood of the Son of God. How remarkably does this ceremony show a lingering knowledge in Israel of the imputation of sin, of the true nature of sacrifice, and of the need of the shedding of blood before sin can be forgiven! And yet so utterly blind are they to the real meaning of the ceremony that the rabbis maintain that it is *not a sacrifice*, but only obtains forgiveness as being obedience to the traditions of the elders. So that the words of the prophet are strictly true, 'The children of Israel shall abide many days without a king, and without a prince, and *without a sacrifice*' (Hosea 13:4).

We left Waslui about two o'clock in the morning, while it was yet dark, and at seven rested for some hours at a wretched khan, large and nearly empty, under a shed. Proceeding northward up a long valley, the summits of the hills being generally covered with trees, the appearance of the country gradually improved, and in the afternoon we came to a really pleasant view. The valley was closed up with hills finely wooded with elms, wild apple trees, and plums, richly laden with fruit. The woodbine and hop-plant were twining round the trees, and many wild flowers gave a charm to this wilderness. Our road was directly over the ridge of hills, and our postilions continued to urge on their horses with their barbarian cries till we reached the summit. A deep wooded ravine now lay beneath and beyond it the vast undulating plain of Jassy. Several miles off the city appeared of great extent, the houses white, spires glittering, and much verdure round.

We entered it before sunset and passed through long streets of artisans, the houses all of one storey, and poorer than those of Bucarest. The Jews were busily employed in shutting up their shops and dressing. Many families were already on their way to the synagogue for no-one would be absent on so solemn an occasion as the beginning of the Day of Atonement. Many of them were fine-looking men, and the Jewesses were beautifully attired, some wearing jewels. Putting up our carriage, we hastened to the synagogue, which we found crowded to excess; even the women's gallery was quite full, and there were many children. The *Absolution Chant*, known by the name of *Col Nidre*, had been sung before we entered. This we wished much to have heard, the tune being plaintive and beautiful, and one which the Jews believe was brought from Sinai. Three rabbis stand up dressed in white, and in their own name and in the name of God, absolve all in the synagogue from the sins committed in the year past. The number of large candles lighted and the multitude of worshippers made the atmosphere quite oppressive in all the synagogues we visited; and the perspiration was running down in streams from the zealous devotees whose cries and frantic earnestness might be heard afar off. They clapped their hands, clasped them, wrung them, struck the prayer-book, beat upon their breast, and writhed their bodies, again reminding us of the Jews of Saphet and Tiberias. On this occasion, the Jews keep up prayer all night and all the next day, till the time of evening when 'the stars appear'.

We left them for the present and found our way to the house of the British Consul-general, Mr Gardner, who received us with great kindness. We afterwards found a lodging in the Hotel St Petersburg, a large establishment kept by a baptized Jew of the Greek Church.

Early next day *(September 18)* we sought out the synagogue again. The Jews come up to the solemnity of the Atonement from the country, as they did to Jerusalem in former days. We visited twelve of their synagogues and found all crowded with men, women, and children, in the same manner as the previous night. At one of them we saw many mothers with their children at the breast or in cradles, sitting on the outside dressed in their finest clothes. It reminded us of the fast described by Joel, 'Assemble the elders, gather the *children, and those that suck the breasts*' (Joel 2:16). As there was not sufficient room within, many men were sitting under the shade of the walls, looking with their faces towards Jerusalem and praying along with those inside. The floor of the synagogue was for the most part strewed with straw or hay, to add to the comfort of the worshippers in their long service; for most of them put off their shoes, the day being so holy. All day the synagogue is full of immense lighted candles. Each family provides one, and each member has a thread in the wick of the candle. These represent the soul of each person according to their interpretation of the Proverb, 'The spirit of man is the candle of the Lord' (Proverbs 20:27). On so solemn a day as this, no Jew will touch one of these candles, even were it to fall and endanger the safety of the synagogue. To do so would be accounted servile work, and therefore they employ a Gentile servant, who is called in when any lights require to be trimmed.

In the prayers they go over the greater part of Leviticus 16, in which the sacrifices of the Day of Atonement are described. The rest of the service consists in reading a Hebrew poem, of which we were assured that most of the worshippers scarcely understood one word, because it is most difficult Hebrew. Yet all were engaged in reading it aloud. Sometimes they came to a chant, when the deep bass voice of the chanter was contrasted with the tenor voices of a few young men; the effect was often very plaintive, and sometimes ludicrous. Again and again the whole congregation broke in with 'Amen', pronounced 'Omain'. Many of the men seemed already quite wearied with their worship, or rather with their bodily exercise, and many had their eyes red and swollen with weeping: a good number of the married men wore the *halukah*, or white shirt of the rabbis). Among the women, some were weeping and others sobbing aloud. A few boys were as seriously engaged as their elders.

There are 200 synagogues in the town and about thirty of these are large. In one quarter there are twenty, all within the space of a street. Some of the buildings had their roofs fancifully painted with figures, representing Paradise and the Creation – wild beasts, trees, and fishes, the golden candlestick also, and table of showbread. In several parts near the entrance of the town, we noticed the *Eruv*, or string stretched from house to house across the street, to make it *a walled town*, the same as we had observed at Saphet.

We found it impossible to ascertain with accuracy the numbers of the Jews in Jassy. The Consul reckoned the whole population of the city at 50,000, and the Jews at somewhat less than the half, perhaps 20,000. This would coincide with the reckoning of many of the Jews themselves, who gave their numbers at 5,500 families. The highest estimate we heard from a very intelligent Jew was 10,000 families, while the lowest was 3,500, or about 15,000 souls. They are regarded by the Government as a separate community, and the capitation-tax is not levied from them individually, but from their chief men, who are left to gather the sum from their brethren in the way they think most equal and fair. Each family, at an average, pay a *ducat*, equal to ten shillings. The way in which the rulers of the Jews levy the tax is as follows: They lay it not on the provisions of the poor, but on articles of luxury. For example, a goose is sold for about a *zwanzig*, but they put a tax on it of half a *zwanzig* and eight *paras*. Thus the rich, who wish luxuries, pay a high price for them; while the poor, who are content with the necessaries of life, escape. They do not consider themselves oppressed by the Government, but the common people use them ill. As an instance of this, we were told that a Moldavian would often reply, when asked by a Jew to do something for him, 'I would as soon do it for a *Zingan*'. The name 'Zingan', and the epithet 'cursed', is often applied to them. All the Jews here speak a corrupt dialect of German. They follow all trades, except that of a smith; the most are tailors, shoemakers, carpenters, and watchmakers; a few are idle, and sleep in the streets. There have been about twenty converts to the Greek Church. Three of these are persons of respectability, one the keeper of the hotel, another a carpenter, and the third a student at college – but all were very ignorant. The Jews believe that their true reason for seeking baptism was that they might get more freedom. It did not make any difference in regard to their employment. If any of the chief Jews were to profess Christianity, many would follow their example. Some of them expressed their belief that Messiah would come in the year 1840, others think it is to be in the seven-thousandth year of the world, and then a time of Sabbaths is to follow. There is a belief, too, among many of them, that the Russians (whom they suppose to be the *Javan* of Zechariah 9:13) are to have the dominion of the world.

There are many Jewish Schools in Jassy, but none of them good. Six of the principal families have refused to send their children to any of these schools to be taught the Talmud because they think that such studies make them mean and degraded; they either send them elsewhere or employ a private tutor. The severe discipline used in Smyrna is not altogether unknown here; for a Jew who acted as our guide told us that his son often came home with his ears bleeding, his hair torn out, and nose twisted, all by the barbarous treatment of his teacher; so that the father has frequently intended complaining to the police, or sending his boy to be taught in Russia.

About six in the evening we went to two of the largest synagogues to see the ceremonies of the Day of Atonement concluded. When the sun is setting they pray for the last time, and their crying out is intense, far beyond all their previous supplications, for if they do not obtain pardon of their sins before the stars appear, they have no hope remaining of obtaining forgiveness for that year. When about to utter their last prayer, a trumpet is sounded like that of the New Year, but only one blast. Then all is over, and forth they come to the light of the risen moon, pouring like a stream from the synagogue. They stood in groups, all turning their faces toward the moon – for the Jews believe that the spots in the moon are the *Shecinah*. Each group had a lighted candle to enable one of their number to read the prayer addressed *to the Shecinah in the moon*. Some held up their hands, others roared aloud, and all shewed by their gestures the intense feeling of their heart.

It was a grotesque scene, as well as peculiarly novel, to stand amid such a company, each in his high fur-cap, the *tallith* round his shoulders, and generally his beard flowing wide over the book he was reading. As we looked upon the crowds of worshippers that filled the spacious court of the synagogue, and saw their white eyes ever and anon turned up toward the bright moon, we were irresistibly reminded of the days when the fathers of that singular people forsook the worship of Jehovah, and 'served Baal and Ashtaroth', and 'made cakes to the queen of heaven' (Judges 2:13; 10:6; Jeremiah 7:18). This service being done, they appeared as if relieved from the pressure of an overwhelming load, for they had fasted and prayed for twenty-four hours, and now dispersed themselves in all directions. Many went homewards singing with great glee in the open streets, and shouting aloud to each other, 'Peace to thee, and peace to thee !' This is said to be done because their sins are now forgiven. How little they know of pardon! the pardon obtained by God's method of justification, which would sanctify and draw the sinner's heart to Him, instead of making it return to folly. 'There is forgiveness with thee *that thou mayst be feared.*' It is not unusual for Jews to meet the same night in their synagogue and be merry together, and we soon after saw several public-houses open, at whose door we could look in; and there were Jews sitting together drinking *rakee*, and singing merrily. In one a Jew was singing over his cups to the full pitch of his voice. False peace leads to false holiness. Thus ended the Day of Atonement. Alas! how changed from the solemn day, when the high priest entered into the holiest of all! During the whole ceremony we observed that the people of the town never interrupted them in any manner.

We got much general information from the Consul. The expenses of living in Jassy are much the same as at Bucarest. There is difficulty in getting a house at all and the rent is very high. A carriage of some kind is indispensable, for even tailors and shoemakers require these on account of the badness of the roads. It is necessary, also, to keep many servants. But the necessaries of life are very cheap.

Jassy is much improved as a city; the streets were formerly paved with wood, but this is no longer the case. It has no fewer than seventy churches; the climate is much more healthy than that of Bucarest, though there is a Moldavian fever prevalent at a certain season. Divorce is not so common as it used to be; the stream of public feeling is now turning against it. Yet it is too evident that the fear of God is not in this place. Of this the Consul related an affecting proof. One evening in January 1838, a great ball was given at which most of the Boyards were to be present. He and a Moldavian gentleman were preparing to set out – their carriage was at the door – when a dreadful shock of an earthquake startled the whole town. At his house, the tall mast that bears aloft the British flag rocked to and fro. After some minutes' silence, his friend proposed that they should still set out for the ball. The Consul replied that it would be useless, for no one would be there at such an awful time. However, the other pressed, and he reluctantly consented to go. They drove up to the place and entered the room. It was brilliantly lighted, and the gay company were met; but all sat silent, pale as death. A large rent had been made in the wall and the plaster had fallen on the floor. The Consul kept his eye on the door, expecting another shock every moment. In a few minutes, however, one of the company made an effort to strike up an air, the floor was swept, the dance began, and all was mirth and levity. 'The harp, and the viol, the tabret, and pipe, and wine, are in their feasts; but they regard not the work of the Lord, neither consider the operation of his hands' (Isaiah 5:12).

The Prince of Moldavia resides in Jassy; he is very affable to strangers, and was favourable to the circulation of the Scriptures in his dominions; but the Bishop is a bigoted man, and would not allow it. When the Consul informed the Prince of our arrival, he asked what our object was in travelling through Moldavia, and expressed a wish to see us. We delayed our departure a day longer in order to accomplish this visit, but the Prince was taken unwell and could not receive us. There is every reason to believe that the Government will not interfere with the labours of a Jewish Missionary in this province.

Late in the evening, an intelligent Jew called on us by appointment, and from him we received some curious facts regarding the Jews here. Three years ago, a rabbi, the greatest man in Jassy, began to read the Scriptures much and to preach against the Talmud. The Jews were so angry that they drove him and his family from the city, so that he was obliged to go to Brody. They gave him 1,000 ducats as an atonement, for it is considered a great sin to expel a rabbi. A rich Jew here, named Michael Daniel, a man of eighty years of age, has a teacher in his house to instruct him in the *Cabala*. In Kotsin, twenty miles from Jassy, there is a sect of the Chasidim, called *Habad* (that is persons who profess 'wisdom, understanding, and knowledge'). On the night after the Day of Atonement, as a party of them were coming home with singing and other expressions of joy, they found a Jew drunk, and who had fallen asleep. This Jew had a gipsy servant who spoke German and he, for the sake of amusement, dressed himself up in the sleeping Jew's clothes and headed the Jewish party. They took the drunk man and carried him through the streets to another house in their foolish revelry. The gipsy having a grudge at the Jews went to the Moldavians and said, 'they were imitating the ceremony of the Church', when, at Easter, they carry about a large figure representing Christ. The people were excited, and rushed on the Jews; one was killed on the spot; twelve were imprisoned, and afterwards sentenced to be hanged; but Michael Daniel having lent the Prince 6,000 ducats and another Jew having lent 2,000, they offered to make a present of these sums, along with 2,000 ducats out of the Jewish treasury to get their brethren released. This was agreed to, but the guilty persons were sent out of the country. How strikingly these facts show the fulfilment of the threatening, 'Thou shalt grope at noonday, as the blind gropeth in darkness, and thou shall not prosper in thy ways; and thou shalt be *only oppressed and spoiled evermore, and no man shall save thee*' (Deuteronomy 28:29).

We devoted the next day *(September 19)* entirely to visiting the Jews. First we visited a school of thirty children, both boys and girls, with fine Jewish countenances. A poor sick boy lay on a couch in the same room, far gone in consumption. The teacher was busily employed in his work. His method seemed to be to repeat over every syllable, until each scholar could fully pronounce it. The boys and girls got the same tuition and the prayer-book seemed to be the only schoolbook. The children were amazed at the entrance of strangers and ran eagerly round us. We learned from the teacher that the children were taught only *to read*, not *to understand*. Nay, he himself could not explain the words of the passage which they were reading. When asked why he did not explain the words, he referred to Psalm 119:18: 'Open thou mine eyes to see wondrous things out of thy law', and drew from it the inference that it was not to be expected that a teacher should be able to explain all that he taught. Several Jews had by this time gathered round, to whom Mr Calman spoke, trying to show them how ruinous and deplorable their ignorance of the Word of God is. They seemed convinced, only they said it was universal in Jassy.

We went to see the old Jew of whom we had got information, called an Epicurus. He was a fine-looking man, of about sixty years of age, mild and thoughtful and his son, an interesting youth, very like his father, was sitting with him. They were true specimens of the Neologian Jews who have cast off the Talmud, but at the same time reject, or almost reject, the Word of God. The old man said that in youth he had been taught that the Scriptures and the Talmud were both divine; and that now, having been enlightened to see the fables and folly of the Talmud, he was naturally led to doubt the authority of the Bible also. He added 'he was sorry that he could not believe the Bible to be the Word of God'. He told us that he believed none but himself in all Jassy could speak the Hebrew; that scarcely any of the Jews knew their own language grammatically; and that they did not wish their children to be taught. 'They want no change. We are doing all we can to throw in firebrands among the stubble of the Talmud; but *"Der alte stier will nicht lernen mehr"* – the old ox will not learn. If you do any thing for them you must hide the good.' They had employed teachers to teach the young grammatically, but the parents would not send them; the children themselves, however, got so fond of them, that they used to follow them on the streets, seeking instruction. When we turned up to Isaiah 53, he said he believed it referred to Jesus; but that it was written by some Christian *after the event*. As a similar case of interpolation, he referred to Numbers 21:27,28 as written after Jeremiah 48:45,46. He got this idea from Jost's *History of the Jews*, but could not give any proof nor could he answer the arguments that show the authenticity of the passage. When we pressed him about sin and the need of pardon, he said, 'We do not sin against God, because he is infinitely beyond us; but we sin against our neighbours, and the punishment of sin is solely in our conscience.' The young man was much less imbued with Neologian opinions, and said to us 'that he was now more a Christian than a Jew'. He acknowledged that we do sin against God, and that nothing but a sense of pardon can give peace. But when we stated that Christians believe themselves forgiven on the ground of the atonement, he said, 'I may have as much peace as they, if I believe myself forgiven even on other grounds.' He admitted the inspiration of the Pentateuch, but not of the Prophets. The old man told us that both he and his son belonged to a secret society in Tarnapol, a town of Austrian Poland, and that the chief rabbi of the rabbinical Jews there is at the head of it, unknown to his people. They work like Jesuits, conforming externally to Judaism but diffusing their principles in secret as widely as possible. Their young men are teachers of languages and have thus opportunity to leaven the minds of the Jewish youth with their sentiments. This young man himself is tutor in six of the wealthy Jewish families in Jassy, whose children are entirely under his influence, hating Judaism, and keeping the Christian as well as the Jewish Sabbath. Another son of this old Jew lives at Vienna with a brother-in-law, who is baptized and is enjoined to bring up the youth as a Christian. There are a great many in Vienna who have their children baptized, although the fathers like to die Jews. In Galicia many fathers are bringing up their children to Christianity, and it is said that there are more baptisms than births, 'so that in a century (said the old man) there will not be a Jew in all Galicia.' When he heard that we were ministers and Calvinists, he said he had read a great deal and knew the Calvinistic system; that it was the most philosophical and added, 'If I were turning Christian I would become a Calvinist.' Both these Jews were very kind to us, the old man saying that this was one of the happiest days of his life. What an awful scene does this interview lay open – half the nation of Israel tottering on the brink of infidelity! Those who have light enough to see the folly of the Talmud have not grace enough to believe the Word of God. The rusty shackles of Judaism are beginning to fall off, but the withered arms of Israel have no life to lay hold on the Saviour promised to their fathers. Thousands in Israel are in a transition state, but it is not such a change as that spoken of in the Prophets, 'I will go and return *to my first husband*, for then was it better with me than now' (Hosea 2:7). The door is open and the time critical, and it seems plainly the duty of the Christian Church without delay to interpose in their behalf, to allure Israel, and speak comfortably unto her, and to say, 'O Israel, return unto the Lord thy God, for thou hast fallen by thine iniquity' (Hosea 14:1).

We next called at the house of the chief rabbi, where they were beginning to erect a booth for the Feast of Tabernacles. The rabbi was a fine-looking man, but not learned He seemed fatigued with the hard services of the preceding day. We explained our object in general terms, deploring the ignorance which we had seen among the Jews, and urging the need of schools where they might be taught to read the Word of God grammatically. He assented, and professed to desire the improvement of his people, but said that we should apply to influential men, such as the merchants, who must exert themselves if these objects were ever to be effected. While we were with him, a young woman came in with some friends, seeking a divorce from her husband, for this is as common among the Jews as among the Greeks. In the shop of the principal Jewish bookseller we found prayer-books, commentaries and portions of the Talmud, but nothing very interesting.

We were invited in the evening to a Jewish marriage. We went at the hour, but a long delay occurred, for the bridegroom not having brought a string of diamonds for his bride's head-dress – an ornament much valued here – she and her friends refused to let the ceremony proceed till it was purchased. 'Can a maid forget her ornaments, or a bride her attire?' (Jeremiah 2:32) is a natural question in Israel at this day. As we were walking to and fro before the door, Mr Calman spoke with a tall Jew upon the evils of the Talmud. He seemed to be much convinced and said, 'Well, I see that we are a people without a religion. But what shall we do? Shall we become Christians like the Greeks who have not the Word of God?'

Returning to the house some hours after, we found that the marriage ceremony had been concluded and that the company were now seated at the marriage-feast. From Mr Calman we received an account of the previous part of the ceremony. Early on the marriage day the *Bathan*, or poet, who performs a very prominent part, comes to the bride's house and addresses her most solemnly upon her sins, urging her to cry for forgiveness, for marriage is looked upon as an ordinance by which sins are forgiven, just as the Day of Atonement, pilgrimages, and the like; and the Jews believe that it will be destined that day whether her luck is to be good or not. She and her attendant maidens are often bathed in tears during this address, which sometimes lasts two hours. The Bathan next goes to the bridegroom and exhorts him in the same manner. This done, the bridegroom puts on the same white dress which he wears on the Day of Atonement and spends some time in prayer and confession of sins, using the same prayers as on that solemn day. He is then led to the synagogue, accompanied by a band of music. The band next goes from him to accompany the bride. The parties are placed near each other and the marriage canopy on four poles is held over them. The contract is read and the sum named which the husband promises to give the woman in case of divorce. The fathers and mothers, friends of the bridegroom, and the bridesmaids, take the bride by the hand, and all go round the bridegroom, in obedience to the words 'a woman shall compass a man' (Jeremiah 31:22). A cup of wine is produced and seven blessings pronounced over it. The bridegroom puts the marriage-ring upon the bride's finger, saying, 'Behold, thou are consecrated to me with this ring, according to the law of Moses and Israel.' Other seven blessings are pronounced over the cup of wine which they taste, and the glass is thrown down and broken to signify that even in their joy they are no better than a broken shred. They are then led together to the bride's house where we found them sitting at the head of the table in silence. The bride had her face veiled down nearly to the mouth with a handkerchief which she wears during the whole ceremony. Her dress, and that of most of her companions, was pure white (Revelation 19:7,8).

The table was filled with guests, the men being seated on one side and the women on the other. Before eating, all wash their hands out of a dish with two handles (Mark 8:3), so formed that the one hand may not defile the other.

It was singular to see this feast of bearded men, the faces of many of whom might have been studies for a painter. The feast at the marriage of Cana of Galilee was vividly presented to our minds. During the repast the music struck up; several Jews played well on the violin, violoncello, cymbals, tambourine, and a harp of a singular shape which they said was Jewish, not Christian. It was played by beating upon the strings with two wooden instruments and the effect was pleasing. It is remarkable that, beyond the bounds of their own land, Israel should have so many instruments of music, while in Palestine, as the prophet foretold, *The joy of the harp ceaseth*. The *Bathan*, or chanter, frequently interrupted the music, and excited the mirth and good humour of the company by his impromptu German verses on the new married pair and their friends.

We were not invited to sit at table, for had we Gentiles touched their food it would have been unclean, but dishes were handed to us where we sat. Several times a plate went round the company for collections; the first time it was 'for the cook', and this they called *the golden soup*; the next time was, 'for Jerusalem'; and a third time 'for the new married couple' – a present for the entertainment given to the company. The bridegroom should have preached a sermon to the company, but he being unlearned, the chanter did it for him. After supper there was a dance, but not after the manner of the Gentiles. Some little girls first danced together; the uncle, a tall handsome bearded Jew, then danced alone; last of all he danced with the bride, leading her round and round by a handkerchief. This forms the concluding part of the ceremony enjoined by the Talmud. Wine flowed plentifully as at Cana; but, being the simple wine of the country, not the slightest riot or extravagance was visible. When shall that marriage-day come of which the prophet speaks, 'As the bridegroom rejoiceth over the bride, so shall thy God rejoice over thee' (Isaiah 62:5)?

September 20

Our last day in Jassy was mostly spent in conversation with the many Jews who came to visit us. None seemed to be under real soul concern, but all had an open ear for our statements of the truth. They told us that most of their brethren here have little higher motive for adhering to Judaism than temporal advantage, such as the expectation of money from some relative when he dies. We discussed many passages together, and they appeared interested and anxious, though very ignorant. After breakfast two Jews came in, one a very intelligent man named Leb Keri, an *avocat* in the town, connected with the courts of law. His special object in coming was to request a New Testament in Hebrew. When we presented him with a copy, he said that he had long wished for one, and on getting some Hebrew tracts also, he refused to part with them to any other, 'Because', said he, 'I have need of them all in discussions with friends on these subjects.' Several other Jews called; and there were eight in the room at once. Their ignorance of Scripture was such that the commonest Hebrew words often puzzled them. Mr Bonar read over Luke 15 in German with one who sat by him, the same who used to be our guide through the town. On the other side of the table sat another, an elderly man, with his broad-brimmed hat resting on the top of his staff, while another stood behind his chair, listening to all the remarks. Mr Calman was, at the same time, in full discussion with an old Jew wearing a white-flowing beard, whilst two others sat at another part of the table perusing portions of the New Testament and examining the Hebrew tracts. Two more moved about from one group to another, listening and sometimes putting questions. One of them, on being asked to say who was meant by 'the man that is a hiding place' (Isaiah 32:2), said 'that he must consult his commentators'. Another spoke of our believing Christ to be the Son of God and said, 'It is impossible.' A third fixed on 1 Corinthians 7:28 as teaching immorality, grounding his argument entirely on a word used in some editions of the translation and which modern Jews always employ in a bad sense. A boy belonging to the hotel seemed considerably interested in the visits of these Jews, and at last told us that he was himself a baptized Jew. He had lived for some time in a Greek convent, along with five other converts, to get instruction, but both he and his companions were disgusted with the superstition and behaviour of the monks.

This was an interesting day. In the evening, we bade adieu to the Consul, and setting off at nine o clock, left Jassy far behind.

When we woke up in the morning *(September 21)*, we were passing through a fine wooded valley, adorned with pleasant villages. On the left stood a romantic-looking church; and at a row of houses by the roadside, we heard the voice of Jews at prayer, proceeding from a small synagogue, consisting of about ten persons. Over a vast plain we obtained a distant view of Botouchany, with its many glittering spires. Near the entrance stood a large cross, with a full-length figure of the Saviour wearing the crown of thorns. We arrived about 11 am, and by the advice of the English Vice-Consul, Signore Scotto, who greatly assisted us, we determined to take horses direct from this place to a village three hours distant called Teshawitz, on the Moldavian border opposite the Austrian quarantine station. We called at the house of a Jew whom we found willing to lend us horses though it was their Sabbath. He could not send a Jewish servant with them; nor would he either name the hire, or take it, yet he engaged a Gentile to go with us and to be his proxy. He forgot the words, *nor thy cattle, nor the stranger that is within thy gates*. This, however, is the genuine result of the hypocrisy taught by the Talmud. Over the door of his house we noticed a framed ornament, with the single word *mizrach* (The East) in large characters, pointing out the direction in which Jerusalem lies.

Botouchany is a peculiarly clean town, containing 20,000 inhabitants and having eleven Greek churches. It extends over a great space and there are gardens and trees interposed which give it a cheerful aspect. There are from four to five thousand Jews in it. We saw great numbers in their best attire, and they appeared far more clean and comfortable than those of Jassy or Bucarest. Their houses also were clean and whitewashed, with a small verandah before the windows. The Consul said that they have sixteen synagogues; but we neglected to make inquiry of the Jews themselves.

We enjoyed a pleasant evening ride and found that three Jewish horses were equal to eight Gentile ones. Our road lay sometimes through deep shady woods and sometimes through open meadow land. Many herds of swine were feeding in the fields. It was rather a hilly region; but beneath us was a fine plain, beyond which rose the distant Carpathian Mountains in the west. At one point we drove through a long avenue of densely planted willow-trees, till we came to the margin of a broad stream, which we forded. We then descended through a grove of pleasant trees upon the small village of Teshawitz.

The sun was setting upon the peaceful scene, and it was too late to admit of our crossing the river Soutchava, which here forms the Austrian frontier, and getting into quarantine. We therefore took up our lodging for the night in a small inn not far from the riverside, kept by a Jew, named Baruch Ben-Roze; who had erected a booth before his door of the willows that grow by the riverside, the next evening being the beginning of the Feast of Tabernacles. He afterwards shewed us his palm branch, called *lulab*, and his fine fruit called *ezrach* (Psalm 37:35), supposed to be the 'fruit of a goodly tree', spoken of in the law (Leviticus 23:40). It is a fruit like a lemon and grows to maturity only once in three years. It is brought from Italy and from the Holy Land, and sometimes more than a hundred dollars are paid to obtain one for the feast. This man had paid four rubles for his, a sum equal to £1 sterling. The Karaites are not so particular; they use an orange or any fine fruit. The man had also slips of myrtle (Nehemiah 8:15) wrapped in the leaf of the palm. When we entered his house, the Jewish Sabbath was coming to a close. As soon as it was over, the father of the family began to bless the lights, all which are extinguished on the Sabbath as the Jews are not allowed to kindle a fire, or even to mend it on that day; and so, when the Sabbath is done, they light their candle and fire anew, and bless God for it. This Jew blessed also the incense and the drink which was to be used, praying over them all. The reason for blessing the incense is to be found in the ancient custom of using incense at the third meal on the Sabbaths. In blessing the lights, he poured out some *rakee* on the table and set it on fire; then dipped his finger in it, and waved the flaming liquid over his face. This is done to show that 'the commandment of the Lord is pure, giving light to the eyes'.

After we had got some refreshment, the family were full of curiosity to see the strangers, especially on hearing that we had seen Jerusalem. The father, mother, an old aunt, two boys, and a little girl, soon gathered round us. The father (our host) talked freely. He hoped, he said, soon to be at Jerusalem himself. The mother asked if we had seen the remains of the old Temple wall? We described to her what we had seen; and then took out a plan of Jerusalem and pointed out to the boy the various interesting places in and about the city which we had visited; and showed them some of the sketches we had taken. One of them was very ready in showing his acquaintance with Jewish history; and both became more and more free with us, wondering much at our interest in the Jews. 'Do you wear *Tephillin*?' asked one. 'How many commandments do you keep?' said another. Our answer was, 'The commandments which you as well as we ought to keep are two: "Thou shalt serve the Lord thy God with all thy heart" and "Thou shalt love thy neighbour as thyself".' The boy, who had shewed considerable knowledge of Jewish history, then asked, 'Why we travelled on Sabbath?' for they were still persuaded that we were Jews. We told him we were to keep our own Sabbath next day. But he, still believing that we were brethren, said, 'They have not broken our Sabbath; they did not work today; a Gentile drove their carriage, and had anything been broken he would have mended it.' The mother then put in a word, asking if we had heard a prediction which some Jew told them was uttered at Jerusalem, that, next year, in the month of March, a great cloud was to burst and pour out a flood that would drown the world? We said that we had not heard it and that it must be false for God promised to Noah never to drown the world any more by a flood. 'But', said she, 'after the cloud has done this, the earth is to be restored again.' We opened the Hebrew Bible at the passage in Daniel, where Messiah is described as 'coming with *the clouds of heaven*', and shewed it to the father, who read it and said, 'Perhaps that was the source of the prediction.'

The little girl, whose name was Esther, stood near Mr Bonar, behind the rest. Speaking of her name, as the name of a Jewish queen, he asked her if she knew much of the Bible? She said that her mother had taught her all she knew, for she had not read the Bible herself. 'I know about

Abraham, Isaac, Jacob, Joseph.' He asked her to go on, but she said, 'I do not know more.' He asked her what she knew about God? 'God', said the little girl, 'is better than all; better than father or mother, a hundred, hundred times. And if I were ill, my father or mother cannot help me, but God can.' We told her that she ought to love Him indeed; for He had so loved us as to send His Son to save us. We asked, 'Where is God?' She pointed upwards, 'There.' 'But is he nowhere else?' She pointed round the room. 'Yes, here'; and then added, 'In my heart, too, and everywhere.' We asked her if she knew that she was a sinner? She said, 'I have no sin.' Her mother taught her this on the ground of her being a daughter of Abraham. We spoke to her of what the Bible declared regarding her sin and danger. No wonder Jewish females are *at ease* and 'careless ones' (Isaiah 32:11) when they are taught to believe that they have no sin! On getting from us a shell from the Lake of Galilee, she expressed great delight and said that she would wear it round her neck.

The father then brought out a collection-box, which he kept in his own house, for the Jews in Palestine; and another for a particular rabbi, a friend, who had gone there. He next shewed us a lump of earth, which he had brought from a rabbi's grave, a rabbi to whom he used to go to get absolution, and whom he greatly loved. The mother asked us if we could tell anything about the rabbi in Russia whom the Emperor had imprisoned, and wondered why he had been imprisoned. 'It cannot be for his own sins, for he had none; it must be for the sins of the people of Israel.' How strange the ideas that float in the minds of the people of Israel! Their knowledge consists of fragments of truth, and these all tinctured by superstition They own the principle of substitution, and yet apply it wrongly – they apply it to a rabbi; forgetting the Psalm where it is said, *'None of them can by any means redeem his brother, or give to God a ransom for him'* (Psalm 49:7). The boy wondered why God punished the devil for doing evil, since (according to the Jewish belief) he made the devil *as he is*. We shewed him that his opinion was erroneous for God created him a holy angel. But the boy persisted in his own view; and with true rabbinical acumen said, 'He supposed that God punished the devil *for being a hypocrite*, for the devil never tempts any one too directly, but always says, "You will get this or that by doing what I propose".' The father told us that he had been in great doubts about continuing to be an innkeeper, as it often interfered with his observance of the Sabbath; but his rabbi, whom he consulted, told him not to give it up; for if he was in danger of sinning in that way, he made up for the sin by helping poor Jews across the frontier, and assisting them when they did not know the Russian and Wallachian languages. Jesuitical casuistry is as much a feature of Judaism as of Popery! Both systems have one author and are pervaded by the same spirit of deceit. After we had separated for the night, the Jew overhearing us singing the psalm together at our evening worship, asked Mr Calman what we had been doing. On being told that we were worshipping God together before retiring to rest, he was greatly surprised.

September 22

We spent the Sabbath forenoon in a calm, retired spot by the river Soutchava, which flows in front of the house, among alders and willows, which grow on either bank. Herds of cattle were feeding not far off, and two or three whitewashed cottages looked down on us from the opposite side. An Austrian soldier on guard, pacing to and fro upon the northern bank, was the only human being in view.

Towards evening, finding that there was no rest for us in the inn, we resolved to pass the river and enter into the quarantine. Accordingly, we crossed at the ford, entered the Austrian frontier, and, under the guard of a soldier, were in half an hour lodged in the quarantine station called Bossanze. We passed a neat wooden church with its ornamented crosses, but could see no marks of the day of rest. We spent the evening, however, in quietness and peace, and tried to sing the Lord's song in a strange land. We had now entered another of the kingdoms of this world where Satan has his seat, till the time when it shall become the kingdom of our God and of his Christ.

And now looking back over these two provinces of Moldavia and Wallachia, it is impossible not to feel their vast importance and inviting aspect as the scene of a Jewish Mission.

1. The number of resident Jews is very great. In the two capitals there are probably from 25,000 to 30,000, and perhaps as many more in the other towns. So that there is a very extensive field for the labours of a missionary.

2. But farther, the fields are also 'white unto the harvest'. The Jews are in a most interesting state of mind. The greater part of them are very ignorant. We learned that among the many thousands of Jassy, there were only a few who could understand Hebrew grammatically, and in their schools we have seen that even the teachers could not translate the

prayers in the Hebrew prayer-book. In this state of things the Secret Society of Galicia above noticed, whose object is to undermine the authority of the Talmud and the whole fabric of superstitious Judaism, are casting their firebrands among the young Jews of these provinces. Many have had their confidence in the Talmud completely shaken and are standing in this critical situation that they are ripe either for the teacher of infidelity or for the messenger of the gospel. Surely, then, it is the duty of the Christian Church to step in and offer them the truth as it is in Jesus, in the room of their old superstition of which so many are weary.

3. There is reason to hope that the Jewish Missionary may carry on his work without hindrance. There is a British Consul-General in each of the capitals, and Vice-Consuls in the most important towns, who would protect and countenance a missionary from our Church. If a conscientious missionary felt it to be consistent with duty to refrain from any direct attempt at the conversion of the Greek population, and to spend all his energies in seeking the lost sheep of the house of Israel, it seems probable that his labours would not be interrupted by the government. In the happy event of the light beginning to spread indirectly from the Jews to the natives, the eager jealousy of the priesthood would doubtless be awakened and persecution might be expected. But these are dangers attending the success of the gospel in every country and in every age; the cause of a triumphant gospel has ever been through much tribulation; and it is our part to move forward in the path of duty, leaving future events in the hand of God. Vast and ripe unto harvest as these fields are, at the date of our visit no reaper had ever put in his sickle. The Prince of Moldavia needed to ask what our object was in traversing his dominions, for no missionary had ever carried there the words of eternal life. A labourer from the London Society has lately been stationed at Bucarest; and the Rev. Daniel Edward, accompanied by Mr Hermann Philip, a converted Jew, has been sent out by our Church and stationed at Jassy. And many of the Jews would not believe that we were really Christians, because they had never before seen *a Christian who loved the Jews*.

4. Another point of great importance is that it is believed that inquirers and converts could support themselves. Every Jew who arrives in these provinces is obliged to bring with him a certificate that he is able to earn a livelihood by some trade. We have seen that all the necessaries of life are remarkably cheap and that the resources of

commerce are far from being fully occupied, so that an anxious Jew might easily support himself even when cast off by his brethren in the flesh. Workmen are employed irrespectively of their creed, and many Jews who have been baptized into the Greek Church found no difference in their means of living. In this way, one of the greatest difficulties experienced by the Jewish missionary in other countries is removed.

5. Moreover, these provinces border upon Austrian Poland, that land of bigotry and the shadow of death, across whose boundary no traveller dares to carry, except by stealth, even an English Bible. If the Moldavian Jews received the light of the glorious gospel, they might, by means of their constant intercourse with the people, scatter some beams into that dark region where the feet of the gospel messenger cannot go.

Here, then, are probably 60,000 Jews – many of them sunk in ignorance, many of them relating their grasp of old superstitions, and not yet fallen into infidelity, not a few showing friendly dispositions to such Christians as have gone to them in the spirit of the gospel of peace, and some eagerly asking to be shown what the faith of Jesus is. Who can deny that a peculiarly inviting region is here set before the Christian Church – 'an open valley full of bones, very many and very dry' – into which she may send men of the same spirit as Ezekiel, who may cry, 'Come from the four winds, O breath, and breathe upon these slain, that they may live!'

CHAPTER 8

AUSTRIAN POLAND

'Behold, they say, Our bones are dried, and our hope is lost; we are cut
off for our parts' (Ezekiel 37:11).

The Austrian quarantine at *Bossanze*, in which we were to remain five
days, was pleasant and healthy. It stands on high ground, having gardens
and whitewashed cottages in view, and looks down upon a fine country
called Bukovine. The town of Soutchava is about an hour distant. A
Hungarian in the quarantine spoke Latin with us. His pronunciation
differed little from ours, but he seemed to attach a peculiar meaning to
several Latin words. Thus, using *dignatur* in the sense of *is named*, he
said, 'Hæc regio *dignatur* Bukovina'. The doctor, too, spoke Latin with
us and was very attentive to our comfort, after we had undergone the
process of fumigation. Indeed, all the attendants were remarkably civil
and polite. Our books were all examined, but none taken from us.

This was the third time we had undergone quarantine since leaving
Jerusalem, and it was by far the most agreeable. We spent the five days
in making up our journals and writing home; and were glad also to get
a little leisure for reading and study. The doctor often came in and
expressed his surprise at our diligence. In the evenings we always
enjoyed a walk within the enclosures of our wooden prison. We now
also chalked out our future route as far as we could see before us. We
proposed to proceed by Czernowitz, Tarnapol, Brody, Lemberg, and so
out of Austria to Cracow.

On the morning of *September 27* we left our quarantine in one of the
briscas or covered cars of the country, and soon reached the pleasant
town of Soutchava, with eight glittering steeples and a castle in ruins,
and a considerable population of Greeks, Roman Catholics, and Armenians. Its situation is fine, on the high rugged bank of a stream that flows
past, amidst trees of all varieties. The houses are whitewashed, which
gives them a clean appearance, and the tiles are all of wood. Half of the
town is occupied by Armenians, who deal chiefly in cattle. The Jews
here deal much in grain and many of them are rich and respectable.

While waiting for the signing of our passports, we spoke to several of them on the street. They told us that there are 200 families here, and that a school to which they pointed, where German and Latin are taught, was attended by many Jewish children. They expect Messiah and their restoration to their own land. They asked if we were Roman Catholics, and on being told that we were not, and that we came from Britain, they asked if we were Calvinists, which we at once declared we were; and then referring to their Feast of Tabernacles, and the booths that were before their houses, we told them how *God tabernacled among men* in the flesh for us. When we were entering the carriage, one of them came up and eagerly asked, 'How far we were to travel that day?' The object of the question was to ascertain by our answer whether or not we were really Christians, for, as we so often found, they were not accustomed to be kindly spoken to by any who were not of their own nation. We told them how far we were going, and on ascertaining that we must travel after six that evening, when the Jewish Sabbath commences, one of them shook his head, and said to the rest, that 'we were not Jews'. We left a Hebrew tract with them – one of the few which we were to have it in our power to leave in the Austrian dominions.

On leaving the town, our road passed between fences of basket-work, curiously defended from the rain by a coping of the same. The road was macadamized and in excellent condition; the cottages were more comfortable than those of Moldavia, and the aspect of the country was more civilized. Plum and apple trees were plentiful in the gardens. We saw several country churches, somewhat resembling the quiet parish churches of Scotland, and came to a bridge of wood, covered over like a penthouse from end to end, the toll of which, as is the case with most of the tolls of that country, was kept by a Jew. Jews are always to be found like Matthew, 'sitting at the receipt of custom'.

The road after this for three hours ran in a straight line, through a fine meadow, sometimes rising gently, sometimes nearly a plain, with the thickly wooded range of the Carpathians on our left bounding the scene. The fields were fragrant with beautiful autumn crocuses. Two pretty straggling villages situated on a hillside, and a Jewish inn, in front of which were booths for the feast, were the only objects of the least interest for several miles. We passed another toll kept by a Jew and were reminded of home by seeing the country people cutting down a field of oats with the scythe; a little farther on, they were gathering potatoes, and there were occasionally fields of hops.

About two o'clock, we descended upon the neat town of Seret, standing upon the river of the same name which we had crossed twice in Moldavia. There are barracks here, and we now began to be familiar with the blue uniform of the Austrian soldiers and the dark green of their officers, with the ornament of the eagle spreading its wings upwards. In the inn where we rested, many were coming and going, and we had a painful view of the immoral state of the people. When they heard that we were English, they said, 'Ah they have the same noses and eyes that we have!' Many were intoxicated; and one old man came up to us and made a long apology, stating that the funeral of a wealthy resident had taken place that day, which had occasioned the revelry, and hoping that we would not carry away an unfavourable report, as if Austrians were generally given to this vice.

On entering the town, we had met many Jews in their best dress and holiday fur-cap, and observed a company of them dancing at a public-house. We now engaged in conversation with two of them, and one young man became very communicative, kindly consenting to be our guide through the town. There are 300 families of Jews residing here, and they have two synagogues and three places of study or *Beth-midrash*. The largest synagogue, a building of considerable size, was shut; but we entered the other, and there two young men began an interesting conversation. They asked if we were Jews; we said, No, we were Christians. They replied, 'Perhaps you are Jews also', and shook hands smiling. The Jews here expected Messiah that year, or else some great event. They told us of a remarkable rabbi, Haiim, at Chosow, eight miles distant, to whom many thousands of Jews go in pilgrimage at the time of the Feast of Tabernacles. They enjoy more liberty in Bukovine than in Galicia; for in the latter province there is a tax on *lights*, which becomes very severe on the Jews who use so many candles on the Sabbath. On asking if there was much infidelity here, they told us that all were Talmudists, except three Epicuruses – probably members of the Tarnapol Society. In the synagogue where we were standing were several copies both of the Talmud and Mishna, but only a few fragments of the Hebrew Bible were to be found in the library. The young men scarcely knew a word of the Scriptures, and when Mr C[alman] shewed them what a different spirit breathed in the Bible from that of the Talmud, they defended the Talmud and the rabbis. One singular defence of their rabbis was taken from Deuteronomy, 'And thou shalt love *also* the Lord thy God', etc., (Deuteronomy 6:5). For they argued that *eth* meant "also" in this passage.[1] 'And why does it say "also"? Who else is to be loved with all our heart? It must be the *rabbis*.' Mr Calman shewed them that they were thus blasphemously putting the rabbis *before God*; pointed out to them their ignorance of the Hebrew language in regard to *eth*; and pressed them to study their language grammatically – for it is true to an incalculable extent that Talmudism would fall to the ground if the grammatical Hebrew was understood. It would have the same effect on the votaries of the Talmud, that instruction in the sciences has upon the blinded followers of Hindooism. On pressing the young men with the want of sacrifices among the Jews, they urged that repeating the passages where sacrifices are commanded is as good as sacrifice, and quoted Hosea 14:2, 'Take with you *words*, so shall we render *the calves of our lips*'. They did not perceive that the prophet describes Israel as both pouring out the words of confession, and also returning to the blood of the great sacrifice. They listened, however, when we opened Isaiah 53, and spoke of Him by 'whose stripes we are healed', but turned aside its force by saying, 'There is a Messiah who suffers for his people in every generation', referring to such cases as that of the Russian rabbi, of whom we had heard as suffering imprisonment. When Mr Calman told them that he believed in Jesus, they did not understand who or what this meant. But when he explained, and shewed them that he was *'a Christian'*, they started back, and with an air of doubt and fear said, 'And do you still love the Jews?' He replied, 'Yes, indeed, I love the Jews still with all my heart'. And thus we parted.

Crossing the Seret, we continued our journey along a road straight as an arrow. The gentle hills on either hand were well wooded, the plain well cultivated, and the roads excellent, as they are in all the Austrian dominions. A full moon enlightened our way to Czernowitz, which we reached at ten o'clock, and found shelter for the night in a very tolerable inn.

September 28

Czernowitz is a pleasant town, with streets wide, well aired, and clean. The houses are generally two or three storeys high, and there are barracks and other public buildings. Most of the names over the shops were Polish. The market-place is a wide square, having one side lined with stalls or movable shops, like sentry-boxes; and, in the middle, a large cross, with a statue of the Virgin sitting at the foot of it, holding

---

[1] This Hebrew word is a grammatical marker used to designate the direct definite object of a verb.

in her arms the dead body of the Saviour, her head adorned with twelve stars, and two angels at her side. A broad street leads from the market-place, down a steep descent, from the top of which is seen the river Pruth winding through the plain below, with a village on the opposite side of the bank, called Satagora, in which many Jews reside. In this street again there is a figure of the Saviour on the Cross, and the Virgin standing beneath it with a sword piercing her heart, in reference to Luke 2:35. The situation of the town is fine and salubrious, on the top of a considerable elevation, looking down on the neighbouring river and surrounded with fertile plains on all sides.

There are 3,000 Jews here, with eight synagogues, only three of which are large. These three we visited, being all under the roof of one large edifice. The congregations were engaged in worship when we entered, but seemed to have little feeling of devotion, for a group soon gathered round each of us at different parts of the synagogue. On saying to those around us, 'We have been at Jerusalem', they were immediately interested, and asked, 'Are the Jews there like the Jews here?' We said, 'They were, but all could speak Hebrew'. They said, 'None here can speak Hebrew except the rabbi'. 'Do you expect ever to return to your own land?' 'We hope for that every day.' We said, 'We Christians are looking for the second coming of the Messiah every day.' They replied 'What Messiah? Is it Messiah ben-Joseph?' This led us to tell of the only Saviour, 'who is exalted to give repentance unto Israel, and remission of sins'. We told them how Christians in our land loved the Jews. Their reply was, 'Here they do not love the Jews'. This took place in the largest synagogue. In the other two, which belonged to the Chasidim, the worshippers were much more intent upon their prayers and more loud and vehement in their cries. When we were leaving, one of them came after us to ask, 'How much of the temple-wall at Jerusalem was still standing, how high and how broad it was?' The same Jew asked if we had seen Hebron, and if the cave of Machpelah was known?

The Jews here are very ignorant. Their young people are not taught to understand the Hebrew, but only to read it; though many send their children to the public academies where Latin and German are taught. Some have given up their belief in the Talmud and many are so careless that they come to the synagogue only on the Day of Atonement. The Jew who acted as our guide through the town (for we purposely employed a Jew on all such occasions), said that he believed the Old Testament Scriptures, but did not believe in a Messiah at all. The truth is that many of them are so entirely ignorant of Scripture that they fancy the doctrine of a Messiah to be one of the traditions of their rabbis and not a promise of Moses and the prophets. The sight of Israel in this region cannot fail to sadden the heart of those that love them. 'Behold, they say, Our bones are dried, our hope is lost.'

We left the town in the forenoon in an excellent vehicle, resembling an English hackney-coach with springs, belonging to the innkeeper, who also furnished a man and horses to carry us to Tarnapol. Passing some prisoners at work in chains, we soon crossed the Pruth by a long wooden bridge and, looking back, got a pleasant view of the town on the height, surrounded with willows and poplars. The banks of the river also were plentifully clothed with willows. The fields were flat, but appeared fertile, many of them clothed with the plant called *retsky*,[2] which has a stalk of a fine reddish-brown, tinging the face of the country in a beautiful manner. The toll-bars on the road are all after one pattern, consisting of a long beam stretching from side to side, one end of which is made to rise upwards at the approach of a carriage by means of a heavy weight at the other extremity. We were, however, painfully reminded, notwithstanding all the outward fertility, that we were now in 'a land of graven images' by the many tall crosses and representations of the Virgin by the wayside.

We rested the horses at a village called Gertsman, surrounded with trees and near a small lake. In a large grassy area which forms the market-place stood a cross with all its accompaniments, the nails and hammer, the ladder, the spear, and sponge; and near this, under a shed, was an image of a saint holding the infant Jesus in his arms. Surely the people of this land have the same mark as the inhabitants of ancient Babylon, 'They are mad upon their idols'! (Jeremiah 50:38). We found only one Jewish family here, and so careless were they that the boy with whom we conversed had no *tsitsith*, and scarcely knew what the name of Messiah meant.

After leaving this village the country was tame and uninteresting, with few trees to refresh the eye. Crosses and images, however, appeared every now and then. We saw also at every village or cluster of houses indications of the sojourn of some of the scattered sheep of the house of Israel in the *succoth* or booths erected for the Feast of Tabernacles beside the cottage-door.

---

[2] Presumably the reference is to *greczka*, a cereal similar to buckwheat and used by the poorer classes to make a substitute bread.

About half-past five we began to descend into a glen between two hills of considerable elevation, the sides of which were covered with brushwood. As we drew near the mouth of this pass, the spires of Zalesky, shining in the evening sun, appeared through the tall poplars and elms in which the town is embosomed. Before reaching it, a bridge of boats carries you across the river Dniester, deep and rapid, separating the province of Bukovine from that of Galicia, which forms part of Austrian Poland. We rested in the town for a few hours and found it as pleasant as it appeared to be from a distance. The hills through which we had passed form a high barrier on the south, overhanging the town. Their sides covered with shaggy wood, and the impetuous river that sweeps their base, add much to the beauty of the scene. At the entrance of Zalesky, a handsome mansion surrounded with pleasant gardens attracts observation. The Jews told us that this is the residence of a rich Galician, Baron Brownowitch, a Jew baptized into the Roman Catholic Church. His father and brethren also have been baptized, and about twenty Jews, all of the wealthier classes, have followed their example. It is to be feared that worldly advancement formed the leading motives for their change; and even were the motive purer, what is there to comfort the hearts of those who love Israel in conversions from Judaism to Popery? The Baron is still very kind to his Jewish brethren, and has ample opportunity; for the whole of this town and twenty other villages are his property.

There are 3,000 Jews here. Their largest synagogue, however, is neglected and dirty, and the service was gone over in a hasty and irreverent manner. We noticed here, what we had seen in some other places, several Passover cakes *(the Aphikumen)* hung up in the synagogue as a charm against fire, theft, or accident. Here, too, the *Eruv* or string is stretched from house to house, to make Zalesky a walled town. One of the windows of the synagogue had been glazed by the society that buries the dead, called *habrah kedoshah*; and their name was on the stained glass. Many of the Jews to whom we spoke were careless and worldly, and one of them told us of seven German families who never attend the synagogue.

We left this place before it was quite dark and pressed on through a flat and dreary country over which the autumn wind swept cold and sharp. By half-past ten we reached a pleasant village called Jaglinsky, having a good Polish inn, or, in the language of the country, *Hartsmi*. The inmates were all fast asleep, but after much knocking, we found admission, and were hospitably entertained by the *gospadina*, or hostess.

September 29

The Sabbath dawned sweetly upon this retired Polish village. It was one of some extent, stretching up the sides of a deep hollow. On one of the heights stood the principal church, and on the opposite bank a fort and barracks. Crosses of all kinds and sizes were planted at every approach to the village, and in the churchyard every grave had one. Early in the morning all the servants of our khan, clothed in their best attire, set off for church; and we followed after them, in order to witness the service. On our way we heard the sound of music proceeding from a cottage, and Mr Calman, thinking that it was a Jewish marriage, entered, when two young women immediately fell at his feet and kissed his boots, thanking him for the honour he had done them in entering their house. It was a Christian marriage. The church was elegantly fitted up and the walls were painted all over with figures of saints and madonnas. During the service one poor woman came in and, with many genuflexions, presented three pictures, one of a madonna, the two others of saints. The audience was scanty, consisting of five or six young people and a few old men and women, all kneeling on the open floor. All, as they entered or retired, first kissed an image of the Saviour that stood in the porch, and then bowed down and kissed the cold floor. The singing and organ were tolerable, but there was no food for the soul.

We then visited a country church in the suburbs built entirely of wood. It was crowded to the door, and many who could not get in had taken their places by the wall, kneeling and crossing themselves as they listened to the service through the seams of the wooden walls. Within the church, the women occupied the end nearest the door, and the men, who formed the greater proportion, stood nearer the altar. All present were plain rustic people, of uncouth appearance and ungainly figures; the men wearing a surtout of sheepskin, with the wool turned inside, the women a cap with a white kerchief tied over it. Lighted candles glared from the altar, and many of the women held tapers in their hands. At one part of the prayer all knelt except ourselves, and then rose. A plate went round for collecting money, and each gave something. Several pictures, miserably executed, hung upon the walls, among which was one of the Saviour, quite hid by the multitude of flowers that had been thrown upon it by the devout worshippers, and another of the Virgin Mary, decorated with strings of beads suspended round it by her grateful votaries. But the most offensive object of all was an old diminutive figure of the Saviour on the Cross, standing near the door. This was kissed by most of those who came in after they had dipped their hands in a vessel of holy water that stood by. Some kissed it on the feet, some under the feet, some more devout lay down and kissed the floor beneath it. The sight of this simple superstition, over which was spread an air of apparent solemnity on the part of the rough peasants, was really affecting. We contrasted the realms of Popery with our own happy Scotland; and if anything could stir up a Scottish Presbyterian to a sense of the greatness of his privileges, it is a sight like this, where ignorance and superstition are leading souls to hell, in peaceful unresisting quietness! The priest was a respectable-looking man, much above his parishioners in point of culture. Oh that God would raise up another Martin Boos in this region of gross darkness, to proclaim the glad tidings of righteousness by the obedience of One!

We spent the forenoon together in the study of the Scriptures and social prayer, and about sunset resolved to visit the Jews who met that evening to celebrate 'the Joy of the Law' (*simhath torah*). It was the commencement of that day which is called in John *'the last day, that great day of the feast'* (John 7:37). We prayed that we might have an opportunity of proclaiming to them the words of Jesus, 'If any man thirst, let him come to me and drink', and our desire was granted. On our way through the village we noticed that the peasants took off their hats a long way before they met us – not, however, with the cheerful air of a freeborn Briton, but with a sullen servile look, the result of well-remembered oppression; for the Polish Barons used to keep the peasantry in real slavery, and the want of a middle class in Poland who might link rich and poor together, has perpetuated the system. Passing the cottage where the marriage had been in the morning, we saw a large company on the green before the door, dancing to the sound of the violin and tabret. They have no joys but those of earth, and the Sabbath is their chief day of gaiety and mirth.

The Jews have three synagogues here, the best of which is a high and spacious building. On asking a Jewish boy if the building before us was the synagogue of the *Chasidim*, he replied, 'No, it is the synagogue of the *prostakis*', that is 'the common people'. He used the word as a term of reproach, for the spirit of the old Pharisees remains in the heart of Israel, and they say still, 'Stand by thyself, come not near to me, for I am holier than thou' (Isaiah 65:5). Entering the large synagogue, we got into conversation with several Jews while the congregation was assembling. We spoke to them of the way of a sinner's pardon and on our saying that their *Cipporah* was the only remnant they had of sacrifice, one of them replied 'that they did not offer the cock and hen as a sacrifice, for prayer now stood in the place of all sacrifices'. How truly are Israel abiding 'without a sacrifice' (Hosea 3:4), when the only appearance of a sacrifice that anywhere meets the eye in the thousand ceremonies of Judaism is totally disclaimed as such by themselves? We spoke on Isaiah 53 and the office of Messiah 'to give repentance to Israel and remission of sins'. Several were attracted to us when they heard us speak of having seen Jerusalem and of our love to the house of Israel. When we told them that in Scotland, true Christians keep the Christian Sabbath as strictly as the Jews do theirs, never travelling nor doing any work, but reading the Bible and worshipping God in public and private, they were astonished and at first did not seem to believe it. At length one of them made his way round to the spot where Mr Calman was speaking in the midst of another group and put the question to him if it were really so? The man came back and told his brethren that it was true, and all seemed greatly pleased. Some boys read to us a portion of the Law beginning, 'Thou shalt love the Lord thy God', which started another conversation; and when we hesitated not to use the words, 'Hear, O Israel, the Lord thy God is one Lord', telling them of our belief in the *one* God, His wondrous nature, and His becoming incarnate, they stood listening with great attention, and one asked, 'Were you *born* Christians?'

On leaving them, we went to the synagogue of the Chasidim. There we were kindly brought forward to a convenient place for seeing the procession in honour of the Law which was about to take place. Several Jews were very friendly and anxious to hear about Jerusalem. One began to speak of the oppression of their nation, which is felt here in the taxes laid on meat and lights, for they pay nearly half a *zwanzig* for a candle – a heavy burden on them who use so many every week. We told them how different was the feeling toward Israel in our country, for true Christians in Scotland and England loved the Jews, and Messiah enjoined us to bear a special love to them. We then read together some of their prayers, which they asked us to translate into German. After this, we had an opportunity of telling how Jesus, at the very feast which they were celebrating, stood in the Temple and invited sinners to come to him.

At length, the service began. The room by this time was crowded to excess; and the glare and heat of the large candles became very unpleasant. After a short prayer, the persons were called up who were to engage in the procession, to each of whom was entrusted a roll of the Law, which he carried in his arms. They are called up according to the alphabetical order of their names, he who presides using these words as he names each, *ten kavod letorah* (Give honour to the Law). The first company being thus called up and arranged, and all the copies of the *Torah* in the ark being placed in their hands, the old rabbi began the dance. The signal for commencing was given (somewhat profanely) in the words of Exodus, 'Speak unto the children of Israel that they go forward' (Exodus 14:15). Immediately they began to move slowly round the synagogue, all present chanting a prayer. Soon the singing became louder, and the movements of the worshippers more rapid. They clapped their hands, shouted, and finally danced with all their might, dandling the roll of the *Law* in their arms. The old grey-haired rabbi danced with the most vehement gestures, while all sung, leaped and clapped their hands, till the whole synagogue was one scene of indescribable confusion. When one company had danced till they were weary, others were called up to form a second, until all the members of the synagogue had shared in it. Such is a specimen of *the procession of the Law*, intended to give honour to the Word of the living God. But the chief joy is reserved for the morrow. What a caricature is this on David's 'dancing before the Lord with all his might!' and what a contrast to David's calm delight in the Word of God, 'O how love I thy law, it is my meditation all the day.' A religious service more silly or childish could scarcely be imagined. We were again reminded of the sure word of prophecy, 'I will give children to be their princes, and babes shall rule over them' (Isaiah 3:4).

When all was over, the rabbi sent to say that he wished to speak with us. We accordingly went to his house, 'which joined hard to the synagogue' (Acts 18:7), and which was immediately filled to overflow with Jews, all intensely anxious to see the Christians who had been at Jerusalem, and were interested in their welfare. When we had answered several questions as to the condition of their brethren in Palestine, Mr Calman seized the valuable opportunity and beginning with a reference to the principles of the Chasidim, who profess to do everything out of pure, disinterested love to God, shewed them with much affection what Jehovah had done to awaken our love toward himself in the great gift of his beloved Son. We then parted from them in a most friendly manner, and returned to our inn. How affecting is such a visit to Israel! 'The priests said not, Where is the Lord? and *they that handle the law knew me not*' (Jeremiah 2:8). Soon may a better day dawn on Zion, when the promise shall be realized, 'I will give you pastors according to mine heart, which shall feed you *with knowledge and understanding*' (Jeremiah 3:15)!

September 30

Leaving our pleasant *hartsmi,* we swept through the vale and village of Jaglinsky. The morning was clear and fine, but much colder than we had yet experienced. We travelled due north through a vast plain country where all the crops had been gathered in except the *retsky*. The highway was straight as a railroad, so that we could see before us for several miles – a dreary prospect to a traveller on foot.

We came down upon the large but dull village of Zadcow where our attention was attracted by a churchyard planted with black crosses as thickly as a grove, and by a large cross at the entrance ornamented with human skulls and bones. Indeed, it is not uncommon in Poland to see the crosses decorated with human skulls and bones, in order that they may more deeply affect the poor blinded worshippers. Here it was discovered that one of our horses needed a shoe, and as the Polish smith proved to be slow at the use of the hammer, we had opportunity to wander about the place. The *Eruv* and the *booths* at many cottage-doors informed us that some of the seed of Abraham had found a refuge here; and we spoke to two or three on the road who told us that there are 300 Jewish families in this place. All the peasants, and even the women, wore sheepskin to keep out the keen north wind.

The next large village was Copochinsky, clean and thriving, with its church, crosses, and images. One image especially attracted our attention, standing in a shed in the market-place – the uncouth figure of a friar carrying the child Jesus in his arms. After this we passed two very poor villages, the first of which appeared to be altogether Jewish.

The country now became bare indeed, though all under cultivation, till we came down upon Trembowla, a pleasant town on the banks of the Seret, having the ruins of an old castle overhanging it and a square fortress at some distance. It has two very handsome churches and one of the large high Polish synagogues, built of wood, but going rapidly to decay. We met several Jews who told us that there are 1,500 of their brethren here and that their synagogue is 120 years old. They listened to us when we testified of Messiah's atonement for sin.

North of Trembowla the country began to improve. We entered a fine valley, watered by the game stream which runs through the town. The fields on either side were fruitful and almost entirely covered with hemp. At the upper end of the vale was a placid lake, out of which the stream issued. The hills were well wooded and some pleasant cottages overhung the lake.

Ascending higher ground, we drove through woods of beech and elm, and then through an avenue of poplars and came to Gulonitsky, a village having a splendid church with three pointed spires, and an elegant mansion which we understood to be that of the Popish Bishop. Everything around wore an aspect of neatness and culture, and even the crosses and images were of better workmanship. A peculiar looking burying-ground on a slight eminence caught our eye as we entered. It had no black crosses, but white upright stones over the graves. We soon discovered that this was the place were the Jews bury their dead. How many souls of Israel have passed away even from this one country village to the judgment-seat of Christ, hardened in the rejection of his gospel by the surrounding idolatries of the Church of Rome! Shall they not take up the words of their fathers? 'The violence done to me and to my flesh be upon Babylon, shall the inhabitant of Zion say; and, My blood upon the inhabitants of Chaldea, shall Jerusalem say' (Jeremiah 51:35).

About sunset we arrived at Tarnapol, one of the finest towns of Austrian Poland, a hundred miles north from Czernowitz. It is of some extent and finely situated, overlooking an extensive lake on the north-west, out of which flows the Seret, encircling part of the town. The churches and public buildings are large and handsome and there are thriving academies. The Jewish burying-ground is on the right hand of the road at the entrance to the town. Many Jews were upon the streets in their best clothes, and many Jewesses, sometimes six or eight in a company, enjoying themselves upon this night of special festivity.

Putting up our carriage, we set out to visit the synagogue of the New School. The service was not begun, but vast numbers of well dressed Jews were already assembled, walking up and down in the porch. The females, too, in their richest attire, were occupying their quarter of the synagogue. As for devotion, there was not even the shadow of it to be seen; the synagogue seemed to be regarded as a place of public amusement and display; and the words of the prophet might that night have been rung in the ears of the daughters of Zion, 'Tremble, ye women that are at ease; be troubled, ye careless ones' (Isaiah 32:11). Three Jewish soldiers in Austrian uniform were among the crowd that waited for the opening of the doors; and several Jewish boys shewed their courtesy to strangers by offering to take us to a seat. They could talk Latin, having attended the Academy, and seemed not a little proud of being able to make use of a learned tongue. The synagogue was at length opened. It was a commodious and elegant apartment with galleries for the women, handsomely painted and illuminated with wax-candles, resembling the fine synagogue at Leghorn, though not equal to it in size. The Jews were very polite, but the service was uninteresting; the company and their dresses seemed to be the principal entertainment.

We left them and proceeded to a synagogue of the Chasidim. Here were assembled a much poorer class of Jews who read prayers with all the fervour of devotion. In a little after we had entered they began the procession in honour of the Law. A standard-bearer went first, then the rabbi, then six others, each carrying a roll of the Law. Upon the standard was embroidered the Austrian eagle with the words, 'I bare you on eagles' wings' (Exodus 19:4).

From this synagogue we sought our way to the great synagogue of the Rabbinical Jews. We wished to see the joyful procession from the rabbi's house to the synagogue – a scene of uproar and folly. Several Jews were discharging pistols and fireworks in the open street. The doors of the synagogue were not yet opened, and the crowd in the porch were running to and fro in boisterous mirth. Alas! there was none of Jacob's feelings, 'How dreadful is this place! this is none other but the house of God, and this is the gate of heaven'. At length, the old rabbi and his friends arrived, with lighted candles and torches carried before them, and a banner, amidst the shouts of the multitude. The doors were thrown open and the crowd rushed in. The brazen lustres poured forth a flood of dazzling light, revealing a very large old synagogue with a high vaulted roof. It is about 600 years old, and in style bears a resemblance to some of our least ornamented Gothic churches. The gallery of the females occupied one side of the building, entirely closed from view by a lattice-work. After prayer, thirty-six Jews were called up to give honour to the law, and each was intrusted with one of the rolls out of the ark. The lighted standard and a flag with a lighted candle at the top of the staff were carried foremost, then the rabbi, a staid respectable-looking man, with thirty-six bearers of the Law, followed after. There was no dance nor extravagant shouting, but a company of young Jews sang many lively airs, often imitating the sound of trumpets and other musical instruments of a military band; the spectators clapping hands while the procession moved several times round the synagogue. And this is the joy of the Feast of Tabernacles which Israel knows now! Where now are the days of Ezra and Nehemiah, when 'the joy of the Lord was their strength' – when they made booths and sat under the booths, 'and there was *very great gladness*? Also day by day, from the first day unto the last day, he read in the book *of* the law of God; and they kept the feast seven days, and on the eighth day was *a solemn assembly* according unto the manner' (Nehemiah 8:17-18). Surely 'the Lord has caused the solemn feasts to be forgotten in Sion' (Lamentations 2:6)! It is not thus that Israel shall worship on that approaching day, when 'they shall draw water with joy out of the wells of salvation, because the Lord Jehovah is their strength and song' (Isaiah 12:1). Nor shall it be with our feelings that the believing nations shall in that day look on Israel's holy service, when 'they go up from year to year to worship the King, the Lord of Hosts, and to keep the Feast of Tabernacles' (Zechariah 14:16).

October 1
Tarnapol has 15,000 inhabitants, and of these there are 1,800 families of Jews, probably more than half the population. The Academy is said to be a very good one; we met some of the students walking in the meadows near the lake, carrying their books upon their heads. The Jews spent this day in prayer, on account of the anniversary of the death of Moses.

We visited a synagogue of the Chasidim in a part of the town where we had not been before. Our entrance caused considerable commotion among the worshippers; their faces assumed an aspect of terror, their chanting was all but silenced, and they whispered anxiously to one another. The reason for their alarm was that they thought we were officers of the Austrian Government come to spy out their doings and find a pretext for oppressing them. How truly these words have come to pass, 'I will send a faintness into their hearts in the lands of their enemies, and the sound of a shaken leaf shall chase them; and they shall flee as fleeing from a sword, and they shall fall when none pursueth' (Leviticus 26:36). Mr Calman soon relieved their fears, and in a little time we saw the dance in honour of the Law renewed with greater vehemence than ever. At first they danced two and two, then three or four all joined hand in hand; they leaped also as well as danced, singing at the same time, and occasionally clapping hands, in a manner that reminded us of the Arab dance and song in the East. A few seemed quite in earnest, with a wild fanatical expression in their countenances, while others were light and merry. One mild, elderly Jew spoke to us, and after listening to what we said regarding Messiah's once offering himself for sin, kept by us all the time, followed us when we left, and shook hands, heartily wishing us God-speed on our journey.

We paid a second visit to the Jews of the New School. They were finishing 'the procession of the Law' as we entered; for they go through all the ceremonies of the other Jews, although in their heart they despise them. There is great mutual contempt between the Jews of the Old and those of the New School. They told us that the rabbi who founded the New School in Tarnapol had died there that very day, and all the Chasidim were rejoicing at the news. This man had been the means of introducing the new system of education for the Jewish youth of this place by instituting an Academy where the German, Polish, Latin, and Hebrew languages, as well as many branches of science, are regularly taught. He and his party had such influence with the government that at first they were empowered to compel all Jewish children to attend the Academy; but this order was afterwards withdrawn, only they were allowed to put a tax of three *kreutzers* on the oké of meat for every boy who is not sent. In spite of this, the Rabbinical Jews cling as firmly as ever to their old system, and only 200 children have been sent to the Academy, though there are 3,000 Jewish children in Tarnapol. It is not, however, altogether from real attachment to their old system that the majority thus oppose any change; it proceeds in many cases rather from a regard to self-interest, and in some from personal dislike to the present rabbi. It is much to be lamented that even those who are taught in the schools of the New Synagogue do not acquire a grammatical knowledge of Hebrew, which would be of the greatest importance, as it would enable them to read the Word of God with ease and intelligence. The reason for this is that they are not allowed to attend the Academy until they have attained a certain age, so that most of those who go to the teacher there have already been taught in some degree by a private instructor, but have not had a solid foundation laid.

We found much difficulty in ascertaining the real opinions of the New Synagogue here. To some extent they might be called *infidels*, for they do not make the Bible the foundation of their faith. But they differ widely from the infidel Jews of Germany and France in this, that they have great respect for the Bible, and seem to have cast it off rather from a belief that they can arrive at truth without it, than from any positive dislike. They are still interested in whatever regards the Holy Land, though they do not expect to return to it. Many of them, however, believe, like other infidel Jews, that *political emancipation* is the only Messiah they are to look for. It was the rejection of the Talmud that led them to reject the Bible also; and yet they retain the rabbinical ceremonies, though they do this chiefly because the Chasidim have accused them of forming a new sect, which the Austrian Government rigorously forbids. It is plain from this fact that there is little of conscientious belief among them. Self-interest and the favour of the world appear to form their principal rule of life. Several Jews of this class called on us at our lodging and were exceedingly polite. One said, 'The Bible had served its day; there was need of something else now'. Another, on being asked why they retained the ceremonies and forms of Judaism since they rejected the Talmud, gave this Jesuitical reason, 'that by maintaining their profession, they obtained access to the families of other Jews, and thus had opportunity of quietly diffusing their doctrines, and undermining the prejudices of their brethren'. At Odessa, some of their sect have gained the approbation of the Russian Emperor for their schools. Only two have been baptized in Tarnapol, and these were females who were induced by the prospect of being married into good Roman Catholic families. We spent many hours in discussion with these men. At one time we had five in the room. Mr Calman spoke plainly to them of true Christianity, and Mr McCheyne explained and applied Zechariah 12:10 to one interesting Jew who spoke Latin. He said that he was one of about twenty who were able to converse in that language.

In the evening we paid a visit to the chief man of the rabbinical Jews, Rabbi Rapaport, the same of whom we had heard in Jassy as being at the head of the secret Society for undermining Judaism – considered one of the most learned Jews in the world, both in regard to languages and general knowledge. He received us politely, but at the same time with somewhat of the stiffness of assumed dignity. He put many questions regarding Palestine, and seemed to be familiar with the events of the day in that country. He inquired as to the progress and success of Ibraim Pasha, and also concerning the visit of Sir Moses Montefiore. We asked his opinions regarding Messiah, to which he replied very cautiously 'that there was no fixed time for his coming, and that the doctrine of a Messiah was not one of the original articles of the Jewish creed. These (he said) related only to God, the resurrection, and the final judgment of men'. One of his attendants spoke out his opinion more fully, saying, 'It would have been better if Messiah had never been foretold!'

Later in the evening a well-educated young Jew called on us. Hearing that we had been inquiring about the practicability of instituting schools among the Jews, he came to offer himself as a teacher. He thought himself qualified, having taught in the Academy of the Jesuits in the town. He conversed with us in Latin, always addressing us by the title of *'Dominatio vestra'.*[3] When telling us that he had given up all expectation of the restoration of his people to their own land, and of the coming of Messiah, he used this remarkable expression, *'Despero, despero'*, that is, 'I have no hope of it', the very term used by the prophet Ezekiel when he foretold what would be the state of Israel before the breath should enter into them, 'Behold, they say, Our bones are dried and *our hope is lost*' (Ezekiel 37:11). This young man professed still to believe the Bible, and we urged upon him the duty of believing things because God had revealed them, and not because reason suggested them. Nearly one-half of the Jewish population of Tarnapol have joined the new sect; yet the opposition on the part of the Rabbinical Jews, and especially the Chasidim, is very strong. One example of this is curious. The new sect made a proposal to form a colony under the sanction of the Government. The Chasidim, in order to counteract this, distributed among the people *charms*, consisting of small pieces of paper, on which some mystical Hebrew sentences were written, one of which, as a curiosity, we procured.

We visited the Jewish burying-place, a large plot of ground ornamented with trees near the entrance of the town. It is covered with upright gravestones, some of them 200 years old, having inscriptions generally in good preservation, and some elegant monuments over the rabbis. The device upon the stone where a *cohen* or priest lies buried is two hands in the position of one pronouncing the blessing, and below are the words, *'On this wise shall ye bless Israel'* (Numbers 6:23). A cluster of grapes, lighted candles, an eagle and a gazelle were some of the other devices. Several of the inscriptions were poetical, but none were interesting. A little boy was buried while we were there. They

---

[3] 'Your lordship.'

brought him to the grave bound up in a white shroud and lying on a bier. A Gentile dug the grave – it being unlawful for an Israelite to do servile labour on a solemn feast day. A small pillow was filled with earth and laid in the grave to be a resting-place for his head. The face was left uncovered, and a loose board laid over the body to prevent the earth from injuring it when thrown in. The covered board is loose so that the dead may have no trouble in getting out at the resurrection, and sometimes, we were told, they put a staff beside the body to help the person to rise at that day! Before the body was laid in the grave, the attendants went through a miserable superstition; the friends present bending over him and asking the dead to forgive them if they had injured him in any way during his life, and to forgive his father and grandfather or any other friend who had done so.

We were shown the grave of a Jewess, who died 200 years ago, named Galla, the daughter of a rabbi, who is said to have lately wrought miracles on diseased persons who prayed at her grave. Some time ago, she appeared in a dream to several people in town and told them that she had got this power. Many went to the place and, according to the story of our guide, were cured. A heap of twigs lay piled up several feet near her gravestone, each one put there by the hand of some grateful Jew or Jewess who had reaped the benefit of a visit to her grave. Our guide assured us that his grandmother had been completely cured of a desperate disease by coming to pray beside this grave. The prophets of Israel foresaw this feature of Jewish apostasy, 'Should not a people seek unto their God? for the living (shall they go) *to the dead*? To the law and to the testimony, if they speak not according to this word, there is no light in them' (Isaiah 8:19, 20).

In the cool of evening, we enjoyed a pleasant walk on the banks of the neighbouring lake and met a company of about thirty Jews, singing together in a joyful mood. There is a better day coming, when after they have sown in tears, 'they shall return and come to Zion with songs and everlasting joy upon their heads' (Isaiah 35:10).

October 2

Early this morning we observed the young men who attend the gymnasium on their way to the principal church to be present at morning prayers for half an hour. There were perhaps 300, all marching in regular order, with their ushers wearing the dress of the Popish priests. Thus the chains of Popery are riveted on the hearts of the rising generation.

Before the door of the church stood an immense cross, with a small picture of Christ near the foot. As the young men retired, many of them approached the cross and kissed the picture, making obeisance before it. What must Israel think when they see the best educated of the Polish youth worshipping an image in the open street, as well as the blinded peasantry bowing down to huge crosses and uncouth images of saints that disfigure the wayside and are crowded round every village – what can they think in such a land as this, but that Jesus taught his followers to bow down to wood and stone, like the worst of the heathen? Surely, in the skirts of Babylon shall be found not only the blood of prophets and of saints, but the blood of many a Jew. 'As Babylon has caused the slain of Israel to fall, so at Babylon shall fall the slain of all the earth' (Jeremiah 51:49).

Several Jews called and took leave of us in a very kind manner. Before setting out about nine o'clock a great crowd began to assemble round a house opposite to our lodging. It was the house of Rabbi Perl, the great reformer and founder of the New School, who was that day to be buried, and about 500 Jews had met at that early hour to do honour to his remains. We left the town in a Jewish *brisca*, a light waggon without springs, not very comfortable, driven by a bearded Jew, who was not very steady, for he stopped at the first house of entertainment on the road, and when we asked the reason, said very honestly that he wanted *snaps* – the common name in that country for strong drink. The day was warm and fine, but the country bare and uninteresting. The crops were all off the ground, except the potatoes, which the peasants were gathering. Sometimes the road was sandy and heavy, sometimes a pleasant wood of oak or birch relieved the weary eye. At one part, a beggar boy seeing us approach bowed to the ground, kissed the dust before us, and then, with clasped hands and imploring look, asked an alms.

About one o'clock we came to Zalosc, situated like very many of the small towns of Poland on the margin of a lake. Here we stopped at a Jewish khan and partook of *Mit-tag*, or 'midday meal', as it is there called. Pike taken out of the lake was set upon the table, along with some of the remnants of the previous day's repast, at the close of the Feast of Tabernacles. A picture of the famous rabbi, Landau, hung upon the wall, a favourite ornament in all the Jewish houses. We were told that there are 100 families of Jews residing here.

Not far from this is another village called Saretsky on the margin of a considerable lake. A few Jews were in the streets as we passed through. Images abounded on the roadside, and especially round the village. How long shall it be ere the Lord a second time bring to pass the words written, 'Therefore, behold, the days come that I will do judgment upon the graven image of Babylon' (Jeremiah 51:47).

At sunset, we came in sight of a prominent eminence crowned with a beautiful church, and near it a large building in a grove which we conjectured to be a convent. The name of the place is Potkamin, one of the most sightly villages of this part of the country. Many Jews were walking in the large square or market-place, and the *shomesh* or 'beadle' was in the act of going round the village, knocking loudly at the door of every Jewish house to give warning that the hour for worship in the synagogue had arrived. We spoke a few minutes with some of them who said that there are 300 families of Jews.

We told an old man, and a friend who was with him, that we had come from the Holy Land; on hearing which, he asked us, 'If we had prayed over the graves of the saints at Jerusalem?' (see again Isaiah 8:19). Mr Calman replied that the Word of God forbade us to do so. But the old man quoted Ecclesiastes 4:2, 'I praised the dead that are already dead more than the living that are yet alive', and confirmed his interpretation of the passage by referring to the Gemara,[4] which says that Solomon prayed to the dead. Mr Calman showed that in following the Gemara the Jews were trusting to the *word of man* which would ruin their souls. Upon which one that stood by replied, 'How could we know when a spoon or a pot should be used, if we had not the Gemara?' Mr C[alman] answered, that that kind of knowledge was of no consequence, but the knowledge of our true state before God, as taught in his Word, was infinitely important for us all.

With another intelligent Jew, under a shed before his shop-door, we had time to converse a little. We told him we came from Scotland, had been in Palestine and loved the Jews. He spoke freely, and on our saying that he had no atonement for sin to offer, replied, 'All that is required is prayer, not sacrifice.' We spoke of Messiah coming for the very end of making atonement and that we looked also for his coming again the second time. He said that all the Jews of that village were Chasidim and

---

[4] In broad terms the Talmud is a set of books comprising the Mishna ('repeated study') and the Gemara ('completion'). The Gemara consists of interpretations and commentaries on the Mishna. Normally the Talmud is used to refer to the materials called Gemara which is an Aramaic term common in medieval Jewish literature.

that they were all hoping for Messiah's coming. At this place, instead of the common *Eruv* or string at the entrance of the town, there was a gateway of wood across the street.

Soon after leaving Potkamin, the road became rough and irregular, and in many places was made of soft sand. Darkness came on and we saw little more till we found ourselves approaching Brody through an avenue of tall pines. It was late when we arrived at the gate of Brody, but it was opened to us on the ground of our being English travellers and we were soon comfortably lodged in a respectable inn kept by a German Jew. The distance from Tarnapol is eight German, or forty English, miles.

October 3

At an early hour we were disturbed in a most unceremonious way by a series of officious Jewish hawkers coming to our chamber, eager to dispose of their goods. First of all the door was pushed open, then a fur-cap and long beard thrust in, while a voice demanded, in German, if we needed knives or combs. No sooner was this visitor gone, than another similar head was thrust in and a voice asked if we wished to buy soap. This singular kind of annoyance was repeated by eight similar visitors before we were fully dressed and we were obliged at last in self-defence to lock the chamber-door.

Brody is situated in the midst of a sandy plain and is five miles distant from the Russian frontier. So completely level is the country all round that the distant village of Potkamin is the only object beyond the town which arrests the eye. When a traveller approaches Brody there is no city visible, there being only three spires, and all the houses being hid by the trees of the environs. Its nearness to Russia gives it importance and increases its trade. There are no more than three Christian churches in the town, two of which are Greek and one Roman Catholic, while there are 150 synagogues. The streets in general are tolerably clean and there is a side-pavement entirely of wood. The appearance of the population was certainly the most singular we had witnessed. It seemed wholly a Jewish city and the few Gentiles who appeared here and there were quite lost in the crowd of Jews.

Jewish boys and girls were playing in the streets, and Jewish maidservants were carrying messages, Jewish women were the only females to be seen at the doors and windows; and Jewish merchants filled the market-place. The high fur-caps of the men, the rich head-dress of the women and the small round velvet caps of the boys met the eye on every side as we wandered from street to street. Jewish ladies were leaning over balconies and poor old Jewesses were sitting at stalls selling fruit. In passing through the streets, if we happened to turn the head for a moment toward a shop, some Jew would rush out immediately and assail us with importunate invitations to come and buy (see Isaiah 55:1). In the bazaar, Jews were selling skins, making shoes, and offering earthenware for sale; and the signboards of plumbers, masons, painters and butchers all bore Jewish names. In the fish-market, the same kind of wrangling and squabbling heard in our own markets was carried on by Jewesses, buying and selling. Jewesses also presided at the flesh and poultry market and in a plentifully stored green-market. Near these were shambles[5] for *torn meat* to be sold only to Gentiles, Jews being forbidden in the law to eat 'any flesh that is torn of beasts' (Exodus 22:31).

The fondness of the daughters of Zion for a fine head-dress, which called forth the indignant warnings of Isaiah, still lingers in the hearts of the Jewesses at Brody. They wear a black velvet coronet, adorned with strings of precious stones or imitation pearls; and though this piece of finery costs several pounds, yet so devotedly attached are they to their 'round tires like the moon' (Isaiah 3:18) that scarcely can an old woman be found seated at her stall who does not wear one, as if they were queens even in their captivity.

There is indeed a complete air of Judaism over the whole town; and at the Post-office, the notices as to the delivery of letters are printed not only in the German and Polish, but also in the Hebrew language.

The number of Jewish families enrolled at the last census was 5,000. An intelligent Austrian, whom we afterwards met at Zloozow – the superintendent of the district – reckoned that there were 25,000 Jews and 10,000 Christians in Brody. His estimate of the Jewish population is probably very near the truth, though the proportion he assigned to the Christian or Gentile population was perhaps too high. There are a few professed Protestants resident here whom the German minister of Lemberg visits only *once a-year* when he preaches in the hall of the inn where we stayed. How precious would the truth appear to some of our congregations in Scotland were they subjected to such a famine of hearing the Word of the Lord!

The Jews of Brody carry on a considerable trade with Leipsic and

---

[5] A meat market or butcher's shop.

Odessa. They have great influence in the town and often act as spies to the Austrian police. About six years ago, Mr Reichardt, now Jewish missionary in London, with another Christian friend, passed this way and distributed tracts; information was immediately given to the police by whom they were detained two weeks till the authorities at Lemberg had been consulted and then were ordered to be removed forthwith beyond the border.

There are perhaps forty rich Jews in the city who may be worth about £10,000 or £20,000, but the greater part are poor. There are many adherents of the New School, although they have only one synagogue. Most of the rising generation are giving up the study of the Talmud and several have been baptized. There is some learning among them, for in one synagogue we met with several lads who understood and spoke Hebrew. Many of the young men are beginning to attend the Government schools in which they are taught Latin and acquire general knowledge. The rabbi of the New School speaks Latin and French.

We visited one of their finest synagogues. It is like an ancient Gothic church; the roof very elevated, and supported by four immense pillars in the massy Gothic style. Brass lustres in great profusion were suspended from the roof, especially in front of the ark, all handsome and brightly polished. The place might easily contain two or three thousand worshippers. The voice of prayer and the loud Amen of the congregation must sound very solemnly through the vaulted aisles. In the porch stand vessels of water for washing the hands; and the whole prayer-book is pasted up on boards upon the walls for the sake of the poor. In a *Beth-midrash* adjoining the synagogue, we found a company of Jews engaged in study and each of us gathered a group around him. Several were able to speak Hebrew fluently, but there was a reserve about them all that distinguished them from the Jews of Moldavia and Wallachia. They had secret suspicions that our object in visiting them was connected with the Austrian Government; and our inquiries after some of their books excited their suspicion still more, for some of their books, which speak against the idolatry of the Church of Rome, are prohibited.

We visited the Hospital belonging exclusively to the Jewish community, called by them *beth-haholim* (the house of the sick), situated in one of the suburbs. Over the door is a Latin inscription, *Ægrorum saluti.*[6] All the wards were remarkably clean and well arranged, fully equal to those of our own hospitals. There is a commodious kitchen, where the food

---

[6] 'For the cure of the sick.'

is prepared after the English fashion and there are baths and a flower-garden for the use of the patients. The physician, two surgeons and the nurses belonging to the establishment are all Jewish. There were fifty-three cases under treatment at the time, each patient having a board over his bed, with his name and disease written on it. It was a sad sight to look upon the pale faces of dying men of Israel. O that 'the great trumpet were blown for those that are *ready to perish*' (Isaiah 27:13)! The expense of this establishment was stated to us at £25 weekly, which is defrayed by the interest of legacies and by contributions from the town.

We then went to the new burying-ground, opened in 1831, when the cholera made its ravages in this country, at which time, for a space of three months, there were in Brody 150 deaths every day. This extensive burying-ground is already half-filled up although the tombs are thickly planted together. The monuments are of a soft chalky stone and most of them adorned with curious emblems. The stone is generally painted and the epitaph is of a bright colour or sometimes in letters of gold. One had a crown painted on it, with the words *kether shem tov* (the crown of a good name). Another had a cup and platter, marking the grave of a Levite who poured water on the hands of the priests. The outspread hands were frequent, marking the tomb of a Cohen or priest, with the words *kether kohanim* (the crown of the priesthood). One stone had two lighted candles painted on it and another had a golden candlestick. The grave of a lady of wealth, who in her lifetime had gone on a pilgrimage to Palestine, was marked by the figure of a ship on the sea and Noah's dove flying towards it. A gate broken off its hinges and in the act of falling represented the door of the ark in the synagogue rent in mourning for some eminent worshipper who had been mother of a numerous family. A hand holding an open book shewed the tomb of an author. A hand, pouring water out of one vessel into another, was painted on the tomb of a woman who used to carry water for the synagogue. One monument had a painting of Abraham's house in the plains of Mamre, surrounded by oak-trees, with his flocks feeding near; it covered the grave of a man named Abraham. A house and a human heart, a lion, a roe, an eagle, a palm tree and many such like were very common emblems. The whole scene brought forcibly to our remembrance the words of the Lord Jesus to the Pharisees, 'Ye build the tombs of the prophets, and *garnish the sepulchres of the righteous*' (Matthew 23:29). The same spirit remains in Israel to this very day.

Standing with us among the tombs, our Jewish guide gave us an affecting account of the death of Rabbi Landau whose picture we had so often seen in Jewish houses. He came from Lemberg when the cholera was raging and visited this burying-ground, where he prayed very earnestly over the graves of the rabbis, asking of them forgiveness and promising to be with them soon. He returned to town, sickened, and died, and next day was buried.

In the evening, we went to the shop of a Jew and bought *Tephillin* or phylacteries, *the broadest* which he had. These consist of little scrolls of parchment in which are written certain passages of the Law, enclosed in two black leather boxes which are bound by leather thongs on the forehead and left hand during the time of prayer. It was to these that our Lord alluded when reproving the Pharisees, 'All their works they do for to be seen of men; *they make broad their phylacteries.*' We got also the *mezuzah*, a small scroll of parchment, on which a portion of the Law is written, with the name of God on the back in transposed letters, which is folded up and nailed obliquely on the doorpost of every Jewish house. Both of these superstitions are derived from a misinterpretation of the command in Deuteronomy, 'And thou shalt bind them for a sign upon thine hand, and they shall be *as frontlets between thine eyes*; and thou shalt *write them upon the posts of* thy house, and on thy gates' (Deuteronomy 6:8, 9). The natural heart in all ages and in all nations is well pleased to substitute mere external observances in the place of spiritual heart-religion. We afterwards purchased a *Tallith*, a white woollen shawl, striped with blue at the edge and having white fringes called *Tsitsith* at the four corners. The Jews wear this over their head during prayer, while they hold the fringes in their hands and frequently kiss them in obedience to the commandment, 'Speak unto the children of Israel, and bid them that they make them *fringes in the borders of their garments*' (Numbers 15:38,39; Deuteronomy 22:12). The Saviour also alludes to them, 'they enlarge *the borders of their garments*' (Matthew 23:5). Upon the part which comes over the forehead, the Jews often wear a band of silver embroidery. A Jewess who had been employed to prepare the *Tallith* for us, refused to sew the embroidered band upon the robe unless we procured for her a silk ribband to put between them, alleging that otherwise she would be breaking the Law which forbids them to mingle 'woollen and linen' together (Leviticus 19:19).

October 4

Early this forenoon, we were sent for by the Commissary of Police, a sharp bustling Austrian, with a pipe in his mouth, who examined us very roughly. We believe that they had suspicions of our being missionaries, and in order to entrap us, alleged that we were Jews travelling under a false passport. The Commissary held a letter in his hand which he had received from Jaglinsky, stating that we went into the synagogue there and joined in the Jewish prayers, even using 'Hear, O Israel, the Lord thy God is one God'. 'And further', added he, 'why did you buy *Tephillin* last night?'

We were somewhat perplexed as well as amused by this attempt to show that we were Jews and not Christians and were now made aware of the system of jealous espionage maintained in this kingdom of Popish darkness. We answered that we were Protestant pastors from Scotland and that all ministers in our country are instructed in Hebrew; that we had read in the synagogue only to show the Jews that we knew their language; and that we had bought the *Tephillin* as curiosities. This seemed to satisfy him and we received our passports for Lemberg; 'Only', he said, 'you must go by Zloozow.'

In paying a second visit to the two principal synagogues, we met with a young man belonging to one of the best Jewish families who requested an interview at the inn. His name was Moses Weitheit, of a very pleasing appearance, gentle and serious in his manners, and able to speak Latin freely and a little Italian. He said he belonged to the New School and yet believed the Scriptures to be the Word of God. He did not look for the restoration of the Jews to the Holy Land, thought the emancipation of the Jews was to be their Messiah, and that true religion consisted in the natural feeling of love to God. His mind was evidently not at rest; he had never read the New Testament and, though he understood the Law, could not understand the Psalms and Prophets. When we shewed him a small New Testament in German, he earnestly entreated us to leave it with him; and when we told him that were we to do so, the circumstance might come to the ears of the Police, in which event we should be detained and brought into trouble, he immediately declared that he would show it to no-one till we were gone. Hiding it in the bosom of his Polish gown, he said *Nemo sciet, nemo sciet!* (no one shall know!). We complied with his request, and could not but breathe a prayer that he might be enabled to draw living water out of this fountain, in a wilderness where blind guides tremble lest one drop from heaven should fall on the thirsty soul. He kept his promise, but we soon found that our caution was needful and that the suspicions of the Austrians concerning us were not removed.

Having hired a comfortable vehicle to carry us to Lemberg, we intended to set out before the gates were shut for the night and accordingly drove up to the custom-house. But here we were detained for three hours, which the custom-house officers and soldiers spent in making complete search into every article we had with us. Not a corner of the carriage escaped their strict, suspicious search; everything except what was on our person was examined. Every book, in whatever language, was taken from us, even our Hebrew and English Bibles; and we were left the alternative of allowing them to be sent to Lemberg to be examined by the Censor there and waiting for his opinion on their orthodoxy, or of at once allowing ourselves to be deprived of their use until we should be beyond the dominions of Austria. On our preferring the latter alternative, they agreed to seal up our books in a parcel and send them on to Cracow to await our arrival. When we pleaded to be allowed to retain our English Bible, the only answer we received was, *'It is not allowed in Austria'*. We were still farther annoyed by their finding several sealed letters of introduction to Consuls and others lying in our desk and on account of which they imposed a fine upon us. The greater our annoyance, the greater the satisfaction of the officers appeared to be. They seemed to feel that it was not every day two Protestant ministers were in their grasp. We were not allowed to leave that night and therefore lodged in a Jewish khan near the gate. Here we experienced several painful proofs of the rapacity of the Jewish people. The keepers of the khan, seeing our anxiety to depart next morning, threw every obstacle in our way, charging two or three prices for every article we had used and striving in every way to extort money from us. We could only pray that the prophecy of Zephaniah might be soon fulfilled, 'The remnant of Israel shall not do iniquity, *nor speak lies; neither shall a deceitful tongue be found in their mouth*' (Zephaniah 3:13).

October 5
We at last got away about midday and enjoyed a pleasant drive through a well-cultivated plain, with gently swelling hills on the left, the young wheat springing fresh and green. About five miles from Brody the country became more varied. The road lay through the estate of a Polish Count; the woods were finely kept and at that time tinged with the red

and brown of autumn. The castle and neighbouring village are called Potchoritz, and there are two churches, the one a rude structure, the other beautiful, situated on the top of a wooded eminence. In front of the latter there is a whole range of pillars, each supporting the figure of a saint; and the large square of the village has in the midst of it a high pillar with a figure of the Virgin on the top.

At three o'clock, we rested a little in a clean inn belonging to the village of Sassow, where we found a small synagogue of wood, and 200 Jewish families, all of the old school, and hoping for the Messiah. Their burying-ground, filled with plain, white tombstones, was at the entrance of the village. Here, too, was a curious specimen of the old Polish church and belfry, both entirely of wood. At the inn we met a Tyrolese, wearing the tall conical cap of his country, who had lately travelled to Palestine in the service of an Englishman, and was very communicative. The Polish *hartsmi*, or inn, is a curious long building, having a wide entrance at both ends, so that you drive in at the one end and in leaving drive out at the other. Within, there are stalls for twenty or thirty horses on each side of the building, and a few rooms at the one end, affording tolerable accommodation to the weary traveller. The only bed is a heap of straw enclosed in a frame, over which they sometimes spread a sheet, while your own mats and cloaks are your covering.

Leaving this village, the fields were beautifully tinged with a reddish-brown, from the colour of the stalk of the *retsky* which had been here cut down. About six in the evening we came to Zloozow, a large village with three handsome churches. Here we found out that it was not without some design that the Commissary at Brody had caused us to get our passports signed here instead of sending us on direct to Lemberg; for we were met at the entrance of the village by a Government officer who was waiting to conduct us to the *Kreisamter*, or superintendent of police. This person was an exceedingly pleasant, intelligent man and could speak English fluently, having been much in the company of English residents in Vienna. He engaged each of us successively in conversation, and then at once rose and said that we should have our passports without delay. While our horses were getting ready, we wandered through the town. In front of one of the churches stood a pillar, supporting the image of a saint with the child Jesus in his arms, with this inscription '*D. o. m. Ex voto statuam hanc Sancto Joanni erexit Francisca Loewel, anno* 1824' (*i.e.* 'Francisca Loewel, in the year 1824, erected this statue to St John, in fulfilment of a vow'). A poor Polish woman was crossing herself and repeating a prayer as she passed it.

There are said to be 500 Jewish families here. We met a very serious and interesting Jew returning from evening worship who told us that all the Jews of this place are Rabbinists and so superstitious that they had been ill pleased with him for shaving off a small part of his beard. He said 'he was not one of the New School, yet thought that they did good in many ways. As for himself, he hoped that he would be saved if he kept free from whatever his conscience condemned and was honest in his trade, which very few are'. In reply we spoke of its being the first point in religion to find a sin-offering which would cleanse the conscience. He seemed serious and interested, but our time was gone, and we soon left him and the quiet village far behind. Late at night we arrived at Zopka, *a hartsmi* in a very solitary situation, kept by a Jewish family who received us kindly and tried to make us comfortable.

October 6
We enjoyed a calm Sabbath morning, the day warm and pleasant. A range of wooded hills bounded the view on the north and there were but three cottages within sight. After morning worship we separated for lonely meditation, agreeing to meet at a certain hour. We did not at the time know that Galicia has frequently been the scene of violent robberies and atrocious murders; but the little we had seen and afterwards saw of the natives convinced us of their profound ignorance and barbarous habits.

Mr McCheyne having gone about a mile and a half toward the hills, sat down to read in a sequestered spot when two Polish shepherds came and sat down beside him. After trying in vain to exchange ideas with them by signs, Mr M[cCheyne] rose to leave them, but they shewed a determination to detain him by putting themselves in his way and endeavouring to force him up into the woods that crowned the hills. A desperate struggle ensued for about a quarter of an hour, till, exhausted by these violent efforts, Mr M[cCheyne] lay down on the ground. They stood by and spoke together for a few minutes – then suddenly plunged into the woods. It seems every way probable that they intended to plunder him; and some of the people at the inn wondered that they had not drawn their large knives. What moved them so suddenly to depart we could not conjecture. We felt that the hand of God that had delivered us out of so many dangers during our previous wanderings had been eminently stretched out again.

The rest of the day we spent together. Our host provided us with his Hebrew Bible, and we had retained an English New Testament in one of our pockets, so that we enjoyed a profitable Sabbath, realizing the promise, 'Yet will I be to them as a little sanctuary in the countries where they shall come' (Ezekiel 11:16). Waggons, heavily laden with merchandise, were passing along the road all day without intermission; for a Sabbath of holy rest is a thing unknown in the dominions of the Man of Sin.

Our Jewish host told us of a town called Premyslaw, two German miles distant, so thoroughly devoted to Judaism that no Jew dare appear on its streets unless dressed entirely in the Jewish manner, in case the Chasidim should tear him to pieces. Only a short time ago it was a very insignificant town, but prosperity came to it with a certain great rabbi. This rabbi is one of those to whom the people repair from all Bukovine and Galicia in times of sickness and distress, asking him to pray for them. They always go as Saul did to Samuel (1 Samuel 9:9), with some present in their hand, which they call *pedeeon* (a ransom). The week before our arrival one man brought him a sum equal to £6, seeking to be delivered from some calamity, and during the Feasts no less than 3,000 persons have been known to visit him, each bringing a present. He has in consequence become very rich, and frequently entertains 500 Jews at his table, spending even £30 a week in supporting his dignity. He assumes the character of a prophet, pretending to have knowledge of future events and to divine the particular sins of any one by looking steadfastly in his face. How applicable to such a man are the words of Jeremiah: 'I have not sent these prophets, yet they ran; I have not spoken to them, yet they prophesied' (Jeremiah 23:21).

Our host told us also of a visit which the now imprisoned Rabbi of Rugen paid to this part of the country about four years ago. He travelled with three carriages of his own, and the Jews flocked to him in such crowds that more than 700 vehicles were upon the road either accompanying or going to meet him. He slept at this inn on his way from Brody to Lemberg. The crowd of Jews that visited him was such that he could hardly get rest and many came to look upon his face while he was sleeping. So great was the excitement that the Austrian Government became alarmed, and ordered him to leave the country in three days. The mother of the innkeeper had often visited this rabbi, seeking peace to her conscience. We shewed them the Psalm, 'None of them can by any means redeem his brother, nor give to God a ransom for him' (Psalm

49:7); and the command of God, 'Call *upon me* in the day of trouble' (Psalm 50:15).

October 7

We left the place before daylight. During a ride of four hours to Lemberg, there was no object of interest except a beautiful village called Veniky, surrounded by wooded hills, the trees all variegated with the tints of autumn. There were many Jews on the street, and Polish peasants whose hard, unmeaning countenances indicated ignorance and neglect. Before entering Lemberg we were examined at the custom-house, where many waggons were undergoing a strict scrutiny. One man had a cart of sticks; a soldier passing by chose one of the best and carried it off as a prize; the man resisted and entreated him not to take it, but in vain, the soldier only threatened him and beat him off. This little incident shewed us something of the military oppression common in this country. Descending upon the town, we came once more upon paved streets, handsome houses and other marks of European civilization. The upper classes were attired very much after the English fashion, except that the ladies wore no bonnet, but carried a diminutive parasol instead. We found a quiet and comfortable lodging in the Hotel de Russie.

Lemberg is a large city, having 130,000 inhabitants; it lies in a fine valley, running nearly north and south, the hills on either side being of considerable elevation. On the east the hill is laid out so as to form a fine drive or promenade. From the summit we obtained a commanding view of the town and environs. The houses are high and well built; the streets and squares are open and airy. There is one very handsome church on the rising ground to the west, and ten other spires rise over the buildings of the town. There are several pleasant walks and boulevards, adorned with fine trees in the heart of the town. There are barracks and other large and elegant public buildings, especially one with a fountain at each of the four corners, and over each fountain the statue of a heathen goddess. An immense theatre was in the course of being built; the bricks were conveyed to the builders on the wall by a row of boys and women, standing on the steps of a very tall ladder, who handed up each brick from one to another. Looking to the east, we observed the tents of a large body of soldiers who were then under review, all pitched in military order. But the country in that direction appeared bleak and uninteresting. While we were standing here, a train of splendid carriages swept past, containing the Archduke of Austria and several officers, fine-looking men in handsome uniforms, the former wearing a dazzling star on the breast. Returning through the city we passed a church, having a figure of the Virgin, with this truly Popish inscription over it, 'Praetereundo cave ne taceatur Ave. '⁶ Rows of wooden stalls instead of shops are as common here as at Czernowitz. Three regiments of well-disciplined soldiers passed us on their return from exercise. We were told that there were 30,000 encamped within three miles of the city. One painful sight, which reminded us of Italy, was the vast numbers of criminals who are condemned to public infamy by labouring in chains upon the streets. They are used in building and other kinds of hard labour through the day, and we saw 120 of them returning at night to their prison, dragging heavy fetters after them.

We visited the Jewish market-place, but did not find it so clean and pleasant as that of Brody. Israel here looks poor, oppressed, and degraded, dwelling in the dust. The Russian fur-cap or broad black hat and black Polish robe are beautiful on respectable Jews with clean flowing beards; but when they turn poor, dirty, and ragged, then they look squalid and desolate indeed, and such was the appearance of the greater number of the Jews of Lemberg.

There are two large synagogues, four smaller ones, and a great many in private houses. We visited one of the largest, a building in the same Gothic style as that of Brody, the roof supported by four immense pillars, and the walls gaudily adorned; in the porch we observed the whole Prayer-book pasted up in sheets on a board for the use of the poor, as at Brody. We asked, If the Jews ever sent money to the Holy Land? One of them whispered, 'that such a thing is forbidden by the Government, they are not allowed to send money out of the country'.

Near sunset we had the opportunity of witnessing the funeral of an old Jewess. The dead body was carried on a bier, covered with a black pall; the men in their ordinary clothes followed, and a throng of women and children brought up the rear. One Jew walked immediately behind the bier, rattling a tin collection-box, and crying out in Hebrew, every few paces, 'Alms deliver from death'; and the same words were embroidered upon the pall. In obedience to this summons, many Jews put in pieces of money as they went along and the money thus collected goes to the Hebra or burying-society. At the gate of the burying-ground,

---

⁶ 'In passing by, beware, Lest you forget this prayer, Ave Maria.'

one woman uttered a loud and piercing cry, which she continued as they proceeded. Arriving at a small portico or covered walk in the graveyard, they set down the bier and uncovered the face of the dead. All the relations gathered round, and bending over the corpse till their lips almost touched the lips of the deceased, entreated her to forgive them if they had injured her in any way. After this, they proceeded to the grave and the body alone was lowered down into it, with the face uncovered. Several of the women now joined in a loud and bitter wail, but their tears and lamentations were only feigned, for at one time they appeared very lugubrious, then, all of a sudden, they stopped and began to scold, or appeared utterly careless. They were specimens of *the mourning women* mentioned in the Scriptures (see Jeremiah 9:17 and Matthew 11:17). A white linen pillow was next produced, to be laid under the head of the deceased, on which there was a scramble among the women which would be the foremost in filling it with earth. The scene of asking forgiveness from the dead woman was renewed with great vehemence and many besought her when she came before God to pray for them and for their children. The *Hazan* or chanter, being hired by the relatives for the purpose, stood by the open grave and repeated many prayers for the dead. This done, the body was covered in, and the company returned to the portico, where the eldest son, standing in the midst, read from off a board hung on the wall another prayer for his dead mother; in which he was assisted by the chanter, for we were assured that he scarcely understood a word of it. Before leaving the burying-ground, each individual washed his hands in water that stood in earthen jars near the gate for this purpose; for the Jews believe that evil spirits hover about the graveyard and would have access to them if they were at all defiled by the dead body. The Jewish hospital, a large commodious building, looks into the burying-ground, where were several of the sick, walking to and fro before the door and others at the windows, gazing on the sad spectacle of death that had passed.

According to the last census, the number of Jewish families in Lemberg was 3,000, or nearly 15,000 souls; but there is good reason to think that there are far more actually resident in that town. That they are an important class here may be ascertained from the fact that the advertisements at the Post-office are in the Hebrew character as well as in the Polish and German; many of the signboards also in the streets are painted with Hebrew letters. There are some Jews belonging to the New School, but they have no synagogue. In one old synagogue we found in the porch *rings* fixed into the wall to which are attached irons for the neck and feet. They were formerly used for fastening up to public view, persons who had broken the regulations of the Talmud in any material point; resembling very much the *juggs* which are yet to be seen in some of the old parish churches of Scotland.[7]

We were a few minutes too late to see the ceremony of a circumcision, for we met the parents carrying away their child. But we saw the chair of Elias, a comfortable chair beside the table where the circumcision is performed. It gets this name from the singular belief that Elijah comes unseen and sits there at every circumcision – probably in his zeal to see the Law enforced to the letter. On the back of the chair is inscribed *Throne of Elijah – his memory be for good*. We spoke with an affable Jew who said that the meaning of the passage which predicts that in the days of Messiah 'thy people shall be all righteous' was there will be no hypocrites, all will be openly good or openly wicked. Talking of the days when the Talmud was in its full glory, he mentioned to us a Jewish proverb. Two towns in Russia – Kiow and Saradow – were so famous for the study and defence of the Talmud that it used to be said 'From Saradow shall go forth the Law, and the word of the Lord from Kiow'. *'Full well do they reject the commandment of God, that they may keep their own traditions'* (Mark 7:9).

October 8

We left this pleasant town in a tolerable Jewish carriage, an old Jew with a long beard driving us. We might have got places in the *Eil-wagen* or stagecoach, but we wished to be masters of our own time, and therefore preferred the offer of this Jew who undertook to carry us the whole way to Cracow, a distance of nearly 200 English miles, for 45 *gulden,* equal to £4.10s.

The country through which we travelled reminded us of the vast undulating plains of France, fertile but uninteresting with a long level road stretching before. The young crops were springing and the peasants gathering their potatoes as we passed. In three hours we came to Grudak, a pleasant village, containing a council-house and two churches, adorned with shady walks and a fine stream of water. Here we saw several Jews in the street, but had no conversation with any. Three hours more brought us to Sandovawiznia, a large village, also upon a pleasant

---

[7] These were iron collars placed around the neck of criminals and which were attached to walls or posts.

stream, with two churches, and many images of saints under its shady trees. The half of the population appeared to be Jewish. Towards evening we passed through Moschiska where the principal street had an old piazza under which many Jewish children were playing, and we were told that there were 600 resident Jews.

We slept at a Jewish khan, near a small village called Laskovola, where are six Jewish families. Our hostess was a simple Jewess, asking a great many questions and expressing great surprise. The whole family were kind and made us promise if ever we came that way again not to forget to visit them.

October 9

Next morning we turned to the north, leaving the main road to get a nearer way, and came on a rustic village, Bejepee, close to a nobleman's seat. The white-washed mansion, the lawn, gardens, and handsome trees, reminded us of similar scenes at home. But they are rare indeed in Poland. The wicker fences being kept in good condition, formed a neat enclosure and also an excellent protection to the young trees. The wooden shed full of images in the square was absolutely ridiculous. The whole land is polluted with these abominations, sometimes under shady trees, sometimes in glass-cases by the wayside, and it may well be said, 'According to the number of thy cities are thy gods' (Jeremiah 9:13).

Crossing the Saan, a tributary of the Vistula, by a floating bridge, we came to Jaroslaw, a small town containing 1,200 families, with several churches, a few public buildings, and a busy market-place. We saw many respectable Jews upon the street, and many Catholic priests. In the suburb stands a handsome convent with three spires, and above the principal entrance a painting of the Virgin Mary, spreading her hands over the monks of the order kneeling round her, having this inscription, *Sub tuum proesidium* (Under thy protection). How truly may a Jew call such Christianity by the name of foul idolatry!

We now travelled due west, through rows of willows, oaks and elms for miles together, till we came to Zeworsk, a village with a covered walk in the market-place, where Jews were loitering. A neat obelisk marked the entrance to some baron's country-seat, and a temporary triumphal arch, adorned with leaves, intimated the expected approach of some of the royal family. We noticed here a broom erected at several doors to show that a soldier was billeted there. The beggars were very loathsome and deformed, and some, to prove that they were Christian, not Jewish beggars, led a pig behind them by a string! Even a wretched beggar in Poland is careful not to be mistaken for a Jew.

In the evening we drove through Lanshut and late at night crossed a deep stream and entered the town of Rzezow, about halfway between Lemberg and Cracow.

October 10

We left this clean, well-built town very early, and pursued our way through avenues of trees, till we reached the village of Zenzow, where a company of Austrian soldiers were exercising. We saw many idle Jews and signboards in the Hebrew character.

An hour after, we came to Ropsitza, a decayed village. The market-place had (as usual) a piazza all round the square, and a covered well in the centre. At one end of the church was a singular 'house of gods'. There were two figures of Christ on the cross; then images of Christ and the three disciples of Gethsemane; and lastly a painting of the whole scene of the Saviour's agony in the garden; all the figures being as large as life. There are sixty Jewish families here, all poor mechanics.

Before noon we rested at a Jewish khan to partake of *mit-tag*. These khans or inns are everywhere to be met with, and are certainly peculiar in their kind, though comfort is seldom one of their qualities. First, you enter at a large gate and drive into a long dark covered stable among horses and *briscas*; then alighting, you proceed through a large chamber at one end, which includes the guest-room, drinking and smoking rooms, kitchen, bedroom, all in one. The things which strike the eye as peculiarly Jewish are the *mezuza* on the doorpost, the *misrach* hanging on the eastern wall to show in what direction Jerusalem lies, and the brazen lustre or Sabbath-lamp suspended from the roof. In one corner is a fire without a grate, and the dinner boiling in earthenware cans standing beside burning faggots. Brass and earthen kitchen utensils, bright and clean, adorn the wall, and the washing-tub has its corner. Being a family room, there are two tolerable beds – serving for sofas by day, a cradle also, and a fine infant in its little carriage. The mother and daughter are preparing the food, and the married daughter, with fine Jewish features, cares for the children. The cow, unreproved, is drinking out of a tub, and hens are wandering about, finding supply at the feet of the different guests, while one more expert than the rest is catching flies at the window. Such was the khan where we rested. Being also a public room, four Jews with long beards were dining at the end of one long table, while we occupied the end of another, and two others were dining at a chest of drawers. One Jew was sitting idly on the cradle; several others, each with a German pipe in his mouth, wandered in and out; while two Gentiles from Breslau stood trying to make us understand their German. In spite of all appearances, the dinner was excellent, and the cost only 8d. a-head.

In the afternoon we passed through Pilsno and soon after met the royal carriages, accompanied by soldiers. A peasant on the road, looking at the Jew who drove our vehicle, called out to him quite gratuitously, and by way of insult, *Verfluchtet Jude* (accursed Jew) (Deuteronomy 28:37) – showing how completely God's ancient people are 'a proverb and a byword', and how the heathen that are at ease 'help forward their affliction'.

After sunset we arrived at Tarnow, where was another temporary arch, and passed great crowds on the streets who had been hailing the arrival of their nobles; the most were well-dressed Jews. Late at night we arrived at a solitary khan, not even so comfortable as the one described above. Two travellers had already taken possession of one part of the floor and were fast asleep, while a Polish servant was sitting at the bar serving out *snaps* to the postilions and others who called even during the night. We preferred to sleep in the hayloft where we spread our mats for the night. When we were taking refreshment, a Jewish girl, who had brought us bread and butter, on seeing one of us about to take up the knife that lay on the table, rushed forward and removed it lest we Gentiles should pollute the knife which they themselves used. The same damsel, however, in the morning said we must be good men indeed, having visited the Holy Land.

October 11

A thick easterly fog overspread the country, so that we saw nothing till we came to Bochnia, where we remarked that the number of beggars was very great. It was common to meet with individuals of them in the country kneeling by the roadside, but in towns they move about in crowds. We had entered a baker's shop to buy some provision, when forthwith fully twenty assembled at the door and assailed us with their importunities as we came out. Popery brings all sorts of miseries in her train.

We met with a curious instance of superstitious conscientiousness this morning in the Jewish boy who attended his father, the driver of our vehicle. We gave him bread and butter at breakfast, but observed that though he looked eagerly at it, he laid it aside till some hours should elapse. The reason was that he had just eaten *flesh* and if he had immediately tasted *butter*, it would have been considered a violation of the precept, 'Thou shalt not seethe a kid in his mother's milk' (Exodus 23:19).

Leaving the main road, our vehicle moved on, and in the afternoon brought us to Vieliczka, a beautiful village surrounded with gardens and orchards which fill the bosom of a deep valley. It is chiefly famous for its remarkable salt-mines, much visited by travellers. We felt a wish to examine its curiosities and enjoy its scenery, but our one object impelled us forward.

On reaching the neighbouring height, Cracow came full in view about four miles distant, with the deep-flowing Vistula (or Weichsel) winding through the plain. We soon reached Podgorze (which means *'near the boundary'*), the suburb of Cracow on the Austrian side of the river. Our passports having been examined, we crossed the river on a bridge supported by floats, and, entering the ancient capital of Poland, found a good lodging in the Rosa, an inn kept by Joseph Cnoxes. No sooner had we arrived than we were subjected like all other travellers to minute investigation, indicating a state of society not overcertain of its own stability. The following printed questions were put to us by the Police:

1. Your name and surname?
2. Your rank, and office, and employment?
3. Your native country, and place of birth?
4. Your age?
5. Your religion?
6. Your condition in life, unmarried, married, widowed?
7. From what place you have last come?
8. How long you propose to remain here?
9. Did you come alone, or had you companions?
10. Had you a passport?
11. Where do you intend to go after leaving this?

It was easy to answer all these questions, but not easy to forget the suspicious tyrannizing spirit exhibited by the examiners. No country has freedom like our own, because no land on earth has had the truth of God so fully preached and so widely embraced.

The same evening we were guided to the house of the Lutheran minister, Mr Otremba, a benevolent man who received us very kindly, although we afterwards learned that he is neither orthodox in his views nor friendly to the Jewish Mission. From him we learned that Dr Gerlach, the missionary of the London Jewish Society, had been removed from this station to Warsaw and had died there some months ago, but that an English missionary was now labouring among the Jews here.

Cracow was a very considerable city in former days when it was the capital of Poland and it still retains many features of majesty. It has not the handsome look of Lemberg, but it has more of the air of antiquity. The houses are lofty and often massy, the churches old and picturesque. The front of one is adorned with statues of the saints as large as life, and another has the scene of the crucifixion in which the figures are larger than life. The ancient castle and cathedral, built upon the same hill, rise over the city, and these, along with its university and other public buildings, testify its ancient greatness. There is a delightful promenade, of great extent, shaded with tall poplars, quite round the town, adding greatly to its beauty. Cracow is the grand cemetery of the ancient Kings of Poland; but when we saw the hills of Moravia appearing in the distant west, the recollection of the many men of God who had been born there, whose names are inwoven with the triumphs of the gospel in some of the darkest regions of the world, spread a holier interest over the scene than could be done by all its associations with Polish kings.

October 12
With some difficulty we found out the residence of the Jewish missionary, the Rev. Thomas Hiscock, a clergyman of the Church of England, whom we soon found to be 'a brother and companion in tribulation, and in the kingdom and patience of Jesus Christ'. It was truly an agreeable surprise to us when we found ourselves seated as if at home with this valuable missionary, his wife, who seemed to be indeed a handmaid of the Lord, and their two children They had lived for some years almost in perfect solitude in the midst of this great city, hated by the Papists because they were Protestants, and by the Protestants because they had no sympathy with their worldly spirit and Neologian theology, so that our coming made their heart overflow with joy and kindness. Mr H[iscock] laboured first in Westphalia for one year, wandering up and down with a knapsack on his back, visiting the Jews, and not without tokens of the divine blessing. Since that time he has been stationed here, where the hardships which he has been called to endure have been very

great. His enemies have at different times excited tumults among the Jews before his window, that the blame might fall upon him in the eye of the Government. He injured his health by a long period of excessive exertion when teaching German, Hebrew and Latin to young Jews in order to get an opportunity of preaching to them 'all the words of this life'. Intent upon his Master's work, he seldom loses an occasion afforded by a Jew calling upon him in the way of trade, of speaking to his soul; and he addresses the poorest and meanest whom he meets in the street, a thing which no Gentile here would do on any account. Often too, he goes into their shops to purchase small articles, simply in order to gain a hearing.

October 13, Sabbath

In the morning we attended the Lutheran church and, after the liturgy had been read, Mr Otremba preached upon, 'Cast thy burden on the Lord' – a general discourse, without one doctrinal statement. Here our best feelings were shocked by seeing at one end of the church a bronze figure of the Saviour on the Cross larger than life, the veins and bones carved in such a way that they appeared to be starting through the racked body. It was brought from Breslau and placed here by the President of the Senate, a Roman Catholic priest, for the purpose of excluding the Jews from Dr Gerlach's evening lecture by prejudicing their minds against the Protestants in general. The present clergyman used no efforts to prevent its introduction. The altar was covered with a cloth of gold, and had four candles burning on it, with a crucifix on one side, and the brazen serpent on the other. The organ was good, and the singing fine; the audience numbered between fifty and sixty, the men occupying one side by themselves, the women the other. The minister stands at the altar while reading the liturgy, and the people sit during prayer and singing. The minister prefaced his discourse by a short introduction, and then gave out his text, on the reading of which all stood till the words were finished. They rise, also, at the Lord's prayer.

We met for worship in the afternoon in the missionary's room where Mr Hiscock preached to us from Matthew 16:13, 'Whom do men say that I am?' In the evening we joined together in the same place, a small company of five, in the midst of a city given over to the darkness and wickedness of Popery, in 'showing the Lord's death till he come'. Mr McCheyne conducted the service in the Presbyterian form, and it was felt by us all as a time of refreshing from the presence of the Lord – a well of salvation 'in a dry and thirsty land where no water is'. It was four years since Mr H[iscock] and his wife had enjoyed this ordinance. They do not think it right to receive it at the Lutheran church, both on account of the error of that church in regard to consubstantiation, and also on account of its cold dead services. They spend silent Sabbaths, and yet are not alone, for they experience much joy in the midst of their afflictions. The God of the missionary is a covenant-keeping God, and he gives them 'a hundred-fold more' than all they have left behind, 'with persecutions'.

During our stay at Cracow we gathered a good deal of information. In regard to the *Protestants*, there are about 600 in the city and 200 more in the country round, but the most of them, it is to be feared, are inclined to infidelity. For a year and a half previous to our visit their only public worship had been a forenoon service every Sabbath with a sermon of twenty minutes' length. Their minister lately had a ball on Sabbath evening, at which eighty persons were present; and such parties are not unfrequent. On one occasion, an awakened Jew, going to the Lutheran minister to be examined for baptism, found him *playing at cards*, and was invited to sit down and join in the game before proceeding to any serious business. The Protestants often tell the Jews here that it is quite as well for them to remain in their Judaism. What a stumbling-block are such Protestants in the way of Israel! 'Woe unto you, Scribes and Pharisees, hypocrites; for ye shut up the kingdom of heaven against men; for ye neither go in yourselves, neither suffer ye them that are entering to go in' (Matthew 23:13).

The Poles in Cracow are exceedingly depraved, and immorality is not looked on as a crime. They are always seeking revolution and would rise in revolt tomorrow if the Austrians were to retire. Lying, stealing, swearing, drinking, gambling and adultery abound. Not long before our visit, a fearful assassination took place in a quiet part of the town. A young man was suspected as a Russian spy; and his body was found with thirty-five stabs in it. We were often reminded of the dark pictures drawn of human nature in the Holy Scriptures, for every feature of it is realized here. 'There is no truth, nor mercy, nor knowledge of God in the land: By swearing, and lying, and killing, and stealing, and committing adultery, they break out, and blood toucheth blood' (Hosea 4:1, 2). Masters in general strike their servants unmercifully, and menservants are often lashed with the whip. At one time they were even murdered without any investigation ever following. The police publicly flog servants, male or female, that are brought to them by their masters. The nobles oppress their vassals even more cruelly than the Russian conquerors have treated them; and the vassals in their turn oppress their servants not less severely. Popery is very strong here and most intolerant. Monasteries and nunneries abound and the priests are notoriously abandoned in their lives, while many of the people are 'mad upon their idols'. Yet among the upper classes there is much infidelity; for they despise Popery in their hearts; and even among the peasantry, there is scarcely one in a hundred that will now go down on their knees in passing an image, whereas, till within these few years, every one invariably did so. Cracow is governed nominally by a Senate, composed of eight members and a president, two of whom are Roman Catholic priests; but as every matter must receive the sanction of the three Residents of Austria, Russia, and Prussia, the protecting powers, they in reality govern. Indeed, Austria seems to have the whole power in her own hands. The Austrian soldiers took possession of the city three years previously, and have occupied it ever since.

The University is said to be the oldest in Europe, except that of Oxford. It might be a very efficient institution, were it not that the Austrians are unfavourable to it, believing that it sows the seeds of revolution among the young men. Many students belonging to the best Polish families are very desirous to learn English, and Mr Hiscock told us that if we would send him fifty English Bibles, he could distribute them profitably to these young men. Since our return, the Edinburgh Bible Society, at our request, kindly engaged to send this supply to Cracow. We were interested in hearing that Mr Dow, who was deposed some years ago from the ministry in Scotland for following Mr Irving's views, had paid a visit to Mr Hiscock, not long before our arrival;[8] but with what object we could not learn. He had come from Russia and Mr Hiscock believed went to Odessa.

The upper classes are dressed very much after the English manner, but the common people wear a white surtout with red lining, a broad hat, and long boots. The women wear a white coarse stuff, with the

---

[8] It is not absolutely clear which of two brothers is referred to here. William Dow, minister of Tongland and Balnacross, was deposed by the General Assembly of the Church of Scotland on 23rd May, 1832. His brother, David Dow, minister at Kirkpatrick-Irongrey, demitted his charge on 7th August, 1832 and was declared to be no longer a minister of the Church of Scotland because he had adopted views inconsistent with its doctrinal standards.

handkerchief round the head, red or white. The Jews wear the fur-cap and long black robe, generally very squalid and torn, said to be a remnant of the dress of the ancient Polish nobles.

The population of Cracow is generally reckoned at 49,000, of whom 22,000 are Jews. The latter live together in a quarter by themselves, divided from the city by a stream called 'the Little Vistula'. This quarter is named Casimir, from Casimir the Great, King of Poland 500 years ago, who married Esther, a beautiful Jewess, and granted to her nation at her request permission to settle there. There are about 10,000 more in other parts of the republic. They follow all trades and yet have no bread to eat. They are so poor that out of all the Jews in the republic, there are not 10,000 who could afford to pay one shilling for a Hebrew Bible. Twelve families are often lodged in one room in winter, the floor being chalked out into so many portions, and a whole family huddled together in each, the children generally remaining in bed to keep themselves warm as they have no clothes to defend them from the cold. It is no uncommon thing for a Jew to pull aside his long black gown and show that he has nothing to cover his limbs. How truly the Word of God by the mouth of Moses has come to pass, 'When I have broken the staff of your bread, ten women shall bake your bread in one oven, and they shall deliver you your bread again by weight; and ye shall eat, and not be satisfied' (Leviticus 26:26). The Jews here are so strict Talmudists that a man of some abilities who had seen and ridiculed the absurdities of the Talmud was solemnly excommunicated. They universally believe in the coming of the Messiah and would not listen to one who doubted it. The Papists, in their zeal to make the Virgin Mary everything, cast discredit on the doctrine that Christ will come again and try to persuade the Jews that Mr H[iscock] is not a Christian because he believes in Messiah's coming again in glory.

The Government some time ago erected a school for Jewish children and employed a Jew to teach Hebrew, German and Polish; but no Jew would send his children because it had been instituted by the Christians. The university also is open to the Jews, so that they may study there free of expense; and Mr Hiscock has frequently prepared young Jews for attending it. The object in granting this privilege no doubt is to bring them over to Popery. The Government seem afraid, like Pharaoh, lest the Jewish become more numerous than the Gentile population, and have enacted a law that no Jew be allowed to marry unless he can read and write Polish.

Of late years, fifteen Jews have been baptized by the Lutheran minister here, nine of whom were instructed by Mr Hiscock. Of some of these he entertained good hope that they were brought to a saving knowledge of Christ, but still more of others, who were melted under the power of the Word and apparently convinced, but who soon left the place. When a Jew comes to a missionary desiring baptism, if he has good reason to believe that there is a real change in the man's heart, he applies to the Senate for a protocol or examination. Often a delay of six weeks occurs before an answer is given. The examination of the candidate for baptism is then carried on before either a Canon or Roman Catholic magistrate, and the Lutheran minister. If they are satisfied, the Jew is baptized by Mr Otremba, and registered in the Lutheran church. This most pernicious law must be submitted to. As soon as a Jew is known to have applied for baptism, his brethren cast him off; the Papists also, and Lutherans, show him no kindness, so that the missionary has often had to maintain him till the examination and baptism were over, selling his own and his wife's clothes for their support. In such circumstances Jews are obliged, after baptism, to leave Cracow and generally go to Hungary to seek their daily bread, so that in this country they must 'suffer the loss of all things' if they would 'win Christ'. If there were any means by which converts could support themselves, Mr H[iscock] was persuaded that one-half of the rising generation of the Jews would become Christians. At least eighty persons have applied to him for baptism, but as far as he could judge, only from worldly motives, and he accordingly discouraged them. It is an interesting fact that since the Protestant Mission has been established here, very few have been baptized into the Roman Catholic church. A Jewish doctor, who has considerable property, was baptized by the Lutheran minister. He is an Arian, but offered to maintain Jewish proselytes on his estate, provided the London Society would allow them to keep their Jewish festivals.

In labouring among the Jews, the missionary here does not go to the synagogue to reason with them, because if there be an ill-natured Jew present, he easily excites a clamour, of which the police would take advantage in a moment. For the same reason he does not preach to them on the public street. He generally goes into a shop, buys a book for a few *groschen* or pence, and while he is making the bargain he begins to speak on the subject of sin and atonement and the shop is soon filled with Jews.

When Jews or Jewesses come to his door to sell their wares he always detains them till they have heard the gospel of the grace of God. When we were dining with him one day, two Jews came to the house to sell some of their articles. Mr H[iscock] spoke very plainly to their consciences of the true way of peace. They wished to buy a Hebrew Bible between them for 3s., but he gave one to each of them, to their great joy. Often thirty such visitors come in one day. We were reminded of the way in which Paul laboured at Rome. 'Paul dwelt two whole years in his own hired house, *and received all that came in unto him,* preaching the kingdom of God and teaching those things which concern the Lord Jesus Christ, with all confidence, no man forbidding him' (Acts 28:30, 31).

He also invites the young men to come to his house and learn any of the languages he knows – English, French, German and Latin. When they come he puts the Bible into their hands and teaches them out of it. At one time the rabbi pronounced a *herem* or curse of excommunication against all Jews who should visit the missionary's house, and appointed a man to walk round his house constantly for several months to watch if any Jew went near him. But notwithstanding all this opposition, Mr H[iscock] finds them ready to hear in their shops, and sometimes in a quiet retired square. Frequently when he has been addressing a crowd of them, the Popish priests have come past and tried to draw the Jews away. He is allowed by the Government to distribute Bibles and tracts in Hebrew, German, and Polish, *among the Jews*; and in this way the Word of God finds its way indirectly among the Poles also. His passport from Lord Palmerston ensures him protection; but the Government is exceedingly unwilling that any more missionaries should come. The president hinted this to him when he spoke of getting an assistant in the Mission, by saying, 'You know there is not work for any more'.

More than once we crossed the bridge over the Little Vistula and visited the Jews in Casimir, their own quarter. The crowds of bearded Jews, almost all meanly dressed, moved our bowels of compassion. One Jewish lad whom we met said, 'I believe in the God of the Jews and in the God of the Christians; I believe in Jesus, and in Mary, *and in all the gods*'. He afterwards added, that he believed in no heaven and in no hell. Without doubt this is not a solitary case in which Popery has led to profane infidelity.

The Jews here, still more than in Brody, have the custom of pressing you to buy their goods. They rush out of their shop, and stepping up to you, warmly recommend their articles; often coming as far as the middle of the street and sometimes even taking you by the sleeve. Thus earnestly will they one day press men to buy 'the unsearchable riches of Christ' (Zechariah 3:10). We went into a small bookshop and conversed with several Jews. One immediately said, 'You are English'. We asked why he thought so. 'Because', said he, 'you begin at once to talk about religion.' Mr Calman shewed them many of the errors of the Talmud and their idolatrous worship of the moon. They were very eager in their defence, showing more feeling than is common.

Our Jewish factor or guide said once, when we were speaking to him, 'Who knows whether Moses ever lived or not?' This shows that the secret unbelief, so common in Galicia, is spreading here also beneath the surface of Judaism. Yet they frequently boast that they are so steady in their faith, that no Polish Jew has ever been baptized. This, however, is contrary to truth.

One fine evening we walked out together about a mile from town to a large pond called Esther's Pool. It is surrounded by willows, poplars, and beautiful acacia-trees; an old chateau, once her palace, stands near, and there are pleasure-grounds on every side. King Casimir the Great, in the beginning of the fourteenth century, married a beautiful Jewess whose name was Esther. Like Queen Esther in the Scriptures, she loved her nation and procured them all the privileges which they enjoy in Poland to this day. One day the king discovered on her head the marks of a dreadful disease, common among the poor in that country, called *plica polonica*, which mats the hair and produces other disgusting appearances. His love was turned to hatred and in his rage he condemned her to be drowned in this pool, which was immediately done, and all Jewesses were commanded to veil their faces in public lest they should ensnare the king by their beauty. The palace and grounds were all laid out for her. A little way off we climbed an artificial mount, made that Queen Esther might view the surrounding country. From this we saw the high artificial hill raised in honour of Kotsiutzo, one of their greatest patriots and generals, who died in America. His bones were brought home and this hill raised over them, every citizen being commanded to carry a basket of earth to the spot. There is another conical hill of the same kind near the gate, sacred to the memory of King Cracus, founder of the city.

We were deeply impressed with the importance of this city as a field of labour in the cause of Israel. Their vast numbers, their afflictions, and their readiness to hear the truth, seem to invite the efforts of the Gospel Missionary. At the same time the difficulties are very great, from the opposition of a Popish government, the worse than indifference of nominal Protestants, and the want of temporal support for awakened Jews. Since the date of our visit, Mr Hiscock has been removed from Cracow to another station. His residence there was evidently blessed to the Jews, he being a judicious, yet devoted labourer, of a pensive spirit, but full of love to Israel, willing to spend and be spent for Christ. May the smile of the God of Israel be upon all his ways!

CHAPTER 9

PRUSSIA AND HAMBURGH

'From the daughter or Zion all her beauty is departed'
(Lamentations 1:6).

October 15

With unfeigned regret we parted from Mr Hiscock and his family, for we had taken sweet counsel together with these 'hidden ones'. None but those who have experienced the same can imagine the feelings with which true Christians meet and part in such a land.

We had received from the Austrian police the sealed parcel containing our books, of which we had been deprived at Brody; and now, disposing of our sleeping mats – hitherto indispensable articles – we prepared to enter the bounds of more civilized Prussia. At nine am we set out in the Prussian *Schnell-post*, a most comfortable vehicle, which was to carry us to Breslau, a distance of 185 miles, for a sum equal in our money to 19s. each. Our road lay nearly north, through the fine strath in which Cracow lies, ornamented with sheets of water and forests of pine, the Carpathian range bounding the view on our left. The whole territory of Cracow, though very small, is beautiful, hill and dale alternating. A convent, embosomed in wood, several picturesque churches, and an old castle crowning an eminence, were the principal objects till we passed within sight of Zarnow where are 1,200 Jews; and crossing the Vistula entered the Prussian province of Silesia. We met with little trouble at the custom-house, and none of that inquisitorial suspicion that characterizes the authorities of Austria. Indeed, we felt as if we breathed a freer air as soon as we knew we were beyond the dominions of the Man of Sin. Crosses and images, however, on the roadside met our view, the undisturbed relics of Popery, which still prevails in these districts. In the first small village we came to, called Berun, all built of wood, with a graceful spire, there was a shameful image of the Virgin. In the clear twilight we saw the spires of Nicolai, and late at night rested for half an hour at Gleiwitz, a full October moon lighting up the old market-place. Here we were accosted by one of our fellow-travellers, a Jew and

411

relative of our friend Mr Cerf, lately Jewish missionary in Edinburgh and Glasgow. He was curious to hear of our wanderings among his brethren, and very kind. We passed on over an excellent road, macadamized like the roads of our own country; and awoke about five in the morning while entering Oppeln, a large pleasant town with a council-house and other public buildings, a good specimen of the general cleanness and neatness of the Prussian towns. The inns afford every comfort to the traveller, and the boys, with satchel on back, hastening to school showed us that we were in Protestant Prussia. Here we were made aware of a regulation of the Schnell-post worth recording. If one waggon be full, the travellers are forwarded in a second; if that be filled, a third is provided, so that no traveller can be disappointed of a place.

We left Oppeln while the new-risen sun was glancing sweetly along the river Oder, upon which it lies, surrounded with pleasant walks. At a churchyard in the suburbs the funeral service was being performed over someone at this early hour. Men, women and children, a decent company, all kneeling round the grave. It was a cheerful resting-place for the dead, the graves being laid out in the form of small gardens and a beautiful bloom of flowers covering most of them. The drive to Breslau has little to interest a traveller. The road is uniformly lined with trees (often fine poplars) at regular distances; the fields are cultivated with great care and beauty by a peasantry who seem industrious and happy; and on the horizon, we generally caught a glimpse of a thriving village with its spire, and tall poplars vying with the spire. We frequently passed on the road the travelling journeymen, so common in Germany, all covered with dust. They go from town to town to gain experience in their trade. Occasionally, too, we met a travelling Jew. After taking our midday meal at Brieg, a town with an old church, and fountain in the market place, in two hours more we passed through Ohlau with its fields of tobacco and about five o'clock in the evening entered Breslau. Occasionally some of our companions during this journey were Jews. But we could hardly recognise them except by their features. The beard, the dress, the language, the manners, in a word, all that gives them nationality is gone and they seem desirous to imitate the Christian population in every thing. At one place, two Jewesses came into the post-waggon. Mr Calman recognised them at once as belonging to his nation, though their gay dress and manners indicated nothing different from those around them. He told them of the Holy Land but could not get them interested; indeed, they were quite unwilling to be recognised as belonging to Israel.

October 17

Early in the morning, a Roman Catholic monk came to our room in the inn, asking charity for the hospital. We did not refuse him, although we saw that the design of the papists in being thus forward in supporting such institutions is to gain public confidence and credit for humanity. Soon after another came asking us to give a little for the Sisters of Charity, telling us their good deeds to the sick and poor. But this we positively refused to do, telling the monk that we were Protestants and that we could not countenance Popery in any way, however indirect.

Breslau is a fine old town, surrounded by a trench, and containing 90,000 inhabitants. The banks of the river Oder, on which it stands, have pleasant walks, shaded with trees, and there are many trees gracefully planted throughout the town. The oldest houses are built of wood and are strange crazy-looking structures. There is one fine old square used as a market-place, where the houses have the gable end toward the street, some forming a sharp angle, others of a fanciful shape. In the centre is a bronze statue of Neptune standing on dolphins, with a fine jet d'eau bursting forth from his trident. At one place, there is a fine statue of Blücher,[1] with one hand grasping the sword and the other lifted up, as he addresses his army in these words inscribed below, *Mit Gott für Konig und Vaterland* (With God's help for King and Fatherland). There are eleven Protestant and thirteen Roman Catholic churches, several of the latter being ancient and spacious.

We visited the University, a large antique building on one side looking out upon the river. The session was not begun, so that we saw only the classrooms, venerable and spacious, like those of our own Universities. We then visited one of the gymnasia or Prussian schools, so justly celebrated over the world. There were 100 children present in the same room, arranged in three classes – the first containing children from four to six years of age, the second from six to ten, and the third from ten to fifteen. They began by singing a hymn, *'Gott ist gut'*, the girls singing the air, the boys the tenor, while the master accompanied them on the violin. All sang from music books, and the effect was pleasing and delightful. The teacher offered up a short prayer, after which every scholar produced and shewed his pencil, paper-book, etc., and sat down to draw, the girls copying flowers and patterns, the boys

---

[1] Field Marshall G. L. Blücher was a distinguished soldier in the Prussian Army and played an important role in the Battle of Waterloo (1815).

plans of architecture, etc. This was the employment of that hour; and all the scholars are required to provide themselves with pencil, compasses, and rule, which are kept in a case and carried along with them. They learn Luther's '*Kleiner Catechismus*' or 'Shorter Catechism', and read the New Testament. The passages of Scripture to be committed to memory are written upon a black board, and also the lessons for next day. They seemed fine quiet children, very tidy, and several young Israelites were among them. All pay about 8d. per month. On our retiring, they rose and whispered softly with one voice '*Adieu*'.

We now found our way to the house of Dr Neumann, a converted Jew of established Christian character and one of the five professors in the University of Breslau who are of the seed of Abraham according to the flesh. He and his lady and son received us very kindly. His eldest son is minister of some Protestant Germans who settled at Rio Janeiro in Brazil and sent for him to come and labour among them. His second son is a doctor of medicine, a fine young man, who speaks English well.

Of the 90,000 inhabitants of Breslau, there may be 30,000 Roman Catholics and 54,000 Lutherans. Rationalism cannot be said to be on the wane in this quarter, for many of the ministers and professors hold these views and few indeed stand up to oppose its progress. The recent death of Olshausen was a severe loss to those who defend the truth. There are probably 6,000 Jews, although some make their number 2,500 families, and they have twelve synagogues. During this year nine Jews had been baptized, but in other years many more. In 1836 there were twenty-six baptisms. The great majority of the Jews here are casting off the Talmud, and the Bible along with it. They are very careless of their religious observances, the young Jews never observing their own Sabbath, but keeping their shops open, neglecting even the morning and evening prayers which they leave to be performed by the old men. Many, it is said, are baptized without making it publicly known. In the rest of Silesia there are about 10,000 Jews of a similar character, among whom a missionary who could speak German might labour with the full approbation of Government, and with good prospects of success.

In the evening we resolved to visit the Jewish quarter, and on our way met an interesting old Jew from Kempfen who took us to their finest synagogue, a large building with windows of stained glass. There were not more than a dozen Jews met for evening prayer, and one of them was a soldier. Yet few as they were, they seemed to be very devotional. In the shop of a Jewish bookseller, we asked a young Jewess if she liked to read the Bible; she replied at once, 'No'. We purchased here some copies of a prayer-book for travellers. On our way to our inn, we noticed many of the signboards in the Hebrew character.

October 18
We started at 9 am in the *Eilwaagen* for Posen, twenty-one German or one hundred and five English miles due north from Breslau, through a country of the most uninteresting sameness of character, and over roads of loose sand the greater part of the way. About eight miles from Breslau, in another direction, the 400 Tyrolese who lately left their native valleys because of their attachment to the Protestant faith are settled in the Coppal mountains. At three we entered the village of Prausnitz, while the bells were tolling the requiem of some deceased citizen. In the Prussian villages there is always a large square in which the houses have their gable end toward the street, and the broad cross beams are visible, giving the houses a fantastic appearance. Many doors had the *mezuza* on the outside, and a Hebrew signboard appeared here and there. Out of a population of 2,000, there are 100 Jews.

The country is well cultivated, but not interesting. Traenberg is another clean village, with its square, old Popish church, and image at the gate. Ten Jewish families live here, and we spoke to some of their children on their way to the synagogue. There is a fine avenue of poplars close by, a handsome baronial residence, and a stream, being the seat of Baron Hartsfield, whose father was once Prussian ambassador to England. Late in the evening we passed through Rawitz, and during the night through Lizza, an important Jewish town, the native place of the rabbi of Glasgow.

October 19
Next day at noon we reached Posen, the chief city of the Grand Dutchy of Posen. It was the Jewish Sabbath, and as we passed through the pleasant Boulevard, we met numbers of well-dressed people walking for pleasure whom we recognised at once by their features to be children of Israel. Like Popish Christians they make their Sabbath a day of show and parade. In the evening two Jewish boys guided us to the residence of Mr Bellson, the worthy Missionary of the London Society, who, with his wife, gave us an affectionate welcome. He is himself a Jewish convert from Cassel Hessen, and had laboured among his brethren in Holland for four years, in Bromberg for three years, and latterly in

Posen. We called with him on Mr Klee, a true lover of Israel, and a person of influence, and also on Dr Cohen, one of the most eminent medical men of the place, a man of learning, and a sincere convert from Judaism. From both of these men we experienced the kindest reception.

Posen has a population of 34,000, of whom 20,000 are Roman Catholics, 7,000 Protestants and about 7,000 Jews. There are three Protestant churches in the town, but it is only in the Garrison church that the gospel is preached in purity. Rationalism, of a more refined but not less dangerous kind than formerly, is still making progress. Very few even of those who seem to be truly pious people believe in the divine inspiration of the Old Testament and scarcely one among them ever studies the prophets.

The arbitrary attempt recently made by the late King of Prussia to unite the Reformed and Lutheran churches into one was resisted by a body of men who still maintain the ancient doctrine of the Lutherans, that 'the very body of Christ' is present under the elements of bread and wine in the Lord's Supper; but their opposition is grounded mainly upon the principle that the King's interference with the church in matters spiritual is sinful. They are in fact maintaining the great scriptural principle for which the Church of Scotland is now so earnestly contending – that the Church of Christ is free and not to be controlled by any civil power in matters purely ecclesiastical. There are two *gymnasia* in Posen to which the wealthier Jews send their children to be educated, so that they are fast renouncing the Talmud.

The Christians here take no interest in the conversion of the Jews, with the exception of a few pious men, such as those to whom we were introduced. And yet there are in the whole Grand Dutchy of Posen upwards of 73,000 Jews, there being some in every town of the province – a vast field for a Jewish Missionary. At the time of our visit, the London Society had three labourers in this part of the vineyard, none of them ordained, but one of them is a *Candidat Prediger*, or probationer, of the Prussian Church. Their labours are uninterrupted and they find them peculiarly interesting.

There were likewise seven missionary schools for Jewish children in different parts of the Grand Dutchy, under the superintendence of the missionaries and of an influential committee in Posen. Each of these is supported at an average expense of from £36 to £40 yearly. The teachers are required to be men regularly educated at a normal seminary, examined and licensed by Government, as none but such are allowed to teach a school in Prussia. The committee use their utmost endeavour to engage only such as give evidence of personal piety, though this is often matter of great difficulty. They never employ converted Jews, because this would excite a prejudice against the school. Not long ago one of their teachers, who had become very decided in his views of divine truth, joined the Lutherans on which account the Government threatened to displace him. In all the schools the children receive the common Prussian education. Hebrew is not taught, for that would require a teacher of higher attainments; but the Old Testament is used as a schoolbook, and the teachers freely introduce the histories and doctrines of the New Testament. In more than one school the New Testament itself has been introduced, and in one the children are acquainted both with the New Testament and the elements of Church History.

It is a wonderful providence of God that the Jews are willing to send their children to schools conducted on such principles. In towns, where the Jews have schools of their own, it would not be possible to draw away the children and prevail on them to attend a missionary school; but in small villages, where there are no other means of education, the Government oblige the children to attend. There are many such places in the Grand Dutchy where schools might still be planted with good hope of success, and the Jewish children are most anxious to attend and have been known to entreat their parents with tears to allow them to become scholars.

In the town of Posen the school had for a time been nearly dispersed on account of the baptism of two of the girls. After this event it was reduced all at once from eighty-three scholars to thirteen, in consequence of the threats of the rabbis. But storms of this kind have occurred before, are to be expected, and may soon blow over. Our own missionaries in India have several times experienced the same trial after the baptism of native converts. The late King of Prussia, the present King (at that time Crown Prince), and other members of the Royal family, were in the habit of receiving an annual report of these schools, and returning to the missionaries their thanks, along with their subscriptions. This was instrumental in inducing the Jews to treat the missionaries with kindness, because they believed them to be in favour with Government.

October 20, Sabbath
Mr Bellson conducted us to the Garrison church to hear a sermon from Mr Niese, an Evangelical minister, who had lately come. All the serious

people attend there, because it is the only church in Posen where they can hear 'the words of eternal life'. It is also the fashionable church, because the officers of the garrison are to be found there. It was crowded, and we had to stand in the passages along with many others, including some devout men from the country, who wore ear-rings according to the custom of the place. After a very short Liturgy, the congregation joined in a psalm, and though there was a large organ leading, the sound of it was almost drowned in the full swell of human voices, carrying all the parts of music in a way unknown in our churches.

After a short preface, the minister read out the text, Ephesians 6:12, 'We wrestle not with flesh and blood', during the reading of which all stood up. He began by remarking that though some might think this passage suited soldiers best, yet every Christian is a soldier; even in times of perfect peace there is war around him. One of his chief foes is the devil – the leader of a host – the unseen 'ruler of darkness', who is crafty, suiting himself to the dispositions of every man; if he be a poor man, tempting him to murmur, if rich, to be proud. Therefore we must take the 'whole armour of God'. The 'righteousness' here spoken of is Christ's righteousness; for our own could never give us courage to stand. The word of God is 'the sword', as we see it proved to be when Christ used it against the devil, giving him always this stroke, '*Es steht geschrieben, Es steht geschrieben, Es steht geschrieben*' (It is written, It is written, It is written'). We overcome through him in the same way. And (said he) '*Christi Bruder ist Satans überwinder*' (A brother of Christ is a conqueror of Satan). Therefore, watch. A soldier on watch cries to each that passes, 'Who's there?' *(Wer da?)* But is that all? No, he must seek help. Therefore, also 'pray'. He then, in a strain of most animated eloquence, suiting his gestures to the words, spoke of the 'hope of salvation' and made allusion to the battle of Leipsic, the anniversary of which had taken place the preceding week, as a time when for seven years there had been one cry through all Germany, *Mit Gott für Konig und Vaterland* (With God's help, for king and country). So must it be with us till our conflicts are crowned with victory. A short prayer followed, after which he pronounced a blessing, the people sang a hymn, and dismissed. It was an interesting audience, and an impressive service; yet we were told that many were offended, for they are not much accustomed to hear the truth.

In the evening we met together in Mr Bellson's for prayer and conversation on the Scriptures. Dr Cohen and Mr Klee were present and at their request we conducted worship in English. There was also present an interesting young man who is condemned to imprisonment for life in the fortress because in his college days he had joined a conspiracy against kings and governments. He has been lately impressed with the truth and by the influence of Mr Klee has his bonds often loosed.

October 21

We found only eleven Jewish children at the missionary school in Posen, and these very young, the rest being for the present deterred from attendance by the influence of the rabbi. The teacher appeared to be a man of an excellent spirit. He examined his class upon the early life of Christ, and then they sang a hymn, while he led them on the violin; one little girl, named Lina, accompanied him with the voice by herself in another hymn. Up to the time of the baptisms this was a flourishing school. There were at one time twelve children in it of whose real conversion the teacher had every reason to hope well; and two of these were the girls lately baptized.

The average number attending the seven missionary schools in this province in the year 1839 was 267. In several of them an evening class is maintained, which is frequently well attended by elderly Jews, even married men. In Posen as many as forty or fifty have come, induced chiefly by the desire to learn writing, though reading and explaining the Scriptures are always the principal business of the class. All the schools are gratuitous, for if the parents had to pay they would not send a single scholar. Every teacher gives in a monthly report of his school to the missionaries, marking the attendance or absence of the children every day, and stating their progress and behaviour. Subjoined is a specimen of the attendance of the children during five months in 1839:

	April	May	June	July	Aug.
At Margonim	44	42	32	34	40
... Evening Class	27	30	25	21	27
At Storchnest	27	25	26	26	26
... Evening Class	21	16	16	16	15
At Kempen	59	60	61	60	60
At Inaworclaw	21	46	48	34	20
At Schlichtingsheim	24	25	25	....	....
At Posen	58	67	76	39	33
At Rogasin	....	....	24	30	32

The books used are the usual elementary schoolbooks, a book of history for children, and the Old Testament. The evening classes are not considered to be under the charge of Government and therefore the system pursued in them is not so complete, nor the reports so full. In their reports the teachers frequently mention the impressions made on the minds of the children by what they hear of the Saviour.

The girl mentioned as baptized nine months previous to our visit was Bertha Louisa Brache. She was one who had been under deep impressions of divine truth for four years; but the teacher, to whose instrumentality she owed her knowledge of the truth, removed to another station a great way off in Prussian Poland, so that she had no-one to whom she might open her mind. Bertha, however, became very decided in her views. Her mother was dead, and her father being her only companion, she loved him exceedingly; but he was a determined Jew and bitterly opposed her desire to be a Christian, so that she resolved to seek baptism and a refuge elsewhere than in Posen. One morning she set out very early, with her Bible and hymnbook, to find out her teacher who now lived so far off; but her father, suspecting which way she would go, pursued and overtook her. On being brought back, she said that as she went along that morning she was exceedingly happy, singing hymns and reading the Word of God freely. Her father treated her very severely, taking every book from her, even her Bible, and not suffering her to attend school; at last she made her escape a second time, and her case becoming known, a very excellent man, who has an estate at Pinne, six miles from town, took her into his family. She was baptized at Pinne by the worthy pastor of the parish, Dr Klee, and seldom has there been a more impressive scene than that baptism. The other girl, whose conversion is also very decided, is named Maria Charlottina Wilensia.

In the evening a meeting of the committee who superintend the schools was held at Mr Bellson's house. There were present two officers from the garrison, affectionate, Christian men, who embraced us in the German fashion, kissing each cheek. Dr Cohen also attended, and one of the pastors of the Garrison Church, a worthy man, yet like some other of the good people of Germany, totally ignorant of the Old Testament, and not reckoning it inspired. We had some interesting converse with this person in Latin, and surprised him not a little by telling him that in Scotland we all received the Old Testament with the same reverence as the New. We removed some of his objections, but he knew so little that he could scarcely find out the books to which we referred in the common

German Bible. He told us that he had read some of Dr Chalmers's works translated into German and desired much to see his sermons. We had often heard the missionaries remark that those Christians in Germany who take a lively interest in the Jews, are all of the persons who have begun to take an interest in the Old Testament; but this clergyman seemed to be an exception. How defective must be the knowledge, sanctification, and spiritual attainments of many German Christians, since 'all Scripture is given by inspiration of God, and is profitable for doctrine ... *that the man of God may be perfect, thoroughly furnished unto all good works*'. How thankful ought we to be that we live in a land where from our youth we are taught that every word of the Holy Bible is divine.

The teacher's salary in their Jewish schools is only £20 annually, and a present varying from a few dollars to £3. The female teacher who is engaged two hours a-day in teaching the girls knitting and sewing receives £4 a year. The rent of school-room, cost of materials, etc. must be added to this, and about £5 at the outset to fit up the room. So that the whole cost of maintaining a Posen missionary school is from £35 to £40 a year. At how small a sacrifice may Christians in this country open up more of these 'wells of salvation' for Jewish children who are 'ready to perish' in Prussian Poland.

We left Posen at 12 o'clock the same night in company with Mr Bellson, to visit one of the Jewish schools at Storchnest, being anxious to be there next morning *(October 22)* in time to see its operations. The blowing of the bugle in the Prussian *Post-waagen* is a very enlivening sound. The *Suarrow* or driver imitates the sounds of the horses going at different rates of speed. *'Blasen sie "Die Fahr-post"'*, said Mr Bellson, and the driver imitated the sound of the common mail coach. Then *'Blasen sie "Die Schnell-post"'* and he gave us the rate of the express-post.

We retraced part of our Breslau journey for three posts and then turned off to Storchnest. The morning was dull and hazy; we were well wrapped up in cloaks and furs, and Mr B[ellson] occasionally beguiled the way with Hebrew chants, till about 10 in the morning we reached Storchnest, a small quiet village with a green in the centre. We found thirty-eight children in the school, of whom only fifteen were girls, all very poor, but having fine Jewish faces. As there are no other means of education, the Government makes it obligatory on the Jewish children to attend this missionary school, and the Burgomaster of the village is warden and must take care that this is done. The teacher seemed a good young man and the children were reading the life of Joseph in the German Bible as we entered. We afterwards heard them examined on Bible history, grammar, geography and natural history, in all which they answered well. Lastly, they sang sweetly three of Luther's Hymns, the teacher playing the violin. On the whole, we were reminded of a well-conducted small parish school in Scotland; only the singing was far more beautiful.

We then proceeded to Lissa, a town of 10,000 inhabitants, of whom 4,000 are Jews. It was here that Emma de Lissau lived; and her relations are still here. The Jews of Lissa are noted for bigotry and attachment to Judaism, and the missionaries, though they sometimes visit it to discuss the truth with their learned men, have no opportunity to preach to the people because the Protestant clergyman is a rationalist and opposes them.

At evening we came in sight of Fraustadt, said to be one of the cleanest towns in Prussia. The number of windmills erected near the town is quite remarkable. Ninety-nine were in sight, all in active operation grinding corn, which is carried to Berlin and the towns around. We spent the evening at Fraustadt with Mr Hartmann, a probationer of the United Church of Prussia, and one of the missionaries of the London Society. Mr Graff, another of their missionaries, also joined our party, for these two make Fraustadt their headquarters and both seem 'workmen that need not to be ashamed'.

Mr Hartmann is allowed to preach in almost all the churches of the Grand Dutchy of Posen and of Silesia, and this liberty he uses on Saturdays in preaching to the Jews. When the missionaries arrive in a town, they spread among the Jews a few printed notices intimating their arrival, and also that there will be sermon at such an hour, mentioning the text or theme. These sermons in the parish church are attended by a congregation of Jews and Jewesses from 200 to 500 in number. They behave quietly, not answering again, as they would do in a room; only when he quotes a passage of Scripture (which he always does in Hebrew), they repeat the quotation along with him and sometimes correct him if he makes a slip in any word. He preaches to them plainly that Messiah is come, and that Jesus is the Messiah. On one occasion, he preached in the parish church of Krotosheim to an audience of nearly 800 Jews who listened with great propriety and stillness till he came to the end, when he began to declare in the most explicit terms that Jesus Christ was the Messiah. This he had no sooner done than they rose and left the church in great confusion. At Pleschen, where there are only 600 Jews, he had lately a congregation of 300 and at Kobylin there were 200. On such occasions the children attending the missionary schools delight to be present and often bring their friends.

At the three fairs held at Frankfort-on-the-Oder, the missionaries attend and preach to great congregations of Jews, both on the Saturday and Sunday. Mr H[artmann] preaches once a-month at Walstein, and once a-month at Glogau, but if there were more either of *candidats* or of ordained missionaries, they would traverse not only the Grand Dutchy, but Silesia also. These two affectionate Germans told us that they had been labouring for twelve years in this province, and they observe a very marked change in the state of the Jewish mind. Twelve years ago the Jews would not have come near a Christian church, nor were they willing to converse upon matters that affected their soul. But now they seem to be convinced in their heads that Judaism is false and that Christianity may be true; but they feel not the burden of sin, and therefore do not really change. The present is the time for Christians to use every effort to send the gospel to them, otherwise infidelity in some form will occupy their minds. What a sphere is this for missionary labour? Here we might have our Scottish system of a parish school and a parish church realized among the many thousands of Israel! Nowhere have we yet seen such an inviting field to one who feels that the simple proclamation of the glad tidings is a minister's chief duty. He may go through the provinces freely, enter the churches, assemble Israel, and, like another Paul, declare to them 'the hope of Israel' as already come.

Mr Bellson, by way of contrast, related some of the difficulties he had met with in labouring among the Jews of Holland. There are 25,000 Jews in Amsterdam, but many of them being rich and influential are difficult of access and bitter in opposition, while the meaner Jews do not hesitate to show their dislike on the streets. On one occasion, they beset his house and tried to raise a tumult. A man of a peculiar mould might be useful there, one who could face much opposition; and it appeared to us that our Scottish churches in Amsterdam and Rotterdam would render the efforts of our missionaries more easy.

October 23

We left Fraustadt, accompanied by the three brethren, all in the missionary waggon as they called it, a car drawn by two active ponies, and driven by Joseph, a Roman Catholic, but a useful servant in gathering the Jews together when we visit small towns.

We shortened the journey by conversing on Israel and the labours and prospects of the missionaries, and soon reached Schlichtingsheim, a neat Polish village, built in the form of a square, with pleasant grass and trees in the centre. In the school were twenty-three Jewish children, all young. The elder scholars had very lately left the school, after completing their term of attendance, which is eight years. There are only twenty Jewish families in the village, and every child of the specified age was present. The scholars were lively and interested; and the teacher seemed to have the true art of fixing their attention. He examined them on the books of Moses. When they repeated the promise that the seed of the woman should bruise the serpent's head, he asked, 'Who is this?' They replied, 'Messiah.' He then asked for the next prophecy in the Bible in regard to him. They quoted the words of Jacob, 'The sceptre shall not depart from Judah till Shiloh come', and said that Jesus Christ was foretold there. He pointed to a map of Palestine and asked them to show Bethlehem, bidding them tell who was born there. They quoted Micah's prophecy and explained it of the birth of Christ. They then pointed out Nazareth and other places in the Holy Land, telling what had happened at the several towns. The Burgomaster, himself a baptized Jew, turned to us and said, 'These children have more knowledge of Christianity in their hearts than the children of the Christians.' The teacher has an excellent method of dealing with the children, for he rather makes them draw him out to speak to them of Christianity, than forces it upon them. They have frequently asked him to allow them to read in the New Testament, which he sometimes does, and we saw their German Bibles piled up, each containing the New Testament. Each child has also a manuscript book of hymns well thumbed, the music written in figures. The parents are either too indifferent to make objections, or their own faith in Judaism is shaken. The teacher then examined them in mental arithmetic, in which it is said that the Jewish boys always excel. He also shewed us specimens of their writing and drawing; and they ended by singing one of Luther's hymns, *Lobe den herrn*.

At one of these schools, on the day before Christmas, the teacher told the children that there would be no meeting of the school next day and explained the reason. He was surprised in the course of the afternoon when some of them requested to be allowed to come next day and learn about the Saviour whose birth he was to celebrate. He gladly consented; and accordingly next day almost all the children came, and he then enjoyed the fullest opportunity of instructing them in the knowledge of Jesus.

A similar incident occurred to another teacher. When walking in the fields one day with some of the children, they gathered round him and entreated him to tell them about his Messiah. He immediately sat down with them in the field and fully proclaimed the Saviour to his little flock.

In the school at Kempen, we were told that there are children who really appear to have the grace of God in their hearts. The same has been the case in the school at Posen, so that God is pouring out his Spirit on the seed of Jacob.

We set out again in the missionary waggon for Glogau, passing through a village which a few years ago was swept away by the Oder overflowing its banks, but which is now rebuilt. An interesting anecdote here related to us shows what blessed effects might flow forth upon the Jews if the Prussian Christians among whom they live were all Christians indeed. An aged Jew was sitting one summer evening beside a really Christian woman, before her cottage door, as is the custom in Germany. The Jew said to her, 'If you would tell what you really think, you would say that Jesus is not the Son of God.' She answered very solemnly, 'As sure as we are sitting here, and the sun shining from heaven, so surely is Jesus the Son of God, and very God himself; and unless you believe in him you must surely perish.' He made no reply, but went home, and soon after took to his bed and was evidently at the gates of death. The Jews, according to their manner, lighted candles; but once and again he revived. At last he cried, *'Herr Jesu'*, Lord Jesus, 'Have mercy upon me!' Upon this, all the Jews left him, and he died alone, calling loudly on the name of the Lord Jesus.

Another anecdote was told us of a less pleasant nature. Some time ago, when the missionaries were travelling through the Dutchy of Posen, they met a poor Jew who asked alms and told them his history. He had had a large family of daughters, but no sons; and had become excessively anxious that the next birth in his family might be a son. He prayed earnestly for this, and went so far as to say that if God would grant his request, he would submit to any suffering or disease and would even be willing that his wife and daughters should die. Some years after, his wife did bear a son, but she herself was shortly after removed by death. Next one of his daughters sickened, and died; then another, till at last all were taken from him. To crown his misery, he himself was seized with that loathsome disease, so common among Polish Jews, the *plica polonica*, and at the same time was reduced to poverty. He considered himself as a monument of the severe justice of God, who had thus punished him for insisting upon a change in the arrangements of his Providence.

Crossing a wide drawbridge, we entered Glogau, a fortified town on the Oder, having 12,000 inhabitants; of whom 1,500 are Jews. It has several Protestant churches, one of which is built of brick and is 500 years old. Its gymnasium is reckoned one of the best in Prussia for teaching the Latin language. We called upon one of the Evangelical clergy, Pastor Anders, a young but faithful minister, who is exposed to much reproach for his Master's name. He spoke with us in Latin, making many inquiries into the constitution of the Church of Scotland.

We here parted with deep regret from our three missionary friends. Although our acquaintance had been so recently formed, we had nevertheless found each other to be brethren, and our hearts were knit together in love to the same Lord and in compassion for Israel.

And now looking back on the view we then obtained of the field of labour in Prussian Poland, our sense of its importance has been deepened rather than diminished. It has many peculiar advantages:

1. *The Jewish Schools*, under the superintendence of the Missionaries, are not confined in their range of instruction to the common elements of a general education. The aim steadily kept in view has been to give the young Jews such instruction as will lead them to Christ. The Committee have succeeded in finding godly men, trained in the normal schools of Prussia, who are willing for a small salary to devote themselves to this work. There was something in these schools that made us feel as if we were visiting our own parochial schools in Scotland; only they were Jewish villages that sent forth the groups of playful children, and Jewish parents that came to make excuses for an absent scholar. The instances of conversion that have occurred show that they have 'the good will of Him that dwelt in the Bush', for already young olive plants in this soil are partaking of the fatness of Judah's true olive-tree. Many more such schools might be added if the Committee had the means; indeed, they might be multiplied to an indefinite extent. Surely some Christian hearts will be touched with pity for the children of Zion, 'who faint for hunger at the top of every street' (Lamentations 2:19). Since our visit, three additional schools have been set in operation by the contribution of Christians in Scotland; and the ease with which

this has been done, proves how possible it would be to multiply them.

2. Along with these interesting schools, a missionary here has *an open door for preaching the word to the Jews*. Perhaps there is at present no other place where one whose delight is to lift up his voice as a herald of divine truth to Israel, could find such an opportunity of gratifying his desire. The missionary has free access every week to the parish churches, if he be inclined to avail himself of the privilege, and on such occasions may be seen a crowd of Jews and Jewesses, with their children running by their side, moving to church to hear the Word of truth proclaimed. Particular occasions also, such as the Frankfort Fair, furnish them with even wider opportunities. Let a man of apostolic mind and energy arise, and unimpeded by Government, he may stand in the midst of Jewish multitudes, proclaiming, 'Ho, every one that thirsteth, come ye to the waters!'

3. *The state of the Jewish mind* in this province at present is most favourable to missionary efforts. In other places they delight to enter into controversy, here they have patience to listen to the exposition of the Word; and parents manifest an extraordinary, unsuspecting readiness to send their children to the schools. The authority of the Talmud with the mass of Jews is altogether shaken; and yet they have adopted no other system in its room, as if God were keeping open the door for Christian labourers. The fact, too, that there have been more converts from the Jews of this province than from any other country, of itself would confirm the favourable hopes that might be entertained from further exertions among them. And, when to all this we add that the qualifications required for a well-furnished missionary are by no means difficult of attainment, being simply a fluency in the German tongue, and a good knowledge of pointed Hebrew, does there not open to the view a field 'white and ready to harvest'? It is not a controversialist that is here required, but rather one who, having the unction of the Spirit, would, like Paul at Rome, 'expound and testify the kingdom of God, persuading them concerning Jesus, both out of the law of Moses, and out of the prophets, from morning till evening' (Acts 28:23).

After our missionary brethren had departed, Mr Klopsch, Director of the Gymnasium, called upon us, and invited us to spend the evening with his family. We complied, and were received with the utmost warmth of affection. Besides his wife, his three boys were in the room, and his daughter continued to work busily at the spinning wheel all the evening, while taking an active share in the conversation at the same time. With the old Director our whole conversation was carried on in Latin, and we understood one another easily. One of his seven surviving children he had called 'Immanuel', because his mother's life was despaired of at his birth, but God *was with her*; another he named 'Reinardt' *(i.e. pure-hearted)*, to intimate the purity of heart required by God; and so with the others. When we asked why he had not given names to his daughters on the same principle, he replied, 'Because at the time of their birth, I myself did not know the Lord.' At his desire, we described the present state of Palestine, while he and his family put many questions about the towns and places mentioned in Holy Writ. He told us that there are forty Jewish boys attending the gymnasium here; some of whom left the Roman Catholic gymnasium and came to him because he was kind to Jews. Of one Jewish boy he had much hope, for he came of his own accord, like Nicodemus, and asked to be taught concerning the Christian faith. He knew a good deal about Scotland, and said that the visit of a German traveller, Gemba, who described the manner in which the Sabbath is kept by the Scottish people, first drew forth his love to our country. He was interested in the questions at present agitating our Church and had already heard that the *Veto Law* was pronounced illegal. He seemed to appreciate fully the Scriptural constitution of our church in being free from all civil control in matters spiritual, and felt deeply that the treatment of the Lutheran church by the Prussian King was an act of encroachment by the civil power, resulting from their church possessing no spiritual jurisdiction distinct from the State. One of his favourite books was Rutherford's *Letters*, which have been translated into German.

During the evening, a German *Candidat* came in and joined the conversation in Latin, and also a gentle Moravian with his wife, from whom Mr Calman received an interesting account of some of their settlements. The company of believers seems to be very small in Glogau, but they are full of love. They have to suffer many things. Meetings for prayer are not allowed, lest they should be used for political purposes, and when they wished to have a Sabbath evening school in the church, the police prohibited it, on the pretence that the church might be set on fire, though the theatre is open with its blazing lustres every night. We told them how different it was in happy Scotland. Late in the evening, we bade them an affectionate farewell, happy to have had a glance into one of the believing families of Prussia.

October 24

We left Glogau in a raw foggy morning, before dawn, and in two hours were at Klopschen. Soon after we passed through Neusaltz, a Moravian village where Kolmeister lives, a venerable missionary who laboured for thirty years at Labrador. At midday verdant vineyards were on each side of the road, on the sloping hills around the pleasant town of Grunberg. Toward evening we reached Lessen, where the Oder is joined by another stream. The broad river, the opposing hill, mantled with vines, and the handsome church, gave it a beautiful aspect. The dark blue kerchief which the women wear on the head in addition to their white caps, gives them a singular appearance.

By nine o'clock we arrived at Frankfort-on-the-Oder, and next morning by daylight entered the capital of Prussia.

Berlin is now so well known in this country that any lengthened description would be here out of place. It is really a handsome city, situated upon a plain, with the Spree, a tributary of the Elbe, flowing through it, spanned by many bridges. The public buildings have much of the air of royalty about them. The castle, the museum, the dome church, the theatre with a church on each side (a painful combination, and an emblem, it is to be feared, of the state of religion in Prussia), are all handsome buildings, worthy of such a capital. The long walk under the linden-trees, with the king's palace and many fine houses on either side, all the way up to the splendid Brandenburg gate, forms one of the finest promenades in Europe. The streets are wide and lively, without being overcrowded like those of London and Paris.

October 25

Our main object being to acquire information regarding the Jews, we eagerly sought out Mr Becker, missionary of the London Society. We found him engaged with the captain of police, in a consultation about some Jews who had come from Poland without a pass, professing to wish baptism, and one of whom at least seemed really in earnest. Up to 1830 Mr Becker was maintained by the Edinburgh Jewish Society and laboured in Magdeburg until he was compelled by the late Duke to leave that station. He was then engaged at Frankfort-on-the-Maine, and latterly at Berlin. During the year then past, fifty-four inquiring Jews had come to him, of whom he had baptized five, but many had drawn back. There were about 5,000 Jews in Berlin, though others make the number 8,000; and between 900 and 1,000 proselytes. Of the latter, the great proportion are very poor, a few only rich, but these have no concern about the salvation of their brethren. Two Jews came in while we were with Mr Becker, one an inquirer, the other a baptized convert, a rabbi from Galacia, named Abraham, whom he had met in London, and who had been lately sent over to study under Mr Becker's care. He is a very learned man, but proud, and unwilling to submit to the labour of acquiring elementary knowledge at his time of life.

There is a society in Berlin for aiding in the support of poor proselytes and inquirers, and which is thought to be absolutely needful. The plan is not to give help directly, but in return for labour, getting pious men to employ inquirers or proselytes at their different trades. In the evening we met with the Committee of this Society and were introduced to the Rev. Mr Kuntze and Mr Focke, the Secretary. We heard a statement of thirty cases of those who receive support. 'Most of our experiences are sad (said Focke), but some are joyful.' One of their first steps was to advertise for Christian masters, who from love would be willing to take Jewish inquirers and converts as apprentices. Thirty-three masters agreed to this, but it was not all of them that had patience and long-suffering with the young Jews sufficient to lead them to persevere. They thought an *Institution for proselytes* would be advisable, where they might be fed and watched over, and from which they might be sent out as apprentices, for at present they sleep each in the house of his master. They had been instrumental in relieving the wants of about seventy proselytes during that year, the support granted differing in different cases, some requiring clothes and everything necessary; only they never give help directly, but always in return for labour. The '*Basle Freund des Israel*', published at Basle, is conducted on the same principles.

Mr Becker mentioned that he had preached at the gaol on the previous Sabbath to 400 prisoners, among whom were forty Jews. The Director is a good man and has been useful to several of the prisoners, and among others to a young Jew. This youth was confined two years for theft, during which time he learned the catechism and much of the Bible, and now that he is set at liberty, he comes regularly to the missionary asking in good earnest what must he do to be saved. Mr Focke also told us of a man who had murdered his mother and who, during his confinement, appeared to be truly converted. The minister who attended him said that his confession of sin was the deepest he had ever heard.

It was likewise mentioned that three persons of note had lately laid before the King of Prussia a proposal that the European powers should at this time bring Jerusalem again under Christian sway, or give it into the hands of the Jewish nation by a bloodless crusade. The king answered that he highly approved of their object, but that he had no influence and advised them to lay the proposal before the other powers of Europe. They were said not to be religious men, but men moved by general views of philanthropy.

Dr Neander,[2] though himself an Israelite by birth, takes no special interest in his brethren. He cannot be made to see that means ought to be used for their conversion, and his opinion is that the efforts of societies are not to succeed. On the other hand, Dr Hengstenberg[3] has done much for the Jewish cause, and has frequently recommended it to his students.

Walking home with the faithful Kuntze, we received from him an account of the religious state of the capital. Berlin has a population of 250,000 souls, and seventy churches of different denominations. Three ministers and two churches have been added lately upon the principle of our Church Extension Scheme, for the Government discovered that the population had greatly increased, while scarcely one additional church had been built for a hundred years. Some rich people subscribed to the new churches, but the Government was the chief promoter of the scheme. Rationalism is not in fashion at Berlin; only three of the ministers are Rationalists, and these are not attended by more than fifty hearers. The late king was a supporter of all good things, though he did not firmly press on his ministers all that he himself saw to be right. The present King (at that time Crown Prince), was thought to be much more decided, and supported the truth in direct opposition to all his father's Neologian councillors. Three of the King's ministers, of whom Kuntze is one, preach the gospel unflinchingly. There is also some success accompanying the preached word in Berlin, and many come inquiring what they must do to be saved. Gossner, who was brought to the

---

[2] Johann Neander (1789-1850) was born of Jewish parents and he changed his name from David Mendel to Neander (new man) on his baptism in 1806. He taught at Hamburg, Heidelberg, and Berlin but without evangelical commitment.

[3] E. W. Hengstenberg (1802-1869) stood in marked contrast to Neander. From a strongly religious home he was converted while teaching intending missionaries at Basel. Thereafter he devoted his life to evangelical ministry as a professor and editor. He is best known for his volumes entitled *Christology of the Old Testament*.

knowledge of the truth through Martin Boos and wrote his life, is pastor of the Bohemian church here, and has been remarkably blessed in awakening souls. The real Christians of Berlin do take an interest in the cause of the Jews, but not equal to its vast importance, for missions to the heathen are far better supported. Kuntze himself is engaged every week in the instruction of inquirers, both Jewish and Gentile, and has baptized 112 Jews from the commencement of his labours, forty of whom were from the Grand Dutchy of Posen, and almost none from Berlin. 'It is a cause (he said) which needs much patience and long-suffering; but the more they are sunk and degraded, so much the more we should compassionate them. And how cheering is that promise, "As ye were a curse among the heathen, O house of Judah and house of Israel, so will I save you, and ye shall be a blessing"' (Zechariah 8:13).

October 26
Rabbi Abraham called and conducted us to one of the New School synagogues, connected with their seminary for youth. A choir of fine Jewish boys sat on either side; the older Jews, wearing no distinctive dress except the *Tallith* over the shoulders, sat in the middle; the women were placed by themselves, but not concealed by any latticework. After a short prayer, a fine Hebrew psalm was sung by the boys responsively, and then the rabbi, Dr Auerbach, gave an extempore prayer in German, and preached a sermon on Abraham offering up Isaac, enforcing from it the duty of serving and obeying God. His quotations from Scripture were given in Hebrew, but always followed up by a German translation. We spoke with several of the Jews present. One who had travelled with us from Breslau seemed a fine young man and seriously inclined. Another spoke with us in Latin. While leading us to the synagogue, he said that he still studies the Talmud, though he does not receive it as the Word of God, and that he believes the Old Testament to be divine. The old synagogue is a fine large building in the Gothic style, like that of Brody, but not so handsome.

We visited the splendid museum, which is freely open to the public; and afterwards called on Elsner, agent for the Bible and Tract Society, a warm-hearted, godly old German, a truly zealous and useful man, and one of those who are raised up by God to be the helps of the ministry in spreading the glad tidings over the world. He gave us the Reformation Tract, newly printed. The Saturday following was to be held as a sacred festival, in commemoration of the Reformation, it being exactly 300 years that day since first their King publicly owned the Reformed religion by partaking of the Lord's Supper in both kinds in the Old Church of Nicolai (2nd Nov. 1539). The present Royal Family had resolved to partake of the Lord's Supper in the same church on that day. On our way home we did not fail to visit this venerable structure, with its sharp-pointed spire, the Nicolai Kirche, where Bucholzer used to preach.

October 27, Sabbath

At nine, we went to hear Mr Becker preach in the Roman Catholic 'Kloster-Kirche', a dismal old church, built of brick, with galleries covered over with ancient paintings, and an immense image of Christ on the Cross with the women standing by, suspended from the roof. These do not suit our Presbyterian, nor even our Protestant taste, and must be an object of abhorrence to a Jew. There was a small congregation of serious old people, and a few Jews. We first heard the Lutheran liturgy, then a psalm, and a discourse on Exodus 23:21, 'My name is in him'. Mr Becker is in the habit of advertising in the newspapers the day before, the subject on which he is to preach, thus:

ADVERTISEMENT
'Return, ye backsliding children, and I will heal your backsliding.' The Old Testament discourse on Jeremiah 3:22, 23, will be given on the Fast-day, 24th April, at nine o'clock am, by Mr Becker, in the Kloster-Church.'

We next went to the Dom-Kirche, where the King and Royal Family generally attend. It is a modern building with a lofty fretted roof, supported by a range of pillars on either side. The altar is adorned with a beautiful painting, two lighted candles, and a crucifix. Five services are conducted here every Sabbath by different ministers, at different hours. As we entered we saw the conclusion of a marriage ceremony which was performed in front of the altar. A short liturgy was then read by an aged minister, and a fine choir of boys sang a hymn, aided by a noble organ. A younger minister preached on 'The two debtors', with a good deal of animation in his manner. Reading sermons, or even the use of notes, seems unknown among Prussian pastors.

At two we heard Mr Kuntze preach in the 'Waisen-Kirche' (Orphan-Church), to a large and evidently impressed audience. The singing was delightful, and the discourse delivered with great fervour and warmth from the words 'Ye were once darkness, but now are ye light in the Lord'. He referred in the course of his sermon to the Reformation, and the third jubilee of it to be celebrated that week. At every mention of the name of our Lord Jesus Christ, whether in prayer or in the sermon, the greater part of the congregation bowed their head. Most of them sat during prayer, though some kneeled, and some stood. After the blessing was pronounced, all sat still for a minute in deep silence, and then rose to depart home.

The Sabbath desecration of Berlin is most lamentable. It is not like the gay pleasure-day of Paris, nor like the day of show and parade in London, but it is like a common business-day. Most of the shops are open and busily frequented, and most of the people wear their weekday clothes. In the evening it was saddening to see the large theatres open and lighted up. Guilty city! Paris sins in comparative ignorance, but Berlin sins against the light of a faithfully preached gospel and the testimony of many holy believers.

October 28

We visited the Jewish school belonging to the New Synagogue, where 150 boys are educated. There are four classes, of which the highest is taught Hebrew thoroughly; one of the boys translated a portion of Isaiah while we were there. They have a small library apparatus for experiments in natural philosophy, and a piece of ground cultivated for the study of botany. The director, Auerbach, paid us every attention, gave us their printed reports, and conducted us through the orphan-house adjoining, where sixteen orphan children are maintained. When educated, these orphans are sent out to work under Christian masters, and two of them have been baptized.

At four o'clock we went to hear Gossner preach in the Bohemian Church. It was crowded with an audience of peculiarly solemn and devout worshippers. The king's brother and his lady are among his most regular hearers. He preaches with much fervour and great plainness, not sparing the sins of high or low. His remarks were often very pointed. 'Some of you cheat, lie, swear, and come to the Bohemian Church and are among my most attentive hearers, and why? That you may balance your sins with your devotions.' He preached first from the New Testament, and then from the Old, both discourses being very brief. At the close the congregation sang a missionary hymn, with special reference to their brethren who have gone to Australia; Gossner reading the line, and all singing in the sweetest manner.

We spent the evening with Mr Focke and learned something more of the brotherly love of German Christians. Mr F[ocke] is the translator of Rutherford's *Letters* and the works of some other Scottish writers into German.

October 29

We had an opportunity of hearing Dr Neander lecture for an hour to about 400 students. He stood without any gown, carelessly dressed in a brown surtout, leaning over a rude desk. His large shaggy eyebrows and prominent Jewish nose give an expression of depth and power to his face, but his whole manner and appearance are most ungainly. His utterance is very distinct, but with a good deal of effort, and with so many pauses that the students were able to write down every word; and when he came to any unusual proper name, he spelt it to them. The lecture was on the authorship of the Epistle to the Hebrews. In the midst of his dissertation the bell rang, whereupon he immediately closed his papers, scarcely finishing the sentence, bowed to the students, and was the first to leave the classroom. There is no prayer either at the commencement or close, for this would be considered *Pietism*. The Doctor is a singular man. When visitors go to call upon him, they have often to seek about his room in order to find him, for he is hidden behind shelves and folios. In conversation they must draw him out, question after question, for no-one gets from him more than he asks. Yet he is very kind to his students and entertains them twice a-week at tea.

Berlin University is now distinguished in all its branches. The great aim of the late king was to make it the first University in Germany, and he has succeeded by gathering the ablest men to be professors there. Its theology is on the whole the soundest of any in Germany. Hengstenberg is professor of Biblical Criticism and confines himself to the interpretation of the Old Testament. He seems to be the firmest and boldest opponent of Rationalism and German philosophy in all Germany, but there are not many professors who adhere to him. Neander is standing still while others are becoming more orthodox, and his views of inspiration would be condemned by every body of Christians in England.

We called upon Gossner and found him a lively warm-hearted old minister. He does not take a particular interest in the Jews. 'This is the time (said he) for angling them out one by one, but not for the general haul.' He spoke much of Martin Boos, saying, 'He was a man like Luther, but very mild, and I myself am a monument of his success.' He believed that the chief reason why Boos never joined any Protestant church was that he could not bear the coldness and infidelity so widely prevalent among them. Thirty-seven Bavarian priests were the fruit of his labour who continue in the Roman Catholic Church, yet preach the truth as it is in Jesus. Many of his people became Protestants, but others could not stand the trials to which they were subjected. He shewed us a picture which represents him with a cap on his head.

We had afterwards an interesting account of Gossner's own labours in St Petersburg. It is eighteen years since he was forced to part from his people there. Many in the Russian capital were becoming concerned about their souls under his ministry, and for this reason he was suddenly commanded to leave. Chained to a soldier, he was conducted out of Russia, when multitudes of his people followed him weeping as they went for ten miles, till he entreated them to return and implored a parting blessing upon them. Although so many years have elapsed, still some of his people meet together upon his birthday every year to pray that his useful life may be preserved. How lasting is the tie that unites a Christian people to their spiritual father!

We spent the evening with Mr Kuntze and two interesting Jewish converts, one a medical man, who desires earnestly to be employed as a medical missionary among his brethren, the other a useful member of the Berlin Society for Visiting the Sick, and both esteemed as truly Christian men. From them we learned something more of the real condition of Christ's kingdom in Berlin. Faithful ministers are on the increase and they maintain three meetings for ministerial conference and prayer. One of these contains seven pastors who meet every Monday evening for the study of the Scriptures, the Hebrew and Greek Bible and Hengstenberg's *Christology* being before them. After supper they go over each of the sermons of the past Sabbath, and communicate freely ministerial experiences and difficulties. What a salutary influence such meetings must exercise, and how worthy are they of imitation by the faithful pastors of our own beloved Church!

Sabbath schools are not allowed in Prussia. Mr K[untze] instituted them and carried them on quietly for three years, but they were put down by the Government on the ground that the teachers were not licensed. Even meetings for prayer are not allowed, through fear lest republican sentiments should be promoted! Yet Mr K[untze] holds a meeting every Wednesday evening in a large saloon in the house of Baron Kotswitz, a faithful old gentleman of eighty-three years of age, and this is filled to overflowing by an audience of above 400 persons. There are many awakened souls in Berlin asking the way to Zion, with their faces thitherward, and for the most part these are either in the highest ranks or in the poorest, the middle class being the most ungodly.

Several of the faithful pastors visit from house to house through their parish, as amongst ourselves, but generally with the help of a *Candidat*, owing to the vast extent of their parishes. The division of parishes is hindered by the minister's salary depending in great part on the marriage fees, etc., which would be much lessened by diminishing the parishes. The schools are entirely under the care of the clergy, so that they can direct the books to be read and the portions of Scripture to be learned. We parted from this affectionate servant of Christ after solemn prayer.

Next day we visited the Normal Seminary, conducted by Mr Diesterweg, reckoned one of the most skilful normal teachers in all Prussia, and an author on the subject. We found him in the upper room, instructing sixty young teachers in the elements of logic. Oral catechetical instruction seems to be one principle of the system. He proposes a question and all who are ready to answer hold up the forefinger. He names one who answers, then another, with the greatest rapidity, keeping up a continuous stream of lively examination among all. The young men are taught in this way for two years, when they are introduced into the classes below to teach the children, the director privately observing and correcting their faults. We went through six classes of the school in which this process was going on. In one, the children were exercised in mental arithmetic. In others, instruction in French, Anatomy and Natural History was given, all in the same lively manner; and in one class, they read a brief history of the Reformation and repeated a hymn. We were much gratified by this visit and longed to see the same system fully realized in Scotland.

We next visited the Berlin Missionary Institution in Sebastian Street, and were kindly received by the Directors, two gentle Christian men. They have a hall for prayer, comfortable apartments for the students, a small library, and a neat chapel adjoining. Several young men were studying there at the time who have devoted themselves to the missionary cause; one of whom was Jacobson, a converted Jew, full of love to his Lord, and under training to carry the glad tidings to his brethren. The expense for each student is £30 a-year.

The same evening we had the pleasure of calling on Dr Robinson, the American Professor, author of *Biblical Researches in Palestine*, a most valuable work, to which frequent references have been made in a former part of this narrative. He was then residing in Berlin for the purpose of bringing it to a completion.

Our inquiries being now completed in the Prussian capital, we set out for Hamburgh (which is thirty-two hours distant) late at night, good old Elsner seeing us away, and supplying us with tracts for distribution. Passing through Spandau and many villages during the night, we came next day about noon to Perleberg, and shortly after to Ludwigslust. This latter place is surrounded with gardens and pleasure-grounds, having formerly been the residence of the Duke of Mecklesberg, in whose territory it lies. At evening we reached Boitzemburg, then crossed a strip of territory belonging to Denmark and early next morning entered Hamburgh.

The environs of Hamburgh are beautiful; fine avenues of trees afford shady walks, through which the scenery of the river Elbe at different openings meets the eye. Many of the houses are old and picturesque. There are 150,000 inhabitants; and it is reckoned one of the most vicious towns in Europe. The city forms a kind of republic, governed by a senate who seem to be opponents of the truth. The established religion is Lutheran, but the pastors are far from being faithful or even orthodox. A little before our visit, two *Candidats* had been preaching against the Divinity of Christ and nothing was done to check them; whilst another faithful *Candidat*, who printed a tract opposed to Socinian views, was tried, fined and forbidden to preach for three years. In the whole Hamburgh territory, there are twenty-six Lutheran pastors, but of these, only six have come boldly forward to defend the truth. One member of senate, who is a faithful man, has published a protest against the Socinianism of some of the ministers. There are 4,000 English resident in this town, and these have an Episcopal clergyman. Mr Rheder, a minister of the Congregational persuasion and a worthy man, labours quietly among his flock, and is undisturbed. Mr Oncken, the agent to the Edinburgh Bible Society, preaches to a small Baptist congregation, but not without interruption.

We found our way to the house of Mr Moritz, missionary of the London Society, by birth a Jew, who for thirty-two years has maintained a consistent profession of the truth. When he first went to London, before his conversion, he lived at the house of a Jewess. On Saturday, instead of going to the synagogue, he spent the whole day in going through the city, gazing at every novelty. On Sunday morning he was astonished at the quietness of the town and still more when he saw the shops all shut. Inquiring what it meant, his Jewish landlady said, 'The people of England are a God-fearing people, and if we had kept our Sabbath as they keep theirs, Messiah would have come long ago.' This word from the lips of a Jewess was the first arrow of conviction that pierced his heart, for he always thought that Christians were idolaters. The arrow remained, and never left him till he was brought to the feet of Jesus. After his baptism he read in a newspaper one day a proposal by Alexander, Emperor of Russia, to establish colonies of Jews near the Sea of Azoph, whereupon he wrote to a friend in St Petersburg that gospel missionaries should first be sent among the Russian Jews. His letter was laid before the Emperor, by whose desire he was immediately engaged in that work. From 1817 to 1825 he went through many provinces of Russia, Volhynia, Courland and the Crimea preaching the gospel to the Jews with great acceptance and often with success. His own aunt and her two sons were the first fruits of his labours. He was often invited to preach in the synagogues of the Jews, where the Jews listened with deep interest.

Frequently, in order to attract them, he made use of their own style, and conveyed the truth in the form of a *mashal* or parable – for the Jews still delight in this form of speech, as their fathers did (Judges 9:7). Once in the synagogue of Kiow, being asked to preach, he spoke the following parable. 'A poor Jew wanted very much to be rich; he therefore put a bandage on his eyes that he might pray to *Mazal* or Fortune, and went everywhere through the streets, looking up to heaven, and crying, "O Mazal, Mazal, make me rich." At length, Mazal threw down a great bag full of precious treasure which fell right before him. The poor man did not take off the bandage, but ran on and stumbled over the treasure. Neither did he even then turn back to see what it was, but went on, still crying, "O Mazal, Mazal, make me rich." Mazal seeing her gift neglected, took it up again into heaven, and the Jew remained a beggar as before.' The Jews present requested an explanation of the parable which he gave them, by referring to Isaiah 9:6 and the 2nd Psalm. A deep silence followed. At last some young men asked, 'And will the bandage always be on our eyes?' He told them to pray that the Spirit of God might take it away. Five of these young men seemed to receive saving impressions that evening.

In 1819 he was in Dorissow preaching the gospel to the Jews when a rabbi from Kletsk (six German miles distant), accompanied by some of his young men, called and asked why he did not come to their town to preach the gospel to them. Mr Moritz said he was willing to come if they would receive him. The rabbi said, 'We will treat you kindly, I and my people will hear you, and I will tell them to treat you kindly.' Accordingly he went and was well received; he declared the gospel freely to them and gave away all his tracts and New Testaments. He did not hear at the time of any particular result; but a year ago, letters came from Warsaw from forty Jews of Kletsk asking if one Moritz was still living and where he was, offering if he were at Warsaw to come there and be baptized. 'Cast thy bread upon the waters, for thou shalt find it *after many days*.'

This excellent missionary regards Russia as by far the most important field for a Jewish mission. There are at least *two millions* of Jews in European Russia, not including Poland, and all are Talmudists except in Courland, where a little more light has broken in. But there seems little hope of obtaining leave for Protestants to labour amongst Israel there, for the Government are doing all they can to crush Protestantism. The Basle missionaries who went to the Caucasus, obtained permission to baptize their converts, but a year after they were all sent out of the country. In the regions bordering on the Baltic, Protestants marrying Greeks were formerly allowed to bring up some of their children as Protestants, but now all must be Greeks. Before, when Protestants were far from a Protestant minister, the Greek priests baptized the children, allowing the children to remain Protestants; but now all such children must be brought up as Greeks.

From Mr Moritz we obtained the same favourable account of the Karaites in Russia as that given before. There are two colonies of them near Wilna, inhabiting a town and a village, the one having 1,500 and the other 300, who support themselves by cultivating the ground. At a place called Kareimisky Neustadt ('new town belonging to Karaites') in Lithuania, they are employed in agriculture, and the cultivation of hops and cucumbers. In the Crimea there are above 4,000 who are nearly all farmers. They are a very moral and trustworthy people. Once they did not receive the prophets, but only the law, but now they receive both as divine. They keep the externals of the law very strictly, never kindling a fire on Sabbath in the coldest winters; but they are full of self-righteousness.[4]

Jews in Russia are now taken into the army, so that no Jew can leave the country without special permission; yet still they succeed in obtaining passports by bribery.

In Sweden, of which Mr M[oritz] is a native, there are only 250 families of Jews, and these are obliged to live in four cities. At Stockholm there are 600 Jews; at Gottenberg, 450; at Narkoping, 100; and at Carlscrona, 40. Mr M[oritz] had visited them all, and so little hindrance is there in the way of labouring among them, that one of the bishops offered him a church in which he might preach to the Jews. In Denmark it is otherwise; there are 2,600 Jews in its capital, Copenhagen, and the same number in Altona, and about 1,000 more throughout the country; but no missionary is allowed to seek their salvation.

Mr Moritz having also visited other parts of Germany gave us information concerning them. In Baden there are 20,000 Jews; in Bavaria 30,000; and in Wurtemberg 1,200. In Baden, the greater part of the Jews have cast away the Talmud, except those in Carlsruhe. In Bavaria, there is a mixture of Rationalists and Talmudists, and little has been done for the Jews there, two-thirds of the population being Roman Catholics. In Wurtemberg, the most of the Jews are Rationalists, but very friendly. No missionary has ever been stationed there, though it is a most inviting field of labour, and he would find delightful Christian families who love Israel in almost every town and village; and were his labours blessed, might be permitted to establish around him a congregation of converted Jews. The desirableness of forming such a congregation was a subject on which Mr Moritz often dwelt. 'You will never make a deep impression on the Jewish mind', he would often say, 'until you form such a congregation. If your church would lay down her plan, and present it to the King of Prussia, you would, no doubt, receive permission to gather all the converts round the missionary, as in the Moravian settlements, so that they might support themselves, sympathize with one another, and be nourished by sound teaching. I know a great many Jewish families in Wurtemberg who would at once join such a congregation; but, at present, they are kept back in some degree by the feeling that most of those who profess Christianity around them are

---

[4] The Karaites represented a Jewish movement which began in the 8th century A.D. They regarded the written law, not oral tradition, as the true source of religious doctrine and practice. Karaites still exist today in a community near Tel Aviv in Israel.

infidels; while, at the same time, their convictions are repressed by the difficulties and painful struggles that are in the way of converts.'

Hamburgh itself presents a difficult field for missionary labour. There are 9,000 resident Jews and a fluctuating class of travelling Jews from Poland, Bavaria and even occasionally from Constantinople and Asia who come here in the way of trade. The majority are Talmudists, but far from being devout; the New School Jews have an elegant synagogue, where they use an organ and German tunes to their hymns.

When Mr Moritz first arrived, he sent a circular of intimation to the Jews, and immediately great crowds visited him. Many soon threatened to kill him; and the rabbis both of the Old and New School used all their influence, so that in a little while all Jews ceased to come to him. He next opened a school and taught twenty-four poor Jewish children for several months; but the rabbis threatened to withdraw their proportion of alms, and so all were removed from him. At the time of our visit, Mr M[oritz] preached every Tuesday in his own house to about seventy hearers of whom, however, the most were Christians, with four or five Jews occasionally. He has found some fruit of his labours among them. Many of the foreign Jews who visit Hamburgh come to him for a tract or a Bible, when he opens to them the gospel, and often they come again. That very week ten such inquirers had been with him. The Jews have great influence over the Government, two-thirds of them being rich, and holding the greater part of the trade in their hands. They have a police of their own, who permit no foreign Jew to stay more than two days without their leave; if he is suspected of inquiring into Christianity, he is sent off immediately. Still Hamburgh is a most important station, and we heartily thanked God when we found so warm-hearted a missionary there, 'going forth weeping, bearing precious seed'.

On our way to the old synagogue we met Mr Oncken, newly arrived from a visit to Denmark, a kind, intelligent Christian, who went with us. The building was large and well filled with careless-looking Jews, with nothing distinctive in their dress except the *Tallith* worn by some. They have little real devotion and seem to cleave to the superstitions of the rabbis in outward form only.

We next visited the New School synagogue or temple, *a temple without a Shecinah*, as Mr Moritz well expressed it. The rabbi, Mr Klee, dressed with a small Jew cap and *Tallith*, black cloak and bands, was in the pulpit, reciting a German hymn with much energy. He then gave a short preface and read the text in the same way as the Lutheran ministers, and delivered with much elocution a sermon on patience and submission to the will of God. He quoted a Christian author and several hymns and even spoke of Christian patience. There were about 200 present, the ladies occupying the gallery and a side compartment. When the sermon was finished and the blessing pronounced in the mode of the Lutherans, the preacher withdrew, and a German hymn was given out, the organ playing one of the fine national psalm tunes. Another rabbi then began the Hebrew prayer, but most withdrew during this service. The peculiarity of their prayer-book is that *they have erased all mention of Messiah*. 'Have I been a wilderness unto Israel? a land of darkness? wherefore say my people, We are lords; we will come no more unto thee?' (Jeremiah 2:31). It is painfully interesting to remark, that though they borrow so many of the externals of the Lutherans, they have a most bitter hatred at Christianity. Like the father of young Hannibal, they administer an oath to their children at confirmation to the effect that *they will never become Christians*. Mr Moritz had frequently conversed with a young Jewess, who had deep convictions of the truth, but who always waved any decided expression of her views by saying, *'Ich habe geschworen, Ich habe geschworen'* (I have sworn, I have sworn).

The same evening we walked out at the Hamburgh gate, and along the Hamburgh Bar, famous or rather infamous over all the world as a scene of deepest profligacy, where many a British sailor has been hurried on to ruin, and where the poor Jews are too often made to share in the sin of Christians. At the end of this walk we came to Altona, connected with Hamburgh, yet in the province of Holstein and belonging to Denmark, a fine town, containing 30,000 inhabitants, with a shady walk under linden-trees, and a beautiful view of the winding Elbe, and a tributary entering it. It contains 2,600 Jews, and many of the shops were open, though it was their Sabbath.

It was this day that we first heard of the wonderful work of God that had lately taken place in Scotland. Mr Rheder, who shewed us much kindness, brought us a newspaper, containing brief references to the Revivals at Kilsyth and Dundee, thinking that we would be able to give him fuller details; but all our letters having been sent to Warsaw, we were in utter ignorance of what had occurred, God having reserved the good news till our wanderings were nearly done. The notices were of the briefest and most imperfect kind; and though Dundee was named, he did not know how nearly we were interested in the shower of blessing. We

were, however, filled with joy, by hearing that God had poured out his
Spirit as in the days of old; and we felt it a special kindness to ourselves
that the glad tidings should meet us when we were almost in sight of our
native land. It appeared also worthy of special notice and thanksgiving
that God had done this in the very year when the Church of Scotland had
stretched out her hand to seek the welfare of Israel and to speak peace
to all their seed. And we felt that the same promises that had so often
supported us in our trials had been made good also to our Church at
home: 'Blessed is he that blesseth thee': 'Pray for the peace of Jerusalem; they shall prosper that love thee'

Those only who have experienced what it is to have been long
separated from a beloved flock, and in distant solitudes to pour out the
heart to God in their behalf, can understand the feelings with which we
now longed to visit our parishes again and to know if they had shared
in the grace that had dropped on the pastures of the wilderness.

November 3, Sabbath

Mr McCheyne preached in Mr Rheder's chapel on the words 'They
overcame him by the blood of the Lamb, and by the word of their
testimony.' It was the first time he had preached since laid aside by that
providence which had led to our mission being proposed. We afterwards enjoyed the privilege of sitting down at the Lord's Table with a
small company of serious people, among whom were four converts of
the house of Israel. Mr Bonar addressed the communicants and then
preached in the afternoon on Jeremiah 31:3-7, giving a sketch of what
we had seen of God's ancient people. In the evening we had a pleasant
meeting in the house of Mr Moritz, who read the 102nd Psalm, and sent
us away with affectionate prayer.

A little after midnight we left Hamburgh, and came to Shulau, where
we embarked on board the Lonsdale steamer for London.

After a prosperous voyage we entered the Thames on the morning of the
third day *(November 6)* and the same afternoon arrived in London. After
spending a few days there among the many kind friends who had been
interested in our wanderings, we hastened to Scotland and, 'according
to the good hand of our God upon us', arrived in peace.

We were welcomed home by the Committee of our Church who had
commended us to the Lord when we went forth, and solemn thanksgiving was offered for our return, with earnest prayer for our two elder

brethren whom we had expected to find arrived before us, but who were detained by dangerous illness abroad. A few days after, the Commission of the General Assembly received us in the same spirit of love and requested to hear from our lips 'concerning the Jews that had escaped, which were left of the captivity, and concerning Jerusalem'; and 'we rehearsed all that God had done with us, and how he had opened the door of faith to his ancient people'. Not less fervent was the welcome we received from the people of our respective parishes on the day we returned to them.

And now that we can look back on all the way that God led us, we are constrained to say, to the praise of the glory of His grace, that He has blessed this undertaking from the beginning to the end. Both in the towns and rural parishes of Scotland, a deep, and we trust, Scriptural interest has been excited in behalf of Israel; an interest which has penetrated to the very poorest of our people. While going from parish to parish to tell the things we have seen and heard, there is one gratification we have never missed – namely, the presence of the aged, patriarchal-looking men of our Scottish peasantry, seated ofttimes on the pulpit-stairs, that they might hear of 'the seed of Abraham, God's friend' – the nation for whose ingathering their godly sires used fervently to pray, as they dropt a tear over the narrative of their miseries.

It was a considerable time before Dr Black and Dr Keith were able to return. The former was detained some months at Vienna and the latter till the following spring at Pesth in Hungary by severe illness. Both, however, returned by the blessing of God with renovated health, bringing with them much interesting and useful intelligence regarding the countries they had visited.

Immediately on their arrival, a report was drawn up and submitted to the General Assembly of 1840, when it was unanimously resolved *that the cause of Israel should from that time form one of the great missionary schemes of our church.* In July 1841, a similar resolution was passed by the General Assembly of the Presbyterian Church in Ireland. So thus one grand result of this undertaking has been that the venerable Church of Scotland, in days of darkness and perplexity, along with her revived and vigorous offspring in Ireland, has been led to acknowledge herself debtor both to the Jews and to the Greeks, and humbly to imitate the Apostolic Church of Jerusalem by sending forth some of her sons to the heathen and some to the circumcision (Galatians

2:9). True, when we turn our eyes on the millions of the blinded heathen and the scattered bones of Israel that whiten the valley of vision, we feel that absolutely nothing has been done at all adequate to the awful need of a perishing world, and the weight of our responsibility. Yet a beginning has been made; the cry, 'Come over and help us', is now distinctly heard in the remotest corners of our land. And all who take pleasure in tracing the steps of the Son of man, as he walks amidst his golden candlesticks, cannot but thank God that these two Churches have now come forth in their full evangelistic character – preaching Christ and Him crucified to their people at home, and stretching out their hands abroad, with the offer of the water of life to the distant Gentiles and the dispersed of Judah. 'Not unto us, O Lord, not unto us, but unto thy name give glory, for thy mercy and for thy truth's sake.'